100.00

100.00

HISTORY
BEHIND THE
HEADLINES

HISTORY
BEHIND THE
HEADLINES

The Origins of Conflicts Worldwide

VOLUME 1

Meghan Appel O'Meara, Editor

Detroit
New York
San Francisco
London
Boston
Woodbridge, CT

Editor
Meghan Appel O'Meara

Gale Group Staff
Editorial: Bernard Grunow, Project Editor; Kathy Droste
and Nancy Matuszak, Contributing Editors; Jason Everett,
Associate Contributing Editor; Rita Runchock, Managing
Editor.

Permissions: Maria Franklin, Permissions Manager; Debra
Freitas, Permissions Associate.

Composition: Mary Beth Trimper, Manager, Composition
and Electronic Prepress; Evi Seoud, Assistant Manager,
Composition Purchasing and Electronic Prepress.

Manufacturing: Dorothy Maki, Manufacturing Manager;
Rhonda Williams, Buyer.

Imaging and Multimedia Content: Barbara J. Yarrow,
Imaging and Multimedia Content Manager; Randy Bassett,
Image Database Supervisor; Dean Dauphinais, Senior
Imaging Specialist; Dan Newell, Imaging Specialist; Pamela
A. Reed, Imaging Coordinator.

Product Design: Kenn J. Zorn, Product Design Manager;
Pamela A. E. Galbreath, Senior Art Director.

ISBN 0-7876-4951-1
ISSN 1531-7307
Printed in the United States
10 9 8 7 6 5 4 3 2 1

TABLE OF CONTENTS

W

CONTENTS BY SUBJECT

RACIAL

RELIGIOUS

TERRITORIAL

ADVISORY BOARD

Jerry H. Bentley is professor of history at the University of Hawaii and editor of the *Journal of World History*. His research on the religious, moral, and political writings of Renaissance humanists led to the publication of *Humanists and Holy Writ: New Testament Scholarship in the Renaissance and Politics and Culture in Renaissance Naples*. More recently, his research has concentrated on global history and particularly on processes of cross-cultural interaction. His book *Old World Encounters: Cross-Cultural Contacts and Exchanges in Pre-Modern Times* examines processes of cultural exchange and religious conversion before the modern era, and his pamphlet "Shapes of World History in Twentieth-Century Scholarship" discusses the historiography of world history. His current interests include processes of cross-cultural interaction and cultural exchanges in modern times.

Ken Berger received his B.A. in East Asian Studies at Eckerd College and his M.A. in Asian Studies and M.S.L.S. from Florida State University. He has been a librarian at Duke University since 1977, with almost all of his time spent as a reference librarian and bibliographer, including the last several years as head of reference. He is currently the Project Manager for the Library Service Center. He has written hundreds of reviews in East Asian studies, military affairs and history, and library and information science.

Frank J. Coppa is Professor of History at St. John's University, Director of their doctoral program, and Chair of the University's Vatican Symposium. He is also an Associate in the Columbia University Seminar on Modern Italy, and editor of the Lang Series on Studies on Modern Europe. He has published biographies on a series of European figures, written and edited more than twelve volumes, as well as publishing in a series of journals including the *Journal of Modern History* and the *Journal of Economic History*, among others. He is editor of the *Dictionary of Modern Italian History* and the *Encyclopedia of the Vatican and Papacy*.

Bill Gaudelli received his Ed.D. in Social Studies Education from Rutgers University in 2000. He dissertation was on "Approaches to Global Education." He teaches at Hunterdon Central Regional High School (winner of the National Council for the Social Studies Programs of Excellence Award) and Teachers College-Columbia University. Publications include "Teaching Human Rights through Conflict-Resolution" in *Social Science* and "Global Education: a Viable Framework for an Issues-Centered Curriculum" in *ERIC Documents*. He is a member of the National Council for Social Studies and the American Forum for Global Education.

Paul Gootenberg is a Professor of Latin American History at SUNY-Stony Brook. A graduate of the University of Chicago and Oxford, he specializes in the economic, social, and intellectual history of the Andes and Mexico, and more recently, the global history of drugs. He has published *Between Silver and Guano* (1989), *Imagining Development* (1993) and *Cocaine: Global Histories* (1999). Gootenberg has held many fellowships; they include Fulbright, SSRC, ACLS, Institute for Advanced Study, Russell Sage Foundation, the Rhodes Scholarship, and a Guggenheim. He lives in Brooklyn, New York with his wife, Laura Sainz, and son, Danyal Natan.

Margaret Hallisey is a practicing high school library media specialist in Burlington, Massachusetts. She is a graduate of Regis College with a B.A. in English and of Simmons College with a M.S. in Library and Information Science. A member of Beta Phi Mu, the International Library Science Honor Society, she serves on the executive Boards of the American Association of School Librarians (AASL), the Massachusetts School Library Media Association (MSLMA) and the New England Educational Media Association (NEEMA).

Patricia H. Hodgson is the District Librarian for the Aspen School District, in Aspen, Colorado. She is a member of the American Library Association, the American Association for School Librarians, and the World History Association. She received her M.L.M. from the University of Colorado at Denver.

Donna Maier has been with the Department of History at the University of Northern Iowa since 1986. Her research interests are in nineteenth century Asante (Ghana), African Islam, and traditional African medicine. Her extensive lists of publications include "The Military Acquisition of Slaves in Asante," in *West African Economic and Social History, The Cloths of Many-Colored Silks* (1996), and *History and Life, the World and Its Peoples* (1977-90, with Wallbank and Shrier). She is a member of the African Studies Association and the Ghana Studies Council.

Linda Karen Miller, Ph.D., teaches American government, world history and geography at Fairfax High School in Fairfax, Virginia. A twenty-nine year veteran, she has received several national and state teaching awards such as the National Council for the Social Studies Secondary Teacher of the Year in 1996, the Organization of American Historian Pre-Collegiate Teacher of the Year in 1996, the Excellence in Teaching Award from the University of Kansas and the University of Virginia, and the Global Education Award from the National Peace Corps Association. She has traveled to Russia and Armenia under grants sponsored by the U.S. Department of State. She has published several lesson plans and articles for PBS and, most recently, Turner Learning's "Millennium 1000 Years of History." She also serves as a consultant to Newsweek magazine and the Wall Street Journal Classroom Edition, as well as the GED testing service.

Philip Yockey is Social Sciences Bibliographer and Assistant Chief Librarian for Staff Training and Development at the Humanities and Social Sciences Library at The New York Public Library.

ABOUT THE SERIES

In 1991 the world witnessed a political change of great magnitude. The Union of Soviet Socialist Republics (USSR) crumbled, ushering in a new era of democracy and the official end of the Cold War. East and West Germany had reunited just two years earlier; for many people formerly behind the Iron Curtain, now seemed to be a time of unbound freedom and autonomy. Yet ten years later, newscasts and newspapers report of a six year war between Russia and Chechnya, a former state within the USSR. After so much optimism about the future, what caused this instability and unrest? Was the cause based in a fundamental flaw of the initial break-up of the USSR or perhaps from something much further back in the regions' histories? How did the international community react to the USSR's collapse and the strife that was to follow?

History Behind the Headlines (*HBH*), a new, ongoing series from the Gale Group, strives to answer these and many other questions in a way that television broadcasts and newspapers cannot. In order to keep reports both simple and short, it is difficult for these media to give the watcher or reader enough background information to fully understand what is happening around the world today. *HBH* provides just that background, giving the general public, student, and teacher an explication of each contemporary conflict from its start to its present and even its future. This thoroughness is accomplished not just by the in-depth material covered in the main body of each essay, but also by accompanying chronologies, textual and biographical sidebars, maps, and bibliographic sources.

Not only does *HBH* provide comprehensive information on all of the conflicts it covers, it also strives to present its readers an unbiased and inclusive perspective. Each essay, written by an expert with a detailed knowledge of the conflict at hand, avoids taking any particular side and instead seeks to explain each vantage point. Unlike television and newpaper reports, which may only have the time, space or even inclination to show one side of a story, *HBH* essays equally detail all sides involved.

Given the number of conflicts that beg such explication as *HBH* provides, an advisory board of school and library experts helps to guide the selection process and narrow down the selection for each volume. They balance the topic lists, making sure that a proper mix of economic, political, ethnic and geographically diverse conflicts are chosen. Two volumes, each written in an accessible, informative way, will be released each year.

PREFACE

Selection and Arrangement

This volume of *History Behind the Headlines* covers thirty conflicts—including ethnic, religious, economic, political, territorial, and environmental conflicts. The topics were chosen following an extensive review of the conflicts covered in newspapers, magazines, and on television. A large number of potential conflicts were identified. Advisors—including academic experts, high school social study teachers, and librarians—prioritized the list, identifying those conflicts that generate the most questions. Topics were then selected to provide a regional balance and to cover various types of conflicts.

The conflicts covered are complex. Each essay discusses multiple aspects of the conflict, including economic and social aspects to religious conflicts, the interests of other countries, international organizations, and businesses, and the international implications of the conflict. The entries are arranged alphabetically by a major country, region, organization, or person in the conflict. Where this might not be clear in the table of contents, the keyword is placed in parentheses in front of the title.

Content

Each essay begins with a brief summary of the current situations as well as some of the major factors in the conflict. Each essay contains the following sections:

- **Summary of the headline event.** An overview of the contemporary conflict that has brought the issue to public attention. For example, the arrest and conviction of Ocalan by Turkey in 1999 or the battle over Elian Gonzalez.

- **Historical Background.** The "Historical Background" is the heart of the essay. The author provides the historical context to the con-

temporary conflict, summarizing the arc of the conflict through history. Each essay tells the "story" of the conflict, capturing important events, transfers of power, interventions, treaties, and more. The author summarizes the changes in the conflict over time, describes the role of major figures, whether individuals, political organizations, or religious organizations, and provides an overview of their positions now and in the past. Where appropriate the author may draw comparisons with similar situations in the country or region in the past. In addition, the author often attempts to put the conflict in the context of global politics and to describe the impact of the conflict on people around the world. Finally, the author may touch on how historians' understanding of the conflict has changed over time.

- **Recent History and the Future.** The final section brings the conflict up-to-date, and may offer some projections for future resolution.

Each essay is followed by a brief bibliography that offers some suggestions of resources for further research. In addition, brief biographies may accompany the essay, profiling major figures. Sidebars may provide statistical information, a quote from a speech, a selection from a primary source document (such as a treaty), a selection from a book or newspaper article that adds to the understanding of the conflict, or may explore an issue in greater depth (such as the Armenian Genocide in Turkey during World War I or the nature of control of the media during the Chechen war). Images may also accompany the essay, including one or more maps showing the area of conflict.

A selected bibliography providing suggestions for background information and research on the nature of conflicts and a comprehensive index appear at the back of each volume.

History is to be Read Critically

Each of the talented writers (mostly academic authorities) in this volume strived to provide an objective and comprehensive overview of the conflict and its historical context. The nature of contemporary conflict, however, makes it difficult to wholly accomplish this objective. Contemporary history and, in fact, all history—should be read critically.

Acknowledgements

Many thanks for their help to the excellent advisors who guided this project—their attention and feedback was greatly appreciated. Many thanks, also, to the thoughtful and dedicated writers, who lent their expertise to help others understand the complex history behind sound bites on the news. Thanks to Bernard Grunow and the team at the Gale Group that made the manuscript a book. Finally, thanks to my family and friends—especially B.B. Sela—for their support and encouragement.

Comments on this volume and suggestions for future volumes are welcomed. Please direct all correspondence to:

Editor, *History Behind the Headlines*
Gale Group
27500 Drake Rd.
Farmington Hills, MI 48331-3535
(800) 877-4253

THE AFGHAN TALIBAN: EMERGING GOVERNMENT OR CIVIL RIGHTS TRAGEDY?

In 1996 a radical Muslim sect known as the Taliban successfully captured Afghanistan's capital city of Kabul. With this victory, Taliban gained control of three quarters of the nation. Taliban leaders immediately imposed a strict interpretation of Islamic law on the citizens of Afghanistan, requiring women to wear full length veils and men to grow beards, and imposing severe penalties for most crimes. As a result of the Taliban's actions, Afghanistan was thrust into the international spotlight.

In February 2000 an Afghan Ariana Airlines Boeing 727 was hijacked by Afghan citizens. The flight from Kabul, the Afghan capital, to Mazar-e-Sharif, the capital of the Balkh province of Afghanistan (located in the north central part of the nation) was supposed to fly several families to a wedding. The plane never arrived. Shortly after takeoff, six to ten of the passengers armed themselves and demanded that the flight crew fly them out of Afghanistan. The flight finally arrived in London on Monday, February 9, 2000, one day after departure from Kabul.

Upon arrival at London's Stansted Airport early Monday morning, the hijackers released a few hostages, primarily those with medical conditions. However, it soon became clear that this was not a simple terrorist act, as those who left the plane described several passengers not associated with the hijackers "many of the women and children—laughed, tossed aside their veils and received the choicest food and drink from their captors." It appeared that this hijacking was an effort by a group of Afghan families to escape the oppressive Taliban regime. Once the British government negotiated a peaceful settlement with the hijackers, this suspicion seemed to have been confirmed.

THE CONFLICT

From 1978 to 1992, the Afghanistan government was Communist and closely allied with the Soviet Union. The United States funded and armed rebels fighting the Communists—the *mujadin*. The *mujadin* were Islamic fundamentalists, and when the Soviet Union withdrew and the Afghani government fell, the *mujadin* established strict Islamic law, *shari'a*.

Religious
- The Taliban, leaders of the organization ruling much of Afghanistan, believe in strict Islamic law.

Political
- Many people around the world believe the regime is denying its citizens their basic human rights.

- Western nations have charged that Afghanistan harbors and supports terrorists.

- The Taliban believes the U.S. betrayed it by ending funding and support after the end of the Cold War.

CHRONOLOGY

1933–73 King Mohammed Zahir Shah attempts to modernize and Westernize Afghanistan.

1973 Zahir's cousin Daud, stages a coup and declares himself leader of the "Republic of Afghanistan." He relies on Communist supporters to come to power.

1978 Daud attempts to remove the Communists and supporters of the Soviet Union from his government. In response, the Communists takes control of the government.

1978–92 The Communist government, which was closely allied with the Soviet Union, fights a civil war against several groups of *mujadin*—fighters in a Holy War. The United States supports the *mujadin*.

1993 The Rabbani regime comes to power. Rabbani supports the establishment of a separate Islamic state. His forces fight the Taliban.

1996 The Taliban moves to capture all of Afghanistan.

1997 The Taliban captures Kabul, the capitol of Afghanistan.

1998 The Taliban declines to turn suspected terrorist Osama bin Laden over to the United States.

1999 The Taliban controls more than ninety percent of Afghanistan, although they still face considerable opposition. The United States and the United Nations still deal with Rabbani's group.

2000 Afghan Ariana Airlines Boeing 727 is hijacked in what appeared to be a bid for asylum.

The Taliban swiftly sent another airliner to collect their wayward citizens. By Thursday, February 11, seventy-four had requested asylum in England, twenty-one had been arrested for the hijacking (the original six to ten, plus an additional number implicated as co-conspirators), and the remainder (roughly seventy men and women) chose to return home to Afghanistan. Despite the negative publicity of the hijacking, Taliban officials still separated the men and women from each other as they left the plane in Kabul, as required by Islamic law (CNN.com, February 14, 2000, AsiaNow site).

HISTORICAL BACKGROUND

Geography and History

Afghanistan is a small south Asian nation of 250,000 square miles. It is slightly smaller than Texas, which is 261,914 square miles. Afghanistan shares borders with Pakistan to the east, Iran to the southwest, Turkmenistan to the northwest, and Uzbekistan and Tajikstan to the north. Only about 12 percent of Afghanistan's land is suitable for cultivation, and of that 12 percent, almost 50 percent is dedicated to farming or livestock. Afghanistan has a population of almost twenty-six million people—it is almost twice as populous as Texas (population 17,655,650 in 1992), but smaller than California (population 30,866,851 in 1992).

Only about twenty-five percent of Afghans have electricity; for the last twenty years, city services have often been interrupted by war among the various ethnic and religious factions in Afghanistan. Because of the continued conflict, the average Afghan's life expectancy is forty-seven years. In contrast, the average life expectancy for an American is seventy-six years.

The majority of Afghans work on small subsistence farms. Inflation is currently at about 240 percent (roughly one hundred times that of the United States), although it cannot be accurately determined. The few industries that exist in Afghanistan are textiles and soap manufacturers, and, to a lesser degree, woven rugs and oil drilling.

The people of Afghanistan represent several distinct ethnic groups. The Pashtun are the largest group, representing about thirty-three percent of the population. Tajiks and Uzbekis comprise about thirty percent of the rest of the population, with Hazaris totaling another twenty percent. The remaining fifteen percent or so are of various ethnic backgrounds. The people of Afghanistan also speak several unique languages and dialects. Persian represents the most widely used language in Afghanistan, followed by Pashtu.

The majority of Afghans follow the Muslim faith. Islam has two major branches of faith, the Shiite and the Sunni. The Shiite believe that leadership of the Islamic community follows a dynastic succession from Imam Ali (a cousin of the prophet Muhammed) and his children. The Shiite of Afghanistan live in the central provinces and were the first to fight against the Soviets. Shiite followers comprise only about fifteen percent of Afghanistan's Muslim community. The Sunni branch of the Islam faith comprise about eighty-

A TALIBAN SOLDIER RESTS NEXT TO A RUSSIAN-MADE ROCKET LAUNCHER. *(AP/Wide World Photos. Reproduced by permission.)*

five percent of Afghanistan and are considered to be orthodox Muslims. Sunni Muslims are more willing to interact with the West and more likely to interpret the Qor'an (also spelled "Koran") broadly. The members of the Taliban are Pashtun Sunni and their radical interpretation of the Qor'an can be puzzling to outside observers.

The predominant political conflict in Afghanistan in the twentieth century centered on efforts by King Mohammed Zahir Shah (who ruled Afghanistan from 1933 to 1973) to modernize and Westernize Afghanistan. Like many Arab nations in the mid 1930s and 1940s, Mohammed Zahir believed Afghanistan needed close ties to the West. Zahir wanted western tools and modern development to improve the lives of his people. However, the traditional religious leaders of Afghanistan, led by Zahir's cousin Muhammed Daud, rejected Zahir's efforts to liberalize his nation. In 1964 Zahir attempted to reform Afghanistan's government by introducing a parliament instituting open elections and permitting the creation of political parties. These reforms were only moderately successful. Muhammed Daud served in several capacities under his cousin, but in 1973 while Zahir toured abroad, Daud staged a coup and declared himself the leader of "the Republic of Afghanistan."

Daud's coup presented the international community with a dilemma. Zahir's reign was making strides in reform, but he had failed to address the deep-rooted social and economic problems in Afghanistan. Daud, on the other hand, may have had a better chance to remedy the many problems plaguing the nation, but he relied on Communist supporters to come to power. Afghanistan is a strategically important nation in Asia and the Middle East. The Soviet Union wanted it as a buffer from the West. The United States wanted Afghanistan as an ally in the oil-rich region of the Middle East.

Although Daud relied on the Communists in his party, by 1978 he had grown wary of their influence and began to purge Communists and Soviet supporters from his regime. In retaliation, the Communists seized control of the Afghan government in 1978. They assassinated Daud and his family in the Saur Revolution.

From 1978 to 1992, the Communist government of Afghanistan was closely allied with the Soviet Union. But the government soon fought a civil war against the *mujadin* (fighters in a Holy War against infidels), who considered the atheistic Communist regime an affront to their religious beliefs. The United States secretly supported the

A LABORER PULLS HIS CART OF SUPPLIES PAST A COMMON SCENE OF DESTRUCTION IN AFGHANISTAN IN THE CITY OF KABUL. (*AP/Wide World Photos. Reproduced by permission.*)

mujadin in their efforts to overthrow the Communist government. The Afghan-Soviet conflict lasted from 1978 to 1989 when the Soviets finally withdrew their military troops from Afghanistan.

The Factions

The *mujadin* fighters were primarily from seven Sunni groups. Four faction leaders, Burhanuddin Rabbani, Gulbuddin Hekmatyar, General Abdul Rashid Dostum, and Abdul Rasul Sayyaf, would soon find themselves in another conflict over which group would become the legitimate government in Afghanistan after the Soviets withdrew. Consequently, the victory over the Soviet empire merely led to a new kind of civil war, one among the various Afghani groups competing for political control over Afghanistan. This civil war was based on political and ethnic disparities among the leadership. While each of the four main leaders were Sunni, they represented different ethnic factions and ideas about Afghanistan's future ties to the West.

Burhanuddin Rabbani is a Tajik from the northern part of Afghanistan. He leads a party faction known as the Islamic State of Afghanistan (Jamiat-i Islami-yi Afghanistan). Rabbani fought against the Soviet invaders and came to power in 1993. His goal was a separate Islamic state, one that rejected the secularization and Westernization of Afghan society. He was the most successful *mujadin* leader in Afghanistan until the rise of the Taliban. Since the Taliban's 1996 capture of Kabul, Rabbani has united with other groups to form the National Islamic United Front for the Salvation of Afghanistan (NIUFSA). In 1998, Rabbani recaptured much of northeast Afghanistan from the Taliban.

Abdul Rashid Dostum, leader of the National Islamic Movement of Afghanistan (NIMA), is an Uzbeki. He served with distinction as a military commander in Afghanistan's Communist regimes. Dostum is a moderate, and as of 1999 was the last military commander to stand in opposition to the Taliban.

Gulbuddin Hekmatyar (or Hikmatyar) is a Pashtu and an early ally of General Dostum. Hekmatyar began as an opponent of the Taliban and formed an alliance with Dostum. However, in 1996 he betrayed Dostum and joined the Taliban. Hekmatyar then joined Rabbani's forces for a brief time, and now is reported to control a small section of northern Afghanistan. Hekmatyar's goal is a radical Islamic state governed by a strict interpretation of Islamic law.

The most important military figure in the anti-Taliban effort is Ahmad Shah Massoud (or Mas'ud). Massoud is a non-Pashtun supporter of the Jamait (Rabbani's group) who successfully fought Soviet forces until the Soviet Union sued for peace in 1983. Massoud is no longer allied with Rabbani, but controls several provinces in north Afghanistan. In December 1999, Massoud won a small victory against the Taliban, but future prospects are uncertain.

The Taliban

The impact of the war against the Soviet Union and the ensuing civil war has been disastrous to Afghanistan. As a consequence of the war, most public educational institutions were closed or destroyed. This forced students to attend other schools, many of which were religious schools stressing a very strict interpretation of the Qor'an and advocating a radical Islamic government. From these schools (largely Pashtun and located in the southern provinces) arose a new group of extremists whose goal was to overthrow the existing Rabbani government and establish an Islamic State of Afghanistan. This group, known as the Taliban, is actually a coalition of students from south Afghanistan. The leader of the Taliban, Mullah Mohammed Omar, remains an enigmatic figure (Mullah is an honorific which means "teacher"). He appears to be about thirty-eight years of age, is a Pashtu, and fought against and was wounded by the Soviets. Omar's opponents claim that he is ignorant of Islamic law and is not really a Mullah or scholar of Islam. Many claim that he is actually a puppet of the Pakistani intelligence community. Such reports are difficult to confirm, but it is clear that he controls the Taliban organization from his Kandahar province base in the southeastern part of Afghanistan. Omar ordered schools for women closed and enforced severe sanctions against criminals and those who opposed his regime.

The Taliban's rise to power was surprising and rapid. The Taliban first made news in 1995 by rescuing a captured Afghan military truck from Pakistani troops. In 1996 the Taliban began an effort to capture all of Afghanistan, and managed to force Rabbani to flee the city. By 1997 the group was in control of Kabul and began to implement their interpretation of Islamic law. Since then, the Taliban has continued to expand its application of Islamic law. Thieves may have their hands amputated and those who fail to carry out their duties to Islam may face fines or imprisonment.

MULLAH MOHAMMED OMAR

1958– The religious leader of the Taliban, Mullah Mohammed Omar, is mysterious. He refuses to meet with non-Muslims or women, and will speak only through intermediaries or over the radio. Because of the ban on photography and television, very few have ever seen a picture of him. He has been described as heavy-set and unusually tall.

He was born into the Pashtun tribe of Uruzgan, Afghanistan in 1958 or 1959. He arrived in Kandahar Province in 1979, to study at *madrasa* (a religious university). After losing an eye in the war with the Soviet Union, he returned to the province as a village cleric.

In 1994 upset with corrupt *mujadin* soldiers and inspired by a vision of a pure, Islamic Afghanistan, Mullah Omar, the "Commander of the Faithful," gathered fifty men, and began a crusade to enforce shari'a (Islamic) law. This was the beginning of the Taliban movement.

In 1999 an unsuccessful assassination attempt destroyed the Mullah's neighborhood and killed ten people. He is now believed to live in Shahar-I-nau (New Town), Afghanistan, with his three wives, five sons, and one daughter.

The Taliban and Women

Shortly after capturing the capital city of Kabul, the Taliban began to impose strict regulations on women. Women were ordered to quit most occupations and don traditional garb, including veils and clothing that fully covered the body. Moreover, most women were prohibited from attending college or visiting their doctors. In 1997, this order was extended to women working in United Nations offices in Afghanistan. Women working for the United Nations could only continue to do so if they were accompanied to work by a male relative. The U.N. protested, but the Taliban insisted on this requirement. Women were not the only citizens affected by the orders of the new regime. Men were ordered to grow beards, and those who had beards were commanded not to trim or shape them. Men were also ordered to keep away from women in public arenas; a man could not approach a woman unless a male relative first introduced the two. These regulations, according to Taliban leaders, were required by their reading of the Qor'an. The Taliban, a strict Sunni sect of Muslim society, had begun the process of converting Afghanistan into an Islamic State.

OSAMA BIN LADEN

1957– Osama bin Laden was born in 1957 in Riyadh, Saudi Arabia. Although he is accused of financing terrorism throughout the world, many Muslims hail him as a hero. Bin Laden's large family (he is one of fifty-two siblings) is known in Muslim countries as benefactors who finance building projects and endow charitable foundations.

In 1979 bin Laden traveled to Afghanistan. Supplied with American arms and intelligence, he recruited thousands of volunteer fighters, and set up training camps to aid the *mujadin* in the war against the Soviet Union.

In 1991 bid Laden came to conflict with the United States. During the Persian Gulf War he denounced Saudi Arabia for allowing American troops into the country. After he was accused of masterminding bombings at U.S. military installations, the Saudis expelled him and revoked his citizenship.

In 1998 two American embassies in Africa were bombed. Bin Laden denied involvement, but the U.S. was convinced that he was behind the bombings. The U.S. fired missiles at one of bin Laden's training camps in Afghanistan. The U.S. also destroyed a Sudanese pharmaceutical plant that they claimed manufactured chemical weapons, but little evidence has been made public. The U.S. charged bin Laden with inciting violence and demanded that he be deported to the Untied States to stand trial. The Taliban party has since welcomed him to Afghanistan as a guest.

The Taliban's actions led to wide criticism. Most international human rights organizations have condemned the regime's harsh stance on women, particularly the Taliban's prohibition of education and medical care for Afghan women. Despite the 1997 United Nations agreement to open several schools for women, the Taliban has either placed strict limits on what those schools can teach, or has simply closed them once United Nations observers left Afghanistan. While the situation appeared to be improving toward the end of 1999, the liberty Afghan women enjoyed in the 1980s has disappeared under the increasing control and power of the Taliban government. The list of abuse toward Afghan women is appalling: women have been forced to stay at home unless accompanied by a male family member; women cannot ride the same bus as men; women cannot

be examined by a male physician; and few female physicians are permitted to practice medicine.

The consequence of violating these bans is quite severe. Reportedly, women have been shot to death for running home schools, or for attempting to leave Afghanistan without a male family member to accompany them. Women have also been beaten in public for such offense as accidentally permitting an ankle to show below a veil. International medical groups indicate that many Afghan women suffer mild to severe forms of depression as a result of these restrictions. In 1998, a survey reported that over 90 percent of Afghan women had little or no access to health care, and 50 percent had a serious illness but were prevented from obtaining treatment. Many of these same respondents reported moderate to severe physical abuse that would qualify—internationally—as human rights violations.

The United Nations began to insist strongly that the Taliban moderate its stance on women by permitting them to attend school and receive adequate medical attention. Taliban leaders agreed to open eleven schools for women and girls, but soon reneged on these and all other concessions. These actions may reflect Muhammed Omar's position, but some observers believe he took these steps in order to pacify the more radical wing of his coalition.

Osama bin Laden

Throughout 1998 and 1999, the United States and Afghanistan clashed over Afghanistan's harboring of what the United States called a dangerous terrorist. The United States claims that Osama bin Laden was the man responsible for the August 1998 terrorist bombings of U.S. embassies in Kenya and Tanzania. bin Laden, a Saudi multi-millionaire educated in the United States, has been involved in Islamic causes since the Soviet invasion of Afghanistan in 1979. During the Afghan revolution, bin Laden used his family's wealth (estimated to be US$5 billion) to support the *mujadin*. The *mujadin* were Afghan freedom fighters attempting to repel the Soviet Union and to topple the Communist regimes of Nur Mohammed Taraki, Babrak Karmal, and Dr. Najibullah. The United States supported the *mujadin*, but domestic and international pressures often interfered with U.S. aid. As a result, many *mujadin* leaders believed the U.S. helped prolong their ten-year struggle to defeat the Communists.

Osama bin Laden agreed that irregular U.S. aid had prolonged the war and, since the mid-1980s,

MAP OF TALIBAN/NIUFSA HOLDINGS IN AFGHANISTAN IN 1995. *(XNR Productions Inc.)*

has considered the United States to be an enemy of the Muslim religion. Bin Laden has reportedly supported actions against the United States in the Middle East, against American forces in Somalia, against the U.S. embassies in Kenya and Tanzania. In 1996, United States and Saudi Arabian officials reached an agreement regarding prosecution for his actions, so bin Laden fled to Afghanistan where he currently lives under the protection of the Taliban. While the Taliban has endured continued international pressure to turn bin Laden over to either the United States or an international tribunal, thus far Taliban leaders have refused. The situation between the U.S. and Afghanistan deteriorated further in August 1998, when the Clinton Administration ordered missile strikes against suspected bin Laden training camps in Afghanistan. Even though most of the missiles hit their targets, there is evidence that these attacks caused several civilian casualties, which resulted in political controversy in the United States.

In 1998 the United States received evidence that Osama bin Laden was in Afghanistan. The United States demanded that the Taliban government return bin Laden to the United States for trial. The leaders of the Taliban refused, claiming that bin Laden was a respected guest of Afghanistan. In retaliation, President Clinton issued Executive Order 13129 prohibiting all trade with the Taliban and in any Taliban controlled territory. The demand for bin Laden's extradition created a tense political situation in the Middle East. Saudi Arabia, a nation with close ties to the United States, discouraged the Clinton Administration from pushing for the extradition. The Saudis feared that a public trial in the United States of an Islamic leader who has "folk-hero" status in the Arab world would intensify conflict between the United States, the Saudi government, and Afghanistan. The Saudi government could not afford to prosecute bin Laden in Saudi Arabia, either, because of the support he has among the Saudi people.

Afghanistan also faces many problems by continuing to protect bin Laden. The Taliban, despite their control of about 90 percent of

MAP OF TALIBAN/NIUFSA HOLDINGS IN AFGHANISTAN IN 1996. *(XNR Productions Inc.)*

Afghanistan, remain an unrecognized political entity for most of the world. Only a few nations have recognized the Taliban government as legitimate. (The United States does not recognize the legitimacy of the Taliban government. The Taliban has attempted to gain international legitimacy, and in 1998 was making progress toward achieving diplomatic recognition as the legitimate government in Afghanistan.) However, currently Afghanistan effectively exists as a nation without representation in the international community. Harboring bin Laden and suffering U.S. attacks has further delayed recognition.

It was in 1999 that the Taliban claimed to control over 90 percent of Afghanistan, although General Dostum and General Massoud still maintain active opposition forces in the field. Several nations around Afghanistan have formally recognized the Taliban government as legitimate. However, the United States and the United Nations still prefer to deal with Rabbani's Jamait.

Taliban leaders see bin Laden as a hero—he fought with Afghanistan against the Soviets, and now he is leading an international attack against the United States and other nations exerting influence in the Middle East. Moreover, bin Laden is about the same age and has had the same experiences as the Taliban leadership. Support for bin Laden is indirectly a validation of their efforts.

RECENT HISTORY AND THE FUTURE

Since January of 1999, the Taliban has attempted to gain recognition as a true and legitimate state. As a result, the Taliban have moderated their support for bin Laden somewhat and have made efforts to use international rules and procedures. For example, when the United States asked Afghanistan to extradite bin Laden, the Taliban asked for evidence linking bin Laden to the embassy bombings. This request was a departure from the Taliban's previous unconditional support for bin Laden and his actions. The Taliban's political efforts during the February hijacking also reflect a change in tactics. First, the Taliban nego-

MAP OF TALIBAN/NIUFSA HOLDINGS IN AFGHANISTAN IN 1997. *(XNR Productions Inc.)*

tiated with the British for a peaceful settlement to the incident. Second, the Taliban attempted to manipulate public opinion by blaming the hijacking on its opponents, claiming the defections might be a publicity stunt. Third, they cooperated with several international organizations to provide the plane the hostages used to return home to Afghanistan and permitted members of the Western press to observe the homecoming. Finally, in a gesture of good will, the Taliban offered to repair the hijacked plane for Ariana Airlines. These efforts indicate that the Taliban is beginning to learn the lessons of political leadership, as it had learned the lessons of civil war.

The Taliban and its opponents generate the majority of their funds from the sale of opium. Afghanistan is the second largest producer of opium, behind Myanmar (formerly Burma). Afghanistan is also a major producer of hashish. Several military factions, including the Taliban, have built and maintain heroin laboratories. The degree of drug trafficking and drug money gener-

ated cannot be accurately estimated, but it is increasingly clear that Afghanistan's warring factions have come to rely on the drug trade for most of their support and funding and this trend seems unlikely to change soon. In addition, it seems likely that economic dislocations and inflation will continue to harm efforts to create wealth or to stabilize Afghanistan's currency.

The Taliban has a great deal to accomplish before the international community considers it a legitimate government. The international human rights community is likely to demand real reforms for women and changes in the Taliban's criminal justice system. Currently, Muhammed Omar seems unwilling to make even moderate change. Despite recent progress, the Taliban seems more interested in strengthening ties to other Islamic groups that in cooperating with the international community. The Taliban also faces stiff opposition from various freedom fighter factions. In 1997 the Rabbani, Massoud, Dostum and Hezmatyar factions formed an alliance known as

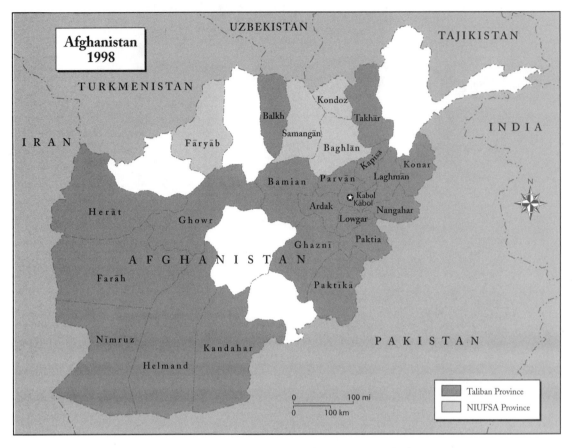

MAP OF TALIBAN/NIUFSA HOLDINGS IN AFGHANISTAN IN 1998. *(XNR Productions Inc.)*

the National Islamic United Front for Afghanistan (NIUFA), but this seems to be a union in name only. The various factions opposed to the Taliban's rule seem willing to fight a low-level guerilla war indefinitely.

BIBLIOGRAPHY

Ademec, Ludwig. *Historical Dictionary of Afghanistan.* Lanham, Md.: Scarecrow Press, 1997.

Auster, Bruce R. "The Recruiter for Hate," *U.S. News and World Report,* 31 August 1998.

Blystone, Richard. "Airline Head Says Hijacking may be Mass Asylum Bid." http://cnn.com/2000/ASIANOW/central (9 February 2000)

Gessner, Bradford D. "Mortality Rates, Causes of Death, and Health Status Among Displaced and Resident Populations of Kabul, Afghanistan," *Journal of the American Medical Association* 272, no. 5 (1994): 382–385.

Hammond, Thomas T. *Red Flag over Afghanistan: The Communist Coup, The Soviet Invasion and the Consequences.* Boulder, Colo.: Westview Press, 1984.

Harpviken, Krisitan Berg. *Political Mobilization among the Hazara of Afghanistan.* Oslo: University of Oslo Press, 1995.

Herbert, Bob. "Fleeing the Taliban," *New York Times,* 25 October 1999, sec. A31.

Keating, Michael. "A Women's Rights and Wrongs," *World Today* 53, no. 1 (1997): 10–12.

MacFarquhar, Emily. "Outlook: Afghanistan," *U.S. News and World Report,* 7 October 1998.

Maley, William, ed. *Fundamentalism Reborn? Afghanistan and the Taliban.* New York: New York University Press, 1998.

Manz, B.F. *Central Asia in Historical Perspective.* Boulder, Colo.: Westview Press, 1995.

Maroofi, Musa M. "The Afghan Taliban: Like it or Not, It Occupies Two-Thirds of Afghanistan and Shows No Sign of Weakening," *Washington Report,* April 1998, 47ff.

Olesen, Asta. *Islam and Politics in Afghanistan.* London: Curzon Press, 1995.

Rasekh, Zohra, Heidi Bauer, M. Michele Manos, Vincent Iacopino. "Women's Health and Human Rights in Afghanistan," *Journal of the American Medical Association* 280, no. 5 (1998): 449–455.

Rashid, Ahmed. "Sister Courage," *Far Eastern Economic Review* 160, no. 48 (1997): 30.

Rubin, Barnett R. "Afghanistan Under the Taliban," *Current History*, February 1999, 79–91.

"The Taliban Virus" *World Press Review* 45, no. 12 (1998): 6–7.

"United Kingdom," *CIA Fact Book*. http://www.odci.gov/cia/publications/factbook.

Wali, Sima. "Repatriation and the Reconstruction of Afghanistan: The Role of Women," *Migration World Magazine* 22, no. 4 (1994): 26ff.

Michael Bobic, Angelen Brookshire, Tim Curry, LaQuisha Hazel, Martha Mengistu, Joy Suza and Kathryn White

DEFORESTATION OF THE AMAZON: ECONOMICS AND BIODIVERSITY

THE CONFLICT

The Brazilian government, Brazilian companies, and multi-national organizations are developing the Amazon rainforest for its timber and other resources, which results in deforestation of the Amazon. In addition to the environmental consequences, the indigenous people are dying out and the long-term viability of the Amazonian rainforest's economy is in question. Small farmers, indigenous people, and environmentalists around the world are trying to limit development of the Amazon.

Economic

- Aggressive development hurts the long-term value of the rainforest and limits the economic viability of small farmers.

- Money for development is required for Brazilians now.

Environmental

- Destruction of the rainforest harms the overall well being of the planet and may destroy future resources, including plants that can provide medicine.

The Amazon Rainforest, which stretches across northern Brazil, Peru, Venezuela, Bolivia, Guyana, and Colombia, is the single largest tropical rainforest, accounting for thirty percent of all the tropical rainforests left in the world. It is estimated that the Amazon is home to one tenth of the world's plant and animal species. The deforestation of this region is perhaps the single greatest environmental risk facing the planet.

Although deforestation in the Amazon has been taking place for decades, the rate of that deforestation reached unprecedented levels in the mid-1990s. Globally, the rate of deforestation is 2.4 acres (one hectare) per second—two football fields of rainforest disappear every second. At that rate, seventy-eight million acres of rainforest (an area larger than the state of New Mexico) are destroyed each year. In Brazil alone, 5.4 million acres of rainforest a year have been destroyed for the past thirty years, decreasing the size of the Amazon by fifteen to eighteen percent. Since 1972 more than two hundred thousand square miles of the Amazon have been cleared; at this rate, the Amazon rainforest will be destroyed in eighty years, according to the environmental organization Greenpeace's 1999 annual report. Recent headlines have indicated that 1999 was a particularly bad year for the Amazon: fires burned out of control across the region and the economic crisis in Brazil disrupted several government and international programs to protect it. The destruction of the Amazon poses significant concerns for global policymakers due to the loss of numerous species, the emission of gases such as carbon dioxide, and the displacement or cultural extinction of countless tribes of indigenous people.

HISTORICAL BACKGROUND

History of Deforestation in Brazil

Before the Portuguese began to colonize Brazil in 1530, it is estimated that the indigenous population of the Brazilian rainforest was six to nine million. Today, less than two hundred thousand indigenous people are left. In the early colonial days, the vast majority of development occurred along Brazil's extensive coast. The greatest deforestation at that time occurred in the Mata Atlantica (Atlantic rain forest), which was cleared for settlements and large plantations of sugar cane, coffee, and cocoa. Only seven percent of the original Atlantic rain forest remains today.

Although there was some early gold and silver prospecting near the mouth of the Amazon as early as the seventeenth century, the Amazon rainforest as a resource remained largely undeveloped for centuries. There was simply little access to the vast untamed region. At the beginning of the twentieth century, the world markets increased their demand for rubber to make bicycle and car tires. Brazilians turned to the Amazon to meet this demand. Unemployed laborers from northeast Brazil began to extract rubber and Brazil nuts from huge forest trees. The laborers were hired by rubber barons who kept them virtually enslaved in indebtedness and poverty. To extract rubber the rubber tappers (as these migrants came to be known) would cut slices into rubber trees and collect the sap. Rubber tappers relied on the health of the forest for their livelihood, so they did not engage in any large-scale deforestation.

In the 1970s the military government of Brazil began to encourage development in the Amazon. Seen as an untapped source of boundless potential, the military government offered incentives for settlers to move into the Amazon rainforest. The government believed that they must develop the resources of the Amazon to help the Brazilian economy and to ensure that Brazil controlled its own territory. The comprehensive development strategy included the building of roads and other infrastructure in the region and tax incentives for cattle ranching, mining and land speculation. Additionally, the government saw the Amazon as a release for pressures caused by a growing urban population in southern Brazil, and developed a series of resettlement programs for urban poor and displaced farm workers. These migrants were encouraged to move into the forest and claim three times the land they could clear in a season. This approach to the development of the Amazon is similar to the U.S. policies regarding

CHRONOLOGY

1530 Portuguese colonize Brazil. Six to nine million indigenous people live in the rainforest.

1970 The government of Brazil begins to encourage development, including development of the Amazon. Projects include the Sobradinho regulating dam (1974), which is estimated to have displaced seventy thousand people.

1975 Chico Mendes starts the Rubber Trappers Union in response to the development and destruction of the forest.

Late 1980s International pressure against deforestation of the Amazon begins to grow.

1988 Chico Mendes is assassinated. Brazilian government, the World Bank, and the World Wildlife Fund announce a commitment to protect sixty-two million acres of Amazon by 2000. The Asian financial crisis hits Brazil. The International Monetary Fund provides a bail-out package that limits "unnecessary" spending, drastically reducing the environmental protection budget.

1992 The first U.N. Conference on the Environment and Development (the "Earth Summit") is held in Rio de Janeiro, Brazil, resulting in Agenda 21.

1994 Brazilian president Fernando Cardoso is elected.

1997–98 El Nino causes a drought that makes the Amazon more susceptible to forest fires.

1999 Fires burn in fifteen of Brazil's twenty-seven states.

2000 An estimated two hundred thousand indigenous people remain in the rainforest.

the American frontier in the nineteenth century. These policies resulted in the massive deforestation in the Amazon that continues to this day.

In the late 1980s international pressure to stop the deforestation of the Amazon began to grow. Internal resistance from indigenous groups and the rubber tappers' union was also on the rise. The military government was also under increasing pressure from a failed economy and a growing gap between the rich and the poor in Brazil. This dissatisfaction led to a new constitution in 1988 and the democratic election of civilian president Fernando Collor de Melo. Although this new government had inherited a host of problems that

THIS AREA OF THE AMAZON RAINFOREST HAS BEEN CLEARED FOR CATTLE OR FARMING USING THE "SLASH-AND-BURN" TECHNIQUE. *(Corbis. Reproduced by permission.)*

made it very unstable, it did begin to focus on the preservation of the Amazon region. In June of 1992, Brazil's government was so interested in addressing environmental concerns that it hosted the first ever Earth Summit in Rio de Janeiro, Brazil. Representatives attended the conference from 182 countries and several international organizations such as the World Bank, Amnesty International and Greenpeace. The outcome of the summit was a series of agreements on greenhouse gas emissions, protection of the rainforest, and sustainable development in developing nations. As a result, Brazil received promises of large sums of money to help with the fight to preserve the Amazon.

In 1994 the current president of Brazil, Fernando Cardoso, was elected. Under Cardoso's leadership, Brazil's economy prospered once again, and many tax incentives and resettlement programs that had caused so much deforestation were rescinded. However, Cardoso believed that the Amazon provided untold riches to help with the economic recovery, and so he continued to make arrangements for infrastructure such as roads and dams to be built in the Amazon basin. When the stock market crash of 1998 reached Brazil, the results were devastating. The government of Brazil felt it could not continue to pay to protect the Amazon and its people, and also saw the Amazon

as the source of much needed resources and development capital. Many protection programs were canceled outright, and those that remain had little money for enforcement.

Like most environmental issues the causes and consequences of deforestation in the Amazon are rather complex. The sources of deforestation include development projects, international financial crises, governmental policies, logging and mining practices, accessibility to forestland, poverty and population pressure, crop choice, and climatic conditions. Each of these contributes in a very real way to the problem of deforestation.

Development Projects

During the 1970s and 1980s, the military government in Brazil made a conscious effort to develop and modernize the Brazilian economy using all available resources within the country including the rainforest of the Amazon basin. For the Brazilian government, the control of the rainforest region was absolutely vital to national security and development plans. They were concerned that the rainforest was being taken over by international environmentalists who wished to prohibit any development. The control of the rainforest was perceived as a key sign of Brazil's sovereignty (the ability to rule over a given territory). To achieve control of the largely undeveloped rainforest, the government began a series of development projects funded by the World Bank and the Inter-American Development Bank. Dozens of large-scale projects such as dam building, mining operations, and road construction were undertaken to build up the infrastructure of the region. Although there were environmental impact assessments made on each project, some consequences were not foreseen.

The Carajas Iron Ore project (1982) is an example of a development project that contributed significantly to deforestation in the region. The original design of the World Bank-funded project was to develop a diversified economy in the Carajas region in the states of Para and Maranhao in northern Brazil. The multifaceted project included funding for railroads and roads networks, mining of iron ore, bauxite, manganese and copper, factories to produce aluminum and pig iron, cash crop plantations for palm oil, soybeans and rice, and thirty thousand acre parcels of land to be cleared for cattle production. The new rail and road networks increased accessibility to the region for even more unemployed farmers and ranchers who engaged in slash-and-burn tactics to clear the forests for farming. While the agricultural aspects of the project required immediate deforestation for land use, the long-term consequences of the mining and manufacturing operations had more devastating effects on the forests. The smelting factories had been designed to be powered by oil, but when the price of oil rose on the international market, oil was no longer affordable. To maintain the profit margin of the operation, the miners turned to charcoal from the rainforest as an energy source—causing massive deforestation in the area.

Since the OPEC oil embargo of 1973, high oil prices have forced Brazil to begin to develop local sources of power by building large dams throughout the Amazon region. Development projects funded by the World Bank, such as the Sobradinho regulating dam (1974) were intended to provide hydroelectric power and irrigation to the farmers of the eastern Amazon. It is estimated that this dam project displaced as many as seventy thousand people living in the area and destroyed thousands of acres of rainforest by the lake created behind the dam. The development of the Amazon basin encouraged more people to move to the area thus increasing population pressure on the rainforest, and furthering the deforestation of the area.

Financial Crises

The Brazilian government began to slow its development plans during the 1990s, and institut-ed a number of environmental reforms to protect the rainforest. In April of 1998, the Brazilian government announced its commitment to join the World Bank and the World Wildlife Fund in a multi-million dollar effort to protect sixty-two million acres of the Amazon rainforest by 2000.

Unfortunately, later that same year the Asian financial crisis crippled the Brazilian economy and altered these plans. The International Monetary Fund (IMF) was forced to put together a forty-one billion dollar bailout package in November of 1998 to save Brazil's economy from collapse. In order to make sure Brazil was able to pay back this emergency loan, the IMF insisted that Brazil adopt "structural adjustment" programs that limited the amount of "unnecessary" spending done by the government. The government proposed to reduce its environmental protection budget by sixty-six percent. Since the Brazilian government did not have the money to enforce new logging and mining bans, they rescinded many of the restrictions on logging and mining. These changes came at a time when the World Watch Institute reported that logging in the Amazon had jumped by thirty percent in 1998. Similarly, structural adjustment programs have enticed Indonesia to lift its ban on logging exports and to slash its export tax from two hundred to thirty percent. Indonesia is also planning to expand its cash crop production by over three million acres (Knight and Aslam 1999). The weak Brazilian economy not only forced a reduction in the money available for forest protection programs, but it also increased the desire to exploit the forest resources in order to earn hard currency through international trade in timber and mineral resources.

Logging and Mining

Logging has been associated with high rates of deforestation in the Amazon for the past thirty years. The environmental group Greenpeace suggests that logging and the road-building to access the resources caused eighty percent of the deforestation in the Amazon. While other sources suggest that the percentage of logging is not quite that high, logging is one of the most important reasons for deforestation in the Amazon. Logging operations in the Amazon continue to increase as other rainforest resources around the world are exhausted. Although an international ban on trade of many species of rainforest hardwoods exists, there is still a tremendous amount of illegal logging. The Brazilian government estimates that as much as eighty percent of the logging done in the Amazon is illegal. The Brazilian Amazon covers 5.3 million square kilometers (roughly the size of Western

Europe), however, the Brazilian Environmental Agency (Ibama) has only twelve hundred technicians to police the whole region. In addition to illegal logging, a variety of products such as charcoal, cardboard and plywood are made legally from logging practices in the Amazon. Asian companies such as Samling Malaysia and the Malasian company WTK have already bought over three million acres for logging and plan to buy another nineteen million acres in the next few years. Currently the Brazilian government does not regulate the amount of forest foreign companies can own.

Mining of precious metals also contributes to the deforestation occurring in the Amazon. The discovery of gold in the upper Amazon basin in the late 1970s sparked one of the largest gold rushes in history. Many miners and mining companies hoping to strike it rich pushed deeper and deeper into the forest in search of precious metals. Brazil is now the world's fourth largest producer of gold; most of this comes from the Amazon region. In order to extract the gold from the surrounding rock, miners use mercury, which is a highly toxic substance posing serious risks to humans and animals, as well as to the environment around the mines. It is estimated that for every pound of gold produced, two pounds of mercury enters the environment.

Government Programs

Many programs instituted by the Brazilian government, particularly in the 1970s and 1980s, have played a role in the deforestation of the Amazon. In an attempt to develop the region, the government offered a number of tax incentives and subsidies to those willing to invest in the Amazon either through land speculation (buying land now in hopes that the price increases in the future) or cattle ranching. Both land speculation and cattle ranching would have been unprofitable in the rainforest without government help. Deforestation occurs when these cattle ranchers clear hundreds of thousands of acres through slash-and-burn techniques in order to provide a range for their cattle. (Slash-and-burn clearing involves cutting down all the tress and burning the land clear of all vegetation.) The rangeland that is created from burnt rainforest is poor in quality and cannot feed the cattle for long; so more forest must be cleared in the future. In the early 1990s, the government stopped many of these incentive programs, but the international market for beef still entices many to raise cattle on deforested lands because the land is cheap.

For investors, land speculation was profitable in the 1970s and 1980s due to the tax breaks given by the government to encourage development, and the high inflation rate that dominated the Brazilian economy at the time. Land prices skyrocketed when World Bank-financed roads were built near the property. In an attempt to resettle the unemployed urban poor from the cities of Sao Paulo and Rio de Janeiro, the government offered incentives for small farmers to develop rainforest land. Under the program, a person could establish their right to land in the forest by clear cutting and developing the land. This encouraged millions to move to the edge of the Amazon and recklessly clear forest through slash-and-burn techniques. The impact of these resettlement programs on the rainforest in the state of Rondonia was significant: in 1975 the annual deforestation rate in the state was 0.3 percent, but by 1988 that rate had risen to 23.7 percent (Anderson 1990).

Access

Increased access to the remote parts of the rainforest has also significantly contributed to deforestation. As new roads are built more poor farmers and migrants move into the rainforest area. The World Bank funded highway (BR-364) attracted 200,000 migrants into the forest along its route in 1989 alone (Miller and Tangley 1991). This trend has been repeated over and over again throughout the Amazon as new roads and rail lines increase access to the undeveloped and forested parts of the Amazon basin. Much of the deforestation caused by the small-scale farmer's slash-and-burn techniques is not accounted for by satellite imagery used to estimate deforestation rates. According to a study conducted by Woods Hole Research Center, the extent of deforestation might be twice that previously thought (published in the April 8, 1999 issue of Nature). These new farmers attempt to plant crops on unusually poor soil, which is exhausted in only a few years, thus driving them further into the forest in search of new land. The land that is cleared at the edge of the forest is also more susceptible to fire in the future from the buildup of dead and dry material (Cochrane 1999). As more of the forest is exposed through road building and agricultural practices, the greater deforestation, fire hazards and greenhouse gas emissions increasingly become concerns.

Agriculture

Another source of the deforestation in the Amazon is cash crop production. Cash crops are those agricultural staple products such as coffee, tea, and soybeans that are produced in large quan-

AREAS OF LUSH, HEAVILY-VEGETATED RAINFOREST SUCH AS THIS ARE GROWING LESS AND LESS COMMON IN BRAZIL DUE TO MISUSE. *(Corbis. Reproduced by permission.)*

tities for sale in world markets. The production of cash crops contributes to deforestation directly as farmers employ slash-and-burn techniques on forests to clear them for cash crop production. Cash crops also impact deforestation indirectly as plantations in southern Brazil employ fewer people on the land that has traditionally been used for subsistence agriculture. Those people are displaced and move to the forest to clear land and farm. It is estimated that as many as twenty-five percent of the migrants in the forest are displaced by the conversion of land in southern Brazil to cash crop production (World Resources 1990-1991). According to the Amazon Work Group a new surge in soybean production by a company called Maggi in the southeastern part of Amazonas State could cause the deforestation of 2.5 million acres. Many small-scale farmers are attracted to cash crop production because of high world market prices for those crops; if those prices fall, farmers abandon these fields and move further into the forest, clearing more land for subsistence farming to survive. They leave the original cash-crop lands fallow in hopes that the prices will rise again and they can resume cultivation. The government used heavy subsidies to encourage the cultivation of soybeans in the 1970s to earn money from exports. During that decade the land under soybean cultivation increased six fold. Brazil became the second largest soybean producer in the world by the early

1980s, accounting for nearly half of the world's supply of the product (Chomentowski et al. 1994).

Climate

Finally, climactic and environmental conditions have significantly contributed to the recent increased rate of deforestation in the Amazon, and the devastating fires that burned out of control across the region in 1999. Forest fires are a fact of life in the Amazon; however, the climactic effect known as El Nino contributed to a prolonged drought from 1997 to 1998 that increased the vulnerability of the rainforest to huge fires. Traditional slash-and-burn techniques employed in forest region farming and a lack of funding for fire suppression (due to budget cuts brought on by the economic crisis of 1998) combined to spell disaster for the forest. Fires burned out of control in fifteen of Brazil's twenty-seven states in 1999. The fires of 1988 and 1999 destroyed an area of the rainforest the size of the country of Belgium.

Consequences of Deforestation

As the trees are removed in a rainforest, there is less transpiration (the releasing of moisture from a tree's exchange of carbon dioxide and oxygen). This means each year less moisture is released into the atmosphere by the forests, thus decreasing rainfall and furthering drought-like conditions

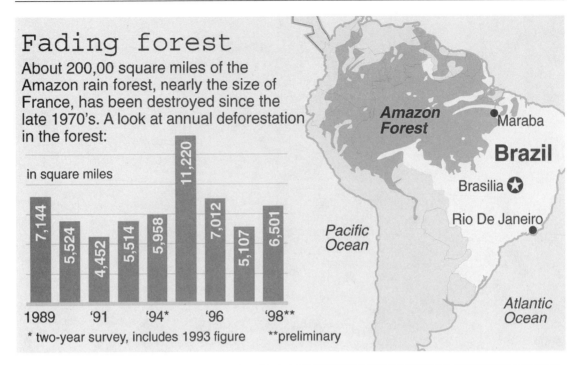

THIS GRAPH SHOWS JUST HOW MUCH OF THE AMAZON RAINFOREST HAS BEEN CONSUMED IN THE PAST DECADE. *(AP/Wide World Photos. Reproduced by permission.)*

across the region. Additionally, most of the nutrients in the rainforest are contained above the soil in the constant process of growth and decay within the forest. When the forest is burned and cleared for agriculture, the remaining soil is of poor quality with few nutrients. Within a few years, the soil is completely exhausted and cannot support crops. The farmers are forced to clear more forests for new lands to plant crops and the deforestation continues. The trees of the forest are also essential to control soil erosion. When the trees are removed, there is nothing to stop the soil from washing away into the rivers. Soil erosion results in the death of fish in those rivers and the eventual filling up of the reservoirs behind new hydroelectric dams in the region. Once the reservoirs are filled with silt (soil deposits) the dams can no longer produce energy and more must be built to maintain the supply of energy for a growing population in the region. More people and forests are displaced with each replacement dam.

The burning of rainforest significantly increases the amount of carbon dioxide (the primary greenhouse gas) released into the atmosphere. The forests in the Amazon basin—while intact—absorb a tremendous amount of carbon dioxide already in the atmosphere. The forests act as a "sink" for greenhouse gases by taking in carbon dioxide and releasing oxygen as they transpire. Some international agreements such as Article 17 of the recent Kyoto protocol on global warming recognize this important function of the Amazon. This protocol sets up the possibility of environmental credits given to Brazil for the protection of the Amazon because of its vital role in balancing the atmosphere's concentration of carbon dioxide.

Another significant consequence of current deforestation in the Amazon is the loss of significant numbers of plant and animal species. Scientists are unclear as to how many species exist in the world (estimates range from seven to twenty million), however, most scientists believe that the Amazon has the largest concentration of species on the entire planet. Species loss is a major consequence of deforestation for a number of reasons. Biotic regions exist in a delicate balance with all species playing a particular role in the health of the overall system; once a species is extinct it can no longer fill this niche and the system as a whole is threatened. Once extinct, a species is lost forever. Currently the world's food supply is based on nine species (Economist 21 March 1998); if disease or changing conditions destroys one of these species, then the biological bank of species in the Amazon might be crucial to ensure food to billions of humans. The Irish potato famine is only one example of the consequences of an over reliance on one species. Species in the rainforest also are a possible source for medicine. In Madagascar, the periwinkle flower has been used to produce medicines that significantly decrease or eliminate certain forms of leukemia.

Major Figures in the Struggle over the Amazon

The government of Brazil has played a major role in both the deforestation and attempts to preserve the Amazon. The government has faced overwhelming pressure from all sides for the last thirty years. In the 1970s and 1980s, the government of Brazil was in the hands of the military. The generals described the undeveloped Amazon in much the same way leaders of the United States viewed the American west during the nineteenth century. The Amazon represented a large area of immense natural resources within the sovereign territory of the country of Brazil. Faced with a growing population in eastern and southern Brazil, the military government saw the rainforest as an opportunity to give their crowded population a new chance. They established reservations for the native population, but just as in the United States, this did not stop conflict and abuse in the frontier. Large-scale cattle barons and small-scale homesteading farmers populated the American west. This was the development plan for the Amazon as well.

The military government also felt that an unpopulated, undeveloped Amazon invited neighboring states and the world community as a whole to take land from Brazil. To prevent the land from being taken it must be developed and this meant some deforestation would have to take place. The enormity of the area made it easy to assume that these actions would not do any long-term damage to the rainforest, an attitude that is still widely held among Brazilians today.

When Fernando Cardoso was elected president in the early 1990s, Brazil had begun to realize that unchecked development and exploitation of Amazonian resources could indeed harm the entire rainforest. He began to search out development assistance that would help preserve the unique resources of the rainforest and the people who have historically inhabited those forests. Special parks and extractive reserves (lands held in common for sustainable harvest of forest products such as rubber and Brazil nuts) were set up and millions of acres of the forest were set aside for protection. Many tax incentives for deforesting activities were renounced and fines were increased. Unfortunately, there was little money in the Brazilian budget to enforce all of these new laws. When the economy took a serious downturn in 1998, ambitious projects proposed by Cardoso to save the forest had to be put on hold or dismantled.

The indigenous people are those natives who have lived in the rainforest for thousands of years. Their cultures are based on the forest and the health of the forest is vital to the health of most tribes. Before the Europeans arrived in Brazil, it is estimated that there were as many as six to nine million natives in the rainforest; estimates, today, are barely 200,000. The tribes have been wiped out by increasing encroachment and deforestation of the Amazon. Their cultures have been eroded by prolonged contact with migrants moving into the region to exploit the resources. Diseases previously unknown in the tribes have taken a heavy toll as the indigenous people come into increased contact with "outsiders." In order to protect some of their forestlands, special reservations have been established; however, this has not stopped a tremendous amount of violence and bloodshed as natives clash with miners, ranchers, and loggers.

In the beginning of the twentieth century, many poor Brazilians from the northeast moved into the forest to harvest rubber by tapping the rubber trees, which need a healthy forest around them to survive. The harvest of rubber by the tappers did minimal harm to the forest. In time, these tappers began to peacefully coexist with the indigenous people of the forest, and they developed a culture of their own.

It is into the rubber tapper culture that Francisco "Chico" Mendes was born in 1944 in Xapuri, Acre in the western Amazon. Mendes's father was a rubber tapper and Mendes took up this line of work at the age of nine. The tappers were often exploited by their bosses and pressured off their lands by the expansion of farmers and cattle ranchers. There was no formal education for any of the tappers or their children until 1970. Mendes began to organize the rubber tappers to work together to protect their forestland from the encroachment of roads and ranchers. In 1975 he started the Rubber Tappers Union in the state of Acre. He founded the National Council of Rubber Tappers in 1985. The tappers struggle became international news with the help of sympathetic media reporters such as Stephen Schwartzman (now a senior scientist at the Environmental Defense Fund). Mendes received two international environmental awards and addressed the United Nations General Assembly on forest preservation. Mendes' work was instrumental in increasing global awareness of the issue of Amazonian defor-

Francisco "Chico" Mendes

1944–1988 Chico Mendes was a *seringueiro* (rubber tapper) who became Brazil's most famous crusader for the protection of the rainforest. Born in 1944, near Xapuri, Brazil, Mendes, like his entire family, began working at the age of ten, learning to extract sap without killing the tree.

When Brazil opened the Amazon to development in the early 1970s, millions of acres of rainforest were cleared for cattle grazing. In 1975 Mendes founded the Rural Workers' Union of Xapuri, linking protection of the rainforest and workers' rights. Mendes and the Union organized mass protests, pioneering the use of non-violent resistance to prevent deforestation. Lead by Mendes, *seringueiros* and their families would form human barriers of up to a thousand people to block the bulldozers and chainsaws of developers.

Mendes also traveled extensively, speaking of the plight of the rainforest and its indigenous people, plants and animals, and convincing international developers to halt slash-and-burn development. He lived under constant threat of death. On December 22, 1988, he was murdered by cattle ranchers in his home. His death mobilized international awareness of rainforest destruction, which pressured the Brazilian government to set aside several million acres as protected forest area.

estation. In 1988 Mendes successfully led the Xapuri Rural Workers Union in an effort to stop cattle rancher Darly Alves from deforesting lands that the tappers were hoping to make into an extractive reserve. Darly Alves' son assassinated Mendes outside his home in December of 1988. Both father and son were convicted of murder in 1990, but escaped from prison in 1993. The government of Brazil set up an extractive reserve in Mendes' honor covering over two million acres. In this reserve, the rubber tappers can continue to harvest rubber from the intact forest. They also harvest Brazil nuts for sale to the international market and companies such as Ben and Jerry's Ice Cream (for use in the Rainforest Crunch ice cream).

The principal farmers involved in the Amazon issue are the large-scale cattle ranchers and cash crop plantation owners and the small-scale subsistence farmers. Two percent of landowners in Brazil control over sixty percent of the land (World Resources 1990–1991). Estates over twenty-five hundred acres (used for cattle ranching and cash crop production) account for less than one percent of the registered rural properties but occupy forty-three percent of the land (Worcman 1990). Such farmers insist on their right to develop their own land and to respond to the demands of the Brazilian and international markets for their goods. The small-scale farmers are responsible for a significant portion of the current deforestation as they clear land to grow crops to feed their families. Fleeing from overcrowded urban poverty or displaced by the loss of their farmlands in southern Brazil, these farmers deforest the Amazon to survive. Extreme poverty has become a significant factor in the destruction of the Amazon. Multinational corporations are contributing to deforestation at an unprecedented rate, but a significant amount of the devastation comes from small scale logging operations and wildcat mines driven by the same poverty that encourages millions to engage in small-scale farming in the forest.

Set up after World War II, the World Bank and the International Monetary Fund (IMF) were intended to help the world develop and stabilize trade. These two institutions have very different objectives. The IMF is designed to help out in short-term crises to stabilize threatened economies. The IMF often requires very harsh economic actions within the country intended to help the economy recover quickly, so no long-term damage is sustained. The theory behind IMF loans is that if the crisis is allowed to go unchecked, the poverty of the nation will do more damage to health, welfare, and the environment than the structural adjustment programs ever could. Thus, supporters would argue that even though the IMF programs are blamed for huge environmental setbacks in forest protection in Brazil and Indonesia, the consequences of no action could be far worse in the long run. The World Bank is designed to give more long-term development loans. In the first three decades of its existence, the Bank favored giving loans to large-scale development projects such as dam building or road construction or the Carajas project. Recently the Bank has become more aware of unintended environmental impacts of its projects. This new awareness has prompted the Bank to begin to fund more small-scale local projects and preservation projects such as the 1998 joint project with the World Wildlife Fund and the Brazilian government to establish a sixty-two million acre preserve in the Amazon.

ANOTHER UNFORTUNATE ASPECT TO THE DESTRUCTION OF THE RAINFOREST IS THE LOSS OF RARE AND/OR ENDANGERED SPECIES SUCH AS THIS JAGUAR. *(AP/Wide World Photos. Reproduced by permission.)*

There are a number of non-governmental organizations (NGO), domestic and international, involved in the conflict over the deforestation of the Amazon. Perhaps the most significant domestic NGOs struggling against deforestation are the rubber tappers' unions. Local unions such as Xapuri Rural Workers Union and national unions such as the National Council of Rubber Tappers are actively engaged in slowing the destruction of the rainforest. Their products, rubber and Brazil nuts, can only be harvested within an intact ecosystem. If the forests are destroyed, their livelihood is also likely to be destroyed. In addition to the rubber tappers, there are several Brazilian environmental organizations working to preserve the forest. International environmental organizations such as Greenpeace, World Wildlife Fund, the Rainforest Action Network, and Friends of the Earth have been involved in the conflict over the forest for decades. Recently many of these organizations have begun to team up with developers to establish patterns of sustainable harvest. The recent joint efforts of the World Wildlife Fund and the World Bank have proved a successful model of cooperation, threatened only by the changing international economic situation. Another international NGO involved in rainforest preservation is the U.S.-based Cultural Survival.

This organization is concerned with the impact of deforestation on indigenous tribes in the Amazon. The spread of development and deforestation has an extremely destabilizing effect on native populations—often displacing them from traditional lands, or diluting their culture through interaction. Cultural Survival has been active for several years protecting the homelands of the tribes, and establishing rural cooperatives so that local people might compete effectively in the marketing of potential products from the forest.

The destruction of the Amazon rainforest has clear international implications, not only because the Amazon covers an area that includes parts of several countries, but also because many of the causes and solutions to deforestation take place beyond the borders of Brazil. In the 1960s the eight countries whose territory contains part of the Amazon rainforest signed the Amazon Cooperation Treaty that was intended to resolve disputes and establish cooperation around the resource. In 1983 the major producing and consuming nations of tropical timber signed the International Tropical Timber Agreement that established the International Tropical Timber Organization (ITTO). The goal of the ITTO is to "facilitate discussion, consultation and international co-operation on issues relating to the international trade and utilization of tropical timber and the sustainable management of its resource base" (ITTO Mission Statement). This organization provides a forum for continued cooperation on an international level regarding the timber trade, which is one of the principal causes of deforestation in the Amazon and around the world.

In June of 1992, leaders from 182 countries around the world met in Rio de Janeiro, Brazil for the U.N. Conference on the Environment and Development also known as the "Earth Summit." Hosting the Earth Summit showed the new Brazilian government's commitment to addressing many of the serious environmental harms of the prior two decades. The forty-chapter document that emerged from this summit is known as Agenda 21 and was signed by most of the countries participating. Agenda 21 is a comprehensive agreement to address many of the world's most pressing environmental concerns without destroying the livelihoods of those who depend on natural resources. Many promises have been made, and some positive steps have been taken, especially in the area of deforestation. However, deforestation continues to be a major issue facing the world.

RECENT HISTORY AND THE FUTURE

Headlines around the world have clearly indicated that the problem of deforestation in the Amazon and elsewhere has been getting worse in the past decade. Record levels of deforestation have been recorded in 1997 and 1998, with all indications that the trend will continue. Recent economic problems in Brazil have curbed government spending to stop deforestation. Economic problems have also increased the pressure on the forest by the poor and others who wish to develop the forest in order to earn money.

In the near term, it is likely that deforestation of the Amazon will continue at an unsustainable level. However, there also appears to be signs of hope for the forest. The present government of Brazil is committed to more sustainable development of forest resources and preservation of significant portions of the remaining forest through national parks, extractive reserves, and indigenous reservations.

The world community is not likely to drop such a visible and vital environmental issue, and will continue to apply pressure and aid to help stop deforestation. Recently the seven richest nations in

the world (the G-7) have committed to the "Pilot Program for Protection of the Tropical Forest in Brazil." This program offers much needed funding and assistance to the government of Brazil in its effort to stop illegal timber and mining operations, and provide poverty relief programs for the poor who would otherwise turn to the forest. The United States is sharing more satellite and monitoring technology to help better assess the extent and rate of damage.

Finally, many new resources are being developed from the rainforest such as pharmaceuticals and medicines that might hold the cure for a number of diseases. These new medicines are developed from unique species of plants in the forest, which require a healthy forest to exist. The economic possibilities of medicines and increased tourism to a healthy forest are projected to be far superior to the present uses of the land for timber, cash crop and cattle production. Perhaps the economic pressures that have made such a devastating impact on the rainforest will also be the forces that work to preserve the forests in the future.

BIBLIOGRAPHY

Anderson, Anthony B. "Smokestacks in the Rainforest: Industrial Development and Deforestation in the Amazon Basin," *World Development* 18 (1990): 1191-1205.

Chomentowski, W.H., D.L. Skole, W.A. Salas and A.D. Nobre. "Physical and Human Dimensions of Deforestation in Amazonia," *Bioscience* 44 (1944): 314–322.

"Fires Burning in Much of Country," *Noti-Sur: Latin American Political Affairs*, 10 September 1999.

Flavin, Christopher. "The Legacy of Rio," *State of the World: 1997*. New York: W.W. Norton & Co.

Houghton, R.A. "Tropical Deforestation and Atmospheric Carbon Dioxide," *Climate Change* 19 (1991): 99-118.

Knight, Danielle and Abid Aslam. "Brazil's Bailout is Environmental Time Bomb," *Inter Press Service*, 18 March 1999.

Miller, Kenton and Laura Tangley. *Trees of Life*. Boston: Beacon Press, 1991.

Ossava, Mario. "Environment-Brazil: Soy Production Spreads, Threatens Amazon," *Inter Press Service*, 10 September 1999.

Ossava, Mario. "Brazil-Environment: Glimmer of Hope for Amazon," *Inter Press Service*, 17 December 1999.

Runyan, Curtis. "Amazon Hatchet Job," *World Watch* 12 (1999): 8.

Stone, Roger D. "The Denuded Earth: What is to be Done?" *World Policy Journal* 15 (1998): 50-57.

"Stumped by Trees," *Economist*, 21 March 1998.

Tautz, Carlos. "The Asian Invasion: Asian Multinationals Come to the Amazon," *Multinational Monitor* 18 (1997): 15–16.

"Trees and Laws," *Economist,* 7 February 1998.

Worcman, N.B. "Brazil's Thriving Environmental Movement," *Technology Review* 93 (1990): 42-52.

World Resources 1990-1991. New York: World Resources Institute, 1991.

Timothy T. Casey

BOSNIA-HERZEGOVINA: CIVIL WAR

THE CONFLICT

With the disintegration of the Communist bloc, the Republic of Yugoslavia deteriorated into nationalist and ethnic warfare. The various ethnic groups—including the Serbs, Croats, and Albanians—were supported by varying internal allegiances and foreign powers. Ultimately, the United Nations intervened to stop the warfare and alleged "ethnic cleansing."

Ethnic-Religious

* Conflict between Serbs (Orthodox Christians), Croats (Catholics), and Albanians (Muslims) in the Former Republic of Yugoslavia.

Political

* Serbia wanted to keep the former Yugoslavia together; Serbia had a vision of a "Greater Serbian" empire.

* Croats, Slovenians, and Albanians wanted independence.

* Europe and the United States wanted to avoid brutal ethnic warfare in Europe, and to avoid looking like they are doing nothing to protect a vulnerable people.

In 1992 television and newspaper audiences in many countries around the world saw horrific pictures of men, women and children held captive and apparently starving in Balkan concentration camps. The scenes recalled the German death camps of World War II in which millions of people died. European and U.S. diplomats attempted to understand how this could be happening *again* in civilized Europe. Eventually, the governments of the United States and Europe intervened with military force through the United Nations and NATO.

HISTORICAL BACKGROUND

A multi-religious Bosnia-Herzegovina (or Bosnia) once existed as a province, first under the Muslim Ottoman empire and, later, under the Catholic Austrian Habsburgs. Both the Ottomans and the Habsburgs ruled multi-ethnic empires in the Balkans for centuries. But in the nineteenth century Serbian nationalists began to see Bosnia as part of their ideal nation-state: a Greater Serbia or Yugoslavia.

In 1878 Serbia gained official independence, becoming effectively autonomous from Ottoman Turk rule and established as an Austrian protectorate. In 1908 Bosnia was annexed by Austria-Hungary in order to prevent Serbia from taking control of it. Bosnia was to remain a key issue of contention during the coming world wars.

At the Paris Peace Conferences of 1919 Austria-Hungary was disassembled. The new southern Slav Kingdom of Yugoslavia was created under a Serbian monarch, with an assembly in the Serbian capital of Belgrade. Yugoslavia included three predominant religions, Eastern Orthodoxy,

CHRONOLOGY

1914–18 World War I ravages Europe. Twenty-five percent of the Serb population dies. Many Serbs demand primary status in new state, since they suffered the most during the war.

1919 Royal Yugoslavia is founded.

1919–1941 Fierce internal political debates in Yugoslavia fuel minor rebellions and assassinations but very few instances of "ethnic cleansing."

1941 The Nazis invades Yugoslavia; the Croatian Ustasa faction sides with the invaders.

1944–45 Communist Yugoslavia is formed.

1948 Tito and Stalin split. Yugoslavia becomes "unaligned" with either the United States or the Soviet Union.

1968 Albanians protest in Kosovo.

1969 Slovene "Highway Crisis" over economic development occurs.

1971 Major protests in Croatian government over economic development take place.

1974 A new constitution grants Kosovo and Vojvoidina autonomy and decentralized power to republics. Major foreign borrowing begins.

1980 Tito dies.

1981 Government begins discussing major economic reforms. Albanian protests break out. The unemployment rate in Kosovo is nearly three hundred percent higher than the national rate.

1982–1989 The living standard is falling rapidly in all of Yugoslavia.

1987 Milosevic gains national attention by defending Serbian rights.

1989 Milosevic removes Kosovo's (and then Vojvoidina's) autonomy and institutes martial law. The fall of the Communist regimes in Eastern Europe begin. Inflation is at two thousand percent.

1990 Slovenia withdraws from Communist party elections in Slovenia and Croatia. Tudjman takes power in Croatia. The U.S. CIA warns of impending civil war in Yugoslavia.

1991 Slovenia and Croatia declare independence. Fighting breaks out between JNA and Slovene militias and in Croatia between Serb irregulars and Croatian police. The European Community recognizes Slovenia and Croatia. Albanians declares Kosovo independent. The United Nations begins attempts at a cease-fire in Croatia. Serbs in Krajina declare independence from Croatia. Serbs in Bosnia declare "Serbska Republika" independent from Bosnia.

1991–92 Protests against Milosevic take place.

1992 United Nations brokers a cease-fire in Croatia. UNPROFOR mission begins in Croatia. Some fighting in Croatia spills over into Bosnia. The majority of Croats and Muslims vote for independence. Bosnia declares independence. Fighting breaks out in Bosnia. The European Community and the United States recognize Bosnia. The United Nations places sanctions on the FR Yugoslavia. Serbs control about seventy percent of Bosnian territory. UNPROFOR mission is extended to Bosnia for humanitarian purposes. No-Fly Zone is declared in Bosnia. UNPROFOR troops are stationed in Macedonia.

1993 The United Nations and the European Community attempts negotiations on the Vance-Owens plan to end the violence in Bosnia. NATO planes begin to enforce the No-Fly Zone at the U.N.'s request. The U.N. declare six Muslim cities in the east of Bosnia to be "Safe Areas."

1994 The EU and U.N. push negotiations on the Vance-Stoltenberg Plan for Bosnia. A mortar attack on a market place kill sixty-eight and wound two hundred people, leading to pressure on NATO and Clinton to "do something" to save lives. The U.S. brokers an agreement between Muslims and Croats against the Serbs. NATO air strikes against Serb troops attack Goradze "Safe Area."

1995 Former U.S. president Jimmy Carter negotiates a four-month truce in Bosnia at the request of the warring parties. Croatians overruns western Slovenia and thousands of Serbs flee. NATO bombs Serb artillery; in response, Serbs take three hundred fifty U.N. troops hostage. Srebrenica and Zepa "Safe Areas" fall to the Serbs. NATO threaten air strikes in response to any attack on Safe Areas. Croats seize Serb-held areas in Krajina; tens of thousands of Serbs flee. A cease-fire is called in Bosnia. Dayton Peace agreement is signed between Croats, Muslims, and Serbs in Bosnia.

1996–97 More major protests take place against Milosevic.

1997–98 Albanian guerrillas launch major attacks on Yugoslav police. KLA and FR Yugoslavia begin heavy fighting in Kosovo.

Roman Catholicism and Islam, and eight political regions with various linguistic and religious minorities. Most people spoke Serbo-Croatian but wrote in either the Cyrillic or the Roman alphabet. Catholics, mostly Croatians and Slovenians, dominated the economy, while Orthodox Serbs controlled politics and the military. Albanians were predominately Muslim. This diverse region was splintered and had been the battleground between the Habsburg and Ottoman empires for four hundred years. Yugoslavs initially attempted a Serbian monarchy to unify the country. Religious and linguistic tensions were mostly stifled from 1918 until 1989–91, except during World War II.

World War II

From 1941 until 1945, the German Nazis and Italian Fascists sponsored satellite states in the Yugoslav provinces of Croatia and in Serbia. Meanwhile, adherents of the three major religions fought each other in the name of Croatian, Serbian and Albanian nationalism. World War II weakened hopes of an integrated Yugoslav with one national identity.

In contrast to the Nazis, who considered racial differences important, most members of Yugoslav national groups during World War II did not consider themselves to be biologically different from one another. Serbian quarrels with both Croatians and Albanians originated in historic, political, class, religious and linguistic differences. During the war, the big three Allies (the United States, Great Britain, and the Soviet Union) viewed Serbs as divided between pro-British and pro-Soviet sentiments, while considering Croats as pro-German and pro-fascist, particularly members of the brutal *Ustache* party. The Kosovo province's Albanians welcomed Benito Mussolini's 1939 invasion of Islamic Albania, and hoped for liberation from the Serbs and unification with neighboring Albania. However, the Albanians and Muslim Bosnians were largely ignored by the Big Three. Some Muslims collaborated with the Nazis; they were concentrated in the province of Bosnia-Herzegovina. They remained a relatively powerless minority within Yugoslavia, and were identified in Belgrade with the despised remnants of the former Turkish Ottoman rulers (the Ottomans were also Muslim).

Josip Tito

Josip Tito came to power through a bloody guerrilla war lasting from 1941 to 1945. His Communist government ruled Yugoslavia from 1945 to his death in 1980, from the Serbian capital of Belgrade. A complicated federal system of power sharing lasted until 1989–91. A tough guerrilla fighter, who showed originality by recruiting an army of all nationalities without favoritism, Tito was anti-religious, anti-fascist and anti-monarchist. Though he rebuilt multinationalism via a federalist structure within his police state, the anti-communists of the North Atlantic Treaty Organization (NATO) gave him little credit during his long administration. Tito's regime, like Vladimir Lenin's in the Soviet Union, tolerated nationality and religious differences. Tito gave Muslims more status in the 1970s than they ever had enjoyed under the Hapsburg monarchy. Like Joseph Stalin, Tito tried to create a new "communist man," who would repress certain types of differences, such as religion and nationalism, but after his death in 1980, the nationalities began to assert claims to independence. While Tito was in power, his main foreign policy objective was to maintain independence from both NATO and the Union of Soviet Socialist Republics (USSR or Soviet Union). Fearing both, Tito stockpiled enormous quantities of arms and munitions.

The Disintegration of the Soviet Union

The complex civil war that began in Yugoslavia in 1991 had multiple causes, one factor in the conflict being the disintegration of the USSR. The Soviet Union, another multi-national state, began to unravel in 1985. Mikhail Gorbachev, chairman of the Communist Party of the USSR, eventually relinquished power between August and December 1991; he was being attacked by revived nationalist groups. Pressures from Poland, Lithuania and the Caucasus forced Gorbachev to make major concessions that would have political and economic consequences for the entire world.

Shortly before Slovenia and Croatia claimed their independence from Yugoslavia, the Persian Gulf War erupted. Saddam Hussein of Iraq invaded Kuwait in August 1990. Hussein believed the U.S. and USSR would not interfere. Hussein's miscalculation became clear when the British and Americans assembled a Middle Eastern coalition under the United Nations (U.N.) flag, which restored Kuwait's sovereignty in March 1991. The Soviet Union's friendly neutrality during the Persian Gulf War allowed the U.N. victory and secured the oil supply for the NATO powers. Slobodan Milosevic, the Serbian leader, was confused by the Soviet Union's stance because the previously stable balance of power in Europe was gradually shifting.

A LARGE CROWD PROTESTS THE TREATMENT OF BOSNIA BY THE UNITED NATIONS DURING THE YUGOSLAVIAN CIVIL WAR. *(Corbis. Reproduced by permission.)*

During 1988-1991, the coalition of Eastern European countries—the Soviets' Warsaw Treaty Organization—was falling apart. In 1988, Poland and Hungary established new democratic constitutions. By 1990, a third Soviet satellite state, East Germany (German Democratic Republic, or GDR) and West Germany (the Federal Republic of Germany, or FRG) re-unified. The new German government pressed Europe to adopt a new unified currency, the euro. The German-led European Union nations (at the time called the European Community) were, in 1990, not paying much attention to the deteriorating economic and social conditions in the Socialist Federal Republic of Yugoslavia (SFRY), and neither were trans-

national corporations in Europe and the U.S. Yugoslavia experienced an intense economic crisis, with growing unemployment and rising debts. Banks in Frankfurt and New York regarded Belgrade's emergency as an opportunity to open Yugoslavia's market.

Western states still focused politically and militarily on the decaying USSR. They could scarcely believe that the Russian empire of 1914 and the Soviet empire of 1953 were disintegrating before their amazed eyes. The Lithuanians, Estonians and Latvians, followed by the Georgians, began demanding independence from the USSR. When Gorbachev resigned in December 1991, the Soviet Union ceased to exist.

WAR-TORN SARAJEVO IS FITTINGLY SEEN THROUGH A BULLET-RIDDLED WINDOW. *(Corbis. Reproduced by permission.)*

As faith in and adherence to Marxist ideology declined in both communist USSR and in Socialist Yugoslavia, the people in both countries were again thrown open to nationalist and religious quarrels. Traditional elites instigated a revival of old-time religious sentiment. In 1989–90 the President of Serbia, Slobodan Milosevic, gradually revived Serb nationalism; he asserted Serb dominance in Kosovo, which was ninety percent Albanian-speaking and had enjoyed some autonomy under Tito's system. The six or eight groups that claimed national sovereignty in Yugoslavia became more concerned with Serb nationalism than with the disappearing Soviet threat. Yugoslavia had a system of rotating presidencies, and when Serbian President Milosevic refused to yield the presidency on March 17, 1991, the Yugoslav civil wars of national liberation from Serb dominance began.

A brief war began in Slovenia in June 1991, and fighting quickly spread to Croatia and then to Bosnia. Soon there were confrontations within the Serbian-dominated Yugoslavian army (JNA). The Serbs dominated the JNA in 1990 with an estimated sixty percent of the officer corp. (In 1991–92 the Slovenia and Croatian officers resigned from the JNA and took their units with them. The "JNA" that remains is an estimated ninety percent to one hundred percent Serbian today.) In 1991 Milosevic believed he could dominate a united Yugoslavia; he regarded Croats,

Albanians and Bosnian Muslims as properly sub-servient to a Serbian-led Yugoslav state. He assumed that he could repress the Yugoslavian peoples without outside intervention, specifically that of the U.N. Security Council or NATO.

In February 1992, at the request of the Croats, the U.N. sent a peacekeeping force to the disintegrating Yugoslavia. Inspired by the Croats' assertion of independence, Bosnia declared inde-pendence from the SFRY, and the NATO powers recognized Bosnia as an independent state in April 1992. However, Serbs within Bosnia supported unification with the Serbian portions of the former Yugoslavia, assured that Serbia could provide them with better protection and representation. Threatened by being a minority, these Bosnian Serbs, supported by the Serbian ruler Milosevic, began a bloody campaign against Bosnian Muslims. Since the Serbs had, historically, controlled the military, the Bosnian Serbs were heavily armed. Soon U.N. peacekeepers were trying to protect Bosnian Muslims from the Bosnian Serb minority within the Bosnian state.

The United Nations Peacekeeping Force

The U.N. is an updated version of the "collec-tive security" attempted by its predecessor, the League of Nations. After years of military passivi-ty, the Persian Gulf War of 1991 spurred an Anglo-American revival of a United Nations role in keeping international peace. This role expanded further with the intervention by the United Nations in Yugoslavia, which constituted a bold assertion of authority within a country torn by civil war. However, the 1991–1992 enthusiasm for U.N.-supervised "peacekeeping" would not survive the Bosnian Civil War and the mission in Somalia.

Slovenia, Croatia, and Bosnia had not enjoyed sovereignty historically. However, the Germans and Austrians recognized breakaway Catholic Slovenia and Croatia in June 1991. Germany took the lead in recognizing both as independent nations, probably for economic reasons, including trade, banking, tourism, and the purchase of cheap materials. Economics aside, Slovenia had historic ties to the Holy Roman Empire and Austria that dated from 1648, while Croatia's links to the Habsburgs and Austria-Hungary date at least from the 18th century. (The Deutschmark had served as the leading currency for investment and foreign trade in all of the old Yugoslavian territo-ries. Most of the "Yugoslavs" who had worked in Germany since the 1950s were actually Slovenians or Croatians.) By 1991 Slovenia and Croatia were

the most economically advanced states of the Yugoslavian federation. By becoming indepen-dent, they could increase their wealth and leave their poorer South Slav neighbors in Bosnia and Serbia to fend for themselves. Germany ignored the potential for nationalist, religious and social conflict that multi-ethnic Bosnia could suffer by the premature recognition of Slovenia and Croatia.

In 1991 Bosnia was nominally 44 percent Muslim, 31 percent (Orthodox Christian) Serbian, 17 percent (Roman Catholic) Croatian and 8 percent mixed or other groups (prior to the disintegration of the state and the rise of national-ism, there was some intermarriage and economic integration among the religious groups in Yugoslavia). Bosnian geography made it difficult to found a new nation of these diverse religions. Serbs dominated the hills and valleys, while Muslims dominated most major towns. The Bosnian Muslims had sought to be protected by the United Nations and NATO powers from Catholic Croats and Orthodox Serbs who wanted to partition the territory of Bosnia. Bosnian Serb and Croat nationalists chafed under the fear that they would become minorities in a multi-religious Bosnia dominated by Muslims of Sarajevo rather than part of a nation-state of their own religious-ly-defined nationalism. There seemed no fair way to draw new boundaries that could satisfy all par-ties inspired by nationalism, particularly the Serbs and Croats.

The administration of U.S. President George Bush and the U.S. Department of State first inter-vened in Bosnia because the major countries of the European Union—Germany, France and Britain—had already supported economic and political intervention, through the United Nations, in Yugoslavia. When Bush recognized Bosnia's sovereignty in April 1992, it was not, in fact, inde-pendent because a Serbian army actually con-trolled most of Bosnia's territory. Eventually, the Clinton administration would lead a six-power coalition, consisting of the United States, Great Britain, France, Germany, Russia and Italy, to intervene in the Yugoslavian civil wars. The pow-ers sought to rescue the Bosnian Muslims and Bosnia's multi-religious capital, Sarajevo.

The United States in Bosnia

Bill Clinton, then Governor of Arkansas, first supported the independence claims of Bosnian Muslims in August 1992, during that year's presi-dential campaign. Later, as president, he would make the Balkan conflict a centerpiece of U.S. for-

MAP OF BOSNIA-HERZEGOVINA. *(United Nations. Reproduced by permission.)*

eign policy during his first term. From 1991 to 1995, the U.S. took the lead intervening in Bosnia. However, politically and ideologically the U.S. was confused as it attempted to define its interests in the Balkan region.

The Clinton Administration proclaimed it was trying to stop "ethnic cleansing" and was defending the Bosnian Muslim cause in the name of multiculturalism. The very term "ethnic cleansing" is broad, and covers murder, arson, rape, expulsion, eviction, extortion, burglary and arbitrary arrest. The JNA and paramilitary Serbian troops were accused of expelling, murdering, robbing, and terrorizing villages to drive out Muslims in order to make certain districts more

homogeneous. Despite these brutal attacks, unlike in Hitler's Germany, the Serbs did not engage in the systematic cremation and gassing that characterized the concentration camps. However, the brutality and racial-religious nature of the attacks led some journalists and politicians to draw parallels to Hitler's Germany. The lightly armed Muslims were vulnerable and endangered in comparison to the heavily armed Serbs. Washington focused on Serb atrocities, suspecting that President Slobodan Milosevic was behind them, and overlooked similar brutal actions by Croat and Muslim Bosnians.

In the shadow of the Holocaust, major Jewish-American leaders have been the most consistent interventionists with respect to Yugoslavia. Most Jewish journalists, practically all Jewish Senators and many think tank leaders and lobbyists, had taken up an anti-Serbian position in the name of "stopping ethnic cleansing," which had been blamed almost exclusively on the Serbs. Yet, few American voters learned from the press or TV that forty-four percent of the Bosnians were nominally Muslim. Nor did they learn that Belgrade, like Sarajevo, was and still is an ethnically diverse city.

The Vance-Owen Plan

A bloody summer of civil war erupted in Bosnia after independence was declared. In September 1992, Lord David Owen, in London at a European Community (EC) Foreign Ministers informal meeting, joined Cyrus Vance's U.N. mediation team. Cyrus Vance, former U.S. secretary of state under President Jimmy Carter, was serving the U.N. as a mediator in the Croatian-Serbian war. Owen, formerly a member of the Labour Party who had become a Social Democrat in the 1980s, agreed with Vance in asking the combatants in Bosnia for a quick end to the hostilities.

The British government supported Lord Owen in representing the European Union. His mission was to work with U.N. peacekeepers in mediating a quick peace between the Bosnian Serbs and Muslims. But Owen's hopes for peace were privately dashed by May 1993. He found the Americans more difficult to work with than the Russians and thought the French were the most cooperative. The Russians, traditional allies of the Serbs, were satisfied with Serbian military gains made in the Bosnian campaign since April 1992; the French and British did not want to sacrifice men and machines to force Serbian military units out of Bosnia. While the British government was able to persuade Russia to send U.N. peacekeepers to Bosnia in February 1994, the move was most likely intended to forestall a U.S. and NATO threat to bomb Bosnian Serb territory. The Serbs had been a strong ally of Russia, Britain, and France for much of the century, and those countries were reluctant to turn on the Serbs.

In January 1993, just as the Clinton Administration was assuming office, Owen and Vance proposed new Bosnian borders based on ethnicity and nationality. Under this new, decentralized Bosnian state, Sarajevo's government would be very weak, rather like the Swiss government of 1815. The plan also allotted substantial territory to the Serbs. U.N. Secretary General Boutros Boutros-Ghali viewed the Vance-Owen

Plan as viable. However, the State Department, under the leadership of Clinton's Secretary of State Warren Christopher and U.N. delegate Madeleine Albright, did not move forward with the Vance-Owen plan. Vance resigned from his U.N. post in Bosnia in frustration in May 1993.

In May 1993 at a plenary session on Bosnia-Herzegovina in Athens, Greece, the unrecognized rebel Bosnian Serbian President, Radovan Karadzic conditionally signed the Vance-Owen Plan to partition Bosnia. The Bosnian Serbs set up their "capitol" at Pale, only twenty kilometers (twelve miles) from Sarajevo.

The Arms Embargo

The EU-UN plan of May 1993 aimed to enforce a total ban on the import of arms to all sides in Yugoslavia. However, a powerful arms lobby in Washington wanted the U.N. arms ban against the Sarajevo government lifted so that Muslims could better fight the heavily armed Serbs. European countries with volunteers serving in Bosnia as U.N. peacekeepers rejected this idea; they felt that more arms would cause the war to escalate. To avoid offending the British and French, U.S. Secretary of State Christopher could not openly advocate providing arms to the Muslims.

Meanwhile, Muslim states in Southeast Asia and the Middle East were donating money and arms to Sarajevo's cause. Private lobbies and hawkish Senators in the U.S. campaigned for lifting the arms embargo. Some individuals in the State Department privately wanted Muslims in Sarajevo to control all of Bosnia and to force the Croats and Serbs in the land-locked republic to accept minority status. Therefore, the State Department never agreed to the Vance-Owen Plan, which favored the Bosnian Serbs.

Most Americans, with little understanding of Balkan history, perceived Catholic Croatians and Muslim Bosnians as victims of Orthodox Serbian aggression. The better-armed and militarily more successful Serbs were portrayed as more brutal by the mass media. They also suspected that an "evil dictator" and "aggressor" in Belgrade—Milosevic—was behind the expulsion policy of the Bosnian Serbs under Radovan Karadzic and Ratko Mladic. The press claimed that the urban, Muslim-dominated Bosnian government treated people better than did the Bosnian Serbian military. Meanwhile, secularized elites in the NATO countries, but even more so in the U.S., dismissed discussion of religion as politically irrelevant to the conflict.

Mass media attitudes were re-enforced by a large faction in Congress that favored military action. Leading Republicans and Democrats both advocated bombing Serbian positions. They talked about "morality" and "pragmatism" rather than religion, since in a predominantly Judeo-Christian America, some found it difficult to advocate for a Muslim community against Christians. Yet the charge of "aggression," separate from religion, became a call to arms for both Congressional and Administration hawks.

Richard Holbrooke, a former Foreign Service Officer who volunteered to re-join the State Department in 1992, deeply desired to save the Sarajevo regime. A Democrat and a part time banker, he was a long-time supporter of Tennessee Senator Albert Gore, Jr., and Gore's presidential ambitions. Upon returning from an August 11, 1992 trip to Croatia on behalf of the International Rescue Committee, Holbrooke urged air strikes against the Serbs. After the 1992 U.S. election, he tried unsuccessfully for a brief period to get rehired by incoming Secretary of State Warren Christopher. In June 1995, Clinton and Christopher finally gave Richard Holbrooke the responsibility of bringing an end to the civil war in Bosnia as a special ambassador. Having inherited a set of maps from the Owen committee, Holbrooke became the chief negotiator responsible for the conclusion of some kind of cease-fire.

On the other hand, General Colin Powell, of the Joint Chiefs of Staff, former Secretary of State Cyrus Vance and much of the Pentagon counseled Clinton to stay out of Bosnia because they saw no particular American interest there. The Pentagon was reluctant to intervene in the Bosnian Civil War for fear that U.S. military involvement in the Yugoslav wars could become another Vietnam or Somalia, an intervention in an internal conflict with no clear goal or end in sight. And the generals realized that it would be hard to convince most Americans to fight in the remote Balkans for the idea of "multi-culturalism." With a majority of the U.S. Congress generally indifferent, President Clinton wavered for two years. He made conflicting statements about the U.N., the EU, the Serbs, the Croats and the Bosnians, before ultimately giving a green light to the State Department to expand the NATO alliance.

The Dole-Lieberman Bill

On May 14, 1994, hawkish Senators demanded that Clinton lift the U.N. arms embargo imposed on Bosnia by passing a bill called the Dole-Lieberman Amendment in the U.S. Senate. The Senators did not specify who would pay for the weapons and who would train the anti-Serb Bosnian army. The Dole-Lieberman bill gave the Bosnian government new hope at a time when it was also expecting an infusion of Arab and Iranian arms and money. Moreover, the State Department proposed a new Bosnian map in July 1994, which would make a fifty-one to forty-nine percent split of the territory, a major reduction in Serb territory compared to Owen's partition plans.

The NATO nations, in the name of the U.N., had already been dominating the Dalmatian coast through a naval embargo and a quasi-blockade, together with control of Bosnian air space, during the 1992–1995 campaigns. Croatia, with its lengthy coastline and private financial ties to Germany, Canada and the U.S., could smuggle in quantities of arms to land-locked Bosnia. The U.S. military assisted a U.N. effort of hindering Serbian arms with naval and air patrols.

Meanwhile, the Croatians were building up their armed forces. On May 1, 1995, the civil war in Bosnia began to escalate when the Croatians launched their first small-scale offensive against Krajina, the Serbian-speaking region of Croatia. With 3,500 troops and twenty tanks, president of Croatia Tudjman's forces took a minor Serbian town, Okucani, from the Serbs in the Krajina region. Overconfident Serbs in Belgrade and in Pale, the Bosnian Serb capital, ignored the defeat. As a test case, Okucani demonstrated to the Croatian Army that Serbian General Mladic had over-extended his lines in Bosnia. This military action was a foretaste and warning of a much bigger offensive to come.

On 4 June 1993, U.N. Secretary General Boutros-Ghali proclaimed several cities "safe havens," including Sarajevo, Bihac and Srebrenica. The cities were islands of Muslim surrounded by Bosnian Serbs. The safe haven proclamation meant that U.N. peacekeeping forces would endeavor to protect these cities from the anticipated Serbian invasion. Many criticized the military basis for safe havens—safe havens allowed Muslims to make raids into the Serbian countryside. Then, they claim "aggression" if Serbs counterattacked and drove out Muslim urban inhabitants.

Pale Serb forces invaded Srebrenica on July 6–11, 1995. A siege of the Muslim city of Srebrenica had been going on since February 1993, but had not yet produced U.S. headlines. The Srebrenica attack by Mladic directly challenged the safe haven concept. Rumors of Serbian massacres of innocent Muslims soon followed, causing the American public to commiserate further over the plight of Muslim refugees.

Dutch peacekeepers were defending the vulnerable city of Srebrenica with a battalion of only 450 men when General Mladic began his attack on July 6. French General Bernard Janvier, NATO's field commander, asked the U.N.'s Japanese advisor in the field, Yasushi Akashi, about sending in American F-16 fighter-bombers. In Amsterdam, Dutch Defense Minister Joris Voorhoeve grew anxious over whether the F-16s might unintentionally hit Dutch troops. Voorhoeve soon asked Akashi to suspend the air operations.

Mladic took Srebrenica by capturing the Dutch U.N. peacekeeping enclave first and holding the peacekeepers hostage. The Dutch then helped the Serbs organize the evacuation by bus of Muslim women and children. Muslim men of military age were segregated and then systematically murdered. Following Mladic's occupation of Srebrenica, the overconfident Serbian general moved on to attack the strategically important town of Bihac, another safe area, near the Croatian frontier.

The Battle of Krajina

From August 4th to 8th, 1995, the Croats waged the Battle of Krajina, resulting in a stunning Serb collapse. Serbian president Radovan Karadzic and General Ratko Mladic had been maintaining the siege against Sarajevo for three years from Pale, only twelve miles from the Bosnian capital. But by the summer of 1995 their supply lines were simply overextended. During the Krajina offensive, a Croatian army of 138,500 men attacked a 31,000-man Serb army, killing an estimated 8,000-15,000 Serbs. In addition, Western news services reported that more than a quarter of a million Serbian civilians were forced out of Krajina. The Croatian army marched deep into Bosnia and turned large sections of conquered territory over to the Sarajevo government as a gift.

During the Battle of Krajina, the U.S. provided air cover and helped jam the radios of the Serbians, while the CIA and the Defense Information Agency (DIA) provided vital intelligence to Zagreb. Sometime in July, U.S. secretary of state Christopher and German foreign minister Klaus Kinkel, meeting secretly in London with a representative of the Croatian government, gave permission for the campaign. The deal included an American suggestion to Croatian President Tudjman that he accept the minority status of Croats living in Bosnia and abide by the rules of the March 1994 "Federation plan" of the Bosnian Muslims and Croats.

The Serb Pale government had rejected the July 1994 American partition plan until the decisive battle of July and August 1995. Clinton now had the choice of a quick peace leaving the Serbs with forty-nine percent of Bosnia's land, or of fighting on into 1996 for the sake of unifying the whole country under Sarajevo. Few in the U.S., Britain, France, or Germany wanted to march up into the hills of Bosnia to arrest "president" Karadzic or General Mladic.

NATO Intervention in Bosnia

As an international body, the North Atlantic Treaty Organization (NATO) moved rather cautiously into the Yugoslav civil wars. A Berlin Ministerial meeting of NATO countries had created a new Combined Joint Task Force (CJTF), which set up the new military command structure in June 1991. This decision was made at the same time that the Germans had pressed the EC to recognize the independence of Slovenia and Croatia. The new strategic effort of CJTF influenced the future structure and planning at NATO headquarters in Brussels. It provided for more flexibility and the possibility of expanding the use of NATO troops.

NATO in 1949 was primarily a defensive alliance directed against Soviet Russia. This was indicated particularly by Article 5, which stated, "an attack against one is an attack against all." NATO membership had expanded between 1951 and 1986, a period during which anti-communism was its primarily justification. But by 1991 NATO leadership was somewhat in disarray. France and Britain were suspicious of the strength of reunited Germany. Some Americans began talking of withdrawal once the USSR disappeared. For several years the State Department, the Foreign Office, and the Auswärtiges Amt in Bonn found in Yugoslavia a cause to re-unite and expand the alliance while enforcing the blockade.

From August 29 to September 14, 1995, NATO bombed the Bosnian Serb Army's technical services. The point of the air raids of "Operation Deliberate Force Action" was to force peace negotiations that would include concessions to Holbrooke by the Pale Serbs. For two weeks, NATO planes launched from Italy and from air-

RADIO FREE EUROPE

Behind the American mass media's simplistic concepts of the Yugoslavian civil wars was the formidable organization of billionaire and philanthropist George Soros. His Soros Foundation influenced public opinion about and throughout the Balkans and the territory of the former Soviet Union.

America's containment strategy of the 1950s, in response to what the U.S. perceived as the Soviet threat, had applied pressure on the Soviet Union in the form of anti-Communist ideological warfare and propaganda—they broadcast reports critical of the Soviet Union and supportive of democracy. The American Committee for the Freedom of the Peoples of the USSR was founded in January 1951, under the general direction of Frank Wisner of the CIA's Office of Policy Coordination. When Radio Liberation first went on the air in March 1953, broadcasting from Germany to the parts of Germany and Austria occupied by Soviet forces, American management proclaimed it to be the "Radio Station of the Coordinating Center for the Anti-Bolshevik Struggle." By the summer of 1954, the Coordinating Center was dissolved, and any idea that the émigré groups would run their own radio station faded into history. Radio Liberation eventually took the name Radio Liberty and broadcast as a separate "entity" until consolidation took place with Radio Free Europe as RFE/RL in Munich in 1976.

In acquiring Radio Free Europe, Soros inherited a gigantic government-run agency with tremendous language skills. RFE/RL was moved to Prague in the 1990s. After the USSR collapsed in 1991, anti-Communist journalists focused their attention on the sins of the Milosevic regime in Belgrade. George Soros purchased Radio Free Europe in 1992 and set up the press organization Open Media Research Institute in Prague. The Soros Media Center was established in Sarajevo at about the same time. The Hungarian-born Soros (with unusual citizenship status—part American, part British, part Hungarian) owned much of the Internet news services in Eastern Europe.

Since the 1980s, Soros had influenced the Warsaw Treaty Organization and Yugoslavia. Through the media and educational donations, he helped to undermine several totalitarian states. Soros established the Open Society Fund in New York in 1979, his first Eastern European foundation in Hungary in 1984 and the Soros Foundation-Soviet Union in 1987. As of early 2000, his foundations were working in twenty-five countries, with a focus on Central and Eastern Europe and the Soviet Union's successor states. Until August 1998, the financier lent Boris Yeltsin's Russian government Eurobond issues to refinance its debt, and he had a large stake in a new Russian telecommunications holding company. Soros' network of foundations and organizations has given away hundreds of millions of dollars, and he has made billions from his many corporations.

---

craft carriers in the Adriatic Sea made 750 attacks on Mladic's positions.

Although some thirty-five previous cease-fire declarations had failed, the cease-fire after this bombing proved to be firmer. Three Serbian leaders, Karadzic, Mladic, and Milosevic, had all been defeated, although sporadic shooting continued.

The Dayton Accords

By September Holbrooke's broad peace settlement program included (1) mutual recognition of each other by the three Yugoslav governments, Bosnia, Croatia and Serbia; (2) endorsement of the State Department's proposed fifty-one to forty-nine percent split of Bosnia, with exact borders as drawn on a detailed map, to be worked out in the future by the three nationalities of Bosnia; (3) retention of unified Bosnia's sovereign status at the U.N.; and (4) a constitution of autonomous rights for the Bosnian Serbs to be determined by further negotiations. These "confederation rights" could in theory be comparable to the rights granted to the Croat minority of Bosnia in March 1994. However, any rights the Bosnian Serbs had in 1995 would be slowly whittled away in the coming years.

After further "contact-power" (the mass media's new name for the six Great Powers) talks in Paris, Moscow and New York, Clinton invited the three Yugoslav Presidents—Alija Izetbegovic of Sarajevo, Franjo Tudjman of Zagreb and Slobodan Milosevic of Belgrade—to Wright-Patterson Air Force Base near Dayton, Ohio, on November 1. The Pale Serbs were only represented in Dayton by two unofficial observers within the Belgrade delegation.

Because of the August-September Croatian invasion of Bosnia, the Pale government, which in 1993-1994 controlled 70 percent of the territory of Bosnia, came out of the Dayton talks holding only 48 percent of Bosnia's land. On the eve of the Dayton Conference, Bosnian Croats controlled some 20 percent of the State of Bosnia, mostly territory in largely Catholic Herzegovina, conveniently contiguous to the Croatian Republic. The Bosnian government forces of Izetbegovic actually controlled less than one-third of the Bosnian territory, a largely fragmented area.

At Dayton, Holbrooke presented his plan for Yugoslavia. The major feature of the treaty was that it followed Holbrooke's conception of Bosnia as a single state comprised of two entities ruled from Sarajevo and Pale. Diplomats from the three nations made an enormous advance over prior agreements in that they generally accepted a final map. After twenty-one days of secret negotiations and hard bargaining, Secretary of State Christopher adjourned the Dayton Conference on November 21 before a major press conference. Milosevic, Izetbegovic, and Tudjman, in that order, made speeches in English endorsing peace and compromise. The Dayton Plan was, in December, endorsed at a Paris gathering of "the 16 conferring powers." However, the future of the Pale entity remained cloudy. Gradually in 1996–1997 any power Pale had was transferred to the new "capital" of Banja Luka.

IFOR/SFOR

To keep peace in Bosnia, a new Implementation Force (IFOR) was created, composed of military representatives from thirty-nine countries, including Russia. IFOR occupied Bosnia. Pledged to come to the aid of Sarajevo, IFOR would be more of an arm of the Organization on Security and Cooperation in Europe (OSCE), rather than a NATO force. A number of Muslim countries also sent volunteers to IFOR. After IFOR began taking over in November 1995, the 34,000 U.N. peacekeepers (27,000 in Bosnia and 7,000 in Croatia) were transferred back to their national armies. Seventeen thousand of these troops, under NATO command, were available for the new IFOR units.

FRANJO TUDJMAN

1922–1999 Franjo Tudjman, history professor, author, and Croatian nationalist, was born May 14, 1922. After serving in World War II, he attended the Military Academy in Belgrade. Upon graduating in 1957, he continued his education at the University of Zagreb, where he earned a Ph.D. in History. Although Tudjman had joined the Communist League of Yugoslavia, he was expelled from the party in 1967 for promoting Croatian nationalism. He was imprisoned twice for his political activities and pro-Croatian writings—the first time from 1972–74 and again from 1981–84. Running on a Croatian nationalist platform, he was elected president of Croatia in 1990, and led the Croatian struggle for independence from Yugoslavia in the 1991–92 civil war. Croatia's independence was formally recognized by the United Nations in January 1992. Tudjman was reelected president that August, and then again in October 1995. After being diagnosed with stomach cancer, he was once again reelected in June 1997, and served as president until his death on December 10, 1999.

Late in 1996, IFOR was renamed the Stabilization Force for Bosnia. SFOR officially replaced IFOR on December 20, 1996, when a new American general replaced the retiring American admiral. Clinton had promised a skeptical Congress in 1995 that IFOR would only occupy Bosnia a year, and by changing the name in 1996, he "kept his promise." However, SFOR would continue to occupy Bosnia indefinitely; it was still there in 2000.

The OSCE has been charged with monitoring the Dayton Accord. Originally founded at Helsinki in 1975 as the CSCE and renamed in the 1990s, at one time it had fifty-five members. By 1995 it had lost a member because Milosevic's Yugoslavia was excluded by the NATO powers at the U.N. The original intent of the 1975 treaty had been to freeze the boundaries of both East and West Europe, bringing the Soviet and Western blocs a sense of security. Twenty years later Milosevic could claim that OSCE had betrayed the idea of a united Yugoslavia. The OSCE General Secretary maintains headquarters in Vienna, with the chairmanship rotating among the member nations. Its function now seems mostly to protect the Muslim Bosnians and Kosovars from attack by Belgrade.

EXCERPTS FROM THE UNITED NATIONS RESOLUTION ON "THE SITUATION IN BOSNIA AND HERZEGOVINA"

Resolution Adopted by the General Assembly. 54/119.

Expresses its full support for the General Framework Agreement for Peace in Bosnia and Herzegovina and the annexes thereto (collectively known as the "Peace Agreement"), which constitute the key mechanism for the achievement of a durable and just peace in Bosnia and Herzegovina, leading to stability and cooperation in the region and the reintegration of Bosnia and Herzegovina at all levels . . . .

Recognizes the role of the international community remains essential, welcomes the readiness of the international community to continue its efforts towards a self-sustaining peace, and recalls that the responsibility for consolidating peace and security lies primarily with the authorities of Bosnia and Herzegovina . . . .

Welcomes the vital contribution of the multinational Stabilization Force in providing a secure environment for the implementation of civilian aspects of the Peace Agreement, calls for the fullest cooperation by all parties in this regard, expresses its full support for the efforts of the United Nations International Police Task Force in carrying out its mandate, and commends its efforts in the establishment of the rule of law in Bosnia and Herzegovina . . . .

Underlines the fact that the assistance provided by the international community remains strictly conditional upon compliance with the Peace Agreement and subsequent obligations . . . .

Insists upon the need to surrender all indictees to the International Tribunal for trial, notes that the Tribunal has the authority to address individual responsibility for the perpetration of the crime of genocide, crimes against humanity, and other serious violations of international humanitarian law in Bosnia and Herzegovina, and demands that all parties fulfil their obligations to hand over to the Tribunal all indicted persons in territories under their control and otherwise to comply fully with the orders of the Tribunal and to cooperate with the work of the Tribunal, including with exhumations and other investigative acts . . . .

Encourages the acceleration of the peaceful, orderly, and phased return of refugees and displaced persons, including in areas where they would be in the ethnic minority, strongly condemns all acts of intimidation, violence, and killings, including those acts designed to discourage the voluntary return of refugees and displaced persons, and demands that such acts be investigated and prosecuted . . . .

Welcomes the report of the Secretary General . . . commends him for its thoroughness and candour, condemns the brutal acts described therein, deplores the appalling magnitude of the human tragedy that occurred before and after the fall of Srebrenica and Zepa, notes with deep concern the findings contained in the report, and therefore encourages the Secretary-General and member States to address these concerns so as to prevent them from recurring in the future . . . .

Reaffirms once again its support for the principle that all statements and commitments made under duress, in particular those regarding land and property, are wholly null and void, in accordance with the relevant provisions of the Peace Agreement, and supports the effective engagement of the Commission for Real Property Claims of Displaced Persons and Refugees in compliance with its mandate . . . .

Stressed the need for timely information about the level of cooperation and compliance with the International Tribunal and its orders, the status and programme for the return of refugees and displaced persons to and within Bosnia and Herzegovina and the status and implementation of the Agreement of Subregional Arms Control . . . .

Decides to include in the provisional agenda of its fifty-fourth session the item entitled "The situation in Bosnia and Herzegovina."

The Dayton Conference created a new Office of the High Representative, OHR, a Sarajevo-based OSCE subcommittee first headed by a Spaniard, Carlos Westendorp. His office is partly comprised of American and British officers charged with implementing the Dayton Treaty. In 1999 Westendrop was replaced by Wolfgang Petritsch, an Austrian. The Sarajevo office worked closely with the three headquarters of OSCE, SFOR and U.N. Their daily routine consisted of exercising the chief executive and supreme court powers for a united Bosnia. President Izetbegovic's authority has been protected by the U.S., NATO and the EU.

Western European ambitions to return the hundreds of thousands of Bosnians who had fled north to Germany, Austria, and Switzerland turned out to be ineffective. However, the Dayton Treaty did enable some refugees to return to their homes over the next five years. SFOR limited its mission to keeping the highways, airports, and railroad stations open. The job of policing the villages was left to local authorities with some token supervision from the OSCE.

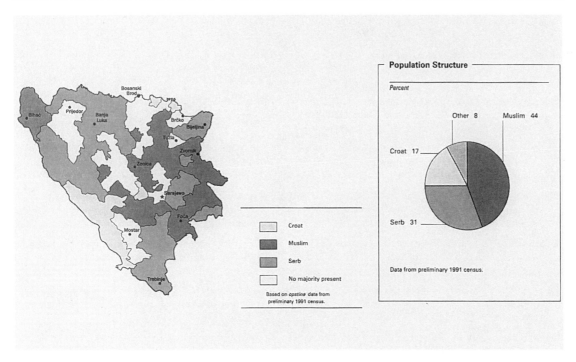

Population Structure

Percent

Other 8   Muslim 44

Croat 17

Serb 31

Data from preliminary 1991 census.

Croat

Muslim

Serb

No majority present

Based on *opstine* data from
preliminary 1991 census.

THIS MAP ILLUSTRATES THE WIDE-SPREAD NATURE OF THE ETHNIC MAJORITIES IN BOSNIA-HERZEGOVINA.
(Central Intelligence Agency. Reproduced by permission.)

RECENT HISTORY AND THE FUTURE

After the November 1995 Dayton truce, most American voters mistakenly assumed that the war had been resolved. However, by the spring of 1999 during the Kosovo bombing campaign, people could see that the Dayton accord had been in fact merely a truce in a wider war. Milosevic continued to be regarded by Washington officials as a menace and a criminal, and officials called for his overthrow and arrest. NATO occupied Kosovo in the summer of 1999 in much the same way as Bosnia had been taken over by IFOR in 1995. As of 2000, unemployment, inflation, and poverty rates remained high throughout the successor states in the Socialist Yugoslavia.

Thanks partly to its military victory over Serbia, NATO became interested in expanding. By 1999 NATO agreed to allow Poland, the Czech Republic, and Hungary to join the military alliance. Hungary borders Yugoslavia, and since 1919 Serbia has been ruling over a large number of Hungarian speakers in Vojvodina, just north of Belgrade. Much of the support of NATO intervention in Bosnia and expansion was by Jewish-Americans and other supporters of Israel who hope that NATO jurisdiction could be expanded to protect Israel.

The new roles the U.N. and NATO seemed to have developed since 1995 are quite different from the old NATO, which was formed originally in 1949 to oppose the Soviet Union. By 1999, most Serbs and Russians viewed the new expanded NATO as imperialist, interventionist, and anti-Orthodox.

The future of American policy toward the Balkans is tenuous. A gradual, ten-year replacement of United States money and troops in NATO by Germany is a possible outcome of the simmering Balkan crisis. Next to Americans, the Germans have been the most eager to expand NATO's jurisdiction into Eastern Europe. Bosnia has actually become a sort of NATO protectorate, primarily occupied by NATO forces. The U.N. Security Council has turned most of the responsibility for resolving nationality problems over to NATO. Bosnians, who dreamed of independence in 1992, seem in 2000 to be willing to remain a de facto NATO protectorate as long as that alliance continues to contain a possible restoration of Serbian power.

BIBLIOGRAPHY

Abramowitz, Morton. "Ominous Rumblings from the Balkans," *The Washington Post*, 16 February 1998.

Ash, Timothy. "Cry, the Dismembered Country," *New York Review of Books*, 46 (14 January 1999): 29–33.

Banac, Ivo. *The National Question in Yugoslavia: Origins, History, Politics.* Ithaca, N.Y.: Cornell University Press, 1984.

Bennett, Christopher. *Yugoslavia's Bloody Collapse: Causes, Course, and Consequences.* New York: New York University Press, 1994.

Bethlehem, Daniel L. and Marc Weller, ed. *The 'Yugoslav' Crisis in International Law: General Issues.* New York: Cambridge University Press, 1995.

Burg, Stephen L. and Paul S. Shoup. *The War in Bosnia-Herzegovina: Ethnic Conflict and International Intervention.* New York: M.E. Sharpe, 1999.

Cohen, Philip J. *Serbia's Secret War: Propaganda and the Deceit of History.* College Station, Tex.: Texas A&M University Press, 1996.

Danner, Mark. "Clinton, the U.N. and the Bosnian Disaster," *The New York Review of Books,* 44 (18 December 1997): 65–85.

Dunn, Seamus and T.G. Fraser, eds. *Europe and Ethnicity: The First World War and Contemporary European Conflict.* New York: Routledge, 1996.

Glenny, Misha. *The Balkans 1804–1999: Nationalism, War and the Great Powers.* New York: HarperCollins, 1995.

Igatieff, Michael. "The Balkan Tragedy," *The New York Review of Books,* 40 (13 May 1993): 3–5.

Lampe, John R. *Yugoslavia as History: Twice There was a Country.* New York: Cambridge University Press, 1996.

Mojzes, Paul. *Yugoslavian Inferno: Ethno-religious Warfare in the Balkans.* New York: The Continuum Publishing Co., 1994.

Pfaff, William. *The Wrath of Nations: Civilization and the Furies of Nationalism.* New York: Simon and Schuster, 1993.

Poulton, Hugh. "The Balkans: Minorities and States in Conflict." In *Minority Rights Group.* London: Cambridge, 1993.

Ramet, Sabrina Petra. *Balkan Babble: Politics, Culture and Religion in Yugoslavia.* 2d ed. Boulder, Colo.: Westview Press, 1992.

Sells, Michael. *The Bridge Betrayed: Religion and Genocide in Bosnia.* Berkeley, Calif.: University of California Press, 1996.

Udovicki, Jasminka and James Ridgeway, eds. *Yugoslavia's Ethnic Nightmare: The Inside Story of Europe's Unfolding Ordeal.* New York: Lawrence Hill Books, 1995.

Robert H. Whealey

Brazil: Racism and Equality

In February 2000 an Associated Press wire-service story about a racially charged incident in Brazil made headlines across the nation. The story described an angry young black woman, Venusemar Andrade, who tried to join one of the all-white carnival parade groups in the northeastern Brazilian city of Bahia. They laughed her off, asking her, "Are you crazy? Blacks don't get into this carnival group. What are you trying to do? Dirty the group?" Venusemar did not politely withdraw from the scene. Instead, she retaliated by bringing criminal charges against the group. She based her case on the Brazilian Constitution of 1988 that classified racism as a crime punishable by up to three years in prison. Interestingly, this constitutional provision was the first effective anti-racism legislation ever adopted by Brazilian lawmakers.

The coverage of the incident raised the question of how such a racist act could have occurred in Bahia—a Brazilian state whose population is eighty percent black. The world-view of Brazil as a land of "racial democracy" has long been held. In the early 1940s, for example, the prominent African American sociology professor E. Franklin Frazier visited Brazil and announced "there is no race problem in Brazil." Frazier could not have been more impressed: "The Brazilian Negro, to use the term in the American sense, first of all is a Brazilian. He is loyal to Brazil and harbors no resentment against whites. He has faith in the justice of the courts and he is convinced his abilities and achievements will be recognized." Even the United Nations authorized a special research project in 1949 to study Brazilian race relations because that country had allegedly escaped the racism that had ravaged Europe under the Nazis.

The Conflict

Historically, Brazil has prided itself on being an integrated community free from racism. Spanish colonists and African slaves co-existed with indigenous people. However, recent conflict has developed regarding racial discrimination.

Racial

- Appearances of racial harmony are masks for a deep separation, where the small white community dominates blacks and native people.

- Individuals are judged by the degree of color in their skin.

Cultural

- The integration of non-white culture has been superficial. Black people and native people are only valued for food and music and dress, not for other contributions.

Economic

- Whites are the wealthiest, and blacks and native people are the poorest. Educational and economic opportunities perpetuate this.

CHRONOLOGY

1500s Portugal colonizes Brazil. Over the next three centuries, 3.5 million African slaves arrive in Brazil.

1822 Portuguese colonial rule ends.

1824 Brazil adopts its first constitution, which guarantees full citizenship to all people, including former slaves (though the constitution does not abolish slavery).

1871–88 The Brazilian Congress enacts several laws that resulted in complete abolition of slavery in 1888.

1930s A militant "Black Front" emerges predominantly in Sao Paulo.

1933 Gilbero Freyre writes *The Masters and the Slaves,* which emphasizes the positive contributions that native Brazilians and former slaves have made to mainstream (white) Brazilian culture.

1988 The Brazilian Constitution establishes racism as a crime.

Why, then, did it take a carnival protestor to show the world that all is not well with race relations in Brazil? In fact, the racial antagonism goes back to 1974, when some Bahians started a black-only carnival group in response, they said, to the long-standing all-white policy of the established carnival groups. But the issue of race relations is not limited to incidents such as this one. Brazil has a long history of suppressing the truth about the treatment of non-whites.

HISTORICAL BACKGROUND

The explanation for the seeming contradiction between appearance and reality in race relations in Brazil begins in Africa. Portugal, which had begun colonizing Brazil in the early sixteenth century, had before that time explored Africa and enslaved its inhabitants. For example, by the mid-sixteenth century, the population of the Portuguese city of Lisbon was twenty percent African slaves. The Portuguese in Brazil—who came from a small European country with a population of two million—were incapable of settling the new colony alone. They used enslaved Africans to solve their labor shortage. Over the next three centuries, 3.5 million African slaves arrived in

Brazil, crossing the Atlantic under appalling conditions. Once in Brazil the African slaves labored in support of Brazil's export economies of Brazilwood (in the sixteenth century); sugar (in the seventeenth and eighteenth centuries); gold, diamonds, and cotton (in the eighteenth century); and coffee (in the nineteenth century).

Although some 4.5 million enslaved Africans started for Brazil, a quarter or more died on the way of disease and maltreatment. The scale of the Brazilian slave trade far exceeded that of the slave trade to the United States. Though the death rate of the slaves from the voyage was high in Brazil, one factor led to a rapid increase in the Afro-Brazilian population: manumission—the practice of releasing slaves to become free laborers. Slaves who became free were healthier and lived longer lives, on average, than captive slaves. Thus, by the mid-seventeenth century African slaves outnumbered the Portuguese colonists. As the African population increased, they became artisans, merchants, messengers, peddlers, scribes, mule drivers, road builders, and a host of other workers within the Portuguese plantation system.

Given the racist foundations of the society, one might have expected poorer white colonists to take these jobs, as was happening in the United States. However, Brazil didn't have enough whites to fill these positions. As a result, there was economic space for the non-whites, who came from the growing ranks of freed slaves and their descendants. This population was often of mixed race, the result, at least in part, of slave master relations with female slaves. Out of such roots was born Brazil's mulatto population. These non-whites (as Brazilian demographers now refer to Brazilians with visible evidence of African descent) soon filled many of the available occupations.

As a result, Brazilian colonial society developed a multi-racial social system—one based on more than two racial categories—in which the growing (mostly free) mixed-race population tempered the division between black and white. The original racist bias of Portuguese colonization never reached the absolute black-white distinctions that plagued U.S. society. The definition of Brazilian racial categories became ambiguous— what were the lines between black and mulatto or white and mulatto? Determining these distinctions came to depend in part on other, non-physical factors such as social demeanor, dress, vocation and wealth. Of course these factors were conditioned by racial prejudices of the time and place, causing a certain circularity that has contin-

SLAVES FROM AFRICA HAUL GOODS TO PLACE AT THE FEET OF THEIR EUROPEAN MASTERS. THE PRACTICE OF SLAVERY IN BRAZIL WAS COMMON FROM THE SIXTEENTH CENTURY TO THE NINETEENTH CENTURY; IT WAS FINALLY ABOLISHED IN 1888. *(Corbis. Reproduced by permission.)*

ued to trouble discussion of race relations in Brazil to the present day.

The racial variables created what anthropologists later called "social race"—physical features modified by the contextual factors mentioned above. Yet the blurring of white racial categories did not change the fact that whites remained at the top of the Brazilian hierarchy while blacks were at the bottom, with the mulatto falling somewhere in between. It was therefore never, at least after the earliest sixteenth century, a matter of absolute differences between races. The English

colonists of North America also imported masses of enslaved Africans to work their plantations. But they categorized these slaves, at least from the eighteenth century on, as subhuman. The U.S. Constitution defined a slave, for purposes of taxation and representation, as worth only three-fifths of a white man. Even after emancipation, the English colonists continued to regard African Americans as less than human. These biases sowed the seeds for the Ku Klux Klan, which maintained a major presence into the 1960s. It also created the racial paranoia that led to segre-

SLAVE LABORERS ON BRAZILIAN PLANATATIONS OF THE EIGHTEENTH AND NINETEENTH CENTURIES PERFORMED SIMILAR TASKS TO THIS BANANA WORKER IN THE CITY OF MANOAS. *(Corbis. Reproduced by permission.)*

gated schoolrooms and laws banning intermarriage among the races in many U.S. states. Beneath this open turmoil ran deep racial hatred—any form of racial "mixture" was a threat to white "purity."

Brazil was different. By the time Portuguese colonial rule ended in Brazil in 1822, its multiracial system was firmly established. As a result, when the independent Brazilians adopted their first constitution in 1824 it guaranteed full citizenship to all former slaves—persons of color were not branded as less than human.

The nineteenth century welcomed milestones in the evolution of Brazilian race relations, such as the abolition of slavery. Brazil continued to import slaves longer than any other country in the Americas, with the exception of Cuba, maintaining their commerce until 1850. The campaign for ending slavery was spearheaded by a coalition of enlightened white lawyers, planters, and politicians along with mulatto business leaders. The Brazilian Congress favored a gradual process, involving successive laws for partial emancipation in 1871 and 1885, before enacting total abolition in 1888. Slaves escaping in mass numbers from plantations propelled the movement, especially in its later years. Although the process sometimes provoked localized conflicts between rebellious slaves and the authorities, "peaceful" resolution of

the slavery issue reinforced Brazil's image as a society that solved its problems with a minimum of violence.

Unfortunately for those who wanted a swift reintegration of ex-slaves into society, these were years during the late nineteenth and early twentieth centuries when "scientific racism" dominated social thought in Europe and the U.S. Proponents of this view claimed to have physical and historical evidence proving a strict hierarchy of races was the inevitable, natural state of man. Brazilian politicians and intellectuals repeated the doctrines of "innate superiority and inferiority of the races" (of whites and blacks, respectively) that dominated learned circles in the United States and Europe. Ironically, in Brazil these theories had minimal impact upon social policy because popular thought and practice in race relations had already ruled out the application of such racial absolutes. The earlier belief that Africans were less than whites, which had facilitated the impact of scientific racism in the United States, was notably absent in Brazil.

The stage was now set for the creation of Brazil's modern multicultural society. The key figure in that process was the anthropologist and historian Gilberto Freyre. This native of the Brazilian northeast (a region that included Bahia), who studied in the United States at Baylor and Columbia universities, published *The Masters and the Slaves* in 1933. The volume was an in-depth study of the social life on the Brazilian colonial plantation. Freyre's book emphasized the relations between many of the house slaves and their white masters, and his argument was that Africans and native Indians had made a positive contribution to Brazilian society through their culture, their labor, and their children. Freyre painted an exuberant portrait of a new race emerging through miscegenation—the mixture of the races—in the tropics. In the subsequent century, Freyre's predictions have not been realized. Brazil continued to be ruled by an overwhelmingly white elite.

Freyre's work was translated into French and English and by 1950 had established itself as the prevailing scholarship on slavery and race relations in Brazil. He was the principal authority cited by those Brazilians who claimed their country was a "racial democracy." Freyre himself became a cultural hero, in-demand for lecture appearances in the United States and western Europe.

However it is important to realize the limits of Freyre's work. Inherent in his analysis was an implicit racial scale that placed whites on top and blacks on the bottom. When Freyre praised the contributions of African cooking, dance, and music, for example, he was really praising Africans and Indians for having contributed to creating a more viable, mostly white, Brazilian elite. Freyre's new "tropical" Brazilian might dance the samba and master African cooking but he was still likely to be white. In fact, the non-European contributions remained largely in the realm of folklore.

Notwithstanding this contradiction, Freyre and his followers helped to convince a generation, both at home and abroad, that Brazil was uniquely non-racist. In reality this was not the case. In the 1940s and 1950s Brazil's power structure—congress, courts, universities, and military commands—were overwhelmingly white. The top ranks of many of those institutions did not include a single Afro-Brazilian. The presence of the occasional mulatto among the politicians and the military officers was enough to reassure the Brazilian elite that social mobility was not racially determined, but some Afro-Brazilians disagreed. In the 1930s a militant "Black Front" emerged, predominantly in Sao Paulo. This front celebrated blackness and challenged the largely white establishment. It was suppressed by the dictatorship of Getulio Vargas (1937-45), only to reappear in different form in the late 1970s, when there was a brief flurry of Afro-Brazilian mobilization. In both cases the black challenge was limited to very small numbers with little impact on the power structure.

RECENT HISTORY AND THE FUTURE

The year 1988 marked the centenary of abolition in Brazil. Many Brazilians were moved to take a new look at the reality of race relations a hundred years after the end of slavery. They saw a society where whites still dominated most institutions, with some exceptions in sports and the arts. They saw, too, that the United States had abandoned segregation and initiated programs to attempt to compensate for past discrimination. African Americans were on the Supreme Court, in presidential cabinets, and among the ranks of university presidents and army generals. One U.S. scholar produced a study in 1992 that showed with copious statistics that from 1950 on the United States had become a more racially egalitarian society than Brazil.

Few of the white Brazilian elite were ready to believe these findings, but it did raise doubts and questions about race relations and began to erode the illusions that still masked social realities in Bahia. Despite all the hype surrounding Afro-Brazilian culture in Bahia, a virtually all-white elite governed that city (and the state). When the Afro-Brazilians began to question the white dominance, the focus of conflict became "carnival." This quintessentially African festival had been co-opted by the white elite beginning in the 1930s. Its existence helped to project the image of racial harmony, but power remained in white hands. The division of races underlying the Bahian carnival, and in Brazilian society, is evident. The racial democracy touted by Gilberto Freyre was more dream than reality.

The concepts of "white" and "black" have long been subject to redefinition and negotiation. Early in Brazilian history such terms proved to be more adaptable than in North America, where, for many years, "one drop" of African blood made an individual black. Although whites maintained social, economic, and political dominance throughout Brazilian history, those of mixed blood ancestry found a degree of upward mobility not available to their counterparts in the United States. This fact allowed the Brazilian elite to claim that their society was uniquely tolerant, especially in comparison to the United States. In recent years, Brazil has

AFRO-BRAZILIANS, SUCH AS THIS GIRL IN THE CITY OF SALVADOR, SUFFER FROM THEIR PLACE AT THE LOW END OF THE SOCIAL AND ECONOMIC SPECTRUM. *(Corbis. Reproduced by permission.)*

begun to change in response to change in the United States. When legal segregation ended and affirmative action began in the United States, the white Brazilian elite lost a powerful rationale to justify their country's system of race relations. Because of the need for historical revisionism, history has never been more relevant for understanding contemporary Brazil. The myth of racial democracy that has long been extolled must be dispelled. Brazil is not and never has been a racial paradise. Despite its fearful legacy of slavery, twentieth-century Brazil has never exhibited the unremitting savagery of lynching in the U.S. or the twentieth-century massacres of blacks in the Dominican Republic and Cuba.

BIBLIOGRAPHY

Andrews, George Reid. *Blacks and Whites in Sao Paulo Brazil: 1888-1988.* Madison, Wisc.: The University of Wisconsin Press, 1991.

Burdick, John. *Looking for God in Brazil.* Los Angeles: University of California Press, 1993.

Butler, Kim. *Freedoms Given, Freedoms Won.* New Brunswick: Rutgers University Press, 1998.

Conrad, Robert Edgar. *Children of God's Fire.* University Park, Penn.: The Pennsylvania State University Press, 1994.

Crook, Larry and Randall Johnson, eds. *Black Brazil: Culture, Identity and Social Mobilization.* Los Angeles: UCLA Latin American Center Publications, 1999.

Freyre, Gilberto. *The Masters and the Slaves.* Trans. by Samuel Putnam. New York: Alfred A. Knopf, 1956.

Skidmore, Thomas E. "Bi-Racial U.S. vs. Multi-Racial Brazil: Is the Contrast Still Valid?" *Journal of Latin American Studies* 25 (1993): 373–386.

Thomas E. Skidmore

Chechnya and Russia: A War of Succession

The Conflict

Following the disintegration of the Soviet Union in 1992, Chechnya declared independence. Russia viewed Chechnya as an integral part of Russia, and there was a significant minority of Russians within Chechnya. Chechnya and Russia went to war over the issue of Chechnya's independence from Russia.

Ethnic

- Chechens view themselves as distinct from Russians.

Political

- Chechens believe they have a right to self-determination.

- Russians believe they must protect the Russian minority in Chechnya.

- Russian officials believe that if they let Chechnya become independent, other ethnic groups in Russia will rebel.

In February 2000, Russian military forces retook the city of Grozny, capital of the breakaway republic of Chechnya. Chechen separatists, who had declared Chechnya's independence in 1991 from the Union of Soviet Socialist Republics (USSR) as it was dissolving, fled once again into the surrounding Caucasus Mountains. Anxious to restore a sense of normality to the besieged capital, Russian officials quickly began to plan a government to replace the one established by Aslan Maskhadov who had been elected to the Chechen presidency in 1997 and who had also fled the capital. The recapture of Grozny, the capital of Chechnya, was a significant victory for Russia whose army had crossed into Chechnya in October 1999 and restarted a war that the outside world had hoped was ended three years earlier.

The Russian army, which had been run out of Grozny in August 1996 by a much smaller band of Chechen separatists, effectively reversed what had been an embarrassing loss. Russian President Vladimir Putin was able to declare Grozny liberated from the "Islamist militants" whom he claimed had been responsible for the series of terrorist bomb explosions in Russia and in Chechnya's eastern neighbor Dagestan. The victory also allowed Putin to temporarily quell mounting international criticism of Russia's handling of its renewed war with Chechnya. Promising immediate relief for the civilians of Grozny, Russian officials rapidly delivered a water purification system and established a number of food kitchens and medical centers. The supplies were desperately needed by Chechen residents, who had endured aerial attacks and a ground assault that retook the Chechen capital street-by-street. As one of only two major cities in Chechnya, Grozny has long been the focal point for both wars between the

CHRONOLOGY

1813 With the Treaty of Gulistan, Persia gives much of the Caucasus, including Chechnya, to Russia. Russian armies fight a forty-year war to secure control over the region.

1917 As the Czarist government falls and the Soviet government rises, Chechnya declares independence.

1920 The Soviet Union reestablishes control over the region. There are several uprisings over the next twenty years.

1936 The Chechen-Ingush Autonomous Soviet Socialist Republic within the USSR is established.

1944 Joseph Stalin deports five hundred thousand Chechens and Ingush to Central Asia; about twenty-five percent of the population dies on the way.

1957 Nikita Khrushchev allows the remaining Chechens to return home to Chechnya.

1988 The Soviet republics of Armenia, Azerbaijan, and Georgia begin to assert their independence.

1990 The Russian portion of the disintegrating Soviet Union declares Russian rule of the Russian portion of the USSR, including Chechnya.

1991 With the dissolution of the USSR, autonomous regions become provinces within Russia. Dzhokhar Dudayev organizes a coup against the local Communist leaders and calls for elections. Elections are held in areas held by Dudayev's forces.

1994 The Russian army enters Grozny, capitol of Chechnya, and is captured by Dudayev's troops.

1995 The Russian army establishes control of Grozny. The Chechen rebels lead a mission into Russia, where they attack a town of one hundred thousand. Later, Dudayev is killed when the Russian army homes in on a cellular phone he was using.

1996 Chechen forces launchs an offensive to re-take Grozny.

1997 Russian president Boris Yeltsin and Chechen president Aslan Maskhadov sign the Treaty of Peace and the Principles of Interrelations Between the Russian Federation and the Chechen Public Ichkeria.

1999 Chechen government officials cut an oil pipeline to Russia, arguing that Russia owes ten million dollars for repairs. Explosions kill three hundred civilians in Moscow; the Russian government blames Chechen extremists. Russian forces invade Chechnya. The IMF puts scheduled loan payments on hold; European nations threaten sanctions if the war doesn't end.

2000 Russian military forces retake Grozny.

---

self-proclaimed Chechen Republic and Russia, which has never officially recognized Chechen independence. Bombarded by both sides as it has changed hands repeatedly, its infrastructure has collapsed, its buildings have been reduced to shells, and its citizens relegated to the cellars.

Moscow's public display of humanitarian aid was not enough to stem the tide of international censure. Since the resumption of hostilities began in October 1999, more than 250,000 civilians have fled to Ingushetia, Chechnya's smaller neighbor to the west. With the flood of refugees came tales of Russian atrocities perpetrated on civilians including stories of mass murder, rape, and torture at detention centers located outside of Grozny. Additional reports have surfaced of villages near Grozny where Russian soldiers have been accused of killing and raping civilians. The steady stream of reports has prompted international organizations including the United Nations (U.N.), the Council of Europe (CE), and the Organization for Security and Cooperation in Europe (OSCE) to urge Moscow to allow an independent investigation into the alleged human rights crimes. Russian officials have denied committing any abuses and have countered the accusations by saying their troops were only responding to attacks by Chechen terrorists. Russian stonewalling has led the Council of Europe to temporarily suspend Russia's voting privileges. Hoping to pressure Russia into calling a cease-fire in Chechnya and to negotiate a new peace settlement, the CE's actions have instead angered Russian officials who have described the suspension as evidence of "Cold War stereotypes and

MAP OF CHECHNYA. *(XNR. Printed by permission.)*

double standards." The vote, which was approved by a clear two-thirds majority of the forty-one-nation body, was meant to embarrass Putin, whose election in March 2000 was in part due to Russian public opinion that he was a "tough leader" and a "heroic winner." Whether or not Putin and the Russian government will respond to the international pressure remains unclear. The scope of the conflict is, however, widening from simply punishing the separatists for alleged terrorist acts against Russian citizens to bringing Chechnya firmly back under Russian control and silencing its 1991 declaration of independence. The Russian government appears to be reasserting its authority over a region it has claimed rule of for nearly three hundred years.

HISTORICAL BACKGROUND

Chechen People and Geography

Chechnya is one of six Russian provinces located in the Caucasus Mountains which stretch between the Black Sea to the west and the Caspian Sea to the east. All six Russian Caucasian

provinces, which in addition to Chechnya include Kabardino-Balkaria, Karacheyevo-Cherkessia, North Ossetia, Ingushetia, and Dagestan, are part of the independent Russian Federation, commonly known as Russia, which came into being when the USSR dissolved at the end of 1991. These Caucasian provinces were previously formed into autonomous regions of the USSR. The Chechen-Ingush Autonomous Soviet Socialist Republic, comprising Chechnya and Ingushetia, was established within the USSR in 1936. It was a somewhat artificial arrangement as the Chechens were at the time more closely allied with the tribes of Dagestan, and appeared to be designed to prevent either Chechnya or Dagestan from becoming a political threat to Soviet power.

With the dissolution of the USSR, the borders of the Caucasus territories were reformed. The three Soviet republics of Georgia, Armenia, and Azerbaijan became fully independent countries. The former so-called autonomous regions were kept with Russia and reformed into provinces. When Chechnya declared its independence from this newly formed Russian Federation, it was arguably taking advantage of the opportunity presented by the Soviet Union's collapse. This opportunistic declaration was, however, what the newly formed Russian Federation feared the most—ethnic groups splintering from the whole and taking with them valuable resources needed by the struggling federation. If they did not prevent Chechnya from becoming fully independent, then how were they to prevent other regions from following suit? To date, Chechnya's declaration of independence and its secession from Russia have not been recognized by either the United Nations or by Russia. The Russian government continues to claim sovereignty over the territory under international law, and the rest of the world considers Chechnya a part of the Russian Federation.

Some one million strong at the end of the twentieth century, the people of Chechnya claim to have lived in the region for six thousand years. They are ethnically and culturally very different from Russians. Chechens are Sunni Muslims who converted to the Islamic faith in the fifteenth and sixteenth centuries. They are also practitioners of Sufism, a form of Islamic mysticism. Russians are Orthodox Christian and speak a Slavic tongue. The Chechen language is part of the Nakh-Daghestanian family of languages, which is indigenous to the Caucasus Mountains and is unrelated to any other language group in the world. Because of their strong historical ties to the land, and the substantial differences between their

IMAM AVER SHAMIL

1797–1871 The legacy of Imam Aver Shamil is a popular subject in the Caucasian Mountains. Claimed by numerous ethnic groups as their own cultural hero, Shamil has become an icon representing different sides of the same story. Although the significance of his life changes depending on the cultural group doing the telling, one point remains consistent—his thirty-year revolt against Czarist Russia foreshadowed every aspect of the current Russian-Chechen conflict.

Imam Aver Shamil was born in 1797 to a noble Avar family of southern Dagestan. A scholar and poet who was respected for his knowledge of the Arabic language, Shamil studied under Muhammad Yaraghi, a Sufi mystic who taught Shamil that the *shari'a,* Islamic divine law from the Koran, must be the ruling law of the Caucasian Mountains. Responding to a call to arms in 1827 by Ghazi Mollah, another student of Yaraghi's, Shamil joined the *jihad,* or holy war, against the Russians. Mollah's *jihad* had come in response to the establishment of Russian military forts, like the one at Grozny, and the repressive regime of Russian General Alexey Ermolov. The revolt was unprecedented as it succeeded in banding together the tribes of the Caucasus Mountains who put aside their legendary vendettas to fight against their common enemy, the Russians. After Mollah was killed in 1834, Shamil was proclaimed *Imam* (leader) and he continued the revolt for twenty-five years. Although his spiritual leadership was significant—the Russians told stories of Shamil's army singing the religious chants he composed for them—his talent as a general was greater. He was famous for swift elusive attacks that often divided the enemy and lured troops into remote mountains and forests where their superior numbers were less of an advantage. While his tactics were successful when meeting the Russians in pitched battle, they were less effective when it came to protecting the aouls (villages) against Russian sieges. It was this inability to maintain control over the settled areas that was to eventually lead to his capture in 1859. After his surrender, Shamil was banished to a small town near Moscow. He was kept there until 1869 when he was allowed to leave and travel to the Middle East where he died in 1871.

Shamil's legacy is significant. In addition to unifying the tribes and clans of Chechnya and Dagestan and defending them against constant Russian attack for twenty-five years, he created a state that was united in Islam and strongly Sufist. His legacy has however, come to have different meanings for each culture. After the USSR dissolved and Chechnya declared its independence, Russian scholars reversed their silence on Shamil and adopted him as a Russian hero. They emphasized the years after he surrendered when he became an admirer of all things Russian. The Dagestanis, of course, still claim him as their national hero but they emphasize the man rather than the struggle and the poet rather than the soldier. For the Chechens, Shamil is a hero and a symbol of what they consider to be their three hundred year-long struggle against the Russians. They frequently point out that even though Shamil was Dagestani, Chechens made up the majority of his army and the capitals of his Islamic state were located in their territory. He is a "legendary Chechen fighter" and an important role model. So significant is Shamil to the Chechen national identity that when Chechnya produced their first series of postage stamps, Shamil's portrait was placed on the 500-ruble stamp.

society and the Russians, Chechens view Russia as a foreign invader on their land.

Chechen society is traditionally divided into family-based clans (called taip); there are roughly 150 taips in Chechnya, each representing three to four villages. During peaceful times, these clans will maneuver for power between themselves; during times of external threat or invasion, they unite to repel foreign invaders. Because of their social structure, Chechens have almost never been effectively governed by a central power, although charismatic leaders have been able to unite the region.

Geographically, Chechnya, along with Ingushetia, occupies seventy-four hundred square miles on the northern slopes of the Caucasus Mountains, north of the Republic of Georgia. Although small, Chechnya is strategically important. Its border with Georgia controls some of the key mountain passes to the southern Caucasus region. More importantly, Chechnya sits on the only existing oil pipeline route out of Baku, a

RUSSIAN SOLDIERS GUARD A POSITION JUST OUTSIDE OF GROZNY, CHECHNYA. *(AP/Wide World Photos. Reproduced by permission.)*

Caspian Sea port in Azerbaijan; it carries oil to Novorossiisk, a Russian port on the Black Sea. International authorities have estimated that the Caspian sea floor may hold as much as two hundred billion barrels of oil which is nearly twenty percent of the world's oil reserves. This capacity makes the Caspian basin nearly as important an oil producer as Saudi Arabia, and twice as large as any other Persian Gulf country including Iraq and Kuwait. The pipeline, built during the Soviet era, can carry twelve million barrels of oil per year and passes directly through the Chechen capital of Grozny. In addition, there is a network of oil wells and refineries within Chechnya itself, which used to provide petroleum products for much of the former Soviet Union. These oil wells and refineries give the region tremendous economic potential today, if they can be put to work on the open market.

Chechnya in Czarist Times

Russian involvement in Chechnya and the North Caucasus region began under Russian Czar Peter the Great. In 1722, Peter laid claim to Dagestan (then a broad region only roughly defined) for the Russian empire. However, Peter was not able to control the area, and Caucasian mountain peoples, including the Chechens, drove out his armies. Nearly a century later, Russia fought a nine-year war with the empire of Persia, which ended with the Treaty of Gulistan in 1813. In that treaty, Persia ceded much of the Caucasus region and the broad north Caucasus territory of Dagestan, to Russia. To establish control over the region, Russia built a fortress at Groznaya (the word means "dreaded" in Russian) in 1818. This fortress would become the modern city of Grozny. From that point, Russian armies fought a prolonged 40-year war with local peoples, including the Chechens, to secure their control over the region. The southern mountainous section of Chechnya was the last area to be conquered around 1859. This first Russian-Chechen war established a familiar pattern for later conflict. Frustrated by the Chechen army's ability to blend into the civilian population, Russian troops used repression and force indiscriminately against local villages. This tended to create new recruits and a desire for revenge among Chechens. Although the last resistance was wiped out by 1860, the Chechen population continued to chafe under the rule of the Russian czars.

New Rulers, Same Rules: Chechnya Under the USSR

When the Russian Revolution of 1917 toppled Czar Nicholas II and placed the socialist Bolsheviks in power, Chechens and Dagestanis

THE POLITICS OF LANGUAGE

Mandarin Chinese is spoken by 726 million people. Four hundred twenty-seven million people use English. Chechen, the language of Chechnya, is today spoken by just under one million Chechens. Chechen is part of the Nakh-Daghestanian language family, a diverse collection of thirty-four languages that have evolved in the north Caucasus Mountains. With six distinct dialects and nearly a million speakers, Chechen is the largest of the Caucasian languages. Unlike the Indo-European group of languages—which spawned English, French, and Russian—Chechen and the Nakh-Daghestanian languages were not brought from other areas of the world as people migrated. They are the unique to Caucasian peoples and the Caucasus Mountains and are unrelated to any other language group. Despite numerous invasions over the centuries by various groups including the Egyptians, Greeks, Romans, Arabs, and Turks, the Chechens, like the other peoples of the Caucasus Mountains, have kept their language pure. In part, this is due to the geography of the region. A culture located within hard-to-reach mountain passes remains relatively isolated from outside influence. Indeed, part of the distinctiveness of the Nakh-Daghestanian languages is their dissimilarity from other language families and even from each other. While Ingush is close enough to Chechen to be generally understood by Chechens, speakers of Chechen do not understand Dargins, or Avars, or many other Caucasian tongues even though all are part of the same language family and all co-exist within an area roughly the size of France.

Like most of the languages in the Nakh-Daghestanian language family, Chechen was not traditionally a written language. It wasn't until the 1930s that an orthography, a method of representing the sounds of language by letters, was created using the Russian Cyrillic alphabet. Unlike many Caucasian languages, Chechen is used in schools, on the radio and television, and in print. The Russian alphabet has allowed Chechens to use their language both publicly and privately, turning their language into a powerful and unifying cultural tool.

Today, ninety-seven percent of Chechens claim Chechen as their first language, their mother tongue. But, like most other cultures of the Caucasus Mountains as well as most cultures of the former Soviet Union, they also speak Russian, which has become the common language of the region. Because the Caucasus Mountains are home to thirty-three languages in addition to Chechen, Russian is used by Chechens to communicate with most other Caucasian cultures. While Russian is the common tongue, it is also frequently a common target of newly independent countries. After the USSR dissolved in 1991, many of its former republics have used language to revive their ethnic and cultural identities. In the former Soviet republics of Estonia and Latvia, local language tests effectively deny citizenship to residents who only speak Russian. Uzbekistan has made Latin script, rather than Cyrillic, the script for their language Uzbek. In Chechnya, three months after the formal peace treaty ending the first war was signed in May 1997, the newly elected Chechen parliament made Chechen its official language.

took the opportunity to declare their independence from Russia and proclaim a new "mountain republic" in the North Caucasus. The rebellion initially challenged pro-Czarist Russian forces and was aided in some places by the Bolsheviks. But, in 1920, after their position was secure, the Bolshevik government turned on the Chechens and the new Soviet Red Army moved to reestablish control over the region. Chechen resistance was largely stamped out by 1923.

Low-level rebellion against Soviet rule continued, however. Over the next twenty years, there were four to five anti-Soviet uprisings, each one suppressed by the Soviet military. In 1944, fearing that the Chechens were collaborating with the Nazi regime of Germany during World War II, Stalin tried to "solve" the Chechen problem by annulling the Chechen-Ingush Republic and deporting almost five hundred thousand Chechens and Ingush to Central Asia—nearly the entire population of both regions. Up to one hundred fifty thousand people—more than twenty-five percent of the population—died during the deportation or in the harsh conditions of the camps in Siberia and Central Asia. In 1957, Soviet leader Nikita Khrushchev reversed Stalin's orders, allowing the remaining Chechens to return to their homeland, and again conferred autonomous status

CHECHNYA'S WAR OF WORDS

As the conflict in Chechnya has evolved, so too has its portrayal in the news media. During the first war, the newly independent Russian news media was instrumental in turning public opinion against the war in Chechnya. Daily reports tallied the heavy Russian losses for its viewers and showed gruesome scenes of street fighting whose victims were primarily civilian. Detailed and sympathetic coverage of Chechen leaders soured Yeltsin's public support and brought about widespread demonstrations in Moscow and St. Petersburg calling for an end to the war.

When the hostilities resumed in 1999, the Russian government went on the offensive early. The recently formed Media Ministry forbade all Russian television networks to publish interviews with Chechen leaders and warned all journalists working in Russia that they would be criminally prosecuted under anti-terrorist legislation if they broadcast interviews with or quoted Chechen leaders. Currently, access to Chechnya by domestic and foreign correspondents requires military credentials, which are highly restricted. Only reporters from pro-Moscow stations are allowed in and then only for carefully orchestrated military tours that toe the line of official reports. Journalists are lectured on how to write and broadcast about the conflict—Chechen fighters for example, must be called terrorists—and those of them whose reports criticize the military operation are subsequently banned from Chechnya. Foreign reporters are rarely given permission to cross into Chechnya and those who attempt to enter the region illegally are arrested and detained. Andrei Babitsky, a reporter from the U.S. funded Radio Liberty that broadcasts to Russia, was arrested and held for six weeks.

Officials at the Media Ministry claim they are trying to prevent terrorist propaganda from being published. They complain that western journalists rarely report on Chechen criminal activities and cite the recent bombings of Moscow apartment buildings and the epidemic of civilian kidnappings as examples. Between the two periods of armed conflict, many Chechen militants did indeed become criminals, and abductions for ransom were a favorite ploy. Over one thousand individuals were kidnapped between 1997 and 1999. At least twenty-one of them were journalists.

The Chechen fighters have countered by setting up information centers outside of both Chechnya and Russia. There are also Chechen information centers in Kiev and in Odessa, Ukraine, and in Poland. They have also established their own web site where they regularly publish what they claim is official documentation of Russian atrocities perpetrated against Chechen civilians. Vladimir Putin acknowledged that their government had "some catching up to do if it was to use the web as effectively as the Chechens." The Russian Media Ministry has declared the documents on the Chechen web site to be forgeries.

to the Chechen-Ingush Republic within the Russian Republic of the USSR. But the damage to Russian-Chechen relations had already been done. The Chechen people have not forgotten their exile and what they perceive as an attempted genocide. Indeed, many of the current and recent leaders of the Chechen independence movement, including Dzhokhar Dudayev and current Chechen president Aslan Maskhadov, were born in Kazakhstan during the period of separation from their homeland.

New Rulers, New Rules? Chechnya and the Breakup of the USSR

The breakup of the USSR brought new hope that relations between Caucasus peoples and Russia might finally change. In 1988 and 1989, the Soviet republics of Armenia, Azerbaijan, and Georgia began agitating for their independence as the Soviet government under Mikhail Gorbachev demonstrated it was increasingly unwilling to intervene with force to restore Moscow's control. In June 1990, the congress of the Soviet Russian Republic passed a declaration of Russian sovereignty over its portion of the USSR. This posed a serious threat to continued Soviet central control as Russia was the largest Soviet republic and controlled roughly seventy-five percent of Soviet territory. In November 1990, the legislature of the Chechen-Ingush Republic passed a similar resolution declaring sovereignty over its own territory and proclaiming independence from Russia. This was the first declaration of Chechen independence since 1920 and is the beginning of the current crisis.

The USSR continued to struggle to hold itself together until August 1991, when hard-line Soviet generals and leaders attempted an abortive coup against Mikhail Gorbachev. Boris Yeltsin, leader of the Soviet Russian Republic, successfully rallied forces that defended the central government in Moscow, earning tremendous popularity. When the coup collapsed, the remnants of the Soviet Union collapsed with it; Gorbachev returned to Moscow to negotiate the breakup of the USSR into fifteen independent republics. During the coup, some Chechens (including current separatist leader Shamil Basayev) went to Moscow to aid in Yeltsin's defense of the White House (the Russian Parliament building) even though in Chechnya itself, the communist leaders of the Chechen-Ingush Republic supported the coup. With Yeltsin's blessing, Dzhokhar Dudayev, a Chechen and a former Soviet air force officer, organized a coup against the local communist leaders, ousted the pro-Moscow political forces, and declared independence for the republic. Dudayev called for immediate elections to establish a democratic government in Chechnya. Those elections were held in October 1991, although only in those parts of Chechnya controlled by Dudayev's forces. The significant territory that was under the control either of pro-communist or pro-Yeltsin forces did not support the move for independence and did not participate in the elections. The elections resulted in Dudayev's movement winning control of the parliament, and Dudayev himself being proclaimed president.

The Russian government in Moscow seemed willing to let the issue stand through 1992. But in March 1993, the Russian government encouraged dissention among the leadership of the Chechen-Ingush Republic. The result was a political division between the Chechen and Ingush portions of the republic. In Ingushetia (the newly-created entity to the west of Chechnya), General Ruslan Aushev, who was initially appointed by Moscow, won elections and became president of the Ingush republic within Russia, leaving Chechnya as a separate autonomous province under the leadership of Dudayev.

The New Russia and the New Chechnya, Round One

The competing claims over who ruled Chechnya could not be ignored forever, and some form of direct contest of power was undoubtedly inevitable. The Chechen government under Dudayev continued to face opposition to its rule in parts of Chechnya as pro-Moscow forces resisted the move for independence. In addition, the Chechen economy suffered severely as Dudayev's anti-Russian policies drove both skilled Russian workers and their money out of the region. After some eighteen months of low-level fighting and counter-accusations between Grozny and Moscow, Russia moved to recapture its authority over the wayward Chechens. On November 26, 1994, a Russian armored column moved into Grozny in hopes of sparking an uprising among Chechen groups opposed to Dudayev's rule. The expected uprising never came, and the Russian forces were captured with little fighting by Dudayev's troops. A few days later, Russian president Yeltsin issued an ultimatum to the Chechen government to disarm and surrender. At the same time, aircraft (possibly from the Russian military, possibly under control of Chechen opposition groups) began bombing Grozny. Less than two weeks later, Russian forces launched a serious ground offensive to retake Chechnya. By the end of 1994, Russian forces deployed in Chechnya numbered near forty thousand.

Despite significant resistance by Dudayev's forces, the Russian army took control of Grozny in January 1995. Over the next several months, Russian troops pushed Chechen fighters southwards; by the summer, Russia had reoccupied most of Chechnya and forced separatists into the mountain strongholds of southern Chechnya. However, these military gains came at a significant cost. While unable to hold territory, the Chechen forces inflicted significant numbers of casualties on advancing Russian troops. During the first half of 1995, protest and dissent against the war increased among Russian citizens, as a free Russian press reported the horrors and damage of war back to Moscow and other large cities. The dissent became so serious that some began to label Chechnya a "Russian Vietnam." The economic costs of war also mounted, pushing an already-ailing Russian economy further into recession.

By the summer of 1995, a stalemate of sorts had developed, with Russian troops holding the plains but unable to dislodge Chechen forces from the mountains. The stalemate was only in conventional military terms, however. Chechen commandos continued to operate behind Russian lines, causing significant damage and sapping the morale of both Russian troops and the Russian public. The most important of these operations came in June 1995, when Chechen rebel commander Shamil Basayev led one hundred heavily-armed commandos seventy-five miles past Chechen borders into Russia to the town of Budyonnovsk.

Once there, his forces attacked several sites throughout the town of 100,000, seized a hospital, and took over fifteen hundred people hostage. Russian forces initially counter-attacked, killing ninety-five and wounding 142 civilians before halting. After a series of negotiations, the commandos were allowed safe passage back to separatist-held portions of Chechnya, and Russia agreed to resume peace talks in Grozny with Dudayev's government. Although the negotiations did not begin immediately, the incident seriously demoralized Russian troops and sent domestic support for Yeltsin's Chechen policy plummeting as Russian citizens worried about their safety from future attacks.

The latter half of 1995 and the first half of 1996 saw little change. Chechen commandos continued to stage occasional raids outside their mountain strongholds. Attacks similar to the Budyonnovsk hostage crisis occurred across the Chechen border in Dagestan, and on a Black Sea ferry—the latter apparently conducted by Turkish citizens of Caucasian descent sympathetic to the Chechen cause. By the middle of 1996, Russia had committed fifty thousand troops to the fight in Chechnya and was using extensive artillery and aerial bombardment in vain attempts to dislodge rebel forces. Their only success came in killing Dudayev in April by homing in on the cellular phone he was using to negotiate with Russian officials. Dudayev's death however, had little effect on either the Chechens' willingness or their ability to continue fighting.

The tide of the war finally shifted in August 1996. On the sixth of August, the day of Yeltsin's inauguration after his victory in the elections earlier in the summer, Chechen fighters launched an offensive to re-take Grozny. Their effort was wildly successful, reaching far beyond the expectations of most military analysts. Russian forces, despite their advantages in heavy armor, air support, and numbers, were driven from Grozny by the end of August and forced to retreat from the surrounding region. In response, Yeltsin sent former Russian general Alexander Lebed to negotiate a cease-fire with the Chechen forces at Khasavyurt. The negotiations were successful; the resulting agreement stopped the fighting, pledged the withdrawal of all Russian troops from Chechen territory, and promised further negotiations to settle the issue of Chechnya's independence within five years. Russian troops had completely left the region by the end of the year, and in May 1997, Yeltsin and new Chechen president Aslan Maskhadov signed the Treaty on Peace and the Principles of Interrelations Between the Russian Federation and the Chechen Republic Ichkeria. Chechnya had achieved independence at least in practice, if not by legal right. This came, however, at a high price: by the August 1996 cease-fire, between fifty thousand and eighty thousand people (mostly civilians) had been killed.

Maskhadov, a moderate nationalist and a former Soviet army colonel of the same generation as Dudayev, was elected president of Chechnya in January 1997. The primary opposition candidate was Shamil Basayev, a hard-line Islamist who had led the raid on Budyonnovsk. Maskhadov had been a commander under Dudayev during the war and had broad support among Chechen voters. After the cease-fire, however, his government had difficulty controlling the region. Organized crime was a serious problem and kidnappings, assassinations, and smuggling became commonplace. Despite Maskhadov's support at the ballot box, much of Chechnya devolved to the control of armed warlords who included in their ranks Shamil Basayev and other separatists.

The initial relationship with Russia appeared promising. Less than two months after the May 1997 treaty was signed, Russia, Chechnya, and Azerbaijan signed an agreement on the shipment of oil from the Caspian port of Baku through Grozny to Russian ports on the Black Sea. But in April 1999, Chechen government officials cut off the oil pipeline between Baku and Novorossiysk, arguing that Russia owed them ten million dollars for pipeline repairs under the 1997 agreement. Russia, in turn, became increasingly concerned about the state of lawlessness within Chechnya, which they claimed threatened Russians still living in Chechnya.

RECENT HISTORY AND THE FUTURE

The most recent round of fighting was sparked by the events of August 1999. Armed Islamist groups based in Chechnya and led by Shamil Basayev, moved into neighboring Dagestan which was still part of Russia. Their intent was to defend Dagestani Muslims from perceived Russian aggression and to establish a larger Islamic state among area Muslims. Basayev's forces were driven back into Chechnya by Russian troops after a few weeks, although the Russian army was unable to keep them from escaping as it claimed it would. A month later in September, a series of deadly explosions in apartment buildings in Moscow, St. Petersburg, and Volgodonsk killed a total of three hundred civilians. The attacks came without warning and no group claimed responsibility, but the Russian government laid the blame explicitly on Chechen extremists.

Using the incursions, bombings, and increasing lawlessness within Chechnya as justification, Russian forces moved across the Chechen border on October 2, 1999. Their initially stated aim was to take a portion of territory in northern Chechnya in order to prevent further attacks like Basayev's incursion, and to protect Russians living on the northern plains of Chechnya. Over the next few months, however, the emphasis shifted to taking more Chechen territory, and then eventually to recapturing Chechnya altogether, despite previous pledges both to avoid using force and to seek a negotiated solution to the question of Chechnya's future status. On December 25, Russian forces begin a new full-scale assault on Grozny, which included extensive artillery shelling, and aircraft assault and was backed by some 80,000 Russian military troops. By the end of 1999, Russians and Chechens appeared to be fighting exactly the same war they had fought three years earlier.

Militarily, this second Chechen war has looked remarkably like the first. By early February 2000, most of Grozny had been recaptured by Russian armed forces, but pockets of resistance remained in the city. By mid-February, Russian armed forces had ordered the city evacuated and its buildings destroyed in an attempt to root out the last rebel forces. As before, the Russians face an additional eight thousand to ten thousand rebel forces in the southern mountains.

Despite similarities, there are important differences between the first and second Chechen wars. The second war in Chechnya has been far more devastating than the first. The Russian offensive has created a new wave of refugees; by the end of 1999 some two hundred fifty thousand Chechens (about twenty-five percent of the population) have been driven from their homes to towns or camps across the border in Ingushetia. An unknown number—estimates are around forty thousand—remain in Grozny, unwilling or unable to leave despite massive Russian bombardment of the city.

For the Russians, this second war has garnered more public support than the previous. An opinion poll taken in November 1999 found that sixty-six percent of Russian respondents thought the war was "successful." The increase is due partly to the genuine fear aroused by the apartment

CHILDREN STARE AT THE DESTRUCTION CAUSED BY THE RUSSIAN SHELLING OF A CHECHEN VILLAGE NEAR THE CAPITOL OF GROZNY. *(AP/Wide World Photos. Reproduced by permission.)*

bombings of September and partly to the increased government control of the media, which has resulted in a tempered view of the war. Similarly, although the war is expensive for Russia—by the end of 1999 it had already cost over one and a half billion dollars—it comes at a time when, because of high oil prices, the Russian government has more revenue and more economic stability. However, the indiscriminate bombardment of Grozny and Russia's apparent lack of concern for civilians in the war zone has cost the Russian government some foreign aid. In December 1999, the International Monetary Fund

(IMF) put scheduled loan payments on hold, and a number of European countries have threatened sanctions if the war continues. Still, Russia appears both more willing and more able to prosecute the war this time, although it is unclear whether they will be any more successful on the battlefield.

The outcome of this Chechen-Russian conflict is currently unclear. Russia appears to be incapable of controlling Chechnya by force as was demonstrated during the first war. But, given increased domestic political and financial support, it may take the Chechen separatists a long time to convince the Russian government to stop trying. In addition, the factionalism that characterizes the current Chechen leadership (demonstrated by the independent actions of President Maskhadov and rebel leader Basayev) make it difficult for Russia to find a negotiating partner who can deliver peace—a fact which the government in Moscow uses to justify its lack of negotiation efforts.

In the long term, there are three possible solutions for Chechnya. One possible outcome is a return to the way Chechnya was governed in the nineteenth century with Russia in nominal control of the region but facing ongoing resistance at a variety of levels. This is probably not a viable long-term situation for Russia unless its economy recovers on more than just temporarily increased oil revenues. Russia simply cannot afford a prolonged and costly struggle; sooner or later, costs will mount, media and public opinion will turn against such a strategy, and the government will be pressured to change course. Another possibility is full Chechen independence. As this would require a near-total collapse of Russian power or a serious crisis in Russia that forces them to redirect their resources elsewhere, this solution is also unlikely. None of the current political parties and factions in Russia support Chechen independence, so even a simple leadership change will not make full Chechen independence any more likely. Russian stubbornness on this point is unsurprising. In addition to the remaining five north Caucasus regions, which could potentially desire to secede from Russia, there are significant separatist sentiments among other non-Russians living elsewhere in the Russian Federation (particularly in Tatarstan, which occupies an important area in the central region of Russia). Full Chechen independence would also take away some of the anticipated oil revenues from Caspian Sea pipelines and this is money, which the Russian government desperately needs. Absent some fundamental change in Russian politics, any future Russian government

will be extremely unwilling to recognize the independence of Chechnya as a separate country.

The third, and most probable, alternative is some form of autonomy within the Russian Federation that provides for substantial local government. This would maintain Moscow's titular control over the region and help it to resist secessionist pressures elsewhere, while satisfying at least some Chechen demands for self-government. Were such an agreement to be created in the next five years, it would probably include a clause on leaving the possibility of future independence open. If, over time, autonomy within Russia is beneficial to the Chechens, particularly if Russian money helps rebuild Grozny, demands for independence may fade. For this solution to last, however, a future Chechen government will have to devise better strategies for dealing with crime and armed opposition within its own government, both of which Maskhadov's government failed to do between 1997 and 1999.

For the rest of the world, the Chechen conflict has two serious consequences. First, its location puts it in the center of efforts to bring more Caspian Sea oil to the international market. If long-term stability can be brought to the area, more oil will flow out of the Caspian basin, through Russia, and onto the world market. This would benefit both Russia, which desperately needs the oil revenue (providing of course that it passes through Russian territory), and the U.S. and European economies, where greater supply would likely lower prices. This prospect insures that the United States and Europe will continue to be interested in a long-term solution to the Chechen crisis.

The second consequence of the outcome of the current Chechen war is in the area of human rights and international law. Chechnya, along with ethnic conflicts in Bosnia, Kosovo, Rwanda, and East Timor, are shaping the world's understanding of the role and limits of international law and its ability to impose standards of conduct on particular countries. Russia's alleged human rights abuses against people it claims as its own have been harshly criticized by international powers, but to date, only moderately punished. If this present war drags on for a long time, as seems likely, the amount of external pressure put on Russia to moderate its behavior will send a powerful signal to other countries with similar problems. If the international community unifies its criticism of Russian tactics, and punishes the Russian government for any abuses, it will strengthen the hand of those who seek to protect human rights globally and increase the likelihood of world leaders using their power to enforce international norms of behavior.

BIBLIOGRAPHY

Arquilla, John, and Theodore Karasik. "Chechnya: A Glimpse of Future Conflict?" *Studies in Conflict and Terrorism* 22 (1999).

Barylski, Robert. *The Soldier in Russian Politics: Duty, Dictatorship and Democracy Under Gorbachev and Yeltsin.* New Brunswick, N.J.: Transaction Publishers, 1998.

Boyle, Francis. "Happy Birthday Chechnya!" *Journal of Muslim Minority Affairs* 18 (1998).

Chesnov, Ian Veniaminovich. "Civilization and the Chechen," *Russian Social Science Review* 37 (1996).

Cornell, Svante. "International Reactions to Massive Human Rights Violations: The Case of Chechnya," *Europe-Asia Studies* 51 (1999).

———. *Small Nations and Great Powers: A Study of Ethnopolitical Conflict in the Caucasus.* Richmond, Va.: Curzon Press, 1999.

Hottelet, Richard C. "Chechnya Redux," *Christian Science Monitor* 92 (1999): 10.

Kagarlitskii, B.I. "Chechnya-Preliminary Results," *Russian Social Science Review* 40 (1999).

Nahaylo, Bohdan and Victor Swoboda. *Soviet Disunion: A History of the Nationality Problem in the USSR.* New York: Free Press, 1990.

Weir, Fred. "Where Rebellion is a Tradition," *Christian Science Monitor* 92 (2000): 1.

R. William Ayers

THE CHIAPAS REBELLION: INDIGENOUS PEOPLE'S RIGHTS IN MEXICO

THE CONFLICT

The indigenous people of Chiapas—natives from before Europeans colonized Mexico—believe they are fighting for their rights and self-determination. The Mexican government believes the indigenous people can have their rights within the context of Mexico. Paramilitary groups are fighting to suppress what they view as terrorist acts by the Zapatistas—one group representing the indigenous people.

Political

- The indigenous people want control over their own destiny.

- Mexican officials—and most Mexicans—want a united Mexico, and want the native people to find a place within Mexico.

Economic

- Conflict over land, and the control of land, increased with the shift from subsistence agriculture to cash crops. The land is now, potentially, very profitable, and so it becomes very important who controls it.

When the North American Free Trade Agreement (NAFTA) went into effect on January 1, 1994, the Zapatista rebellion in the state of Chiapas sent convulsions throughout Mexico as the indigenous people rose up in arms against the government. The Mexican Indians felt that Mexico's neo-liberal (practical, rather than ideological) economic policies had devastated their traditional way of life. In Mexico, and particularly in heavily indigenous Chiapas, rebellions have not been isolated occurrences. Populated by Mayan-speaking Indians, the Mexican state of Chiapas borders Guatemala to the south and is divided between the highlands and lowlands. Regionalism, religion, and the struggle for land are factors that have influenced the historical development of Chiapas and contributed to the ongoing crisis.

HISTORICAL BACKGROUND

Colonial Period

After Fernando Cortés (1485–1547) conquered central Mexico in 1521, he sent out expeditions to settle the rest of the country. Luis Marín initially established the Spanish presence in Chiapas between 1521 and 1524. The indigenous people rebelled in 1527 against the Spaniards, who had brought disease, exploitation, war, and a new religion. In 1528 the conquistador Diego de Mazariegos finally pacified the region and extended Spanish domination, founding Ciudad Real, which became the seat of colonial administration, in the temperate highlands. European diseases, such as measles and smallpox, and labor exploitation decimated the Indians of the lowlands. The Spanish relocated the lowland Indians and shifted their agricultural and livestock production to the area surrounding Ciudad Real.

CHRONOLOGY

1521 Fernando Cortez of Spain conquers Mexico.

1528 Diego de Mazariegos dominates Mexico and pacifies the indigenous population.

1500s Fray Bartolomé de las Casas oversees the conversion of Indians to Catholicism.

1708 The Indians abandon the church in response to a religious belief in the coming end of the world.

1712–13 A three-month rebellion by the Indians is crushed.

1822–23 The Mexican empire disintegrates. Chiapas decides to remain with Mexico to end its subordination to Guatemala.

1854 The Revolution Ayutla defeats Gen. Antonio López.

1961–67 Following the French invasion, the liberals become the champions of Mexican nationalism.

1867 Indians in Chamula establish a shrine to a clay idol; thousands made pilgrimages to the shrine.

1868 The *ladinos* (Mexicans whose ancestors are from Spain) attack the shrine and jail the indigenous religious leader.

1876–1911 The Porfiriato, when Porfirio Díaz rules.

1911–20 The Mexican Revolution occurs; fighting breaks out between the highland elite and the lowland elite in Chiapas.

1936–40 Agrarian reform results in the establishment of an indigenous workers' union—the Union of Indian Workers.

1940–70 The Mexican Economic Miracle.

1974 The government asks Bishop Ruiz to organize an Indigenous Congress.

1975 The government holds the first National Indigenous Congress in Pátzcuaro, Michoacán, Mexico. The National Council of Indian Pueblos is established.

1977 A secular movement, People's Politics, organizes a peaceful struggle for socialism among peasants.

1994 The Zapatista National Liberation Army chooses the date NAFTA went into effect—January 1, 1994—to start their rebellion. The government responds by sending in troops; in the initial fighting 145 people are killed. Later, the National Democratic Convention is held in the Lacandon jungle. The rebels increase their offensive.

1996 The Zapatista Front of National Liberation, a nonviolent political organization, is established. The San Andrés Accord on Indigenous Rights and Culture is signed, containing minimal concessions by the government. Later that year, a new guerrilla group, the Popular Revolutionary Army, emerges.

1997 Indigenous people, organized by the Zapatistas, go to Mexico City for a march. The Zapatista Front of National Liberation is formally founded. The Acteal Massacre takes place late in the year, resulting in forty-five deaths and the creation of hundreds of refugees.

In accordance with colonial policy, the Catholic Church played a dominant role in incorporating the indigenous people into the emerging colonial state. The responsibility for converting the Indians to Catholicism and protecting them from excessive exploitation by Spanish colonists fell on the Dominican order, led by Fray Bartolomé de las Casas (1474–1566). The order reorganized native society but allowed Indians a degree of autonomy. This circumstance contributed to the persistence of indigenous traditions and practices as native religious beliefs and Catholic traditions blended through a process called syncretism. The *ladinos* (people of European descent) and the Indians coexisted until 1712, the year a major rebellion broke out.

An economic depression resulting from a decline in silver production in the viceroyalty of New Spain (Mexico) during the late sixteenth and early seventeenth century affected the region of Chiapas. The Spanish hold on Chiapas was weakened and the dominance of the Dominicans was strengthened. The Crown's need for revenue in the second half of the seventeenth century led to the centralization of colonial administration whereby regional authorities were responsible for collecting the tribute (a payment imposed by government). To weaken the regular orders, such as the Dominicans, the Crown increased the number of bishoprics, which resulted in an increased number of secular clergy (clergy appointed by and loyal to the government). Conflicts between the secular clergy and the regular clergy ensued, weakening the Dominicans hold on the indigenous population. Whereas the Dominicans had demonstrated a modicum of respect toward the Indians' traditional beliefs and practices, the new bishops showed no such restraint. They denounced native religion as paganism and the "work of the devil," and aggressively attacked the spiritual leaders of the Indian communities.

An economic crisis, coupled with excessive exaction (demand for a fee or contribution) by civil and religious authorities, led to a millenarian movement—religious belief in the end of the world—among the region's indigenous inhabitants. The movement, which combined native and Christian ideas, originated among the highland Indians in 1708 as word spread of a miraculous appearance by the Virgin Mary. Abandoning the church, the Indians established their own cult that preached the destruction of the *ladinos* and the beginning of a new life for the indigenous people. In actuality, it was an autonomous movement through which the Indians sought to free themselves from the Church and colonial authorities. In 1712 a three-month rebellion occurred as the Indians slaughtered their Spanish masters and attempted to destroy all vestiges of Spanish rule. Reinforcements from Guatemala crushed the rebellion, but final pacification did not occur until 1713. The authorities mutilated rebels and dispersed them by sending them to lowland haciendas and ranches. Devotion to the Church increased in the aftermath. The brutality of the repression, and widespread epidemics after 1712, quelled major revolts in the region until the nineteenth century.

Early Nineteenth Century

Under the Bourbons, economic reforms benefited *ladino* merchants and landowners, who continued to exploit Indian labor. Economic growth exacerbated regional conflicts between the producers and merchants from the lowlands and royal political authorities from the highlands. During the colonial period Chiapas was subordinated to Guatemala, but in 1821 Mexico achieved independence from Spain, and a chaotic period ensued as various conflicts engulfed the new nation. With the disintegration of the Mexican empire from 1822 to 1823, the Central American provinces broke away from Mexico. In 1824 Chiapas decided to remain with the Mexican Republic in order to end its subordination to Guatemala. In honor of Fray Bartolomé de las Casas, the new republican elites renamed the state capital, Ciudad Real, San Cristóbal de las Casas.

The political chaos of the nineteenth century benefited the new state's elites by allowing for regional control removed from centralized state authority. The state's elites reflected the political divisions of the nation: those from the lowlands adopted a liberal ideology and those from the highlands embraced a conservative one. Regional *caudillos* (civil or military strongmen) emerged and political instability engulfed the state and the nation. As coffee and timber became the primary exports of Chiapas, the liberal and conservative factions became rivals for control of Indian labor and land. The lowlands acquired new economic importance as the highlands gradually lost their political and economic dominance. The liberals sought to wrest control of these economic resources from the Dominicans, who continued to monopolize them. The Church, in general, continued to protect the Indians from rapacious *ladinos*, who resented their lack of access to this labor supply.

The rise of the liberals in Mexico began with the defeat of the *caudillo* Gen. Antonio López de Santa Anna by the Revolution Ayutla in 1854. Liberal reforms were initiated in this period, when laws were passed that sought to create a secular nation and divorce the Church and Indian communities from their land. The promulgation of the Constitution of 1857 codified these reforms, thus provoking the conservatives to invite the French to intervene in Mexican affairs. After the French Intervention (1861–67), the conservatives were discredited in both the nation and the state of Chiapas and the liberals became the champions of Mexican nationalism.

These national events were reflected in the state of Chiapas as the liberal and conservative factions fought for control of the state apparatus. The administration of Angel Albino Corzo (1855–61), implemented the liberal reforms aimed at the Church- and Indian-held lands. Land privatization contributed to conflicts between *ladinos* and the Indian communities, which increased the threat of Indian rebellions. The attack on the Church by liberals contributed to the exile of the bishop of Chiapas and members of the secular orders. The period of the French Intervention brought a conservative government from 1863 to 1864, but after this the liberals regained control of the state government and ushered in a new period of liberal/conservative conflict. This intra-elite conflict came to an end as the two groups united in the face of another major indigenous revolt. Political power devolved to the *caciques* (local political bosses) associated with prominent families that had enriched themselves through the liberal reforms.

The indigenous people suffered through the exaction of labor and tribute demanded by both warring factions to fuel their struggles. Periods of conflict after 1848 had affected the Tzeltal and Tzotzil regions, as the weakening of state and church control contributed to the emergence of native rituals and the rise of Indian authorities within the communities. With the liberal restoration, the Indians were ordered not to pay their tithes to the church. The liberal victory contributed further to the breakdown of the relationship between the church and the Indian communities. The Indians sought autonomy as they established their own religious and market centers free from church control. In Chamula, however, the church continued to demand that the Indians communities pay their tithes and ignore the liberal laws.

In Chamula a new millenarian movement emerged that was reminiscent of the movement that led to the 1712 rebellion. The Indians reaffirmed their identity through the renewed practice of their native culture and religion. In 1867 the Chamulans established a shrine to a clay idol that, according to a community leader, Augustina Gómez Checheb had borne. Indians in the thousands made pilgrimages to the shrine. In 1868 the *ladinos,* frightened of this phenomenon, attacked the shrine and jailed the indigenous religious leader. Indian villagers responded by attempting to defend themselves, which further increased the *ladinos'* paranoia of a major Indian rebellion. In 1869 a schoolteacher convinced the Chamulans to meet with the authorities in San Cristóbal. When they arrived, the *ladinos* massacred them. This massacre allowed the lowland elite to exert their control over the highland Indians' land and labor.

Porfiriato (1876–1911)

During the Porfiriato, when Porfirio Díaz ruled the destiny of Mexico, the nation experienced a period of economic growth spurred on by exports. Once Mexico was thrust into the world market, there was a demand for Chiapas's primary products, especially coffee and cattle. As the

Indians became dispossessed of their land, they were forced to work on ranches and coffee plantations or immigrate to the jungles, away from the state's authorities. When Guatemala's coffee oligarchy built a railroad from the western coffee plantations to the Atlantic coast, the Mexican government, fearing that Chiapas's own coffee elite might secede to Guatemala, built a railway along the Pacific coast to integrate central and western Chiapas into the national economy. Although Porfirian modernization ignored eastern Chiapas, where the Lancandón jungle is located, Chiapas became fully integrated into the world market through its export economy. Mexico's modernization exacerbated the country's internal social problems and led to a wider gap between rich and poor, and the elite and the masses, a gap that eventually gave rise to the circumstances that contributed to the Mexican Revolution.

Mexican Revolution (1911–1920)

Francisco I. Madero (1873–1913) initiated the Mexican Revolution when he issued his Plan of San Luis Potosí in 1911. In the first phase of the Mexican Revolution in Chiapas, the liberal lowland elite supported Díaz while the highland elite, in order to regain control, declared themselves *maderistas* (supporters of Madero). The highland elite raised an Indian army, the Brigada de Las Casas, to combat the lowland elite. While the highland elite sought to regain their former political and economic power, the Indians sought to rid themselves of the harsh taxation and labor obligations exacted by the *porfirista* authorities. The lowland *porfiristas* crushed the highland elite's rebellion after three months. Meanwhile, the Indians continued to struggle against authorities, thus prompting the highland elite to unite once more with their brethren in the lowlands to defend their interests.

The second phase of the Revolution in Chiapas began in 1914, initiated by the revolutionary government of Venustiano Carranza (1859–1920). That year Gen. Agustín Castro, representing the constitutionalist forces, entered Chiapas with the intention of elevating the indigenous people and freeing them from exploitation. The arrival of Castro threatened the political and economic power of Chiapas's elite, who banded together in order to confront this outside threat. Carranza's new revolutionary government instituted laws to benefit the Indian masses but that jeopardized the continuing dominance of the *ladinos.* A new labor law abolished debt servitude—where a worker is de facto enslaved to pay off a debt that never goes away—and gave workers other rights. The law allowed the Indians toiling on the plantations and ranches in the western lowlands to return to their villages. In the more remote region of eastern Chiapas, these reforms did not alter the exploitative relations between landowners and workers. The elite, perceiving the revolutionaries as an occupying army determined to divest them of their privileges, responded by organizing a counterrevolution. The large landowners signed the Act of Canguí and organized an army, to combat the revolutionary regime. The army was known as the *mapaches* (raccoons) because they operated at night. In 1915 the *carrancistas* (supporters of Carranza) also battled a reconstituted Brigada de Las Casas. The Indian and *mestizo* (mixed ancestry) workers utilized this period to challenge the local authorities and throw off the yoke of oppression. In 1917, when Carranza sent in reinforcements, the Indians of Simojovel seized land from the plantation owners. The Brigada finally defeated both the *carrancistas* and the Indians, allowing for a reassertion of *ladino* domination. Once more, the *ladinos* brutally suppressed the Indians by destroying their crops and villages and by executing many of them. The conflict engaged the government for six years until 1920, when the carrancistas departed, leaving the state in the hands of the counterrevolutionaries.

Institutionalizing the Revolution (1920–1940)

Gen. Alvaro Obregon (1880–1928), Mexican president from 1920 to 1924, arrived at a settlement with the *mapaches* once they declared themselves *obregonistas* (supporters of Obregon). This settlement ensured the continued rule of *ladino* political bosses and landowners, who would operate free from federal intervention. Some hope for a progressive government emerged with the founding of the Socialist Party of Socunusco in 1921. Soconusco, a region of coffee and banana plantations located on the southwest coast of Chiapas, depended on contract workers from the highlands. These workers, hoping to realize some of the revolution's ideals for the working class, began organizing and held several strikes to demand basic rights. Carlos Vidal won in the 1925 gubernatorial elections with the support of the workers. In 1927 the *mapaches* assassinated Vidal, and power reverted to them. Agrarian reform, one of the major demands by the Mexican peasantry and Indian communities during the Mexican Revolution, would not reach Chiapas during this period, as the landowning elite prevented its full implementation.

It was not until the administration of Gen. Lázaro Cárdenas (1895–1970) from 1934 to 1940 that substantial changes in land distribution were made. Despite a period of renewed conflict that ensued between the federal government and the regional *caciques* over Cárdenas land distribution, Cárdenas promoted the occupation of plantation lands by the landless and in this way gained the support of the peasantry and Indian communities. Cárdenas also actively promoted the organization of the peasantry into agrarian committees associated with the Confederación Nacional Campesina (CNC) (National Peasant Confederation) so they could be brought into the national political party and the Partido Revolucionario Mexicano (PRM) (Mexican Revolutionary Party), the precursor to the present Partido Revolucionario Institucional (PRI) (Institutional Revolutionary Party).

Cárdenas utilized this political support to intervene in the gubernatorial elections of 1936 and achieve the election of his candidate, Efraín Gutiérrez. He subsequently established the Department of Social Action, Culture and Protection of Indigenous Peoples (DPI) and named as its head Ernesto Urbina, a Tzeltal- and Tzotzil-speaking organizer among the Indians. During his tenure (1936–40), Urbina benefited the indigenous people by vigorous implementation of agrarian reform through the redistribution of land in the highlands and Soconusco. He also established an indigenous workers' union—the Union of Indian Workers (STI)—to represent the plantation workers and to coordinate the contract labor and local agrarian committees. These actions incorporated the indigenous people into the state and further solidified the loyalty of the indigenous people and peasants to the national party.

The Mexican Economic Miracle (1940–70)

Heightened demand for agricultural exports during World War II reversed some of the gains achieved by Cárdenas's administration in that large estates benefited from new government policies. In order to survive, peasants not only cultivated their own plots but also sought wage work on the plantations. Searching for land and livelihoods, some peasants began to immigrate to the eastern jungle, a movement that would have tremendous ramifications for the environment. In the 1950s the government shifted its policy toward the Indians as it promoted new developmental projects among the indigenous people. These projects were undertaken by the National Indianist Institute (INI), which channeled government funding to the municipalities. The INI worked with local indigenous leaders to implement these programs and thus strengthened their political power. These policies reinforced the identity of the indigenous people and strengthened localism among them.

The colonization of the eastern jungles, known as the Selva Lacandona, increased after the 1950s. Attracted by the abundance of workers, colonists bought marginal plots from rich landowners and established themselves along the periphery of large estates. These colonists provided labor for the estates and ranches that dotted the jungles. The colonists came from Chiapas and other parts of Mexico as a result of land pressures. The government promoted colonization of the eastern jungles because the region acted as a pressure valve by absorbing the growing population. Conquistadors established this pattern of colonization—from the highlands to the lowlands—during the colonial period. Immigration and colonization resulted in an uprooted population and exacerbated conflicts between rancher and peasant, and between peasant and peasant, for land and other resources. In the highlands, as a result of agrarian and other revolutionary reforms, Indians controlled the local government, but in the lowlands ranchers and large landowners controlled the local government, while the peasant majority were disenfranchised from political power.

The Roman Catholic Church

Further conflicts ensued when Chiapas became a field for proselytizing by the Catholic church and Protestant missionaries, which contributed to the building of social movements. During the 1930s, a period of intense anticlericalism in Mexico, Protestant missionaries were allowed to enter various remote regions in order to weaken the power of the Catholic church. These missionaries were also utilized in the government's literacy campaigns. Initially, their activities were negligible but with economic growth and social dislocation, their message reached more of the Indian communities. As the Protestants left traditional Catholic communities, migration to eastern Chiapas increased and squatter camps outside of San Cristóbal were established. By 1990 the Protestant members of the communities of eastern Chiapas made up a substantial number of the population.

In its effort to counteract the rising Protestant influence, the Catholic church played an important role in Chiapas. In 1962 Pope John XXIII held Vatican Council II, which strongly influenced the church's policy toward the poor and oppressed. Samuel Ruiz, the bishop of Chiapas, attended this conclave and was profoundly affected by its message. When he returned to Chiapas, he invited the Dominicans energized by the church's social teachings to help him attend to the problems of the poor and the indigenous people. He established schools, a health center, workshops, and a communal farm. His most controversial act was creating schools intended to teach Indians how to engage in grassroots organizing. They were responsible for educating Indian communities about their rights and the steps necessary to protect them. Subsequently, Ruiz attended the Second Conference of Latin American Bishops, held in Medellín, Colombia, in 1968. At this conference Ruiz learned of the Theology of Liberation, a theory of Marxist (communist) analysis combined with the teachings of the church. Liberation Theology was a way for the church to dedicate itself to working with the poor and the oppressed in their peaceful struggle for social change.

In 1974 the government asked Bishop Ruiz to organize an Indigenous Congress in commemoration of the five-hundred-year anniversary of the birth of Fray Bartolomé de las Casas. Ruiz asked the catechists to go into the communities and elect representatives who would express their demands to the government. Many consider this grassroots organization the precursor to the radical peasant movements of subsequent decades. The Congress allowed the Indians to express themselves to the government. In the past, the government had held meetings with the Indians in order to inform them of preordained government policies and programs. After the Congress was terminated, the catechists took the message into the communities and continued their organizing activities.

Social Movements

In 1977 a secular movement known as People's Politics (PP) began to replace the catechists in eastern Chiapas. PP was made up of political organizers from northern Mexico who practiced Maoism and sought to organize peasants for a peaceful struggle for socialism. Many of its members had participated in the 1968 Mexican student movement, which was violently suppressed by the government. PP worked with the peasants to obtain credits from the federal government. Subsequently, other peasant organizations emerged. The Emiliano Zapata Peasant Organization (OCEZ), operating in the town of Venustiano Carranza, helped the peasants to oppose the ranchers who attempted to evict them from their

SUBCOMANDANTE MARCOS

1959– Zapatista leader Rafael Sebastin Guillen Vincente is better known by his alias, Subcomandante Marcos. Although not Mayan himself, Subcomandante (sub-commander) Marcos has championed the rights of indigenous Mexicans in the southern state of Chiapas.

For several years, Marcos's origins were uncertain. It is now known that he was born into an upper-middle class Mexican family. After studying in Mexico City and Paris, Marcos taught sociology at the Autonomous Metropolitan University of Mexico. In 1984 he moved to Mexico's poorest state, Chiapas, to work among the local indigenous population. During the 1980s, he led literacy and health care programs, and worked to link the plight of indigenous groups throughout the world, often using Mayan mythology to explain contemporary issues.

After a constitutional amendment removed indigenous Mexicans' land rights, Marcos led an uprising in protest. On January 1, 1994, Marcos and an army of Chiapans temporarily took over the town of San Cristóbal.

Although considered a terrorist by the Mexican authorities, Marcos has become part of popular culture. In 1996 he met with film director Oliver Stone to discuss a movie about the uprising. His masked and pipe-smoking image is a popular icon throughout Mexico and the slogan "Viva Marcos!" appears on dolls, t-shirts, and even underwear.

In 1999 the United States' National Endowment for the Arts cancelled support for an award-winning bilingual children's book, *The Story of Colors,* when it was discovered the book was written by Marcos.

mittee—that was named after the revolutionary peasant leader Emiliano Zapata's 1911 plan for agrarian reform.

The Economy

Economic factors shaped the direction of many of these political events. After 1940 the Mexican government under the PRI pursued a policy of industrialization, which contributed to Mexico's "economic miracle." In agriculture, peasants shifted from the production of subsistence crops to export crops, a shift the government promoted. During the late 1970s and early 1980s Mexico experienced an oil boom that allowed it to contract huge loans from international funding organizations. Over-borrowing contributed to the problems of the 1980s, when Mexico entered into its debt crisis—a time known as the "lost decade." In 1982 a major economic crisis sent shock waves through the country and policymakers, financiers, and industrialists decided to restructure the Mexican economy. In the 1990s, a neo-liberal model of free trade dominated the government's policies. (Neo-liberalism is a policy guided by pragmatism, not ideology.) The implementation of this model by the government contributed directly to the Chiapas rebellion.

The election of President Carlos Salinas de Gotarri (1988–94), amid charges of electoral fraud, signified the ascendancy of the neo-liberal technocratic elite (pragmatists reliant on technology). They implemented free trade policies that directly influenced the peasant and Indian communities of Chiapas. NAFTA—the North American Free Trade Agreement—would be the result of this shift away from PRI's ideals of the Mexican Revolution. Uppermost in the plans of technocrats was the establishment of a market economy by commercializing land and labor. In 1992 they modified Article 27 of the Mexican Constitution, the principal article that stimulated the agrarian reform and protected the *ejidos* (communal land ownership). The modification not only allowed individual farmers to grant themselves title to the land and to sell or rent their plots but it also allowed for large scale agribusiness ventures and land concentration. Subcomandante Marcos, one of the leading spokespersons for the Zapatistas, specifically identified this modification as the spark that led to the armed struggle.

In Chiapas, land seizures by large landowners and ranchers were common but peasants also seized land from the large landowners and ranchers. Other resources, especially oil and timber, attracted companies and investors to the eastern

lands. In northern Chiapas, the Independent Confederation of Agricultural Workers and Indians (CIOAC) organized rural workers into unions to combat abuses.

The federal government vied with these organizations for control of the peasantry and the Indians. In 1975 the government held the National Indigenous Congress in Pátzcuaro, Michoacán. Afterward, it established the National Council of Indian Pueblos (CNPI), which was responsible for funding regional programs. The government disbanded the CNPI when it lost its control to independent organizers. The independent organizers created their own organization—the *Plan de Ayala* National Coordinating Committee

THE FACE OF REVOLUTIONARY EMILIANO ZAPATA ADORNS THIS EDUCATIONAL AUDITORIUM IN CHIAPAS, MEXICO. *(AP/Wide World Photos. Reproduced by permission.)*

jungles. The demand for land, as well as the exploitation of timber, has caused the destruction of the Lacandon rain forests. The government also exacerbated this situation by establishing bio-reserves in areas already occupied by peasants.

The federal government implemented policies to increase the production of coffee, one of Chiapas's primary export commodities. When international coffee prices increased, the government provided land and credits to large landowners for coffee production. The peasants also shifted their production from subsistence crops to coffee. In 1979 INMECAFE (the Mexican Coffee Institute) agreed to transport eastern Chiapas's coffee to national markets. The institute not only provided credits and loans for coffee production but also warehoused, processed, and merchandised coffee. In 1989 the federal government, in keeping with its policies, privatized INMECAFE by handing over its functions to private industry. At this time, the price of coffee collapsed in the world market, affecting many of the small- and medium-sized coffee producers. Solidarity (a national antipoverty program) provided those in need with some funds, but it utilized political criteria in its distribution, alienating many peasants who supported neither the government nor the PRI.

THE POPULARITY OF SUB-COMMANDER MARCOS AMONG THE INDIGENOUS PEOPLE IS SHOWN BY THIS DOLL, DRESSED IN HIS LIKENESS, AT A STAND IN MEXICO CITY, MEXICO. *(Corbis. Reproduced by permission.)*

The Zapatista Rebellion

In response to the contradictions created by these economic and political factors, the peasants and the Indians took up arms against the government and its policies. The Zapatista National Liberation Army (EZLN) chose January 1, 1994—the date that NAFTA went into effect—as the date for the rebellion. NAFTA represented to them a system of globalization that had hurt the indigenous and peasant communities of Chiapas. The Zapatistas rebelled in numerous towns, even taking and holding San Cristóbal de las Casas for a few days. The government responded to the initial armed rebellion by sending twelve thousand troops into the region. After two major skirmishes the Zapatistas retreated to the eastern forests. In the initial fighting, 145 individuals were killed, and the military continued to repress the Indian villages implicated in the rebellion.

On January 12, the government declared a unilateral cease-fire and established a Commission for Peace and Reconciliation as it sought negotiations with the rebels. Salinas feared both national and international public opinion because 1994 was an election year. This cease-fire allowed the peasants to seize town halls in protest against the fraudulent elections of local officials and to invade land. While some landowners fled, others armed themselves and organized private militias. The government recruited Bishop Ruiz to negotiate, and on February 21 peace talks began in the Cathedral of San Cristóbal de las Casas. The image of Subcomandante Marcos emerged as the embodiment of the Zapatista rebellion nationally and internationally. Spreading the Zapatistas' message, Marcos released a series of poetic communiqués and declarations, even utilizing the Internet, to explain the circumstances for the rebellion and the rebel demands.

The EZLN presented thirty-four demands, encompassing political, social, and economic reforms, to the government negotiators. When the talks recessed, the two sides had agreed on thirty-two tentative accords. The EZLN delegates went back to the communities to discuss these accords. Meanwhile, on the national level, the government entered into crisis with the assassination of the PRI's presidential candidate, Luis Donaldo Colosio Murrieta, on March 23. Many observers concluded that internally the PRI was in disarray as two wings of the party fought for control. The Zapatistas believed the assassination signified that the hard-liners within the party had the upper hand. Mass protests against the government's use of the military in Chiapas also troubled the federal government. The EZLN rejected the government proposals on June 12 and called for a National Democratic Convention, to be held in August, for the creation of a transitional government and the writing of a new constitution. The convention, held in the Lacandon jungle, was modeled on the 1914 Convention of Aguascalientes that had brought together the revolutionary forces to air their demands. The Zapatistas also sought to gather all of the forces of opposition to the government's neo-liberal policies. The PRI's replacement, Ernesto Zedillo Ponce de León, won the presidential elections that year.

The new year, 1995, began with a major economic collapse that deepened the crisis nationally and in Chiapas. In late 1994 the rebels continued their offensive by establishing four autonomous zones—called "zones of rebellion" by the Zapatistas—and by seizing more land, blocking roads, refusing to pay taxes, and expelling government officials. PRI hard-liners, along with foreign investors and landowners, wanted the government to take decisive and forceful actions by sending in the army. While Zedillo made peaceful overtures, he unleashed the army on February 9, 1995, on the pretext that the Zapatistas had stashed weapons in Mexico City and Veracruz. He ordered the arrest of the Zapatista leadership. The rebels and their supporters fled across the border into the Guatemalan jungles. The government's actions provoked a major demonstration of one hundred thousand people in Mexico City. In response, on February 14, Zedillo ordered a cease-fire, suspended the arrest order, and called for new negotiations. In October the government and the EZLN resumed peace talks in San Andrés Larráinzar. During this period, violent land evictions by the government, with the support of the ranchers' association, continued.

On January 1, 1996, the Zapatista Front of National Liberation (FZLN), a civil nonviolent political front, was established. On January 18, the negotiations came to a close with the signing of an accord between the two parties, the first since the January 1994 rebellion. The San Andrés Accord on Indigenous Rights and Culture contained minimal concessions by the government. The accord recommended certain reforms in the Constitution concerning municipal boundaries and the ability for indigenous people to run for political office independently of any national political party. Achieving regional autonomy for the indigenous people remained an important goal even after the signing. The repression of the indigenous people continued as paramilitary groups, organized and supported by the PRI, operated in Chiapas against the communities supporting the Zapatistas and participated in defending the ranchers' land

against invasions. Violence within the indigenous communities, especially in the north, emerged as those Indians who supported the PRI accused other Indians with whom they disagreed of being "Zapatistas," whether they were or not.

Under these adverse circumstances, the Zapatistas began a second major event, the Continental Encounter for Humanity and against Neo-Liberalism, on April 3 in La Realidad. This meeting included important international writers, political activists, movie stars, and other well-known personalities. These personalities ensured international media coverage for the Zapatista struggle, the plight of the indigenous people, and the continuing repression in Chiapas. Nationally, the breakdown of order in Chiapas focused attention on the weakness of President Zedillo, and rumors abounded that he would soon resign. Military pressure on the communities intensified and land evictions increased. The Zapatistas announced that the Intercontinental Encounter on Humanity and Against Neo-Liberalism would be held in late July, once again in La Realidad. In June, twelve villagers of different political persuasions were assassinated in various towns. On June 28 a new guerrilla group, the Popular Revolutionary Army (EPR), with no apparent links to the Zapatistas, emerged in the Mexican state of Guerrero.

The economic crisis—the Mexican crash of 1994–95—had hurt not only the indigenous people but also members of the middle-class. Many placed the blame on free trade and high-interest rates for their economic predicament. Members of the rural and urban middle-class, as well as *ejidatarios* (members of communal landowning communities) established their own organization, El Barzón. El Barzón had goals similar to the Zapatistas and the two formed an alliance to resist neo-liberalism in a meeting held from July 19 to 21 in La Realidad. The Intercontinental Encounter opened on July 27 and concluded on August 3, with three thousand delegates from Mexico and other countries attending.

The July 1997 congressional elections in which opposition political parties won a majority of the seats demonstrated the weakness of the PRI and the resistance of the majority of Mexicans to its neo-liberal policies. In Chiapas, the Zapatistas abstained from participating in the elections. A state of civil war existed in Chiapas's northern indigenous villages, and the army continued its forays into Zapatista territory. The Zapatistas sent delegates to attend the Second Intercontinental

ZAPATISTA SUB-COMMANDER MARCOS LEAVES A MEDIATION MEETING IN LA REALIDAD, HIS STRONGHOLD WITHIN CHIAPAS, MEXICO. *(AP/Wide World Photos. Reproduced by permission.)*

Encounter for Humanity and Against Neo-Liberalism, held in Spain from July 25 to August 2. With the return of the delegates, the EZLN announced that eleven hundred Zapatista men, women, and children would march on Mexico City to attend a founding congress for the FZLN, which had not taken place since its inception in January 1996. Javier Elorriaga, a Zapatista, was responsible for the organization of the congress, which would try to achieve Zapatista goals through nonviolence. On September 8, the marchers left San Cristóbal on buses, collecting supporters along the way to Mexico City. They entered Mexico City on the September 12 and on September 15 FZLN was formally founded.

The bloodiest incident of the civil war—the Acteal Massacre—occurred in Chiapas on December 22, 1997. Before the massacre, skirmishes between PRIistas (supporters off the PRI) and Zapatista supporters led to the political killing of individuals, burning of houses, and expelling of villagers. This situation contributed to the creation of refugee camps around Acteal. On December 22, in an act of revenge for the murder of a PRIista, sixty armed men attacked the peaceful unarmed villagers engaged in their daily activities. Forty-five people were killed in the attack, most of them women and children. As news of the massacre spread, it reached the government and the

Zapatistas. The Zapatistas issued a communiqué blaming the massacre not only on Zedillo but also on federal and state government officials. The government sent in five hundred troops of its U.S. trained Airborne Special Forces Group to restore order and protect against reprisals. Government supported paramilitaries were implicated in many of the political assassinations as well as in the massacre. The refugee problem increased as a result of this wanton violence, as thousands of Zapatista supporters, fearing more attacks, fled their villages.

RECENT HISTORY AND THE FUTURE

In 1998 and 1999 the government continued its offensive, utilizing the military and the police against the Zapatistas. The government has also targeted and expelled foreign supporters of the Zapatistas operating in Chiapas. Making use of rumor and innuendo, it charged the Zapatistas with cultivating and trafficking drugs, a charge denied by Subcomandante Marcos. In September 1999 the government announced a new initiative for peace in Chiapas. The Zapatistas responded by blocking roads and accusing the government of continuing their military buildup while talking about peace. U.N. officials visiting the region have concluded that the military should suspend its patrols, the guerrillas should lay down their arms, and both sides should engage in a peaceful dialogue to find a solution to the region's problems.

Recently in Chiapas, Bishop Felipe Arizmendi, from the Tapachula diocese in southern Chiapas, replaced Bishop Ruiz in the diocese of San Cristóbal de las Casas. Many supporters of Ruiz felt that his deputy, Bishop Raul Vera, should have been chosen by the Vatican, since he, like Ruiz, is a vocal supporter of the indigenous people and a critic of the government's treatment of the Indians. Arizmendi, considered a conciliator by many, promises to continue Ruiz's work and mediate between the government and the rebels in order to resolve the standoff.

The Zapatista rebellion has transformed the political landscape in Chiapas and throughout Mexico. The Zapatistas voiced the indigenous people's demands for land, rights, and autonomy. It has not only empowered the indigenous people but also transformed the role of women within the Indian communities. Women are major supporters of the Zapatistas, as demonstrated by the brief occupation by several thousand women of a state-run radio station in Chiapas on International Women's Day 2000.

Since 1994 the Zapatista rebellion has clouded Mexican politics, as evidenced by the 1997 congressional elections. The year 2000, a presidential election year, appears no different. The opposition candidate from the National Action Party (PAN) has promised to begin peace talks with the Zapatistas, if elected. Protests continue against the government's policies and privatization of the economy, which continue to deeply affect the peasantry. Concerning the Acteal Massacre, a year after the government's investigation, eighty-eight people, mostly supporters of the PRI and opponents of the Zapatistas, were arrested. In July 1999 twenty individuals were given long prison terms for their role in the massacre. These terms were subsequently overturned in January 2000. The situation remains tense in Chiapas, as many of the political, social and economic problems that contributed to the rebellion are unresolved.

BIBLIOGRAPHY

"Acción Zapatista." http://www.utexas.edu/students/nave/ (20 September 2000).

Benjamin, Tom. *A Rich Land, A Poor People: Politics and Society in Modern Chiapas.* Albuquerque, N.Mex.: University of New Mexico Press, 1989.

Clarke, Ben and Clifton Ross, eds. *Voice of Fire: Communiqués and Interviews from the Zapatista National Liberation Army.* Trans. By Clifton Ross, et. al. Berkeley, Calif.: New Earth Publications, 1994.

Collier, George A. and Elizabeth Lowery Quaratiello. *Basta! Land and the Zapatista Rebellion in Chiapas.* Oakland, Calif.: Food First Books, 1994.

Gosner, Kevin. *Soldiers of the Virgin: The Moral Economy of a Colonial Maya Rebellion.* Tucson, Ariz.: University of Arizona Press, 1992.

Harvey, Neil. *The Chiapas Rebellion: The Struggle for Land and Democracy.* Durham, N.C.: Duke University Press, 1998.

Krauze, Enrique. "Chiapas: the Indians' Prophet," *The New York Review of Books* 16 December 1999: 65-73.

MacLachlan, Colin M. and William H. Beezley. *El Gran Pueblo: A History of Greater Mexico.* 2d ed. Upper Saddle River, N.J.: Prentice Hall, 1999.

Meyer, Michael C. Meyer, William L. Sherman and Susan M. Deeds. *The Course of Mexican History.* 6th ed. New York: Oxford University Press, 1999.

O'Brien, Karen L. *Sacrificing the Forest: Environmental and Social Struggles in Chiapas.* Boulder, Colo.: Westview Press, 1998.

Rus, Jan. "Whose Caste War? Indians, Ladinos, and the Chiapas 'Caste War' of 1869." In *Spaniards and Indians in Southeastern Mesoamerica: Essays on the History of Ethnic Relations.* Edited by Murdo J. Macleod and Robert Wasserstrom. Lincoln, Nebr.: University of Nebraska Press, 1983.

———. "The 'Comunidad Revolucionaria Institucional': The Subversion of Native Government in Highland Chiapas, 1936-1968." In *Everyday Forms of State Formation: Revolution and the Negotiation of Rule in Modern Mexico.* Edited by Gilbert Joseph and Daniel Nugent: Durham, N.C.: Duke University Press, 1994.

Wasserstrom, Robert. *Class and Society in Central Chiapas.* Berkeley, Calif.: University of California Press, 1983.

Womack, Jr., John, comp. and trans. *Rebellion in Chiapas: An Historical Reader.* New York: The New Press, 1999.

"Zapatistas! Documents of the New Mexican Revolution." http://lanic.utexas.edu/project/Zapatistas/ (20 September 2000).

"Zapatistas in Cyberspace: A Guide to Analysis and Resources." http://www.eco.utexas.edu/Homepages/Faculty/Cleaver/zapsincyber.html (20 September 2000).

Carlos Pérez

COLOMBIAN DRUG WARS: GUERRILLAS, PARAMILITARY GROUPS, AND THE GOVERNMENT

THE CONFLICT

Colombia produces seventy-three percent of the world's coca leaf—the plant from which cocaine is made. In Colombia, drug organizations (cartels), militias, and paramilitary groups fight each other for profits and protection. Cartels fight the extradition of drug dealers to the United States for prosecution.

Political

• Drug dealers want to sell drugs and don't want prosecution of their members—in Colombia or in the United States.

• The militias are guerrilla movements that are attempting to overthrow the government, and are often funded by drugs.

• The paramilitary groups are fighting to establish order in Colombia—often using assassinations and torture.

• The Colombian government has been unable to prosecute law breakers; if they attempt to prosecute, government officials and judges are murdered by the cartels and militias.

• The United States, in an attempt to end the influx of drugs into the U.S., wants to extradite drug dealers to the U.S., where they can be tried in a court of law.

At the end of the twentieth century, Colombia was the largest producer of cocaine in the world, and was quickly becoming a major grower of opium. Drug consuming nations, chiefly the United States and other wealthy countries, annually spend between five and ten billion dollars for these elicit pharmaceuticals. Colombian drug cartels, principally Cali and Medellin, named after the cities where they originated and are headquartered, and Colombian guerrilla rebels, particularly the Revolutionary Armed Forces of Colombia (*Feurzas Armadas Revolucionarias de Colombia* or FARC), M-19 (Nineteenth of April Movement), and the National Liberation Army (*Ejercito de Liberation Nacional* or ELN) which control perhaps forty percent of the Colombian countryside, have struggled to maximize their share of the global drug market. The cartels and rebels have fought and cooperated with each other, battled and corrupted the beleaguered Colombian government in Bogota, and countered and frustrated the United States and other foreign efforts to destroy their illicit trafficking activities. Much of traffickers' success stems from the terror their ruthless killing and kidnapping of opponents induces. Not only are government officials assassinated in retaliation for attempting to suppress the drug trade, but cartel and rebel competitors and erstwhile allies frequently get cut down in turf wars. This violence has resulted in the deaths of tens of thousands of Colombians since the late 1970s.

The global marketing of Colombian drugs has extended cartel-related affairs beyond that South American country. Other Andean nations which produce cocaine, especially Peru and Bolivia, and countries through which drugs make their way to the United States, notably countries in Central

America and the Caribbean and Mexico, in addition to the consuming nations themselves, are subject to corrupting influences and persistent violence. That these traffickers have likely penetrated a vast cross-section of institutions in Colombia and abroad can be concluded from the following titles of newspaper articles of the 1990s: "Tentacles of Latin Drug Lords Extend Well Beyond Borders," "Drug Cartel's Miami Lawyer Sentenced," "German 'Cocaine Chemicals' for Colombia Worry U.S.," "Banker's Drug Bust Spotlights Colombians' Hidden Habits," "Cocaine Barons May Fall, but Industry Will Survive," "Murderous Drug Cartels Endanger the Continent," "In South America, Drugs Are a Political Force," and "Will Narco-Guerrillas Become the Rulers?"

The relationship between Colombian cocaine dealers and the outside world has been established in the case of Panamanian President Manuel Noriega, the Contras in Nicaragua, and Fidel Castro in Cuba, noting three of the most prominent examples. Cocaine connections cut across ideological lines both before and after the end of the Cold War and the collapse of communism. That these traffickers have likely, directly and certainly indirectly, contributed to drug-related violence can be seen in the killing of an Irish reporter, a Mexican cardinal, the Tijuana chief of police and scores of other notables, as well as innocent bystanders and innumerable nameless participants in the drug trade.

HISTORICAL BACKGROUND

One factor in Colombia's drug wars is the nation's lengthy tradition of coca production and consumption. Long before American baby boomers began using cocaine in the 1970s as a presumably safe alternative to heroin, amphetamines, Quaaludes, and LSD, South American farmers in Argentina, Bolivia, Colombia, Brazil, Ecuador and Peru cultivated and ingested the coca leaf. The Incan elite—South American natives—chewed the coca leaf, and by the time the Spanish arrived in the late fifteenth century, the practice had spread to commoners. Economic, medicinal and recreational considerations account for the coca leaf's popularity.

Many factors contribute to the economic viability of coca leaf farming. The crop can be grown on land that is nutrient poor and geographically unfavorable, such as steep hills, and on land that is climatically hostile because of too much rainfall,

CHRONOLOGY

1930 Guerrilla movements, such as FARC, M-19, and ELN are founded and, over the next seventy years, flourish due to government weakness.

1980 Colombia cultivates an estimated four percent of the world's coca leaf crop.

1981 Jorge Ochoa's sister is kidnapped by leftist guerrillas. Ochoa and other Medellin leaders organize a paramilitary group, Death to Kidnappers, which capture and kill guerrillas and their families until Ochoa's sister is freed. Paramilitary groups emerge all over Colombia.

1987 Colombia cultivates an estimated eleven percent of the world's coca leaf crop.

1991 Colombia cultivates an estimated nineteen percent of the world's coca leaf crop.

Mid-1990s Colombia cultivates an estimated seventy-three percent of world's coca leaf crop.

1995 The Palace of Justice is attacked in order to prevent the extradition of drug dealers to the United States. More than one hundred people, including nine justices of the Supreme Court, are killed.

and thus ordinarily unsuitable for other crops. The coca leaf can be harvested as early as eighteen months after planting and can produce as many as a half-dozen harvests per year, a productive potential much greater than nearly any other crop. Moreover, by the late twentieth century, drug traffickers encouraged coca cultivation by providing farmers with money, seed, fertilizer, and protection. Most significantly, the coca crop yields the cultivator a higher return than other crops. In the mid-1980s, it earned nineteen times as much as citrus crops and an amazing ninety-one times as much as rice! Coca leaves have been used medicinally over the centuries to ward off the effects of hard labor, cold weather and assorted other physical maladies. By the end of the second millennium the recreational use of cocaine (a manufactured alkaloid of coca) in the Andean nations had reached epidemic numbers. Particularly destructive was the spreading practice among Colombians of paste smoking, which involves lacing cigarettes with *basuco* (cocaine), and which can produce brain damage.

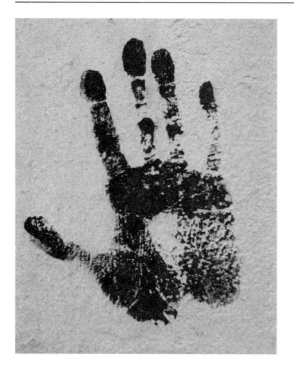

THE CALI DRUG CARTEL USES THIS BLACK HAND-PRINT TO INDICATE ITS PRESENCE. *(Corbis. Reproduced by permission.)*

Another element contributing to the drug wars in Colombia is that country's unstable and weak political establishment, which has produced ten constitutions since 1811. The mid-twentieth century witnessed *La Violencia,* an armed conflict between the liberal and conservative political parties that resulted in the deaths of two hundred thousand to three hundred thousand people in a country of eleven to twelve million people. One of the principal issues surrounding this ordeal of violence, which existed on a smaller scale before the late-1940s eruption and continued beyond the official end of *La Violencia* in 1953, was liberal support for guerrilla bands and conservative attempts to eradicate the rebels. The United Nations consistently placed Colombia among the top ten nations in the world with the highest homicide rates between 1955 and 1988, and a 1989 Colombian government commission (*Comision de Estudios sobre la Violencia*) concluded that the principle perpetrators were the cartels, the guerrillas, paramilitary units and the government. So long as authorities in Bogota are unwilling or unable to defeat the cartels, guerrillas and paramilitary units, law and order will continue to be an unrealistic dream.

The History of Cocaine Use in the United States

The huge demand in the United States and other industrial nations for cocaine fuels the drug industry in Colombia. Between the passage of the Harrison Act in 1914, which restricted drug use in the United States, and the counterculture movement of the 1960s, drug consumption largely was confined to artistic and minority communities. However, a broad cultural revolt occurred in the 1960s that produced a vocal defiance of the older generation, best evidenced in Vietnam War protests, civil rights demonstrations, and the re-emergence of the women's movement. Baby boomers questioned authority, loudly proclaiming in the words of a 1960s song, "there's a whole generation with a new explanation." Movies, songs, the news media, and the academic world seemed to cheer on this challenge to established norms, especially as it applied to drug experimentation. But as the young adults approached middle age in the early 1970s, they sought drugs which did not produce the "bad trips," associated with LSD, or "final trips," as seen in the drug-related deaths of Jim Morrison of the Doors, Alan "Blind Owl" Wilson of Canned Heat, Jimi Hendrix, Janis Joplin and others. Marijuana continued to be a popular high; some people were looking for a more intense, yet safe, chemical experience.

Cocaine seemed to be the perfect drug. Nearly everywhere one turned in the 1970s, cocaine was extolled as the drug with many advantages and few drawbacks. Popular cultural magazines like *Rolling Stone* labeled cocaine the "drug of the year." *New York Times Magazine* proclaimed that users got a good high "without the forbiddingly dangerous needle and addiction of heroin." *Newsweek* stated that medical authorities believe "cocaine probably causes no significant mental or physical damage;" two Harvard University psychiatrists in their book *Cocaine: A Drug and Its Social Evolution* seemed to sanction the popular notion that the drug is "a relatively innocuous stimulant, casually used by those who can afford it to brighten the day or the evening." The Chicago Bureau of Narcotics claimed "You get a good high with coke and you don't get hooked;" and at the very top of the establishment, President Jimmy Carter's drug policy advisor, Dr. Peter G. Bourne, wrote that cocaine "is probably the most benign of illicit drugs currently in widespread use." It appeared that using coke could also provide the creative energy and insight that LSD users had celebrated, but without the negative side effects.

IN AN EFFORT TO FIGHT THE DRUG TRADE AT ITS ROOT, THE COLOMBIAN NATIONAL POLICE SPRAY POPPY CROPS, THE RAW INGREDIENT OF HEROIN, WITH A STRONG PESTICIDE. *(AP/Wide World Photos. Reproduced by permission.)*

For the remainder of the twentieth century cocaine use in the United States rose and fell in popularity. During the 1970s cocaine was considered chic. By the late 1980s, with popular support behind the "Just Say No" Campaign, consumption dipped. The 1990s witnessed a decline in consumption of cocaine, but not of most other drugs. Statistics on illicit cocaine imports and consumption are at best rough approximations, and they sometimes provide mixed signals. Thus, between 1976 and 1988, cocaine imports consistently increased, from 20 to 230 tons per year, dipping in 1989 to 200 tons. Meanwhile, estimates suggest that in 1995 1.5 million Americans used cocaine regularly and 2.5 million were occasional users, down from 5.7 million regular and 7.1 million occasional users in 1985. Certainly the news associated with cocaine use made people rethink its "innocuous" nature by the 1990s. Cocaine deaths, notably that of basketball star Len Byas, appalling stories about "crack" babies, which regularly made the television news, and the arrest of prominent actors and politicians, such as Charlie Sheen and Washington, D.C. mayor Marion Berry, reversed the more sanguine assessments and trendy appeal of the drug two decades earlier. Nonetheless, two

MAP OF COLOMBIA. (© *Maryland Cartographics. Reprinted with permission.*)

hundred tons of cocaine had customers. One consumer growth area was crack cocaine, which became popular in the 1980s, and regular users probably numbered about a half a million a year during the last decade-and-a-half of the millennium. Crack, or freebase, made by removing the hydrochloride base of cocaine hydrochloride, became particularly preferred in the inner cities of the United States because it produced a more intense high than regular cocaine and was much cheaper.

Cocaine as Big Business

Coca cultivation and cocaine manufacturing followed the demand patterns in the United States. In June 1953, then United States Commissioner of Narcotics (predecessor of the current "drug czar") Harry J. Anslinger published *The Traffic in Narcotics*. The index of that book contained only one reference to Colombia: "coca-leaf chewing." Until the 1970s, in fact, most illicit cocaine activities were centered in Chile. When General Augusto Pinochet came to power in Chile, he eradicated the cocaine business in Chile, and it then moved north to Colombia, which had only a small cottage industry for cocaine at the time. During the 1970s Colombian drug entrepreneurs began importing coca from Bolivia and Peru, processing it in Colombia, whence it was shipped north to consumer markets. It is estimated that in 1980, Colombia cultivated only 4 percent of the world's coca leaf crop; in 1987, 11 percent; and four years later, 19 percent. Approximately 73 percent of all cocaine manufacturing was done in Colombia by the early 1990s. And until that time, Colombians also directed most of the distribution to, as well as much of the dispersal within, the United States. As U.S. drug interdiction efforts increased in the Gulf of Mexico and along the east coast in that decade, Colombian cartels sub-contracted much of the trafficking activities to Mexican drug cartels. But at the end of the second millennium, Colombia remained the center of the global illicit cocaine enterprise.

Colombian cocaine cartels and leftist antigovernment guerrillas control the cultivation, processing and distribution of coca and cocaine. The first organization to produce cocaine on a business-like basis was the Medellin cartel. It began in the 1970s by smuggling coca into Colombia from Bolivia and Peru and sending it north by individual couriers or mules (*mulas*), usually to Florida or California (one flight from Bogota to Los Angeles was labeled "the cocaine special" in the late 1970s). By the next decade the Medellin leader-

ship—Pablo Escobar, Jorge Luis Ochoa, Gonzalo Rodriguez Gacha, and Carlos Lehder—had not only put together a solid organization capable of producing large profits and protecting its interests, quite often with violence; but it had also created an image of legitimacy and philanthropy, at least at home. Lehder began a newspaper and a political party, *Movimiento Nacional Latino*; Escobar set up a newspaper, was elected to Congress, and spent lavishly on benevolent projects for the poor in Medellin. As the government captured, killed, extradited, or drove into exile the Medellin leadership by the late 1980s, the Cali cartel emerged to fill the cocaine trafficking vacuum. Until then a small organization, under brother bosses Miguel and Gilberto Rodriguez Orjuela, the cartel came to control most of Colombia's cocaine manufacturing and commerce (estimated at eighty percent of the global trade) by the late twentieth century. Much of the cartel's success seems to have been the result of a conscious policy of maintaining a low profile and keeping public violence to a minimum. The Spanish term, *convivencia*, is used to describe how the people of Cali coexist with the cartel and suggests a working relationship whereby the citizens ignore the situation in exchange for jobs, economic growth, and an acceptable level of killing. The Colombian government has attempted to root out cartel kingpins, and by the late 1990s had been successful in imprisoning much of the Cali leadership, but other *narcotraficantes* (drug traffickers) commenced operations, including Jesua Amayak Russa, head of the Atlantic Coast drug cartel, and the guerrilla-based traffickers.

Guerrilla movements in Colombia date back to the 1930s and, like the cartels, survive and often flourished due to the central government's weakness. FARC, M-19, and ELN all have revolutionary agendas informed by Marxist theory—which is not uniformly taken seriously. However, the chief item on their programs is the overthrow of the government in Bogota. Controlling nearly half of the country and growing rich from the coca cultivated in their territory—amounting to eighty-five percent of the world's coca leaf production in the year 2000—the guerrillas can field armies of more than twenty thousand well-armed soldiers and have regularly done battle on the outskirts of the capital. The national army rarely scored a win when engaging the guerrillas, due both to the government's timidity and also to the guerrillas' popularity (the guerrillas—and cartels and paramilitary groups—protected coca farmers' crops and thus their incomes). Most of the nation's coca is produced in territory controlled by FARC, the largest of the rebel groups, which charges the cartels and other growers a fee for crop protection, as well as for the right of transporting the manufactured cocaine. As with the cartel leaders who labored hard to acquire a humanitarian image (many drug lords sponsor beauty queen contestants), so too, FARC leader Mario Marulanda Velez cultivates a freedom fighter image that many peasants, intellectuals, and even some foreign journalists, embrace.

The paramilitary groups, fielding about ten to fifteen thousand troops, emerged to protect landowners and merchants in guerrilla-infested territory from kidnapping and extortion, and to organize criminal activity and terrorism in the cities. When leftist guerrillas kidnapped Jorge Ochoa's sister, Marta Nieves, in 1981, he and other Medellin leaders organized Death to Kidnappers, which captured and killed guerrillas and their families until Marta Nieves was freed. Carlos Castano leads the largest of the rural groups, United Self-Defense Forces of Colombia. Controlling about five thousand troops, Castano appears to view himself to be on a mission to eradicate the rebels, which he claims kidnapped and killed his father. The organization La Terraza, named after a bar in the Manrique neighborhood of Medellin that cartel leader Pablo Escobar's men frequented, dominates the urban areas. Just as impoverished farmers looked to the cocaine business for economic relief, the poor youth of the cities viewed La Terraza and other such organizations as vehicles out of the *barrio*. The paramilitary groups believe that if they can increase the level of violence until the guerrillas cannot protect the people they claim to be serving, rural support for the Marxist rebels will dissolve. Meanwhile, as the paramilitary right and the guerrilla left do battle, the Colombian army can watch them destroy each other removing both elements of government opposition. This analysis assumes perpetual mutually antagonistic relations between the warring groups, a supposition that does not take into account the power of money, which has resulted in the sometime cooperation between them.

The violence resulting from the turf wars among the various combatants makes living anywhere in Colombia hazardous. Thirty-five thousand people have died during the last decade of the twentieth century as a result of what amounts to a civil war. Perhaps the most striking example of savagery occurred on November 6, 1985, when the Palace of Justice was attacked to prevent the extradition of Colombian drug dealers to the United States. (Extradition is the legal method of removing a suspect from one jurisdiction—in this case Colombia's—in order to bring him to trial in another—in this case the United States.) In the ensuing clash between the army and the attackers, M-19 guerrillas, nine justices of the Supreme Court and nearly one hundred civilians died. Although M-19 leader Alvaro Fayad claimed his rebels took no part in the attack, it appeared to be yet another example of the informal collaboration between drug lords and guerrillas. Less than a year later, Supreme Court justice Hernando Baquero Borda was gunned down as he was in the process of revising the nation's constitution regarding extradition. Not coincidentally, the extradition treaty between the United States and Colombia was declared un-constitutional in June 1987, following the extradition of cartel leader Carlos Ledher earlier that year. In May 1989, M-19 kidnapped diplomat, presidential candidate, and newspaper editor Alvaro Gomez Hurtado, in order to exchange him for Carlos Ledher. Colombian ambassador to Hungary, Enrique Pareja Gonzalez, narrowly escaped assassination in Budapest, where he had been sent to get him out of harm's way at home for his support as Justice Minister for the extradition treaty.

Journalists have been special targets of *narcotraficantes*. Since 1980, scores of investigative reporters, editors and publishers have been murdered, including *El Pais* editorial writer Gerardo Bedoya in 1997. Although some newspaper people regularly censored their writings to avoid criticizing the *narcotraficantes*, many journalists stood their ground and paid the ultimate price. Even the star of Colombia's soccer team, Andres Escobar (no relation to Pablo), could not escape the wrath of the drug lords, when he was executed in 1994 for kicking the soccer ball into his own goal. When satirist Jaime Garzon was slain in 1999, La Terraza was the prime suspect but any *sicarios*, or hit men, could have been hired.

RECENT HISTORY AND THE FUTURE

The past can very likely give us a good view of the future of Columbia's drug wars, and it does not bode well for those hoping for a government victory and an end to drug trafficking. Cocaine production is increasing along with the quality as the price decreases. Imports of cocaine into the United States continue to rise even as its government claims to be pursuing a vigorous war on drugs at home and abroad. There are clear signs that this war's progress is being evaluated mainly statistically, a tonnage count of confiscated cocaine as the index of victory. The capture, incarceration or killing of cartel or rebel leaders is touted as a sign that the drug war is making headway, when in fact a new leader emerges as an old one is eliminated; a new cartel replaces an old one; a new cocaine manufacturing plant sprouts up after the destruction of an old one; new land comes under coca cultivation as other productive ground is sprayed or confiscated. America's attempt to aid the Colombian government in its eradication efforts has often produced as much hostility in that country as support. Thus the spraying of coca crops has enraged coca farmers; collateral damage to non-coca farmers from anti-drug operations has generated ill will too. The attempt to extradite drug lords to the United States has spawned a nationalist reaction. Since 1998, the government in Bogota has been pursuing a policy of negotiating with the rebels and guerrillas. The people are tired of the violence and peace is popular.

Nor are the drug war campaigns outside of Colombia succeeding. The same poverty that attracts young men in Colombia lures youth elsewhere to transport or distribute the cocaine. The Caribbean, Central America and Mexico have been corrupted by drug money, as has the United States, where most of Colombia's cocaine is consumed and much of cocaine's profits are laundered. As in Colombia, so too elsewhere: the death of this gang leader or the confiscation of that cocaine shipment makes no discernable impact on trafficking and consumption patterns.

One possible consequence of Colombia's drug wars is the military involvement of the United States. In 2000 only a few hundred United States servicemen were stationed in Colombia, serving in support and training capacities. But as the position of the Bogota government weakens, political pressure increases for the United States to do "something." Yet the Colombian government is skeptical about the United States' political commitment to eradicating coca production.

The likelihood is that conflict will continue, that the United States will work to prevent the collapse of the Bogota government and the possible victory of the guerrillas, who could then aid Marxist movements in other South American nations. It is equally likely that continued demand for cocaine in the United States will keep the cartels and guerrillas in excellent economic and military shape, which in turn will require Washington to increase military aid. Potentially, if enough pressure is brought to bear on the government to negotiate an end to the fighting, then perhaps a sort of *convivencia* will be worked out—the government winking at trafficking and accepting the guerrillas' de facto political control of nearly half the country in return for a minimum of violence.

BIBLIOGRAPHY

Jonnes, Jill. *Hep-Cats, Narcs, and Pipe Dreams: A History of America's Romance With Illegal Drugs.* Baltimore, Md.: Johns Hopkins University Press, 1996.

Lee, Rensselaer W., III. *The White Labyrinth: Cocaine and Political Power.* New Brunswick, N.J.: Transaction, 1990.

MacDonald, Scott B. *Mountain High, White Avalanche: Cocaine Power in the Andean States and Panama.* New York: Praeger, 1989.

Scott, Peter Dale and Jonathan Marshall. *Cocaine Politics: Drugs, Armies, and the CIA in Central America.* Rev. ed. Berkeley, Calif.: University of California Press, 1998.

Smith, Peter H., ed. *Drug Policy in the Americas.* Boulder, Colo.: Westview Press, 1992.

Thoumi, Francisco E. *Political Economy and Illegal Drugs in Colombia.* Boulder, Colo.: Lynne Rienner, 1995.

Walker, William O., III. *Drug Control in the Americas.* Rev. ed. Albuquerque, N.Mex.: University of New Mexico Press, 1989.

Thomas D. Reins

THE DEMOCRATIC REPUBLIC OF CONGO (CONGO-KINSHASA): THE AFRICAN WORLD WAR

THE CONFLICT

Conflict continued in the Congo following the 1997 civil war that brought Laurent Kabila to power. The many different ethnic groups in Congo and the large refugee population led to general unrest and periodic brutality. A large number of countries neighboring the Congo were involved, leading the war to be labeled the "African World War."

Ethnic

- Many different ethnic groups live in Congo, and most of the political affiliations are based on ethnicity.

Political

- The Rwandan massacre created a huge influx of refugees, many of which supported Kabila's bid for power.

- Angola's interest in the war is to protect its own security. Uganda is concerned about protecting its own borders and about protecting its allies, the Rwandan Tutsi. Many other neighboring countries are involved in the war.

In early 2000, the conflict in the Democratic Republic of Congo (or DRC or Congo) continued. The most recent phase of the conflict began in July 1998 when Congo President Laurent Desire Kabila ordered his former allies out of the country. Kabila's allies, mainly Rwandan government troops and ethnic Congolese Tutsis (known as the Banyamulenge), had been the main forces that brought Kabila to power in May 1997 after an eight-month rebellion against former ruler Mobutu Sese Seko. The rebellion in eastern Congo against the Mobutu government, begun in October 1996 and led by Laurent Kabila, was prompted by ethnic tensions in eastern Congo. The roots of the rebellion occurred during the previous two and a half years in neighboring Rwanda.

The current conflict in the Democratic Republic of Congo can only be understood within its regional and historical context. Since independence from Belgium in 1960, the Congo has experienced several secessionist attempts—break away attempts by a region—(in Katanga Province) and periods of ethnic conflict (in Katanga, Kasai and the Kivu provinces) that resulted in thousands of deaths and the displacement of tens of thousands of Congolese. Congo, the second largest country in sub-Saharan Africa (Africa below the Saharan desert), is home to some two hundred different ethnic groups, four hundred language dialects, and vast resources. The country is situated in central Africa and borders nine states, many of which have also been embroiled in intense internal, often ethnically based, conflict over the past forty years.

HISTORICAL BACKGROUND

Colonial Rule and Independence

Belgium colonized present-day Congo in the nineteenth century. (The capital of present day Congo is Kinshasa and the country is sometimes referred to as Congo-Kinshasa to distinguish the country from the Republic of Congo, otherwise known as Congo-Brazzaville.) At the Berlin Conference of 1884–85, the European powers recognized the claim of King Leopold II over the central African territory. He ruled what was then called the Congo Free State as his personal kingdom, using forced labor to extract rubber, ivory, and minerals. Leopold's harsh treatment of the Congolese people led to international outrage, and he was forced to turn over the administration of the colony to the Belgian government. Most of the worst abuses against the people ended under Belgian rule, yet Belgium continued to extract the resources without making any effort to develop the country. During the 1940s, the Belgian government increased the extraction of resources from Congo in order to finance Belgium's war effort. In addition, Belgium moved the Banyarwandans, ethnic Hutus or Tutsis, originating from the area known today as Rwanda, into the two Kivu regions to farm. Banyarwandan refers to either Hutus or Tutsis from the historical Tutsi kingdom that encompassed areas of Rwanda, Burundi and Congo. Before the genocide, Congolese did not distinguish between Hutus and Tutsi, but thought of both groups as outsiders. It was only after the Rwandan genocide that non-Banyarwandan Congolese started to refer separately to Banyamulenge (Tutsis) and Hutus. Other Banyarwandans had already been living in the area when Congo's borders were drawn at the Berlin Conference. The Belgians also relocated the ethnic Luba of the two Kasai provinces (south-central Congo) into the Katanga region (also known as Shaba, in the southeast) in order to work the mines there. Both of these moves increased ethnic tensions in the country and caused resentment within the communities who were native to the Kivu and Katanga regions.

The movement for independence of the country began in the Katanga region, and political parties were formed, largely along ethnic lines. In the late 1950s, the separatist party Conakat (Confederation of Katangan Associations) was established and headed by Moise Tshombe. Conakat drew support from the Lunda and Yeke ethnic groups of Katanga. The Congolese National Movement also emerged as an important actor in the independence movement. It split into two

CHRONOLOGY

1800s Belgium colonizes the Congo.

1884–85 At the Berlin Conference, the European powers recognize the claim of King Leopold II to central Africa, including the Congo.

1950s Parties fighting for independence emerge, including the Conakat, headed by Moise Tshombe, and the Congolese National Movement, one faction of which was headed by Patrice Lumumba.

1960 Congo wins independence from Belgium, its army mutinies, and Belgium uses the mutiny to reestablish itself in the country.

1961 Power is returned to Congolese president Kasavuba. Former prime minister Lumumba is murdered. Power struggles continue.

1965 The military takes over, installing Mobutu Sese Seko as head of state.

1971 Mobuto changes the country's name to the Republic of Zaire.

Mid-1990s The Katanga region is operating as a separate entity, with its own currency and trade agreements.

1994 The killings of Tutsi in Rwanda leads to more than one million refugees flooding into eastern Zaire.

1996 The Congolese government advocates the removal of ethnic Tutsi from Congo; the Tutsi form militias, including the Armed Forces for the Liberation of Congo-Zaire, led by Laurent Kabila.

1997 Mobutu is driven from power. Kabila declares himself leader and changes the country's name back to Congo.

1998 Kabila decides he no longer needs the support of the Tutsi who brought him to power; he orders all Rwandans to leave the country. Tutsi rebels fight Kabila's forces.

1999 A cease-fire agreement is signed between Kabila and the Tutsi.

camps in 1959. One faction, led by Patrice Lumumba, was supported primarily by the ethnic Lulua of the Kasai provinces. The other faction, led by Joseph Ileo, Cyrille Adoula, and Albert Kalonji, drew support from the Luba of Kasai.

Independence from Belgium was granted June 30, 1960. Patrice Lumumba became prime minis-

PATRICE LUMUMBA. *(Source unknown.)*

ter and five days later, the Congolese army mutinied. Belgium used the army mutiny to reestablish itself in the country and to support the movement to break away from the Congo underway in Katanga. United Nations troops were sent in to maintain order. In September 1960, President Joseph Kasavubu fired Lumumba. The military took over temporarily and Lumumba was arrested. Order was restored to Congo and power returned to President Kasavubu in February 1961. Former Prime Minister Lumumba was murdered shortly thereafter. Power struggles continued in the early 1960s, this time between President Kasavubu and Katangan leader Moise Tshombe. In November 1965, the military took over, and Mobutu Sese Seko became head of state.

Mobutu Sese Seko

During the Cold War, Mobutu was seen by the West as a key ally in the fight to contain the spread of communism in southern Africa. Mobutu wielded absolute power during his thirty-year reign, yet he faced a serious challenge from secessionists in Katanga in the 1970s and eventually lost control of much of the country. He implemented policies aimed at "Africanizing" Congo. He renamed the state the Republic of Zaire in 1971. Under Mobutu's policy of "authenticity," all colonial or Christian names, public and private, were changed to Zairean ones. Mobutu tried to

encourage nationalism based on loyalty to the state rather than loyalties to specific regions. However, regional rivalries remained and were expressed as ethnic conflict.

Mobutu was able to hold onto power for so long both because of support from the West and because he refined kleptocracy (the systematic theft of state funds). It is estimated that he took millions of dollars from Zaire's state coffers and put the money in personal bank accounts in Europe. He also developed a system of patronage whereby he rewarded powerful friends within the state with a share of the stolen wealth. Not only did he steal state funds from the mining sector, he also stole millions from World Bank and International Monetary Fund loans that were designed for development of Zaire. Because of this extensive plundering of state wealth, there was little development of Zaire's infrastructure, industry, or people. In addition, basic services like health and education were not provided to the Congolese, and low-level civil servants remained unpaid for long periods of time.

Mobutu's unwillingness to share the wealth of the state with the majority of the population eventually contributed to his downfall. Another factor which led to Mobutu's downfall was the lack of infrastructure itself. In a country about one-third the size of the continental United States, the lack of usable roads hampered the ability of the government to control its territory. By the mid-1990s, for example, the Katanga region was operating as a separate entity from Zaire with its own currency and trade agreements with neighboring states. Finally, after the collapse of the Soviet Union in 1989 and the end of the Cold War, the United States was much less tolerant of Mobutu's repressive and corrupt activities and largely withdrew U.S. support for his government.

Ethnic Relations in Congo

Several of Congo's ethnic groups have played a prominent role in Congo's political development. Because of its vast mineral resources, Katanga produces a great proportion of the wealth of the country. The Katangans felt marginalized under the Mobutu government because the wealth taken from Katanga was not returned to it in the form of development assistance. The Lunda of Katanga Province (about two percent of the total population) were leaders in the secessionist attempts of that region just after independence and again in the 1970s. In 1977 and again in 1978, rebels in Katanga attempted to secede from Zaire, but were repulsed each time by Mobutu's

LAURENT KABILA

1939– Laurent Kabila was born in 1939, in Luba, Katanga, and educated in France and Tanzania. In 1960, he fought in the civil war as a protege of nationalist leader, Patrice Lamumba. After Premier Lamumba's assassination, Kabila tried unsuccessfully to overthrow Mobutu in 1965. During the 1970s and 1980s, Kaliba organized anti-Mobutu factions, which were financed by kidnappings for ransom and mineral mining operations. Kabila organized the Alliance of Democratic Forces for Liberation of the Congo, which was made up of Congolese and refugees from neighboring countries. The Alliance began its rebellion in 1996, and within seven months had conquered the capital, Kinshasa. Kabila declared himself president, and changed the name of Zaire back to The Democratic Republic of the Congo.

Kabila inherited a country that was financially bankrupt and torn by war. Since 1965 the population has tripled to forty-six million in 1999. Rwanda, Uganda, and Burundi have invaded the Congo. In addition, the Congo hosts over one million refugees of the civil war in Rwanda. Its borders are considered unstable, with several surrounding countries staging raids for the Congo's strategic resources.

In 1999 Kabila signed the Lusaka Accord, a ceasefire agreement with seven surrounding countries,

PRESIDENT LAURENT KABILA. *(Drawing by Bill Bourne. Gale Research.)*

which has, so far, proven ineffective. Opposition parties are banned, and hundreds of thousands of refugees, largely Rwandan, have been killed in refugee camps.

forces with the help of Belgian, French, and U.S. support or troops. These secessionist invasions were launched from Angola and were among the greatest challenges to Mobutu's regime. The people of Katanga, including the Lunda and Yeke, had long demanded greater control over their region.

In addition, the Lunda have a history of ethnic conflict with Congolese from other regions, especially the Luba, who were brought to Katanga to help with mining. The Luba were resented by the Katangans because they had become business and civil leaders in Katanga, and the Katangans viewed them as interlopers, not native Katangans. During the early 1990s, the Katangans drove out nearly all the Luba from the region, even those who had lived in Katanga for generations. The expulsion of the Luba from Katanga was in reaction to the appointment of Etienne Tshisekedi, a

Luba, as prime minister in 1992. Tshisekedi has long been one of the leaders of the opposition movement, and his appointment as prime minister was an attempt by Mobutu to placate the opposition. Instead, the people there were unhappy that Mobutu did not appoint an opposition Katangan to the post of Prime Minister instead of a Luba.

The Luba (four percent of the population) of East and West Kasai provinces became an indigenous elite under Belgian colonial rule. They took advantage of missionary education opportunities, and became administrators in the colonial government. Many migrated to other regions under Belgian rule, which caused resentment among natives of these regions, especially in Katanga. During the late 1950s, clashes over land were fought between the Luba and Lulua. When the Luba were expelled from Katanga in the mid-1990s, they returned to the Kasai provinces but they no longer had access to land in those regions and so they suffered hardships.

Hutus and Tutsis

The Banyarwandans are people of Hutu and Tutsi ethnicity that were part of the greater Tutsi kingdom in pre-colonial times. The Banyarwandans are in three countries: Congo, Rwanda and Burundi. Tutsi in particular have long been resented by other ethnic groups because of their relative prosperity first under the Tutsi kingdom and then under colonial administrations. At present, the minority Tutsis run the governments of both Rwanda and Burundi even though they make up only fourteen percent of the total population of each country. In 1972, the Banyarwandans in Congo were granted citizenship by the Mobutu government. However, their citizenship was withdrawn in 1982 through legislation barring citizenship from "immigrant" ethnic groups. There is some question as to whether the withdrawal of citizenship was ever codified in law, but effectively the Banyarwandans did not have Zairean citizenship under Mobutu and were even forced to pay additional taxes to local Bantu chiefs. Prior to the influx of refugees from Rwanda in 1994 in response to the genocide there, the Banyarwandans—both Tutsi and Hutu—lived together in peace but were subjected to discrimination from Congolese and other ethnic groups. After the influx of the Rwandan refugees, non-Banyarwandan Congolese began differentiating between Congolese Hutus and Tutsis, and some tensions between the two groups also surfaced.

In 1994, Rwanda experienced genocide of its Tutsi population. The ethnic Hutus who make up eighty-five percent of the Rwandan population murdered at least eight hundred thousand ethnic Tutsi men, women and children. Moderate Hutus who did not believe in killing the Tutsis were also killed during the genocide. The well-planned massacre occurred over a period of one hundred days, and most of those killed were hacked to death with machetes. Neighbors were incited to kill neighbors by the extremists who declared the Tutsis the enemies of Rwanda. The extremist Hutus, known as the Interahamwe ("those who attack together") began their campaign of elimination of the Tutsis after the presidents of Rwanda and Burundi were killed when their plane was shot down in April 1994. Shortly after the genocide began, a Tutsi rebel group, the Rwandan Patriotic Army (RPA), which had been active in the country and had bases in neighboring Uganda, executed an effective campaign against the Interahamwe, defeating them quickly. In the aftermath of the genocide, close to one million Rwandans fled west into eastern Congo out of fear of retaliation from the victorious RPA. Among the million refugees were thousands of Interahamwe and ordinary Rwandans who had taken part in the murder of the Tutsis; they settled into refugee camps in Congo. From mid-1994 until the end of 1996, the Interahamwe, through intimidation and extortion, controlled the Rwandan populations in the refugee camps in eastern Congo. The influx of refugees proved to be a huge burden on the Congo government, at that time called Zaire.

In March 1996, the local government in Congo's Kivu province advocated the removal of ethnic Tutsis from the country. At the same time, tensions within the refugee camps were also high because the people were living in squalid conditions and were prevented from leaving the camps by the Interahamwe. Hutus feared retaliation for the genocide by the new Tutsi-dominated Rwandan government. Meanwhile, the ethnic Tutsi Congolese fought against the local government's campaign to remove them, forming militias that were organized as the Armed Forces for the Liberation of Congo-Zaire (AFDL). In October 1996, the AFDL rebellion, consisting mainly of Congolese Tutsis and Rwandan soldiers, was launched. Soon, it controlled much of eastern Congo, and Laurent Kabila came to be seen as the organization's leader. AFDL also picked up allies within the Congolese population (who opposed Mobutu's government). Though allied with veteran rebels from Angola's UNITA (National Union for Total Liberation of Angola) movement, Mobutu's forces were ill trained and ineffective against the rebel AFDL and many soldiers abandoned their posts or joined the rebels. Mobutu himself was ill and receiving cancer treatment in Europe during the early stages of the rebellion. He returned to the Congo in December 1996 only to be driven from the country in May 1997 when the AFDL was victorious.

With the victory, Kabila declared himself president of the newly renamed Congo. Kabila established a new government and put ethnic Tutsis—both Congolese and Rwandan—in positions of power. In the aftermath of the rebellion, it became clear that the Kabila's Rwandan troops, in an attempt to wipe out the Interahamwe, had committed atrocities against the Rwandan Hutu refugees who were scattered from their camps shortly after the rebellion began. The majority of the refugee population returned to Rwanda in late 1996 and early 1997, but many thousands remained unaccounted for and no one knows how

MOBUTU SESE SEKO

1930–1997 Joseph Desire Mobutu was born in 1930 and educated in the Congo and Brussels. In 1956 he joined the Nationalist Movement. In 1960 he led a coup against nationalist leader Patrice Lamumba, who was assassinated. Mobutu became the army chief of staff, and staged another coup in 1965, installing himself as prime minister in 1966. In 1967 Mobutu oversaw the creation of a presidential form of government, which didn't take affect until Mobutu became old enough to assume power under the provisions of its constitution.

The Congo changed its name to Zaire in 1970 as part of Mobutu's National Authenticity program. In 1971 Joseph Mobutu changed his name to Mobutu Sese Seko Kuku Ngbendu wa za Banga ("the all powerful warrior who, because of his endurance and inflexible will to win, will go from conquest to conquest leaving fire in his wake"), and encouraged all citizens to Africanize their names. Mobutu received large amounts of Western aid (about 8.5 billion dollars between 1970–94); the United States considered Zaire an important Cold War ally. Mobutu also participated in France's "La Francophonie" program, which encouraged the spread of French language and culture, in exchange for French aid.

Civil unrest was constant in Mobutu's Zaire. Revolts in the Katanga Province (now Shaba) took place in 1970 and 1978. As the civil war of 1996–97 was taking place, Mobutu refused to acknowledge the exis-

PRESIDENT MOBUTU SESE SEKO. *(Archive Photos. Reproduced by permission.)*

tence of either the war or of rival leader Laurent Kabila. On May 18, 1997, as Kabila and the Alliance of Democratic Forces for the Liberation of the Congo entered the capital Kinshasa, Mobutu and his family fled to Morocco, where he died of cancer on September 7, 1997 at the age of sixty-six.

many were killed by Rwandan troops in Kabila's rebel army. In the aftermath of the Rwandan genocide, the Rwandan government continued to fight Interahamwe and ex-Armed Forces of Rwanda (ex-FAR, the forces of the pre-genocide Hutu government), particularly in northwest Rwanda, which borders on the Congo. After defeating the extremists from Rwanda in 1994, the Rwandan government extended its fight against its Hutu opponents to Congo. In addition, the Rwandan government wanted to help its Tutsi brethren in the Congo who were subject to discrimination and violence at the hands of other ethnic groups under Mobutu's rule.

However, Kabila's reliance on Tutsi support during the rebellion, especially the Rwandan Tutsis, disturbed the rest of the population of Congo, particularly the population in the east of the country. Further, Kabila proved to be an autocratic leader, banning political parties and putting all the power and resources of the state in his presidency. He was charged with being dictatorial and oppressive. His regime was accused of committing many human rights violations, including jailing journalists and opposition politicians, and carrying out extra-judicial executions and torture. After some months in power, Kabila found that he had no support base and that many in the country were dissatisfied with his rule. In July 1998, Kabila strategically decided that he no longer needed the support of the Tutsis who had brought him to power.

Kabila ordered all Rwandans to leave the country. Days later, Kabila's former allies—the Rwandan Tutsis—launched a new rebellion in eastern Congo in an attempt to remove Kabila from power. Since August 1998, the Tutsi rebels have been fighting Kabila's forces, and they currently hold at least fifty percent of Congo. The rebel group called itself the Congolese Rally for Democracy (RCD), and was led by a scholar, Ernest Wamba dia Wamba. The rebels split into two factions in May 1999. Wamba was ousted for being ineffective and replaced with Emile Ilungu. Wamba regrouped, calling his faction RCD-ML (Liberation Movement), while Ilungu continued to lead the main RCD faction, renamed RCD-Goma (after a city in eastern Congo). A third rebel faction emerged in November 1998. Led by a businessman, Jean-Pierre Bemba, and originating in Equateur Province, it is called the Movement for the Liberation of the Congo (MLC).

Kabil's Foes and Friends

Several neighboring states have been pulled into the conflict as active participants. These include Uganda, Rwanda and Burundi on the side of the rebels and Angola, Zimbabwe, Namibia, Libya, Sudan, and Chad on the side of Kabila's government. Each regional government has its own motivation for involvement in the conflict. Rwanda and Burundi, both led by minority Tutsi governments, have security concerns since extremist Hutus from both countries maintain bases in eastern Congo. Since 1994, Burundi has been engaged in a low-intensity war against Hutu insurgents which has claimed at least two hundred thousand lives. Burundi government forces conduct counter-insurgency operations in the Congo against Hutu extremist groups (the Palipehutu and the Forces for Democracy and Development (FDD)), sometimes in conjunction with Rwandan and Ugandan forces. Burundi's presence in Congo is almost entirely aimed at hunting down extremist Hutus from Burundi, and the government of Burundi does not challenge the Kabila government. In fact, Kabila's government has supported the Burundi government against a regional economic embargo. Rwanda, on the other hand, feels betrayed by Kabila since, without Rwandan Tutsi aid, he would never have been able to take over Congo. Also, there are assertions by governments in the region that Rwanda hopes to enlarge its territory into Congo because it faces acute land shortages. Without secure borders, these two states are unlikely to disengage from the fighting in Congo.

Uganda supported the initial rebellion against Mobutu, a long-time foe. Uganda continues to support the rebels against Kabila out of concern for Ugandan security and out of allegiance to its long-time allies the Rwandan Tutsis. The Rwandan Tutsis had aided current Ugandan President Yoweri Museveni in his rebellion against then-president Milton Obote in the 1980s. Uganda is also concerned that Congo soil has been used as the launching pad for Ugandan rebels (The West Nile Bank Front) who are supported by the Sudanese government. The humanitarian and security situation in Uganda's Rwenzori mountain region has deteriorated since the conflict in Congo began, and Museveni feels that Kabila is not a strong enough leader to secure the border region between their two countries.

Kabila's allies are, for the most part, states that border the Congo and who do not want to see the disintegration of sub-Saharan Africa's second largest country. Zimbabwe has some economic motivations in allying with Kabila's government and has begun to profit from the mineral wealth of a small area of eastern Congo that Zimbabwe controls. However, Zimbabwe's participation in the conflict is very unpopular in Zimbabwe itself and the government of Robert Mugabe appears to be looking for a way to exit from the war. Angolan interest in the conflict in the Congo is mainly because of its own internal security concerns. In Angola, UNITA rebels renewed their war against the government of Jonas Savimbi in late 1998. Since then, the Angolan government has been concerned with UNITA's use of Congo soil as a base. Kabila's government has allowed the Angolan government to launch attacks against UNITA on Congo soil, and in return Angola has supported Kabila in his fight against Congolese rebels. In fact, when the second Congo rebellion began in August 1998, the government of Kabila was saved by Angolan government forces who kept the Congolese rebels from taking over Kinshasa. Namibia, Chad, Libya and Sudan have played lesser roles in the conflict, mainly supplying Kabila's government with arms and other supplies.

Aside from regional governments, Kabila also has traditional militia groups in eastern Congo fighting the rebel forces. These militias, known as Mai-Mai, are fighting the rebel forces mainly because they dislike the presence of foreign troops on Congo soil. The Mai-Mai particularly dislike the domination of the region by Congolese or foreign Tutsis. The Mai-Mai have been involved in other ethnic clashes in eastern Congo. They have no overarching administrative structure, recruit among village youth, and are organized by local leaders.

CONSTANT CIVIL WAR IN CONGO AND THE SURROUNDING COUNTRIES HAS LEFT MANY CHILDREN HUNGRY AND PARENTLESS, LIKE THESE BOYS IN THE VILLAGE OF MBANDAKA. *(AP/Wide World Photos. Reproduced by permission.)*

The Lusaka Accords

Finally, in September 1998, a peace process, the Lusaka Accords, began. The governments of South Africa, Zambia, Mozambique, and Tanzania, under the auspices of the Southern African Development Community (SADC), played key roles in the peace process that culminated in the signing of a cease-fire agreement in July 1999. Under the terms of the accord, all rebel and government attacks were to cease and the military forces were to disengage. Violence against civilians was to cease and parties were to help with the delivery of humanitarian assistance through the opening of aid corridors. A Joint Military Commission was also to be established to investigate reported cease-fire violations, work out mechanisms to disarm militia groups, verify the disarmament of civilians, and monitor the withdrawal of foreign forces. A U.N. peacekeeping force is to be deployed at an unspecified future date. Since its signing and implementation, however, the accords have not brought about a stable peace in the conflict zone, and tensions remain high. Neither the government and its allies nor the rebels and their allies trust each other. Additionally, the sides are far apart in their vision for the future of the Congo.

In the months since the Lusaka Accords was signed by the Congo government and the main rebel factions, there has been little progress in moving toward a sustainable peace in the country. The main accomplishment of the Lusaka Accords was the establishment of a cease-fire among all parties. Yet, the cease-fire has been broken numerous times since its implementation, and the situation in eastern Congo has worsened since the beginning of 2000. In December 1999, the three rebel factions met under the guidance of Uganda and Rwanda in order to try to resolve their differences and present a united front against Kabila's forces. They agreed to set up a leaders' forum and a joint political and military commission. The military commission would work to form a united Congolese military while the political commission would work to develop common goals and policies. The rebels have come under fire from human rights organizations for committing human rights abuses in their territories, as well as for failing to stop inter-ethnic fighting between two groups, the Hema and Lendu, which has led to approximately 5000 deaths. According to the United Nations Office for the Coordination of Humanitarian Affairs, the humanitarian situation in eastern Congo, and the Great Lakes region in general, has deteriorated greatly since the summer of 1999. Congo has not only produced thousand of refugees and internally displaced people, it has also been the recipient of thousands of refugees fleeing fighting in Angola.

In January 2000, former Botswana president Sir Ketumile Masire was appointed to oversee the Lusaka process. Also in that month, the U.N. Security Council met to discuss the security situation in the Congo and give a boost to the Lusaka peace process. The Security Council said it intended to move quickly to approve a resolution authorizing the deployment of military observers to the country. Presidents from the countries involved in the conflict met with the Security Council in an attempt to further the peace process; however, no new agreement was reached. Rebel leaders, because they are non-state representatives, could not be officially invited by the Security Council to attend the meetings. However, the U.S. government made it known that they would be welcome in New York during the talks so that informal negotiations could take place.

The United Nations recommended a mission of about 5,500 people, including 500 military observers and 3,400 security personnel. However, the Security Council stopped short of committing itself to a timetable to send the mission and did not commit itself to a full-fledged peacekeeping force as recommended by the African heads of state. A proposal on the mission was circulating within the U.N. in early February 2000. The United States Congress would have to approve any resolution authorizing U.N. troops sent to the Congo before the U.S. could give its approval in the Security Council. Fresh offensives in the conflict were reported in early 2000, and the prospects for continued fighting were high.

The Conflict and the International Community

Tolerance for autocratic rulers within the international community decreased greatly after the end of the Cold War. Further, the liberation of Eastern European countries provided a model for the people of Africa and elsewhere who had long suffered under dictatorial and corrupt leaders. In addition, Western governments and financial institutions were becoming tired of providing funds to African governments without seeing any real progress in the economic development of their states. The culmination of all these factors in Africa was a push towards democratization in the early 1990s. Opposition groups throughout the continent became more vocal, and conflicts broke out in many states as rulers tried to maintain their hold on power.

Mobutu managed to manipulate the democratization process in the early 1990s and continued to wield significant power, even with the adoption of a Sovereign National Congress that was intended to oversee the move to a more democratic government. He agreed to end one-party rule and to allow multi-party elections. In April 1994, Mobutu and the opposition agreed to transitional government. However, it functioned poorly, and before elections could be held, the rebellion broke out in eastern Congo in October 1996.

The recent conflict in the Congo has many facets, including a struggle for power within the Congo, an ethnic conflict pitting Banyamulenge against other ethnic groups, and a regional conflict with security as the main concern. Kabila has not ruled Congo under democratic principles and opposition to his regime has been extensive. However, opposition to Kabila has been slowed as "native" Congolese focus their resentment on the presence of Banyamulenge rebels. Many Congolese prefer the autocratic rule of Laurent Kabila to the perceived domination of the ethnic Tutsis. They fear that if the rebels take over the country, Rwanda will take control of their country. Other countries in the region have supported Kabila out of security concerns related to conflicts in their own countries, out of the hopes for economic gains by tapping into Congo's vast resources, and out of support for the general principal of sovereignty. Sovereignty is the notion that a government is the supreme arbiter of affairs within its own borders, and that those borders are inviolable.

African governments have long supported the integrity of their states' borders, despite the arbitrariness of their creation. Even though the European powers carved up Africa at the end of the nineteenth century with no regard to historical kingdoms or ethnic relations, African governments have been reluctant to accept any rebellion that has led to the disintegration of their states. Most governments in Africa would rather fight decades-long wars (and many have) in the name of national unity than accept peace under the condition of redrawing their borders. Only Ethiopia has voluntarily given up part of its territory in order to create a new state, Eritrea.

The regime of Laurent Kabila has been at least as oppressive as the worst years under Mobutu Sese Seko. Amnesty International reports that after he took power, Kabila's government arrested hundreds of people, including human rights activists, journalists, opposition party members, and those associated with the Mobutu government. Kabila's government also attempted to prevent a United Nations team from investigating alleged mass killings of Hutu refugees and Congolese Hutus by the AFDL. The U.N. was eventually allowed to enter the country to investigate the allegations of mass killings, but it was hampered in its efforts to visit massacre sites by the government.

The African Association for the Defense of Human Rights in Congo-Kinshasa (ASADHO) was also highly critical of Kabila's first year in power. In a statement on the first anniversary of Kabila's rule, the organization reported that ethnic tensions are exacerbated in the country, especially in the Kivu provinces, that arbitrary arrests take place routinely, that security forces operate with unlimited power, and that political trials are conducted in military rather than civilian courts. Kabila has also deliberately excluded the traditional opposition from political consultations with his regime. He has arrested their leaders, including Etienne Tshisekedi, a long-time Mobutu foe, who was arrested twice under Kabila and banished to his birthplace in Kasai. Since the second rebellion began in October 1998, Kabila appears to be cultivating the support of regional governments more than the support of the people of Congo.

RECENT HISTORY AND THE FUTURE

The conflict in Congo is of grave concern to the governments of central Africa who are directly affected by the conflict. Not only are many states involved directly in the conflict fighting with either the rebels or the Kabila government, but many more states are involved indirectly as a result of refugee migrations and arms flows in the region. A sense of insecurity in the entire region prevails because of the Congo conflict. African governments are very concerned about the integrity of Congo's borders. They do not want to see the disintegration of the state because of the humanitarian consequences and because a change of borders in one African state could set a precedent for other rebels groups who wish to secede from their states and create newly independent states. There are so many ethnic groups in Africa, many with nationalist sentiments, that African governments find it essential to stand firm in their commitment to the integrity of African borders. Finally, African governments are concerned with who controls the vast resources of the Congo. Some of those allied with Kabila hope to profit themselves from their loyalty to him during the rebellion.

International leaders have similar concerns regarding the conflict in Congo. International leaders do not want to see Congo further destabilized because of the potential for great humanitarian disaster. Already, thousands of people have lost their lives and hundreds of thousands have been displaced from their homes. The entire region is affected by the mass movements of people, and the capacity of humanitarian organizations to deal with the crisis is limited by the insecurity of the region within which they are working.

Crises in Africa are so pervasive and involve such great numbers of people that Western governments appear overwhelmed by the problems and seem unsure how, exactly, to intervene. Western governments have been reluctant to intervene directly in African crises since the humanitarian intervention by the U.S. in the Somali civil war in 1993 led to the deaths of U.S. military personnel. The international community is also concerned about the Congo conflict because of the vast wealth of the country. Western governments are the main beneficiaries of the mineral wealth extracted from Congo, and they would be reluctant to lose their partnerships with those who control the resources. Finally, the Western governments would like to see movement towards democracy in the Congo and the rest of Africa because they feel that democratic governments are better able to deal with the economic, social and political problems facing African states.

The conflicts of the region are so interwoven that resolving one without addressing the others will almost certainly lead to renewed conflicts. In addition to addressing the immediate goals of the combatants, it is also necessary to address the social and economic problems confronting the states of central Africa. Congo is fortunate in that it has the resources to develop into a viable state if it can implement policies that encourage economic growth and equitable distribution of wealth; other countries in the region have a greater challenge ahead of them in trying to bring about economic growth and a better quality of life for their people.

In early 2000, it appears that the Congo conflict will continue for some time. The peace process has begun, but at the same time, rebels and government forces continue to break the cease-fire agreement. The recent reconciliation between the rebel factions may prove to be troublesome for President Kabila and his allies, especially if Kabila's allies withdraw their support out of the need to address their own domestic concerns. Rwanda is not likely to abandon its support for the rebels until it feels the threat of the extremist Interahamwe has disappeared. With the availability of arms in the region, and the extensive resources of the country, both sides could continue their fight for years to come.

BIBLIOGRAPHY

African Association for the Defense of Human Rights in Congo-Kinshasa. *Statement on the First Anniversary of the New Regime.* Kinshasa (15 May 1998).

Ajulu, Rok. "Congo is Back! Congo is Gone! The Congo Crisis Again!" *Africa World Review* (February-April 1999): 6–12.

Amnesty International. *Annual Report 1998.* New York: Amnesty International, 1998.

———. *Zaire: Collapsing Under Crisis.* New York: Amnesty International, 1994.

"Congo Talks Wind Down, No Pact," *Washington Post,* 26 January 2000.

Currey, James. *The Creation of Tribalism in Southern Africa.* Berkeley, Calif.: University of California Press, 1989.

"The Democratic Republic of the Congo." In *The Europa Year Book* Vol. 1. London: Europa Publications, Ltd., 1999.

International Crisis Group. *Central Africa Project.* http://www.crisisweb.org (20 September 2000).

Prendergast, John and David Smock. *Reconstructing Peace in the Congo.* Washington, D.C.: United States Institute of Peace, 1999.

United Nations Office for the Coordination of Humanitarian Affairs. *Integrated Regional Information Network (IRIN) daily reports.* http://www.releifweb.int/IRIN (20 September 2000).

Zaire: A Country Study. 1994. Washington, D.C.: Library of Congress.

Anne Pitsch

CUBA AND THE UNITED STATES: REVOLUTION, NATIONALISM AND ENEMIES NEXT DOOR

In late 1999 a young Cuban boy, Elian Gonzalez, was picked up clinging to a life raft in the waters between Cuba and Florida. He was the latest in a long line of refugees seeking to escape Cuba and make their way to America. As it turned out, Gonzalez had taken to sea in a small boat with his mother and a number of other refugees. The boat sank in rough weather; Gonzalez's mother and the others were killed. After the U.S. Coast Guard rescued Gonzalez, he was taken to the United States in preparation for return to Cuba. Gonzalez's parents had divorced, and his father remained in Cuba. He sought the boy's return.

Typically, Gonzalez would have been returned to Cuba. He was only six years old and by most accounts was not old enough to make a decision to immigrate for himself. In the United States, as in many countries, there is a presumption that the interests of the child are best served by living with one of his parents, if not both. Given Gonzalez's mother's death, it seemed appropriate that he be returned to his father. Certainly if Gonzalez had come from Mexico, Nicaragua, Haiti, or Jamaica, he would have been returned to his remaining parent with little fanfare. But things would be different in the Gonzalez case.

Gonzalez had relatives in the United States. These relatives were part of a large Cuban exile community who left the island after the Communist takeover in 1959 led by Fidel Castro. Instead of returning the boy to Cuba as one might expect, the Gonzalez relatives fought to have him remain in the United States. The Gonzalez relatives were adamant that Elian not be returned to Cuba. They, and others like them, represented the

THE CONFLICT

Cuba, a Communist country just ninety miles off the coast of the United States, has a long history of conflict with the United States. Cuban immigrants in the United States have, with the support of its government, attempted to invade Cuba and overthrow its president, Fidel Castro. The United States has a long-standing economic embargo of Cuba. In 1999 a small group of people attempted to escape Cuba; most drowned on their voyage. But a small boy, Elian Gonzalez, lived, and the resulting legal and political maneuvers highlighted the continuing conflict between Cuba and the United States

Political

- The United States is vehemently anti-Communist.

- Cuba is anti-Capitalist, though without a protector due to the disintegration of the Soviet Union.

- Cuba does not want to be dominated by the United States

- Cuban immigrants, a strong political force in the United States, hate the idea of any compromise with Castro. They feel that returning Elian Gonzalez to his father in Cuba relegates the child to living a life under tyranny.

Economic

- The United States has a long-standing economic embargo of Cuba.

- Many of the Cuban immigrants, especially those who immigrated immediately following the revolution, were wealthy in Cuba, and resent Castro for expropriating their wealth.

CHRONOLOGY

1492 Cuba is discovered by Columbus.

1511–13 Diego Valasquez conquers Cuba in the name of Spain.

1895 Jose Marti launches a revolution against Spanish rule. Though it was unsuccessful, it encourages the growth of Cuban nationalism. Spain responds to the revolt brutally. The U.S. battleship U.S.S. Maine is sent to Havana, Cuba to protect Americans. While there, it mysteriously explodes, causing two hundred American deaths. Shortly thereafter, the United States intervenes in what becomes the Spanish-American War.

1899 After winning the Spanish-American War, the United States establishes control over Cuba.

1900 The United States allows Cuba limited elections and the drafting of the first Cuban constitution. It requires inclusion of the Platt Amendment, which limits Cuba's autonomy.

1902 Cuba gains independence, subject to the restrictions in the Platt Amendment.

1906–12 Control of Cuba goes back and forth between the United States and Cuba.

1924 In the Monroe Doctrine, the United States states that interference of European powers in the western hemisphere will not be tolerated.

1933 A group of non-commissioned officers, led by Fulgencio Batista, mutiny and take control of the military in what is known as the "Sergeants' Revolt." The military installs Ramon Grau as president.

1953 A group of young revolutionaries, led by Fidel Castro, attacks the Moncada army barracks but are captured and sentenced to prison.

1955 Batista grants amnesty to Castro. Castro goes to Mexico to train a rebel army.

1958 Castro and his followers, including Che Guevara, overthrow the government.

1959 Castro institutes significant reforms, including nationalization and central planning.

1960 The Soviet First Deputy Premier visits Cuba.

1961 The United States breaks diplomatic relations. The United States sponsors a failed invasion of Cuba by Cuban immigrants, called the "Bay of Pigs."

1962 The United States establishes an embargo to cover any product containing material from Cuba. The placement of Soviet missiles in Cuba leads to the Cuban Missile Crisis.

Mid-1980s During the Mariel boatlift, thousands of Cuban refugees leave for the United States, including some criminals and mentally ill patients.

1999 A young Cuban refugee, Elian Gonzalez, is picked up clinging to a raft in the waters between Cuba and Florida. The ensuing custody battle between his Cuban and Miami relatives brings the issues of Cuba and the United States, and Cuban-American immigrants, to the headlines.

best of Cuba's entrepreneurial community. They lost everything they owned to Communist Cuba, which seized private property for the state in order to build a socialist regime. Their hatred of Castro remained intense even after more than forty years. With more than one million compatriots in the southern Florida area, this group of exiled Cubans is a significant political force in American politics. They often vote as a block against anyone they perceive as unfriendly to their interests.

In spring of 2000, Elian's father, Juan Gonzalez, came to the United States to claim his child.

As the case wound its way through the courts, the Miami-based Gonzalez family refused to return the boy to his father. The Immigration and Naturalization Service—the U.S. agency responsible for the boy—retrieved the child at gunpoint, and he was united with this father. Meanwhile, the Cuban immigrant community in Miami exploded. Their anger at Cuba—at Fidel Castro—emerged with claims of Cuban brainwashing, persecution, torture and abuse.

The uncompromising attitude of Cuban-Americans is reflected in the larger context of

U.S.-Cuban relations. The two states have been bitter enemies since Castro's revolution. To truly understand the chasm between these two countries, one must understand the history of U.S.-Cuban relations.

HISTORICAL BACKGROUND

Understanding Cuba

Cuba's relationship with the United States is partially determined by its geo-strategic location. Cuba is located approximately ninety miles south of Florida. It commands the eastern approaches to the Caribbean, as well as to Latin America. Thus control of Cuba allows one to influence access to Latin America and the Caribbean. The value of the location increased with the opening of the Panama Canal a century ago. The importance of Cuba was realized when it was occupied by Spain from approximately 1511 to 1898. So long as Spain controlled Cuba the United States would always worry about European intervention in the Western Hemisphere. In 1823, through the Monroe Doctrine, the United States stated that the interference of European powers would not be tolerated in the Western Hemisphere. With the Monroe Doctrine it became apparent that a key goal of the United States was to eject Spain from the Western Hemisphere, and, thus, from Cuba as well.

The lack of diversity in the Cuban economy is also important for understanding Cuban-American relations. Partly because of its colonial history and occupation by Spain, Cuba developed and relied upon very few crops. Tobacco and sugar came to dominate Cuba's economy during the colonial period. This problem was magnified in later years and even today sugar dominates the Cuban economy. This is a weakness for Cuba, because it makes Cuba heavily dependent upon external economic factors beyond its control, such as the demand and international prices for sugar. If sugar demand goes down, if prices fall, or if Cuba's primary trading partners refuse to purchase sugar, then Cuba's economy suffers.

The third factor in understanding Cuba is Cuban nationalism. While Cuban nationalism was initially directed toward Spain, over the last one hundred years it has clearly become focused on the United States. Distrust of the United States unites many Cuban people. At the same time, thoughtful Cubans recognize that they must reach some accommodation with the United States if they are to maximize their own self-interest: the United States can make the lives of all Cubans difficult. Yet Cuba does not have the ability to make the

A STRONG ANTI-U.S. SENTIMENT EXISTS AMONG SOME CUBAN-AMERICANS; THIS MAN HOLDS A SIGN WITH A PICTURE OF ELIAN GONZALEZ THAT READS, "KIDNAPPED BY THE USA AND THE CUBAN AMERICAN NATIONAL FOUNDATION." *(AP/Wide World Photos. Reproduced by permission.)*

United States equally miserable. Consequently, while it might make sense for Cuba to reach some agreement with the United States, since Castro's revolution, Cuba has sought to avoid all contact with or weaken the United States so as to avoid American domination (Suchlicki, 1997).

The interaction of geography, economy and nationalism is found throughout the history of U.S.-Cuban relations over the past one hundred years.

History

Columbus discovered Cuba in 1492. At least three native tribes occupied Cuba at this time. Between 1511 and 1513, Diego Velasquez conquered Cuba in the name of Spain. This initiated the colonial period, which was to last until at least 1898. During this time, the native Cubans were essentially wiped out. The population was largely replenished by Spaniards and slaves brought from Africa. Throughout the eighteenth and nineteenth centuries Cuba moved increasingly to an economy based on sugar. Consequently, Cuba became more and more dependent upon those states that purchased sugar.

Meanwhile, as Cuba became increasingly reliant on sugar, other changes were occurring in the world's economy. For example, U.S. investment in Cuba was expanding every year. At the same time, Europeans were becoming less dependent upon Cuban sugar and thus withdrawing from the market. Increased U.S. investment and European withdrawal made Cuba more vulnerable to the United States. The United States was rapidly becoming the only large market in which Cuba could sell its sugar.

In the latter half of the eighteenth century Spain continued to refuse to grant either autonomy or independence to Cuba. Spain was attempting to retain its colonial empire in a time of massive economic and political change. Cubans were increasingly bitter as they saw independence sweep Latin America during the mid-1800s. Not surprisingly then, the Cubans tried to revolt in the Ten Years War (1868–78). Though the war was long and bitter, Spain managed to defeat the rebellion because the Cuban forces were divided on a number of issues, especially slavery. Large landowners in Cuba did not wish to see the institution of slavery abolished because they thought they needed a source of cheap labor to remain competitive in sugar production. A successful revolt against Spain, however, demanded the assistance of all elements of Cuban society, including the slaves, and this lack of cooperation doomed the rebellion. A second rebellion, known as the Little War, occurred between 1879 and 1880. This rebellion relied more heavily on slaves, but without the other elements of Cuban society, also failed.

The years after the Little War were characterized by political discontent and a lack of unifying leadership in Cuba. The issue of slavery continued to divide Cubans. Nationalism became the unifying factor; nationalism refers to a sense of pride and loyalty toward one's country, and is often created by an outside source. A charismatic leader was required—one who could unify all Cubans under the banner of Cuban nationalism. Jose Marti was that leader.

Jose Marti and the Revolution

Marti was a poet, a journalist, a lawyer, a leading intellectual, a humanitarian, and a nationalist. He spent significant time traveling the world and lived in New York for years. He attempted to organize the Cuban revolution from New York. He knew that he must unite Cubans in order to overthrow the Spanish. He also knew that such a rebellion was doomed without U.S. support. At the same time, Marti was fearful of replacing Spanish domination with U.S. domination. He was forced to walk a thin line between seeking U.S. support in his revolution, but not so much U.S. involvement that they would simply replace the Spanish and still deny Cuba self-determination (Suchlicki, 1997).

Marti launched his revolution in early 1895 with the help of other leaders such as Juan Gualberto Gomez, Maximo Gomez (a Dominican by birth), and Antonio Maceo. Marti was killed in his first battle with the Spanish on May 19, 1895. However, he had encouraged the growth of Cuban nationalism, a nationalism that rejected foreign domination by any power, including the United States.

The revolution went on without Marti. The Spanish reacted brutally, killing, torturing, and placing people in detention camps. In turn, Cuban immigrants in the United States publicized this information and turned the Spanish atrocities into propaganda. Maceo was killed. But as more and more information reached America, public opinion turned squarely against the Spanish. The U.S. battleship U.S.S. Maine was sent to Havana to protect Americans, where it mysteriously exploded causing over two hundred American deaths. Shortly thereafter, the United States intervened in what became the Spanish-American War (much to the chagrin of Cubans, who were fearful of just this sort of interference by outside powers). The Cuban revolution took too long, allowed U.S. intervention, and Marti's very fears came to pass (Suchlicki, 1997).

The explosion of the Maine served as an excuse for U.S. involvement. The United States entered into war on April 25, 1898. America was an expanding power at the time: it had grown to include California and developed to the point that it was the economic equal of any state in the world. The Cuban revolution provided occasion to remove the remaining Europeans from the Western Hemisphere. The geo-strategic value of Cuba would only grow with the Panama Canal (1914). Socially, manifest destiny, or the notion that the United States had a duty to expand its way of life and culture, justified such actions. Finally, America had a strategic doctrine, as set forth by naval strategist Alfred Mahan, which demanded acquiring coaling stations for its growing navy. Again, the spoils of war with Spain satisfied this need.

The war itself was brief. The United States was a new and growing power, while Spain an old and feeble power. The United States defeated Spain in a few battles and Spain requested peace. Spain left Cuba and the United States entered. As Marti had feared, rather than freeing Cuba, U.S. intervention seemed simply to replace one colonial power with another.

Cuban Sovereignty and the Platt Amendment

On January 1, 1899, the United States established military rule over Cuba. Cuban revolutionaries were disappointed by the U.S. move. Still, the initial U.S. administration restored public services, improved sanitation, and successfully worked to decrease disease. In 1900 the United States began to prepare Cuba for independence by allowing limited elections and the drafting of Cuba's first constitution. The United States also drafted certain language to be attached to the Constitution better known by its American legislative name: the Platt Amendment.

The Platt Amendment put various restrictions on Cuban sovereignty. For example, Cuba was forbidden from entering into any treaty with any foreign power that might impair Cuban independence (in U.S. eyes). Cuba could not allow any other foreign power to obtain control over any portion of the island. Cuba was not allowed to contract for any public debt that could not be covered by its current revenues and Cuba was required to allow the United States to lease naval basing rights, providing the United States with the naval base at Guantanamo Bay. But probably the most offensive language to Cubans was that Cuba agreed to allow the United States to intervene in Cuban affairs in order to assure Cuban independence or to protect life, property, and individual liberty. The Platt Amendment was not repealed until 1934 and served to humiliate Cuba and irritate U.S.-Cuban relations for years to come. It

would also have long-term consequences on the maturity of Cuba's political process.

On May 20, 1902 Cuba was granted independence, subject to the Platt Amendment. At this time, Cuba's economy was strong and Cuba was guaranteed a tariff (importation tax) preference to sell sugar in the U.S. market in return for which the United States was granted preferential treatment for its products in Cuba. Politically, however, Cuba's fears were realized: pursuant to the Platt Amendment the United States began intervening in Cuban affairs almost immediately. The United States first intervened in 1906, only four years after Cuba gained independence. In early 1909 self-rule was once again handed over to the Cubans, but U.S. Marines returned in 1912. United States intervened less overtly between 1910 and 1920. In addition to military intervention, the United States continued to dominate the island's economy, controlling more and more economic enterprises throughout the 1920s. Anti-American feelings grew.

Machado

In 1925 Gerardo Machado was inaugurated as Cuba's president. Initially, Machado's administration was characterized by improvements to Cuba's economy and increased spending on the domestic infrastructure. However, these benefits were gained at the expense of freedom and democracy. Machado systematically made it more difficult for his political opposition, while at the same time increasing his own powers. Not surprisingly, Machado was reelected in 1928 to a six-year term; his term began inauspiciously, as the Great Depression occurred in October 1929.

As with everywhere else in the world, the Great Depression created exceptionally hard times in Cuba. Cuba was heavily dependent on exports and trade suffered grievously during the Great Depression. As the general population began to suffer, Cuba's suffering impacted the political arena. Protests spread and crime grew. Assassinations occurred on a regular basis, with the opposition and government forces using gangs of thugs to battle one another. Out of this cauldron arose the "1930 Generation" comprising students who believed the United States frustrated Cuban hopes in 1898. The 1930 Generation sought to complete the Cuban revolution, and ultimately provided the foundation upon which Castro later built his revolution (Suchlicki, 1997). Machado was forced to flee Cuba in August 1933 and was replaced by Carlos Manuel de Cespedes. Yet the turmoil was such that Cespedes was unable to govern.

FIDEL CASTRO RUZ

1926– The future "maximum leader" of Cuba was born on a sugar plantation August 13, 1926 (possibly 1927). Castro was raised Roman Catholic, and attended Catholic schools. Politically active while a student at the University of Havana, he graduated with a doctorate in law in 1950. In 1953 after contesting the legality of the Batista regime in court, Castro led an unsuccessful attack on an army post. Originally sentenced to fifteen years in prison, he was soon released and exiled. He traveled to the United States, where he briefly played for an American baseball team and appeared in a Hollywood film.

After regrouping with revolutionaries in Mexico, Castro returned to Cuba and launched a guerrilla war in 1956, overthrowing Batista in 1959. Under Castro, radical economic and land reforms caused many professionals and prosperous Cubans to emigrate. Castro was elected chairman of the Nonaligned Nations Movement in 1979 and has dispatched Cuba troops in numerous international disputes. Running as the sole candidate; he was elected to a fifth term as president in 1998.

Partially as a result of continuing instability, on September 4, 1933 a group of noncommissioned officers (NCOs or sergeants) mutinied, arrested their commanding officers, and took control of the military in what became known as the "Sergeants' Revolt." They were led by Fulgencio Batista and were soon joined by influential student revolutionaries. The military installed a nationalist, reformist government led by Ramon Grau, a former university professor. Grau instituted a number of reforms, some of which were not supportive of U.S. business interests. Grau's reforms irritated groups within Cuban society, and in early 1934 Batista was able to force Grau from power. Batista then handpicked Cuba's political leadership, while maintaining all significant political power for himself. Batista's regime was characterized by some real reform efforts. In May 1934 Batista's handpicked president signed the Treaty of Relations with the United States, which among other things got rid of the Platt Amendment. Later that year the Treaty of Reciprocity was signed, granting Cuba certain commercial preferences with the United States.

Batista continued to control the presidency and powerful positions in Cuba by providing military support and by driving his rivals from power when they threatened him. Batista finally ran for president himself in 1940 and defeated Grau. Throughout his tenure Batista maintained friendly relations with the U.S. government. He cooperated closely with the United States during World War II and provided stability in Cuba. Still, signs of discontent remained. Gang warfare, or "gangsterism," appeared more fully at this time as a tool of social, economic, and political warfare. Nationalism also returned to the debate on Cuba's future. In 1944 Grau managed to win the presidency and Batista retired to the United States. In 1948 yet another reformist candidate, Carlos Prio, won the presidency. Like Grau before him, Prio was unable to control corruption and graft. Moreover, his reformist tendencies frightened U.S. commercial interests, and U.S./Cuban relations were becoming increasingly strained. At the same time, Batista had been elected senator in-absentia in 1948, and had recently returned to Cuba. Of those opposing government, current and former radical students were best organized and caused the greatest problems for government. One such opponent was Fidel Castro.

The Fall and Rise of Fidel Castro

Castro planned to run for political office in the 1952 elections. He never had the chance. On March 10, 1952, Cubans awoke to find that Batista had engineered a bloodless coup (rebellion). The coup was supported by the military and caught the rest of Cuba by surprise. Batista appointed himself president and promised elections in the future. Because Batista had allowed elections previously, the opposition did not immediately resist him. When given the chance to run the country, Batista created a prosperous economic environment, but did so by suppressing democracy.

While Batista's Cuba was prosperous economically, it was also highly dependent upon the United States. Batista's repressive political regime combined with growing nationalist sentiments against United States. Batista, too, had changed. He sought far less reform than he had in the 1930s. Rather, by the 1950s, Batista sought to steal money from Cuba and allow his friends to do the same. Assorted opposition parties began rallying against Batista and some clashed violently with Batista's troops.

Meanwhile, the young revolutionary Castro strongly opposed Batista. On July 26, 1953 Castro unsuccessfully attacked the Moncada army bar-

FIDEL CASTRO, SHOWN HERE DURING HIS OVERTHROW OF THE BATISTA GOVERNMENT. *(The Library of Congress.)*

racks, was captured, and sentenced to fifteen years in prison. At his trial he delivered a speech that ended with the line, "history will absolve me." This was to become Castro's rallying cry. Although the attack failed, Castro gained both a stage on which to put forth his views as well as public prestige because of this challenge to the regime. While in prison, Castro published a brief manifesto also entitled "History Will Absolve Me," in which he claimed nationalistic and reformist motives for his rebellion. At this point Castro did not openly advocate communism. In fact, the Communists criticized the barracks attack.

Batista held elections in 1954 that were boycotted by the opposition. Consequently, although Batista won the elections, his legitimacy was lower than ever. As a result of this lack of legitimacy and in response to opposition, Batista granted a general amnesty in 1955, freeing political prisoners, including Castro, who then fled to Mexico.

In Mexico, Castro began organizing a rebel army to return to Cuba. Included in this army were his brother Raul and the Argentine doctor and revolutionary, Ernesto (Che) Guevara. By late 1956, riots and strikes were paralyzing Cuba. In December, Castro and eighty revolutionaries returned to Cuba where they were attacked by Batista's army on landing. Many were killed, but Castro, his brother, and Che Guevara escaped to the Sierra Maestra mountain range.

A stalemate evolved between Batista's army and Castro's forces. Castro's forces were not strong enough to come down from the mountains and directly challenge Batista's army. At the same time, Batista's army could not move into the mountains and dislodge Castro's forces. During the standoff, Castro slowly but steadily gained strength. Since he had some level of legitimacy with the populace based upon his "history will absolve me" speech, he was able to steadily recruit new members and supporters. Moreover, a significant element of Cuban society at the time was dissatisfied with Batista, even if they were not Castro supporters. While these individuals and groups did not necessarily directly support Castro, their actions weakened Batista and therefore indirectly strengthened Castro. Castro's forces occasionally made forays beyond the mountains to strike Batista's forces, demoralizing them. Batista responded with ever-increasing repression, further alienating not only the populace but also his external patron, the United States. Finally, Batista's forces were corrupt and did not really care to fight. With each small battle Batista's army lost, Castro grew a little stronger.

In March 1958 the United States cut off arms shipments to Batista's army, which dealt a serious blow to their morale. With the loss of U.S. support, it seemed no one supported Batista or his army. In November of 1958, Batista held fraudulent elections. Soon thereafter the revolutionaries fought their way out of the mountains. Batista's troops crumbled before them. Batista could see the imminent destruction of his regime and fled to the Dominican Republic on January 1, 1958. Castro's followers (led by Che Guevara) entered Havana victoriously the next day.

The period of time following Cuba's revolution is one of the most confusing in Cuban history, and certainly in U.S.-Cuban relations. The United States and Castro's Cuba quickly grew to despise each other, though it is unclear exactly why. Castro did not initially take control of the Cuban government, but instead acted as commander of the military. Castro also did not immediately embrace communism, at least not publicly, though there is evidence that he had entered a secret alliance with the Communists by the summer of 1959. Castro did, however, move relatively quickly to restrict free speech and establish himself as the sole source of real power in Cuba. He went

about systematically destroying and weakening his enemies. Old power centers such as the military, political groups, and other centers of civic society were also destroyed. Revolutionary bodies, controlled by Castro, replaced the old institutions. Castro dismantled Cuban political culture.

A Swing Left

Economically, Castro quickly became anti-capitalist. In May 1959 the first significant land reform occurred. Pursuant to the Agrarian Reform Law, land tracts were nationalized or otherwise expropriated—they were taken from individuals, often with no compensation, and transferred to the government. The property was put into cooperatives—communally owned and operated organizations—under the dictates of socialism. At the same time, income was redistributed from one group, usually the wealthy, to another, generally the poor, and additional public services were made available to the people. Most of the resources of Cuba, including those owned by Cubans and foreigners, were taken over by the government. In some sectors of the economy, this was more gradual, in other sectors, more rapid, but the direction of change was always toward socialism. In effect, the upper and middle classes suffered in terms of property redistribution, while the lower classes benefited. Central planning, a hallmark of communist governments, was imposed in February 1960. Cuba began suffering almost immediately from its adoption of Soviet-style economic policies. Such policies did not provide the incentives necessary for economic growth. By 1961 food rationing had been "introduced for the first time in the island's history." On July 5, 1960 the United States cancelled Cuba's sugar quota and Cuba responded by nationalizing the assets of U.S. companies in Cuba. Relations between the two states deteriorated.

Politically, too, the United States and Cuba found it difficult to communicate. Communists in the government grew in influence, as other groups were de-emphasized. The Soviet First Deputy Premier visited Cuba in February 1960. The Soviets agreed to provide Cuba with aid and also agreed to purchase Cuban sugar. In retrospect, it appears that Castro was, more than anything else, simply anti-U.S. He did not have to be communist out of conviction. He may have turned to communism because that was the only force that could protect his revolution. He believed America would not attack him as long as the Soviets supported him. By March 1960 the United States was training groups of Cuban exiles to invade Cuba.

THE SHORT DISTANCE BETWEEN THESE TWO NATIONS AT-ODDS IS EMPHASIZED BY THIS SIGN. *(Corbis. Reproduced by permission.)*

Hostility Grows Between the United States and Cuba

The United States did not immediately turn against Castro. But when he began expropriating U.S. property, and then made repeated attempts to arrange revolutions similar to Cuba's in other Latin American countries, the United States became overtly hostile. Through 1960, as the Cuban revolution became increasingly radical, relations between the two states deteriorated further. Cuba nationalized more and more U.S. businesses and the United States increased economic pressures culminating in an embargo in October 1960. On January 3, 1961 the United States broke diplomatic relations with Cuba. By mid-1961 Castro had publicly declared the revolution socialist in nature and himself a communist. Castro thereafter merged the remaining political parties with the Communist Party and a Soviet-style government was installed. The U.S. embargo was tightened further in March 1962 to cover any product that contained any material from Cuba.

To fully understand why the United States reacted so forcefully, one must place the Cuban revolution in the broader context of the Cold War. The United States saw itself as engaged in a zero-sum conflict with the Soviet Union, where any victory for the Soviets was a U.S. loss. Cuba not only represented a U.S. loss, but it was a loss right in America's backyard. Furthermore, Cuba was still viewed as a vital strategic area for the control of Latin America. A hostile Cuba could (and did) support unfriendly revolutions throughout Latin America. On top of this, the 1950s had seen the United States lose some level of its predominant role in world politics. As other countries rebuilt following the devastation of World War II, it caused anxiety among U.S. leaders who sought to maintain the United States' clear superiority. Not only were assorted states moving closer to the United States in terms of power and less willing to comply with its demands, but the Soviets had nuclear weapons and China and other states had "gone Communist." The "loss of Cuba," therefore, appeared to be a significant threat.

The Bay of Pigs and the Repercussions

The United States sponsored an invasion of Cuba on April 17, 1961. This attempted invasion at the Bay of Pigs is often referred to as the "Bay of Pigs fiasco." It was a miserable failure. There was no coordination between the invasion force and local resistance groups, or much support from the U.S. sponsors of the invasion force. Forces that were commanded by Castro defeated the invaders, who were largely Cuban exiles. Not only was this a blow to U.S. prestige and to young U.S.

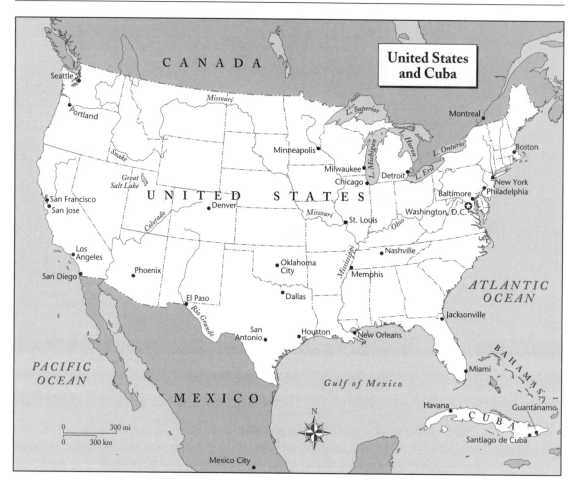

MAP OF CUBA AND THE UNITED STATES. *(XNR Productions Inc.)*

president John F. Kennedy, but also it seemed to prove much of Castro's claims about the United States' intent to destroy Cuba's revolution and Cuban independence. The attempted invasion allowed Castro to crush any remaining opposition, to rally the Cuban people behind his cause, and to justify his military buildup to critics. As U.S.-Cuban relations sunk to an all time low, Soviet-Cuban relations improved, further irritating the United States and discrediting any ideas it might have about accommodating Castro.

There is some evidence that Soviet Premier Khrushchev viewed Kennedy's performance during the Bay of Pigs and at the 1961 Berlin summit as a show of weakness. Whether or not the perceived weakness provided the opportunity, the Soviets introduced nuclear weapons into Cuba in mid-1962; by having nuclear weapons in the Caribbean, the Soviet Union would be able to quickly hit the United States during a conflict. The United States

discovered the weapons through reconnaissance flights over Cuba and a confrontation between the Soviets and Americans ensued. This confrontation is known as the Cuban Missile Crisis (after the Soviet missiles designed to deliver the nuclear weapons). The Cuban Missile Crisis lasted from October 16 until October 28, 1962. The United States imposed a blockade on Cuba on October 22 (referred to as a "quarantine" so as to avoid problems of international law). Shortly thereafter, the Soviets agreed to remove the missiles in exchange for which the United States agreed not to invade Cuba and to remove certain missiles from Turkey, which were probably already slated for removal. The Cuban Missile Crisis is generally regarded as the closest the world has come to nuclear war.

Though the Cuban Missile Crisis is generally regarded as a U.S. victory, Castro got what he had always wanted: a pledge that the United States would not invade and overturn his revolution.

However, Castro was also excluded almost entirely from the management of the crisis; this was probably a good thing since Castro is reported to have urged Soviet use of nuclear weapons. In any event, he was apparently angered by the Soviet removal of the missiles and thereafter distanced himself from the Soviets politically for some time. But the realities of the world political situation were that only the Soviet Union could provide Castro the support his revolution needed if it was to survive so close to the United States. Though the United States had agreed not to invade, it did not ease the economic embargo and remained hostile to Cuba. While Cuba could look elsewhere for help, as it did to China, ultimately only the Soviets possessed the resources Cuba needed.

Nevertheless, for the short term Castro broke with the Soviets and engaged in an aggressive foreign policy including greater support for the "export of revolution" throughout the Americas and elsewhere. Castro also looked to China for support, became involved in Africa (an involvement that would eventually span almost thirty years), and was a supporter of both anti-Israeli efforts in the Middle East and anti-American efforts around the world. Castro's aggressive foreign policy irritated the Soviets because they preferred a unified strategy of foreign policy managed by the Soviets. Castro was not following Soviet orders. While the Soviets had little direct recourse, over time Castro could not get the economic support he needed elsewhere, and he returned to the Soviets.

Castro's need for Soviet support became apparent with the exceptionally poor Cuban economic performance in 1963. One consequence of this poor economic performance was Castro's return to the Soviet fold. But there were other reactions that would impact on U.S.-Cuban relations. For example, Guevara believed that economic success domestically depended upon a favorable international environment. Thus, the reason for failed economic growth at home was the unfavorable international environment imposed on Cuba by the United States. If enough countries could revolt and throw off the yoke of imperialism (as represented by U.S. capitalism), economic success would soon follow domestically. Consequently, Cuba continued to attempt to spread revolution. The U.S. reaction was predictable and hostile. Cuban attempts to export revolution generally failed for the most part as revolutions were crushed throughout Central and South America. Guevara himself was killed with rebels in Bolivia. Cuba needed the Soviet's protection more than ever.

The returning alliance between the Soviets and the Cubans became even clearer when Castro supported the Soviet invasion of Czechoslovakia in 1968. Support for this contradicted Castro's attempts to lead the less developed world and his claims that he represented an alternative to Soviet domination, not to mention his claims that he was not dominated by the Soviet Union. The late 1960s saw détente—a relaxation of tensions—between the United States and Soviet Union. This forced Cuba to reign in its independent foreign policy and become even more subservient to the Soviets, if it desired to retain Soviet aid.

Exporting Revolution

By the early 1970s Castro was still supporting socialist governments worldwide with civilian and military advisors, but he was only supporting revolution where the Soviets allowed. This was Castro's price for continued Soviet aid and support. Ties between the Soviets and Cuba became closer as the Soviets gained naval-base rights in Cuba, operated reconnaissance flights out of Cuba, used Cuba as a listening post on American activities, and sent thousands of advisors and even combat troops to Cuba. High-level delegations traveled between the capitals of Moscow and Havana. Latin American revolution and subversion was set aside for internal development. As détente waned and U.S.-Soviet relations took a turn for the worse, Castro was allowed to resume his activities abroad.

Cuba's foreign policy returned to interventionism in the mid-1970s. These interventions were less haphazard than they had been previously and more in accordance with Soviet grand strategy. In fact, Cuba even admitted its foreign policy was subordinate to that of the Soviets in 1975, quite a change from Castro's claim to lead the nonaligned states. Specifically, in 1975 Cuba intervened in Angola's ongoing struggle for independence on the side of the Marxist and Soviet preferred Popular Movement for the Liberation of Angola (MPLA). This intervention was arguably emboldened by U.S. international paralysis occasioned by the Watergate scandal and the withdrawal from Vietnam. Still, South Africa attempted to intervene on behalf of two Western-favored groups: the National Front for the Liberation of Angola (FNLA) and the Union for the Total Independence of Angola (UNITA). The MPLA managed to get control of the ports as the Portuguese—Cuba's former colonials rulers—withdrew in November 1975. Three Cuban ships with men and materiel had already arrived in Angola in

October of 1975. Shortly thereafter, the Cubans and South Africans, as well as the three Angolan factions, were involved in combat. Initially the Cubans were battered by the South Africans and considered pulling out in December of 1975. But right around this time the U.S. Congress withdrew funding for the other Angolan factions and imposed an embargo on South Africa. These were unrelated to the Cuban intervention, but demonstrated a certain lack of understanding of the implications by the U.S. Congress in the area of foreign policy, at least vis-à-vis Soviet aggression. South Africa thereafter pulled back and the MPLA was able to defeat both the FNLA and UNITA. UNITA, however, turned to guerrilla warfare and, with South African (direct) and later United States (indirect) assistance, was able to carve out a zone free of MPLA influence in the early 1980s.

A second Cuban intervention during this time period occurred with about seventeen thousand troops in Ethiopia from 1977 to 1979. Here, it is reported that Cuban armored forces fought Somali forces. The Cubans were successful in forcing the Somalis to withdraw back over the border. Some Cuban troops initially remained in order to help rebuild Ethiopia and provide both civilian and military instruction. These forces have withdrawn with the end of the Cold War. However, Cuban interventions continued in many other places during the late 1970s and early 1980s. For example, Cuba provided military assistance throughout Africa, the Middle East, and Latin America, either to pro-Communist governments or Communist revolutionaries. Assistance was provided to Algeria, Zaire, Libya, Mozambique, Iran, Iraq, Afghanistan, South Yemen, Nicaragua, El Salvador, and Grenada. Even thus engaged, the Cubans believed that the United States might be willing to form a closer relationship with them because of the election of U.S. president Jimmy Carter in 1976.

The Carter administration initially saw a relaxation of relations with Cuba. Some travel was permitted between the countries, U.S. reconnaissance flights were reduced, certain fishing rights were agreed to, and the countries even opened small diplomatic posts in 1977. At this point, the Cuban exile movement, which had grown in strength and influence since its fleeing to the United States applied political pressure to halt any further normalization of relations. Moreover, continued Cuban export of revolution did little to help the situation. It is useful to examine more closely the renewed Cuban attempts at exporting revolution in Latin America in the late 1970s and forward.

In 1978 the Cubans began arming and training the Sandinista National Liberation Front (FSLN) during its struggle against Anastasio Somoza's dictatorship in Nicaragua. Eventually the Marxist FSLN was victorious. Cuba followed this up by providing extensive military and civilian support for the Sandinistas after their revolutionary victory. In return, the United States armed and supported the Contra army to attempt to overthrow the Sandinistas and their Cuban backers. U.S. president Ronald Reagan's election in 1980 and subsequent policy on Nicaragua and El Salvador prevented any chance of Cuba rapprochement with the United States; the United States even invaded Grenada in 1983 while Cuban troops were there. In response, Cuba's armed forces were upgraded with advanced Soviet weaponry in the mid-1980s. Latin American states, too, attempted to punish Cuba in the early 1980s for Cuba's revolutionary-based foreign policy. However, Cuba was able to regain support from these nations by siding with the Argentine regime in its battle against Britain during the Falklands War.

At any given time during the 1980s an estimated thirty thousand Cuban troops were in Angola. Cuba's involvement in Angola, a number of Soviet interventions (directly in Afghanistan and indirectly in Poland), as well as other interventions helped lead to the election of President Reagan. Reagan sought to confront Cuban elements in Angola by providing greater support to UNITA. With the collapse of the Cold War and the loss of its patron the Soviet Union, Cuba negotiated a withdrawal from Angola, which allowed the MPLA to hold elections under which the MPLA was victorious. In something of a foreign policy coup, Castro was able to demand South Africa's withdrawal from Namibia in exchange for Cuba's withdrawal from Angola, but of course the change to Black African rule inside South Africa meant it would have pulled out of Namibia in any event.

Mariel Boatlift

The mid-1980s saw a new chapter in U.S.-Cuban relations with the Mariel boatlift. This episode began when some ten thousand Cubans invaded the Peruvian embassy in Havana seeking asylum and a life outside of Cuba. In response, Castro agreed to let anyone leave if they would only assemble at the Port of Mariel. With the assistance of Miami-based exiles, several hundred thousand people left Cuba before Castro closed the floodgates. In addition, some 260,000 refugees left the island between 1965 and 1971 in the

United States-Cuban Freedom Flights Program (Lima-Dantas, 1987). This exodus was similar to what happened later in the 1980s when the East European states attempted to let the disaffected leave their Communist homelands—large numbers of people tried to leave. It is noteworthy that Castro attempted to manipulate this apparent rejection of his revolution by inserting assorted criminals and mentally ill patients into the boatlift.

The late 1980s and early 1990s saw the downfall of the Soviet Union and Castro's loss of his patron. The Soviets (first, and later, the Russians) reduced and then eliminated aid to Castro. Meanwhile, as Soviet aggression ended internationally, Cuba too was forced to reign in its behavior if it hoped to retain any aid or positive world opinion. Castro may have felt his regime was threatened from within, because Arnaldo Ochoa, former commander of Cuban troops in both Angola and Ethiopia, was tried and executed. Although Ochoa was officially tried on drug charges, a power struggle or, at least, a perceived threat, may have been the real cause.

Castro is now without a patron. Russia is not in a position to provide aid. Latin American states, as well as European states, are willing to trade with Castro, though the Helms-Burton legislation (a U.S. law which punishes foreign countries that have economic dealings with Cuba) makes this difficult. Yet, Castro has little to offer except barter. The Cuban economy deteriorated during the 1990s. It continues to suffer oil shortages, shortages of industrial products, and of course, food rationing. Yet, Castro opposes market reforms because they require a decentralization of economic power, which tends to lead to an eventual dispersion of political power, and eventually may lead to challenges to his leadership role.

RECENT HISTORY AND THE FUTURE

In early 1996 the Cuban air force shot down an unarmed plane flown by a Cuban exile organization, Brothers to the Rescue, which was involved in searching the waters between Cuba and Florida for refugees. The United States responded by passing the Helms-Burton legislation. While this legislation was criticized as an extraterritorial application of U.S. law, it nevertheless made it more difficult for Cuba to open to trade or for change within Cuba to occur. It allowed Castro to continue to find support for anti-American Cuban nationalism.

The question then arises as to if or when Castro will fall. While many factors seem to mitigate in favor of his overthrow, he has retained power through eight U.S. presidents. His control over the military seems unquestioned. Moreover, Castro's brother, Raul, is the commander of the military. Without military support there is no way for the populace to overthrow Castro. Economic and political penetration could possibly lead to unrest sufficient to generate an overreaction by the regime. But such penetration is difficult if not impossible with the U.S. embargo and the Helms-Burton legislation. So then, it seems only Castro's death will bring change in Cuba. Clearly there is no support in Cuba for U.S. intervention and no other state has the capability to intervene.

BIBLIOGRAPHY

Aguila, Juan. *Cuba: Dilemmas of Revolution.* Boulder, Colo.: Westview, 1994.

Baeza, Mario and Sidney Weintraub. "Economic and Political Constants/Changes in Latin America." In *The United States and the Americas.* Edited by Albert Fishlow and James Jones. New York: W.W. Norton, 1999.

Baloyra, Enrique and James Morris, Eds. *Conflict and Change in Cuba.* Albuquerque, N.Mex.: University of New Mexico, 1993.

Benglesdorf, Carolle. *The Problems of Democracy in Cuba.* New York: Oxford University, 1994.

Blight, James and David Welch. *On the Brink: Americans and Soviets Reexamine the Cuban Missile Crisis.* New York: Hill and Wang, 1989.

Carbonell, Nestor. *And the Russians Stayed: The Sovietization of Cuba.* New York: William Morrow, 1994.

Dominguez, Jorge. *To Make the World Safe for Revolution: Cuban Foreign Policy.* Cambridge, Mass.: Harvard University, 1989.

Fauriol, Georges and Eva Loser, eds. *Cuba: The International Dimension.* New Brunswick, N.J.: Transaction, 1990.

Fishlow, Albert. "The Western Hemisphere Relation: Quo Vadis?" In *The United States and the Americas.* Edited by Albert Fishlow and James Jones. New York: W.W. Norton, 1999.

Gonzalez, Edward. *Cuba: Clearing the Perilous Waters.* Santa Monica, Calif.: Rand Corporation, 1996.

Halperin, Maurice. *Return to Havana.* Nashville, Tenn.: Vanderbilt University Press, 1994.

Horowitz, Irving, ed. *Cuban Communism 1959–1995.* New Brunswick, N.J.: Transaction, 1995.

Jordan, David. *Revolutionary Cuba and the End of the Cold War.* New York: University Press of America, 1993.

Lima-Dantas, Elizabeth. "Historical Setting." In *Cuba: A Country Study.* Edited by James Randolph. Washington, D.C.: Library of Congress. 1987.

Lowenfeld, Andreas. "Congress and Cuba: The Helms-Burton Act," *American Journal of International Law,* July 1996: 419-34.

Moses, Catherine. *Real Life in Castro's Cuba.* Wilmington, Del.: Scholarly Resources, 2000.

Paterson, Thomas. *Contesting Castro.* New York: Oxford University, 1994.

Perez, Louis. *On Becoming Cuban.* Chapel Hill, N.C.: University of North Carolina, 1999.

Preeg, Ernest and Jonathan Levine. *Cuba and the New Caribbean Economic Order.* Washington, D.C.: Center for Strategic and International Studies, 1993.

Robinson, Craig. "The Economy." In *Cuba: A Country Study.* Edited by James Randolph. Washington, D.C.: Library of Congress, 1987.

Sheldon, Liss. *Fidel! Castro's Political and Social Thought.* Boulder, Colo.: Westview, 1994.

Suchlicki, Jaime. *Cuba: From Columbus to Castro and Beyond.* Washington, D.C.: Brassey's, 1997.

———. *Historical Dictionary of Cuba.* Metuchen, NJ: Scarecrow Press, 1988.

Walker, Phyllis. 1987. "National Security." In *Cuba: A Country Study.* Edited by James Randolph. Washington, D.C.: Library of Congress.

Michael Tkacik

ETHIOPIA AND ERITREA: BORDER WAR

Over two hundred thousand troops are massed at the border between Ethiopia and Eritrea, waiting for the next outbreak of violence in a war that has been fought off and on since 1998. Ethiopia and Eritrea are two of the poorest countries in the world. Yet poverty has not prevented a war that appears to be more about sovereignty and national pride than about the few square miles of land around which fighting has been concentrated. Ostensibly at issue is which country controls approximately two hundred square miles of territory along the border of the two states. The land that is disputed is not of great value; it is scrubland, where farmers have traditionally raised a few hardy crops and grazed their goats. For Eritrea, this scrubland represents their claim to sovereignty and the victory they won in a thirty-year civil war against Ethiopia. To the Ethiopian government the issue is one of defending against this and any possible future Eritrean incursions into their territory.

Few people outside of those living in the Horn of Africa, an eastern outcropping on the continent of Africa including the countries of Ethiopia, Eritrea, Somalia and Djibouti, and a few academic experts understand why these countries are fighting, but the whole world has remarked upon the particular brutality of this war. The Ethiopian-Eritrean border war has attracted international attention for the tactics used by each side. After taking a few miles of Ethiopian territory, the Eritrean army dug in and began to use trench warfare to defend their territorial acquisitions. In response the Ethiopian army used the time-honored method for combating trench warfare—rushing the trenches in human waves in order to capture the enemy. This method of fighting has led to a large and mounting death toll on

THE CONFLICT

The war between Ethiopia and Eritrea—two of the poorest countries in the world—began in 1998. Eritrea was once part of the Ethiopian empire, but it was colonized by Italy from 1869 to 1941. Following Italy's defeat in World War II, the United Nations determined that Eritrea would become part of Ethiopia, though Eritrea would maintain a great deal of autonomy. In 1961 Ethiopia removed Eritrea's independence, and Eritrea became just another Ethiopian province. In 1991 following a revolution in Ethiopia, Eritrea gained its independence. However, the borders between Ethiopia and Eritrea had never been clearly marked. Following arguments and skirmishes, Eritrea invaded the area of Ethiopia it viewed as its own. Trench warfare—and the deaths of many soldiers and civilians—has continued since then.

Territorial

- Eritrea believes that Ethiopia has moved border markers to infringe on Eritrean territory.

Economic

- Ethiopia believes that Eritrea charges an exorbitant fee to export Ethiopian coffee through the Eritrean port.

- There is conflict regarding use of the U.S. dollar for transactions, instead of local currency.

CHRONOLOGY

May 6, 1998 Conflict begins as several Eritrean soldiers enter Badme.

May 12, 1998 Mechanized brigades of Eritrean soldiers conquer the town of Badme.

June 5, 1998 Eritrea bombs the town of Mekelle in the Tigray region of northern Ethiopia, hitting a school as well as other targets.

June 9, 1998 War breaks out on a second front around the town of Zala Ambesa, the main road between Ethiopia and Eritrea.

June 11, 1998 Fighting occurs on a third front, close to Assab. Eritrea bombs Adigrat in the Tigray region.

July 1998 Eritrean students studying at the University of Addis Ababa are arrested and sent to a detention camp in Bilate. Other Eritreans living in Ethiopia are forced to return to Eritrea.

August 1998 Ethiopia shoots down a jet en route to South Africa when it enters the no-fly zone along the northern border area. Two European civilians are killed.

November 1998 Ethiopia accepts the OAU Framework Agreement.

February 6, 1999 Ethiopia launches an offensive in which it reclaims Badme and takes Eritrean territory inland from the Badme front.

February 10, 1999 U.N. Security Council passes Resolution 1227, which establishes an arms embargo on Ethiopia and Eritrea.

February 27, 1999 Eritrea accepts the OAU Framework Agreement.

2000 Ethiopia invades Eritrea.

both sides. Though the numbers are disputed, it is estimated that seventy thousand soldiers from both sides have died. The rest of the world has been stunned by methods of fighting that have not been used for such an extended period of time since World War I.

In addition to the staggering death toll, this war has also been characterized by the use of land mines against both combatants and civilians. When the Eritrean army retreated from the terri-

tory it had captured initially, it left fields and scrubland filled with landmines, making farming impossible and a re-establishment of the Ethiopian administration difficult. Ecologically, the effects of this war will be felt for years, both because of the presence of so many landmines and due to the effect that the fighting has had on the fragile, semi-arid ecosystem, now polluted with shell casings, wrecked military equipment and the refuse of two armies.

Prior to the war, relations between the two countries had been friendly enough that many Eritreans lived in Ethiopia—the larger country with more economic opportunities. When the war began, the Ethiopian government became distrustful of Eritreans living within its borders and began to round them up and forcibly expel them, often without even allowing them to gather up other family members. Approximately fifty-five thousand Eritreans living in Ethiopia have been so expelled. Other Eritreans left voluntarily to avoid being forcibly removed.

While the expulsion of citizens has primarily affected Eritreans, an estimated three hundred fifty thousand Ethiopians have been moved from the Tigray region of Ethiopia, where most of the fighting has occurred. During the first year of the war, the Eritrean army bombed towns in Tigray and terrorized the local population. The Ethiopian air force also bombed civilian areas until an agreement between the two sides was reached to stop the air war. The on-again, off-again nature of the fighting discouraged Ethiopians from returning to their homes. The failure of peace talks, and the development of new fronts in the fighting has also discouraged local residents from returning to the areas under dispute or near the disputed areas.

HISTORICAL BACKGROUND

In 1974 the Ethiopian Revolution ended the longest ruling monarchy in African history. Haile Selassie, the well-known emperor and statesman, was deposed in a revolution caused by inequality and lack of development and democracy within Ethiopia. The Marxist government that took over power was called the Dergue, which is the Amharic word for committee. (Amharic is the language of Ethiopia.) But what was supposed to be a committee quickly turned into a dictatorship under the control of Mengistu Haile Mariam. Shortly after the revolution, Mengistu began to purge the country of dissent in what was called the "Red Terror." Many young people died, others

THE WAR BETWEEN ETHIOPIA AND ERITREA SCATTERED REFUGEES TO OTHER AFRICAN COUNTRIES; THESE TWO WOMEN WALK PAST A CAMP IN EAST SUDAN. *(Corbis. Reproduced by permission.)*

fled the country or joined armed opposition groups in the countryside.

Opposition to the state was already going on in the northern province of Eritrea, where fighting dated back to 1961. In 1961 the Ethiopian state abolished any autonomy held by the Eritrean region. Though it was at one point part of the Ethiopian empire, the Italian colonization of Eritrea from 1869 until 1941 gave it a distinctly different history than the rest of the Ethiopian state, which had never been colonized. When Italy was defeated in World War II, it was forced to give up its colonies. A United Nations commission decided what should be done with the Italian colonies in Africa: Eritrea, Libya and Italian

Somaliland. It was determined that Eritrea should be united with Ethiopia, but that it should be allowed to keep its own laws, flag and language. Eritrea, therefore, had some autonomy from 1952 until 1961, when Haile Selassie decided to end what Eritrean autonomy existed. In 1961 Eritrea was stripped of its distinctive government and became simply another province of Ethiopia. It was at that time that fighting began between Eritreans who supported complete independence from Ethiopia and the Ethiopian state.

Armed opposition to the Ethiopian state continued throughout the 1970s and 1980s. Opposition to the Ethiopian government grew during the Ethiopian famine that occurred in 1985. The gov-

HAILE SELLASSIE

1892–1975 Haile Sellassie was born near Harer, Ethiopia on July 23, 1892. His name at birth was Tafari Makonnen. Ras ("prince") Tafari displayed keen intellectual abilities early in his studies, and by the age of fourteen was appointed provincial governor. Upon his coronation as emperor of Ethiopia in 1930, he took the name Haile Sellassie, which means "might of the trinity." He was also granted the title "Conquering Lion of the Tribe of Judah, Elect of God and King of the Kings of Ethiopia."

Haile Sellassie led his country while in exile for a time during World War II. In 1941 he returned to power in Ethiopia. Early in his rule, he was considered a progressive reformer, who outlawed slavery and introduced educational, economic, and social reforms. He helped found the Organization of African Unity in 1963. However, as famine, economic depression, and the Eritrean crises worsened conditions in Ethiopia, he lost support. Sellassie was deposed by military mutiny in 1974, and lived under house arrest until his death on August 26, 1975.

In addition to having served as Emperor of Ethiopia from 1930–74, he is worshipped as a divine being by followers of the Afro-Caribbean Rastafarian religion.

ernment was thought to have responded too slowly and to have favored certain regions with food aid. By the late 1980s, the Ethiopian state was threatened by organized rebel groups throughout the countryside. These groups were organized along ethnic lines with the Oromo supporting the Oromo Liberation Front, the Tigrayans supporting the Tigrayan People's Liberation Front (TPLF) and the Eritreans supporting the Eritrean People's Liberation Front (EPLF).

These rebel groups began to coordinate their offensive actions in the late 1980s, a strategy that proved very successful. The TPLF began reaching out to other ethnic groups to form an umbrella organization called the Ethiopian People's Revolutionary Democratic Front (EPRDF). The EPRDF included groups representing most of the major ethnicities in Ethiopia apart from the Eritreans. Eritreans were not included because it was accepted by the EPRDF that Eritrean independence would become inevitable should the Ethiopian government be overthrown.

In 1999 as a result of coordinating efforts among the rebel groups, as well as the weakness of the government of Mengistu Haile Mariam, the Ethiopian state underwent a "second revolution." Mengistu Haile Mariam fled to Zimbabwe where he now lives in exile and the EPRDF took over the capital city of Addis Ababa. The Eritreans established an independent state in the north, which became officially independent after a 1993 United Nations sponsored referendum. The separation was accomplished in a friendly manner with Ethiopia taking complete responsibility for the foreign debt and the Eritreans being left with substantial resources and control over the port of Assab.

The leaders of the two countries knew each other and had cooperated with one another in the overthrow of the previous state. Both countries realized that the border between them had not been properly demarcated and it was assumed that Eritrea's boundaries would be the boundaries it had prior to its incorporation into the Ethiopian state in 1952. But this proved to be a problem because the borders of Eritrea prior to 1952 were not clearly defined. There were multiple maps of the border area, most of which marked the border as a straight line, in spite of the fact that administration of the areas followed the jagged boundary of a river. Perhaps because the Italians always desired to take over more of Ethiopia, they did not clearly identify the southern border of Eritrea. To resolve the confusion regarding the border, Ethiopia and Eritrea formed a border commission in 1993 to discuss the border problem. The commission met from 1993 through 1997, but conflicts between local peoples in the border areas continued during this period. At issue was the question of who had the right to farm the territory. Eritrean people complained of harassment and fines imposed by Ethiopian officials and the confiscation of animals. Neither side seemed certain which farmers—Ethiopians or Eritreans—should be able to plant crops.

Serious economic problems between the two countries began in 1997. Ethiopia was, at that point, already angry with Eritrea about what Ethiopia viewed to be excessively high port charges to export its coffee crop through Assab. The two countries shared a common currency, the Ethiopian birr, and Ethiopia was upset that Eritrea was using birr to acquire dollars and thereby tightening the money supply in both countries. In 1997, Eritrea came out with its own currency called the nakfa. Ethiopia insisted that interstate transactions be conducted in dollars,

TRENCH WARFARE

Ethiopia and Eritrea are involved in trench warfare—soldiers wait in trenches for the opposition to try to push them back. During World War I, European soldiers fought foot-by-foot over much of their continent. One of the most powerful descriptions of trench warfare is in Erich Maria Remarque's *All Quiet on the Western Front.* In this book, Remarque fully captures the vulnerability of the trenches and the unpredictability of war: "The front is a cage from which we must await fearfully whatever may happen . . . . If a shot comes, we can duck, that is all; we neither know nor can determine where it will fall."

More than just the fear of bullets or bombs, however, resides within the trenches. Dug from the earth and fenced with barbed wire, the trenches are home to man and animal alike. Remarque reports that soldiers, forced to live in narrow, confined spaces gouged out of dirt, facing the enemy across a small expanse of land and wondering where the next shell might land, combat a far closer enemy in the rodents and other animals that make the trenches their homes. Rats, grown fat on the bodies of dead soldiers that no one has the time, energy or ability to bury, travel unmolested as bombs rain from the sky. Trench soldiers are seemingly accosted from all sides.

When the enemy attack begins, the trenches become a horror of chaos and provide little shelter, as this passage from *All Quiet on the Western Front* illustrates: "The bombardment does not diminish . . . . Our trench is almost gone. At many places it is only eighteen inches high, it is broken by holes, and craters, and mountains of earth. A shell lands square in front of our post. At once it is dark. We are buried and must dig ourselves out."

The picture painted by Remarque, who experienced the trenches firsthand, is hardly one of noble soldiers going off to fight and die bravely for their country. It is one of men fighting simply for survival, living with the fears and the horrors of war, trying to be among those who make it out alive. Remarque is straightforward in telling this fact. "Modern trench-warfare demands knowledge and experience; a man must have a feeling for the contours of the ground, an ear for the sound and character of the shells, must be able to decide beforehand where they will drop, how they will burst and how to shelter from them."

---

which put economic pressure on Eritrea as it then had to pay for imports of food and other Ethiopian resources in dollars. By the end of 1997 tensions between the two countries had risen to an all time high.

What Really Happened at Badme?

The confrontation began when armed Eritrean troops crossed the de facto border at Badme. According to the Ethiopian government, Eritrean troops entered Ethiopia in violation of an existing agreement that prohibited the crossing of the border by armed military personnel. Ethiopian police reminded the Eritrean soldiers of this agreement and asked them to leave their weapons if they wished to enter Ethiopia. The Eritrean troops refused to comply and opened fire on the Ethiopian police, killing two police officers.

The Eritreans claim that Badme is their own territory based on maps from the Italian colonial era. The Eritrean government alleges that after

1991 the Ethiopian government had a systematic policy of attempting to expand their northern province of Tigray through the acquisition of Eritrean territory. They claim that in 1992 Tigray administration officials crossed the true border and put new border markers deep in Eritrean territory. Subsequently Ethiopians from the Tigray region moved into this newly reclaimed area and Eritreans living there began to be harassed. Attempts to peacefully resolve the conflict were allegedly met with further territorial aggression and harassment by the Ethiopians until the Eritrean troops were called into protect the interests of the local people.

Ethiopia acknowledged that there are problems with the demarcation of the border between the two countries. However, Eritrean movement into the Badme area was seen as aggressive due to the fact that Badme had never been administered by an Eritrean government, not since 1991 and not during the Italian colonial period. The bilater-

The TPLF is currently the dominant party in the coalition of parties that makes up the EPRDF.

Zenawi is known as being both bright and energetic. He earned a masters degree after the 1991 success of the rebels. He collaborated with Issayas Afeworki, now president of Eritrea, in the attempt to overthrow the Dergue government. The two were reported to be friends prior to the beginning of tensions that ultimately led to the border war.

Issayas Afeworki is also of the Tigrayan ethnic group, though he was raised on the Eritrean side of the border. He is well respected for his intelligence and his 'everyman' quality. President Issayas (the Eritreans have the same naming convention as Ethiopians) is known to drive around Asmara (the capital of Eritrea) in an old Toyota and live modestly with his wife and three children.

Issayas Afeworki was active in fighting for Eritrean independence since 1967. He helped to form the Eritrean People's Liberation Front (EPLF) as a joint effort between Muslims and Christians aimed at the independence of Eritrea. When Eritrea became independent in 1993, the National Assembly elected Issayas head of state. Shortly thereafter, the EPLF dropped its military name and became the People's Front for Democracy and Justice or PFDJ.

The similarity in the backgrounds of these two leaders—they both come from the same region and have both worked their way up in the hierarchies of their groups during an active conflict—could have led to a positive rapport and the ability to communicate amicably. However, this has not been the case. Since the outbreak of active fighting between Ethiopia and Eritrea, speeches and statements by the two leaders have done more to escalate the conflict than to diffuse it. Indeed, both leaders appear to feel justified in the use of force to protect their border and perceived violations of sovereignty.

MAP OF ETHIOPIA AND ERITREA. *(XNR. Printed by permission.)*

al border commission had been established to resolve the border conflicts, but the Eritrean military takeover of Badme moved the dispute from diplomacy to armed conflict.

The Leaders

Meles Zenawi has been the head of the Ethiopian government since 1991 when the EPRDF overthrew the government of dictator Mengistu Haile Mariam. He became prime minister of the current government of Ethiopia in 1995 after his party won elections under the new Ethiopian constitution. Prime Minister Meles, as he is properly called in Ethiopia where a person's last name is simply their father's first name, was born Legesse Zenawi. He comes from the Tigray region of Ethiopia, from the town of Adwa, a historic and revered site in Ethiopia. Adwa is the place where the Ethiopian army was able to fend off Italian colonization efforts in 1896.

Zenawi went to high school in Addis Ababa and started college where he studied medicine. The Ethiopian Revolution occurred in 1974 and Meles interrupted his studies to fight against the government of Mengistu Haile Mariam. He joined an organization that was later to become the Tigrayan People's Liberation Front or TPLF.

RECENT HISTORY AND THE FUTURE

Efforts at Resolution

The Organization of African Unity (OAU) has developed a three-pronged peace agreement that has been supported by the United Nations, the European Union and the United States. The three prongs of the agreement consist of the Framework Agreement, the Modalities, and the Technical Arrangements. The agreement was developed in consultation with Eritrea and Ethiopia and adopted by the OAU in July of 1999. However, it has not yet led to peace, because Ethiopia has refused to sign the Technical Arrangements.

Both parties to the dispute have agreed that the United Nations will determine the demarcation of the border. However, though the end result is decided, obstacles to a formal agreement remain. Ethiopia objects to the Technical Arrangements document that would lead to the final settlement, because it does not entail a return to the situation before the outbreak of fighting. The primary obstacles to conclusion of the process and an Ethiopian/Eritrea agreement are: the specific identification of all areas that are currently occupied and agreement on the movement of troops out of the areas of conflict; the alteration of the Technical Arrangements so that a U.N. Peacekeeping Force would be replaced by a much smaller OAU observer mission and; the restoration of civilian control in all areas from which troops withdraw. Ethiopia is adamant that it will not agree to the Technical Arrangements until there is a guarantee in place to return control of all territories to what they were before the whole conflict began.

The peace agreement has been on the table now for over a year with little evidence that Ethiopia is ready to sign the Technical Arrangements in their current form. Frequent diplomatic interventions and appeals from the United States and other countries have had no success. Eritrea appears frustrated by Ethiopia's demands and argues that the Technical Arrangements are not open to amendment. Eritrea appears to be afraid that if it accepts the changes to the Technical Arrangements that Ethiopia is demanding, Ethiopia will get the disputed territory back and reestablish control of the area. In this scenario, Eritrea will ultimately be the loser, as the problems that initiated its incursions into Ethiopian territory will not be solved.

Several countries have made efforts to mediate the conflict and achieve agreement on the Technical Arrangements. Libya, Algeria and the United States have all sent high-level diplomatic missions to shuttle between the two leaders in an effort to bridge the gap between the positions of Eritrea and Ethiopia regarding the Technical Arrangements. However, each side has refused to budge from his position and none of the international diplomatic missions have so far been successful. Mediators are frustrated by the fact that both countries have agreed to the eventual U.N. demarcation of the border, but are unable to take

MILITARY SPENDING

Fighting a war is expensive. Both Ethiopia and Eritrea have used precious resources and valuable foreign currency to improve their military capabilities since the fighting began in 1998. Prior to 1999, both countries used airplanes, artillery and tanks that were supplied to them, primarily by the Soviet Union, during the Cold War. Once the conflict began, Ethiopia purchased fifty-five new tanks from Ukraine as well as Sukhoi-27 fighter planes. The Eritreans have purchased new Mig-29 jets and surface-to-air missiles.

Between their new purchases and the daily expenses of war, such as ammunition, salaries for soldiers, and food and medical equipment, both sides have significantly increased their military spending. In May, 2000 the United Nations Security Council passed a resolution imposing an arms embargo on both Ethiopia and Eritrea. The arms embargo occurred both as a result of renewed fighting and because of estimates that both sides in the conflict were spending a million dollars a day on military purchases.

Both countries have raised funds for the war through an increase in taxation, enforced "contributions" by citizens, and donations to the cause from Ethiopians and Eritreans living abroad. In addition, Eritrea has received contributions toward its military budget from the governments of Qatar and Libya. Eritrea does not make the figures pertaining to its military spending public. Estimates are that both countries were spending around $100 million dollars per year on defense prior to the outbreak of the war in 1998. Recent data from the Institute of Strategic Studies in London suggests that the 1999 spending by both countries had skyrocketed with Ethiopia increasing its budget to $480 million and Eritrea to $306 million.

The U.S. State Department estimates that Eritrea spent 7.8 percent of its Gross National Product (GDP) on military expenses in 1997, and Ethiopia spent 1.9 percent on military expenses in 1997. These percentages can be tripled or quadrupled to account for military spending since the outbreak of the war in 1998. This makes Eritrea, a poor country, one of the largest spenders for ME/GDP (military expenses per GDP) in the world.

the steps needed to calm the military conflict and enable the demarcation to take place.

While attempts are ongoing behind the scenes to bring the conflict to resolution, both Ethiopia and Eritrea have been engaging in a war

THE ERITREAN PEOPLE'S LIBERATION FRONT (EPLF), WITH SOLDIERS SUCH AS THESE ENGAGED IN TRENCH WARFARE, WAS THE MAIN MILITARY GROUP RESPONSIBLE FOR ERITREA'S INDEPENDENCE IN 1993. *(Corbis. Reproduced by permission.)*

of words that mirrors the war on the ground. Ethiopia has repeatedly referred to the "aggression" of Eritrea. The foreign minister of Eritrea has argued, "For our part, we will condemn and challenge any force or power which forces us to withdraw from our own land and sovereignty" (Tseghenay 1/27/99). It does not appear likely that they will reach a settlement soon.

Extension into Other Countries

While Asmara and Addis Ababa (the capital of Ethiopia) have made no further progress toward peace after the initial OAU agreement, the border conflict has expanded into other countries in the Horn of Africa. In an attempt to destabilize Ethiopia by encouraging conflicts within it, Eritrea has supported rebel movements by several different groups opposing the Ethiopian state. The Eritrean government has been funneling money and arms to the Oromo Liberation Front (OLF), which has been fighting the Ethiopian state in southern Ethiopia. It has also been supporting Al-Ithad Al-Islami, an Islamic group that supports the secession of the Ogaden area of Ethiopia. Aiding these groups is a deliberate and somewhat successful attempt to destabilize Ethiopia and engage Ethiopian security forces in places other than Eritrea.

However, Eritrea's funding of rebel groups has resulted in an extension of the Ethiopian/Eritrean conflict to parts of Kenya and Somalia. Ethiopian forces have pursued OLF rebels over the Ethiopian border and into both Kenya and Somalia. In addition, Ethiopian troops have attacked the forces of Somali warlord Husain Aideed inside the Somali border because of his alliance with Eritrea. The Somalis have lodged a complaint with the U.N. Security Council and the Organization of African Unity, protesting Ethiopian involvement in their territory, but because of the conflict with Eritrea and with the rebel groups, Ethiopia is unlikely to stop. Ethiopian relations with Djibouti remain strong because all Ethiopian exports are now passing through the port there.

There is a great deal of international pressure for Ethiopia and Eritrea to solve the border conflict. Any lasting solution must include a way for both the Ethiopian and Eritrean leaderships to save face by claiming victory. Since both sides have agreed that a U.N. team should survey the border area and determine where the border should be, the only obstacle to resolving the dispute is to develop an agreement on the terms of the ceasefire and troop withdrawals. However, after eighteen months of negotiations and third party interventions there is no progress toward agreement on these issues. The chief obstacle to achieving troop withdrawals is a lack of trust on each side. The Ethiopians do not trust the Eritreans to withdraw to the positions they held prior to the outbreak of fighting and the Eritreans do not trust that the Ethiopians will negotiate a new border in good faith once they give up the armed conflict. A solution to this conflict has been in sight virtually since the beginning of fighting. These two countries have been unable to see past their immediate security interests and distrust of one another to achieve that solution. The Eritreans fought Ethiopia for thirty years to achieve their independence. Both countries are capable of fighting a long war driven by issues of pride and perceived threats to sovereignty in spite of their relative lack of resources.

BIBLIOGRAPHY

EIU Country Report, Ethiopia, 2d Quarter 1999. London: The Economist Intelligence Unit Limited, 1999.

International Monetary Fund. *International Financial Statistics.* 1995–1997.

"No respite in the Horn," *The Gazette,* 9 February 2000.

Plaut, Martin. "Horn Conflict: Devil in the Detail," London: BBC Worldservice, 13 March 2000.

Tekle Fessehazion. "Genesis of the Border War," mimeo, 1999.

U.S. Department of State. *Human Rights Reports for 1999. Ethiopia.* http://www.state.gov/www/global/humanrights/1999_hrp_report/Ethiopia.html (25 February 2000).

Sandra Fullerton Joireman

THE GAZA STRIP AND WEST BANK: STATEHOOD AND SECURITY

THE CONFLICT

The Gaza Strip and West Bank were given to the Palestinians in the United Nations 1948 decision that established Israel. The land was captured by Jordan and Egypt in a war that started the day after the U.N. decision. Israel captured the territory during the Six-Day War in 1967. Since then, Israel has held the territory.

Political

- Israel has felt that it needed control of the West Bank and Gaza Strip to protect its borders.

- Israel has charged that the West Bank and Gaza Strip supported guerrilla attacks against Israel, and that Israel needed to control the areas to limit attacks.

- The Muslims in the Gaza Strip and West bank want a Palestinian state. In the past, there has been talk of unification with Jordan, however, because of the large, radical population in the "occupied territories," Jordan is not interested in unification.

- Until, perhaps, recently, the Palestinians, including those in the West Bank and Gaza Strip, have not recognized Israel's right to exist.

When the Israeli prime minister, Ehud Barak, assumed office in July 1999, the world, especially the Arab states, watched with cautious optimism. Prime Minister Barak vowed to find a lasting peace between the Palestinians and Israelis and with its other Arab neighbors. But over the last fifty years the peace process between the Palestinians and Israelis often made little progress. It appeared almost insurmountably difficult for the groups to reach an agreement regarding the West Bank and Gaza Strip. The current strife between the Israelis and Palestinians is vastly changed from what it was when the State of Israel was created in 1948.

The history of the Palestinian-Israeli conflict is complex and includes many different political forces. The hostility between the Israelis and Palestinians has its roots in the claim by two different national groups to the same territory. In the nineteenth century, Jewish groups, known as Zionists, emerged, advocating a Jewish state in the biblical land of Israel. At the same time, in the Middle East, with the decline of the Ottoman Empire (the Turkish empire that ended in the 1920s), a movement toward a distinct Arab identity was growing. This Arab nationalism competed with political Zionism and led to the increasingly violent conflict between the two groups for statehood in Palestine. The Jews claimed historical, biblical and ideological connections to the land, while Palestinian Arabs attributed their right to Palestine to continued habitation in the land for hundreds of years, along with promises—from Britain and the other major powers—for Arab independence after World War I. The potency of these historical and emotional connections has created one of the most complex questions of the twentieth century.

CHRONOLOGY

1800s Jewish groups, known as Zionists, advocate a Jewish state in the Biblical land of Israel.

1915–1916 The Husayne-McMahon correspondences, between the British and the Arabs, specify that if the Arabs help the British defeat the Ottomans, the British promise to support the Arabs request for independence after World War I. At the same time, the British negotiate the Sykes-Picot agreement with the French, which divides up the Middle East between the French and the British.

1917 The Balfour Declaration by the British states that Great Britain favors the establishment of a national home for the Jewish people in Palestine.

1920 The San Remo Peace Conference gives Britain a mandate over Palestine, Transjordan (known as Jordan, today), and Mesopotamia (modern day Iraq). The French receive control of Lebanon and Syria.

1947 The U.N. General Assembly votes to partition Palestine between the Jews and the Arabs.

1948 David Ben-Gurion declares the creation of the state of Israel. The following day, the first Arab-Israeli war begins. When it ends, Israel has more land than they started with—and more than had been promised them under the U.N. resolution.

1956 The Suez Crisis occurs.

1964 The Palestine Liberation Organization (PLO) is founded.

1967 The Six-Day War results in Israel again obtaining more territory.

1973 The Yom Kippur War (The 1973 War) takes place. To put an end to the hostilities, the U.N. passes a resolution that specifies direct negotiations to implement the previous resolution on the partition of Palestine.

1978 Egyptian president Anwar Sadat and Israeli prime minister Menachem Begin sign the Camp David Accords.

1987 The Intifada—the Uprising—in the Gaza Strip and West Bank takes place.

1988 The Palestine National Council votes to establish an independent state (as opposed to creating a federation with Jordan).

1993 The Israelis and the Palestinians sign the Oslo Accords, a "Declaration of Principles on Interim Self-Rule for Palestinians."

1994 The Israelis and the Palestinians sign the Gaza-Jericho Accord.

2000 Israel withdraws from occupied Lebanon.

HISTORICAL BACKGROUND

Migration of European Jews

During the late nineteenth century many Jews began to immigrate to Palestine, primarily because of growing anti-Semitism—anti-Jewish sentiment—in Europe. Mass attacks on Jews in Russia in the early 1880s forced many to leave their homes in Europe in search of new, more peaceful lives. The majority of emigrants went to the United States, while those Jews with strong religious and nationalist feelings went to Palestine, a small area in the Middle East. Once in Palestine, the Jews began to build a strong community with political, social and military institutions. They were preparing to form a state.

British Promises

Although some Arabs were apprehensive about the number of Jews entering Palestine at the end of the nineteenth century, the Arabs were not necessarily anti-Zionist. They were more concerned about the economic implications of the growing influx of Jews. Yet the situation worsened in 1917 with the proclamation of the Balfour Declaration by the British. The declaration stated that the British monarch "views with favor the establishment in Palestine of a national home for the Jewish people." The Arabs within Palestine felt betrayed.

Prior to this declaration, the British had made a deal with the Arabs regarding Palestine.

EHUD BARAK

1942– Ehud Barak was born on February 12, 1942, on Kibbutz (a farming commune in Israel) Mishmar HaSharon. He was raised in this community, near the Lebonese border, which his parents had helped found. At the age of seventeen he enlisted in the army and eventually became Israel's most decorated soldier. As the commander of an elite commando unit, he led the successful liberation of hijacked airliners in 1972 and 1976. In 1973, dressed as a woman and carrying a purse full of explosives, he raided a Palestinian group responsible for the murders of Israeli athletes at the Munich Olympic Games. He earned a degree in physics and mathematics in 1976 from the Hebrew University of Jerusalem, and received a Master's Degree in economic engineering from Stanford University in 1978.

After a thirty-five-year military career, Barak resigned as army chief of staff in 1995 and joined the Labour party, serving first as interior minister, and then foreign minister. He was elected prime minister in a landslide victory in May 1999. His centrist goals have focused on meeting Israel's security concerns while making peace with Israel's neighbors and cautiously preparing his country for Palestinian statehood.

In communications with the Arabs, the British promised to support their request for independence after WWI if the Arabs agreed to help the British defeat the Ottomans, who had sided with Germany. These letters, which were written between July 1915 and January 1916, became known as the Husayn-McMahon correspondences. The British left the boundaries of the region guaranteed to the Arabs deliberately ambiguous. As such, both the Arabs and Jews believe that they were promised statehood in the same territory. Simultaneously, the British were negotiating a deal with the French called the Sykes-Picot agreement. The agreement defined the areas that would be under French and British control after the war. These included areas both the Arabs and Jews believed the British pledged to them. All of these arrangements conflicted with one another and continue to play a large role in the tensions that remain today.

As expected, with the end of World War I, the San Remo Peace Conference of 1920 created a series of mandates designating that Britain would control Palestine (modern day Israel), Transjordan (modern day Jordan) and Mesopotamia (modern day Iraq). The French received control of Lebanon and Syria. Since their agreement with the Arabs was vague, the British claimed that the area did not include Palestine. The Arabs interpreted the bargain differently. The British could not keep their promises to all groups, but managed to appease the Arabs by creating the modern states of Jordan and Iraq with Arabs in control.

It was only after the Balfour Declaration in 1917 that a distinct Palestinian nationalism began to develop. Previously, the Arabs who lived in Palestine considered themselves an inseparable part of the Arab community, while simultaneously maintaining a special connection to the territory in which they resided. During the early twentieth century, the people of the Middle East were unfamiliar with the modern state concept. Because of this fact, it is not peculiar that neither a strong nor distinctly separate Palestinian identity existed at this time. They viewed themselves as part of the larger Arab community.

The United Nations Intervention

As more Jews immigrated to Palestine, the enmity between the Arabs and Jews grew, as did a separate Palestinian identity. As Jewish immigration continued to climb, larger and more violent protests and riots began to occur in Palestine. Despite the increasing hostilities, the Zionists continued to build a political, economic, and military infrastructure in preparation for statehood. The Arabs, on the other hand, chose not to cooperate with the mandatory power and felt that violence could rid the areas of both the Jews and the British. By 1947 the British could no longer contain the fighting between the Arabs and Jews in the territory under their control. Therefore, the British decided to let the United Nations decide who should have the territory. On November 29, 1947, the U.N. General Assembly voted to accept a partition of Palestine. Both the Palestinian Arabs and Jews received territory in which to create two separate states.

The partition of Palestine by the United Nations in 1947 was an attempt by the international community to alleviate the tensions between the two groups. This U.N. action, however, only heightened the level of violence in the region. The Arabs flatly rejected the proposal to create two states, while the Jews reluctantly accepted the U.N.'s decision. Notwithstanding repeated Arab threats to declare war on the Jews if a Jewish state was erected, David Ben-Gurion proclaimed the creation of the state of Israel on May 14, 1948 and became the nation's first Prime Minister. The following day, the first of many Arab-Israeli wars began.

The First Arab-Israeli War

The Palestinians' attempted to capture all of Palestine. However, during the 1948 war following the formation of Israel, Israel conquered territory that had been allotted to the Palestinians by the U.N. partition. Additionally, both Jordan (Transjordan) and Egypt took control of areas that had been given to the Palestinians. Jordan gained the West Bank and Egypt administered the Gaza Strip. Thus, the 1948 war left the Palestinians with no state of Palestine as they had been promised in the U.N. partition. At the time, the Palestinians expected the Arab states to help retrieve the land allotted to them by the U.N. Instead, the other Arab states took the land from them.

This shift in control by Jordan and Egypt of the border of the new state of Israel left Israel with three specific security challenges. First, the area of the West Bank that Jordan occupied almost cut Israel in half. The fact that Israel was only ten miles wide at its narrowest point caused considerable concern for the country's security. This security issue continues to be a crucial factor in the current negotiations between the Israelis and Palestinians. Second, the Syrians controlled the strategic position of the Golan Heights. Domination of this area allowed Syria easy access to bomb the Israeli settlements below. Third, Israel acquired a very long border with the Egyptians, along the Sinai desert. Israel was concerned that if the Egyptians massed troops on the border, they could cut Israel off from Eilat, its Red Sea port. The Israelis viewed each of these problems as serious threats to their existence.

The early history provides crucial background for understanding the claims of both the Palestinians and Israelis today. It is also important for grasping the difficulty in finding agreements acceptable to both sides. For example, in 1948 many Palestinians were either forced to leave the newly declared Israeli state or they fled from Israel in fear. Many escaped to the West Bank and Gaza Strip. This exit of Palestinians led to a significant refugee problem. One of the most complex issues in the current Palestinian-Israeli negotiations concerns the fate of these refugees. The region being negotiated for a Palestinian state, however, deals only with the West Bank and Gaza Strip. Many of the refugees left what is today Israel proper. This land is not part of the negotiations for a Palestinian state. With the current peace process,

these refugees will have to relinquish their dream of returning to their homes.

The Suez Crisis of 1956

Tensions continued after the 1948 war. Palestinian groups attacked Israel from both the West Bank and Gaza Strip. The Israelis retaliated by bombing both Jordan and Egypt, the states that controlled these areas. By 1956, Israel wanted to stop the infiltration into Israel from the Gaza Strip. During the same period, the British and French worried about Egypt's nationalization of the Suez Canal. (In July 1956 Egypt took control of the Suez Canal—an important waterway for trade and military activity.) For the British, nationalization meant a significant decrease of influence in this strategically important area. Therefore, Israel—in cooperation with the British and French—attacked Egypt on the Sinai Peninsula. Although Israel's attack was successful militarily, the U.S. forced the British and French to stop the attack and demanded that Israel pull out of the Sinai and Gaza Strip. The military was forced to withdraw from the Gaza Strip and a small U.N. force was stationed there to monitor the activities of Israel and Egypt. Throughout the Arab world, and especially in Egypt, Egyptian president Gamal Abd al-Nasser was seen as standing up to the Western forces.

Following the Suez war of 1956, the Palestinians relied on other Arab countries to get the land back from Israel. Since Nasser had stood up to the West, the Palestinians hoped that soon Palestine would return to their control. At this stage in the conflict, the Arab states and the Palestinians were interested in destroying Israel and regaining all of Palestine, not just the area allotted to the Palestinians by the U.N. partition.

The Creation of the PLO

While the Egyptians controlled the Gaza Strip, they wanted to curtail Palestinian guerrilla attacks from Gaza. The Egyptians knew that Israel would not hesitate to retaliate for guerrilla attacks by attacking Egyptian territory. Since the Arab states were unable to control the Palestinian guerrilla groups, the Arab states created the Palestinian Liberation Organization (PLO) in 1964. The Egyptians, the main proponent of this organization, believed that the creation of the PLO would allow them some control over Palestinian activities. Egypt hoped the PLO would unify the various guerrilla groups under this new umbrella organization, uniting all Palestinians, wherever they were located.

YASSER ARAFAT

1929– Yasser Arafat was born August 1, 1929 in either Jerusalem or Egypt. At birth he was named Mohammed Abadul-RaOouf Qudwa Arafat Al-Husseini, but called Yasser ("easy") by the relatives who raised him after his mother died. In 1956 he earned a degree in civil engineering at the University of Cairo, and began to organize Arab guerrillas to combat Israel. He became chairman of the Palestine Liberation Organization in 1968.

After Arafat (with a pistol at his side) addressed the U.N. General Assembly in 1974, the PLO was recognized as the representative of the Arabs of Palestine.

In 1988 Arafat recognized Israel's right to exist. The PLO's endorsement of Iraq during the Gulf War temporarily interrupted the peace process. However, on September 13, 1993 Arafat and Israeli prime minister Yitzhak Rabin signed a peace agreement. They received the Nobel Peace Prize for their efforts.

The 1993 peace agreement created the Palestinian Authority to oversee limited self-rule. Arafat was elected the Palestinian Authority's first president in January 1996. Arafat's recent attempts to curtail militaristic, anti-Israel groups have caused him to lose credibility among militants. However, he continues to maintain popular support as Palestine prepares for statehood. Arafat lives in the Gaza with his wife Suha At-Taweel, and young daughter, Zahwa.

One of the groups that Egypt wanted to control was Fatah, an organization founded in the late 1950's by students in Cairo. Fatah became one of the main branches of the PLO. Yasir Arafat, who was involved in Fatah's creation, is currently the president of the Palestinian Authority in the West Bank and Gaza Strip.

By 1965 Fatah was frustrated with the Arab states' reluctance to take immediate action regarding the call for an all-out battle to destroy Israel. The Palestinians tried to lure the Arab states into war with Israel by continuing their guerrilla attacks on Israel, relying on Israel to strike back. However, after the Suez crisis, even though Egyptian president Nasser had stood up to the West, he recognized the enormous military power of the Israelis. He was not interested in being drawn into a conflict with Israel until he was prepared. Unfortunately, Nasser made a series of moves that Israel

viewed as hostile including closing the Gulf of Aqaba to Israeli shipping and removing U.N. forces from Egyptian soil. Believing itself threatened, Israel attacked Egypt in what Israel claimed was a preemptive strike—attacking Egypt before Egypt could attack Israel. The Arab states believed that it was an unprovoked attack.

Six-Day War

During the Six-Day War, Israel fought Egypt, Jordan and Syria. As in 1948, the end of the Six-Day War left the Israelis in control of more Arab territory. The Arab states' defeat during the Six-Day War resolved several problems for Israel while creating others. Israel's acquisition of the Golan Heights, the Sinai Desert, the West Bank and Gaza Strip produced more secure borders for Israel. Yet the capture of the West Bank and Gaza Strip left Israel in control of 1.3 million Palestinians who were hostile to the notion of Israeli domination. Once the Israelis controlled these areas, the Palestinians and Israelis were in daily contact in both the territories and in Israel proper. This increased contact fashioned a very different relationship than the one between the Arab states and Israel.

Furthermore, the present negotiations discussing the delineation of borders for a Palestinian entity or state are closely linked with the results of the Six-Day War. Many Palestinians in the West Bank and Gaza Strip advocated their independent state have the borders that existed prior to the 1967 war—the Palestinians want a state comprised of the West Bank and Gaza Strip. After the 1967 war, the U.N. passed Resolution 242 calling for "withdrawal from territories occupied in the recent conflict." Acceptance of the resolution implied acceptance of the concept of "land for peace"—giving up control of the land in exchange for peaceful co-existence. In addition, the resolution called for the recognition of the "sovereignty, territorial integrity and political independence of every state in the area." This suggested a mutual recognition by the Israelis and Palestinians. This mutual recognition did not occur until 1993.

By gaining control of the West Bank in 1967, the Israelis also attained control of all of Jerusalem. Prior to the Six-Day War, Jerusalem was under Jordanian rule. During that period, Jews were not permitted to visit their holy sites, particularly the Western Wall. Once the Israelis captured the city, the Jews vowed never to let it be divided again. The Israelis have allowed open access to all holy sites. The issue of Jerusalem is one of the most difficult issues that the Palestinians and Israelis must negotiate. Both groups claim Jerusalem as their capital and want full control of their sacred places.

An overwhelming change in the Palestinians' philosophy and tactics occurred after the horrible defeat of the Arab armies during the Six-Day War. It was following this stunning debacle that the Palestinians recognized the need to discover a more effective strategy to gain independence. The conflict then shifted from one between the Arab states and Israel to a separate one between the West Bank and Gaza Strip inhabitants and the Israelis.

The 1973 War (Yom Kippur War)

In 1973, by executing a surprise attack, the Arab states made an attempt to defeat the Israelis and retrieve the land lost during the Six-Day War. Although the Arab states inflicted severe casualties on the Israelis, they were unable to regain control of Israeli-held territories. To put an end to the hostilities, the U.N. passed Resolution 338 that specified direct negotiations between the parties involved to implement Resolution 242.

The war in 1973 again convinced the Palestinians that they could not depend on the Arab states to liberate their land. Moreover, the PLO was becoming increasingly interested in pursuing both diplomatic and military strategies. Real movement toward an Israeli-Palestinian agreement, however, did not occur until the uprising in the Gaza Strip and West Bank in 1987.

The Intifada

The Palestinian uprising in the Gaza Strip and West Bank, also known as the Intifada, reflected a changed Palestine. The Palestinians within the territories were ready to take matters into their own hands to create an independent Palestinian state. The outbreak of violent demonstrations and riots in December 1987 had several causes. After 20 years of Israeli control of the West Bank and Gaza Strip, Palestinian frustration peaked. Many had grown up under Israeli control and had never experienced democratic freedoms. The increased contact with the Israeli population because of employment opportunities in Israel proper allowed the Palestinians to view a different lifestyle. Additionally, the improved standard of living as a result of higher wages in Israel without a corresponding increase of political and social freedom escalated the Palestinians' frustration. The growth of a more educated Palestinian population also heightened many Palestinians' expectations for better opportunities and civil rights.

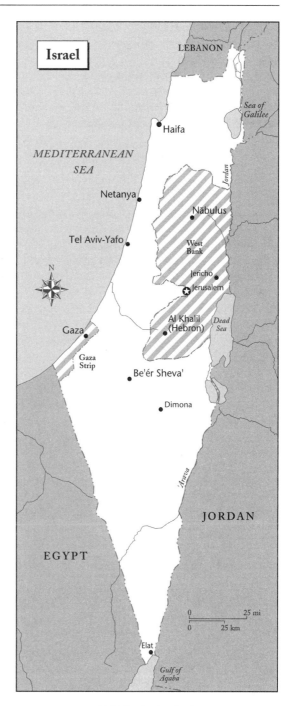

MAP OF ISRAEL. (XNR Productions Inc.)

Furthermore, the Palestinians became severely dependent on Israel due to the lack of an economic infrastructure. This dependence increased both the population's frustration and hastened the growth of a strong Palestinian national identity, one separate from being Arab. The development of a potent national identity was crucial in influencing the eruption of the Intifada.

Another factor that led to increased hostilities in the territories was the war in 1973. It was viewed in the Arab world as a victory. The Arab states were able to launch a surprise assault on Israel and inflict a large number of casualties. In the eyes of the Arabs, especially the Palestinians', Israel's deterrent power was waning.

President Anwar Sadat of Egypt made an historic visit to Jerusalem in 1977. In 1978 President Sadat and Israeli president Menachem Begin signed the Camp David Accords, which secured peace between Egypt and Israel in exchange for Israel returning the Sinai desert. This event had a profound effect on the Palestinians. The Palestinians had assumed that any peace treaty with an Arab state would contain a comprehensive agreement for a Palestinian state. The Palestinians expected the Egyptians to force the Israelis to return the West Bank and Gaza Strip as part of any peace deal. Sadat attempted to maintain the connection between the return of the Sinai with the Palestinian state, but he was unsuccessful; once again, the West Bank and Gaza Strip were brushed aside. The Palestinians, frustrated by both Israeli actions and those of their Arab brethren, sought a path with which to push the issue of their statehood back into the foreground.

One of the most controversial issues and a large contributor to the Intifada in 1987 was Israel's settlement policy. When the Likud, Israel's center-right party, assumed power in 1977, its policies were based on the ideology of Greater Israel. This meant that retaining parts of the biblical land of Israel was a key political platform. The Likud was more interested in holding onto territory than in conducting a peace process. Many Israelis contended that settlements would provide added protection for Israel; consequently, Jews moved into the Arab portions of Israeli-held territory and established towns. The new Jewish communities, however, only incited resentment among the Arabs.

From 1977–87, many settlements were established close to Arab villages. Prior to 1977, the Jewish settlements were relatively isolated from the Arab areas. Until the Likud Party's defeat in 1992, the settlement policy continued to incite anger. Some academics argued that the policy was not shortsighted, but was implemented precisely to gain permanent control of the region.

Israel created policies to control the inhabitants, including deportations. These policies contributed to the inability of the moderate West Bank or Gaza Strip Palestinians to establish a political party to negotiate with the Israelis. While the Israelis did not grant Palestinians freedom of political activity on the West Bank and Gaza, the PLO also refused to permit the West Bank Palestinians to found an independent political party. Yasir Arafat's major interest was to prevent the emergence of an independent Palestinian leadership in the territories. The PLO feared that any separate authority would diminish its power and legitimacy as the "sole representative" of the Palestinian people. Because many Palestinians were scattered in other countries, the PLO wanted to maintain its influence over matters concerning *all* Palestinians. Therefore, the existence of the Intifada indicated a rift between the Palestinians in the territories and the external Palestinian leadership.

Because of Palestinian frustration with Arafat and the PLO for not being able to deliver on their promises of liberating Palestine or at least in making progress diplomatically, the West Bank and Gaza Strip Palestinians concluded that they should act independently. The Intifada, however, was a not a well-thought-out, calculated event. The uprising was a spontaneous reaction to specific triggering events including an incident during which a Palestinian terrorist crossed the Israeli border using a hand-glider, entered an army base in northern Israel, and killed six soldiers. This action was a victory for the terrorists and proved that the great Israeli army, which had dealt the conventional Arab armies a devastating blow in 1967, was vulnerable.

Thus, there were several factors that led to the outbreak of violent demonstrations and riots in December 1987. The Intifada forced the policy makers to reevaluate Israel's objectives within the territories. The Intifada reflected a new self-reliance for the Palestinians in the occupied territories. They no longer trusted the other Arab states or Palestinians from outside the territories to retrieve the land promised to them by the U.N. in 1947.

Furthermore, during the Intifada Israel frequently sealed the territories to contain protesters and did not allow the Palestinians access to their jobs in Israel. As such, they were forced to become more self-sufficient. When the Palestinians could not work, their anger increased. The Israelis realized that they could not continue to control the occupied territories without great cost.

As has been the case throughout the Arab-Israeli conflict, global events have influenced the direction of the discord. With the collapse of the Soviet Union, the Gulf War between Iraq and

Western nations, including Israel and Saudi Arabia, in 1991, and the continuation of the Intifada, conditions became more conducive for a peace settlement.

The Conflict in Global Context

The Israeli-Arab and Israeli-Palestinian conflict has always concerned external players. Although the Soviet Union supported the creation of the State of Israel, it shifted its support to the pro-Arab camp by the 1950s. The United States extended solid support for the security of Israel, yet has always had an interest in maintaining good relations with the Arab states, especially the oil-producing states. Therefore, the United States has frequently attempted to broker comprehensive peace settlements between Israel and the Arab states.

RECENT HISTORY AND THE FUTURE

Recently, the Palestinians in the Gaza Strip and in various parts of the West Bank have gained some autonomy over their region. Important changes occurred in the Middle East landscape that helped the peace process. Since 1967, Israeli, American and even Jordanian officials had frequently expressed that the Palestinians should not have their own state, but should join a federation with Jordan. Yet in 1988, King Hussein of Jordan declared that his country would no longer fund salaries of civil workers in the West Bank and would support an independent Palestinian state in the West Bank. This reflected Jordan's changed view that the Palestinians should have their own country. With his declaration, King Hussein recognized Palestinian national identity.

Another important transformation for the Palestinians occurred in 1988 when Yasser Arafat renounced terrorism and accepted Resolutions 242 and 338. Most Palestinians were no longer seeking to gain all of Palestine and destroy Israel, but to achieve independence in the West Bank and Gaza Strip. On November 15, 1988, the Palestinian National Council (PNC), the Palestinian's government-in-exile, voted to establish an independent Palestinian state as opposed to creating a federation with Jordan. Despite the fact that they did not possess territory, the declaration of Palestinian statehood in December 1988 paved the way for new diplomatic initiatives.

Yasser Arafat would not state explicitly that Israel had a right to exist. Likewise, the Israelis would not recognize the PLO as the "sole repre-

AN ISRAELI SOLDIER CHECKS THE IDENTIFYING PAPERS OF A PALESTINIAN PASSING INTO THE GAZA STRIP. *(AP/Wide World Photos. Reproduced by permission.)*

sentative of the Palestinian people." No meaningful peace process could occur without this recognition. However, Arafat's acceptance of Resolutions 242 and 338 seemed to imply the acceptance of Israel's existence. Although the Israeli-Palestinian dialogue did not begin in 1988, the door was left open for future contacts.

Another significant event that furthered the peace process occurred in August of 1990. Iraq, led by President Saddam Hussein, invaded its tiny neighbor, Kuwait. A U.S.-led coalition sent troops to the Gulf to help liberate Kuwait. The Palestinians supported Hussein's invasion, especially after Hussein linked his withdrawal from Kuwait

FREQUENT WARRING WITH ISRAEL HAS LEFT SOME PALESTINIANS DESTITUTE; THESE THREE GIRLS SEEK FOOD FROM A PALESTINIAN REFUGEE CAMP ON THE WEST BANK. *(Corbis. Reproduced by permission.)*

to Israel's departure from Palestine. But the Arab countries were divided on Iraq's invasion of Kuwait, with many states, such as Saudi Arabia, condemning the invasion. Due to this endorsement of Hussein, the PLO's position in the Arab world and with the United States declined after the war. Many Palestinians who had lived in and received considerable financial support from Gulf states were expelled.

With the conclusion of the Gulf War, the United States took advantage of this altered political scene and pushed for peace negotiations. By forcing Hussein to withdraw from Kuwait, the United States had new credibility within the Arab world. Moreover, the end of the Cold War between the U.S. and the Soviet Union enhanced opportunities for peace. With the Soviet's weakened global position, they did not oppose the U.S.-led coalition's war with Iraq. This left the U.S. in a strong position to advance the peace process.

The United States pressed for an international peace conference in Madrid, Spain to resolve the conflict between the Israelis and the other Arab states. Prime Minister Yizhak Shamir who governed Israel until 1992 was adamant about not negotiating with the PLO. Shamir declared that he would not attend the Madrid conference if PLO representatives were present. He resolved to partic-

ipate if a joint Palestinian-Jordanian delegation and not the PLO represented the Palestinians. Little progress was achieved during these negotiations until Israel elected a new government.

The Oslo Accords

In June 1992, Yitzhak Rabin was elected Prime Minister of Israel. Unlike his predecessor, he was willing to make territorial concessions to the Palestinians to achieve peace. Although initially he did not want to deal directly with the PLO, he eventually modified his position. In late 1992, Israelis and officials from the PLO began meeting secretly to forge an agreement dealing with the West Bank and Gaza Strip. These negotiations took place in Oslo, Norway, and are referred to as the Oslo Accords. As a result of these mediations, on September 13, 1993 the Israelis and Palestinians signed an agreement at the White House called the Declaration of Principles on Interim Self-Rule for Palestinians (DOP). This was a momentous step for the peace process.

The agreement had several important components. The two groups agreed that within ten months of the signing, the Palestinians would elect a Palestinian council. This council would then replace the Israeli military and civil administration and would run the affairs of Gaza and the West

Bank for five years until a final agreement could be reached. A permanent agreement was supposed to be implemented by December of 1998.

So why has the final status of the West Bank and Gaza Strip not yet been determined? Again, events occurred that altered the timeline agreed upon by both groups. With every negotiation and deal, both the Israelis and Palestinians had disagreements. For example, the DOP stated that both groups would decide upon the structure and size of the Palestinian council. The five-year interim period to resolve the final status arrangement would not begin until the council was elected. The Israelis and Palestinians differed as to the size of the Palestinian Council. While issues were being negotiated, Israel dominated many areas of Palestinian life. Therefore, the longer the negotiations continued, the longer Israel maintained control.

Additionally, a key component of the Oslo accords was that the Palestinians and Israelis would negotiate an agreement by December 13, 1993 outlining the withdrawal of Israeli military forces from the Gaza Strip and the West Bank's "Jericho Area." Both groups disagreed as to what constituted the "Jericho Area." Despite missed deadlines for both the negotiations and withdrawal, the Gaza-Jericho Accord was signed on May 4, 1994. While the Israeli army began its withdrawal from these areas, the Palestinians in the Gaza Strip and West Bank had begun their dream of having a state.

The Role of Terrorism

Yet other impediments to concluding the peace negotiations continued to arise. Opposition groups on both sides tried to derail the process. In 1994 a Jewish extremist gunned down forty Arabs who were praying in a mosque in Hebron, an area that is also sacred to Jews. The PLO suspended peace talks for several months. Later that year, HAMAS, an Islamic extremist group from the territories that opposes the peace process, killed many Israelis with car bombs and suicide attacks. Although both sides tried to keep the process alive, the Israelis suspended talks after more suicide bombings occurred in early 1995.

A critical event on November 4, 1995 put the peace process on even shakier ground. A Jewish extremist who opposed the negotiations assassinated Prime Minister Rabin. The new elections in Israel in 1996 brought the Likud government back into power after a four-year hiatus. The Likud Party fundamentally disagreed with the idea of territorial concessions. This change in government

did not bode well for the negotiations between the Israelis and Palestinians.

Progress

Notwithstanding long periods of stalled negotiations under the Likud Prime Minister, Benjamin Netanyahu, some progress did occur. In January 1997, the Israelis legally divided the West Bank City of Hebron and put the Palestinians in charge of most of the city. In Hebron, four hundred Jewish settlers live in the midst of one hundred twenty thousand Palestinians; in the Gaza Strip there are more than one hundred thousand Jewish settlers. Although Israel's army still maintains a presence to protect the Israeli settlers, the Palestinians control eighty percent of the area.

Additionally, Arafat and Netanyahu concluded the Wye Agreement under the sponsorship of the U.S. in 1998. This agreement dealt with additional Israeli troop withdrawals from the West Bank. It also contained a commitment from President Arafat that he would crack down on terrorism in areas under Palestinian control. Currently, the Palestinians control about forty percent of the West Bank. Furthermore, the Palestinians formally rescinded the call for the destruction of Israel from the Palestinian National Charter.

The defeat of Netanyahu by Barak in 1999 was a welcome change for the peace process. The international community, especially the Arab states, did not view Netanyahu as willing to negotiate a real settlement with the Palestinians. Barak's arrival on the scene infused new life in the peace initiatives. Although the process has stalled under Barak's leadership, there is renewed optimism that final status talks can be completed.

Today, the Palestinians in the Gaza Strip and most West Bank cities have control over many aspects of their daily life. They control taxation, health issues, tourism, education and culture. They also maintain a civil police force. Notwithstanding their new power, the Palestinians want a state with complete control over all aspects of their lives including maintaining a military, providing security for their population and conducting foreign affairs. They also want Jerusalem as their capital.

Although significant progress has been made on the road to peace between the Israelis and Palestinians, complex issues remain and have been deferred until final status talks. One issue is whether Jerusalem be controlled jointly by Palestinians and Israelis, or divided, since they both claim it as their capital. Another issue regards

Palestinian refugees and whether they will be allowed to return to Gaza and the West Bank. Many of the refugees' families were from Israel proper. Will they receive reparations? Will the Israelis curtail the number of Palestinians allowed to enter Palestinian areas due to security reasons?

Moreover, the final borders of the Palestinian entity have yet to be resolved. A controversial issue remaining concerns the amount of territory that should be returned to the Palestinians. The Palestinians insist they should receive all of the West Bank and Gaza with few border adjustments. They claim that the Israelis must accept the boundaries that existed prior to the Six-Day War. The question of Jewish settlements within the West Bank and Gaza, however, continues to add a complex dimension to the issue of borders, as negotiators decide if the Israeli army should continue to protect these settlers, if the settlements should be incorporated into the area given to the Palestinians, and if the settlers should be forced to leave.

Connected with the settlement problem is the issue of water use. The West Bank contains water aquifers that the Israelis have controlled since the occupation of the West Bank in 1967. The Israelis have limited Palestinian use of this water, while utilizing a disproportionate amount in the Jewish settlements. The two sides need to agree upon a mutually acceptable formula for sharing resources.

Additionally, what will be the nature of a Palestinian entity? Israelis and Palestinians interpret the Oslo Accords very differently. For many Israelis, the five-year interim period specified in the agreement does not necessarily mean that Palestinian statehood will result. Many Israelis fear the notion of an independent Palestinian state on their borders. They continue to believe that an autonomous entity linked with Jordan would provide Israel greater security. Prime Minister Rabin never supported the idea of statehood, but rather a type of self-determination short of statehood. It is clear, however, that the Palestinians will accept nothing less than an independent state.

Several possibilities remain for the future. The Palestinians have vowed to declare a Palestinian state by September 13, 2000. At best, Israelis and Palestinians will have decided the final status issues including Jerusalem, borders, refugees and division of resources by that date. Ehud Barak and Yasser Arafat contend that they are committed to ending this conflict. At worst, if the Palestinians declare statehood without the final status issues

decided, violence might ensue. In the Palestinian's view, they have been patient and flexible since the 1993 Oslo accords. They had expected the final status of their state to be determined by 1998.

The issue of Jerusalem poses a great challenge for both the Israelis and Palestinians. It appears from statements that neither side will compromise. Israel opposes any plan to divide the city and the Palestinians insist that Jerusalem will be the capital of a Palestinian state. Nonetheless, there is a glimmer of hope that some accommodation can be reached. During the Palestinian elections in 1996, the Israelis allowed the Palestinians from East Jerusalem to vote for representatives in the Palestinian National Authority. This action illustrates willingness on the Israeli's side to afford the Palestinians in Jerusalem a separate status even though Jerusalem is a united city under Israeli control. As such, there might be a way to compromise on Jerusalem in the future. Additionally, the fact that the issue of Jerusalem was even broached for negotiations means that there is some room for discussion.

Furthermore, the PLO may lose legitimacy in the eyes of its followers if they believed that the PLO accepted too large a compromise on key issues. Palestinian opponents of the peace process agree that Arafat has sacrificed too much already. If Arafat loses followers, they might turn to HAMAS, with a corresponding resumption of violence.

Nonetheless, there is hope that the peace process will continue and a permanent solution will be found. The process has gained an extraordinary momentum and real progress has been achieved. Outside players such as Egypt, Jordan and the United States can provide important guarantees to bring the two players to a lasting agreement. Ultimately, however, only the two sides can secure peace through difficult compromise and a genuine desire for success.

BIBLIOGRAPHY

Bickerston, Ian J. and Carla L. Klausner. *A Concise History of the Arab-Israeli Conflict.* 2d ed. Upper Saddle River, N.J.: Prentice-Hall, 1995.

Harkabi, Yehoshafat. *Arab Strategies and Israel's Response.* New York: The Free Press, 1977.

Jabber, Fuad and Ann Mosely Lesch and William Quandt. *The Politics of Palestinian Nationalism.* Berkeley, Calif.: University of California Press, 1973.

Kelman, Herbert C. "The Palestinianization of the Arab-Israeli Conflict," *The Jerusalem Quarterly* 46 (Spring 1988): 3–15.

Mandel, Neville J. *The Arabs and Zionism Before World War I.* Berkeley, Calif.: University of California Press, 1976.

Nakhleh, Emile A. "The West Bank and Gaza: Twenty Years Later," *Middle East Journal* 42 (Spring 1988): 209–226.

Rubenstein, Alvin, ed. *The Arab-Israeli Conflict: Perspectives.* 2d ed. New York: HarperCollins Publishers, 1991.

Smith, Charles D. *Palestine and the Arab-Israeli Conflict.* 3d ed. New York: St. Martin's Press, 1996.

Ruth Margolies Beitler

GERMAN RIGHT WING EXTREMISM: ANTI-FOREIGNER VIOLENCE IN THE COUNTRY OF THE HOLOCAUST

THE CONFLICT

In the 1990s there were reports of increases in violent attacks against foreigners in Germany. In addition, there were several high-level scandals involving neo-Nazi or right-wing supporters. With the reunification of the two Germanys (East and West), some people feared the re-emergence of the old militaristic, Nazi Germany that resulted in the Holocaust.

Political

- The right wing in Germany glorifies a German past of power and military might.

- Because of the Holocaust, many Nazi activities and paraphernalia are illegal in Germany. Many Germans are horrified that they would continue to be thought of as Nazis.

- Surrounding countries fear a strong, militaristic Germany.

Economic

- Economic tension, especially lack of economic opportunity in the eastern part of Germany, led to frustration—and the search for someone to blame.

- The right wing in Germany blames foreigners, especially asylum seekers and foreign workers who were invited to Germany in better economic times, for lack of jobs.

During the 1990s, headlines from Europe splashed around the world's newspapers alerted citizens to growing right wing extremism. Throughout the European continent, right wing political parties had a varying, but chilling, effect on politics and culture. Jean-Marie Le Pen's National Front in France and Jörg Haider's Freedom Party in Austria are among two of the most successful extremist parties of the decade. The National Front averaged fifteen percent in the election in France while the Freedom Party entered an Austrian governing coalition in 2000. Given the stigma of Nazism, the alarm with which observers viewed these political trends was most significant in Germany.

Right wing extremism, which conjures images of Adolph Hitler's regime in Germany (1933–45), which implemented policies of racial superiority, including the mass extermination of Jews, gypsies, homosexuals, and other groups they viewed as "inferior," has molded anti-immigrant, anti-asylum seeker, and anti-foreigner attitudes. The result has been violence against Germany's large foreign resident and asylum-seeking populations. The violent anti-foreigner events have garnered significant journalistic and academic attention since the late 1980s and have been exacerbated by the aftermath of the Cold War and German reunification. The discovery of significant neo-Nazi inroads in the military, the firebombing of Turkish residences in the German towns of Mölln and Solingen, the attack of refugee hostels in Hoyerswerda and Rostock, the increasing incidence of violent attacks in the early 1990s (including 336 arsons and 2,427 recorded incidents in 1991), the success of specific political parties, and other events highlighted a growing trend toward right wing extremism in Germany.

Violence against foreigners has been particularly unsettling and has prompted protest and response from the government. For example, in light of 569 right wing crimes in the German state of Brandenburg in 1997, including 152 labeled "xenophobic,"—the intense dislike of foreigners—the Brandenburg government created a forty-five-member mobile commando force to combat both the growth in neo-Nazi attacks and the expanding identification among East German youth with Nazi paraphernalia. While the political violence of neo-Nazis, or the radical right, is worrying, the most ominous sign of the advancement of the radical right appeared at the ballot box in eastern Germany. In Saxony-Anhalt, the German People's Union (DVU) polled thirteen percent of the vote in regional elections in 1998, doubled pre-election estimates, and entered the regional parliament.

HISTORICAL BACKGROUND

The Nature of Right Wing Extremism

While German right wing extremism is unsettling, it must be placed in a proper historical and environmental context. Since World War II, German right wing extremism has generally appeared in the form of violence. Over the years, there have been numerous right wing extremist parties that have fielded candidates, but not one of these political parties have been able to sustain success in the political arena. One- or two-election success has been the norm with these political parties, often fading out of the limelight due to internal conflict and public ostracism. Unlike their counterparts in France, Austria, and Italy (among others), the German radical right has never received representation in the German national legislature, *Bundestag*, since World War II. Instead, the radical right has been confined to particular *Länder* (states) and local government.

When exploring right wing extremism, it is important to understand its nature. In academic literature, universal agreement does not exist about both the essence of right wing extremism, its goals, and whether all political parties and organizations that are labeled as such display similar traits. Contemporary right wing extremism is generally seen as a reaction to the change that has evolved in advanced industrial societies since the 1960s. These movements are largely anti-democratic, nationalistic, and reject the social and cultural changes of the past thirty years. While it is not entirely accurate to label all groups "neo-Nazi," German right wing extremists often engage in historical revisionism and diminish the significance

CHRONOLOGY

1919–33 Weimar Germany.

1933–45 Nazi Germany under Adolph Hitler.

1990 East and West Germany are reunited.

1991 There was a drastic increase in the number of violent incidents by right-wing extremists.

1997 The Germany army is rocked by scandals, including studies that determined that young officers are overwhelmingly right wing.

and importance of the Holocaust. Extremists reject multiculturalism and diversity and argue that Germany's large non-German population has irreparably harmed their nation.

Some experts have suggested that labeling all parties and movements under a single umbrella is both misleading and problematic. Other experts have suggested that, in fact, there are two different types of right wing extremists. The first type, including such parties as the National Democrat Party of Germany (NPD) and the DVU reflect conflicts from the first half of the twentieth century. During this same time period, social groups violently fought against one another over control of production, the nature of democracy, and the nature of the economy. The second group of extremists, embodied in the Republikaner Party, formally rejects fascism and the Nazi tradition, though some supporters may not express this belief.

Whereas the first group emphasizes owner-worker conflict, the latter extremist groups emphasize post materialist (non-economic) values and orientations. They focus on fighting the social and cultural changes of the last three decades, the question of national identity, and immigration issues in order to protect the cultural character and identity of the past. This New Right has sought to fill the vacuum created by a society where traditional community and national ties are weakening. Thus, one would expect that support for the Republikaner will cut across income and occupation, and attract those who feel insecure and marginalized within society. While there are differences, there are also similarities regarding their opposition to immigration, asylum seekers, a

NEO-NAZI VIOLENCE AGAINST FOREIGNERS

	1992	1993	1994
Attempted Murders	6	20	8
Bombings	11	3	1
Arson	656	284	80
Terrorism	*	36	27
Bodily Harm	585	727	494
Prop. Damage	1019	539	250
Total	2277	1609	860

* Acts of Right-Wing terrorism were not tabulated before 1993.

TABLE OF NEO-NAZI VIOLENCE AGAINST FOREIGNERS. *(Copyright © 1996 by Praeger. Reproduced by permission of Greenwood Publishing Group, Inc., Westport, Conn.)*

strong sense of national pride, and a large degree of political alienation. In fact, many scholars would argue that, while there is indeed a strain of extremism in Germany historically, it would be fundamentally wrong to equate the extremism of the 1990s with the 1920s since the context, political, and social environments spawning the new groups are very different from that of the 1920s.

1991: Violence of Right Wing Extremism Increases

Splashed on the front headlines of newspapers throughout Germany and the world have been many stories about neo-Nazi resurgence, including statistics on violence toward asylum seekers and other non-Germans, and the apparent success of rightist parties. Since German reunification in 1990, and the subsequent economic problems encountered in the former communist eastern Germany, right wing extremism has risen, fallen, and risen again during the 1990s. Almost immediately after unification, attacks against asylum seekers and foreigners increased.

The year 1991 was a watershed. There were 2,427 incidents of violent right wing extremism, including 336 arson attacks. In one week in May, German authorities recorded the beating of a Zairian, an arson attack directed at a Turkish kindergarten in Bonn, vandalism at a Jewish temple, five arson fires at a single refugee shelter, and twenty-six arrests of individuals shouting the Nazi

slogan "*sieg heil.*" The violent events between 1991 and 1993 at Hoyerswerda and Rostock, where hostels sheltering asylum seekers were besieged, and arson attacks resulting in deaths at Mölln and Solingen were horrific events captured headlines throughout the world; however, throughout eastern Germany, neo-Nazi skinheads have made entire neighborhoods unsafe for foreigners.

Increased right wing extremist attacks appear to catch many politicians off guard. The incidents in the early 1990s were, according to German governmental sources, clearly linked to the revolutionary changes in Europe and contributed to the deaths of thirty people. Throughout the mid-1990s, partially as a result of a government clampdown, right wing extremist attacks consequently declined from 1992 to 1996 for four consecutive years. From over 2,000 incidents in 1991, there were only 624 incidents in Germany associated with right wing attacks by 1996.

Government Countermeasures and Historical Context

In response to the brutality between 1991 and 1993, the German government carried out intensive countermeasures. Germany's constitution created a militant democracy emphasizing the need for the government to vigilantly protect the constitution by prohibiting anti-democratic political parties and organizations. Because of the rise of Hitler during Weimar Germany (1919–33), coupled with the government's suppression of civil liberties, the Holocaust, and other forms of totalitarianism, the Federal Republic of Germany sought to enshrine in its 1949 constitution the Basic Law, principles and provisions to protect the country against similar occurrences. First, there was a five percent threshold for political parties to receive representation in regional and national legislatures—political parties must receive a minimum of five percent of the vote—in order to create a barrier against extremist political parties with little support. Second, the Federal Republic of Germany created a constructive vote of confidence to make it difficult to remove chancellors through negative majorities if, for example, extremist left and right parties held significant representation in the legislature. Third, the revised constitution enabled the government to ban political parties and organizations that did not support democratic principles or organize themselves democratically.

While extremist violence increased in the early 1990s, it bore little resemblance to the right wing in the 1920s. For example, while support increased marginally for right wing extremist political parties, the parties did not have charismatic leaders with communicative powers to capitalize on the potential reservoir of support. Additionally, public support for right wing extremist parties was low. Whereas parties of the extreme right garnered 10.5 percent of the vote in the first post-World War II elections, no political party of the extreme right has surpassed five percent in a national election. Finally, right wing extremist behavior has caused outrage in the German population.

In order to combat right wing extremism, the government has invoked numerous countermeasures both before and since 1991. For example, the government prohibits employment of extremists in public service, and has created an Office for the Protection of the Constitution that annually prepares statistical and analytical reports about the growth and decline of extremism. In 1994, the government banned right wing extremist political parties that did not comply with democratic principles. The three main extremist political parties, the Republikaner, German People's Union (DVU), and the National Democrat Party of Germany (NPD) were put under close surveillance by governmental authorities.

New criminal laws were created. Statements defaming entire groups of citizens were made illegal. Nazi-like flags, badges, uniforms, slogans, and gestures were outlawed. Penalties for extremist violence were increased. Special anti-extremist police units were created at the national and regional levels. Holocaust denial became punishable by up to five years in prison. Production and distribution of Nazi memorabilia and propaganda, leaflets, posters, and newspapers were made illegal.

One controversial element of governmental countermeasures was asylum law reform. Harkening back to Germany's Nazi past, the Basic Law created a lenient asylum policy making the country a safe haven for those fleeing persecution. While Germany's economy boomed, the asylum policies garnered little public opposition. However, with economic slowdown and widespread unemployment, coupled with social costs encountered since reunification, asylum laws have attracted significant public attention. Combining asylum laws with the large number of non-German workers recruited to help Germany's economy during the 1960s and 1970s, non-Germans account for nine percent of the total population (more than seven million). The right wing has seized on the large non-German population, according to the chairman of the North Rhine-Westphalia Republikaner party, claiming, "Each Turk entering this country

ASYLUM SEEKERS AND PRIMARY ORIGINATION STATES

Year	Total Asylum Seekers	Primary Origination State	
1979	51,493	18,044	Turkey
1980	107,818	57,913	Turkey
1981	49,391	9,901	Poland
1982	37,423	6,630	Poland
1983	19,737	2,645	Sri Lanka
1984	35,278	8,063	Sri Lanka
1985	73,832	17,380	Sri Lanka
1986	99,650	21,700	Iran
1987	57,379	15,194	Poland
1988	103,076	29,023	Poland
1989	121,318	26,092	Poland
1990	193,063	35,345	Romania
1991	256,112	74,854	Romania
1992	438,191	122,666	Yugoslavia
1993	322,599	73,717	Romania

Source: Jansen (1994).

TABLE OF ASYLUM SEEKERS AND PRIMARY ORIGINATION STATES. *(Copyright © 1997 by Greenwood Press. Reproduced by permission of Greenwood Publishing Group, Inc., Westport, Conn.)*

will either burden our empty social welfare coffers or take away a scarce job."

Given the sizeable non-German population, it is no surprise they are an easy scapegoat for right wing extremists. Anti-foreigner prejudice has fluctuated in Germany from fourteen percent maintaining negative attitudes in 1980 at the beginning of an increase in rightist violence, to less than six percent in 1990. After unification and economic problems, anti-foreigner prejudice increased.

Although Germany is twenty-five times smaller than the United States geographically and has approximately one-third of its population, it took in the same number of immigrants in 1992, before asylum reform. This influx of asylum-seekers created tension and anti-foreigner sentiment and, even with the most lenient asylum laws in Europe, Germany faced insupportable immigration growth given the dramatic transformations occurring throughout eastern Europe. The disintegration of the Soviet Union and its satellite countries caused large numbers of people to migrate to western

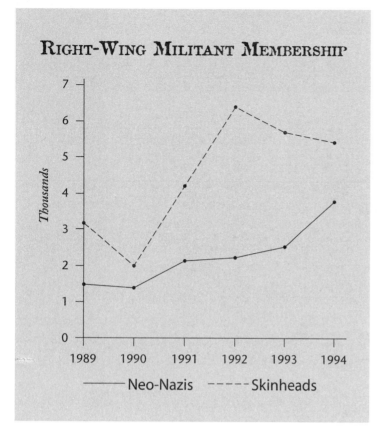

RIGHT-WING MILITANT MEMBERSHIP

Neo-Nazis ——— Skinheads - - - - -

GRAPH OF RIGHT-WING MILITANT MEMBERSHIP. *(Copyright © 1996 by Praeger. Reproduced by permission of Greenwood Publishing Group, Inc., Westport, Conn.)*

Europe. In 1993 the government reformed the law, requiring foreigners coming to Germany through other countries to seek asylum in those countries first rather than in Germany. In effect, this change would cut asylum growth dramatically and bring Germany closer in immigrants to other western nations, though Germany still accepted fifty percent of all European asylum seekers in the 1990s. An impetus driving change of asylum laws was to blunt the appeal of right wing extremists and to ease political tensions in Germany.

Rise in Extremism in the Late 1990s

While reform of the early 1990s cut right wing extremism dramatically, activity increased late in the decade. After four years of decline, 1997 saw a significant increase in right wing extremism. There were 790 violent incidents, with 462 hate crimes directed against foreigners. Violence escalated by twenty-six percent, including thirteen attempted murders, 677 assaults, thirty-seven arson attacks, and two bomb attacks. Though encompassing only seventeen percent of Germany's total population, over half of all the violent acts occurred in eastern Germany. In total, there were 11,719 right wing offenses in Germany in 1997, two-thirds related to the distribution of propaganda and anti-Constitutional symbols.

While extremist offenses have increased, it is important not to exaggerate the scale. Whereas rightist groups are particularly strong in other European countries, such as Italy, Austria, and France, their numbers appear relatively small but growing in Germany. Reportedly, there are approximately thirty-five thousand members of the three main political parties in Germany and nearly fifty thousand members of rightist organizations, representing less than 0.1 percent of the population. This number includes twenty-four hundred people who are classified neo-Nazis and nearly eight thousand hardcore extremists willing to use violence to achieve their purpose.

Particularly unsettling to policymakers is the age of people engaging in right wing extremist violent behavior. In past decades, supporters of extremist political groups were overwhelmingly older. Presently, the increased extremist behavior has been concentrated among the young. Seventy-five percent of all violent incidents were committed by those under twenty-one, fifty percent were under eighteen and a full ninety percent by those under twenty-five.

Eastern Germany and Extremism

The problem is particularly apparent in eastern Germany—it is estimated that 33 percent of all eastern German youth are prone to the extreme right—where economic and social conditions of the former communist state are worse. In Gelsenkirchen, German youths as young as thirteen firebombed immigrant hostels because, according to one, "we hate black people." Hence, thirty-eight percent of western Germans agreed that foreigners lived at the expense of Germany, while fifty-five percent of eastern Germans agreed; twice as many eastern Germans than westerners think that a dictatorship could solve Germany's problems.

A majority of violent acts occur in formerly communist eastern Germany. Consequently, the overall increase in extremist attacks was twenty-seven percent from 1996 to 1997, and in some other eastern states, the figures were higher. Berlin saw an increase of 78 percent, while Brandenburg increased 35 percent, Saxony-Anhalt 57 percent, and Mecklenburg-Western Pomerania 70 percent. Overall, there were 2.7 violent acts per one hundred thousand people in eastern Germany, 385 percent higher than in western Germany. Individually, the six eastern states had the highest rates of extremist motivation and five saw increased activity. While extremist tendencies continue to exist in western Germany, most notably in Baden-Württemburg and Bavaria, which combined in 1997 was responsible for one hundred violent extremist acts, many western German states decreased in violent offenses in 1997.

Various explanations attempt to clarify the increased extremism in eastern Germany. Originally, while Germany has encountered significant economic problems since reunification, much of the brunt of reunification has fallen on eastern Germany. Unemployment rates have occasionally exceeded twenty-five percent, increasing the ranks of potential supporters for the extremist parties who seek either a scapegoat or strong government intervention to alleviate the economic problems.

Second, there is a lack of democratic tradition in eastern Germany therefore lending to the success of authoritarian political parties on the left and the right. Thus, while eastern Germany provides fertile ground for increased rightist extremism, the former Communist Party, the Party of Democratic Socialism (PDS) is also very strong in eastern Germany.

Third, the former East German state did not debate its Nazi past, generally blaming western Germans for fascist and Nazi orientations. To this extent, the socialization process in eastern Germany did not educate citizens in the same fashion as the western German authorities.

Fourth, some scholars argue that extremists are likely to be recruited from the economically vulnerable social classes. Additional influences including difficult economic conditions and bleak employment outlook, the declining importance of churches and unions in the socialization process (especially true in eastern Germany), changing technology, and the inability of many eastern German youth to keep up with modernization contributes to an environment conducive to the rise in extremist success.

Right Wing Parties

There are three major right wing extremist political parties, each with varying levels of strength and control. Right wing political parties have contested elections since the end of World War II, though their significance has been confined to brief periods and the sub-national level. From 10.5 percent in the first post World War II

election, to the end of the 1950s a democratic consensus existed and right wing extremist political forces lost voters at every election. Since the 1950s, right wing revivals have occurred three times. The first, during the mid to late 1960s, saw dramatic political gains by the National Democratic Party followed by stagnation and failure of the right wing to coalesce behind a single party. The second and third waves occurred, respectively, in the late 1980s and early 1990s when the Republikaner Party entered state and European parliaments. While the right went through considerable turmoil in the mid 1990s, it rebounded in the late 1990s with striking gains by the German People's Unions in eastern Germany.

The oldest of the three, the NPD, was created in 1964, and has received the least support in recent elections. The party rose to prominence during the mid-1960s when the two largest mainstream German political parties, the Christian Democratic Union/Christian Social Union (CDU/CSU) and the Social Democratic Party (SPD) entered into a "Grand Coalition" to combat economic and political problems. Extremist forces on the right lambasted the CDU/CSU for its willingness to compromise with the left-wing SPD. The NPD appealed to right wing voters, emphasizing nationalism and made apparent gains in regional parliaments. Between 1966 and 1968, the NPD entered seven regional parliaments passing the five percent threshold in Bavaria (7.9 percent) and Hesse (7.4 percent) in 1966, Rhineland (6.9 percent), Schleswig-Holstein (5.8 percent), Lower Saxony (7.0 percent), and Bremen (8.8 percent) in 1967, and Baden-Württemburg (9.8 percent) in 1968.

While mainstream German politicians viewed this success with apprehension and fear, the NPD's quick ascendance was followed by a quick demise. Although the party attracted twenty-eight thousand members in the late 1960s, membership fell to eight thousand in 1979, and stood at little more than four thousand in the late 1990s. In elections after 1968, the party failed to receive representation at either the regional or national level.

The party's decline in the late 1960s is attributed to a variety of factors. First, mainstream political parties acted quickly to isolate the NPD and its message; accordingly the party was wracked with internal dissension and factionalism. Then, national economic conditions improved, diminishing the protest appeal of the right. Finally, the party lacked effective leadership to communicate their message to the voters.

While the NPD declined in prominence, the party continues to contest elections. By some accounts, while support is not high, the party has great penetration in the eastern German youth scene and has attracted large numbers of skinheads. Stressing nationalism, xenophobia, opposition to asylum seekers, and revision of the history of the Nazi period, the NPD remains an important player and, by some accounts, was rejuvenated by the success of other rightist parties in the late 1990s.

Led by party chairman Udo Voigt, a former member of the German Army (the *Bundeswehr*), the NPD party is headquartered in Stuttgart. Previously an officer in the German Army, Voigt is a controversial figure who has compared German democracy with the former East German communist state. During his tenure, beginning with his appointment in 1996, he has sought to revitalize the fortunes of the NPD. In elections in the late 1990s, party support was marginal. The NPD received 0.3 percent (126,428 votes) in the 1998 German national elections, finishing with the lowest total of the three nationalist parties. Their percentage increased slightly in the European elections of 1999 with 0.4 percent, while receiving 0.7 percent in the 1999 Brandenburg elections and 0.8 percent in Berlin.

While the NPD has declined in significance since the party's initial success in the 1960s, the Republikaner Party rose to prominence in the late 1980s. Created in 1983, the Republikaner was created as a regional party headquartered in Bavaria. In 1984 the party had two thousand members but rose to twenty-five thousand after electoral successes in 1989. In the Berlin 1989 city elections, Republikaner support rose to 7.5 percent. The party built on this success with 7.1 percent in the European elections in 1989, a whopping 14.6 percent in Bavaria, and 8.6 percent in Baden-Würtemmburg. The upsurge in support strongly suggested that the Republikaner would enter the Bundestag after the national elections in 1990. Polls showed support for the Republikaner hovering at ten percent in early and mid 1990; however, with unification, there was a precipitous drop in support and they captured only 2.1 percent in the national election.

Four years later, the Republikaner was unable to rediscover its success of the late 1980s. After government crackdowns, its support dropped significantly. From 10.5 percent in the 1992 Baden-Würtemmburg elections, the Republikaner was insignificant in the 1994 elections, capturing just 1.9 percent of the vote in the national elections

and dropping to only 3.9 percent in its stronghold in Bavaria. After its debacle in Bavaria, party chief Franz Schönhuber, a former officer in the *Waffen SS* during Nazi Germany, was deposed due to both its loss in the elections and his flirtations with the officially shunned German People's Union. His successor, Dr. Rolf Schlierer, has attempted to present the party as a mainstream right-conservative party.

The Republikaner is considered ideologically related to France's neo-fascist National Front. The party denies any nostalgia for Nazism. Though eschewing the Nazi past, a significant percentage of Republikaner members openly reject democracy. A Saxony-Anhalt party board member has likened parliamentary democracy to a "mass murder system." They have walked a fine line between pro-democracy and anti-democracy official positions. They reject voting rights for non-Germans, including citizens of the European Union in local elections, and call for an immediate end to immigration. The party does not officially recognize Germany's borders with Poland and refers to the new eastern German states as Middle Germany.

Reunification harmed the Republikaner in the short term, diminishing its appeal. However, with the integration of eastern Germany, the party has expanded opportunities for electoral success in the economically underdeveloped east. In recent elections, Republikaner has experienced some success and failure. In 1996, it scored 9.1 percent in Baden-Württemburg, down nearly 2 percent from its 1992 mark. During the elections of 1998, it scored a disappointing 3.6 percent in Bavaria and 1.8 percent nationally. While achieving success in European elections in 1989, in the 1999 European elections they received 1.7 percent, while polling 2.7 percent in Berlin, and only 0.8 percent in the Thuringian regional election. Whereas the DVU made formidable gains in 1998 and 1999, the Republikaner has been unable to repeat its political success of the previous decade. However, by the end of the 1990s, its membership rolls were 15,500, placing it as the largest of the nationalist parties.

The most successful nationalist party in recent history is the DVU. Created as a "club" in 1971 by Gerhard Frey, a millionaire Munich-based publisher, the party was relatively unknown and unimportant until its re-creation as a political party in 1987. Relying upon the subsidy of Dr. Frey, the party published two newspapers with a weekly circulation of thirty-five thousand copies, down from a high of one hundred ten thousand in 1989. In the late 1990s the party's membership also witnessed a similar trend, declining from a high of approximately twenty-six thousand early in the decade to fifteen thousand by 1997.

While denying any overt links to Nazi ideology, the DVU sent subtle anti-Semitic messages woven through its two weekly publications. The publications downplay the Holocaust and relativize its importance. Campaigning for a "Germany for the Germans" and the expulsion of criminal foreigners, the DVU has attempted to build a base in the eastern German states where unemployment is rampant and the public outlook is bleak.

During the 1990s, the DVU had limited success. Like the Republikaner, its support peaked when it received 6.3 percent of the vote in Schleswig-Holstein in 1992. For the next five years, the DVU dropped off the political scene. Inevitably, right wing success in the political arena was limited. During this time, the government employed aggressive measures to curtail right wing extremism.

In the late 1990s, the DVU was beginning to perform well in the public opinion polls in eastern Germany. One major breakthrough occurred in Saxony-Anhalt in regional elections in April 1998. Tallying thirteen percent, double pre-election polls, the DVU's success was viewed with alarm by mainstream politicians. Its achievement was due in large measure to the economic conditions in the troubled state along with the large influx of spending by Dr. Frey. Also in Saxony-Anhalt, the DVU spent more money than either of the two mainstream political parties, suggesting that a well-publicized extremist message has significant potential resonance in eastern Germany.

Attempting to build on the triumph in eastern Germany, the DVU heavily contested regional elections in Mecklenburg-Western Pomerania in September 1998. It was unable to repeat its victory in the regional and national elections in 1998, scoring only 2.9 percent in the depressed eastern state, while polling only 1.2 percent in the national election. In 1999, it fared better, capturing five seats in the Brandenburg legislature with 5.3 percent of the vote, although it was unable to make a breakthrough in Thuringia (3.1 percent). The DVU's support, while regionally significant, is confined largely to the eastern German states of Saxony-Anhalt and Brandenburg. They fail to contest elections in most areas of the country, leaving those contests to the Republikaner or the National Democratic Party of Germany.

IMMIGRATION AND ELECTORAL SUPPORT FOR THE NEW RIGHT

Variable	Coefficient	T-value	Standard Error
Foreign Population	-1.932*	-4.380	0.441
Crime	3.561*	11.031	0.219
Unemployment	-0.024	-0.112	0.219
Intercept	-7.252	-12.618	0.575
Adjusted R-squared	.705		
F-value	21.894*		
N	122		

* $p < .001$

TABLE OF IMMIGRATION AND ELECTORAL SUPPORT FOR THE NEW RIGHT. IT SUGGESTS THAT WHILE THERE IS AN ASSOCIATION BETWEEN FOREIGNERS AND VOTES FOR THE NEW RIGHT, THE VOTE IS LOWER WHERE THERE ARE MORE FOREIGNERS. *(Copyright © 1997 by Greenwood Press. Reproduced by permission of Greenwood Publishing Group, Inc., Westport, Conn.)*

Demographics of Right Wing Extremism

While important to chart the success and failure of right wing extremist political parties, it is equally important to look beyond the numbers and analyze the supporters of these parties. Examining exit polls gives a clear picture of the type of voter that is most likely to support extremist arguments. Supporters of the three parties are overwhelmingly male. For example, in Saxony-Anhalt, the DVU scored sixteen percent among male voters while polling only ten percent of women. A gender gap exists for the other rightist parties, including the Republikaner, whose voters are reportedly two thirds male and one third female.

Supporters of the nationalist parties are very young, although the difference is clear between support levels in eastern and western Germany. In Saxony-Anhalt, the DVU captured 32 percent support from 18–24 year olds and 23 percent from those aged 25–34, though they attracted only 3 percent of voters over 60. Among Republikaner voters, their appeal is primarily to older nationalists. In 1996 the western German state of Baden-Württemburg found 56 percent of Republikaner voters were over 45, while 29 percent were under 35. Emphasizing the young male support for the DVU, the party captured 38 percent of the 18–24 male vote in Saxony-Anhalt in 1998. The key for nationalists is to coalesce joint appeal and find a unifying force to capture the support from both

ACTS OF RIGHT-WING VIOLENCE AND AGES OF PARTICIPANTS

Ages	1991	1992	1993
Under 18	21.2%	23.9%	16.8%
18–20	47.8%	43.3%	39.1%
21–30	28.3%	29.9%	36.5%
31–40	2.2%	2.5%	4.9%
40 Plus	0.5%	0.4%	2.7%

TABLE OF ACTS OF RIGHT-WING VIOLENCE AND AGES OF PARTICIPANTS. *(Copyright © 1996 by Praeger. Reproduced by permission of Greenwood Publishing Group, Inc., Westport, Conn.)*

older and younger voters. However, while this goal would seem obvious, there are severe inter-party differences and animosities that have thwarted various attempts to form a united front among the extremist parties.

In addition, nationalist supporters tend not to be religious. While the DVU scored eight percent in Saxony-Anhalt among Protestants and Catholic voters, they polled sixteen percent among non-religious voters. Finally, while economic conditions are important for providing an environment encouraging rightist parties, there is little evidence to suggest that nationalist parties perform better among the unemployed, though support for nationalist parties is slightly higher among the unemployed, blue-collar workers, and those involved in employment training programs.

RECENT HISTORY AND THE FUTURE

Rightist Military Scandal

The right wing attacks and electoral successes were not the only threatening sign of the revival of extremism. Though never free of incidents related to charges of right wing extremism, the German military, with universal male conscription, was never viewed as a hotbed of political extremism; however, the 1990s witnessed increasing signs of right wing extremist penetration in the military. For example, in 1994 there were seventy-four soldiers cited for extreme right wing offenses including brawling, spreading illegal propaganda, and meeting with right wing groups.

During 1997, the German army was rocked by two scandals. First, public television broadcast homemade videos of the German army showing several eastern German soldiers, including two officers giving the Nazi salute, making disparaging comments about Jews, simulating rape and torture, and singing along to far right music. On the heels of these videos, there were reports of a dramatic increase in the number of cases of rightist extremism among service personnel, and the incidents were growing more violent. Anecdotal evidence by one ex-soldier quoted in a German newspaper states that about fifty percent of new recruits in 1997 in eastern Germany were extremist. While that number may be exaggerated, a military university study found that the younger officer class was overwhelmingly right wing and there was some use of Nazi mottos and paraphernalia by select superior officers.

The second scandal, which caused shock from politicians of all political colors, came to light in December 1997 when convicted neo-Nazi Manfred Roeder, who served eight years in jail for racist bomb attacks that resulted in the deaths of two Vietnamese, was invited to lecture on nationalism to soldiers at an elite military academy. The German Defense Minister suspended a lieutenant general and ordered disciplinary hearings against a colonel regarding this circumstance. The uproar was part of a growing public awareness that rightist violence was increasing in Germany after years of decline.

Scholars are split about both the nature and future of right wing extremist violence and political parties in Germany. There is a reservoir of alienation from the political system, and disillusion with the aftermath of reunification in eastern Germany. However, in the past thirty-five years there have been three waves of extremism in Germany. The first of these waves, those of the 1960s, late 1980s and early 1990s, gave way to crackdowns, ostracism, and declining support and incidence of violence. If history provides a gauge for judging the future, extremist parties should rise and fall in both extremist violence and success at the polls.

The lack of sustained success for nationalist parties is due to a variety of factors. For example, the mainstream political parties have joined forces to isolate these groups. The German constitution also gives the government great leeway in cracking down on anti-democratic political parties to ensure that the conditions that led to Nazi seizure of power do not occur again. In addition, violence has caused a backlash against the right and spawned anti-extremist protest and demonstrations throughout Germany. Lastly, the three main extremist political parties view each other with scorn that has undermined the attempts to form a united front political party.

The 1980s and 1990s have witnessed the rise in various right wing extremist political parties throughout Europe. Their success has varied from inclusion in a governing coalition in Austria via the Freedom Party, significant regional inroads for Italy's Lega Norda (Northern League), and vital and stabilized national support for France's National Front (averaging fourteen percent over recent elections). While Germany was fertile ground for fascism and the growth of Nazism during the 1920s and 1930s, due to the psychological impact of the Treaty of Versailles ending World War I and the severe economic downturn, the German political environment has changed considerably and represents both opportunities and limits to the growth in German nationalism. The opportunities for German nationalism include significant right wing attitudes among a minority of the electorate, the depressed economic conditions in eastern Germany, and Germany's large non-native population that cause tensions with socioeconomic lower class Germans.

However, there are severe limits. In addition to considerable factional fighting, the right bears the stigma of Germany's Nazi past. While the Republikaner disavow Nazism, and the German People's Union and National Democratic Party of Germany chart a course between pro-system and anti-system tendencies, the rightist movements continue to be publicly linked with Nazism. Unlike its neighbors Austria and France, the link between the past and the present is clear and unambiguous, though they do limit the opportunities even for the Freedom Party and National Front. This was apparent during the mass protests after inclusion of the Austrian Freedom Party in the governing coalition in 2000, given the positive past comments of the party's leader, Jörg Haider, toward Nazi policies. Thus, unless the nationalists can overcome these rigid limitations, they are likely to continue to be a nuisance in German politics but remain a fringe element. They are likely to continue to play a significant role in eastern Germany and cause disturbances through violence. However, given the vigilance of the mainstream public and political parties, they are not likely to make sustained advances for the foreseeable future in western Germany.

BIBLIOGRAPHY

Betz, Hans-Georg and Stefan Immerfall, eds. *The New Politics of the Right: Neo-Populist Parties and Movements in Established Democracies.* New York: St. Martin's Press, 1998.

Cheles, Luciano, Ronnie Ferguson, and Michalina Vaughn, eds. *Neo-Fascism in Europe.* New York: Longman Press, 1991.

Chapin, Wesley D. *Germany for the Germans?: The Political Effects of International Migration.* Westport, Conn.: Greenwood Press, 1997.

Cowell, Alan. "Pro-Nazi Incidents in German Army Raise Alarm," *New York Times,* 5 November 1997, sec. A.

Drozdiak, William. "Right Wing Extremist Violence Surges in Germany," *Washington Post,* 7 May 1998, sec. A.

"Echoes of an Evil Past," *Economist,* 28 September 1991, 58.

Federal Office for the Protection of the Constitution. *Annual Report—1997.* Bonn, 1997.

Lewis, Rand. *Neo-Nazis and German Reunification.* Wesport, Conn.: Praeger, 1996.

Merkl, Pail and Leonard Weinberg, eds. *The Revival of Right Wing Extremism in the Nineties.* Portland, Ore.: Frank Cass, 1997.

Roberts, Geoffrey. "Extremism in Germany: Sparrows or Avalanche?" *European Journal of Political Research* 25 (1994): 461–82.

Schiller, Bill. "Cancer of Right Wing Extremism Spreading in Germany," *Toronto Star,* 6 December 1992, sec. H.

Schönwälder, Karen. "Right Wing Extremism and Racist Violence in Germany," *West European Politics* 18, no. 2 (1995): 448–56.

Stöss, Richard. *Politics Against Democracy.* New York: St. Martin's Press, 1991.

Warren, Marcus. "Germany Fears Nazi Revival in Army." *Daily Telegraph (London),* 21 September 1997, 27.

Michael Levy

HUMANITARIAN AID: COMPASSION AND CONTROVERSY

THE CONFLICT

The provision of humanitarian aid—food, medicine, shelter, and economic assistance—has grown considerably in the last several years. The International Red Cross and Doctors Without Borders provided aid during almost every conflict. The U.S. Marines distributed food during a famine in Somalia. Much of the world community sees humanitarian assistance as an obligation of being human and humane. However, humanitarian assistance and the organizations providing it are often charged with prolonging conflict, aiding warriors who will fight again, and providing inappropriate, and ultimately harmful assistance.

Territorial

- Some countries see aid provision as interfering with their right to manage their country and control their people. Some countries deny aid organizations access to their land and people.

Economic

- Economic assistance may be inappropriate for the development level, and may be unsustainable without additional aid.

Political/Ethnic

- Doctors and other aid workers, providing medicine and food, may be making the war longer and bloodier, as they patch up soldiers to keep on fighting.

International relief organizations are a relatively new phenomenon in modern international relations. Functioning independently of any government and motivated by humanitarian concerns, international relief groups have made a considerable impact on crisis situations caused by almost every type of human and natural disaster. At the turn of the twenty-first century, their growing number and importance influenced global politics and world opinion more than ever before. In October 1999 international relief gained worldwide attention when the medical relief organization Doctors Without Borders (known internationally by its French name, Médecins Sans Frontières) won the Nobel Peace Prize for its humanitarian work.

The concept of international relief has not been without controversy, however. While international relief organizations have provided great amounts of material aid to suffering people, their activities have also been widely criticized. At many times, especially in the twentieth century, international relief groups have been unable to assist in some of history's worst humanitarian catastrophes. Many states have viewed the activities of some groups as undue interference in their internal affairs and have as a result taken drastic actions to undermine their credibility and cast doubt on their intentions. Other regimes have been accused of co-opting humanitarian organizations for their own selfish propaganda purposes. Some instances of fraud and waste have created cynicism about both the effectiveness and the intentions of international relief organizations. Perhaps most disturbingly, relief organizations have been accused of prolonging war and suffering by nursing combatants back to health—and to the battlefield. In many ways, the concept of international relief is

CHRONOLOGY

1859 The Battles of Solferino and Magenta, fought by French Emperor Napoleon, are witnessed by Swiss-born Henry Dunant. The memoirs of his experience caring for the the wounded French soldiers leads to the founding of the International Red Cross.

1864 The Geneva Conventions, the first international code of conduct regarding the treatment of prisoners of war, are established.

1875 The Red Cross sponsors an international conference to abolish slavery.

1875–78 In response to the Balkan Crisis, Great Britain calls for armed intervention on humanitarian grounds.

1901 Dunant is awarded the Noble Peace Prize.

1944 Nazi Germany hides the brutality and suffering of the concentration camps from Red Cross officials.

1945 The U.N.'s Convention on Human Rights is established.

1948 The U.N.'s Convention on the Prevention and Punishment of Genocide is established.

1961 Amnesty International is founded.

1972 In the United States, the Jackson-Vanick amendment links trade to the Soviet government's promise to permit emigration of persecuted Jewish citizens.

1977 U.S. President Jimmy Carter promises to incorporate human rights as a defining principle of U.S. foreign policy.

1992–93 U.S. President George Bush authorizes the use of U.S. Marines to distribute food and other aid during a famine in Somalia.

1999 Doctors Without Borders (Médecins San Frontières) wins the Noble Peace Prize for its humanitarian work.

intimately associated with modernity. The intellectual climate of the mid-nineteenth century, when international relief truly began, was characterized by a revival of the Enlightenment ideal that humanity is ultimately perfectible. Constant advances in science, technology, and quality of life convinced many that the days of the world's problems were numbered. The Enlightenment's focus on humanism thrived in the nineteenth century's belief that growing knowledge and prosperity throughout the world would end the suffering that corrupted the inherent goodness of humanity and caused all evil. The classical liberal tradition of democratic government, civic equality, a free civil society, the consideration of human rights, and emphasis on humanity's standard of living made tremendous strides, especially in the Western European nations that dominated global politics.

One of the most striking contrasts to this worldview was the manner in which technology affected the development of modern warfare. Along with its material progress, the technological advancements of the nineteenth century created conditions that made war systematically much more bloody than it had ever been before. While the murderous battlefields of World War I have been identified as the prime example of old-fashioned tactics against newly mechanized warfare, the scientific ability to kill efficiently and in greater numbers dates from an earlier period. Indeed, the same observation about old tactics and new methods of warfare had been made about the American Civil War (1861–65) and the development of the rapid-fire rifle and Gatling Gun.

HISTORICAL BACKGROUND

Dunant and the International Red Cross

The worst excesses of this new warfare had become apparent several years earlier, however. In the most important case for international relief organizations, it actually brought a war to a premature conclusion. While the French Emperor Napoleon III promised to support the Italian kingdom of Piedmont-Sardinia in its drive for Italian unification in 1859, heavy French losses in only two battles, Solferino and Magenta, persuaded Napoleon to conclude a separate peace with his principal opponent, the Austrian Empire, and take back his pledge to fight until Italy was unified.

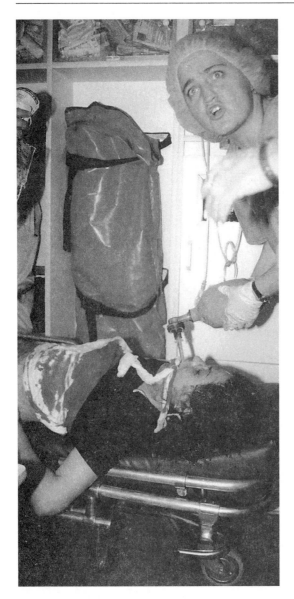

HUMANITARIAN GROUPS SUCH AS DOCTORS WITHOUT BORDERS PROVIDE VALUABLE ASSISTANCE TO LOCAL HOSPITALS WHEN EMERGENCIES ARISE. A DOCTOR TRIES DESPERATELY TO SAVE A TURKISH WOMAN AFTER AN EARTHQUAKE IN IZMIT, TURKEY. *AP/Wide World Photos. Reproduced by permission.*

The losses at Solferino, the first of these battles, were so serious that they prompted the Swiss-born businessman Henry Dunant (1828–1910), who had been following Napoleon III to acquire a business concession in Tunisia, to become personally involved in caring for some nine thousand wounded French soldiers who were largely unattended. Dunant's example and subsequent memoir of his three-day experience caring for the French wounded led to the creation of an international organization to ease the burdens of human suffering inflicted by war and other forms of disaster,

the International Red Cross. In addition to its direct relief activities in the wars that followed, the International Red Cross also gave a great deal of attention to the achievement of international agreements to respect what a later generation would call basic human rights. In 1864 the fruits of Dunant's personal and philosophical reaction to the horror of modern warfare led to the Geneva Conventions, the first international code of conduct for the treatment of prisoners of war and enemy civilians in wartime. In 1875 the Red Cross sponsored an international conference to abolish the last vestiges of slavery and the slave trade. Though a financial scandal effectively removed Dunant from the organization's leadership, he was raised from poverty and obscurity in 1901, when he was awarded the Nobel Peace Prize.

If the idea of international relief was implanted in the mind of one progressive individual in 1859, additional technological innovations spread both the power of conscience and the horror of war to populations on a mass scale. Even before the sight of the wounded at Solferino had moved Dunant to set an example that led to the creation of the first organization devoted to international relief, the invention of the telegraph, the increased circulation of cheaply produced popular newspapers, and increased literacy among the populations of developed countries combined to create a popular international consciousness of human suffering. The Crimean War of 1852–55 actually introduced the first professional war correspondents, who for the first time could relay their reports from battlefields in a distant part of European Russia to audiences throughout Western Europe. Mass politics and mass media encouraged the distribution of these reports, especially in widely circulated newspapers that were printed cheaply to ensure large-scale readership.

The spread of such reports in the 1850s began to have a serious impact on European diplomatic relations. The first Balkan Crisis of 1875–78 became a concern for all of Europe largely because of Western press reports of Turkish atrocities against the Ottoman Empire's Bulgarian Christian subjects. These reports were available in vivid detail and the people of Western Europe were horrified. In Britain, a country that traditionally based its entire foreign policy on the concept of its national interests, the opposition Liberal Party called for armed intervention against the Turks purely on humanitarian grounds. The concept of the world's first international relief organization also played a significant role, as representatives of the International Red Cross attempted to encourage all parties in the conflict to adhere to the Geneva Convention. Similar overtures were made in every other international conflict of the age.

Famine in the Soviet Union

As technology improved, however, humanitarian groups faced challenges. Although popular consciousness of human suffering had been raised by the more peripheral wars of the latter half of the nineteenth century, the collapse of the European order in 1914 presented international relief with a huge challenge. The scale of conflict and the adaptation of military technology in World War I, resulted in more casualties in four years than European armies had sustained in the previous eight centuries. Nevertheless, the Red Cross embraced the human catastrophe of war, working to ease the suffering of the wounded and to ensure the rights of prisoners of war. The International Red Cross's headquarters in Geneva and national Red Cross organizations throughout the world made notable and frequently successful efforts to assist the families of soldiers who were missing to determine what had happened to their sons on the battlefield. Red Cross officials also helped bereaved families locate bodies and even arranged for transportation and burial.

World War I and its tragic losses, however, were only the prelude to the horrors of the twentieth century. In addition to technological advancement in warfare and military technology, the application of science to human society brought with it two important, and very catastrophic, new factors with which humanitarian organizations would have to contend. Science and politics began to mix in ways that unleashed some of the most terrible tragedies in human history. Marxists—communists and socialists who believed in the theories of Karl Marx—believed that the concept of humanitarian charity of any kind was a trick to keep the "toiling masses" in a state of oppression. In other words, the exploiting classes temporarily eased the suffering of the oppressed to solidify their control. This theory led the young Russian Marxist Vladimir Ilyich Ulyanov (known to history by his alias Vladimir Ilyich Lenin) to refuse to participate in famine relief in Czarist Russia (1890–92).

Despite these ideologically charged objections to the principles behind humanitarian aid, a successful demonstration of international relief during World War I came in the world's first socialist state, Lenin's Soviet Russia (also known as the USSR). After suffering the death and dis-

A MEMORY OF SOLFERINO (UN SOUVENIR DO SOLFERINO)

J. Henry Dunant (1828–1910)

Here is hand-to-hand struggle in all its horror and frightfulness; Austrians and Allies trampling each other under foot, killing one another on piles of bleeding corpses, felling their enemies with their rifle butts, crushing skulls, ripping bellies open with sabre and bayonet. When they have no weapon left, they seize their enemies by the throat and tear them with their teeth.

Brains spurt under wheels, limbs are broken and torn, bodies mutilated past the point of recognition . . . .

The convoys brought a fresh contingent of wounded men . . . every quarter of an hour . . . . Men of all nations lay side by side on the flagstone floors of the churches. They called out in their distress . . . and writhed in desperate convulsions that ended in tetanus and death . . . .

With faces black with the flies that swarmed about their wounds, men gazed around them, wild-eyed and helpless. Others were no more than a worm-ridden, inextricable compound of coat and shirt and flesh and blood.

Another . . . with his skull gaping wide open, was dying, spitting out his brains on the stone floor.

Another . . . was not yet twenty, but he was quite white-haired. His hair had gone white in the battle . . . .

The women of Castiglione, seeing I made no distinction between nationalities, followed my example, showing the same kindness to all these men . . . all of whom were foreigners to them.

ruption of the world war, two revolutions, a brutal civil war, and extreme communist policies, the new Bolshevik regime ruled over a country devastated by serious famine in the years 1921–22. Following a policy designed to rebuild his country before fully socializing it, Lenin appealed to the world for humanitarian relief and the United States responded in abundance. Headed by Commerce Secretary and future president Herbert Hoover, the American Relief Administration distributed food and other supplies, which most estimates (including Soviet ones) credit with having saved some ten million lives.

Despite its willingness to accept American help at that time, the Soviet regime acted much differently when its people faced a later disaster. When the brutal policies of Josef Stalin caused another massive famine in 1930–33, the Soviet Union's authoritarian state actively prevented international relief. Convinced that it was engaging in a campaign against the forces of a "class

WHILE RED CROSS VOLUNTEERS OFTEN FIND THEMSELVES IN THE MIDST OF MILITARY CONFLICTS, THEY ALSO ASSIST DURING TIMES OF NATURAL DISASTERS. HERE RESCUE WORKERS SAVE SEVERAL PEOPLE IN ECIJA, SPAIN, AFTER THE GENIL RIVER OVERFLOWED. *AP/Wide World Photos. Reproduced by permission.*

enemy" (i.e. the Russian peasantry) that had to be controlled and coerced, the communist regime systematically deprived much of the countryside of food. In highly ideological statements, Soviet officials criticized appeals for moderation, material assistance, and even simple compassion as "saccharine liberal humanitarianism." The Soviet Union, they firmly believed, was carrying out history's inevitable progression toward communism, a goal for which any human sacrifice was acceptable.

In addition to depriving their own people of sustenance, the Soviet government refused assistance from the outside world when it served its purposes and, during the famine and for decades after, denied the existence of the famine. Soviet citizens who mentioned it (including those who were starving) were subject to prison sentences for engaging in "anti-Soviet propaganda." Government control of the Soviet media encouraged the publication of "open letters" from Soviet farmers that told concerned Westerners how wrong they were to believe that people were starving in the USSR. Western press correspondents were forbidden to travel to rural areas affected by famine, though some partial reports appeared in the Western media. Stalin denied the International Red Cross permission to operate within Soviet borders. Alternative relief organizations estab-

lished by Cardinal Innitzer, the Archbishop of Vienna, and by ethnic Ukrainians living in eastern Poland, were also ineffectual because of Moscow's refusal even to acknowledge a need for their help. Even the USSR's official history of American relief activities in 1921–1922 was rewritten to show that Hoover's relief mission had been an elaborate hoax to establish a counterrevolutionary espionage network. Conservative estimates from demographic studies (the first Soviet census after the famine was suppressed and its compilers purged, presumably because of the sharp, unnatural population decline which it showed) suggest that the famine claimed at least eleven million lives. A majority of the victims belonged to large and historically independent ethnic minorities (especially Ukrainians) who were purposely targeted for that reason. A majority of the victims were children.

World War II and Nazi Germany

During World War II, Nazi Germany used its totalitarian powers to block international relief organizations. While international relief organizations were relegated to the sidelines, Hitler's Germany established a system of concentration camps whose main purpose was to murder the declared enemies of the Nazis while extracting whatever wealth they might possess or forced labor they might provide. All told, more than sixteen million people perished in such camps in the name of political ideology, social prejudices, and, most importantly for the Nazis, racial purity. More than six million of those who perished were Jews who were condemned simply because of their ethnic and religious background. Large numbers of Poles, Russians, and other Slavic peoples also perished at the hands of the Nazis.

Although some details of Nazi atrocities were reported in the West only a short period of time after they happened, the Nazi police state successfully excluded all unwanted international humanitarian assistance from the areas under its control until the end of the war. At one point, Nazi officials even justified allowing large numbers of Soviet prisoners of war to starve to death with the callous legal argument that the USSR had never signed the Geneva Convention. There were even some instances in which the Nazi government used neutral humanitarian representatives for its own selfish purposes. Even as the horror of German atrocities became known, the Nazis allowed the Red Cross to help German civilians who had suffered from Allied air raids.

The Nazis also tried to use international humanitarianism to try to convince the world that allegations of human rights violations against it were baseless. In 1943 the German army discovered a mass grave of Polish officers in the Katyn forest, near Smolensk in the occupied USSR. Although we now know that the massacres of these and other Polish officers discovered later were atrocities committed by the Soviet Union in 1940, Nazi Germany nevertheless invited International Red Cross officials to prove that only the barbarous Soviet communists indulged in such inhumane behavior. All the while, of course, nearly 1.5 million Soviet Jews and millions of other Soviet citizens lay in mass graves due to German actions.

Nazi authorities used humanitarian aid workers in an attempt to disprove accusations about organized mass murder in concentration camps. In the 1930s, before mass extermination began in earnest, Red Cross officials and others were allowed to visit the camps at Dachau and Buchenwald, but evidence of brutality and suffering were deliberately hidden from them. In the summer of 1944, International and Danish Red Cross officials were invited to tour the Nazi concentration camp at Theresienstadt (Terezin) north of Prague. Described as the "Paradise Ghetto," Theresienstadt was in reality a dressed-up transit camp designed to lure prominent West European Jews from their homes in order to send them to their deaths in the extermination camps further east. After an elaborate effort to "beautify" the camp, dramatized in detail in Herman Wouk's novel *War and Remembrance*, the Red Cross visitors were shown around a camp that hid the murderous and genocidal realities. After their visit the Red Cross delegation gladly issued statements claiming that nothing was amiss in the treatment of Theresienstadt's Jews. Even the Third Reich's largest death camp at Auschwitz, where more than two million Jews perished, was visited by Red Cross officials later in 1944, and once again the Germans successfully pulled the wool over their eyes. Even as Auschwitz reached the height of its mass killing operations, the Red Cross' report had nothing to say about the camp's gas chambers, crematoria, forced labor, and appalling living conditions.

To the credit of international relief groups in this era, however, they did insert themselves into disaster situations as soon as it was practicable. Several humanitarian Zionist groups were able to rescue small numbers of Jewish refugees from German-occupied regions and to send support to those who remained. Red Cross field workers entered liberated concentration camps on the heels of the Allied armies to aid the survivors. In many instances, humanitarian groups successfully intervened on behalf of the Jews even before the Germans had left. The Swiss Red Cross managed to persuade the Swiss government to allow the emigration of several hundred Jewish children from France in 1942. Red Cross pressure led directly to the release of twelve thousand Jewish children from the Jasenovac camp in Croatia in 1943. A joint appeal from the president of the Red Cross, Pope Pius XII, President Franklin Roosevelt, and the King of Sweden persuaded the Hungarian government to cease its cooperation in the Holocaust in July 1944, though deportations of Hungarian Jews to concentration camps continued after the country was placed under German military administration. After the end of the war, United Nations relief officials established successful refugee camps for so-called Displaced Persons (DPs) who had lost their homes as a result of the conflict and were desperately in need of humanitarian aid.

Despite these successes and their good intentions, in the age of totalitarian states obsessed with ideology and population control, international relief was of little help to the millions who died. Largely as a result of this sad fact, international relief since the end of World War II has focused on attacking government policies that cause

Geneva Conventions

Article 12—Members of the armed forces and other persons mentioned in the following Article, who are wounded or sick, shall be respected and protected in all circumstances. They shall be treated humanely and cared for by the Party to the conflict in whose power they may be, without any adverse distinction founded on sex, race, nationality, religious, political opinions, or any other similar criteria. Any attempts upon their lives, or violence to their persons shall be strictly prohibited; in particular, they shall not be murdered or exterminated, subjected to torture or to biological experiments; they shall not willfully be left without medical assistance and care, nor shall conditions exposing them to contagion or infection be created.

Article 14—The wounded and sick of a belligerent who fall into enemy hands shall be prisoners of war, and the provisions of international law concerning prisoners of war shall apply to them.

Article 13—Prisoners of war must at all times be humanely treated. Any unlawful act or omission by the Detaining Power causing death or seriously endangering the health of a prisoner of war in its custody is prohibited, and will be regarded as a serious breach of the present Convention. In particular, no prisoner of war may be subjected to physical mutilation or to medical or scientific experiments of any kind which are not justified by the medical, dental or hospital treatment of the prisoner concerned and carried out in his interest. Measures of reprisal against prisoners of war are prohibited.

Article 26—The basic daily food ration shall be sufficient in quantity, quality and variety to keep prisoners of war in good health and to prevent loss of weight or the development of nutritional deficiencies. Sufficient drinking water shall be supplied to prisoners of war. Collective disciplinary measures affecting food are prohibited.

Article 30—Every camp shall have an adequate infirmary where prisoners of war may have the attention they require, as well as appropriate diet. Isolation wards, shall, if necessary, be set aside for cases of contagious or mental disease.

Prisoners of War suffering from serious disease, or whose condition necessitates special treatment, a surgical operation or hospital care, must be admitted to any military or civilian medical unit where such treatment can be given.

---

humanitarian catastrophes while still addressing the need for immediate aid.

Since World War II

While the creation of the United Nations in 1945 was spurred by a desire to prevent international conflict, the international community also greatly expanded notions of human rights and international law that were designed to prevent humanitarian disaster. If authoritarian states actively worked against direct international relief, humanitarians argued, political pressure might persuade them to reverse policies that created such disasters. The victorious powers in World War II brought German and Japanese officials to trial in international courts for crimes against humanity to demonstrate how seriously the international community would now regard humanitarian considerations. Sanctions against humanitarian disasters were formalized with the U.N.'s General Assembly adoption of its Convention on Human Rights in 1945 and the Convention on the Prevention and Punishment of Genocide in 1948, measures which condemned violent abuse of national, ethnic, and religious groups.

In an era that was dominated by the Cold War, humanitarian considerations played a considerable role in international politics. In the United States, such organizations as the Peace Corps and the Alliance For Progress were established to provide direct aid and assistance to people in the developing world. While developing countries doubtlessly benefited from American generosity, the activities of these organizations were also intended to serve American political purposes. In a world where the ideological competition between the United States and the Soviet Union had become the dominant feature in international relations, the developing world became one of the principal battlegrounds. Since the nuclear age discouraged direct military conflict between the superpowers, diplomatic leverage played a considerable role. Often the balance was influenced by or even turned on Washington or Moscow's ability to convince developing nations that it had the more noble humanitarian aspirations.

RECENT HISTORY AND THE FUTURE

While direct aid from the Red Cross and other international relief groups continued and multiplied after the war, humanitarianism also began to find expression on political grounds. The growing realization that human catastrophes were linked to economic difficulties led the international community to establish world financial institutions like the World Bank and International Monetary Fund (IMF) to assist nations beset by financial chaos. The IMF and the World Bank were developed to provide economic assistance—including loans—to countries to help them develop. However, the IMF and World Bank have been criticized for providing support that undermines local economies and human rights, and for slowing development by encouraging chronic indebtedness.

Despite the increased awareness of the international community, however, some of the previous shortcomings of international relief persisted. The success of the communist revolution in China in 1949 set the stage for perhaps the largest human tragedy in modern history, as an estimated thirty-five million people in that country perished in another government-manufactured famine. Chinese leader Mao Zedong actually based his program on Stalin's policies of the 1930s and sought to establish control over the peasantry and eliminate potentially disloyal elements in the population. Other politically driven human catastrophes, like Pol Pot's genocidal regime in Cambodia in the 1970s and the massacre of Rwandan Tutsis by the majority Hutu population of that country in the 1990s, have been exacerbated by governments' unwillingness either to acknowledge what was happening or to allow humanitarian groups to assist the suffering. In East Timor in the 1990s, humanitarian organizations, including Médecins Sans Frontières, were kicked out of the country as rebels fought with the military in support of independence from Indonesia. In the Democratic Republic of the Congo, the Congolese government denied humanitarian organizations access to specific areas, reportedly because government officials did not want independent observers to see evidence of massacres.

Occasionally the assistance provided by humanitarian organizations is criticized. In the 1990s, humanitarian organizations provided aid to hundreds of thousands of refugees from the

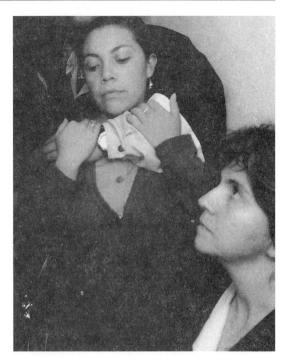

RED CROSS STAFF, DESPITE THEIR PEACEFUL MISSION, OCCASSIONALLY FALL VICTIM TO ATTACK OR CAPTURE. THIS GROUP OF RED CROSS WORKERS WAITS TO BE RELEASED AFTER BEING DETAINED BY PROTESTORS IN BOGOTA, COLOMBIA. *AP/Wide World Photos. Reproduced by permission.*

Rwandan genocide. In 1994, the majority Hutus attacked and killed hundreds of thousands of minority Tutsi. When the Tutsi fought back, hundreds of thousands of Hutu fled to what would become refugee camps. Among the refugees were—almost certainly—Hutus who had participated in the genocide. Humanitarian organizations were challenged for providing medical and food relief for killers, and for healing killers so they could continue the war. In some cases it appeared that the Interhamwe—the Hutu organization responsible for the genocide—had taken control of food distribution at the camps as a way of controlling the people.

Furthermore, many critics felt that international humanitarian organizations represented an alarming move toward globalization. Critics charged that the organizations were often ill informed regarding the nature of the crises and providing inappropriate and unsustainable solutions. They were charged with prolonging refugee crises by preventing or, through food and shelter, discouraging refugees from returning home. Some critics charged that the organizations were often fronts for political opportunists; teachers have been charged with inciting rebellion.

Political Solutions to Humanitarian Issues

Such cases as these caused many humanitarians to realize that direct political pressure might be a solution. The 1961 arrest of seven Portuguese students who publicly toasted freedom became a cause célèbre for human rights advocates who subsequently founded Amnesty International. Amnesty International focuses on correcting human rights abuses by appealing directly to the offending governments and to international public opinion for support. Many imprisoned human rights and political activists have been released or had their sentences commuted because of Amnesty International's activities. In 1977 the organization was awarded the Nobel Peace Prize.

The politicization of human rights by Amnesty International and other groups has succeeded in effecting national foreign policies, especially in the West. As Cold War tensions began to relax, humanitarian concerns impacted many of the new commercial and arms control agreements between the United States and the USSR. For example, the Jackson-Vanick amendment of 1972 linked East-West trade agreements to the Soviet government's promise to permit the emigration of many of its persecuted Jewish citizens to the United States and Israel. Other agreements between Washington and Moscow were predicated specifically on the release of Soviet political prisoners from labor camps, house arrest, or psychiatric hospitals. In 1977 U.S. President Jimmy Carter promised to incorporate human rights concerns as the defining principle in American foreign policy and criticized many American allies for their human rights violations. Humanitarian principles have occasionally caused U.S. intervention in countries the United States might not otherwise have gone. President George Bush's decision to use American Marines to oversee the distribution of food and other aid to Somalia during a famine in 1992–93 demonstrated American commitment to humanitarian relief as a matter of policy. American military intervention in possibly genocidal conflicts in Bosnia in 1995 and in Kosovo in 1999 also stand as examples of political commitments driven by humanitarian concerns.

The concept of direct humanitarian relief has also become an important principle in international politics. The collapse of the Soviet Union and its communist satellite nations in 1989–91 created large-scale opportunities for the United States Agency for International Development (USAID) and for many international financial organizations, (such as the World Bank and IMF), to sponsor development and recovery. Through the 1990s this often took the form of direct aid programs that provided material assistance and sophisticated political and economic advice. Although there have been instances of corruption and financial scandal associated with these relief activities, they nevertheless mark the dramatically increased role of humanitarian relief as a means of promoting international peace and stability.

After what was perhaps humanity's most disastrous century, the original idea of providing direct aid to the suffering, as Dunant did at Solferino, has expanded into a high-level political issue that many governments have now incorporated into their foreign policies. Largely in response to the growing power of oppression, humanitarian relief has greatly expanded in scope and manifested itself in a number of new ways— political, military, and technological, as well as medical—that attack the political sources of human catastrophes as well as their results.

BIBLIOGRAPHY

Robert Conquest. *The Harvest of Sorrow: Soviet Collectivization and the Terror-Famine.* New York: Oxford University Press, 1986.

Stephane Courtois, et. al. *The Black Book of Communism: Crimes, Terror, Repression.* Cambridge: Harvard University Press, 1999.

Jean-Claude Favez, et. al. *The Red Cross and the Holocaust.* Cambridge: Cambridge University Press, 1999.

John F. Hutchinson. *Champions of Charity: War and the Rise of the Red Cross.* Boulder, Colo.: Westview Press, 1997.

Walter LaFeber. *America, Russia, and the Cold War, 1945–1996.* 8th ed. New York: McGraw Hill, 1997.

Caroline Moorehead. *Dunant's Dream: War, Switzerland, and the History of the Red Cross.* San Francisco, Calif.: Publisher's Group West, 1999.

Leni Yahil. *The Holocaust: The Fate of European Jewry, 1932–1945.* New York: Oxford University Press, 1991.

Paul du Quenoy

IRAQ: ECONOMIC SANCTIONS

In January 2000, the United States navy seized a Russian oil tanker as it headed out of the Persian Gulf. Officials in Washington claimed that it was carrying oil from Iraq and was thus in violation of the sanctions imposed on that country in 1990 and of the 1996 agreement that allowed it to sell a limited amount of oil to purchase food, medicine, and other humanitarian supplies. The Russian government claimed that the privately owned ship had picked up its oil in Iran, but subsequent tests showed otherwise. The United States planned to sell the oil on the international market and turn the proceeds over to the United Nations to use in compensating individuals and companies that had made claims against Iraq since the 1991 Gulf War.

HISTORICAL BACKGROUND

Early History of Iraq

As recently as the thirteenth century Iraq was the heart of the Arab world and was as advanced as any culture of the time. Since then, however, the country has been far weaker. Iraq began the twentieth century as a province in the Ottoman Empire, the Turkish empire that ruled the Middle East and southern Europe from about 1500 to 1920. From the 1920s until the late 1960s, Iraq was dominated by the British and was governed by a succession of weak rulers. In 1968, the Baath (or Ba'ath) Party seized power and established one of the most powerful and ruthless regimes in the world, which has been headed by Saddam Hussein since 1979. At about the same time, money from oil began pouring into Iraq—about fifteen percent of the world's proven reserves sit under Iraqi soil.

THE CONFLICT

Iraq has been in conflict with much of the rest of the world since it invaded the small country of Kuwait in 1990. Following the war, the United Nations demanded that Iraq destroy any facilities for producing weapons of mass destruction—chemical, nuclear, and biological weapons. Iraq has not cooperated with the required inspections and has accused the United Nations, and in particular the United States, of spying. In response, the United Nations has instituted economic sanctions. Iraq can sell a specified amount of its oil for food and medicine; otherwise, Iraq may not trade with other countries.

Territorial

- Iraq believes that U.N. inspectors are infringing on Iraq's right to do as it pleases within its own border.

- The United Nations fears that Iraq will attack neighboring countries if it has weapons of mass destruction. The United Nations suspects that Iraq has used such weapons on its own Kurdish population.

Economic

- U.N. sanctions make Iraq poorer and less able to conduct war.

- Saddam Hussein and his family and friends have adequate food and luxuries. Intense poverty makes the general public angry at the West, not at their own government.

Political

- Saddam Hussein resents Western wealth and Western calls for democracy. He wants to rule Iraq with no interference from Western governments and human rights organizations.

CHRONOLOGY

1990 Iraq invades Kuwait. Operation Desert Shield is formed. U.N. resolutions authorize sanctions and use of force.

1991 The Gulf War is launched by Desert Storm. Uprisings by Kurds and Shiites occur in Iraq. UNSCOM is created.

1992 Iraq violates U.N. restrictions regarding the development of weapons of mass destruction (WMD).

1993 Iraq formally accepts U.N. conditions on WMD.

1994 Iraq acknowledges major WMD programs. Saddam Hussein's children, Saddam and Hussein Kamal, and their families defect, return, and are then executed.

1996 Limited oil sales are permitted for purchases of humanitarian aid.

1998 Iraq stops cooperating with UNSCOM. UNSCOM leaves Iraq. Air strikes begin and continue into 2000.

1999 Iraq rejects plans for a new U.N. inspection team.

From 1980 to 1988, Iraq fought a bitter and bloody war with its neighbor Iran. During the war, the United States and its allies drew closer to the regime in Baghdad, the capital of Iraq and headed by Saddam Hussein, because of Iraq's willingness to take on the new Islamic republic in Iran. After the Iran/Iraq war, Iraq was in serious economic trouble. Despite the billions of dollars it made from the sale of oil and the significant progress it had made in the 1970s, for instance in increasing the literacy rate, Iraq was once again one of the poorest countries in the region.

As a result of its poverty, the Iraqi regime began demanding aid from other oil-rich countries in the Persian Gulf. The Iraqi government claimed with some justification that it had borne tremendous sacrifices in the war with Iran and that those other countries benefited and they should, therefore, help defray Iraq's costs. Iraq was especially insistent that its neighbor, Kuwait, provide aid. Before 1918 the two had been administered together in the Ottoman Empire, and some scholars and politicians felt that the tiny country should have been incorporated into Iraq following the disintegration of the Ottoman Empire after World War I.

In 1990 Baghdad also claimed that Kuwait was stealing Iraq's oil by drilling diagonally under the border and pumping oil that was properly Iraq's. Since oil lies in large reserves under the surface of the earth, it is possible to remove oil from deposits that are not directly under a country's land. As that spring and summer of 1990 wore on, Saddam Hussein's government grew ever more menacing toward its neighbor.

Meanwhile, the United States and other Western powers watched the growing tension in the Middle East warily. They faced other, seemingly more important, issues, most notably the ongoing collapse of communism in Europe and what would soon be the former Soviet Union. Furthermore, the administration of U.S. President George Bush did not have a firm or fixed view on Iraq. As noted above, the Western powers had aided Iraq during the war with Iran. For example, Iraq was the largest recipient of U.S. agricultural aid during most of the 1980s. Finally, most Western analysts were convinced that, despite his harsh rhetoric, Saddam Hussein was one of the more pragmatic and moderate leaders in the Middle East. After all, Iraq had one of the most secular, or least religious, regimes in the Middle East and, among other things, allowed women to hold positions of authority in government and professional life.

As the tensions mounted, Iraqi authorities looked to the United States to gauge how it would react to Iraqi aggression against Kuwait, but Iraq did not get a clear message. In the most notorious event, Iraq came away from a meeting with U.S. Ambassador April Glaspie believing that the United States would not act if Iraq invaded Kuwait. Members of the Bush administration insist that they made it as clear as possible to the Iraqis that any aggressive action would bring a swift and strong reply from the United States and its allies. However, it appears that, in the last days before the invasion, the United States intelligence community was split down the middle. About half of the Bush administration analysts were convinced that Iraq would invade; the others were convinced that officials in Baghdad were bluffing.

The Gulf War

Iraq was not bluffing. On August 2, 1990, Iraqi troops poured over the border into Kuwait. Within a matter of hours, they occupied all of tiny Kuwait. The Kuwaiti royal family and many other members of the elite fled.

MAP OF IRAQ. (© Maryland Cartographics. Reprinted with permission.)

Following its rapid victory over Kuwait, Iraq seemed poised to invade Saudi Arabia as well. Conquering Saudi Arabia would have given Iraq control of well over one quarter of the world's oil reserves, which it could have used to threaten the economic security of the entire Western world.

Because of the threat to Saudi Arabia, the Western world reacted much more quickly and much more firmly than Baghdad expected. Within weeks, a United States-led coalition began assem-

bling what it called Operation Desert Shield—a force that would ultimately number over eight hundred thousand troops. The hope was that Operation Desert Shield would both deter the Iraqis from any further aggressive behavior and would compel Iraq to withdraw from Kuwait—a phenomenon that political scientists call "coercive diplomacy."

During the rest of 1990, intense activity occurred on the diplomatic and military fronts. The United States worked through the United

SADDAM HUSSEIN

1937– Born on April 28, 1937, in Tikrit, a poor town about one hundred miles from Baghdad, he is known in Iraq as Saddam Hussein Al-Takriti. His father died before he was born, and he was raised by relatives who reportedly abused him. At the age of eighteen, he moved to Baghdad and became politically active, later participating in an attempt to assassinate the Iraqi prime minister.

He fled to Egypt and studied law. Returning to Iraq in 1963, he attended Baghdad School of Law. Later that year, Hussein was imprisoned, escaped, and became the leader of the Baath party, leading a coup that returned the party to power in 1968. As vice president, Hussein directed the nationalization of Iraq's oil reserves in 1972.

In 1979 Hussein became president, and quickly appointed himself to multiple governmental positions. Legally, the Baath Party, through the Revolutionary Command Council, runs Iraq. In fact, Iraq is now run, largely, by Saddam Hussein, his sons, and a few close confidants, many of whom are also from Tikrit.

Nations to put together an unprecedented coalition of countries in opposition to the Iraqi invasion. The coalition included not only the traditional U.S. allies such as the United Kingdom, Canada, and France but a number of Arab states including Saudi Arabia, Egypt, and Syria, marking the first time that any major Arab power allied with the West against a fellow Arab state. The coalition also spearheaded a diplomatic effort around the world to try to find a solution to the crisis. The French and Soviets, in particular, were particularly active and hoped to use their history of good relations with Iraq to act as intermediaries.

Meanwhile, the United Nations Security Council imposed economic sanctions to deny Iraq access to the world's oil market and thus cut off Iraq's supply of cash. With the sanctions, the U.N. tried to eliminate Iraq's ability to import needed goods to keep its economy and, especially, its military going.

But the sanctions didn't work as planned. Therefore, on November 29, 1990, the United Nations Security Council passed Resolution 678, authorizing the coalition of allies to use force to compel Iraq to withdraw from Kuwait if it did not

do so before January 15, 1991. Iraq failed to comply with the ultimatum from the United Nations. Therefore, on the morning of January 17, Operation Desert Shield became Operation Desert Storm. For thirty-nine days, bombs from allied planes and missiles rained down on Iraq, inflicting tremendous damage. But the initial damage did not prompt the Iraqi government to surrender. On February 24, the allied ground attack began. The allied ground forces encountered surprisingly weak resistance from what were thought to be well trained and disciplined troops. Within three days, the Iraqi forces had pulled out of Kuwait, and U.S. President George Bush announced a cease-fire that the Iraqi government accepted. By doing so, Iraq agreed to abide by all the resolutions passed by the U.N. Security Council in the months following Iraq's invasion of Kuwait.

U.S. President Bush and his colleagues accepted a cease fire rather than continuing to pursue the retreating Iraqis to Baghdad and, possibly, overthrowing Saddam Hussein himself. They justified their decision by stressing that the U.N. mandate did not extend beyond forcing Iraq out of Kuwait. The pursuit to Baghdad would likely prove very costly for allied, as well as Iraqi, forces, and such a campaign might not have led to the creation of a more democratic or human regime.

The allies' decision was questioned, however, in the months after the war ended. Uprisings began among the Kurds in the north and the Shiites in the south, who are minorities within Iraq. Allied governments were able to mount a massive campaign to help the Kurds, who had set up what can only be considered a de facto state of their own. On the other hand, the allies were unable to help the Shiites. The regime in Baghdad cracked down ruthlessly, killing thousands of people and draining the marshes, which are vital to the regional economy and way of life.

Economic Sanctions and Weapons of Mass Destruction

Saddam Hussein remained in power. The Iraqi government was killing thousands of its own citizens. The war had settled little other than reversing the Iraqi invasion of Kuwait. The regime in Baghdad seemed more like that of a rogue state than it had before Iraq invaded Kuwait.

As a result of the situation within Iraq, all the resolutions passed by the United States before the war and accepted by Iraq at the time of its surrender remained in effect. Others resolutions were later added. The limits imposed on Iraq in an attempt to force it to leave Kuwait were largely still in place nearly ten years later.

These resolutions placed limits on Iraqi behavior. The economic sanctions initially imposed by U.N. Security Council Resolution 661 were passed in August 1990. The resolution bans almost all foreign trade with Iraq and prohibits U.N. member states and companies working in them to import to or export from Iraq. In 1996, the Security Council passed Resolution 986 which modified these rules and allowed Iraq to sell up to $2 billion of oil a year on the international market. The proceeds from those sales could be used to buy much-needed food, medical supplies, and other humanitarian goods. The funds were to be controlled by the United Nations, though once the material got to Iraq, the food, medical supplies and other goods would be distributed to the people primarily by the Iraqi government.

When the sanctions were initially developed they were tied to explicit goals—unconditional withdrawal, paying for damage done in Kuwait, and eliminating the Iraqi programs to develop weapons of mass destruction (WMD). In April 1991, following Iraq's withdrawal from Kuwait, the U.N. modified the conditions of Resolution 687 and tied the conditions to Iraq ending the WMD program. This resolution introduced the second category of sanctions, which barred Iraq from developing "nuclear weapons or nuclear-weapons-usable material" and stated that UNSCOM (United Nations Special Commission) would: "Carry out immediate on-site inspections of Iraq's biological, chemical and missile capabilities, based on Iraq's declaration and the designation of any additional locations by the Special Commission itself." Once it was satisfied that the Iraqi government was not developing weapons of mass destruction, negotiations about ending the economic sanctions could begin.

Many observers are convinced that the Bush and, later, the Clinton administrations, had a different agenda. Some observers believe that the United States was prepared to use its veto in the Security Council to keep sanctions in place as long as Saddam Hussein was in power. This meant that, most likely, the sanctions would remain in effect until Saddam Hussein died or was removed from power.

The U.N. and allied officials appeared to expect the inspection of Iraq for WMD material to be a brief operation. Iraq was given fifteen days to provide information on the location of all its WMD facilities. UNSCOM would then have four

THE U.N. EMBARGO OF IRAQ HAS LED TO NATION-WIDE FOOD RATIONING; CITIZENS SUCH AS THIS MAN IN THE CAPITOL OF BAGHDAD PICK UP THEIR MONTH-LY ALLOTMENT BUT SAY THAT IT IS NOT ENOUGH. *(AP/Wide World Photos. Reproduced by permission.)*

months to devise a plan for making certain that Iraq was in compliance with the resolution.

By linking the ending of sanctions to the weapons inspections, the U.N. gave tremendous responsibility to the people who were responsible for conducting the inspections. While the inspectors officially worked for the U.N. and other international organizations (including the International Atomic Energy Agency), virtually all of them came from the United States, Great Britain, and other advanced industrialized countries. Generally the only people with the necessary technical skills

HIGH OIL PRICES AND INCREASING IRAQI FRUSTRATION WITH U.N. EMBARGOES HAVE LED SOME TRADERS TO GO TO GREAT LENGTHS TO EXPORT OIL FROM IRAQ. THIS RUSSIAN VESSEL HAS BEEN DETAINED BY THE U.S. NAVY AFTER IT WAS DETERMINED THAT THE SHIP CARRIED SMUGGLED OIL. *(AP/Wide World Photos. Reproduced by permission.)*

for conducting the investigations were from industrialized nations. The fact that the inspectors were from the West—Iraq's former military foe—has not made reaching an agreement between the inspectors and Iraq easy.

UNSCOM had anything but a brief mission. UNSCOM and Iraq have been negotiating and posturing for seven years. Meanwhile, the sanctions and, to a lesser degree, the inspection requirement grew ever more controversial outside of Iraq.

Iraqi officials appeared to do what they could to make UNSCOM's work difficult. Time and

again, the Iraqi government refused to turn over information or allow the UNSCOM inspectors into "presidential sites" and other facilities that UNSCOM thought housed WMD facilities. In 1997, UNSCOM was still trying to conduct thorough inspection and Iraq was still claiming the inspections were an unwarranted invasion of privacy and national sovereignty. In 1998, Iraq finally forced UNSCOM to leave once it became clear that the inspectors were closing in on what inspectors were convinced were biological weapons facilities. The Iraqi government accused the inspectors of spying. In late 1999, the U.N. instituted a new weapons inspection system. Iraq once again refused to cooperate making the lifting of sanctions anytime soon unlikely.

The Iraqis and what is left of the 1990–91 coalition have come close to war on several occasions since the cease-fire in 1991. In 1993, the U.S. twice launched cruise missiles, the first time targeting a factory thought to be part of the nuclear weapons program. British and American planes have routinely fired on Iraqi fighters that allegedly violated the no-fly zones in the northern and southern parts of the country. Last, but not least, the allies launched four hundred fifty cruise missiles and carried out six hundred fifty bombing raids after UNSCOM left in 1999.

The allies and UNSCOM did make considerable progress in limiting Iraq's capability to wage war. Iraqi military forces are no more than about forty percent of what they were in 1990. Most of Iraq's chemical and nuclear facilities have been destroyed, though both could be re-started fairly quickly and easily should the Iraqi government choose to do so. Less progress was made on dismantling Iraq's biological weapons and missile programs, but even these programs have been seriously limited.

The standoff over weapons inspections continues and, therefore, sanctions remain in effect. The British and American governments do not appear to be willing to accept anything less than complete proof that the WMD programs have been permanently dismantled and will, in all likelihood, require the removal of Saddam Hussein from office before they seriously consider lifting sanctions. The other three permanent members of the Security Council—China, France, and Russia—seem willing to ease and perhaps fully lift the sanctions. However, the United States and United Kingdom seem likely to use their veto power to keep sanctions in effect without major changes in Iraq.

RECENT HISTORY AND THE FUTURE

Humanitarian Impact of the Sanctions

While the standoff regarding weapons inspections continues, and the U.S. and British governments appear unwilling to accept anything less than absolute proof that WMD capability has been dismantled, there has been criticism of the sanctions. Since the mid-1990s, international attention has focused on the social and economic impact in Iraq of the sanctions. Critics of the

sanctions have chronicled the human toll the sanctions have taken while noting that the sanctions have not moved Iraq noticeably closer to complying with the 1990 and 1991 resolutions.

Iraq has not allowed outside observers to systematically study living conditions in Iraq and so accurately assessing the impact of the sanctions is difficult. Available statistics are unreliable and should be treated as estimates. However unreliable, the statistics still describe a tragedy of massive proportions.

Before the Gulf War, Iraq gained the hard currency—money—it needed to import food and other consumer goods primarily by selling oil. Sanctions all but completely cut off the flow of oil and, hence, of cash. One estimate suggests that Iraq lost about $130 billion in oil revenues during the 1990s.

The most reliable estimate is that approximately five hundred thousand people have died directly or indirectly as a result of the economic sanctions. Some estimates put the total deaths at a million people, though most observers think that figure is unlikely to be true. However, even if the million-person figure is twice the actual number, the sanctions-related deaths would still be several times the number that occurred during the fighting of the Gulf War itself.

The sanctions have hit Iraq's health care system particularly hard. The death rates for infants and children under five are both more than twice what they were before the war. There are unconfirmed reports that single syringes are sterilized and reused up to seventy times. In 1997, human organs—kidneys, livers—could be sold for $2,500 on the black market. Water purification supplies are not routinely available, which increases exposure to cholera and other diseases. A 1997 U.N. report found that more than ten percent of Iraqi children were acutely malnourished and a third had had their growth stunted due to a lack of food.

The industrial infrastructure of what had been one of the most advanced economies in the Middle East is in ruins. There is some food processing and clothing manufacturing, but otherwise, the country produces very little. Indeed, in 2000, it could not maintain its pipelines well enough to pump the full amount of oil it is allowed to sell. The salary of an average worker dropped from $300 a month before the war to just $7 a month. Once middle class, many Iraqis have been forced to sell such luxuries as their furniture.

Moreover, revenue from the sale of oil has not brought relief to Iraqi civilians, at least as envisioned

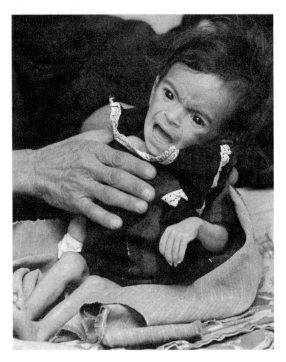

DUE TO A SHORTAGE OF FOOD AND MEDICINE, THIS YOUNG IRAQI GIRL NEEDS MORE THAN THE COMFORTING OF HER GRANDMOTHER. *(AP/Wide World Photos. Reproduced by permission.)*

by the U.N. Much of the material bought under the program has been diverted into the hands of the Baath Party elite and not reached the intended population. Iraqis who can take advantage of the black market still live luxuriously. Most of the elite, of course, are close to Saddam Hussein and his family. Even more galling to critics of the Iraqi regime is the fact that the "Iraqi people" gave Saddam Hussein a sumptuous new palace to celebrate his sixtieth birthday in 1997. Two years later, the regime opened the new city of Saddamiat that had a theme park with a 30-foot-high statue of the dictator.

And, as critics of sanctions in general frequently point out, they have not had much of an impact in forcing Iraq's compliance with U.N. resolutions. As noted earlier, the Iraqi government has never more than grudgingly complied with UNSCOM inspectors. While Iraq did publicly accept the territorial integrity of Kuwait in 1993, it has taken few other steps to ease the international community's fears that it might return to an aggressive policy once sanctions were lifted.

Yet, advocates of continuing the sanctions assert that the Iraqi regime is largely responsible for the suffering and that the poverty and health care crisis would have occurred even if the international community had allowed Iraq to sell as much oil as it wanted. Without sanctions the authorities in

Baghdad would not have cooperated as much as they have with the weapons inspectors. And the supplies available to Iraq have undoubtedly reduced the disease and death to some—unfortunately unquantifiable—degree.

Sanctions seem likely to remain in place for the foreseeable future. Despite increased U.S. and British support for exiled Iraqi dissident groups, there seems little chance that they—or anyone else—can force Saddam Hussein from power at this time. And, it is hard to see any future American or British administration changing its policies as long as he is still in office. Meanwhile, criticisms of sanctions mount, while their supporters have a hard time demonstrating that the sanctions are effectively addressing concerns regarding weapons production. In the end, the sanctions against Iraq also point out one of the most unsettling conclusions about international relations today. Sanctions and other forms of coercive diplomacy are at best imperfect policies.

BIBLIOGRAPHY

Batatu, Hanna. *The Old Social Classes and the Revolutionary Movement of Iraq: A Study of Iraq's Old Landed and Commercial Classes and of its Communists, Ba'athists, and Free Officers.* Princeton, N.J.: Princeton University Press, 1978.

Bengio, Offra. *Saddam's Word: Political Discourse in Iraq.* New York: Oxford University Press, 1998.

Byman, Daniel. "A Farewell to Arms Inspections," *Foreign Affairs.* (Jan/Feb 2000): 110–132.

Cockburn, Andrew and Patrick Cockburn. *Out of the Ashes: The Resurrection of Saddam Hussein.* New York: HarperCollins, 1999.

Dawisha, Adeed. "Identity and political survival in Saddam's Iraq," *Middle East Journal.* 53 (1999): 553–567.

Fuller, Graham and Ian Lesser. "Persian Gulf Myths," *Foreign Affairs* 76 (May-June 1997): 42–53.

Gordon, Michael and Bernard Trainor. *The General's War.* Boston, Mass.: Little, Brown, 1995.

Herrmann, Richard. "Coercive Diplomacy and the Crisis over Kuwait, 1990-1991," in *The Limits of Coercive Diplomacy.* Boulder, Colo.: Westview Press, 1994.

Karsh, Efraim and Inari Rautsi. *Saddam Hussein: A Political Biography.* New York: Free Press, 1991.

Al-Khalil Samir. *Republic of Fear: The Inside Story of Saddam's Iraq.* New York: Pantheon, 1990.

Marr, Phebe. *The Modern History of Iraq.* Boulder, Colo.: Westview, 1985.

United Nations. *Report of the Secretary General Pursuant to Paragraph Three of Resolution 1111 (1997).* 28 November 1997.

Charles Hauss

KASHMIR: WAR IN THE HIMALAYAS

In May of 1998, India surprised the world by detonating a nuclear explosive device. Pakistan, India's neighbor and long-time adversary, responded with its own series of nuclear detonations. With these events, both countries joined the "nuclear club" of publicly acknowledged nuclear-capable states, and drew international attention to the decades-long hostility which has dominated their relationship since both received their independence from the British Empire in 1947. Newspapers and television journalists reminded us that India and Pakistan have fought three wars in their short history. As the century drew to a close, South Asia seemed destined to take the place of Europe as the mostly likely spot on the planet for a devastating nuclear war.

A landmark summit between the leaders of India and Pakistan in early 1999 seemed to ease tensions, and reassured the world that a nuclear conflagration may not be inevitable. For the first time, a direct bus service between Delhi, India and Lahore, Pakistan was established, allowing daily contact between the citizens of long-time enemies. But in May of 1999, tensions reached new heights when armed forces from Pakistan infiltrated a mountainous area of the disputed Indo-Pakistani border. Indian armed forces responded with an all-out ground and air assault; the resulting fighting raged for eleven weeks, and left around one thousand dead. The fighting ended when Pakistan, which maintained that the infiltrators were militants fighting against Indian rule in the state of Kashmir, pulled those forces back across to its side of the line. The confrontation left both India and Pakistan—and the international community—badly shaken. During the eleven weeks of fighting, Indian and Pakistani armed forces had come into

THE CONFLICT

Kashmir, a mountainous area best known for the famous Himalayan Mountains, has been the site of considerable warfare during the last fifty years. The Kashmiri population is two-thirds Muslim and one-third non-Muslim. Before 1947 Kashmir was part of the larger, British-ruled India, including modern-day India, Pakistan, and Bangladesh. Since the partition into predominately Muslim Pakistan and predominately Hindu India in 1947, there is virtually constant conflict over whether Kashmir should be with India or Pakistan, or independent.

Religious

*   India believes that is must protect the large number of Hindus living in Kashmir. Moreover, India is a secular democracy with many religions living within its borders. If it admits that there is not room in India for Muslims—by allowing Kashmir independence or unification with Pakistan—minority religious groups all over India may rebel.

*   Pakistan believes that the Muslims in Kashmir are being denied self-determination. Muslims from all over the world come to fight on behalf of Kashmir.

Economic

*   Kashmir contains numerous important trade routes.

*   At the time of partition, Kashmir's transportation and trade links were primarily with western Pakistan.

CHRONOLOGY

711 Arab Muslims come to India, bringing Islam to a predominately Hindu region. Eventually, the region is ruled by the Caliph of Islam, located in Baghdad in modern day Iraq.

1400 The British establish a trading company, the British East India Company, which won the rule of India, working through local leaders.

1857 The Sepoy Rebellion.

1885 The Indian National Congress is formed.

1886 The All-India Muslim League is founded.

1947 India and Pakistan are partitioned and received their independence from the British Empire. Fighting breaks out over the province of Jammu and Kashmir; it is eventually divided into Indian-held Kashmir and Pakistani-held Azad ("free") Kashmir.

1949 A cease-fire is called between the sides.

1962 India loses the Sino-Indian War, over territory disputed by China and India.

1963 Riots in the Vale of Kashmir (India-held Kashmir).

1965 India and Pakistan fight in the Rann of Kutch.

1971 Bangladesh is created following another India-Pakistani war.

1972 The Simla agreement.

1989 The Jannu and Kashmir Liberation Front kidnap the daughter of an official in exchange for the release of prisoners.

1990 An estimated one hundred guerrilla and paramilitary groups in Kashmir carry out actions during the 1990s. Some join together in the All-Party Hurriyat Conference.

1998 India detonates a nuclear device and Pakistan responds in kind.

1999 A summit raises hopes of reduced tensions, but Pakistani troops infiltrate part of the disputed territory, resulting in an eleven-week ground war.

direct conflict, with Indian and Pakistani air force jets—some capable of carrying nuclear weapons—dueling each other over the skies of the disputed territory. While the nuclear crisis was averted, the international community saw the fighting as a reminder of how dangerously close to total war the two new nuclear powers might have been.

The nuclear tests of 1998 and the crisis of 1999 also brought back to international attention the key issue which continues to divide India and Pakistan: the province of Jammu and Kashmir, generally referred to as Kashmir. The portion of border that still needs to be defined between the two neighbors divides the territory in two, with each side's army facing the other across a Line of Control (LOC) that neither recognizes as a permanent border. As the only Muslim-majority territory in Hindu-dominated India, the Indian portion of Kashmir also poses serious internal threats to Indian security and politics. An internal rebellion, which India asserts is supported and encouraged by Muslim-dominated Pakistan, has claimed some twenty-five thousand lives since 1989. Militant groups of Kashmiri Muslims opposed to

Hindu Indian rule frequently bring Indian and Pakistani forces into conflict near the LOC, and sometimes engage in high-profile international actions, like the hijacking of an Indian Airlines jet in December of 1999. Armed groups operating inside Kashmir demand union with their Muslim brethren in Pakistan or independence for the province. The territory thus presents a challenge for both South Asia and the world: to get India, Pakistan, and the Kashmiris to agree on a future that will insure the stability of the region and defuse the tension between two nuclear-armed neighbors.

HISTORICAL BACKGROUND

Kashmir: Geography and People

The territory of Kashmir is located in the northwest corner of India, at the northern end of the border between India and Pakistan. It is nearly eighty-six thousand square miles in size, roughly equivalent to the state of Minnesota. Of this area, some sixteen thousand square miles in the Aksai Chin region is claimed by China in a separate dispute between India and China, and has been occupied by China since the Sino-Indian war of 1962. Of the remaining territory, approximately thirty thousand square miles are on the Pakistani side of the LOC, and constitute what Pakistan calls "Azad Kashmir", meaning Free Kashmir; India refers to this area as Pakistan-Occupied Kashmir, or POK. India controls the balance of roughly forty thousand square miles, including the Vale of Kashmir, the heart of the entire Kashmir region and the location of its traditional capital, Srinigar.

The Indian and Pakistani portions of the territory each play a different role in their state's political system. India has attempted to incorporate its portion of Kashmir into its federal system, which resembles the United States' arrangement in which regional territories are given a measure of self-government and allowed to elect local parliaments and leaders. For Kashmir, as for other potential problem areas, India created the concept of "special status" federalism, enshrined for Kashmir in the Indian constitution under Article 370. In essence, this status was meant to guarantee Kashmir its distinctiveness as a Muslim-majority area and give it greater freedom and self-rule than other regions in the Indian political system. In practice, India has often overridden or dismissed Kashmir's regional government and imposed direct rule by the central government as a means of restoring order and combating separatist rebellion and Pakistani involvement in Kashmiri politics. Kashmir's last elected government was dismissed in 1990, and the Indian portion of the province has been under direct rule from Delhi since.

Like India, Pakistan has a federal system that devolves some power to regional governments while running national affairs from the central government in the capital of Islamabad. The Pakistani-controlled areas of Kashmir are divided into two parts: the Northern Areas, a sparsely inhabited region in the northernmost portion of the territory that is ruled directly by the Pakistani central government in Islamabad; and Azad Kashmir, a crescent-shaped region wrapped around the Indian-controlled Vale of Kashmir, whose provincial capital is in Muzaffarabad. Azad Kashmir has a provincial government similar to those in the four Pakistani provinces (Sind, Punjab, Balochistan, and the Northwest Territories), but it does not have the same status within the federal government as the four larger regions. Traditionally, within the central government there has been a Minister for Kashmiri Affairs and Northern Areas responsible for overseeing policy in those regions. Thus, Azad Kashmir holds a "special status" within Pakistan similar to Indian Kashmir's constitutional status. However, while the Indian government often feuds with local Kashmiri rulers, the Pakistani government has generally enjoyed a good relationship to the leadership in Muzaffarabad.

Physically, the territory of Kashmir is important for both India and Pakistan. One of the most mountainous regions of the world, it sits astride a number of important transportation routes through central Asia, linking India, Pakistan, Afghanistan, and China, including the Karakoram pass, one of the main routes between the southern Himalayas and western China. It is the last area of undefined border between India and Pakistan, and is thus a potential security threat to both sides. The northern end of the LOC is completely undefined in the region of the Siachen Glacier, which has pushed both India and Pakistan to maintain a substantial military presence in an otherwise inhospitable region. For Pakistan, Kashmir's geography is particularly important. Both the Indus and Jhelum rivers—Pakistan's main sources of fresh water—pass through the province; in 1948, during the first Indo-Pakistani war, India cut off portions of Pakistan's water supply, devastating Pakistani agriculture. Finally, the Vale of Kashmir, in the center of the region between the Pir Panjal and Great Himalaya mountain ranges, holds tremendous potential as a tourist site; even during the current unrest, travelers from around the world come to visit every year, bringing an important income source to the region.

Beyond the region's physical importance, however, the conflict in Kashmir has always been at its heart about the people who live there. There are roughly eight million residents in the Indian portion of Kashmir, and an additional two million in Pakistani-controlled Azad Kashmir. The population in Indian Kashmir is roughly two-thirds Muslim and one-third non-Muslim; most of the latter are Hindus, although there are also Sikhs and members of other religions. In Azad Kashmir, the population is overwhelmingly Muslim. In Indian-held Kashmir, the Muslim and non-Muslim populations are largely, although not completely, separated by the Pir Panjal mountain range. The Muslims tend to be concentrated in the Vale around the traditional capital, Srinagar, while the Hindu population is concentrated south of the mountains around the city of Jammu. Most Kashmiris, regardless of religion, speak the Kashmiri language, which is one of eighteen officially recognized languages in India. Because of the tremendous diversity of languages in both India

A PAKISTANI SOLDIER GUARDS THE CHULUNG GLACIER, AN AREA MUTALLY CLAIMED BY INDIA AND PAKISTAN. *(Corbis. Reproduced by permission.)*

and Pakistan, and their history of creation as modern states, language has often been less important politically than religion in determining political loyalties.

South Asia and the Coming of Islam

The relationship between Hindus and Muslims is a very old one, dating back to 711 A.D. when Arab Muslims first made their way over Persia to the Indian subcontinent, bringing the new religion with them. Prior to this point, India was dominated primarily by Hindu rulers, or rajas, who presided over a feudal structure based largely on the Hindu caste system, which divided peoples by birth into different social classes. The Islamic invasion introduced a different value system; the Islamic faith taught that all were equal in the eyes of Allah, although early Muslim rulers often discriminated between Arabs and non-Arabs. The initial Muslim incursions brought control of the Indus valley—the regions of Sind and Punjab— under the control of the Caliph of Islam in Baghdad, in modern day Iraq. There the new rulers converted substantial portions of the population to the new faith. Muslim rule continued even as the central Islamic empire, run from Baghdad, began to loosen; in 871 Arab princes in Sind and Punjab established independent dynasties of their own, thus beginning the history of local Muslim rule in South Asia.

Over the next three hundred years, relations between Muslims and Hindus consisted mainly of warfare, as Muslim rulers in central Asia staged raids into Hindu territory to plunder the kingdoms there. The most infamous (to Hindus) of these rulers was Mahmud, who established an empire centered near what is now Kabul in Afghanistan, and who conducted some seventeen campaigns of plunder into northern India between 1000 and 1025. In 1175 Muhammed of Ghur, a central Asian leader, began a determined conquest of northern India. By 1236 his son had been established as Sultan of Delhi, representative of the caliph in Baghdad, and had extended his rule as far east as Bengal. This early empire collapsed some one hundred years later, but was replaced in the mid-1500s by a unified Mughal empire led by Muhammed Akbar. By the end of the sixteenth century, Akbar had conquered everything from Afghanistan through present-day Pakistan and northern India to the Bengal region, and brought a unified Muslim rule to much of the Indian subcontinent.

The Mughal empire generated more converts for Islam, but also ushered in a period of relative peace between the religions. Prominent Hindus were invited to take part in Akbar's administration, and some 15 percent of the administrative class were Hindus. Hindu literature and art were encouraged, and some important Hindu customs and beliefs (like the stricture against slaughtering cows) were incorporated into Mughal law. By incorporating elements of both Muslim and Hindu culture, the Muslim Mughal rulers who succeeded Akbar were able to maintain their rule over a majority Hindu population through the seventeenth century. During this period, the Taj Mahal—simultaneously a monument to Islam and one of the most enduring symbols of Indian culture—was built.

By 1700 however, the policy of tolerance by the Muslim rulers had been abandoned in favor of a strict Islamic rule. Hindu lords and peasants alike rose in rebellion against their Islamic rulers, draining the resources of empire and tearing it apart from within. The descendants of Akbar fell to fighting amongst themselves, and by the middle of the 1700s the Mughal empire was in tatters, having sown the seeds of discontent and distrust between the Muslim and Hindu communities, and giving the newly arrived British the opportunity to add India to their growing world empire.

South Asia and the Coming of the British

The first British, French, and Portuguese arrived in India as traders and merchants as early as the 1400s. The British were the first to establish a significant presence, primarily in coastal cities like Bombay and Calcutta. These first outposts were primarily private ventures, organized under the British East India Company, although with substantial support from the British government. By 1700 some twelve hundred Englishmen were living in Calcutta, working for and overseeing the factories of the Company. The British soon became involved in local politics as a means of enriching themselves further; as they did in other places around they world, they allied themselves with local rulers and used the tendency of local nobility to struggle for power amongst themselves (particularly as the Mughal empire was collapsing) to become the "power behind the throne" in large areas of India.

In their process of extending political influence, the British learned to make full use of caste and religious tensions in Indian society. Rival groups, whether within families, local nobility, or religious communities, were pitted against each other, with each needing British backing to insure victory in the local struggle for power. In the process, British East India Company representatives exacerbated existing tensions between Muslims and Hindus across India. By the time the remaining Mughal leaders united in 1764 to attempt to push the British out of their realm, their empire had been significantly weakened; the resulting British victory at Baksar on the Ganges spelled the end of the Mughal empire and the beginning of British dominance in India.

The British quickly learned that they could not rule the entire subcontinent themselves, and that any attempt to do so would lead to more uprisings against their rule. Correspondingly, they developed a system of efficient administration to work with local leaders and the existing power structure, making sure to spread the benefits of empire among Indians as well as British merchants. The result was an increasingly large empire in India, still run mostly by representatives of the British East India Company. By 1850 British holdings in India stretched from Bengal in the east to the Indus river in the west, Kashmir in the north, and all the way to the southern tip of the peninsula and across to the island of Ceylon in the south. Within this empire, some local leaders were permitted to retain titular control of their lands, so long as they acceded to British rule. But as the British extended their control over more and more of India's land and economy, conflict and rebellion were, perhaps, inevitable.

Indian Nationalism, Muslim Nationalism, and the Anti-Colonial Struggle

The first serious anti-British revolt in India had the effect of strengthening, rather than weakening, British control over the colony. In 1857 after a series of British social reform laws which offended Hindu and Muslim practices, a rebellion broke out among the ranks of "sepoys"—native Indians who were paid or pressed into service with the British Army. The rebellion was sparked by a cultural blunder on the part of the British: in introducing the new Enfield rifle to native troops, the British attempted to force sepoy troops to bite the tips off of paper ammunition cartridges which had been smeared with animal fat. To Hindus, for whom cows are sacred, and Muslims, for whom the eating of pigs is profane, this proved the final piece of evidence to convince them that their British masters were betraying them into defiling their religion, in an effort to weaken the people for conversion to Christianity. The resulting rebellion briefly wrested control of much of India from British forces. By the end of 1858, however, the rebellion had been crushed, and control of India passed from the East India Company to the British government itself. One of the British crown's first acts was to return local rule to some 570 local princes and nobles—including a Hindu *maharaja*

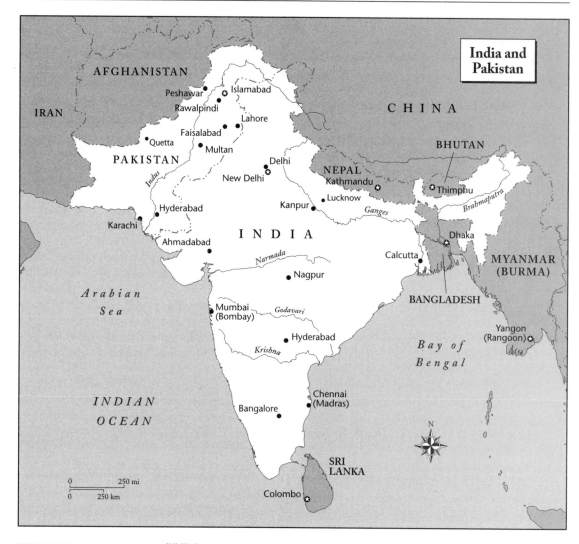

MAP OF INDIA AND PAKISTAN. *(XNR Productions Inc.)*

(a prince) in Kashmir—in exchange for their alliance with British power. The British government also tightened its grip on India and began to implement the educational and administrative systems of British rule across India.

The consolidation of British rule also brought modern education and ideas to the elite of India, and thus helped to spur the development of a pan-Indian identity and Indian nationalism. The growing sense of injustice in the wake of the Sepoy Rebellion and tightened British control led to the formation of the Indian National Congress in 1885, with representatives from across the subcontinent. From its inception, the Congress was overwhelmingly Hindu, leading disaffected Muslim leaders to seek other avenues to protest British rule. Britain exacerbated this difference by dividing the administrative province of Bengal in 1905,

creating a Muslim-majority East Bengal and a Hindu-majority (but non-Bengali-speaking) West Bengal. The partition convinced both Hindus and Muslims of the destructive nature of British rule, while 'proving' to the Hindus that the British were siding with the Muslims and granting the Muslim community a new potential base of power from which to organize. A year later, the All-India Muslim League was created in Dacca, the capital of the newly created East Bengal.

With the creation of the Muslim League as an alternative to the Indian National Congress, a clear choice was created within the anti-British movement over India's future. As British rule continued after World War I, each organization became increasingly identified with its leaders: Muhammed Ali Jinnah of the Muslim League, and Mohandas Gandhi and Jawaharal Nehru of the

Indian National Congress. Although the League and Congress briefly allied in 1916 in a call for Indian self-rule, cooperation collapsed in the early 1920s as violence and tensions rose between Hindus and Muslims, both of which were increasingly convinced that the other was in league with the British in maintaining foreign repression over India. By 1928 Jinnah and other Muslim elites had totally ruled out any formula for India's future which did not allow for a separate Muslim electorate; in 1930 the Muslim League began calling for a separate Muslim state, to be named Pakistan (meaning "Land of the Pure"). Nehru and Gandhi continued to press for a unified, secular India that encompassed peoples of all faiths, but as World War II approached it became increasingly clear that this was an unlikely outcome.

The arrival of World War II brought further crises to the relationship between Britain and India. The British needed Indian support, but had neither time nor resources to command it against the Indian will. Both the Indian National Congress and the Muslim League sensed that the war presented an opportunity, but they continued to argue about the future shape of the subcontinent. During the war, Britain attempted to negotiate with both groups by offering future independence in exchange for Indian support of the British war effort. While some Indians supported Britain, many did not, and the end result was that by 1945, Britain was little closer to solving its "India problem" than it had been in 1930.

The Tragedy of Partition: British De-Colonization, and the Origins of the Kashmir Crisis

With the end of World War II, it became clear that Britain had neither desire nor ability to maintain control of India for very long. The continued division between the INC and Muslim League over one-state versus two-state solutions, however, presented the British with a thorny problem: to whom would they turn over authority and control? In 1946, the British government made one final attempt to bridge the divide, bringing together leaders from both sides to suggest a unified, federal structure for India that would give Muslims, and other minorities, local and regional autonomy. The agreement collapsed, and by August 1946 waves of violence began to sweep across India, resulting in thousands of deaths.

Having failed to create an agreement on a unified India, Britain accepted the Muslim League's demand for partition and announced on July 15, 1947 that one month later "two independent Dominions" would be created and would be called India and Pakistan. The announcement set off a massive migration, as Hindus and Sikhs fled the areas to become Pakistan and Muslims fled India. Approximately ten million people fled across the new boundaries; of these, one million were killed, as Muslims killed trainloads of Hindus fleeing east and Hindus and Sikhs vented their anger on Muslims fleeing west.

In the chaos of partition, the state of Jammu and Kashmir posed a particular problem. As part of the partition process, Britain decreed that the leaders of the 570 nominally independent princely states would have to accede to either India or Pakistan, as geography and demographics dictated. Kashmir, by far the largest such state, stood on the boundary between the two new countries. Its population, some four million in 1947, was three-fourths Muslim, but its ruler, *maharaja* Hari Singh, was Hindu, as were most of the civil servants in his government. Singh's family, the traditional Hindu rulers of Jammu, had gained control of Muslim Kashmir in the 1840s from the British, who had sold it to the family in exchange for their recognition of Britain's ultimate authority. At the time of partition, Kashmir's transportation links and trade connections were largely directed to the west, to what became Pakistan. During the 1930s, the *maharaja* had faced a growing challenge from his population for a greater share in the government, led by Sheikh Muhammad Abdullah, who was allied more with the Indian National Congress than the Muslim League. These efforts Singh had largely rebuffed, loosening his grip on power only slightly after the end of World War II.

When the British announced the partition plan, the *maharaja* hesitated, fearing that he would be swept aside if he acceded—consented—to Pakistan. He initially signed a "stand-still" agreement with Pakistan, putting off the final decision and hoping to gain independence from both India and Pakistan. But in August of 1947, Muslim peasants in Kashmir revolted against their Hindu landowners. The revolt was supported by large numbers of volunteer fighters from Pakistan, shipped to the border in Pakistan's British army trucks. In October, volunteers from Pakistan swept across the border into Kashmir, seizing western Kashmiri cities and driving towards the capital of Srinigar. Four days later, *maharaja* Singh formally acceded the rule of Kashmir to India and appealed for military support. The British governor-general insisted that India's acceptance be conditioned on the will of the Kashmiri people, to which Nehru, India's first prime minister, agreed.

Indian troops were quickly dispatched to Kashmir, arriving just in time to save Srinigar from falling into the hands of the Muslims. The fighting eventually stabilized along a front between Srinigar and Uri, leaving roughly a quarter of Kashmir's territory in the hands of Muslims. The Muslims declared Azad ("free") Kashmir as a new state, with its capital at Muzaffarabad, and acceded to Pakistan. The front was eventually stabilized by a United Nations-arranged cease-fire, which took effect January 1, 1949. Despite the agreement in principle on the need for a plebiscite to determine the final status of the territory, no vote was ever held across all of Kashmir, and the province remained divided. The first (though undeclared) Indo-Pakistani war ended in stalemate, leaving open the key issue that would generate hostility between the new countries for the next fifty years.

Kashmir as Spark: India & Pakistan, 1949–1989

The 1949 cease-fire froze Kashmir in a state of partition that appeared increasingly permanent, although both India and Pakistan continued to insist that a plebiscite be held. India, in control of three-quarters of the province, integrated Kashmir into its own government structure, but kept very careful control over its local politics. Although it initially supported Sheikh Abdullah Muhammed, the Indian government threw him in jail in 1953, and replaced him—through tightly controlled elections—with a new government led by Bakshi Mohammed, who ruled the state with an iron grip. Bakshi's government was both corrupt and oppressive, further alienating much of Kashmir's population, although the Indian federal government invested significant sums of money on social reforms and economic development. Despite local tensions, Kashmir remained relatively calm throughout the 1950s.

In the early 1960s, tensions between Muslims and Hindus across India resulted in rising intercommunal violence. In 1963 Indian police forcibly put down riots in the Vale of Kashmir. India released Abdullah from prison and formed a new government in Kashmir, but negotiations with Pakistan over the Kashmir issue continued to make no progress. Sensing India's weakness in Kashmir and as a result of India's loss to China in their 1962 war, Pakistan began to pressure India on the Kashmir issue, stepping up its activity along the cease-fire line. In April of 1965, Indian and Pakistani forces came to blows in the Rann of Kutch, a mostly deserted salt marsh at the southern end of their border near the Arabian Sea.

Emboldened by its successes in that battle, Pakistan determined to wrest Kashmir from India by force, first by sending Pakistani-trained guerrillas across the cease-fire line into Kashmir in July and August of 1965 to support Kashmiri unrest. A war of words between India and Pakistan quickly escalated to armed force, and by the beginning of September India had sent forces into Kashmir to push back the perceived Pakistani aggression along the cease-fire line, while Pakistan's army had invaded across the border farther south, headed for Jammu. The war, which lasted for three weeks and came to encompass most of the Indo-Pakistani border, left India in control of more of Kashmir than before. In late September, both sides accepted a United Nations cease-fire, and entered into negotiations in Tashkent, in the Soviet Union. The agreement reached there, in January of 1966, essentially restored the previous cease-fire line but did nothing to resolve the larger of issue of Kashmir's future.

India and Pakistan returned to war six years later, this time over Bengali-speaking east Pakistan, which after years of domination by the less-populous, Urdu-speaking west had decided it wanted its independence. After massive refugee migrations into eastern India, the Indian army intervened in November 1971, and less than four weeks later the independent state of Bangladesh was created. During the fighting, Indian troops engaged Pakistani forces in the west as well, including in Kashmir. But India's forces had no intention of making significant new gains in the west, and Pakistan was too weak to take new territory from India. At the subsequent peace conference in Simla in 1972, India and Pakistan agreed to some minor adjustments to the cease-fire line in Kashmir, recognized it as the "Line of Control," and agreed to forgo the use of force in any attempt to resolve the question in the future. The Kashmir issue returned to the background of Indo-Pakistani relations, as a constant—but low-level—threat to their relationship.

Kashmir as its Own Actor: 1989–Present

Tensions remained in Kashmir following the 1972 Simla agreement, but the issue received little attention for another ten years. In the 1980s India began a series of political maneuverings in the province in an attempt to find a stable and legitimate government that could bring peace and stability to the province. These political changes were the result of the death of Sheikh Abdullah in 1983. His son, Farooq Abdullah, was elected in that year to head a government for the state under the National Conference party. The Indian government initially backed Farooq, then brought down his government a year later in favor of a rival movement, only to switch its support back to Farooq in 1986, enabling him to win state elections in 1987. These political games served to discredit Farooq in the eyes of many Kashmiris, who rallied behind the rival Muslim United Front party. Farooq's victory in the 1987 elections was widely perceived as the result of Indian election rigging, which further alienated the Muslim population.

These tensions exploded into outright violence in late 1989 and early 1990. In December of 1989, a previously ineffective guerrilla force that named itself the Jammu and Kashmir Liberation Front (JKLF) took the daughter of a high government official hostage. She was released after the JKLF's primary demand—the release of five of their jailed leaders—was met. Kashmiris took to the streets in celebration, and were met with police gunfire, which left several Kashmiris dead. These deaths only served to further enflame the population, which launched massive protests across the state. India, sensing that Farooq had lost control, dismissed the provincial government and declared direct President's Rule over Kashmir.

Insurgency movements broke out across Kashmir, killing hundreds in 1990 and, over the decade of the 1990s, thousands. The rebellion was complicated by charges on both sides of massive and brutal human rights abuses, and by persistent accusations by India that Pakistan was fomenting the rebellion by infiltrating military personnel across the border. These charges led to a brief crisis in Indo-Pakistani relations in 1990, when moves by both sides suggested the possibility of a nuclear war; but both subsequently backed away from confrontation with each other, although their involvement in Kashmir continued. Increased repression by Indian security forces brought heightened struggle by Kashmiris and sympathetic Muslims who came from other parts of Central Asia to aid their Islamic brethren. While the JKLF initially enjoyed both local popular sentiment and some measure of international support, by the mid-1990s the insurgency had fragmented into over one hundred different guerrilla and paramilitary groups. Some of these were able to come together and cooperate under the banner of the All-Party Hurriyat Conference, although such cooperation has been limited by continued disagreements among groups.

In general, these insurgency groups have tended to be of two types: those that proposed independence for Kashmir, led by the JKLF,

which were generally more secular in orientation, and those that proposed immediate union with Pakistan, such at the Jamaat-i-Islami, which tended to be more Islamic in ideology. Although it has been difficult to tell (foreign access to the region has been limited since the imposition of direct rule by India), the former, more secular groups appear to be primarily Kashmiri, while the Islamic groups appear to have received substantial support (including fighting personnel) from Muslims elsewhere in Central Asia. Much of this support has come through Pakistan, although the Pakistani government has consistently denied any involvement. Many of the arms and fighters came from Afghanistan, where the conclusion of the war with the Soviet Union in 1988 and continued civil war within the country have generated substantial supplies of both weapons and fighters willing to risk their lives for Islamic causes.

Even as the insurgency movement fragmented through the 1990s, Indian security forces continued to be unsuccessful in restoring order to the Kashmir region. Over the decade, fighting ebbed and flowed around the state, focusing most frequently on Srinigar but also occurring throughout the Vale and in Jammu. In 1996 India restored local rule by holding elections, which were again won by Farooq's National Conference but boycotted by the All-Party Hurriyat. By decade's end, over twenty-five thousand people had been killed in the fighting, with no obvious end in sight.

RECENT HISTORY AND THE FUTURE

While the cycle of suppression and insurgency continued throughout the 1990s, by 1998 the issue had largely disappeared from international headlines, as new tensions in Iraq and the Balkans came to the fore of western attention. In 1999, however, Kashmir once again became an area of concern as renewed tensions between Indian and Pakistani military forces flared along the Line of Control. The year began on a hopeful note, as Indian prime minister Vajpayee and Pakistani prime minister Nawaz Sharif met in Lahore for the first time, pledging to intensify their efforts to find a political solution to the ongoing Kashmir crisis. The February meeting also produced a cease-fire agreement for the LOC, across which Pakistani and Indian troops engaged in periodic shelling. This cease-fire ended three months later, however, when a substantial number of Muslim militants, and possibly some Pakistani troops, infiltrated across the LOC near the town of Kargil and took control of strategic peaks and highlands. India retaliated with substantial force, and the ensuing battle quickly escalated to involve the regular army and air force of both sides. The fighting lasted for eleven weeks, during which all negotiations were broken off, and roughly one thousand people were killed. Coming almost exactly one year after India and Pakistan's nuclear weapons tests, the Kargil fighting quickly took on the aura of an international crisis; as the fighting escalated, concerns about a nuclear exchange grew. The crisis abated in July, when Pakistani prime minister Nawaz Sharif agreed to withdraw the militants— which he continued to maintain did not include Pakistani regular forces—after meeting with U.S. President Clinton in Washington. Although it avoided a wider war, the outcome was widely seen as a victory for India.

The crisis and its outcome had significant political implications in both India and Pakistan. After the fighting subsided, Kashmir returned to its previous status quo—continued sporadic violence and occasional cross-border shelling. India attempted to press its apparent advantage by restoring a semblance of normal politics to Kashmir, holding local elections in September. The elections were boycotted by nearly all Kashmiri groups, and resulted in both low turnouts (less than one percent in some districts, and perhaps fifteen percent overall) and violence. The apparent defeat at Kargil did little to lessen Kashmiri militant activity, which continued throughout 1999 and into 2000. Nor did it bring a halt to the periodic back-and-forth artillery battles by Indian and Pakistani forces. Within the Indian portion of Kashmir and along the LOC, the Kargil crisis solved nothing, but raised tensions by reminding the world how close nuclear-armed Pakistan and India are to conflict.

The Pakistani retreat from Kargil did significantly alter the balance of power within Pakistan, however. Prime Minister Sharif's apparent surrender—deeply unpopular with people across Pakistan, as well as the Pakistani military—added fuel to an already-growing opposition movement against Sharif's government. Opposition rallies and government crackdowns created unrest, which threatened to destabilize Pakistani politics entirely. In October, Sharif attempted to fire his military Chief of Staff, General Pervez Musharraf, who was believed to have masterminded the initial Kargil operation. In response, the Pakistani army organized a bloodless coup and ousted Sharif from power. Since then, Musharraf and a military-appointed government have led Pakistan. They

have pledged to continue pressing the Kashmir issue with India and the international community. This, combined with continued violence within Kashmir and fighting along the LOC, largely halted further political progress with India through mid-2000. President Clinton's visit to both India and Pakistan in March 2000 failed to break the logjam; Pakistan continued to call for international mediation, but India refused it, and Clinton took the position that he could not interject American mediation where it was not wanted by both sides.

As of the middle of 2000, the Kashmir situation appeared to have returned to the impasse that has dominated the region for the past ten years. Although they shocked the world, the 1998 nuclear tests by both India and Pakistan did little to change the overall situation. India first tested a "nuclear explosive device" in the early 1970s, and Pakistan has openly claimed to have nuclear capability since the early 1990s, a claim most outside analysts agreed with. The military reality is that an all-out war between India and Pakistan would clearly devastate both, while India retains enough conventional military superiority to deny Pakistan any significant territorial gains in Kashmir. The 1990s also demonstrated that India lacks the capability to permanently suppress either Kashmiri militancy, or external infiltration by Islamic groups bent on wresting control of the province away from India. Finally, the political positions of the various sides have not changed at all in the last ten years. India refuses to discuss the issue outside of bilateral talks with Pakistan, and refuses to consider giving up control of Kashmir; Pakistan continues to insist on the opposite of India's position; and a range of groups in Kashmir continue to advocate either independence or union with Pakistan.

Given these realities, the possibility of a resolution in the near future appears unlikely. In the long run, the three theoretical possibilities are union of some or all of the Indian-held province with Pakistan; independence for Indian-held Kashmir, either in part or in whole, which Pakistani-controlled Azad Kashmir might join; or normalization of politics in Indian-controlled Kashmir as a permanent part of India. The first and second possibilities would require the Indian government to voluntarily relinquish control, probably to some form of vote or plebiscite to determine the wishes of the population of Kashmir. Events in 1999 in Indonesia and East Timor, in which Indonesia did exactly that, led the All-Party Hurriyat Conference to hold up the East

IN A REGION WROUGHT WITH CONFLICT, THERE HAVE BEEN OCCASIONAL SPELLS OF PEACE, LIKE THAT BROUGHT ON BY THIS SIGNING OF A 1971 TRUCE BETWEEN INDIAN AND PAKISTANI OFFICIALS. *(Corbis. Reproduced by permission.)*

Timor case as a model which would allow a plebiscite, originally promised in 1947, to determine the province's final status. The analogy between India and Indonesia is not a perfect one, however; Indonesia was going through a transition between authoritarian rule and democracy in 1999, while India has been a democracy since its independence. Moreover, India was founded on the notion that Muslims and Hindus can live peaceably together in South Asia; to relinquish its one Muslim-majority province, some say, would be to repudiate the entire exercise and call India's fundamental identity into question. Hence, it appears that voluntary Indian withdrawal of their claim to Kashmir is unlikely in the absence of radical political changes there.

The third possibility, however, is also problematic. Kashmir is unlike East Timor in another way: the Kashmiris receive substantial support from the outside world for their struggle, while the East Timorese fought more or less alone for nearly three decades. India has proved inept at convincing the Muslims of Kashmir that they should give their political allegiance to the Indian government. Given the scale of violence over the last decade—most of the over twenty-five thousand killed in Kashmir have been civilians—they appear unlikely to do so in the near future. A relatively porous

border along the LOC, and a ready supply of weapons and willing Islamic fighters, guarantee that Kashmiri groups will be able to continue their campaign against Indian rule for the foreseeable future. If India wishes to retain its control, which appears likely, she will have to be prepared to pay a significant price over time.

Ultimately, progress on Kashmir will come only when one of the main players—Pakistan, India, or the indigenous Kashmiris—change their minds about the conflict. Of these three, Pakistan is least important. Even if a new Pakistani government were to decide to stop supporting Kashmiri independence, they would likely not be able to stop continued infiltration by private armed groups across the LOC. Pakistan possesses some ability to change the balance of power between different Kashmiri groups, either in favor of those who want union with Pakistan or towards those who advocate Kashmiri independence, but they cannot, on their own, resolve the conflict, even by surrendering.

Progress, then, depends on the continued contest of wills between India and the Kashmiris themselves. Either could decide—although not without significant cost—to accede to the wishes of the other. Each side perceives that to do so would put its very survival at stake. This situation will change only when one side redefines its identity in such a way as to allow the other to "win" without it committing suicide. Thus, India could redefine itself away from the religious vs. secular debates of the 1940s, and accept the notion that this particular group of Muslims does not want to belong to India any longer. Likewise, the people of Kashmir could come to redefine their identity, not to repudiate Islam, but to see it as fitting within a broader India where they felt welcomed and at home. Both of these are distant, remote possibilities, and neither is guaranteed to ever happen. In the meantime, we can expect Kashmir to continue much as it has been for the past decade: plagued by violence, instability, and tension between two South Asian nuclear powers.

BIBLIOGRAPHY

Barnds, William J. *India, Pakistan and the Great Powers.* New York: Council on Foreign Relations, 1972.

Desmond, Edward. "The Insurgency in Kashmir (1989–1991)," *Contemporary South Asia* 4 (1995): 57–17.

Evans, Alexander. "Kashmir: The Past Ten Years," *Asian Affairs* 30 (1999): 21–35.

Ganguly, Sumit. "Wars Without End: The Indo-Pakistani Conflict," *Annals of the American Academy of Political and Social Science* 541 (1995): 167–179.

India: A Country Study. 5th ed. Washington, DC: Library of Congress, 1996.

Krishan, Y. "The Unfinished Agenda of the Partition," *Asian Affairs* 29 (1998): 278–287.

Kulke, Hermann and Dietmar Rothermund. *A History of India.* 3rd ed. New York: Routledge, 1998.

Lamb, Beatrice Pitney. *India: A World in Transition.* 4th ed. New York: Praeger Publishers, 1975.

Pakistan: A Country Study. 6th ed. Washington, DC: Library of Congress, 1995.

Schofield, Victoria. "Kashmir—Today, Tomorrow?" *Asian Affairs* 28 (1997): 315–325.

Sikand, Yoginder. "For Islam and Kashmir: The Prison Diaries of Sayyed Ali Gilani of the Jama'at-I-Islami of Jammu and Kashmir," *Journal of Muslim Minority Affairs* 18 (1998): 241–250.

Wolpert, Stanley. *A New History of India.* 3rd ed. New York: Oxford University Press, 1989.

R. William Ayers

THE KURDS IN TURKEY: THE CAPTURE OF OCALAN

Until his capture by special forces in February 1999, Abdullah Ocalan was the most wanted man in modern Turkish history. Over the years, the authorities in Ankara, Turkey's capital, have labeled him "a communist," "a bandit," "a murderer," a "threat to national unity" or, their preferred epithet, "terrorist." They have said he was responsible for the deaths of up to thirty thousand people, including fifty-five hundred soldiers, that he had drained the national treasury of $100 billion, cost Turkey a coveted membership in the European Union, and humiliated a proud people in the eyes of the world.

But to the vast majority of Turkish Kurds—an impoverished and culturally oppressed minority that inhabits the southeastern part of the country—Ocalan (pronounced OH-jah-lahn) was simply known as Apo, an affectionate nickname. Most Kurds probably did not share his Marxist ideology; some even disagreed with his calls for an independent Kurdish state. But it was a rare Kurd who did not look up to him as a great *"peshmerga,"* or warrior (literally, "those who stare death in the face")—a respected title among this martial people—and a leader who stood up for the Kurdish people and against what the Kurds see as the mighty Turkish war machine and the repressive Turkish state.

What both sides could agree on was that Ocalan and the Kurdish Workers Party that he founded as a student in 1979 (PKK is its Kurdish acronym) had plunged the Turkish republic into the greatest political crisis since Turkey's founding in the years after World War I.

From 1984 when Ocalan and the PKK launched their first guerrilla attack against government forces, southeastern Turkey has been host to

THE CONFLICT

Abdullah Ocalan's arrest in February 1999, followed by his trial and death sentence, made front-page news of the long conflict between Turkey and the Kurds. While hostility between the Kurds and the Turks has simmered for centuries, the modern conflict dates from the Treaty of Versailles in 1919 which ended World War I. This treaty divided the lands where the Kurds lived among several countries including Turkey, Iraq, Iran, parts of the former Soviet Union, and Syria. In Turkey, the Kurds were ruled in an environment of Turkish nationalism; in 1937, Mustafa Kemal Ataturk proclaimed a secular country, outlawing public, cultural, and religious expression, including the very word "Kurd."

Ethnic and Religious

- Kurds are not allowed free religious and cultural expression within Turkey.

- Turks view a secularized society, free from symbols of religious and cultural differences, to be key to a stable society.

Nationalistic

- Kurds are scattered over a mountainous region that spans several different countries; they view themselves as a people without a state.

- Turks view the Kurdish Workers Party (PKK) as a terrorist organization trying to destroy Turkey.

Economic

- Kurds are generally poorer and have fewer opportunities than Turks in Turkey.

- A few Kurds have had very influential positions.

CHRONOLOGY

2000 B.C. Kurds migrate to the Middle East, including Turkey.

1000 A.D. Turks migrate to the Middle East, including Turkey.

1915–18 Massacre of the Armenians in Turkey by both Turks and Kurds.

1919 At the Versailles peace conference, the lands where the Kurds live are divided into several different countries, each ruled by a non-Kurd majority.

1923 Ataturk's modernization and securalization effort outlaw all religious expression in public, including Kurdish culture. The name "Kurd" is banned; all Kurdish people are officially referred to as "mountain Turks who have forgotten their language."

1937–38 A Kurdish revolt in the Dersim highlands results in the deaths of more than forty-thousand Kurds.

1979 Ocalan founds the Kurdish Workers Party (PKK).

1984 The PKK's first attack on Turkish forces leaves twenty-four soldiers and nine civilians dead.

1999 Ocalan is captured in Kenya, returned to Turkey, tried and sentenced to death. Ocalan denounces violence and supports a peace effort. Turkey weighs its desire for admittance to the European Union, which does not permit the death penalty, against its desire to execute a man it regards as a terrorist.

a brutal civil war. To combat a guerrilla army that has never numbered more than fifteen thousand, the Turkish government dispatched up to three hundred thousand troops to the disputed region, destroyed thousands of villages, and forcibly relocated hundreds of thousands of Kurds. Its army has invaded northern Iraq—where the PKK maintains bases—a half dozen times in as many years and Turkish officials have threatened to cut off the water supply to neighboring Syria, which had also supported the PKK. In response, say the Turks, the guerrillas assassinated government officials, forcibly recruited Kurdish peasants, and launched terrorist attacks in Turkish cities. Thus, to many Kurds and Turks in February 1999, it hardly seemed possible that Ocalan was now in the custody of Turkish authorities. As it turned out, the end game—the final four month-long pursuit and

capture of Ocalan—was as rife with intrigue as the fifteen year-long war with his organization was rife with brutality.

HISTORICAL BACKGROUND

The Capture of Ocalan

The final days began in October 1998, when the Turks got the Syrians to cease all support for the PKK and expel Ocalan from his base in Syria. But when Syrian forces showed up at PKK bases near the Turkish border, Ocalan was nowhere to be found. Rumors placed him in various places all over the world. Turkish Prime Minister Mesut Yilmaz said he was in Moscow. In a telephone interview, Ocalan said he was in Kurdistan but that could mean Turkey, Iraq, Iran, Syria, Armenia or Azerbaijan since there are significant Kurdish enclaves in all of those countries (Kurdistan is a region that encompasses parts of all of these countries). As it turned out, Yilmaz was right. But by December, the PKK chief had shown up in Rome.

There, under heavy Italian guard, the fifty-year-old Kurdish leader made a shocking announcement, denouncing the very struggle he had launched. "If the guerrillas want to continue what they have been doing for fifteen years," he told an interviewer with Kurdish TV in Europe, "then I have nothing to do with them." If the renunciation was meant to placate the Turks, it didn't work. They continued their pressure on Rome, but Italian law did not allow extradition to any country—such as Turkey—that maintained the death penalty. Still, the authorities made it clear that they wanted the embarrassing refugee out and, in January 1999, Ocalan fled for destinations unknown, after being refused asylum by Germany, the Netherlands and a host of other countries.

A month later, Turkish special agents flew to Africa. Acting on information provided by the American government—and, some say, Israeli intelligence—the Turks had learned Ocalan's whereabouts: the Greek embassy in Nairobi. Under intense pressure from the Turks and NATO ally the United States, the Kenyans and the Greeks—the latter long-time foes of the Turks and, according to Ankara, long-time supporters of the PKK—told Ocalan he would have to leave and arranged for him to fly to the International Court of Justice in The Hague, Netherlands on February 16. But the Kenyan security agents charged with bringing him to the airport turned him over to the

THE FORGOTTEN GENOCIDE

During World War I, the Turkish Ottoman Empire perpetrated one of the largest acts of genocide in world history, systematically deporting and massacring more than one million of its minority Armenian population who lived primarily in the eastern regions bordering Russia. Turkey's unlikely ally in the genocide was the Kurds, long considered the mortal enemy of the Armenians. The World War I genocide followed two decades of repressive Turkish rule under which the Armenians were gradually stripped of their property and their civil rights and over two hundred thousand of them were murdered.

After the start of the war, the Armenians, who were mostly Christian, were considered by Turkey to be an "internal foe" because of their potential loyalty to Russia and to the Russian Orthodox Church. Ordered to turn over all their weapons, the Armenians were left defenseless and the very weapons they turned in were then used as evidence of their complicity with Russia. Claiming they were a risk to national security, the Turks began deporting the Armenians. It was during these deportations that hundreds of thousands of Armenians were murdered by bands of Kurds and Turks. Those that weren't deported were tortured and murdered in their villages, again by Kurdish and Turkish troops. Some were bludgeoned to death, others shot, and still more were herded into churches, which were then burned. Most of the men, defined as any male over fourteen, were killed almost immediately. Women often survived the initial ambush only to be abducted, raped, and often murdered. Infants were abandoned along roadsides and older children were frequently given to passing Turks and Kurds in hopes of enhancing their chances of survival. Many of these children were later adopted into Turkish families who converted them to Islam and assimilated them into the Turkish culture. The marches and massacres were devastating and effective. In total, one and a half million were deported. Just over three hundred thousand survived.

On the surface, the Kurds fought alongside the Turks in order to purge Turkish soil of a Christian populace. However, by siding with the Turks against the Armenians, the Kurds were allowed to unleash decades of pent-up tension caused by the migration of Kurdish tribes into the predominantly Armenian region that bordered Turkey and Russia. By exploiting these tensions, the Turks were learning a valuable lesson in how to expel an unwanted minority. Many of the tactics used during the World War I genocide were used in later decades against the Kurds including forced relocations, the systematic repression of culture, and the exploitation of existing tensions between tribes. To this day, Turkey denies the Armenian genocide. Its official position is that the murders were in response to an opportunistic Armenian uprising against the Turkish majority. The deportations were simply an act of civil defense.

Turks instead, who quickly whisked him back to Turkey, where he was held as the sole inmate at a remote maximum-security prison on the island of Imrali. While Turks celebrated in the streets and called for the death penalty, the Kurdish population—both in Turkish cities and in the huge exile communities of Europe—exploded in anger, with the Greeks, Kenyans and Israelis being the primary targets of their rage. In Berlin, Israeli guards fired on Kurdish protectors who were trying to occupy the Israeli embassy, killing three and wounding sixteen.

Responding to the violence—which included rioting in Istanbul and other Turkish cities—Ecevit hinted that his government might consider easing martial law in the southeast if guerrillas laid down their arms, though he added that Kurdish autonomy, or independence, of any sort was out of the question. "If and when conditions become more conducive to solving certain problems, then new approaches may prevail," he told a gathering of newspersons five days after Ocalan's capture. "A substantial decrease in terrorism would be conducive to improvements and reforms in the social, economic and political life of the country." But, he added, nothing could be done until the rebel leader had been put on trial. "At the moment," he noted, "public opinion is very sensitive because every day our soldiers are being killed." That was an understatement. Within a week, one of Ocalan's lawyers quit the case, fearing for his life after demonstrators pelted his van with stones and threatened his life, while another was arrested for previous contacts with the PKK, an act of treason under Turkish law.

ABDULLAH OCALAN. *(Photograph by Jamal Saidi. Archive Photos. Reproduced by permission.)*

Ocalan's Trial

On May 31, Ocalan's trial began with an extraordinary statement by the accused. In forty minutes of testimony, the PKK leader apologized for the war he and his organization had fought against Ankara and said, if freed or even allowed to live, he would pursue democratic change only and would do everything in his power to turn the PKK into a regular political party. He then issued a plea to his followers to give up the armed struggle. "Now is the time to end this conflict, or else it will get much worse," he said. "I want to dedicate my life to bringing Turks and Kurds together." The declaration was met by skepticism from Turks and Kurds alike, though for very different reasons. Most Turks simply did not trust him. While Kurds—remembering the way the courts and security forces had always outlawed or crushed any party that advocated their cause too strongly—put little faith in the political system. The Kurds had little faith in the system despite the fact that their latest attempt at party politics—the People's Democracy Party (parties with the name Kurd in them remain illegal)had just performed well in Kurdish regions in the national elections in April 1999.

But the Kurds understood one thing—and most foreign experts agree with them—that, for all the trappings and even substance of democracy in Turkey, the real power in the country lay with the military, which considers itself the protector of the Turkish state and which has seized power three times since World War II to fulfill that self-proclaimed role. Moreover, and not unexpectedly, it has been the Turkish generals—more than any other group in the country—that has insisted on a military solution to the Kurdish problem. Still, just two days after Ocalan issued his remarkable declaration came an equally extraordinary statement from PKK headquarters somewhere in the mountains of southeastern Turkey: "Our entire party organization, with supreme unity and cohesion, is bound to and fully supportive of the efforts of our leader." The offer, however, came with a warning. "If the Turkish republic and the various interlocutors in the region and the world think this is weakness, they are badly mistaken," the statement added. "We have made every preparation and are ready to fight on in the same way we have fought for fifteen years."

The prosecutors were not impressed. Just a week after Ocalan's extraordinary opening statement, they insisted on the death penalty, based on charges of treason and advocacy of separatism, both capital offenses in Turkey. After a two-week recess, the PKK leader offered a political defense. It was, he said simply, Turkish restrictions on the Kurdish language and Kurdish cultural expression that had led him and his followers to violent resistance and their insistence, first, on a separate state from Turkey and, then, for autonomy within the Turkish republic. "These kinds of laws give birth to rebellion and anarchy," he said. "Even the smallest obstacle is enough to spark an uprising. The most important of these is the language ban. It provokes this revolt. The way to resolve this problem is to develop Kurdish as a normal language for private conversation and broadcasting."

But, like the prosecutors before them, the judges in the trial were not impressed. On June 29, they sentenced Ocalan to death. Unlike the days following his capture, there were no violent demonstrations on the part of the Kurds and only muted statements of satisfaction on the part of Turkish authorities. The absence of violence and elation, experts said, was not hard to explain. For Turks and Kurds alike—indeed, for anyone who has studied the long and troubled history of the region—the verdict and sentence seemed almost inevitable.

The Kurds and the Ottoman Empire

The Kurds—some twenty-five million strong and inhabiting a mountainous swath of the

KURDISH DEMONSTRATORS PROTEST WHAT THEY FEEL IS THE UNFAIR DEATH SENTENCE LEVIED AGAINST ABDULLAH OCALAN. *(AP/Wide World Photos. Reproduced by permission.)*

Middle East from southeastern Turkey through northwestern Iran—are among the longest-lived cultures on the planet. In a depiction that would remain remarkably consistent for four thousand years, a Kurd is featured in the *Epic of Gilgamesh*, the world's oldest written epic, as a wild man from the mountains who is eventually tamed by, and comes to serve, a civilized hero from the plains. Most scholars cite the Kurds' origins in the vast movement of Aryan peoples into the Middle East that occurred roughly two thousand years before Christ. Indeed, the various Kurdish languages and cultures are most closely related to those of the Persians, a fellow Aryan people, rather than Semites who originally inhabited the region or the Turks who arrived there after the year 1000 A.D. Named by the Babylonians—who called them the Qardu—the Kurds eventually found themselves by the Christian era under the rule of the Parthians to the east and the Romans to the west. Indeed, it was the *pax romana* in Anatolia—the peace enforced by ancient Rome the heartland of modern Turkey—that encouraged the Kurds to migrate north and west into that vast peninsula.

By 700 A.D., the Kurds found themselves increasingly drawn into the orbit of the great Arab civilizations of the Middle East. And for the next seven hundred years the Kurds—now converted to Islam (although retaining vestiges of their ancient

"cult of the angels")—thrived politically and economically. Among their number was the great Saladin, the general who drove the Crusaders from Jerusalem in the twelfth century. Situated along the great silk road between Europe and Asia—but protected by their mountain home against the Mongol hordes—the Kurds exploited their position by either becoming suppliers and drivers of the great caravans or by robbing them.

The conquest of much of the Middle East by the Ottoman Turks in the fifteenth and sixteenth century represented a mixed blessing for the Kurds. Economically, it was a setback. By closing off the overland trade routes between Europe and Asia, the Ottomans denied the Kurds access to outside goods and money. At the same time, the Turkish sultans worked out alliances with the various Kurdish principalities, granting them various levels of autonomy depending on how geographically accessible they were. The sultans also recruited Kurds—renowned for their martial abilities—as defenders of the empire against encroachments from the north and east.

But the rise of Christian Europe and the decline of the Ottoman Empire in the eighteen and nineteenth century had a devastating effect on Kurdish fortunes. By the early 1800s, the Ottomans found themselves under siege by France in North Africa, Britain in the Persian Gulf and

Russia from the north. In response, several reformist sultans decided to modernize their empire through political and—what would now be called—market reforms. The autonomy of the Kurdish principalities was ended and the region placed under direct Ottoman rule. Kurdish communal lands were parceled out as private property. While these reforms helped keep the dying Ottoman Empire alive for another century, they destroyed Kurdish political institutions and turned independent Kurdish shepherds and farmers into agricultural workers, forced to work on farmlands that belonged to non-Kurds, including Armenian merchants and Turkish bureaucrats, or increasingly autocratic Kurdish *aghas*, or chiefs. The dire conditions led to desperation and, in the 1870s, the first Kurdish rebellion of the modern era. The first rebellion was crushed by Turkish forces and *jash*, a Kurdish word for turncoats that also means "little donkeys." Many among the *jash* would be recruited to serve as *hamidiye*, a Cossack-like force recruited by the sultan to guard the empire's frontier with Russia and maintain control against the restive Armenian population.

With the Ottomans entry into World War I on the side of Germany, the empire's fate was sealed, although not before the *hamidiye* and other Kurdish forces were unleashed, alongside Turks, in an onslaught against the Armenians that resulted in one of the great genocides of the twentieth century. Signing a separate armistice with the allies on October 31, 1918, the Ottoman Empire ceased to exist. The hated Greeks occupied the southwestern part of Turkey, while the British seized control of Constantinople and the Dardanelles. All of the Ottoman holdings throughout the Middle East were turned over to the British and French as mandates, despite the fact that the Europeans had promised their Arab allies independence once the war was over.

The Kurds, locked away in their mountain villages and devoid of political leadership for nearly a century, failed to come to grips with the nationalism that was enveloping the region until it was too late. Ignored at the Versailles peace conference of 1919, where the winners of World War I divided regions of the world among themselves, the Kurds found themselves divided into several lands, each ruled by a non-Kurd majority. In Iraq and Syria, they would eventually find themselves ruled over by a dominant Arab population. In Iran, they come under Persian rule. But it was in Turkey that their destiny proved particularly miserable as the Kurds came to be the principle victims of a rising Turkish nationalism.

The Rise of Turkish Nationalism

Following World War I, Turkey was humiliated and nearly destroyed as a nation, a memory which has scarred the Turkish people ever since. But under the leadership of Mustafa Kemal, or Ataturk ("father of the Turks"), they rallied, throwing the invaders out of their Anatolian homeland. At first, the Kurds supported the Turks in the struggle, believing that the new state would be a multicultural one with Turks, Kurds and other ethnic groups sharing political power and enjoying cultural autonomy. This hope was based on two precedents. Whatever the sultan (the head of the Ottoman Empire) had visited on them over the centuries, the Kurds had always been committed to the Ottoman Empire since it was, by definition, a multicultural state that placed loyalty to the sultan and the empire above nationalism. Moreover, with the sultan serving dual roles as both emperor and caliphate—that is, spiritual head of all Islam—the Kurds would be protected as members of a faith that emphasized equality among all believers.

But the Kurds were mistaken in their belief that the new Turkish state would offer the same protection as did the Ottoman Empire. To unify his new Turkish state and revive Turkish cultural pride, Ataturk not only modernized the country (among other measures, he outlawed the traditional fez and changed the Turkish alphabet from an Arabic- to a Roman-based one), he secularized it as well, ending the more than one thousand year-old caliphate. Worse, as far as the Kurds were concerned, Ataturk also banned all expressions of non-Turkish culture. Over the next ten years, the Turkish government would outlaw Kurdish schools, organizations and publications—even the language itself. All references to Kurdish regions were wiped from the map. The very name "Kurd" was expunged and all Kurdish peoples were now officially referred to as "mountain Turks who have forgotten their language." Virtually every administrative and military post in the Kurdish parts of Turkey was staffed by Turks, and they pitted tribe against tribe and stole Kurdish land and property.

The result of these measures was a series of Kurdish revolts that rocked southeastern Turkey in the 1920s and 1930s, and led to even more repressive measures by the Turkish military. Kurdish rebelliousness against the state began modestly enough when several former *hamidiye* officers formed a nationalist organization known as Azadi, Kurdish for "freedom." But most Azadi members were urban-based intellectuals, with few links to Kurdish peasants. To reach out to the masses, they

MUSTAFA KEMAL ATATURK

1881–1938 As a young military officer, Mustafa Kemal became a national hero during World War I by showing military cunning and leadership. Following Turkey's loss in the war, Turkey was divided among conquering nations, and Kemal became the central voice of Turkish nationalism. In June 1919, Kemal issued a declaration of independence calling for a united Turkey. Turkey attained recognition as an independent country through the Treaty of Lausanne after which Kemal quickly began to modernize the country.

The secularization of Turkey dictated that men could no longer wear a fez and women were pronounced legally equal to men. Religious expression was also prohibited. Kemal viewed the secularization of Turkey as a necessary requirement for its modernization and its participation in the bounty of Western economic development. A secular state would also be undivided by cultural and religious differences. As part of Kemal's modernization effort, all Turks had to adopt surnames, as are used in the West; Mustafa Kemal chose "Ataturk," which means "Father of the Turks."

MUSTAFA KEMAL ATATURK. *(The Granger Collection. Reproduced by permission.)*

recruited a popular political and religious leader named Sheikh Said whom, they thought, they could use to build an independence movement. But Said had other plans. Ambitious and headstrong, he immediately launched a rebellion against the Turkish state in February 1925 that brought down the full wrath of Ankara. Within two months, Said was captured, put on trial and condemned to death, exactly seventy-four years to the day before Ocalan himself would be sentenced.

Other, smaller revolts in more remote areas of Kurdistan followed. The last—in 1937–38 in the Dersim highlands—would result in the deaths of over forty thousand Kurds. While the revolts of the interwar period varied in size and effectiveness, they shared common goals, as well as a common fate. They combined appeals to traditional faith and modern nationalism, but were defeated not just by the armed might of the Turkish state, but by inter-tribal suspicion and the antipathy of traditional Kurdish leadership. The brutal defeat of the Dersim revolt would bring a troubled peace to Turkish Kurdistan for almost half a century. And when Kurds rose up again—as the PKK in 1984—it would be a very different revolt: anti-tribal and

anti-religious, with a strong nationalist agenda and Marxist ideology.

The Rise of the PKK

Three trends marked the decades between the end of the Dersim rebellion in the late 1930s and the rise of the PKK in the early 1980s and shaped the modern struggle for Kurdish nationalism. First, of course, was the continuing war on Kurdish culture and language, as Kurdish dance, costume, music, art, even the use of the Kurdish language in private, was ruthlessly suppressed. Second was economic modernization. First railroads and then highways pushed into the region, bringing commercial agriculture, mining, and some industrial development in their wake. But little of this economic activity benefited the Kurds. Virtually all business and land was owned by Turkish or foreign capitalists and few Kurds were hired in any but the least skilled, lowest-paid positions. The Kurdish regions of Turkey were transformed, in the opinion of Kurdish intellectuals, into a kind of internal colony. In the decades following World War II, hundreds of thousands fled to cities in western Turkey and Western Europe, looking for education and work.

Finally, many Kurds—particularly those who had migrated to urban areas—found themselves caught up in the troubled and violent politics of the Turkish state. From the 1960s onward, Turkey has been torn by struggles between right and left (the conservative and the progressive, or socialist/communist), with most Kurds gravitating toward the left. On no less than three occasions—in 1960, 1970 and 1980—the Turkish military intervened, took power away from civilian politicians for a time, ended political strife through martial law, and then handed the reins of government back to the civilian politicians.

In 1979 amidst a wave of leftist agitation, the Kurdish Workers Party was formed by Ocalan and a group of young, radical, urban-based Kurdish students, intellectuals, and labor organizers. They were heavily influenced by Marxist-Leninist ideas and Maoist rhetoric—theories involving the economic relationship of workers and owners and of a worker-peasant revolution. Their goal was a socialist Kurdish-Turkish federation. Traditional politics, as far as the PKK was concerned, was ineffective. Indeed, Kurdish political options were very limited. Any political party bearing the name Kurd or advocating the Kurdish cause in any way was illegal and the Turkish government has banned several over the years, leaving Kurdish supporters of parliamentary solutions marginalized. Instead, the PKK decided to take to the streets and organize direct action, including strikes and demonstrations. But the coup of 1980 and the intense repression that followed—more than thirty-three thousand Kurds were arrested and 122 sentenced to death—made that form of protest unwise.

For the next few years, then, the PKK set itself a new task, recruiting guerillas and guerilla supporters in the Kurdish enclaves of Turkish cities and in the Kurdish countryside. On August 15, 1984, they launched their first attack on Turkish forces, killing twenty-four soldiers and nine civilians in the southeastern Turkish towns of Eruh and Shemdinli. Through the rest of the decade and into the early 1990s, the war intensified, as Kurdish guerrilla forces—supported by Iraq, Iran, Syria, and, according to Ankara, Greece and the Soviet Union as well—continually launched hit-and-run attacks against Turkish outposts and towns throughout the southeast. At first, the Turkish military was caught off-guard. Organized to serve as NATO's southeastern protection against a possible Soviet attack, they had little training, experience or equipment for fighting an anti-guerrilla war.

Gradually—under U.S. tutelage—they adapted, turning the war—in some ways—into an Anatolian version of Vietnam. Indeed, many of the tactics employed by the Americans were taken up the Turks, including strategic hamlets—whereby villagers who represented potential guerrilla supporters were relocated to government-controlled camps—free-fire zones, and rapid, helicopter-borne troop deployments. The Turkish military also pursued the enemy into neighboring countries, particularly Iraq. But, like Vietnam, the army faced a formidable foe—highly motivated, highly mobile, and situated in a guerrilla's ideal topography of nearly impenetrable mountains. By 1990 the war had reached a stalemate, with the guerrillas unable to wear down the army and the army unable to deliver a knockout blow to the guerrillas.

The Gulf War and the "Safe Haven"

Then, in 1991, came the Gulf War between the United States and its allies against Iraq. As the war ended, hundreds of thousands of Iraqi Kurds fled Iraqi President Saddam Hussein's army seeking refuge in the Kurdish parts of Turkey. In and of itself, this temporary influx might not have affected Turkey's own Kurdish war. Ocalan and the Iraqi Kurd leadership had little but contempt for each other; the PKK leadership saw the latter as tribal and reactionary and the Iraqi Kurds viewed Ocalan as a communist agitator. There was little chance of an alliance. But it was exactly that antipathy that intrigued the Turks, specifically President Turgut Ozal, a brilliant strategist and moderate reformer who had come to power in 1986. Indeed, Ozal recognized that the Gulf War and the subsequent chaos in Iraq represented both a challenge and opportunity for Turkey. And he proposed several measures to take advantage of the fast-moving situation.

As early as December 1990, a month before Desert Storm, Ozal broached the idea of creating some kind of a quasi-independent Kurdish entity in the Iraqi north and under the protection of Turkey. While at first glance the idea seems to run counter to everything Turkey and its struggle with its own Kurds stands for, it actually made some sense. Officials in Ankara, the capital of Turkey, would establish a protectorate over a region that the PKK used to launch attacks against Turkey. In addition, the Turks could recruit the Iraqi Kurds to fight the PKK. As the old regional adage had it: "who better to fight a Kurd than a Kurd?" Then, in March 1991, as Saddam Hussein turned his military against the Kurdish rebels, setting off a humanitarian catastrophe that captured the world's attention, Ozal—hoping to head off any western criticism of Turkey's treatment of its own Kurds—ended the ban on the Kurdish language, albeit legalizing it for private conservation only. Slight as this concession was, it represented the first time the government of Turkey had recognized the existence of a Kurdish people within its borders.

At first, Ozal's strategy worked: a quasi-independent "safe haven"—with Turkish-based NATO air protection—was established. In October 1992, the Turks launched their largest military offensive against PKK based in northern Iraq. And this time, they had the support of the Iraqi Kurds. Unfortunately, for the Turks, the Iraqi Kurds soon reverted back to form. In May 1994, following disputes over land and smuggling rights, the two main parties, the Kurdistan Democratic Party and the Patriotic Union of Kurdistan, fell into bitter factional fighting that has lasted—with various ceasefires—through the present day.

Despite the difficulties with their Iraqi Kurd allies, however, the Turkish army began to get the upper hand by the mid-1990s, launching numerous offensives against the PKK both within Turkey and within Iraq. And while the Turkish military and government remain committed to a military solution to the Kurdish problem, Ocalan and the PKK began to moderate their position. Statements from the organization appeared devoid of calls for a Marxist-Leninist revolution. And, in place of demands for an independent Kurdish state, there was talk of Kurdish cultural autonomy and Kurdish rights with the Turkish republic. In December 1997, Ocalan once again renewed calls for direct negotiations between the PKK and the government, saying "we are ready to declare a cease-fire to find a peaceful solution to the national Kurdish problem and open a way to dialogue."

RECENT HISTORY AND THE FUTURE

Mutual Distrust

Ankara, however, has brushed aside all such overtures. The military maintains the PKK is not to be trusted and that it would use any ceasefire to replenish its supplies and its recruits. Conversely, the generals argue, PKK calls for a peaceful settlement indicate that the military campaign against it is working and should be continued until the organization ultimately surrenders. Moreover, the

SECULAR TURKEY

Turkey believes that the foundation of a stable multicultural society is lack of religious and cultural expression in public. They believe that symbols of religious and cultural differences divide people: Christians from Muslims and religious Muslims from secular Muslims. Therefore, Turkey has outlawed religious symbols in public—including the word "Kurd" and, as in the article below, the Islamic headscarf.

"Turkish Court Rules on Head Scarves," New York Times, *9 December 1999.*

ANKARA, Turkey—Turkey's appeals court ruled Thursday that a university had the right to bar a female student who wears an Islamic head scarf from classes.

A local court had earlier ruled that it was Esra Ege's democratic right to wear a head scarf while attending classes at 19th of May University in the Black Sea city of Samsun.

Turkey, a predominantly Muslim country, has strict laws that forbid religious dress at schools and public offices.

A court in Samsun had earlier challenged those laws and ordered the university to accept Ege in classes and pay her $200 in compensation.

The appeals court in Ankara said the court's decision violated the secular constitution, the Anatolia news agency reported. The court's decision is final.

Strict Muslims consider it obligatory for women to cover their heads, but the secular government regards head scarves as a political statement.

In May, legislators forced a deputy from parliament's chamber after she tried to wear a head scarf to parliament.

Turkish military knows it has an unwavering supporter in the United States. During the Cold War, Turkey was critical to NATO defense; since the fall of the Shah of Iran in 1979, Turkey has also become the United States' closest and most trusted ally in the Islamic world. With the U.S. continuing to supply arms—a supply now bolstered by Turkey's new ally, Israel—and willing to turn a blind eye to Turkish atrocities against the Kurds, there has been little need of talk of amnesty and no talk of negotiations on the part of Ankara, before or after Ocalan's capture.

There are also more fundamental reasons for Turkish reluctance to pursue a peaceful settlement. First, the vast majority of Turkish politicians argue that there really is no Kurdish problem. Indeed, Turkish law is explicit on the question of the unity and equality of all Turkish citizens. There is no

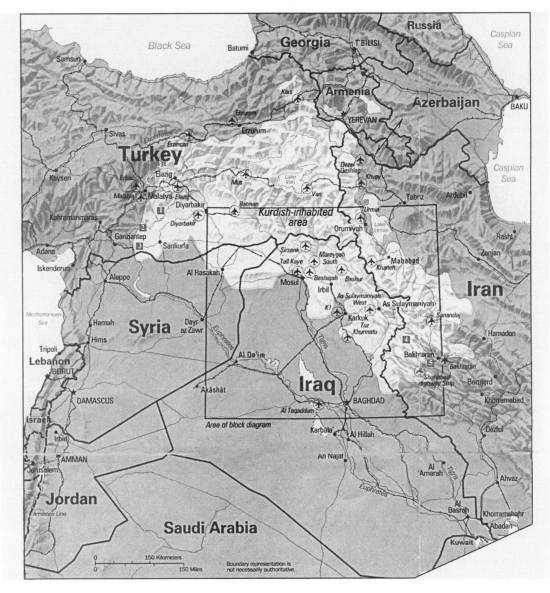

MAP OF KURDISH-INHABITED AREA. *(University of Texas. Reprinted by permission.)*

official discrimination and many Kurds have risen to the highest ranks of the Turkish political, business and cultural worlds. Many, if not most, Kurds now live in urban areas side-by-side with the Turkish compatriots, intermarrying and intermingling easily.

But this picture of happily integrated Kurds is not a complete picture. Kurds—both in the southeast and in urban Turkey—are generally poorer, less educated, and less healthy than Turks. While it is true many Kurds succeed in Turkish society, that success comes at a great cost. To make it, they must give up their Kurdish-ness—their language, their culture, even their very names. Finally, there remains a deep suspicion of Kurds. Many Turks

harbor a prejudice of Kurds, seeing them as ignorant, dirty, violent, and prone to crime. And, it is arguable, few Turks really trust the patriotism of Kurds, believing that, deep down, they would prefer a state of their own—a fact that many Kurds, in private, would agree with.

This question of patriotism is critical to an understanding of the mutual distrust that has perpetuated the current conflict. The Kurds are a distinctive people—arguably, the largest ethnic group in the world—occupying a geographically coherent region—without a state of their own. They are intensely proud of their culture, their heritage and their history—much of which consists of their millennia-long struggle for independence from lowland regions from Babylon to modern-day Turkey. Turkish nationalism is a newer thing but one that is no less intense. Within the body politic is the traumatic memory of lost power and prestige. Having once ruled much of the Middle East and southeastern Europe, they saw their sovereignty successively whittled down to the Anatolian heartland itself. Then, in the wake of World War I, they saw Turkey itself humiliated, occupied, and threatened with dismemberment by outside powers.

Out of that catastrophe, they arose to build a modern state and a modern national identity, the components of which were the unity of the republic and pride in Turkish accomplishment. The presence of a significant minority—Kurds represent about twenty to twenty-five percent of sixty-four million people—that refuses to identify with that state and nationality calls into question the Turkish nation itself. This explains why Turkey officially refused to recognize the existence of Kurds until 1991 and why it maintains—to this very day—that Kurdish demands for autonomy are encouraged by foreign powers bent on destroying the Turkish state. Thus, as far as Ankara is concerned—and despite the clear evidence to the contrary—Ocalan and the PKK are foreign-sponsored terrorists with little real appeal or support among the Kurdish masses of Turkey.

Yet, so far, Turkey has shown no signs it plans to carry out the death sentence against Ocalan anytime soon. There are two reasons—one internal and one external—for this hesitation. The European Union—which abhors and bans the death penalty—has made it clear that Turkish membership—much coveted by the country's political and economic elite—would be postponed indefinitely if Ankara executes Ocalan. And even the most hardened Turkish generals admit that executing Ocalan would turn him into a martyr and set off new violence. Indeed, the PKK has vowed an unprecedented campaign of urban terrorism should its leader be put to death.

As for the future, there are signs of hope. Turkish hopes for membership in the European Union may force it to grant modest concessions to its Kurdish population on matters of culture, education and language. While the Kurds—war-weary and brutalized—would probably prove willing to accept this recognition and space for their way of life. If Turkey can find peace, then it may find prosperity. And there is nothing like economic growth—equitably shared—to put the demons of nationalism and history to rest.

BIBLIOGRAPHY

Arfa, Hassan. *The Kurds: A Historical and Political Study.* New York: Oxford University Press, 1966.

Bruinesscn, Martin van. *Agha, Shaikh and State: The Social and Political Structures of Kurdistan.* London: Zed Books, 1992.

Bullock, John and Harvey Morris. *No Friends but the Mountains: The Tragic History of the Kurds.* New York: Oxford University Press, 1992.

Chaliand, Gerard, ed. *A People Without a Country: The Kurds and Kurdistan.* New York: Olive Branch Press, 1993.

Gunter, Michael M. *The Kurds and the Future of Turkey.* New York: St. Martin's Press, 1997.

———. *The Kurds in Turkey: A Political Dilemma.* Boulder, Colo.: Westview Press, 1990.

Helsinki Watch. *Freedom and Fear: Human Rights in Turkey.* New York: Helsinki Watch, 1986.

———. *State of Flux: Human Rights in Turkey (December 1987 Update).* New York: Helsinki Watch, 1987.

Hitchens, Christopher. "Struggle of the Kurds," *National Geographic,* August 1992.

Hotham, David. *The Turks.* London: John Murray, 1972.

Izady, Mehrdad. *The Kurds: A Concise Handbook.* Washington, D.C.: Taylor and Francis, 1992.

Kreyenbroek, Philip G. and Christine Allison. *Kurdish Culture and Identity.* Atlantic Highlands, N.J.: Zed Books, 1996.

Kurdish Life, Brooklyn, N.Y.: The Kurdish Heritage Foundation, 1991.

McDowall, David. *The Kurds: A Nation Divided.* London: Minority Rights Publication, 1992.

Meiselas, Susan. *Kurdistan: In the Shadow of History.* New York: Random House, 1997.

"Turkish Rule on Head Scarves," *New York Times,* 9 December 1999.

Vryonis, Speros. *The Turkish State and History: Clio Meets the Grey Wolf.* Thessalonica, Greece: Institute for Balkan Studies, 1991.

James Ciment

LIBERIA IN CIVIL WAR: HAVEN FOR FREED SLAVES REDUCED TO ANARCHY

THE CONFLICT

Blacks from America—former slaves—colonized Liberia in 1822. Since 1989 Liberia has been fighting a bloody and brutal civil war. In addition to the deaths and mutilations, the war has created thousands of refugees, and virtually decimated the infrastructure of the country.

Political

• The Africans from America (Americo-Africans) established a government in Liberia and for much of the history of Liberia, ran the government. The native-born Africans were not allowed to fully participate.

• Many rebel groups, such as ULIMO, led by Samuel Doe, emerged to fight the Liberian government and each other.

• The war in Liberia destabilized neighboring countries.

Economic

• Americo-Africans are significantly wealthier and have more opportunities than Africans whose ancestors have always been African.

Nowhere has the severity of conflict been more dramatically evident than in West Africa. Liberia was the first to suffer. On Christmas Eve in 1989, insurgent leader Charles Taylor invaded the country with only one hundred irregular soldiers armed primarily with AK-47 assault rifles; within months, he had seized mineral and timber resources and used the profits to purchase additional light weapons. In 1990, Taylor's ill-trained and undisciplined insurgents toppled the government of President Samuel Doe (who had come to power in a conventional, albeit bloody, coup ten years earlier). Civil war broke out and fighting continued for seven more years before a tentative peace was made.

As a result of the civil war, approximately one half of a population of 2.4 million became refugees in bordering countries. The number of dead is in the thousands, without having a realistic headcount. Within Liberia, those who stayed have swarmed into the cities, causing overcrowding and massive unemployment. At this moment, even though aid is given to Liberia, with its corrupt government, the future outlook for the country is dim.

HISTORICAL BACKGROUND

The country of Liberia, which is on the southern west coast of Africa, has a unique history as it was founded to promote emigration of freed slaves to Africa. The modern political history began in 1816 with the formation of the American Society for Colonizing the Free People of Color in the United States. This was an organization designed to facilitate the resettlement of freed slaves in African colonies patterned after America, many of

CHRONOLOGY

1816 The American Society for Colonizing the Free People of Color in the United States, the purpose of which was to establish a country for freed U.S. slaves, is founded.

1822 The first group of freed U.S. slaves establish a colony on land in Africa—named Liberia.

1862 The United States recognizes Liberia as an independent nation.

1870 E.J. Roye is elected president of Liberia.

1884 The Americo-African group, the True Whig Party, seizes control.

1972 William Jenkins Tolbert becomes president.

1980 A group of non-commissioned officers, led by Master Sergeant Samuel K. Doe, overthrows the True Whig government.

1989 Civil war erupts.

1990 Liberia is in chaos; the Economic Community of West African States intervenes. ECOMOG establishes a neutral zone around the city of Monrovia, the capital of Liberia.

1992 Yamoussoukro IV Agreement.

1993 Cotonou Agreement.

1994 Accra Acceptance and Accession Agreement and Accra Clarification.

1996 Civil war ends with the signing of the Abuja II Peace Accords.

1997 Presidential elections are held for the first time.

1999 Liberian refugees are repatriated by United Nations organizations.

---

whom had been in the U.S. for hundreds of years. In 1822, the first group of freed slaves established a colony on a small parcel of land bought for three hundred dollars from a local chieftain. The colony was named Liberia, meaning "land of liberty," and the capital city of Monrovia after the American President, James Monroe. In 1847, the Free and Independent Republic of Liberia was proclaimed. Ironically, European countries were the first to recognize the new country, and it was not until 1862, that the United States formally recognized its own creation as an independent nation.

For about 133 years, Liberia was thought to be a relatively stable country. Nevertheless, under the surface, tension between the Americo-Africans (blacks whose ancestors came from the United States) and the indigenous people were brewing. Since the purchase of the new colony, there were ongoing bitter racial struggles. The indigenous people—the Manding, Kru and Gola, who were part of sixteen groups that lived there when the blacks from America arrived—were from the onset completely against the arrival of the new immigrants. When the American government bought the land, these three groups revolted and tried to throw out the newly arrived settlers by force. The

initial number of freed slaves who settled in the new country was about fifteen thousand people. However, the revolt was unsuccessful. Thereafter, unable to keep the land for themselves, those who were native to the region tried to carve out for themselves both an economic and a political place in the new country.

Among the new arrivals, there was also a lot of tension. There were two distinct groups of freed slaves: mulattos—people of mixed race parentage—and African-Americans of pure African descent. There had been an intense rivalry between them since the beginning of the colony. Those of African-American heritage, who constitute about five percent of the present population, have dominated both the political and economic scenes, while the balance of the population has engaged in subsistence farming with a relatively lower standard of living. Most Americo-Africans lived in the city; most of the indigenous African population lived in the rural areas.

Trouble could be seen as early as 1870 when E. J. Roye was elected president of Liberia. He was the first African-American of pure descent to be elected to this office. In 1871, after only one year in office, Roye was assassinated in a civilian

LIBERIA WAS FORMED IN THE EARLY 1800S BY AFRICAN-AMERICANS, SUCH AS THESE ILLUSTRATED WHO ARE WAITING FOR TRANSPORTATION, WHO FELT COMPELLED TO RETURN TO THE HOME OF THEIR ANCESTORS. *(AP/Wide World Photos. Reproduced by permission.)*

coup. The coup was led by Joseph Jenkins Roberts and a group of distinguished leaders from within the mulatto community. They managed to hold political power for thirteen years; in 1884 the True Whig Party, the Americo-African coalition named after a political party in the United States, seized permanent political control. Political power and wealth had been in the hands of the small minority of Americo-Africans for so long that, in 1930, the League of Nations condemned the country as being a republic of twelve thousand citizens with one million subjects. The imbalance between the two groups was constant until 1944. From 1944

until 1980, the administrations of both William V. S. Tubman and William R. Tolbert tried to lessen the differences between the indigenous people and the Americo-Liberian groups.

William Tubman took the office of president in 1944 and is regarded as having brought his country into the modern age. He held an "open door" policy in order to encourage foreign investment into the country, which was successful. He undertook a unification policy aimed at closing the divide between those indigenous people and the African-American community. He gave indigenous people representation in Liberia's House of

Representatives and redistributed land to them. This representation in the House, however, did not create a balance as it was designed. The Americo-Africans still held the majority of votes in the government and the money that came from foreign investments went more to the urban areas than the interior regions that needed development.

President Tubman died in 1971 and William Jenkins Tolbert took office in 1972. He was the first Liberian president who spoke a dialect of the interior indigenous people, and his rule was characterized by a more casual, open style of government. In order to promote reforms, Tolbert brought non-True Whig Party supporters into the government, expanded educational opportunities and introduced universal suffrage. Previously, only those who lived in cities and were educated had the right to vote. Some critics claimed he "let peasants into the kitchen." Yet, Tolbert was confident in Liberia's history of political stability, so he permitted political parties to emerge, with one of the first being the Progressive Alliance of Liberia. Rural communities organized self-help groups and university students started to organize a radical student union.

The administrations of both Tubman and Tolbert tried to remedy both the political and economic problems that were dividing the people. However, Liberia's people of lower status were already committed to more rapid change. The first signs of unrest occurred in 1979. Supplies of rice, which was a main staple of the people, dropped below what was necessary for sustaining the population. It dropped because many growers went to work for the large rubber plantations. In order to give an incentive to the people to increase rice supplies, the government proposed that the price of rice be raised from $22 to $26. Instead of encouraging more production, the proposed price raise infuriated the people and they called for a rally to protest the rise. The government refused to grant permission for the rally, which set off populist riots in the capital of Monrovia. The riots caused wide spread looting and when it finally ended, fifty people were killed and more than five hundred were injured. Furthermore, the riot brought about almost total destruction to businesses, with ninety percent in the capital either partially or completely destroyed. It was estimated that the cost of the damage was about fifty million dollars. The Liberian Congress granted President Tolbert emergency powers wherein he immediately imposed a curfew on the city. These measures did not work as the rebellion continued.

PRESIDENT WILLIAM RICHARD TOLBERT, JR. *(Corbis. Reproduced by permission.)*

On April 12, 1980, a group of non-commissioned officers led by Master Sergeant Samuel K. Doe overthrew the True Whig government. Samuel Kanyon Doe, who was semi-literate, was a member of the Krahn cultural group and entered military service at the age of eighteen. Throughout his service in the army, there had been long-standing tensions between the Krahn and the other rural indigenous groups. Thomas Weh Syen of the Kru people and Thomas Quiwonka of the Gio people supported Doe's takeover. They stormed the Executive Mansion, assassinating and disemboweling President Tolbert. Along with the assassination of Tolbert, Samuel Doe and his men executed thirteen other senior members of Tolbert's administration. With this act, the group seized power and set up a Peoples' Redemption Council (PRC). Samuel Doe then positioned himself as Commander-in-Chief and Chairman of the PRC.

The first signs of rivalry and discontent within the Doe administration came a year after power changed hands. Weh-Syen, now a major-general and Vice-Chairman of the PRC, along with four others, was executed for plotting to assassinate Samuel Doe. Doe's other accomplice in the downfall of the Tolbert administration, Thomas Quiwonkpa, tried to initiate his own coup in 1983. He was granted clemency, but later fled the coun-

SAMUEL K. DOE

1950–1990 Samuel Kenyon Doe was born May 6, in either 1950, 1951, or 1952. After attending school until the eleventh grade, he dropped out and enlisted in the army. He rose through the ranks of the military, and was appointed a master sergeant in 1979. Shortly thereafter, Doe joined a group of rebels and participated in the violent overthrow of the Liberian government in 1980. In 1981 he became the first Liberian head of state not descended from the Americo-Liberian elite when he assumed the rank of general and appointed himself commander in chief of the army.

Doe was elected to another term as president in a 1985 election that was widely believed by international observers to be fraudulent. After an unsuccessful coup attempt shortly before his inauguration, Doe launched attacks on those whom he viewed as political opponents, as well their associates and families.

After suppressing another uprising in April 1990, Samuel Doe was killed by rebel leaders in Monrovia, on September 9, 1990.

try when it became apparent that his life was in danger. Two years later in 1985, Quiwonkpa returned, staged another attempted coup and was finally executed and dismembered. Doe then set out to destroy all of Quiwonkpa's ethnic group, the Gio, and a nationwide attack was waged against them.

Ironically, despite the violence of the coup waged by Samuel Doe, the people welcomed it. The majority of the indigenous people embraced the new Doe administration. However, the enthusiasm for the new government did not last. Within months most of the new members of the government were either fired or forced to resign. Any opposition to the policies of Samuel Doe was not tolerated. Although the new regime claimed to represent the entire country, it was evident that power was in the hands of only those who were from the Krahn ethnic group. In 1985, Doe was re-elected to the presidency in an election that was widely accused of being fraudulent. From that point, Samuel Doe was repeatedly accused of brutality and corruption, while at the same time his administration faced declining national production, declining economic conditions, and animosity from neighboring countries. His Krahn ethnic

group was encouraged to respond by repressing any opposition to his administration with complete open brutality. Atrocity after atrocity as executions, castrations, rapes, floggings and dismemberment became a common theme in Liberia as the country deteriorated into civil strife.

Civil War

In 1983 Charles Taylor, who is currently the president of Liberia, was charged with corruption. He managed to escape the country, but was captured by the American government and put in jail in Massachusetts. While in jail, Taylor managed to escape and made his way back to Africa where he joined forces with Colonel Muamar Qaddafi and trained in a Libyan terrorist camp. Qaddafi, who had troops in Chad, was interested in west African nations, thus wanted to institute friendships among those potential leaders.

In December 1989, civil war broke out. Charles Taylor, who had been assembling a small army trained in Libya, led an invasion from the Ivory Coast (Cote d'Ivoire). The invaders called themselves the National Patriotic Front of Liberia (NPFL) and received support from Libya, Burkino Faso, the Ivory Coast and Liberians living abroad. Charles Taylor's tactic was to exploit the hostility already aroused by the fraudulent 1985 elections. It was not, however, his intention to install the person who was actually considered to have won the election: Jackson Doe from Nimba county. In fact, Jackson Doe was later put to death by the NPFL. This tactic succeeded and Taylor gathered the support he needed. However, the Krahn Armed Forces of Liberia (AFL) retaliated with more brutal slaying of people from Nimba county, and drove the Gio and Manos ethnic groups far back into the brush country. Additionally, the AFL began killing Gios and Manos within its own ranks who were suspected of sympathizing with the rebels. In response to the savageness of the AFL, the NPFL mounted its own campaign to slaughter any member of the Krahn, Mandingo, or other group that was a Doe government supporter.

ECOWAS

By July 1990, the capital of Monrovia was in absolute chaos. There was widespread looting and killing. Taylor's troops had overrun the country and anarchy was widespread. In August, the situation had become so depraved that the Economic Community of West African States (ECOWAS) decided to intervene militarily. They created a military force called the ECOMOG or ECOW-

AS Monitoring Group. At this point, the NPFL split in two when Prince Yormie Johnson, one of Taylor's main aids, formed his own rebel group called the Independent National Patriotic Front of Liberia (INPFL). In September 1990, the INPFL succeeded in capturing Samuel Doe as he left the Executive mansion to meet with the president of the ECOWAS. He was severely tortured, mutilated, and executed—all of which was recorded on videotape. On August 30, 1990, a national conference took place. All groups sent representatives except the NPFL. The conference elected Dr. Amos Sawyer, leader of the Liberian Peoples' Party, as head of the interim government.

Yamoussoukro Agreement

In October 1990, the ECOMOG established a neutral zone in the boundaries of the city of Monrovia. The idea behind the neutral zone was to create a situation in which a cease-fire and peace talks could be pursued. The following month, a cease-fire agreement was signed in Bamako, Mali. For the next two years, a shaky peace existed in Liberia. The ECOMOG and Dr. Sawyer's government exercised control over the region of Monrovia. At the same time, Charles Taylor's National Patriotic Reconstruction Assembly government, based in the city of Gbarnga, regulated activities in the rest of the country. An uneasy quiet was achieved while the ECOMOG sponsored a series of negotiations that eventually ended in the signing of a peace agreement. The agreement was signed in Yamoussoukro, the capital city of the Ivory Coast, and became known as the Yamoussoukro IV Agreement. Under it, rebel factions were to be secluded temporarily and disarmed before full-scale national elections could be held under the supervision of the ECOWAS. The Yamoussoukro Agreement was never executed as the NPFL refused to agree to give up its weapons. They argued that the ECOMOG was in reality not a neutral organization, rather it was under control of a newly armed force: the United Liberation Movement of Liberia.

United Liberation Movement of Liberia

Al-haji Kromah organized the United Liberation Movement of Liberia (ULIMO) in March 1991, along with former followers of the AFL. ULIMO was supported by the government of Sierra Leone, but the group broke into smaller factions. These fragmented groups were organized according to ethnic backgrounds: the ULIMO-K for Kromah's Mandingo supporters, and the ULIMO-J for those who supported Roosevelt Johnson and the Krahn. In August 1992, fighting

CHARLES TAYLOR

1948– Charles Ghankay Taylor was born January 27, 1948 in Monrovia, Liberia, into the elite Americo-Liberian ethnic group descended from freed American slaves. He was well educated, and received degree in Economics in 1977 from Bentley College, in Massachusetts in the United States. He returned to Liberia to become director the the General Services Administration, but fled in 1984, after being accused by the Liberian Government of embezzlement. He was arrested in the United States, but escaped from a Massachusetts prison while awaiting extradition. After living in exile in several African countries, he founded the National Patriotic Front of Liberia (NPFL) in 1989. At the end of that year, he led an invasion of Liberia from the neighboring Ivory Coast. The NPLF became one of many warring factions in Liberia.

In 1995 under the terms of the peace accord that ended the civil war, Taylor joined the transitional government. He and his party, the All Liberian Coalition, won seventy-five percent of the vote in July 1997 multiparty elections. In August 1997 he was sworn in as president with absolute power over both houses of parliament.

broke out between the two major factions, the ULIMO and the NPFL. Many people fled to the protected capitol of Monrovia, but in September the NPFL massacred about 450 people. In October, the NPFL began what was known as Operation Octopus, which was an attempt to take over the capital. Their assault was stopped by the ECOMOG, along with the AFL and ULIMO. Yet, bloodshed did not stop here. In June of 1993, more than five hundred more people were slaughtered by the NPFL.

Since ULIMA held the capitol, Charles Taylor was forced to negotiate with the U.N. Special Representative to try to find a settlement. After a series of meetings that took place in Geneva, Switzerland, another peace agreement was signed. This agreement was signed in Cotonou, the capital of Benin, on July 23, 1993. The conditions of the Cotonou Agreement were basically similar to those in the Yamoussoukro Agreement, but with several important exceptions. A new interim government was to be made up of all major parties, which was called the "Liberia National Transition Government." Additionally, the United Nations,

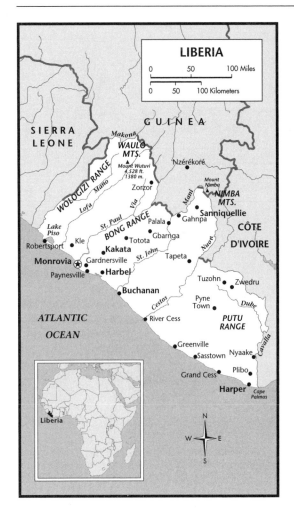

MAP OF LIBERIA. (© *Maryland Cartographics. Reprinted with permission.*)

along with other African states, was to oversee the disarming of all factions involved. In September 1993, the Security Council of the United Nations passed Resolution 866. This created the United Nations Observer Mission in Liberia. The Mission brought 651 people to Liberia that included 303 military observers, 20 military medical personnel, 45 military engineers, 58 U.N. volunteers, and 89 civilians, and also incorporated 136 Liberian civilians.

The Cotonou Agreement was no more effective than the previous agreement. A time limit of seven months had been set for disarming the different factions and holding elections, which proved unrealistic. In addition, none of the groups had any intention of abiding by the various provisions. Another agreement, the Akosombo Accord, brought about by Charles Taylor, Alhaji Kromah, and General Hezekiah Bowen, was signed in

September 1993 to augment the Cotonou Accord. This, too, was opposed—not only by civilians and other factions, but the ECOMOG as well. The overall sentiment was that the new accord granted too much power to the NPFL, ULIMO-K and AFL, thus, in essence, splitting up Liberia among the three different factions.

By April 1994, Nigeria, which was one of the primary countries providing troops in the ECOWAS Monitoring Forces, had become completely frustrated with the situation. In addition, Nigeria had problems of its own that it needed to address and, therefore, decided to pull out of Liberia. The U.N. was able to get Nigeria to agree to postpone its withdrawal.

Accra Agreement

At the end of 1994, the rebel groups signed another agreement. It was called the "Accra Acceptance and Accession Agreement and Accra Clarification." This agreement included more of the rebel factions than had been included in the Akosomba Accord. In order to calm the fears of renewed fighting and torture, an indigenous leader from the north, Chief Tamba Taylor, was chosen to represent his fellow citizens. Following this agreement, the interim government formed a Rapid Response Unit to try to put a stop to the random murders and robbery in Monrovia. However, by this time, Monrovia had become desolate, with destroyed buildings and random killings, and even the ECOMOG troops were attacked by rebel forces whenever they came out in the open.

The civil war formally ended on August 17, 1996, with the signing of the Abuja II Peace Accords, and a cease-fire took effect on August 31, 1996. This agreement established a six man Council of State to run the country until national elections could be held. The Council included Wilton Sankaawulo, who was Chairman of the Council and Chief Tamba Taylor, who was Vice-Chairman. Other members were Charles Taylor of the NPFL; Alhajii G. V. Kromah of the ULIMO-K; Oscar Quiah of the LNC; and George Boley of the Coalition. All former members of the various rebel factions signed the Ajuba II Peace Accord.

In July of 1997, the Liberian civil war actually came to an end when legislative and presidential elections were held for the first time since 1985. Charles Taylor and his National Patriotic Party took over seventy-five percent of the vote, thus insuring them control of both the legislature and presidency. Although international observers have

A LIBERIAN WOMAN STANDS ATOP THE REMAINS OF A MONROVIAN HOSPITAL, YET ANOTHER CASUALTY IN LIBERIA'S CIVIL WAR. *(AP/Wide World Photos. Reproduced by permission.)*

said that the elections were run fairly and openly, some groups have contended that the election was really carried out under a great amount of intimidation. There have even been accusations that the election was fixed. The government was now in the hands of a man who had been responsible for much of the destruction.

The Aftermath of Civil War

The destruction that has taken place in Liberia is of huge proportions. Liberia had a pre-war population of 2.4 million people. It is estimated that over one hundred fifty thousand people were killed during the war, and fifty thousand of that number were children. In addition to those killed, about seven hundred thousand have fled the country. About fifty percent of the population has been displaced as well. Most of these refugees have fled to Monrovia and the city of Buchanan for protection. There were so many displaced that when elections came, the traditional system, which was based on geographical representation, had to be discarded and replaced by a country wide party-based system of proportional representation.

The country today has taken on the appearance of a security state: there are military and security agencies everywhere. Charles Taylor has his own presidential security force; this force is known as the Special Security Service and is extremely large and heavily armed. Taylor's son, Charles Jr., is the head of a secret military group that is said to have six hundred members. This unit includes not only Liberians, but men from Gambia, Sierra Leone, and Guinea. Besides the President's security forces, many of the ministers and legislative members have their own personal security forces. Because there is now an increased sense of security in the country, many refugees have returned or expressed their desire to be repatriated.

Because so many people have indicated their desire to return, the United Nations High Commissioner for Refugees began a large-scale effort at repatriation starting in December 1997. By May of 1999, more than one hundred nine thousand Liberians have been repatriated by the U. N. organization, with as many as two hundred thousand more returning on their own.

The civil war in Liberia has ruined Liberia's economy. Before the civil war broke out, Liberia was the second largest exporter of iron ore in the world. Their exports in this market accounted for more than two-thirds of the country's export earnings. During the war, the industry has completely fell apart and it has yet to be reinstated to its former capacity. Aid to rebuild Liberia's metal industries has been offered. For example, in 1997, Commonwealth Gold, which is part of a South African international consortium, apparently went into a joint venture with the Liberian government. For exclusive rights to Liberia's minerals, Commonwealth Gold pledged to give $7.5 billion dollars in reconstruction aid over a ten-year period. Without the aid, the industry did not stand a chance of being rebuilt. However, it was unclear that money from the deal would actually go for national reconstruction or if it would go to personal use.

The agricultural economy also was destroyed during the civil war. The national staple crop of rice fell in production to as low as ninety thousand metric tons. This is about twenty-three percent of the total national requirement to feed the people within the country. Many of the stockpiled seeds and equipment disappeared during the war, making it virtually impossible for farmers to re-start production after the war. Rubber farming and lumber production also dropped drastically. Because many people have returned to rural regions due to the violence in the cities, the need to rebuild the agricultural sector is greater than ever.

International organizations such as the United Nations Food for Agriculture, the European Union and various non-governmental organizations (NGOs) have provided seeds and equipment in an emergency effort to aid communities. In the past year, efforts have increased to make seeds available to the poor rural regions so that farmers can plant rice. Statistics show that rice production has climbed seventy percent over pre-war levels and another staple, cassava, has jumped one hundred percent. With the efforts of outside sources, it is estimated that food has been made available for more than 1.5 million Liberians. There is also an emphasis on educating the Liberian farmers on new agricultural methods. Although great strides have been made, Liberia still requires food and food aid.

A major problem in Liberia since the onset of the civil war has been the destruction of its health care system. Ninety-five percent of its healthcare infrastructure was destroyed during the war. Because of this, more than ninety percent of Liberians do not have any access to health care at all. Even those that do, find that it is extremely inadequate. In the majority of the Liberian counties, there are no healthcare facilities, and many of the people die from routine diseases that are completely preventable including malnutrition, tetanus and measles. Again with outside aid, many of the counties have just barely begun to receive the most basic services.

One area of the economy that has not suffered as greatly is the shipping industry. Liberia still gets a considerable income from ships flying the Liberian flag. Many countries that wish to avoid health and safety regulations find flying the Liberian flag is a way to get around many strict rules in other countries.

Another casualty of the Liberian war has been indigenous cultural traditions. Descendants of freed slaves continue to live a life that is relatively luxurious, while those who live in rural areas have been relegated to subsistence farming practices. It is quite easy to distinguish between the two, as rural people favor the wearing of traditional African garments, while Americo-Africans tend to dress extremely formally, in the Western style. Before the war, many of the indigenous people received an education, but that rarely happens now. Most have left the country. There is little or no electricity, even in Monrovia; few have running water and garbage collection is non-existent. Although aid organizations have provided some healthcare, most hospitals in the city, along with most of the banks, have been closed.

BIBLIOGRAPHY

Africa Contemporary Record. New York: Africana Publishing Co., 1969–1989.

Bever, Edward. *Africa.* International Government and Politics Series. Phoenix, Ariz.: Oryx, 1996.

Unger, Sanford J. *Africa The People and Politics of an Emerging Continent.* New York: Simon & Schuster, Inc., 1989.

Africa Watch. http://www.Africawatch.org.

Barbara DeGorge

NAGORNO-KARABAKH: SELF-DETERMINATION AND ETHNIC IDENTIFICATION

THE CONFLICT

Nagorno-Karabakh, which is primarily Armenian, was a province of Azerbaijan for much of the time it was part of the USSR. Nagorno-Karabakh is fighting for its independence from Azerbaijan, with support from Armenia.

Ethnic

- The people of Nagorno-Karabakh are primarily Armenian and Christian; the people of Azerbaijan are primarily Azeri and Muslim.

Political

- Armenians and Armenians in the United States support Nagorno-Karabakh.

- Turkey and Iran periodically aid Azerbaijan.

Economic

- Oil has been discovered in Azerbaijan, so many countries have an interest in settling the war.

Between 1988 and 1994 an undeclared war raged in the small, mountainous territory of Nagorno-Karabakh (pronounced Na-Gore-No Car-a-Bach, and often referred to as Karabakh). Nagorno-Karabakh is a seventeen hundred square-mile enclave that lies within the borders of Azerbaijan. Azerbaijan and Armenia each claim Nagorno-Karabakh as a significant part of their respective histories. In 1988 when the contemporary conflict started, Armenia shared no common border with Nagorno-Karabakh, but roughly seventy-five percent of the territory's two hundred thousand people were ethnic Armenian. Bloodshed erupted, in fact, when the Karabakh Armenians expressed their desire to unite with Armenia. A series of violent conflicts followed in Nagorno-Karabakh, Azerbaijan, and Armenia. They ranged from disorganized persecutions and organized massacres, to, by early 1992, full-scale war. By 1994 an estimated twenty-five thousand people had been killed in the conflict. Many of the dead were civilians and non-combatants, including women and children. The war was fought with ethnic cleansing, human rights violations, and torture taking place on both sides. The fighting also made refugees of four hundred thousand ethnic Armenians who lived in Azerbaijan and of seven hundred thousand ethnic Azeris and Kurds who once lived in either Armenia or Nagorno-Karabakh. As late as the spring of 2000 almost one million refugees of the conflict lived in camps in Azerbaijan, Armenia, Turkey, or Iran.

The main participants in the war and in the present dispute are Karabakh Armenians, Azerbaijan, and Armenia. Armenians in Karabakh, who initially sought to unite with Armenia, now demand independence from Azerbaijan and the right to self-determination. Azerbaijan, however,

CHRONOLOGY

1813 Treaty of Gulistan gives Nagorno-Karabakh to Russia.

1905 Revolutions throughout Russian empire spread to Azerbaijan and Armenia. Thousands die over several months of fighting and rioting in cities.

1915 Azerbaijanis in the "Army of Islam" commit genocide in Armenia and massacre 1.5 million Armenians.

1918 Armenia declares independence.

1920 The Soviet Union establishes control over Azerbaijan and Armenia.

1921 Josef Stalin decides to grant control of Nagorno-Karabakh to Azerbaijan.

1937 Nagorno-Karabakh is given the official name Nagorno-Karabakh Autonomous Oblast.

1985 Mikhael Gorbachev announces *glasnost* and *perestroika* in the Soviet Union.

1988 Armenians in Karabakh declare independence. Violence erupts in Nagorno-Karabakh and in Azerbaijan.

1990 "Bloody January" opens the year of escalating violence.

1991 Communist government collapses and the Soviet Union disintegrates. Conflict over Nagorno-Karabakh is no longer an internal Soviet problem but a conflict between two independent states. War escalates in Nagorno-Karabakh as Azerbaijani and Armenian nationalism fuels conflict and Soviet military disarray leads to the transfer of arms to both Armenians and Azerbaijanis.

1994 Cease-fire; peace and resolution, however, remain elusive.

believes Armenia is behind the Karabakh independence movement and sees Armenia as its principal enemy and main combatant. Azerbaijan seeks to maintain its territorial borders and protect its sovereignty, and thus, refuses to allow Karabakh independence. For its part, Armenia showed complete support for Nagorno-Karabakh's independence movement and provided financial and military assistance during Karabakh's war with Azerbaijan. In addition, at least eight thousand volunteer Armenian soldiers came to the aid of Nagorno-Karabakh during the war. At present, Armenia has waived all territorial claims to Karabakh and now professes a policy of non-engagement.

Complicating matters further has been the role that outside influences have played in creating the conflict and in trying to mediate its end. The war escalated during and after 1991, in large part because of the disintegration of the Soviet Union. Armenia and Azerbaijan, both former republics of the Soviet Union, are in many ways the victims of Russian and Soviet imperial policies that date back into the nineteenth century. Living under Russian and Soviet rule, for example, meant that Azerbaijanis and Armenians lived within territorial boundaries not of their own making. Russian and Soviet government officials, in fact, drew and re-

drew the national boundaries of Armenia, Azerbaijan, and Nagorno-Karabakh, creating large pockets of ethnic minorities in each area in the process. With the breakup of the Soviet Union, Azerbaijan, Armenia, and Nagorno-Karabakh inherited borders that had not been drawn along ethnic lines. In the absence of Soviet rule, nationalism and ethnic conflict emerged in the region. The war between Armenians in Nagorno-Karabakh and Azerbaijan was not the only ethnic war of the post-Soviet era, but it was the bloodiest. In 1994 Armenians in Karabakh and Azerbaijan agreed to a cease-fire and the negotiation process began. A solution to the Karabakh problem had not been found as late as mid-2000.

HISTORICAL BACKGROUND

Early Nagorno-Karabakh

Like all conflicts, there are long and short-term factors that contributed to the war in Nagorno-Karabakh. Geography, invasion, colonization by foreign conquerors, Soviet policy, nationalism, and intolerance are but a few of the notable sources of conflict. Armenians and Azerbaijanis both feel a strong, historic connection to Nagorno-Karabakh that makes a peaceful

NATIONALISM

In modern history, nationalism has been a powerful idea and movement. It refers to the belief that the nation-state is the supreme form of political, social, economic, and cultural organization of a people. A basic assumption is that individuals owe loyalty to the nation-state. It is characterized by feelings of community and is based upon the belief that people of nation-states share common things, such as languages, religions, as well as a common historical past and experience. Prior to the emergence of nationalism in the eighteenth century, people tended to base their personal identities (how they see themselves) and their loyalties on religious, provincial, village, clan, or tribal affiliations. There was little connection to the nation-state. Nationalism can also contain a strong sense of ethnic chauvinism as people often define themselves and their community against what they are not. In Armenia and Azerbaijan, two nation-states that do not have long histories as independent states, nationalism revolves around ethnic identity.

solution difficult to find. Many of the present circumstances in the area are a reflection of how the region developed historically. The present day states of Armenia, Azerbaijan, and Nagorno-Karabakh are geographically located between Europe and Asia in a region known as the Caucuses. Historically, these lands provided a land bridge between Asia and Europe. Rich in resources, the Caucuses served as a crossroads of human movement. Over thousands of years countless merchants, travelers, and nomads passed through the region. Some stayed, others did not. Among those who stayed were an Indo-European people whose descendents are Armenian, as well as a Turkic people, from today's Middle East, whose descendents are Azerbaijanis or ethnic Azeris.

The area was subjected to a large number of invasions and eventually succumbed to foreign colonization. The Mongols of Central Asia invaded the area in the thirteenth and fourteenth centuries. The Persian, Ottoman, Roman, and Russian Empires, moreover, all considered the Caucuses as part of their empires at various points of time. Many of these empires, in fact, rivaled one another to dominate the rich natural resources and cultures of the region. Some empires had a lasting effect on the development of Armenians and Azerbaijanis.

One notable example comes from the diverse religions that are common in the Caucuses. Armenians adopted Christianity in the fourth century AD while under Roman rule. Azerbaijanis converted to Islam while under Turkish control.

Therefore, because of thousands of years of invasions, settlements, and migrations the Caucuses developed a very diverse population with different languages, religions, cultures, and customs. In fact, an 1897 census of the Caucuses found twenty-two different ethnic groups living in the region. The territory was always changing. Ethnic groups could be counted as a majority population in one century and a minority population the next. This same ethnic and religious diversity has continued into the twenty-first century and it has provided a source of tension and conflict between Armenians and Azerbaijanis.

The population of Nagorno-Karabakh also changed over time. Yet, Armenians and Azerbaijanis both claim that historically, Karabakh belongs to them. Armenians assert that Karabakh has been Armenian since the seventh century BC. They contend that in the mountainous region of Karabakh Armenian princes never came under the rule of foreign conquerors until the Russian Empire took control of the region in the nineteenth century. Armenians, therefore, see Karabakh as a stronghold of Armenian autonomy and culture. By contrast, Azerbaijanis claim that the area historically belonged to ancient Azeri people and that the large population of Armenians in Nagorno-Karabakh is a recent development. They assert that in the eighth century AD Armenians moved into the area and forced Christianity, the Armenian language, and Armenian culture on the population living there. The Armenians in Nagorno-Karabakh, according to Azerbaijanis, are not true Armenians but are the descendents of converted Azeris. In addition, Azerbaijanis claim that only after the Russian annexation of Nagorno-Karabakh did Armenians migrate there in large numbers. More importantly, Azerbaijanis consider Nagorno-Karabakh as a cradle of their civilization because it has produced distinguished Azeri poets, writers, musicians, and composers who encouraged Azeri cultural pride.

Russia and the Soviet Union

The current ethnic tensions between the Armenians and Azerbaijanis were also once exaggerated and exploited while both people lived under Russian, and then Soviet, rule. In the early nineteenth century Russia subsumed Armenia and Azerbaijan into the Russian Empire. In 1813

Russia also acquired Nagorno-Karabakh from Turkey with the Treaty of Gulistan. Russia wanted the entire region for many reasons. Economically, the area is rich in mineral resources and in oil. Strategically, the area also provided a buffer zone between Russia and a rival empire to the South, the Turkish Ottoman Empire. Russia and the Ottoman Empire rivaled one another for control of the Caucuses for centuries, but in 1867 Russia finally established five different governing territories that extended political control over present-day Armenia, Nagorno-Karabakh, and Azerbaijan.

The Russian Empire had a lasting effect on the development of Armenians and Azerbaijanis. When Russia began to industrialize and diversify its economy in the nineteenth century Armenians living in Azerbaijan became more prosperous than the native Azerbaijanis. Armenians tended to live in cities like Baku, the present-day capital of Azerbaijan. They had a great deal of property and wealth and controlled many of Baku's oil companies. Azerbaijanis, in turn, tended to be agriculturists and more rural. Azerbaijanis were also, in general, poor unskilled workers. When Russia expanded its control over the region and started to extract raw material such as oil from cities, including Baku, Armenians prospered and received better treatment from Russian government officials. After all, they controlled the flow of a precious resource. Many Armenians rose to political and economic power in this system. In general, Azerbaijanis did not. Animosities thus developed over economics and political power.

Russia not only sought to dominate Karabakh, Azerbaijan, and Armenia economically, it also sought to "Russify" the local population. Russian educational policies and the Russian language joined the Russian government and economic policies in the Caucuses. In Azerbaijan "Russification" also meant trying to convert Azeris to Christianity. The spread of the Russian language and attempts to establish "the Cross of Christ" in the Islamic Azerbaijan were the two main policies Azerbaijani patriots fought hardest against. Armenians also had to cope with Russification. When they resisted, Russia used force to put down Armenian insurrections, just as they did in Azerbaijan.

These Russian policies fueled the ethnic and religious differences between Armenians and Azerbaijanis. The Russian government knew that ethnic disparity was pronounced in the Caucuses so it used a "divide-and-rule" policy that intentionally relocated and mixed ethnic groups togeth-

STATEMENT OF THE CAUCASIAN BUREAU, USSR, 1921

In 1813 Russia acquired Nagorno-Karabakh from Turkey. Following the Communist revolution in Russia, Nagorno-Karabakh was ruled by the USSR. The Caucasian Bureau oversaw the states in the Caucasus, including Nagorno-Karabakh. Initially the Caucasian Bureau decided to transfer Nagorno-Karabakh to Armenia. The decision below, however, came following a meeting in 1921 between the Caucasian Bureau and the Soviet Commissar for Nationalities, Josef Stalin, later ruler of the Soviet Union.

Proceeding from the necessity for national peace among Muslims and Armenians and the economic ties between upper and lower Karabakh, of its permanent ties with Azerbaijan, mountainous Karabakh is to remain within the borders of Azerbaijan Soviet Socialist Republic, receiving wide regional autonomy with administrative center Shusha, becoming an autonomous region.

er as a way of discouraging the national demands of any single group. Divide-and-rule pitted ethnic groups against one-another, and it intended to keep each group weak and dependent on Russian authority. It was a policy that often contributed to violence between Armenians and Azerbaijanis. In 1905, for example, an Armenian police officer killed an Azeri civilian, sparking months of violence that the Russian government did nothing to stop. When it was over six hundred Azeris and nine hundred Armenians lay dead. Later that year violence surfaced again, this time leaving over one thousand dead.

Russia's rule over the Caucuses had another lasting effect on Armenians and Azerbaijanis. It contributed to the development of an intense nationalism for both groups. For Azerbaijanis, nationalism began to emerge in the nineteenth century when a pan-Turkic movement swept through much of the Islamic World. Pan-Turkism called for the unification of all Turkic people, including Azeris, who spoke similar languages, had similar historical experiences, common origins, and who practiced the Muslim faith. This seemed a better alternative to Russian rule for Azerbaijanis, who believed that they were exploited under the Russian colonial system.

For Armenians, an intense form of ethnic nationalism led to demands for self-reliance and self-government. Armenian nationalism grew

EXCERPTS FROM AN INTERVIEW WITH GALINA STAROVOITOVA, DEPUTY IN THE SUPREME SOVIET OF THE USSR

Haratch, Paris, 20 September 1990 (in Armenian).

. . . There are numerous problems linked to the modifications of borders . . . .; But it seems to me that the problem of Artsakh should not be placed in this category. It is not, in fact, a territorial question . . . . In reality, it is a question of self-determination by one part of a people. It is a matter of the defence of the political, cultural, and religious rights of an ancient people

I believe it is necessary to outline three criteria which can be employed to decide to whom a group belongs.

1. The historic background of a given region: here it is undeniable that this region is Armenian. There exist, to be sure, several falsifiers of history (such as Ziya Buniyatov) who sow doubts on Karabagh's past. This allows the passions of the Azerbaijani people to be churned.

2. The actual demographic profile of the region: this profile does not always correspond with the historic background as we can see today in the case of Nakhichevan, or the Abkhazians who do not constitute more than 17 percent of the population on their historic lands. Fortunately, and despite the policies of all these years, Armenians still continue to constitute 80 percent of the population of Artsakh.

3. The will of the people: the population must say with whom it wishes to be unified. Its will must be expressed in a constitutional manner, be it through the ballot box or by means of a decision by the legal authorities in the territory concerned. Since 1988, the people of Artsakh have expressed their will five times by means of decisions by the Soviet of the Autonomous Region.

I would like to stress that these three criteria rarely coincide, but this is precisely the case for Artsakh. That is why, if one considers that problem from a democratic and humanitarian point of view, there can be no doubt as to the legitimacy of the demand.

. . . In February 1998, the population of Artsakh expressed its desire to be unified with Armenia. It was not necessary to explain to me the nature of the problem. I recognized the legitimacy of this demand immediately, and I have expressed my solidarity at every opportunity.

I am sometimes criticized for taking the side of one people against another. Sometimes, I am also the object of threats by the Azerbaijanis. Azerbaijani newspapers smear me by saying that I am in the pay of the Dashnaks . . . . I do not respond to this level of criticism . . . .

I hope that the development of democracy in Azerbaijan will raise it to a level where the Azerbaijani people will understand that errors have been made, which have taken them on an ill-chosen path.

To defend the cultural interests of an ancient people can only honour those who chose this path. But I believe that in the case of the Artsakh, it is a matter of the defence of democracy in general . . . .

Starovoitova, Galina. From an interview in The Caucasion Knot: The History & Geopolitics of Nagorna-Karabagh. *Zed Books, Ltd., 1995. Copyright © 1995 by Zed Books. Reproduced by permission.*

---

tremendously during the early twentieth century because Armenians believed that only independence guaranteed survival. For example, during World War I, Armenia, Karabakh, and Azerbaijan each declared independence from Russian rule. Azerbaijan, however, then joined with the Turkish Ottoman Empire and marched an "Army of Islam" into Armenia. Between 1915 and 1922 roughly 1.5 million Armenians were killed in a policy of genocide. Adult Armenian males were killed instantly while elderly men and women, as well as children, were marched to death in Syria. Russia did nothing to defend Armenia. In fact, by 1918 Russia had pulled out of World War I and was confronted with a civil war of its own between the Czarist government and Bolshevik (Communist) revolutionaries. Armenians, therefore, demanded self-determination as a way of safe-

guarding their existence. They believed they could not trust Azerbaijan, nor could they trust Russia. A few short years later, however, Armenia, as well as Azerbaijan, came under the control of a new foreign government. This time it was the Soviet Union.

The Soviet Union established control over Azerbaijan, Karabakh, and Armenia in an opportunistic and piecemeal fashion. After striking a deal with Turkey the Soviet Red Army marched into Baku in April 1920, and on the next day established the Soviet Socialist Republic of Transcaucasia. The Red Army proceeded into Karabakh and by the end of May brought the Armenian population there under its thumb. The Soviet government then set its sights on Armenia, which was at the time engaged in a war with Turkey. The

Red Army closed in on the Armenian capital of Yerevan and by the end of 1920, Armenia became a Soviet Socialist Republic. The status of Nagorno-Karabakh now became an internal Soviet matter.

Under Soviet rule the divide-and-rule policy returned to the Caucuses. In 1921 Josef Stalin (1929–53) began to redraw the borders of two new Soviet Republics when he confronted the complexities of the situation in Nagorno-Karabakh. Stalin was one of the principal revolutionary leaders in the Communist take-over of Russia. As the new Bolshevik government began to extend its administrative control over its new republics, Stalin was appointed Soviet Commissar of Nationalities, a position that gave him control over the new ethnic groups living within the Soviet Union. Stalin believed that it was important to take sides in the dispute between Armenia, Karabakh, and Azerbaijan—and he sided with Azerbaijan. A separate administrative group called the Caucasian Bureau, however, had already decided that Karabakh should be transferred to Armenia. Yet in a strange turn of events, the committee reversed that decision a day later and agreed with Stalin that Nagorno-Karabakh should be in Azerbaijan. Stalin then established Karabakh as an autonomous *oblast*, administrative territory, within Azerbaijan, despite the region's clear Armenian majority. Stalin drew new territorial boundaries around Nagorno-Karabakh, which divided Armenia from Karabakh by a six-mile strip of land called the Lachin corridor. By keeping Armenians inside Azerbaijan Stalin insured the cooperation of the new Soviet Republic of Armenia. In effect, the Soviet government held the fate of Karabakh Armenians hostage to Soviet policies in the Caucuses. Stalin's decisions had the twin effect of devastating Armenians while elevating Azerbaijanis. The way the decision was made also insured future hostilities. Unsurprisingly, when Karabakh Armenians sought unification in 1988, they used Stalin's decision as a justification for their pursuit.

The Soviet Union ruled over Azerbaijan and Armenia for the next seventy years. During that period the status of Nagorno-Karabakh, and tensions in general, were quieted by strong authoritarian rule that silenced any questioning of national policy. Yet, as historian Ronald Suny wrote in his 1983 study *Armenia in the Twentieth Century*: "The single most volatile issue among Armenians is without a doubt the question of Karabakh, the autonomous region heavily populated by Armenians living within the Azerbaijani Soviet Republic." That volatility began to show itself

after 1985. In 1985 Soviet Premier Mikhail Gorbachev announced reforms in the Soviet Union called *glasnost*, "openness," and *perestroika*, "restructuring." These reforms eventually unleashed the nationalist forces that had been hiding for decades under Soviet rule.

Glasnost allowed for a degree of public debate to emerge within the Soviet Union over questions concerning environmental, economic, and nationalist policies. Gorbachev himself criticized Stalin's arbitrary 1921 decisions. Gorbachev's call for reforms and his encouragement of national debate inspired the creation of several grassroots democratic movements within the republic. In late 1987, for example, Armenians in Karabakh publicly protested the poor environmental conditions and the political corruption in Nagorno-Karabakh. They then moved dramatically to push for independence because of two important events. First, in late 1987, Heydar Aliyev, the Communist Party Chief of Azerbaijan, was removed from office. Historically, he opposed any Armenian autonomy in Karabakh. Second, Gorbachev's chief economic adviser, Abel Aganbegyan, stated publicly that Moscow was sympathetic to Armenian wishes. These two events signaled the possibility for change in Karabakh. By the end of 1987 tens of thousands of Armenians in Karabakh and in the Soviet Republic of Armenia began mass demonstrations calling for the unification of Karabakh and Armenia. For the first time in seventy years Armenians believed momentum was on their side.

In early 1988 the momentum for secession from Azerbaijan grew steadily in Karabakh and Armenia. Demonstrations erupted in January when five hundred thousand Armenians in Yerevan began to protest Stalin's 1921 decision to transfer Karabakh to Azerbaijan. Increasingly, Armenians began to associate Soviet decisions with Azerbaijani exploitation in the territory. Armenians also reminded the public of the 1915 massacre in Armenia and of the loss of national independence after World War I. At the same time, Armenians in Karabakh entered a new round of protests over Azerbaijan's policies in the region. They complained that under Azerbaijan, Armenians in Karabakh were denied access to higher education, were barred from traveling to Armenia, and that Azerbaijan spent little money on developing Karabakh. Armenians claimed that Azerbaijan's policies were the equivalent of cultural genocide.

Azerbaijan countered these accusations, arguing that Azerbaijan was forced to accept Karabakh as an independent territory rather than have it

EXCERPTS FROM AN INTERVIEW WITH ELENA BONNER, WIDOW OF ANDREI SAKHAROV

Le Figaro, 26 July 1990.

Karabagh was, it seems, the first to believe in the slogan 'All power to the Soviets,' and by the resolution of its Soviet followed the path chosen by her people—the 75 percent of the people living in the territory—which is to say reunification with Armenia. Armenia supported this movement which was the expression of *perestroika* and only opposed the type of Stalinist power which decides where each people should settle and live. Not having understood that, the government has defended the Stalinist constitution above all, even above its own existence. Nowhere else in the country and at no other time was there such a level of support for *perestroika* and its leader as there was in Armenia and Karabagh.

Let us recall the main slogan of those day, 'Yes to Gorbachev.' But fear of all mass, popular, spontaneous movements is characteristic of our government. It is afraid. That gave unsupervised forces the opportunity to organize Sumgait.

. . . In December 1988 a group from Moscow accompanied Sakharov to the Caucasus. There they met with the First Secretary [of the Communist Party of Azerbaijan], Vezirov. Like an actor, he gave us a lecture on Armenian-Azerbaijani friendship. Andrei Sakharov was hard pressed to interrupt this rumbling voice of a trained orator. We explained why we had come. No reaction. Once again he started up on

friendship. 'We are fraternal peoples.' Then I said that even among brothers there are disputes, but in the midst of tragedy they forget the past. For example, the earthquake—that was a tragedy! 'You are upset that the world has not noticed your kindness. Return Karabagh to the Armenians since, over there, there isn't even a single piece of land on which to settle. Then the entire world will come to its knees and thank your people.' You should have seen his face when he cut in, 'Land is not give. It has to be conquered. With blood.' And he repeated it with great satisfaction, 'With blood!' That ended our talk with the authorities in Baku. Vezirov promised blood. There you have it.

. . . Two world wars, the civil war, the Armenian genocide of 1915, the genocide of the Jews, Cambodia, our Gulag. Isn't that sufficient? All these young Azerbaijanis, Armenians, and Russians who have tinted the pink rocks of the Caucasus with their blood? Isn't it enough for the president of the largest country in the world—a sixth of the planet? And if he listened? . . . But he will not listen, not any more than he listened to the words of Andrei Sakharov in the Supreme Soviet: 'For Azerbaijan, Karabagh is a question of prestige; for Armenia, it is a question of life and death . . . .'

Bonner, Elena. From an interview in The Caucasion Knot: The History & Geopolitics of Nagorna-Karabagh. *Zed Books, Ltd., 1995. Copyright © 1995 by Zed Books. Reproduced by permission.*

incorporated directly into the republic. It also pointed out that the Soviet Union intentionally created an artificial Armenian majority in Karabakh by including Armenian villages in the boundaries, while excluding Azeri villages. Armenian, moreover, was designated the official language of instruction in Karabakh, and Armenians tended to control the educational and cultural institutions of Karabakh as well. Azerbaijanis, therefore, never believed Karabakh's Armenians had legitimate complaints.

Tensions escalated when, on February 20, 1988, the Armenian-dominated Soviet Deputies of Nagorno-Karabakh passed a resolution by a vote of 110 to 17 calling for the transfer of Karabakh to Armenia. This was the first time that a vote of transfer had been made. Hundreds of thousands of Armenians took to the streets of Yerevan and Stepanakert, the capital of Nagorno-Karabakh, celebrating the vote and demanding

unification. This vote, however, also signaled the return of ethnic violence to the Caucuses. In Sumagit, a town north of Baku, Azeri mobs attacked Armenians in response to the vote's results. Local Azeri authorities did not respond and over thirty Armenians were murdered, dozens of women were raped, and several hundred others were severely hurt. Azeri officials attempted to cover up the violence.

The movement for unification and the violence in Sumagit led to the creation of an Armenian nationalist organization called the Karabakh Committee (KC). Its membership was comprised primarily of prominent Armenian intellectuals, who served as a political opposition group to the Armenian Communist Party, which many believed always complied with Moscow's policies. The Karabakh Committee advocated union with Nagorno-Karabakh as a national goal, promoted the democratization of Armenia, and sought economic reform, as well as some form of national independence. The Karabakh Committee met with Mikhail Gorbachev in pursuit of these objectives and pressured the Armenian Communist Party to change its position regarding Karabakh. The Armenian Communist Party eventually conceded and asked Gorbachev to transfer control of Karabakh to Armenia—a recommendation Gorbachev roundly denounced as an "abuse of *glasnost*." Gorbachev never intended for *glasnost* to create shifts in territories or ethnic violence. He tried to mediate the conflict but was ultimately unable to chart a long-term resolution. By the end of 1988 Gorbachev ordered the imprisonment of eleven members of the Karabakh Committee. To settle the increasingly tense situation in Karabakh, Gorbachev then created a small administrative group to oversee the governance of the territory and recommend policy decisions in the future. The imprisonment of the KC, combined with the slow-pace of change in Karabakh, led to the formation of another Armenian nationalist organization, called the Armenian National Movement (ANM), in early 1989.

Attempts to unify Armenians woke Azeri nationalism. By the fall 1988 Azerbaijanis increasingly feared the loss of national sovereignty if Karabakh was lost. Azerbaijani's openly condemned both the governments in Baku and in Moscow for not settling the question of Karabakh once and for all. In November 1988 hundreds of thousands of Azeris (Azerbaijanis) poured into the streets of Baku in a public expression of their demands. By early 1989 Azerbaijani nationalism became more organized with the formation of the Azerbaijan Popular Front (APF). The APF operated much like ANM. Its leadership came primarily from the intellectual community and was intensely nationalistic. The demands of the APF directly contrasted with what Armenian nationalists wanted. The APF called for complete control over Karabakh, and they publicly criticized decisions in Moscow and Baku. The Azerbaijan Popular Front also found a great deal of popularity among Azeris, while the Azerbaijan Communist Party increasingly lost the confidence of the people. The APF, in fact, managed to organize strikes and direct an economic blockade of Armenia. The blockade, which was still in place in early-2000, cut Armenia off from nearly eighty-five percent of the food and fuel it needed. The intense nationalism also led to the creation of armed militia groups in Azerbaijan. These militias were typically loosely organized groups that were not under the control of the official government. They played a prominent role in the escalating fighting of 1990.

Bloody January

In 1990 the government of Armenia began discussing the budgetary demands that were necessary to deliver economic and social reforms in Karabakh. Azerbaijani's saw this as meddling in their national affairs. In response Azerbaijani militias attacked three Armenian towns in Karabakh on January 11, 1990. This violence paled in comparison, however, to what would happen in Baku later during "bloody January." The series of disorganized conflicts began on January 13 when Azeris took to the streets in mass protests of Armenian "interference" in Karabakh. Many Azeris turned to violence when a rumor circulated through the massive crowds that an Armenian man living in Baku had used an axe to kill an Azeri. Azeris quickly descended into the Armenian section of Baku seeking vengeance. Two nights of carnage followed as Azeri mobs beat, raped, and murdered Armenians. Seventy-four Armenians were murdered in the two days and fifty thousand Armenians fled Baku fearing for their lives. The Soviet Union responded to the violence by sending over ten thousand additional troops into Baku to try to restore order. The situation, however, worsened during the next few weeks. Soviet forces marched into Baku and took control of the capital city after five hours of fighting. After the Azerbaijan Communist Party denounced the Soviet intervention, Soviet soldiers arrested leaders of the APF, broke through several Azerbaijani blockades, and established military rule, or martial law, in the city. The Soviet Union then dismissed the Azerbaijani government and replaced it with its own leaders.

Bloody January had a lasting effect on the Armenian-Azerbaijani conflict. Not only did it heighten ethnic tensions between both sides, but it also led to the creation of several Armenian militia groups. The largest of these was the Armenian National Army, which recruited over five thousand soldiers. In addition, Armenia and Azerbaijan deepened their distrust of the Soviet Union. Azerbaijanis, of course, resented the open conflict with the Soviet soldiers. Armenians, in turn, believed that Soviet soldiers stood by in Baku while hundreds of Armenians were beaten, killed, and forced to leave their homes. Armenian suspicions were reinforced when, during the summer of 1991, Soviet forces joined with Azerbaijan military troops in conducting passport and arms checks on Armenian villages in Nagorno-Karabakh.

Declarations of Independence

Armenians believed that Soviet actions—the passport and arms checks and the deportations of

Armenians that followed—were all in anticipation of full-scale war in Nagorno-Karabakh. In response, several important developments occurred in Armenia during 1990 and 1991. First, Armenian militias started attacking Soviet troops in order to steal weapons. These militia groups often set out at night and assaulted border checkpoints and weapons depots in order to obtain automatic rifles, grenades, and rocket launchers. There were as many as 115 separate militia attacks between January and May 1991 alone. Second, Armenians elected their first non-Communist government in August 1990, when Levon Ter-Petrosyan was elected to head the new government. Ter-Petrosyan was one of the founding members of the Karabakh Committee and was the leader of the Armenian National Movement. Under his rule Armenia began to make plans to secede from the Soviet Union. On August 23, 1990, Ter-Petrosyan made Armenian intentions public when he called for the creation of a "United Armenia" that included Nagorno-Karabakh.

Armenia's desire for independence was similar to independence movements throughout the Soviet Union in 1990. The Soviet government had slowly started losing control of many of its republics, and, Armenia and Azerbaijan were not the only republics to break into violence during this period. When the Soviet Union did collapse in December 1991, the conflict over Nagorno-Karabakh was already becoming the bloodiest affair in the region. The fall of the Soviet Union, moreover, changed the nature of the conflict. The Soviet government lost control over many of its commanders and troops stationed in the Caucuses. Many of those ex-Soviet troops resorted to selling their artillery, weapons, and military supplies to the highest bidders. Initially, Azerbaijan benefited from the sales and began shelling Nagorno-Karabakh with Soviet artillery. As the Soviets withdrew from the region Armenians and Azeris stood in direct conflict with one another. The dispute was no longer an internal Soviet problem between two republics. Rather, it became an undeclared war between two newly independent national states, with Nagorno-Karabakh at stake. For Armenians the war remained a struggle for self-determination by the Karabakh Armenians. For Azerbaijan the war was a struggle to maintain its territorial boundaries. Both sides saw Karabakh as vital to the future of independence in their respective countries.

War

Beginning in late 1991 the war went through four bloody stages, each punctuated by human rights violations on both sides. The first phase opened with Azerbaijan's military offensive on Karabakh between December 1991 and May 1992. Baku began mobilizing Azerbaijani forces in December 1991, but Nagorno-Karabakh's declaration of independence in January 1992, prompted those forces to move into Karabakh. Azerbaijan then launched a full military offensive on Stepanakert, with the intent of driving Armenians out of Karabakh. Equipped with armored vehicles, rocket launchers, and artillery fire Azerbaijan's military moved in, but to their surprise, they were beaten back by Karabakh Armenians. From there, the attack deteriorated into a series of disorganized and indiscriminate artillery shellings that killed several hundred Armenian civilians. This action, apparently designed to break the will of Armenians, did not achieve its objective. In fact, it had the opposite effect: Armenians in Karabakh rallied to respond with force.

This initial phase of the conflict ended with a Karabakh Armenian counter-offensive in North and West Karabakh. Armenian forces first captured the Azeri village of Malybeyli and then began a full-scale offensive toward the Azeri village of Khojaly. After several days of intense fighting, which witnessed the slaughter of one thousand ethnic Azeris in Khojaly, Armenians took control of the village on February 25, 1992. They did so with the help of former Soviet troops. For Azerbaijanis the loss of Khojaly was a major military and symbolic defeat. Prior to its downfall Khojaly was the second largest ethnic Azeri village in Nagorno-Karabakh. Its loss meant that it would be very difficult for Azerbaijan to regain control of all of Karabakh. Following the victory in Khojaly Armenian forces next seized control of the Azeri town of Shusha, which had rich historic and cultural value to ethnic Azeris. Finally, the Armenian counter-offensive managed to seize control of the town of Lachin. The Armenian victory at Lachin changed the conflict because Lachin is located in the strip of land that once divided Nagorno-Karabakh from Armenia. Controlling Lachin meant controlling the six-mile boundary that separated the two territories. From that point forward Karabakh Armenians controlled the borderlands with Armenia, which meant they could be resupplied by their western neighbor. It also meant that the territory would become a major sticking point in any future peace talks.

The initial phase of fighting set several precedents for the future. Azerbaijan's military established a pattern of futility and disorganization that lasted the next two years. In addition, the failure to achieve military objectives sparked repeated political crises in Azerbaijan. On March 5, 1992, Azerbaijan's president Ayaz Mutalibov stepped down amidst massive public demonstrations calling for his removal. Between 1992 and 1994 the Azerbaijan government changed hands several times because of Karabakh. The initial phase also reinforced the practice of slaughtering civilians in the conflict. This was not to be a war of soldiers and armies; civilians were targeted as well.

The next major phase of the conflict began in the summer of 1992 when Azerbaijan launched a second major offensive on Nagorno-Karabakh. This stage began with the election of Abulfaz Elchibey as president of Azerbaijan. Elchibey was a hard-line nationalist and a member of the Azerbaijan Popular Front. He vowed to reverse the policies established by Mutalibov and to liberate the "Turkic homeland" of Karabakh. Elchibey diverted large sums of money into rebuilding and reorganizing the Azerbaijani military. Five days after his election, moreover, Elchibey ordered the launching of a large Azerbaijan offensive on Karabakh. With more than one hundred tanks and armored personnel carriers, and with air support, Azerbaijan aimed to split Karabakh in two and then take each half one-by-one. Karabakh's Armenians were caught off-guard by the sudden coordinated attack and they suffered significant losses during the summer and fall of 1992. The war tipped in Azerbaijan's favor for the first time.

The Karabakh Armenian counterattack, beginning in October 1992, marked the third phase of the war. During this period Karabakh Armenians took back Nagorno-Karabakh and ultimately occupied 20 percent of Azerbaijan by mid-1993. Azerbaijani forces, weakened by years of fighting and disorganization, could not hold-off the Karabakh Armenians despite their superior numbers. Karabakh Armenians pushed Azerbaijanis out of Karabakh and eventually managed to invade and occupy parts of Azerbaijan.

This decision to expand the terrain of battle into Azerbaijan and, in particular the Karabakh war against Azeri civilians, sparked an international response to the war. The United Nations and the United States expressed concern over human rights violations, demanded an immediate cease-fire, and the withdrawal of Karabakh Armenians from Azerbaijan. In addition, a dangerous situation emerged when Armenian victories led Azerbaijan's ally, Turkey, to mobilize its military and express public support for Azerbaijan. This was the first indication that the conflict could potentially spread into a region-wide war involv-

STATEMENT OF THE FOREIGN MINISTER OF NAGORNO-KARABAKH

On March 16, 2000, the Foreign Minister of Nagorno-Karabakh included the following passage as part of a statement in response to the Azerbaijan's position in the conflict. It shows the degree to which suspicions and tensions remain strong.

We are convinced that the irreconcilable position of Azerbaijan has proved who is actually and not declaratively seeking for the peaceful settlement of the conflict. It has disclosed the real intentions of official Baku—to isolate Nagorno-Karabakh, to preserve and aggravate the economic and humanitarian crisis with the aim of displacing the autochthonal [indigenous] Armenian population from the region.

ing Turkey, Iran and potentially Russia. Turkey, Iran and Russia watched the war closely. By the end of 1993 Karabakh Armenians counted major victories in the war. They drove Azeris out of Karabakh, occupied at least twenty percent of Azerbaijan, and established a territorial connection with Armenia.

The final military phase of the war opened with another Azerbaijani military offensive on Karabakh. In the winter of 1993 Azerbaijani forces poured into the occupied territory seeking to liberate it from Armenian control. Under orders not to retreat, and with the aid of foreign mercenaries from Afghanistan and advisors from Turkey, the Azeri military made significant gains in re-taking lost territories. The effort came to an end, however, because heavy snowfall and the military offensive proved too costly in terms of lost personnel and armored vehicles. With military conflict at a standstill by the spring of 1994 both sides agreed to a cease-fire so that a negotiated peace process over Nagorno-Karabakh could begin.

RECENT HISTORY AND THE FUTURE

The cease-fire has been in place since May 1994 and, while there has been sporadic fighting, there have been no major military actions by either side since then. Unfortunately, there has also been no major movement in peacefully settling the con-

MAP OF NAGORNO-KARABAKH. *(XNR Productions Inc.)*

flict, and both sides appear so far apart in the negotiations that some observers see another war on the horizon. The sides are deadlocked on one fundamental issue: Karabakh wants complete autonomy but Azerbaijan refuses to let it go.

Several developments have made the conflict over Nagorno-Karabakh more complex and, in many ways, more dangerous. The first factor is the role of outside influences on the war itself and in the peacemaking process. As mentioned earlier, ex-Soviet troops and military weapons have found their way into the hands of both sides, making the conflict deadlier. Turkey and Iran, two Islamic nations, have at various times felt pressure to aid the Muslim Azeris. Thus, as quoted in Michael Croissant's, *The Armenia-Azerbaijan Conflict* (1998), the presence of foreign states prompted Azerbaijan's President Elchibey to state in 1993, "To my great regret, the war between Armenia and Azerbaijan long ago ceased to be a war between two rivals from the Caucasus. This is a war in which the combating peoples have become the pawns of mightier powers."

Much of the international attention stems from human rights violations and the huge number of refugees created by the conflict. There has

been a general "humanitarian crisis" in the Caucuses since violence started in 1988. According to the non-governmental group Human Rights Watch the war in and around Karabakh witnessed horrific violations of human rights and of the rules of war, including forced removals, execution of prisoners of war, looting and burning of civilian homes, hostage taking, bombing of hospitals, medical transports, and rescue missions, and the indiscriminate use of military force against civilian targets. These violations took place on both sides, especially during the bloodiest years of the conflict between 1992 and 1994. As a result the international community has increased efforts to settle the dispute peacefully and to provide medical supplies and food to refugee camps.

Outside influences have also intervened out of their own national self-interest. After the break-up of the Soviet Union, Russia has sought to maintain a powerful and active role in the Caucuses. Russia is motivated by a strong desire to maintain its historic influence in the region, and it has economic interests as well. Russia wants to maintain a leadership role in the Caucuses and has been trying to mediate a peaceful solution since 1992. It is also trying to block Turkish influence in the region. This is especially true because Azerbaijan refused membership in the Commonwealth of Independent States (CIS) in 1992. The CIS is a loose federation of former Soviet republics; Armenia belongs to the CIS. Turkey and Iran are in competition with Russia for influence in the Caucuses and both are concerned with the close proximity of war to their own respective borders. Both nations fear that if the conflict opens again, military actions will spill over into their states. Iran also contains a sizable Azerbaijani minority and fears that any additional conflict will add to the number of refugees pouring into Iran. Finally, the Organization for Security and Cooperation in Europe (OSCE) is also trying to negotiate an end to the conflict in order to elevate its own status as a peacemaking organization.

In addition to efforts to secure a negotiated peace plan, a round of negotiations were taking place in Baku that did not concern the war, but rather the oil in Azerbaijan. On September 20, 1994, Azerbaijan negotiated an $8 billion oil contract with companies from the United States, the United Kingdom, Russia, Japan, Turkey, Saudi Arabia, and Norway. The foreign companies project that over the next thirty years 650 million metric tons of oil will flow out of Azerbaijan, translating into roughly $100 billion in profit for the companies and Azerbaijan. This contract, which calls for the drilling of oil in the Caspian Sea just off the coast of Azerbaijan, near Baku, further complicates the peace process. Karabakh and Armenia fear that Azerbaijan will use oil profits to buy arms and weapons in order to attack Karabakh. In fact, since 1994, both sides have, at various times, purchased arms from foreign countries in anticipation of renewed warfare. Armenians also fear that because many of the countries brokering a peace settlement also have an interest in Azerbaijan's oil, Karabakh will be forced into a settlement it does not want. So, Karabakh has resisted all attempts to negotiate a peace settlement that do not allow for complete independence in Karabakh.

Another factor that has complicated matters is the role of Armenians outside of Karabakh. Armenians in Armenia, motivated by the prospect of Karabakh's independence, volunteered by the thousands to fight against Azerbaijan. In addition, Armenians living in the United States have raised money to supply and fund the independence effort in Karabakh. Armenians in Los Angeles, California, held a telethon, and raised close to eleven million dollars to construct a road from Karabakh to Armenia. The Armenian lobby in the United States also supported an American law that prevents the United States from using government funds to provide medical aid to Azerbaijan.

The prospect for the return of armed conflict does not seem likely, if only because both sides lack the present will or the military means to accomplish victory. Peaceful resolution, however, seems equally remote. The real danger, therefore, lies in the future. The Caucuses have a long history of ethnic divisions that, during various points in history, have been exploited and served as catalysts to violence and war. As long as the Karabakh Armenians and the Azerbaijanis see their very survival as the main issue in the territorial dispute over Karabakh, there are few chances for a negotiated settlement. Both sides remain inflexible on very fundamental issues. Both sides believe the other has victimized them, and both sides argue that history is on their side in claiming the diverse territory of Nagorno-Karabakh.

BIBLIOGRAPHY

Alstadt, Audrey. *The Azerbaijan Turks.* Palo Alto, Calif.: Stanford University Press, 1992.

Betts, Wendy. "Third Party Mediation: An Obstacle to Peace in Nagorno Karabakh," *SAIS Review* 19, 2 (1999): 161–183.

Chorbajian, Levon, Patrick Donabeian and Clark Mutatian. *The Caucasian Knot: the History and Geo-Politics of Nagorno-Karabakh.* London: Zed Books, 1994

Croissant, Michael. *The Armenia-Azerbaijan Conflict: Causes and Implications.* Westport, Conn.: Praeger, 1998.

Helsinki Watch. *Bloodshed in the Caucuses: Escalation of Armed Conflict in Nagorno-Karabakh.* New York: Human Rights Watch, 1992.

Human Rights Watch/Helsinki. *Azerbaijan: Seven Years of Conflict in Nagorno-Karabakh.* New York: Human Rights Watch, 1994.

Rieff, David. "A Case Study in Ethnic Rife," *Foreign Affairs* (March-April 1997): 232–244.

Suny, Ronald G. *The Revenge of the Past: Nationalism, Revolution, and the Collapse of the Soviet Union.* Palo Alto, Calif.: Stanford University Press, 1993.

Mark A. T. Esposito

OIL: PROTECTIONIST PRICING AND FUEL DEPENDENCE

THE CONFLICT

The countries belonging to the Organization of Petroleum Exporting Countries (OPEC) control almost sixty-seven percent of the world's estimated crude oil reserves and forty percent of the world's production of crude oil. When OPEC limited production in order to drive up prices, Western nations—highly dependent on oil—protested. In the spring of 2000, OPEC increased production, but prices continued to rise.

Economic

- The countries that have a lot of oil want to make money off of the scarce resource—and want to continue to make money for a long time.

- Industrialized countries are highly dependent on oil, and high oil prices effect their economies.

During 1999 and 2000 gasoline prices rose more rapidly than at any other time in history. Fed-up citizen groups throughout the United States organized "Gas-Out Days," when millions of drivers refused to purchase gasoline in hopes of influencing oil companies' pricing. Undeterred, prices continued to rise and with them went the prices of goods transported using petroleum. The situation revealed a basic truth of American life: The United States is a chemically dependent nation—it is dependent on fuel.

After the Gas Crisis of the early 1970s there was a steady decline in prices. The trend was reversed in 1996, due mainly to the steady increase in the world demand for oil. The price-increase was an outcome of decreased supply brought on by the slowing of production, particularly among members of Organization of Petroleum Exporting Countries (OPEC). This was a dramatic shift from the early years of the petroleum industry, when the substance could barely be given away. More than possibly any other resource, petroleum has become intertwined with the modern way of life. This national dependence fuels the importance of petroleum in global economic and political affairs.

HISTORICAL BACKGROUND

Creating Petroleum

The intricacy of petroleum to American life in the 1990s would have shocked nineteenth century users of "Pennsylvania rock oil." Most farmers who knew about oil in the early 1800s knew seeping crude as a nuisance to agriculture and water supplies. These observers were not the first people to consider the usefulness of petroleum, which had been a part of human society for thousands of years. Its value grew only when European-Americans directed their commodity-making skills to the resource.

Crude oil was found and used in some fashion in various locales throughout the world. However, the area that is credited with first noticing petroleum is a mountainous area in western Pennsylvania, nearly one hundred miles above Pittsburgh. The oil occurring along Oil Creek was named initially for the Seneca people, who were the native inhabitants of this portion of North America at the time of European settlement. There were, however, earlier users of this same supply.

Northwestern Pennsylvania served as a temporary home to the mound builder society living centuries prior to the Seneca. Paleo-Indians of the Woodland period, before 1400, ventured from their original homelands in the Ohio Valley and along the Great Lakes on frequent journeys to Oil Creek, where they collected oil on a fairly large scale for use in their religious rituals. Although no written accounts remain, it was well known that initial European explorers in the area found long, narrow troughs that had been dug along Oil Creek. Early use of the crude oil reveals interesting contrasts between Native and European cultures. The Seneca skimmed the oil from the water's surface, using a blanket as a sponge or dipping a container into the water and used the collected crude as ointment or skin coloring. European explorers designated this Pennsylvania stream as Oil Creek beginning in 1755. Tourists and soldiers passing through the area were known to soak aching joints in the surrounding oil springs and even to imbibe the crude as a castor oil variation.

As the oil's reputation grew, settlers to the region gathered oil from springs on their property by constructing dams of loose stones to confine the floating oil for collection. In the mid-1840s one entrepreneur noticed the similarity between the oil prescribed to his ill wife and the annoying substance that was invading the salt wells on his family's property outside Pittsburgh, Pennsylvania. He began bottling the waste substance in 1849 and marketed it as a mysterious cure-all available throughout the northeastern United States. He only acquired the oil by skimming, but Samuel Kier's supply quickly exceeded demand due to the constant flow of oil from the salt wells. With the excess, he began the first experiments with using the substance as an illuminant, or substance that gives off light. The culture of expansion and development began to focus on petroleum.

CHRONOLOGY

1851 Francis Brewer enters the first lease for extraction of oil.

1855 George Bissell incorporates the Pennsylvania Rock Oil Company of Connecticut.

1870 John D. Rockefeller forms the Standard Oil Company of Ohio.

1911 Standard Oil has grown so large that it is broken into subsidiaries. The pieces will grow into Mobil, Exxon, Chevron, Amoco, Conoco, and Atlantic, among others.

1948 U.S. consumption of oil is 5.8 million barrels a day.

1960 In order to be able to negotiate better with oil companies, countries producing oil form the Organization of Petroleum Exporting Countries (OPEC).

1972 U.S. consumption of oil is 16.3 million barrels a day.

1973 Disturbed that the oil companies are making huge profits, OPEC declares an embargo of shipments to unfriendly states, including the United States.

1990 Iraqi President Saddam Hussein invades Kuwait. The resulting war and economic sanctions feed a production imbalance, ultimately contributing to price increases.

1999–2000 Gas prices rise more rapidly than any other time in history.

The discovery of petroleum usefulness to the industrial age required the influence of outsiders. Dr. Francis Brewer, a resident of New Hampshire, traveled to Titusville in 1851, to work with a lumbering firm of which he was part owner. During the visit Brewer entered into the first oil lease ever signed with a local resident. Instead of drilling, however, the lessee merely dug trenches to convey oil and water to a central basin. Upon his return to New England Brewer left a small bottle of crude with Dixi Crosby, a chemist at Dartmouth College, who then showed it to a young businessman, George Bissel.

Petroleum's similarity to coal oil immediately struck Bissell. He signed a lease with Brewer to develop the petroleum on the lumber company's land, but first Bissell needed to attract financial backing in the amount of $250,000. This would not be easy since neither he nor anyone else knew of what utility petroleum would have. Some of the risk could be assuaged by scientific explanation of the odd curiosity, petroleum. Benjamin Silliman, Jr., of Yale University provided such backing in his report released in April 1855. Silliman estimated that at least fifty percent of the crude could be distilled into a satisfactory illuminant for use in camphene lamps and ninety percent in the form of distilled products holding commercial promise. On September 18, 1855, Bissell incorporated the Pennsylvania Rock Oil Company of Connecticut, the first organization founded solely to speculate on the potential value of the oil occurring naturally beneath and around the Oil Creek valley.

From this point forward petroleum's emergence became the product of entrepreneurs—except for one important character: Edwin L. Drake of the New Haven Railroad. In 1857 the company sent Drake to Pennsylvania to attempt to drill the first well intended for oil. The novelty of the project soon wore off for Drake and his assistant Billy Smith. The townspeople irreverently heckled the endeavor of a "lunatic." During the late summer of 1859 Drake ran out of funds and wired to New Haven, Connecticut, for more money. He was told that he would be given money only for a trip home—that the Seneca Oil Company, as the group was now called, was done supporting him in this folly. Drake took out a personal line of credit to continue, and a few days later, on August 29, 1859, Drake and his assistant discovered oozing oil.

The technological scope began to shift within two years of Drake's discovery. Portable steam engines became the norm for drilling in the Oil Creek valley and allowed wells to reach new depths. Natural gas within these deeper wells created the first "flowing" wells, sending a rush of oil upward in a gush of escaping natural gas. Gushers vastly increased the amount of crude on the market. The *Venango Speculator* discussed the effects of the massive increase in the oil supply from twelve hundred barrels a day in 1860, to over five thousand in 1861, and then to more than double that amount by 1862.

Pennsylvania oilmen classified the collection and distribution of crude oil as their most pressing technological quandary. Trying to solve this problem, engineers with little training devised the precursors of many contemporary technologies, including off-shore wells, pipelines, tanker rail cars, and increasingly complex refineries. Entrepreneurs quickly identified development and control as the portion of the oil industry that was most likely to endure, outlasting Pennsylvania's diminishing supply.

After the American Civil War the oil industry consistently moved toward the streamlined state that would allow it to grow into the world's major source of energy and lubrication during the twentieth century. Oil was a commodity with so much potential that it attracted the eye and interest of one of the most effective businessmen in U.S. history, John D. Rockefeller. Working within the South Improvement Company for much of the late 1860s Rockefeller laid the groundwork in his effort to control the entire industry. Rockefeller formed the Standard Oil Company of Ohio in 1870. Oil exploration grew from the Oil Creek area of Pennsylvania in the early 1870s and expanded from Pennsylvania to other states and nations during the next decade. By 1879 Standard controlled ninety percent of the U.S. refining capacity, most of the rail lines between urban centers in the northeast, and many of the leasing companies at the various sites of oil speculation. Through Rockefeller's efforts and the organization he made possible, petroleum became the primary energy source for the nation and the world.

Defining Modern Business

John D. Rockefeller and Standard Oil first demonstrated the possible domination available to those who controlled the flow of crude oil. Rockefeller's system of refineries grew so great at the close of the nineteenth century that he was able to demand lower rates and eventually even kickbacks from rail companies. One by one he put his competitors out of business and his own corporation grew into what observers in the late 1800s called a trust, what today would be termed a monopoly. Standard's reach extended throughout the world and it became a symbol of the "Gilded Age" when businesses were allowed to grow too large and benefit only a few wealthy people. Reformers vowed things would change.

President Theodore Roosevelt, who took office in 1901, led the Progressive interest to involve the federal government in monitoring the business sector. In the late 1890s "muckraking" journalists wrote articles and books exposing unfair and hazardous business practices. Ida Tarbell, an editor at *McClure's* who had grown up the daughter of a barrel maker in Titusville, took aim at Rockefeller. Her *History of the Standard Oil Company* produced a national furor over unfair trading practices. Roosevelt used her information to enforce anti-trust laws that would result in

WHEN OPEC DECIDED TO RESTRICT ITS FLOW OF OIL TO UNFRIENDLY NATIONS IN 1973, MANY GAS STATIONS RAN COMPLETELY OUT OF GAS. THOSE THAT DIDN'T, LIKE THIS ONE IN FORT LEE, NEW JERSEY, WERE SWAMPED WITH CUSTOMERS. *(AP/Wide World Photos. Reproduced by permission.)*

Standard's dissolution in 1911. Rockefeller's company had become so large that when broken into subsidiaries, the pieces eventually grew into Mobil, Exxon, Chevron, Amoco, Conoco, and Atlantic among others.

Even after Standard's dissolution in 1911 the image of its dominance continued. Standard had led the way into international oil exploration, suggesting that national borders need not limit an oil controlling entity. Throughout the twentieth century large multinational corporations or singular wealthy businessmen attempted to develop supplies and bring them to market across national borders. In the 1960s, however, nations began to

draw from Rockefeller's model to devise a new structure. Massive international companies managed the import and export of oil regardless of the country of origin. The importer—often companies in Western, industrialized nations—in many cases, was most in control of supply and demand, and, therefore, of the prices.

This situation began to shift in the late 1950s. The Eisenhower Administration decided to implement quotas on the import of crude oil. Quotas—when only a specified amount of oil could be imported from outside the country—were designed to protect the sale of domestic oil. Begun in 1959 such quotas infuriated oil-producing coun-

THE COST OF OIL

The costs of gasoline includes the costs to produce and delivery it to consumers. These costs include the cost of crude (unrefined) oil (about thirty-seven percent of the cost of a gallon of oil), the cost to refine and process the oil (about thirteen percent of the costs), the costs of marketing, distributing, and selling the gas (about fourteen percent). Federal and state taxes vary from state to state, but generally represent about thirty-six percent of the price of a gallon of gas. The price of a gallon of gas reflects these costs, as well as profits or losses by each company at each stage.

Gasoline prices change due to local competition—multiple gas stations in a small area must compete for business. In addition, good weather and vacations generally cause gas prices to rise an average of five percent—or 3.5 cents per gallon—because consumers are traveling more frequently. The largest cause of gas price fluctuation is the price of crude oil. In general, when prices go up $10 per barrel of crude oil, the price at the gas station goes up $.25 per gallon. Finally, because of differences in the costs of distribution, gas can cost different amounts in different areas of the country.

In 1999 the Organization of Petroleum Exporting Countries (OPEC) limited production to drive the price (and their profits) up. Though they increased production in 2000, other factors conspired to keep prices high in the United States. Industrialized countries in Asia were recovering from a substantial Asian financial crisis; as the situation in Asia improved, there was a higher demand in Asia for oil. In addition, the booming U.S. economy increased the demand for gas. The increased demand raised prices around the world.

It is difficult to assess the actual impact of higher gas prices on the economy. Higher gas prices can depress the sale of certain consumer items; in 2000 truck manufacturers were worried about that high gas prices would slow the sale of trucks. However, the countries that sell oil—at higher prices and higher profits—often recycle the profits into the industrialized country's economy by purchasing equipment, manufactured goods, and services.

---

tries throughout the 1960s. By September 14, 1960, a new organization had been formed with which to battle companies making money through the extraction oil around the world. The Organization of Petroleum Exporting Countries (OPEC) had a single clear intent: to defend the price of oil. OPEC would from this point forward insist that companies consult them before altering the price of crude. They also committed themselves to solidarity, and they aspired to a day when oil companies and Western nations would come to them to negotiate. The founding members of OPEC were Saudi Arabia, Venezuela, Kuwait, Iraq, and Iran.

Hitting the Road

Commodities such as petroleum are culturally constructed: A market must first place a value on them before they are worthwhile. In the earliest years of petroleum it was refined into kerosene, an illuminant to replace whale oil. After 1900, when electricity became the source of most lighting, petroleum's greatest value was derived from transportation, mainly the automobile.

First developed in Europe in the late 1800s the automobile was marketed successfully begin-

ning in 1894. Inconvenience from a lack of roads and infrastructure precluded Americans from rapidly accepting the new "horseless carriage." The manufacturing and marketing efforts of Henry Ford and others changed this attitude by 1913, when there was one motor vehicle to every eight Americans. Henry Ford's model of mass production made sure that by the 1920s the car had become no longer a luxury, but a necessity of American middle class life. The need for additional infrastructure—roads and bridges—was growing, but it was unclear who would pay for the development.

After the Federal Road Act of 1916, federal, state, and local governments began using taxpayer funds to construct roads. This process of road building began what some historians have called the "largest construction feat of human history," and the American road system unfolded throughout the early twentieth century. Beginning in the 1920s legislation created a Bureau of Public Roads to plan a highway network to connect all cities of fifty thousand or more inhabitants. Some states adopted gasoline taxes to help finance the new roads. These developments were supplemented in the 1950s when President Dwight D. Eisenhower included a national system of roads in his preparedness plans for nuclear attack. This development cleared the way for the Interstate Highway Act to build a national system of roads unrivaled by any nation.

In the United States the construction of roads initiated related social trends which added to Americans' dependence on petroleum. Most importantly, between 1945 and 1954, nine million people moved to suburbs. The majority of the suburbs were connected to urban access only by the automobile. Between 1950 and 1976 central city populations grew by ten million while suburban growth was eighty-five million. Housing developments and the shopping/strip mall culture that accompanied decentralization of the population made the automobile a virtual necessity. Shopping malls, suburbs, and fast-food restaurants became the American norm through the end of the twentieth century, making American reliance on petroleum complete. Americans now were entirely wedded to their automobiles, which allowed prices of petroleum to impact American life more than any other nation.

A Truly Global Commodity

OPEC's five founding members were the source of over eighty percent of the world's crude oil exports. The members argued that its formation represented a shift of control of the natural resources to the states or nations in which they were located. Despite such proclamations OPEC had little united power to wield in its early years. The existence of OPEC ensured that the companies would not act without consultation, but political power had not yet been mobilized.

During succeeding years OPEC gained political clout through some activities of its own, but also through American fuel dependence. Between 1948 and 1972 oil consumption in the United States grew from 5.8 million barrels per day to 16.4. This three-fold increase was surpassed by other parts of the world: Western Europe's use of petroleum increased by sixteen times and Japan by 137 times. Throughout the world this growth was tied to the automobile: Worldwide automobile ownership rose from 18.9 million in 1949 to 161 million in 1972. The U.S. portion of this growth was significant, from 45 million to 119 million. New technologies enabled some refiners to increase the yields of gasoline, diesel and jet fuel, and heating oil from a barrel of petroleum, but the needs remained unlike anything the world had ever seen.

Such reliance on fuel forced the U.S. federal government to question relevant policies. In 1969 the administration of U.S. President Richard Nixon began debating the quota program. In April 1973 Nixon delivered the first-ever presidential address on energy, in which he announced that he would abolish the quota system, capping the import of crude oil into America. Domestic production, even with quotas, could not keep up with American needs. Clearly, quotas were meant to manage and limit supplies of crude oil in a surplus market, not in the world of shortages that was taking shape. When there is a surplus—too much oil—some countries, such as the United States, limit the amount of oil imported from foreign countries to protect the sale and price of oil found in the United States. If there is a shortage of oil—not enough—prices will stay high and U.S. oil will almost certainly be purchased.

Without the import barriers the United States was a full-fledged and very dependent member of the world oil market. By the summer of 1973 American imports of petroleum had doubled. As prices began to rise OPEC realized that the companies, not the countries who owned the oil, were reaping huge profits. This contradicted the ideology of their arrangement, and some members began demanding action. Throughout the early 1970s OPEC demonstrated that it would not only be concerned with commodity pricing, but that regional politics would also have a bearing on the organization's practices. In fact, pricing was soon to become a weapon in a new breed of international economic warfare. Anwar Sadat, president of Egypt, proposed a simple idea to the other ministers of OPEC in October 1973: an embargo on shipments of crude oil to unfriendly states, including the United States. As approved, the plan reduced shipments by 5 percent each month. In the United States the embargo came as an almost complete surprise.

Petroleum had become a tool of diplomacy. The "OPEC Oil Embargo" fed national panic, which contributed to gas prices rising by as much as forty percent. Gas lines and stations with empty tanks became common sights. "Sorry, No Gas Today," read signs in front of many stations. The gas crisis required rationing and cultural changes from the American public. The embargo was a resounding lesson of "living within limits" for many Americans. Throughout the 1970s their ideas helped to define the modern environmental movement's tenets regarding the conservation of natural resources. In terms of world power the equation had been permanently altered. Following the embargo, a stable supply of crude oil had been placed undeniably with "matters of national interest."

At the same time, there was an effort to develop America's domestic oil reserves. This effort centered on developing a formerly taboo location: Alaska. In the late 1950s, British Petroleum and Sinclair Oil began investigating deposits of oil in Alaska. High costs precluded further development, except by Richfield, a California-based independent producer, which later became ARCO. Their first oil strike came in 1965 on the North Slope's Prudhoe Bay, at the northern-most point of Alaska—an area locked in ice for much of the year. The harsh conditions and isolation made such development difficult. Environmentalists resisted the idea of running a heated pipeline south to a transshipment center in Valdez on Prince William Sound; however, the gas crisis of 1973 seemed to make the pipeline a matter of national necessity. The eight-hundred-mile Trans-Alaska Pipeline helped to ease some of the oil import pressures on the United States, but debate continued throughout the twentieth century regarding to what extent the Alaskan wilderness should be opened to drilling.

Taking Extreme Measures

By the mid-1980s OPEC was faced with a dilemma: It had control of world oil prices, but what was in its bests interests, high or moderate prices? In particular, the Middle East sat on 660 billion barrels of oil, representing almost two-thirds of proven oil reserves. It produced an average of twenty million barrels per day—approximately thirty-three percent of world production—and had forty-five percent of the world's trade in oil. And yet, leaders of these nations still felt unappreciated by the Western world.

At his inauguration in 1989 U.S. President George Bush seemed to speak directly to the Middle East when he said, "They got a President of the United States that came out of the oil and gas industry, that knows it and knows it well." They also got a leader who clearly believed in the strategic importance of U.S. influence in the OPEC-dominated Middle East, which was at that time responsible for producing two-thirds of the world's oil. OPEC was wrestling with the idea of fixing petroleum prices for the good of all its members, but many individual nations were unwilling to limit production due to their own economic limitations. Kuwait repeatedly rejected the directives of other OPEC member-nations' and continued production that would lower oil prices worldwide. On August 2, 1990, Iraqi

President Saddam Hussein showed the world that Iraq had had enough of Kuwait's lack of allegiance. One hundred thousand Iraqi forces stormed into the small nation of Kuwait and quickly took control of it and its oil supply.

Strongly influenced by oilman and U.S. President George Bush, United Nations forces held the line before quickly defeating the Iraqi forces. As Iraqi forces fled Kuwait they lit many of the small nation's oil wells on fire. This created an environmental hazard and debilitated Kuwait's immediate ability to produce oil. Most damaging, however, was Saddam Hussein's miscalculation presented by a United States with a military presence in the world's main oil region. Bush accomplished his goal of creating a mutually dependent relationship between Persian Gulf nations and the United States. This, however, did not necessarily mean that price stability would last. The late 1990s brought more problems related to underproduction. The production imbalance fed the tripling of gasoline prices in 1999–2000.

RECENT HISTORY AND THE FUTURE

While prices in 2000–2001 are estimated to set records in purely numerical terms, they will still be roughly forty percent lower when adjusted for inflation than they were at their record in March 1981. Adjusted prices will be sixteen percent lower than they were in 1990, during the Persian Gulf War. OPEC met in March 2000, and agreed to raise production quotas by two million barrels per day. International companies also stepped up efforts to develop new supplies. Most observers believed that nations in the former Soviet Union would uphold the most promise. The construction of pipelines around the Caspian Sea promised to unlock new supplies of crude oil to the world over the next ten years. While such oil booms were not open to individual speculation, as were the early oil fields in Pennsylvania, Texas, and elsewhere, they will dramatically alter lives in nations such as Azerbaijan and Armenia, as well as in many African nations. Many observers hope that such supplies will also lessen global reliance on OPEC nations.

Regardless of the location of future supplies, the fact remains that petroleum is a finite resource. The petroleum age, as most scientists agree, will near its end by 2050. Modern technology, unfortunately, allows us to account rather exactly for this certain demise: We have guzzled 800 billion barrels during the petroleum era; we know the location of 850 billion barrels more, which are termed "reserves;" and we expect that 150 billion barrels more remain undiscovered. Simply, there is an end in sight. New energy sources will need to be found.

BIBLIOGRAPHY

Black, Brian. *PETROLIA: The Landscape of the America's First Oil Boom.* Baltimore, Md.: Johns Hopkins University Press, 2000.

Olien, Roger M. and Diana Davids Olien. *Oil and Ideology: The American Oil Industry, 1859–1945.* Chapel Hill, N.C.: University of North Carolina Press, 2000.

Yergin, Daniel. *The Prize: The Epic Quest for Oil, Money & Power.* New York: Simon and Schuster, 1992.

Brian Black

THE EXTRADITION OF CHILEAN GENERAL AUGUSTO PINOCHET: JUSTICE DELAYED?

THE CONFLICT

General Pinochet led a coup in Chile in 1973 following which there were killings, torture, and "disappearances" of dissenters. Then Pinochet, no longer the head of the government, traveled to London, England; Spanish government officials sought to extradite him from England for crimes committed by him and his administration.

Political

- Political leaders are responsible for the crimes committed by their governments.

- It is the world's responsibility, including international courts or country-specific courts such as Spain's, to make sure suspected criminals—including heads of government—are held responsible.

- If political leaders are held responsible, any leader traveling outside his or her country could be charged and tried.

- It is the responsibility of Chile to decide whether to charge Pinochet with crimes.

Efforts to extradite General Augusto Pinochet (pronounced Pin-O-Shay) to Spain captured the attention of the world from late 1998 through early 2000. Charges of human rights abuses by Pinochet's administration, which governed Chile from 1973 to 1989, revived the interest of international observers. Many had long questioned the activities of military dictatorships in repressing their own citizens, as well as foreign visitors, for alleged political crimes. Amnesty International and the families of the "disappeared," who were victims of Pinochet's military and paramilitary forces, actively sought the former dictator's extradition for trial. Supporters of Pinochet clashed, sometimes violently, with those who supported the extradition proceedings. Protests took place in London, England, in Santiago, Chile, and in several other cities worldwide. The conflict reopened painful wounds of the Chilean people, who had been struggling for a decade to reestablish the rule of democratic government and bury their memories of a barbarous and all-too-recent past.

HISTORICAL BACKGROUND

Chile's economic development hinged on the exploitation and export of an abundant and very profitable natural resource: copper. The three largest copper mines in Chile, together called the "Gran Minería," were developed during the twentieth century through investment capital and technology from the United States. The U.S. multinational corporations that controlled these mines were called the Anaconda Company and Kennecott Copper Company. Many Chileans resented the control these companies exercised over copper production, pricing, and sales. Chileans also alleged that the U.S. government tried to domi-

CHRONOLOGY

September 3, 1970 Salvador Allende Gossens is elected president of Chile. This marks the first democratic election of a Socialist to the office of president of a Latin American country.

September 11, 1973 Augusto Pinochet Ugarte heads four-man *junta* that overthrows Allende government.

October 5, 1988 A "No" vote reveals a popular mandate of fifty-five percent voting against Pinochet's continued leadership of the country.

December 14, 1989 Patricio Aylwin wins a democratic election for presidency of Chile and assumes the office in 1990. Pinochet steps down from the presidency but remains in charge of Chile's military forces.

March 10, 1998 Pinochet resigns as head of the armed forces after twenty-five years but the following day assumes that the post of "senator for life," a title that carries with it immunity from prosecution for acts committed during Pinochet's term as president of Chile.

Septemer 21, 1998 Pinochet travels to Europe on a private visit and is later detained in London pursuant to formal indictments and an arrest warrant handed down by Spanish judge Baltasar Garzón.

October 1998 The Chilean Foreign Ministry protests the detention, saying that Pinochet enjoys diplomatic immunity. The British Foreign Office does not agree.

November 25, 1998 Pinochet celebrates his eighty-third birthday. The House of Lords' magistrates rejects his claim of immunity.

December 1998 Pinochet appears before the Bow Street Magistrate's Court, at the start of his extradition hearing. The court accepts the defense argument and annuls the November 25 ruling.

March 24, 1999 Britain's House of Lords dismisses all charges against Pinochet except the charges of torture and conspiracy to torture after December 1988.

April 15, 1999 Britain's Interior Secretary Jack Straw states that extradition proceedings may go forward.

October 8, 1999 British Magistrate Ronald Bartle says that Pinochet could be extradited to Spain for trial on charges of torture and conspiracy to torture dating from the last fourteen months of his military regime.

October 14, 1999 Chile asks Britain to free Pinochet on humanitarian grounds, citing his deteriorating health.

October 22, 1999 Pinochet's attorneys lodge a formal appeal against decision to extradite him to Spain and apply for a writ of habeas corpus for his release.

January 11, 2000 Britain's Home Office announces its decision to allow Pinochet to return home to Chile on "humanitarian grounds." Straw grants seven days to submit an appeal for his consideration.

March 2, 2000 After hearing arguments from both sides, Straw announces his decision to set Pinochet free, deeming the eighty-four-year-old too frail to be extradited to Spain, or any other country, to stand trial for human rights abuses.

April 26, 2000 Appeals Court of Santiago begins hearings on whether to lift Pinochet's immunity from prosecution. Indictments brought by Chilean judges total fifty-eight as of Pinochet's release from London on March 2, 2000 and jump to ninety-five by May 3, 2000, the date on which the appeals court concludes its hearings on immunity.

nate Chile through its influence over the copper companies or by fixing the prices or amounts of copper that the companies sold. A large percentage of Chile's treasury receipts came from taxes on the production and sale of copper, so these allegations meant that many Chileans felt that their government had been unjustly deprived of revenues as a result of the actions of these companies. Chile's dependence on the copper industry caused many nationalists to push for "nationalization," or government takeover and administration of these economically important mines.

SALVADOR ALLENDE GOSSENS

1908–1973 Salvador Allende was born July 26, 1908 in Valparaiso, Chile. He became politically active while studying medicine at the University of Chile. Although his education was disrupted by frequent suspensions and two arrests, he earned an M.D. in 1932, and the next year helped organize the Chilean Socialist Party. Elected to the Chilean legislature in 1937, he developed a reputation as a champion of the poor. As the minister of health from 1939 to 1943, Allende addressed social causes of poor health. He served four terms in the Senate, from 1945 until 1970. That year, he became the first popularly elected Socialist head of state in the western hemisphere.

As president, he developed the "Chilean Road" to socialism, a combination of economic reform and democracy. Striving to improve the conditions of most Chileans, Allende diminished the role of private corporations through institution of land reform policies and nationalization of Chile's banks and major industries. Other programs froze food prices, subsidized milk, increased the minimum wage, and provided medical care and education programs for children.

On September 11, 1973, a military *junta* overthrew and, possibly, assassinated him, though it was claimed he "committed suicide after refusing to step down."

The Chilean people lived at both ends of the economic spectrum. Chilean elites in the manufacturing or agricultural sectors made up the "bourgeoisie," and enjoyed a comfortable or even prosperous standard of living. The Chilean middle class sought to obtain the benefits held by the bourgeoisie, and many of them worked as bureaucrats, ran small businesses, or owned small to mid-sized farming properties. The lower class in Chile, however, lived a life of hunger and deprivation. Shantytowns, built from scrap lumber, corrugated tin, and even cardboard, housed many of the poor; their tiny dwellings were often poorly furnished with dirt floors and no electricity or running water. The need for reforms in housing, education, working conditions and compensation, and land distribution was most strongly felt among the members of the lower class. Nutrition and health among the poor suffered as a result of their meager earnings.

When the conservative administration of Jorge Alessandri gave way in 1964 to the presidency of Eduardo Frei, the hopes of the middle and lower classes rose. The Frei administration fulfilled some of its promises of labor and agrarian reform, and its social welfare programs drew the attention of the Alliance for Progress, which deemed Chile a "showcase" of its policies. The original intention of the Alliance for Progress, created by U.S. President John F. Kennedy in 1961, was to offer funding and incentives for reform in Latin American countries as a way to deter them from turning to Communist-inspired social and economic reforms. U.S. policymakers feared the alternative that could result from these pressures for reform: a revolution that could follow the example set by Fidel Castro's Cuban revolution.

Salvador Allende Gossens

Frei's policies proved insufficient to meet the demands of Chile's hungry and exploited masses, and the election of 1970 offered them an opportunity to elect a candidate whose agenda more closely matched their own desires. Chile's democratic systems and traditions, which encompassed a multitude of political parties, often required candidates to form alliances between parties, or coalitions, in order to obtain the necessary number of votes to win elections. Salvador Allende Gossens, a member of the Socialist party and perpetual contender for president, ran as the candidate of the Popular Unity coalition. Allende's coalition included several parties, including dissident factions of the long-established Radical party, certain reform-minded splinter groups, the Socialist party, and the Chilean Communist Party. Allende's philosophies positioned him as a moderate reformer, attempting to "ride herd" over a stampeding coalition of reformers and revolutionaries who cried out for rapid fundamental change. The Popular Unity coalition platform included sweeping agrarian reforms, nationalization of the foreign-dominated Gran Minería, labor reforms, and far-reaching social welfare and economic programs.

Richard M. Nixon, then president of the United States, was an avowed anti-communist. His resolve against Latin American revolutionary sentiment had grown since Castro's takeover of Cuba. His strong anti-Communist stance had become a personal issue following an attack on his motorcade by an angry mob of Venezuelan students (later labeled by the U.S. State Department as "communist-inspired") protesting his "good will" visit to South America in 1958. Nixon had been pelted with rotten tomatoes, spat upon, heckled, and nearly killed by an angry mob. This experience shaped his view toward Latin America and Nixon became more determined that ever to fight the spread of communism in the western hemisphere. Nixon set out to prevent Allende's election and, when it later became necessary, to destabilize his regime with the intent of removing him from office. One operation, called Track II, encouraged a military coup before Allende could be inaugurated. Henry Kissinger, then national security adviser to Nixon, and several other officials linked the Socialist Allende with the communist members of his Popular Unity coalition. According to Harold Molineu in *U.S. Policy Toward Latin America*, Kissinger echoed Nixon's desire to prevent Allende's election and, later, to ensure his ouster, when he was reported to have said, "I don't see why we have to let a country go Marxist just because its people are irresponsible."

Richard Nixon, the CIA, and the funding of the U.S. multinationals such as AT&T, combined with conservative elements within Chile, were unable to prevent Allende's election to office in 1970. He quickly introduced an amendment to nationalize the Gran Minería. Congressional approval in July 1971 was unanimous, with 158 senators and deputies voting to ratify the congressional amendment that would be necessary for nationalization. In response, and with the aid of several U.S. multinationals affected by Allende's nationalist policies, Washington intensified its covert activities to undo Allende's regime. Nixon ordered that the Chilean economy "should be squeezed until it screams," and attempts were made to strangle Chile's economy, to create panic among the people, and to disrupt normal life. The United States imposed an "invisible" economic blockade aimed at creating economic chaos and destabilizing Chile's Marxist government. Allende protested this "grave aggression" aimed at his government in the international arena, but his December 4, 1972 speech before the United Nations failed to elicit sufficient support to halt U.S. efforts.

The Allende administration proved incapable of coping with the onslaught. The economic chaos caused by the invisible economic blockade led to hoarding of goods and the growth of a black market; the conservative sectors of society staged protests; and labor responded with general strikes that plunged the population into turmoil. Parliament blocked Allende's reform attempts at the same time that members of the Popular Unity coalition urged him to speed up the pace of

EXCERPT FROM THE FINAL PUBLIC SPEECH OF SALVADOR ALLENDE GOSSENS

Surely this will be my last opportunity to address you . . . . My words are not spoken in bitterness, but in disappointment. They will be a moral judgment on those who betrayed the oath they took as soldiers of Chile . . . . I shall pay with my life for the loyalty of the people . . . . The seed we have planted in the worthy consciousness of thousands upon thousands of Chileans cannot remain forever unharvested . . . . They have the might and they can enslave us, but they cannot halt the world's social processes, not with crimes nor with guns . . . . These are my last words, and I am sure that my sacrifice will not be in vain. I am sure that this sacrifice will constitute a moral lesson, which will punish cowardice, perfidy, and treason.

change. Chilean owners of small to mid-sized properties and business feared that the seizure of their lands by peasants and workers through *tomas*, or takings, such as those that had already taken over larger enterprises. The conservative right encouraged these fears, and newspapers such as *El Mercurio*, which received millions of dollars in support from Chilean conservatives and the CIA's "front" organizations, heightened the sense of impending disaster. Chilean society became polarized between left and right, leaving the country without the stabilizing influence of a middle political sector.

While its economic manipulation wrought havoc with Chile's economy, the United States continued to maintain close ties with those organizations that it deemed to be most susceptible to U.S. influence. The Chilean military, which had been the beneficiary of increased U.S. military aid to the region since the 1960s, did not suffer the same fate as the Chilean government. Although all loans and credits to Chile's Popular Unity government were cut off in the "invisible" blockade, the United States continued to spend massive amounts in military aid to Chile during the Allende regime. At the same time, the United States continued to assert that it had been merely a disinterested bystander since Allende came to power, except for protests against his expropriation policy. A *New York Times* article the day after Allende's overthrow alleged that this increased military aid had been the central element in Washington's attempts to demonstrate cooperation and even-handed treatment of the Allende government.

Chile's military plotted to overthrow the Allende regime in order to halt further disintegration of Chile. The Allende administration's food rationing program, begun in response to widespread hoarding of staple goods such as meats, milk, diapers, bread, and coffee, only worsened the panic, and a black market trade in these commodities flourished. General strikes in 1972 and 1973 crippled the nation's transportation industries and virtually shut down Chile's major cities. Several coup attempts failed in 1973; some called for Allende's resignation. The sense of impending doom was not dispelled by a parade of more than one million peasants and workers to commemorate the third anniversary of Allende's election to the presidency. Many of the marchers requested that they be given arms with which to defend the government, but Allende refused, fearing that it would lead to a massacre. Allende intended to call for a national plebiscite, or people's vote, on September 11, 1973, which, he was sure, would reveal the widespread support for his government's programs and dampen the military's enthusiasm for another revolt.

Despite Allende's optimism, the military attacked La Moneda, Chile's presidential palace, on September 11, 1973. Allende's first reaction to news of the impending attack was disbelief, then defiance, and finally resignation to the inevitability of battle. His final address to the Chilean people, broadcast over the radio as the army began its assault on the palace, was a moving defense of political principle and a poignant expression of his personal commitment to the betterment of Chile.

The attack on La Moneda was the first of many attacks by the Chilean military in an effort to "extirpate the Marxist cancer from the body politic" of the country. As thousands fled to friendly embassies seeking protection from the military's excesses, thousands more were rounded up and taken to interrogation centers for detention and "questioning." A rash of "disappearances" became a bloodbath of vindictiveness and rage, as bodies were found floating in the Mapocho River, lying in the blood-stained streets, or hanging as examples to the unwary political left. These methods became, as Hernan Valdés described them, part of a very effective campaign of "political detergency" aimed at silencing all attempts at protest.

General Augusto Pinochet

Gen. Augusto Pinochet was one of the members of the military junta that overthrew Allende; within days of the coup it was clear that Pinochet was in charge. He ruled Chile for the next seven-teen years. Thousands of deaths occurred in the early weeks following the coup, among them Victor Jara, a well-known Chilean folk singer, and two U.S. citizens, Charles Horman and Frank Teruggi. Even Chileans who fled into exile were targeted by the Chilean secret police forces; former Allende cabinet officer Orlando Letelier was killed by a car bomb in Washington, D.C. in 1976. Evidence pointed to the direct involvement of Pinochet's secret police, and six persons were imprisoned for their part in the car bombing. The U.S. Justice Department reopened its grand jury investigations into the matter in March 2000.

International pressure to stem the tide of human rights abuses combined with domestic protest against the dictatorship restored democracy to Chile; in October 1988 Pinochet held a plebiscite to extend his term of office. When the result was overwhelmingly against his continued rule, Pinochet agreed to hold democratic elections in 1989. General elections led to the election of Patricio Aylwin, a moderate conservative, as president. Democratic government in Chile paved the way for conciliation, and Chile's civilian president Aylwin appointed an eight-member commission in 1990 to investigate the extent and nature of the human rights violations. The commission, headed by Raul Rettig, issued its formal report in February 1991; that report was followed in 1996 by the report of the Reparation and Reconciliation Corporation. The two reports brought the number of "disappearances" to 1,102 and deaths by execution or torture to 2,095, for a total of 3,197 cases that were officially recognized by the Chilean government. Thousands more cases of torture remain unrecognized, and the totals continue to climb as mass graves containing the bodies of bound and tortured victims are found and additional cases are brought to light.

In 1978 Pinochet decreed an amnesty (Decree 2191) designed to shield those responsible for human rights violations committed between September 11, 1973 and March 10, 1978 (including himself). The Chilean Constitution drafted during the Pinochet dictatorship included a provision that created certain parliamentary positions called "senators for life;" these parliamentarians have complete immunity under Chilean law. When Pinochet negotiated the transition to democracy and later agreed to step down as head of the armed forces, Pinochet guaranteed himself a position as senator for life. He could not be prosecuted for any of the executions or torture within Chile unless a constitutional amendment lifting the decree was passed.

AUGUSTO PINOCHET UGARTE

1915– Augusto Pinochet was born November 25, 1915 in Chile. After graduating from Chile's Military Academy in 1936, he rose through the ranks of the army. Shortly after appointment as commander of the army, Pinochet led a military coup, which overthrew the Chilean government.

With the support of the army, he installed himself as head of the military junta and assumed sole authority as head of state in June 1974. He repressed civil liberties and, in 1977, his regime was condemned by the U.N. Human Rights Commission for torturing detainees. An assassination attempt in 1986 resulted in further oppression and disappearances of suspected critics of Pinochet's government. Following a 1989 referendum, he was denied the right to continue as president. However, he retained command of the army until 1998 and was appointed a "senator for life."

Although the constitution provided him with immunity from prosecution within Chile, he was arrested in Britain while seeking medical attention in September 1998. A judge had requested his extradition to Spain to stand trail for human rights violations. He was released March 2, 2000, on humanitarian grounds, and returned home to Chile.

AUGUSTO PINOCHET. *(AP/Wide World Photos. Reproduced by permission.)*

The victims of human rights violations in Chile and their relatives, with the support of international organizations, lawyers, and judges, had campaigned for a quarter of a century for justice. The whereabouts of many of *desaparecidoes*, the Spanish term for "disappeared ones," remain unknown because the immunity granted to so many has prevented discovery and prosecution. The Chilean Constitution appears, therefore, to guarantee the rights of those in power to commit human rights abuses and other crimes with without fear of punishment.

Human rights abuses were not committed only against Chilean citizens. Victims included citizens of Spain, Belgium, France, Italy, Luxembourg, and Sweden, among many others. In those countries, criminal proceedings were instituted in national courts against Pinochet. The Spanish courts, for example, wanted to bring Pinochet to Spain, to be prosecuted for crimes against Spanish citizens committed by the dictatorship. The

Spaniards did not believe that Pinochet could receive a fair trial in Chile due to the constitutional immunity provisions. In October 1998, Spanish judge Baltasar Garzón issued a provisional arrest warrant alleging that Pinochet had been responsible for the murder of Spanish citizens in Chile. A supplemental warrant was issued a few days later alleging that Pinochet was responsible for systematic acts against Spanish citizens including murder, torture, "disappearance," illegal detention, and forcible transfers in Chile and other countries.

The Appeal for Extradition from London

While he was in Chile, however, Pinochet was outside the reach of these foreign courts; Chile would not extradite him for trial in another country. When he went to London for back surgery in October 1998, Pinochet was served with the first warrant and placed under arrest by a Scotland Yard official. Pinochet's lawyers immedi-

THE CHARGES AGAINST PINOCHET

Britain's Crown Prosecution Service (CPS), acting on behalf of Spain, introduced the charges against former Chilean dictator Augusto Pinochet at the beginning of the extradition hearings. The charges included thirty-four claims of torture, for which individual victims were named, and a more general allegation of "conspiracy to torture," arising between December 1988 and December 1989.

The allegations included graphic descriptions of beatings, electric shocks, sexual abuse, and intimidation. In five of the cases, the alleged torture eventually led to death. Twenty-seven of the victims were men; seven were women.

Agence France-Presse's September 27, 1999, listed the allegations: "One woman was beaten and threats made to rape her sister. Several victims were suspended, beaten, electrocuted and suffocated. One man was forced to take hallucinogenic drugs, another was locked into a small cage and suffered electric shocks, and another had a tube inserted into his anus. In another case, a woman was allegedly interrogated while she was naked and threats were made against her nine-year-old daughter. Other victims were deprived of sleep, food and water. Some were threatened with death or disfigurement."

The allegations also included a count of "conspiring to abduct and torture known or suspected political opponents. It was agreed some of the victims would be killed and others tortured, the charges said. The policy would be operated through public officials, either in the military, or another state authority, under the general's command." The conspiracy charge alleged that the aim of this policy was not only to elicit information, but to frighten other potential critics. It also accused Pinochet of deliberate efforts to conceal the whereabouts of "the disappeared."

Alun Jones, on behalf of the CPS and Spain, argued that although the charges did not actually accuse Pinochet of inflicting the torture himself, he was a "secondary party, counseling or procuring them."

Pinochet's Response

In a statement read to the magistrate court in April, Pinochet declared, "I do not agree with this . . . I have nothing to do with any of these charges . . . . I am being humiliated. I am a general with sixty-four years service and I am a gentleman who knows about honor."

Barrister (lawyer) Clive Nicholls argued in Pinochet's defense that because the legal definition of torture was the infliction of severe pain and suffering, "instantaneous death cannot amount to torture," as the victim had not suffered. Similarly, he argued, the cases of people still classified as disappeared did not amount to torture—for them or for their relatives—as they were not "victims."

ately brought a petition before the English courts, asserting his immunity from arrest and extradition as a former head of state. The High Court for England and Wales agreed, but the British government, acting on behalf of the Spanish authorities, appealed to the judicial committee of the House of Lords. The House of Lords originally ruled 3-2 in favor of the extradition, but that decision was annulled a few weeks later when it was revealed that a conflict of interest existed. Lord Hoffman, who had voted with the majority in favor of extradition, had ties to Amnesty International, one of the international groups involved in the case. The annulment led to a second hearing in January 1999, by a panel of seven British judges. The panel considered alleged offenses committed in Chile as well as assassinations of escaping leftists committed in Italy, Argentina, the United States, and elsewhere. The government of Chile was permitted to intervene in the case on behalf of Pinochet.

On March 24, 1999, the panel issued its ruling that Pinochet had no immunity but that he could not be extradited to Spain for acts committed before Britain enacted the International Convention Against Torture in December 1988. This effectively reduced the number of charges for which Pinochet could be extradited to Spain for trial to thirty-four. Further, the House of Lords suggested that British Home Secretary Jack Straw review his earlier decision allowing the extradition to proceed.

Pinochet's supporters in Chile and in Britain began to lobby for his release. Former British prime minister Margaret Thatcher, a long-time friend of Pinochet, joined in the appeal for his release. Straw encouraged both sides to present their written positions and considered the findings of a team of doctors who examined Pinochet to determine his fitness to stand trial. Pinochet, who suffers from diabetes and depression, wears a pacemaker, and has difficulty walking, was found to have suffered brain damage as a result of several strokes during September and October 1999. Straw concluded that Pinochet was unfit to stand trial due to his poor physical and mental health, as well as his advanced age, and ordered his release on "humanitarian grounds." Pinochet was released and returned to Chile on March 2, 2000.

The decision set in motion a series of efforts in Chile to strip Pinochet of his immunity from prosecution for human rights abuses committed during his regime. Claims were brought before Chilean judge Juan Guzman for criminal complaints including torture, "disappearances," execution, and murder. Among them is the most famous case picked by Guzman to seek the lifting of Pinochet's immunity: the so-called "caravan of death," in which a group of high-ranking military officers toured several Chilean cities shortly after the coup, dragging political prisoners from jail and executing them. The number of claims continues to climb as the victims and families of victims seek justice for the human rights abuses committed during the 1973 to 1990 dictatorship.

International Interest in a Trial for Pinochet

The magnitude of the human rights abuses in Chile cannot rival the numbers of "disappeared" in Argentina between 1976 and 1983, where official figures acknowledge more than ten thousand people killed for their opposition to the military government, and human rights organizations estimate three times that number. The dismal theme of the "Dirty War" waged by the Argentine military against subversive elements in its own country is being replayed in recent years as Argentina, like Chile, investigates the theme of justice versus national reconciliation. Many senior military officers who served in the Argentine dictatorship are currently imprisoned or involved in legal battles over the cases of babies who were born to imprisoned political prisoners, taken from their mothers, and placed for adoption. Spanish judge Baltasar Garzón has been active in preparing charges to include terrorism and torture against many of the leading figures in the Argentine military dictatorships.

AT THE BOW STREET MAGISTRATE'S COURT IN LONDON, SCENE OF MUCH OF THE LEGAL DECISION-MAKING REGARDING THE FUTURE OF AUGUSTO PINOCHET, DEMONSTRATORS HOLD SIGNS AND A CARICATURE TO PROTEST THE POSSIBILITY THAT PINOCHET WOULD NOT FACE CHARGES FOR THE CRIMES HE MAY HAVE COMMITTED IN OFFICE. *(AP/Wide World Photos. Reproduced by permission.)*

Brazil and Uruguay, too, are grappling with similar issues of past military repression and the need for retribution for their crimes. The military forces of Brazil, Argentina, Uruguay, Paraguay, and Chile even cooperated in the 1970s and 1980s to target and detain escaping leftists in an effort called "Operation Condor." Since the Pinochet extradition case has thrust the issue of human rights abuses into the international arena, Brazil

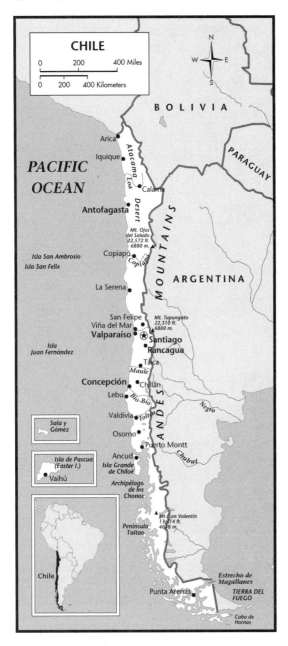

MAP OF CHILE. (© *Maryland Cartographics. Reprinted with permission.*)

others say that the true motivation behind the international justice movement is revenge. They say that the "key player" nations, motivated by organizations like Amnesty International and Human Rights Watch, have set aside the rhetoric of the Cold War to seek, instead, a sense of international community that is acutely aware of its new role as moral police officer to the world.

RECENT HISTORY AND THE FUTURE

Chile promises today to eliminate the mere suggestion that authoritarian dictators can act with impunity. Yet, it rejects the notion that international means can or should be used to enforce the principles of human rights (or to bring retribution for violations of human rights). Chile, which was willing to submit its appeals before the World Court in order to free Pinochet from extradition proceedings in Britain, now alleges that the Chilean judiciary should be left alone, without undue pressure (domestic or international), to resolve issues that should properly be addressed within Chile's borders. It defines the key issues, therefore, as autonomy and Chilean nationalism, rather than human rights and the global community.

Chile faces many compelling issues. How will the recently elected Socialist president, Ricardo Lagos, handle conflicts between Chile's right, left, and centrist parties? What impact will the economic instabilities of the global market have on the tenuous state of calm that exists among these sectors? In addition, the middle and upper classes that supported the Pinochet government and its policies must now reconcile their newfound economic prosperity with an awareness of crimes against humanity. These issues have received increased news coverage since the Chilean judiciary's decision to lift Pinochet's immunity from prosecution. Pinochet's legal team has appealed the decision, but the toll of legal cases brought against him in Chile continues to climb; over one hundred claims were filed in Chile within the first three months after Pinochet's release from Britain. Sporadic public demonstrations, both in favor of and against Pinochet, disrupt daily life in the capital. Finally, with the Chilean military staging demonstrations of its power as recently as 1993 (after the election of a civilian president), conflict over the Pinochet issue could lead to a deterioration of relations between the government and the armed forces. This could be a source of major worry in a country still deeply divided over the legacy of military rule.

recently agreed to open its archives on Operation Condor. The United States, too, has pursued a policy of active declassification and released of many of its files on the Chilean 1973–78 era, when the worst of the abuses took place. As the Pinochet conflict is played out in Chile and the world arena, these countries as well as the international human rights community have reopened the debate on the issue of human rights abuses by military governments. Opponents argue that the core issue is accountability for crimes committed, while

BIBLIOGRAPHY

Agosin, Marjorie. *Tapestries of Hope, Threads of Love: The Arpillera Movement in Chile, 1974–1994.* Albuquerque, N.Mex.: University of New Mexico Press, 1996.

Koonings, Kees and Dirk Kruijt. *Societies of Fear: The Legacy of Civil War, Violence and Terror in Latin America.* New York City: Zed Books, 1999.

Oppenheim, Lois Hecht. *Politics in Chile: Democracy, Authoritarianism, and the Search for Development.* Bolder, Colo.: Westview Press, 1998.

U.S. Congress. Senate. *Covert Action in Chile, 1963–1973, Staff Report of the Select Committee to Study Governmental Operations with Respect to Intelligence Activities,* 94th Cong., 1st sess., 1975 (Washington, D.C.: Government Printing Office, 1975).

U.S. Congress. Senate. *Hearing Before the Subcommittee to Investigate Problems Connected with Refugees and Escapees of the Committee on the Judiciary,* pt. 1, 93d Cong., 1st sess.; pt. 2, 93d Cong., 2d sess.; pt. 3, 94th Cong., 1st sess. (Washington, D.C.: U.S. Government Printing Office, 1973; 1974; 1975).

Wright, Thomas and Rudy Oñate. *Flight from Chile: Voices of Exile.* Albuquerque, N.Mex.: University of New Mexico Press, 1998.

Valenzuela, Arturo, et al. "Chile." In *The Breakdown of Democratic Regimes.* Baltimore, Md.: Johns Hopkins University Press, 1978.

DeeAnna Manning

Roma in Eastern Europe: The Wall in the Czech Republic

The Conflict

In 1999 a town in the Czech Republic built a wall to separate the white, ethnic Czechs from the Roma, or Gypsies. Roma live all over the world, but particularly in eastern Europe. Tensions between the Roma and the ethnic groups with which they share a country have been around for hundreds of years; in recent years this has taken the form of persecution, discrimination, and, occasionally, violence.

Cultural

- The Czechs view the Roma as dirty, thieving, and disruptive.

- Roma were, historically, nomadic trades people and peddlers of tin.

- Roma have different beliefs about property and behavior than their white, ethnic neighbors.

Political

- Tensions regarding how best to integrate a very different culture—especially one that may want to remain separate.

- Disagreement about how much of the cultural difference is caused by historical laws limiting the education and behavior of Roma.

Religious

- Roma have specific religious practices, which include separation from unclean people, the *gadze*.

On October 24, 1999, an editorial appeared in the *New York Times* entitled "Europe's Walls for Gypsies." The article reported recent efforts by the Czech city of Usti nad Labem to erect a wall to separate the city's Gypsies, or Roma (pronounced RO-ma), from white, ethnic Czechs. It also noted the recent persecution of the Roma in Kosovo and the ongoing persecution of this minority throughout central and eastern Europe. Fourteen months earlier the U.S. Congress's Commission on Security and Cooperation in Europe heard testimony (from this author and others) regarding European policies and treatment of the Roma. The panelists agreed that there were varying degrees of bad treatment of Roma. According to these panelists, the best country for a Roma to live would be Hungary, followed by Bulgaria, Romania, and finally, the Czech Republic. Since that time, Kosovo has replaced the Czech Republic as the worst region in central and eastern Europe for Roma to live.

Yet historically, this was not always true. Bohemia and Moravia, as well as parts of Silesia, the historic provinces that make up the Czech Republic, traditionally had few Roma, while Kosovo, a province of Serbia, was not known as a place of persecution and mistreatment of the Roma. In fact, historically, it was Romania where the Roma have suffered the most persecution even though Romania was the home for most Roma since they entered Europe. The Roma in Kosovo, the Czech Republic, Romania, and elsewhere in central and eastern Europe share a history of persecution that goes back for centuries and still exists today. The hatred of the Roma was and is so deep that they were the only group other than the Jews to be included in Nazi Germany's Final Solution during the Holocaust. Hatred and prejudice of the

CHRONOLOGY

1300s First historical documentation of Roma in Europe.

Late 1700s Maria Theresa, empress to the Hapsburg empire, implements a policy designed to force the assimilation of Roma by, among other things, kidnapping their children and placing them in foster Catholic homes.

Late 1700s and 1800s Emancipation of Romania's Roma slaves, the *robi*.

1899 The Gypsy Information Agency, a special anti-Roma unit, is created by the German police.

1906 "Combatting the Gypsy Nuisance" is issued. It establishes a partnership among several European countries to stop Gyspies' nomadic lifestyle.

1928 Germany issues a law that all Roma in Germany be placed under police surveillance.

1933 Adolf Hitler comes to power in Germany. German officials use the "Law for the Prevention of Genetically Diseased Offspring" to sterilize Roma.

1935 The Nuremberg Laws give full German citizenship only to Aryans.

1936 A concentration camp for Roma is established in the Berlin, Germany suburbs to hide the Roma from visitors to the 1936 Olympics.

1942 Himmler orders all Roma of Germany departed to Auschwitz.

1944 All of Birkenau's Roma are gassed, in the night known as *Zigeunernacht* (Night of the Gypsies). An estimated two hundred thousand to five hundred thousand Roma die during the Holocaust.

1999 Usti nad Labem, a city in the Czech Republic, builds a wall to separate the city's Roma, or Gypsies, from the white, ethnic Czech population.

Roma lie deep in the history of the region and have endured for centuries.

HISTORICAL BACKGROUND

The Roma of Central and Eastern Europe

The Roma (singular Rom), or as they are more commonly known in the English speaking world, the Gypsies, entered Europe from India in the Late Middle Ages (900–1500 A.D.). Some Europeans referred to this dark-skinned group as "Egyptians," which became the source of the word "Gypsy." In the non-English speaking parts of Europe, however, the Roma are referred to as *cigán, tsiganes, zigeuner,* and other similar terms. These terms come from the Byzantine Greek word, *Atsinganoi,* which means itinerant wanderer or soothsayer. Because of the stereotypes and prejudice that surround these words, the Gypsies prefer a name of their own choosing, from their language, *Romani*. Today, Roma prefer to be referred to as *Rom* or *Roma,* a *Romani* word meaning man or husband, rather than Gypsies. Rom is singular and refers to an individual, while Roma refers to a group. It is also appropriate to use the word

Romani as an adjective to refer to someone who is a Rom (male) or a Romni (female).

The origin of the Roma is controversial. According to Dr. Ian Hancock, a prominent scholar, Europe's Roma originally came from India, where they belonged to the Rajput class of warriors. The Roma gradually made their way across Central Asia, Persia, and the Byzantine Empire before they settled in the Balkans (southeastern Europe) during the Middle Ages.

Historical records from the fourteenth century document the presence of the Roma in Europe. The "Egyptians," as they were called, were highly prized as gunsmiths, metal smiths, horse specialists, and musicians. Despite this, the Roma remained at the bottom of the region's socioeconomic ladder. In Romania's historic provinces, Wallachia and Moldavia, the Roma were enslaved. Since Romania has always held Europe's largest Roma population, this status helped enforce the negative stereotypes that have haunted the Roma.

In other parts of the Europe, the Roma remained free. The gradual takeover of the Balkans in the fifteenth and sixteenth centuries by the Ottoman Empire, ruled from Damascus, saw the

MAP SHOWING THE AREAS ACROSS WHICH THE ROMA ARE SPREAD. *(XNR Productions Inc.)*

movements. Austrian rulers, the Hapsburgs, in the early eighteenth century forbade the Roma to enter their kingdom, which included much of central and part of western Europe. For a first offense of entering the kingdom, a Rom was branded. If caught in Hapsburg lands a second time, the Rom was executed. Similar policies existed in many German states during this period.

Hapsburg policies changed in the second half of the eighteenth century under emperors Maria Theresa and Joseph II, though they remained insensitive to Roma culture and traditions. The seventeenth and eighteenth centuries were the time of the Enlightenment in Europe, when science, religious tolerance, and intellectual exploration were revered. Spurred by distorted Enlightenment ideas, Maria Theresa implemented a series of policies that tried to force Roma assimilation into society by forbidding them to live as nomads and by kidnapping their children and placing the children in foster Catholic homes. Other aspects of these policies sought to destroy any Roma sense of their own past and heritage. Maria Theresa's son, Joseph II, continued these policies, though by the end of his reign in 1792, he was reconsidering the policies, particularly after forty-one innocent Roma were executed in his Slovak lands for crimes they did not commit. One good thing to come from Hapsburg policies was a census that provided a complete overview of Roma life in the Hapsburg Empire at the time.

Though traditionally looked upon as groups of impoverished, illiterate nomads, the Roma evolved as a complex group of clans with various dialects of *Romani* and a diverse set of social and cultural values. Many of Europe's Roma could trace their origins to traditional occupations or regions of origin. Some of the most important Roma groups or tribes in Europe were the Vlach, whose European roots were in Wallachia and Moldavia, what is now modern Romania, and the Kalderása. All Roma shared was a deep commitment to the family and clan, and an almost universal distrust of the non-Roma or *gadzé*. Centuries of mistreatment and persecution by the *gadzé* helped create this distrust and strengthen the Roma view that to deal with the *gadzé* is a violation of strict hygenic codes known as *marimé*.

In the late eighteenth and nineteenth centuries, some Roma began to move out of the Balkans, particularly after the emancipation of Romania's Roma slaves, the *robi*. They were encouraged to leave by the military, political, social, and economic upheavals that swept the region during this period. Yet with the exception

status of the Roma decline further because their European neighbors often incorrectly associated them with the hated Muslim Ottomans. They were also victims of the broader social and economic upheavals that swept central and eastern Europe at this time. The Roma, like many crafts and trades people of that era, offered their highly prized skills to rural settlements and towns on a seasonal basis. The Roma faced growing restrictions on the amount of time that they could stay in certain areas, so they moved frequently. These restrictions were combined with an increasing prejudice against the Roma based on stereotypes that became an integral part of the fabric of not only central and east European society, but of the entire Western world. These stereotypes—that Roma were dirty, deceitful, and thieving—fostered prejudices that continue to dog the group to this day.

By the mid-sixteenth century, most of the world's Roma lived in central and eastern Europe, particularly the Balkans. They found themselves increasingly trapped in a lifestyle of forced nomadism—constantly moving from place to place—which pushed them to the edge of society or even to enslavement. Their condition worsened over the next two centuries as governments throughout the region sought to restrict their of Hungary, Roma throughout most of central and eastern Europe continued their nomadic way of life. When given the opportunity to integrate, the Roma quickly adapted. Unfortunately, they often continued to be haunted by the age-old prejudices and stereotypes that depicted them as untrustworthy thieves and irresponsible wanderers.

For a brief period after World War I, Roma in central and eastern Europe enjoyed a cultural and historic awakening as the postwar democracy took hold in the region. Some of Europe's various Roma groups tried to adapt their nomadic traditions to this new environment. Roma intellectuals hoped to create a greater sense of Rom self-awareness throughout Europe and to develop political influence. They also sought to preserve their heritage. Unfortunately, whatever modest gains Roma leaders made in the 1920s and early 1930s were swept away by the new, fascist-oriented dictatorships that took control of much of central and eastern Europe.

Germany, the Roma and the Holocaust

In Europe's German states efforts were made in the eighteenth century to halt Roma nomadism. Particularly sinister was the practice of kidnapping Roma children and placing them in non-Roma Christian homes. The goal was to destroy the all-important Roma family unit and prevent the development of future generations of Roma. Roma efforts to resist these attempts were met with harsh reprisals.

Anti-Roma violence became the norm throughout the German states. After German unification, efforts were made to force Roma who were foreign to Germany out of the country. Authorities also expected Roma native to Germany to give up their nomadic way of life. In the spring of 1899, Bavarian police created a special anti-Roma unit, the Gypsy Information Agency, or *Nachrichtendienst in Bezug auf die zigeuner*, which began to collect fingerprints, family information, photographs, and other data on the Roma in Bavaria. This data became the basis of the infamous *zigeuner-Buch* (1905), which contained detailed genealogies on five thousand Roma, and criminal data on those who had been arrested. It also included photographs of Roma drawn from police records throughout Germany.

In 1906 the Prussian Minister of the Interior issued "Combating the Gypsy Nuisance" (*Bekämpfung des zigeuner unwesens*), which linked agreements with a number of countries throughout Europe to domestic German efforts aimed at preventing Germany's Roma from continuing their nomadic lifestyle. A large number of Roma fled Germany for other parts of Europe, where they were equally unwelcome. After World War I, some German states revisited the "Gypsy Question." Several passed laws that required that the Roma be fingerprinted, photographed, and carry travel documents with them. Other laws forced the Roma to stop moving from place to place. Any Roma or other itinerant person who had no gainful employment could be punished with up to two years in a state work facility. Roma could not own guns, and those without proper identification papers could be deported.

In 1928, a national law ordered that all Roma in Germany be placed under police surveillance. In 1929, authorities transformed Bavaria's special Roma affairs office into the National Central Office for Fighting the Gypsy Nuisance, headquartered in Munich. The new organization established ties with an international police organization in Vienna, Austria to share information on the Roma.

After Adolf Hitler came to power in Germany on January 30, 1933, Nazi officials felt that the various anti-Roma laws and decrees put into force by the earlier German states were sufficient to oversee the "Gypsy menace." There were only thirty thousand to thirty-five thousand Roma in Germany in 1933, and they were divided into several groups. The largest group was the Sinti, though there were also the Rom, the Gelderari, the Lovari, the Lalleri, and groups of Balkan Roma.

Though Hitler's new regime did not enact any specific anti-Roma legislation, pre-1933 laws as well as the "Nazi Denaturalization Law" (1933) and the "Law Regarding Expulsion from the Reich" (1934) gave the Nazis the legal authority to begin to force foreign Roma out of the country. In addition, German officials used the "Law for the Prevention of Genetically Diseased Offspring" (1933) to sterilize Roma, though there are no exact figures as to the actual number of Roma sterilized from 1933–45. By 1935, local pressure prompted German officials, particularly Kripo, the criminal police, to begin to place Roma into special camps known as *zigeuner lager* . The first Roma concentration camp was established outside of Cologne in the summer of 1935, followed by similar facilities in other parts of the Third Reich. The largest Roma concentration camp was in the Berlin suburbs at Marzahn and was set up on the eve of the 1936 Olympics to hide the Roma from the view of visiting athletes and spectators. Prior to the opening of the Nazi Olympics, police throughout Prussia raided Roma camps and homes and forced marched them to Marzahn.

The Nuremberg Laws (September 15, 1935) further strengthened the Nazis' persecution of the Roma. The Nuremberg Laws gave full citizenship only to Aryans and forbade marriage and extramarital sexual relations between Aryans and Jews. Legal commentaries soon added the Roma and Afro-Germans to these restrictions because the Nazis argued they had *"artfremdes Blut,"* or alien blood. Authorities also viewed the Roma as criminal "asocials" who were a threat to Aryan German society.

In 1936 the Reich Ministry of the Interior issued a report that said that despite international efforts against the "Gypsy plague," it did not seem as though any immediate solution was in sight. Though the study talked of forcing nomadic Roma to settle, it noted that this would cause Roma assimilation with Aryans, a fact that was racially unacceptable in Nazi society. Moreover, the report argued, the settlement and possible integration of Roma into German society would increase the crime rate in Germany. Other options were to create special "reservations" for Roma, though Roma criminality would make such facilities unacceptable to the communities around them. They could also be forced to leave the Third Reich, though, legally, only foreign Roma could be forced to leave. The report concluded that the best way to deal with the Roma was to do what had been done for years—keep an eye on them and force them into concentration camps. By the time World War II broke out, the Roma of the Third Reich had been deprived of many of their civil, social, and economic rights. Moreover, war also brought a wave of Roma deportations, usually in conjunction with action against Jews.

Yet by 1941, however, there were still Roma registered for the draft and marrying non-Roma. Some Roma children still attended public schools. This was soon to change. In 1941–42 new anti-Roma regulations began to remove many of these remaining privileges. The first major wave of Roma deportations began in 1941, when German authorities shipped over five thousand Roma to the Lodz ghetto. In the summer of 1942, the Wehrmacht (German armed forces) prevented Roma from serving in the military. On December 16, 1942, Heinrich Himmler, head of the Gestapo, ordered all Reich Roma deported to Auschwitz. The first German Roma were sent to Auschwitz in the early fall of 1942, where they helped to build the Gypsy Family Camp at Birkenau.

Himmler's decree was not all-inclusive, and provided temporary exemptions for pure Sinti and Lalleri Roma. He later appointed a number of Sinti and Lalleri leaders to identify those who were "pure-blooded," with the idea of allowing those selected to live within specially confined areas. Martin Bormann, Adolf Hitler's private secretary, strongly objected to Himmler's efforts to save this handful of Roma and protested to Hitler. Himmler countered Bormann's arguments in a personal conversation with the Führer, and the Sinti-Lalleri exemptions held. In reality, the criminal police paid little attention to this special list of Roma.

The Roma and the Final Solution

Planning for the Final Solution began in the early months of the German invasion of the Soviet Union in the summer of 1941. The plan to murder all of the Jews in Europe, and later the Roma, involved the development of new methods of mass murder and body disposal that were more efficient than the shootings and mass burial techniques used by the *Einsatzgruppen* and other German occupation units in the Soviet Union. By the end of 1941, the construction of death camps and the opening of new gassing facilities at existing concentration camps were well under way. Once the Germans completed these facilities by mid-1942, they began to ship Jews, and later Roma, out of the Greater Reich and the ghettos of occupied Poland to the major death camps. Along with these efforts were plans to expand operations into central and Western Europe, and finally to those nations allied with the Third Reich. Those Jews and Roma not designated for mass murder survived in slave labor conditions designed for slow death.

Auschwitz, which consisted of separate concentration, death, and forced labor camps, was the primary symbol of the evil of the Holocaust. The Germans murdered over one million people here, ninety percent of them Jews. Auschwitz II-Birkenau, the death camp, had gas chambers and crematoria. A small number of Roma prisoners had been brought to Auschwitz in the fall of 1942, though they did not begin to arrive in large numbers until Himmler ordered that all German and Austrian Roma be sent to Auschwitz later that year. Theoretically excluded were the pure Aryan Roma—thirteen thousand German Sinti and 1,017 Austrian Lalleri Roma. On January 29, 1943, the SS Race and Settlement Main Office ordered the deportation of German and Austrian Roma to Auschwitz, with some exemptions.

Beginning in late February 1943, large transports of Roma began to arrive in Birkenau.

Almost eleven thousand arrived during the first month; seventeen hundred were gassed immediately upon arrival. Six thousand Roma were sent to Auschwitz II over the next three months. The number of Roma arrivals then slowed until early 1944. Most of Auschwitz's Roma lived in the Gypsy Family Camp.

Like other groups who survived *Selektion*— the process of deciding the placement or disposal of prisoners—at the entrance to Auschwitz II-Birkenau, Roma inmates had numbers tattooed on their arms. Life in the Gypsy Family Camp was as horrible as elsewhere in Auschwitz, and disease and starvation were rampant. Though the SS used some Roma as slave laborers, most were not subject to it, which gave other prisoners the impression that camp authorities were giving the Roma special treatment. Josef Mengele, the chief SS physician at the Gypsy Family Camp, and other SS physicians used some Roma, particularly twins and those with the skin disease *noma* in their medical experiments.

By the summer of 1943, Himmler had decided to eliminate the Gypsy Family Camp. By the end of that year, 18,736 Roma were living in the family camp. The official decision to eliminate the Gypsy Family Camp came on May 15, 1944. The following evening, SS units moved on the Roma barracks but they were challenged by Roma prisoners armed with crude weapons. The well-equipped SS troops backed away and delayed the destruction of the camp. The ongoing process of taking able-bodied Roma for slave labor continued. By the time that the Germans again decided to act against the Gypsy Family Camp on August 2, 1944, only 2,898 Roma remained in Birkenau. Another 1,408 Roma lived in Auschwitz I and were sent to the Buchenwald concentration camp. Beginning on the evening of August 2, the SS gassed and cremated all of Birkenau's Roma. This was the infamous *zigeuner nacht*, Night of the Gypsies, remembered as a special time of horror for the Roma.

The fate of the Roma throughout Europe during the Holocaust varied from country to country and region to region. In those parts of Europe that were part of the Greater Reich— Germany, Austria, Bohemia and Moravia, northern Slovenia, and parts of Poland—Roma usually suffered significantly due to the direct application of Nazi racial laws and implementation of the Final Solution. The level of suffering the Roma in countries under German or German-satellite military or civilian occupation suffered depended on who was the occupying power. Though estimates vary widely, between two hundred fifty thousand and five hundred thousand Roma died during the Holocaust. A far greater number were persecuted or forced to work as slave and forced laborers by the Germans and their allies.

The Roma After the Holocaust

Dr. Ian Hancock, a prominent Roma scholar and member of the United States Memorial Council in Washington, DC, has given the Roma experience in the Holocaust a *Romani* name—*O Porrajmos*—the Great Devouring. Christian Bernadac, author of *Holocaust oublié: Les Massacre des tsiganes*, has called this time of Roma suffering "*l'Holocauste oublié*," or "the forgotten Holocaust." Both of these phrases capture the pain of Roma suffering during this horrible period.

At the end of World War II, the Allied occupying powers treated the Roma (as they did the Jews) as "homeless" or "stateless" displaced persons. The Roma who survived the death and concentration camps were often too weak to leave them, and many died in the days after liberation. The Roma, like other Holocaust victims, were often forced to live in Displaced Persons Camps where, occasionally, they were housed together with former SS members and other ethnic groups, which created a great deal of tension. Efforts by Allied officials to gather information from the Roma about their families were met with deep suspicion caused by centuries of discrimination. The Roma had learned over time that most official information gathered on them would later be used against them. This deeply ingrained distrust of the *gadžé* made it difficult for Allied relief agencies to gain any detailed facts from the Roma about their experiences in the Third Reich or the fate of their families.

Germany was divided into two zones at the end of the war, which later became the Allied-oriented Federal Republic of Germany (West Germany) and the Soviet-dominated German Democratic Republic (East Germany). The West Germans refused to recognize the German Roma—the Roma and the Sinti clans—as victims of "racial persecution," which initially neutralized any Roma claims to compensation for their suffering. In fact, all of the Allied powers adopted this position: that the Roma had suffered because the German Nazi government had viewed them as "criminal and asocial elements." In response, the West German Roma formed the Committee of German Gypsies to fight for reparations, but without initial success. A small number of Roma cases were presented to West German courts in the first decades after the Holocaust. Usually, the cases were rejected by the courts because the judges argued that the Roma had been persecuted by the Nazis not because of race, but because they were asocials or criminals. In 1963 the West German Federal Court of Justice finally backdated the beginning of "racial" discrimination against the Roma in the Third Reich to 1938. This did open the door to a modest number of new claims for Roma reparations. What few claims have been paid to the Roma in Germany and elsewhere have been made on an individual, not a collective, basis.

It is difficult to determine how many Roma Holocaust survivors exist today, though Ian Hancock, author of *The Indian Origin and Westward Migration of the Romani People,* once estimated that the figure could be as high as five thousand. Though most Roma Holocaust survivors have chosen to remain silent about their persecution, the recent decision of a number of Swiss banks to pay up to $1.5 billion in reparations to Holocaust victims has stirred some hope that Roma Holocaust survivors may now receive some compensation for their suffering and losses. Jewish survivors will get eighty-eight percent of the Swiss funds, while the remaining twelve percent will be available to non-Jews, including the Roma.

After the Holocaust, under the region's new communist governments in central and Eastern Europe, the fast growing Roma populations suffered from extreme impoverishment and high illiteracy rates. Moreover, Roma prejudice continued to be the principle stumbling bloc to Roma integration into central and Eastern European societies. Since the plight of the Roma contradicted communist claims that they had created societies free of "capitalistic" injustice, prejudice, and discrimination, leaders throughout the region mounted expensive campaigns to force the Roma to assimilate. Roma nomadism was outlawed and their children were rapidly mainstreamed into public schools without consideration of language, social, or economic differences. Roma children who exhibited educational difficulty were often labeled mentally retarded and sent to special schools, a practice that continues to this day. Roma settlements were destroyed and their occupants forced into government housing projects without regard to Roma desires or needs, and job training programs were created to help move the Roma from traditional jobs to skilled positions.

Many of these policies were driven by fear of high Roma birth rates compared to almost zero population birth rates among non-Roma throughout central and Eastern Europe. Efforts to curb Roma growth centered around forced assimilation and, in Czechoslovakia, efforts to sterilize Roma women. Though some remarkable gains were made in Roma education, housing, and employment from the 1960s through the 1980s, the policies were implemented without consultation with the Roma themselves.

With these policies, anti-Roma prejudice resurfaced, driven by jealousy over what many *gadzé* saw as expensive government policies that favored the Roma over others. This prejudice intensified throughout the 1980s, a period when the economies throughout Central and Eastern Europe suffered tremendous declines. When communism began to collapse in the late 1980s, the more open environment that replaced it saw a new, more virulent form of anti-Roma prejudice surface that had not been seen since the Holocaust.

During the communist era, prejudices against the Roma were seen as the single greatest barrier to the improvement of the quality of Roma life. Democratization has offered the Roma new opportunities for economic, social, cultural, and political growth that were not possible under communism. Unfortunately, the continued deep impoverishment of the Roma, coupled with continued prejudice and discrimination, created an explosive situation that was potentially politically destabilizing. As Czech president Vaclav Havel has noted, the plight of the Roma is the litmus test of the democratization experiment in the Czech Republic. The same could be said for the rest of central and eastern Europe.

RECENT HISTORY AND THE FUTURE

The Roma in the Czech Republic

The Czech Republic was part of Czechoslovakia from 1918 to 1939 and from 1945 to 1993. Traditionally, the majority of Czechoslovakia's Roma lived in the Slovak portions of the nation. Prior to the formal separation of Czechoslovakia into two nations on January 1, 1993, there were one hundred fifty thousand Roma in the Czech lands and four hundred thousand in Slovakia. Though estimates vary widely, there were between two hundred thousand and three hundred thousand Roma in the Czech Republic at the end of 1999. Part of the increase from 1993 figures came from Slovak Roma who fled to the Czech Republic prior to the 1993 split and partly from the high birth rate of the Czech Roma.

Though the Czech Republic was once viewed as a model post-communist state, its discriminatory policies toward the Roma have tarnished this image. Time and again, stories have appeared in the Western press detailing various acts of discrimination and violence against the Czech Republic's Roma. Skinhead violence has been a serious problem since 1989. Though estimates vary widely, between 1989 and 1999, scores of Czech Roma have been killed or injured in skinhead attacks. A minor international crisis took place between the Czech Republic and Canada in 1997 after hundreds of Czech Roma fled to Canada to escape persecution. The mayor of the Czech town of Ostrava offered to help pay for the airfare of any Roma who wanted to go to Canada. The Canadian government halted the immigration into Canada because of the tremendous influx of Czech Roma.

The Skinhead attacks and the attempted Roma exodus to Canada represented two extremes of the Czech Republic's difficulties with its Roma population. Today, the Roma in the Czech Republic are an impoverished and ill-educated group that has not been allowed to enjoy the fruits of Czech democracy. From the moment the Czech Republic was created in 1993, discriminatory citizenship and other laws were put in place that insured that the Roma would have fewer rights than other Czechs. This discrimination is so pervasive that, according to a 1999 report by the European Roma Rights Center in Budapest, "Roma in the Czech Republic live in general exclusion from the opportunities enjoyed by the majority community." According to the report, the Roma face social, economic, and educational barriers due to their race. They are segregated in an educational system that disproportionably sends a very large number of Roma children to schools for the mentally handicapped.

Discrimination against the Roma is so widespread that several Czech cities have discussed building walls to separate the poorer Roma sections of the communities from the non-Roma portions. In Usti nad Labem, the city council voted to build a seventy-foot concrete "noise barrier" to separate a poorer section of the city with a predominant Roma population from the rest of the community. The city's decision was met by widespread domestic and international protests. In Plzen (Pilsen), the city council approved plans to move the city's Roma to portable cabins outside of the city that would be watched 24-hours a day by the police. Though authorities agreed to delay their plans for the move, they were never com-

MAP SHOWING CITIES OF IMPORTANCE TO THE ROMA PEOPLE IN THE CZECH REPUBLIC. *(XNR Productions Inc.)*

pletely abandoned. These decisions were followed by skinheads across the Czech Republic.

When officials in Usti nad Labem finally decided to begin construction of the wall on October 5, 1999, the city's Roma occupied the construction site. Czech president Vaclav Havel, the European Union, and others appealed to city leaders to reconsider their decision. Stubbornly, the city's leaders argued that the wall was a "symbol of law and order" and was designed to protect Czech citizens from "noise, garbage, and crime by their Gypsy neighbors." The Roma countered that the wall reminded them of the walls of Holocaust concentration camps. The protests had no effect on city leaders, and in the early morning hours of October 13, 1999, construction began and the wall was quickly completed. Petr Uhl, the Czech government's human rights commissioner, has vowed that the wall will somehow be removed.

The Roma in Kosovo

Until recently, few people other than Balkan specialists knew anything about the Serbian province of Kosovo. About eighty-eight to ninety-two percent of Kosovo's two million people were Albanians. Most of Kosovo's population is Muslim. The 1991 census showed a Kosovor Roma population of forty-three hundred, though the European Roma Rights Center has said that the Roma could make up as much as five percent of the Kosovo's population.

The Serbs, who consider Kosovo the cradle of their civilization, gradually lost it to the Ottoman Empire after the fateful battle at *Kosovo Polje* (Field of the Blackbirds) in 1389. Kosovo remained under Ottoman control until 1913. After World War II, Yugoslavia was recreated

WORKERS TAKE DOWN A WALL THAT HAD BEEN USED TO KEEP ROMA GYPSIES SEGREGATED FROM THE REST OF THE POPULATION. *(AP/Wide World Photos. Reproduced by permission.)*

under Marshal Tito, Yugoslavia's great wartime guerilla leader, as a communist state. Kosovo was incorporated as a province of Serbia, which had been the dominant force in Yugoslav politics from 1918 to 1941.

In the late 1980s, there was a gradual decline of communist control over Yugoslavia's six republics, and the threat of collapse for the Yugoslav confederation. If Yugoslavia fell apart, it would dramatically impact Serbian influence and power in the confederation. Serbian leader Slobodan Milosevic used historic references to Kosovo to inflame Serbian national sentiments. When the confederation began to collapse in the

early 1990s, the Serbs tried to draw Roma leaders in Kosovo into an alliance with Kosovor Serbs. Initially, many Kosovor Roma supported Milosevic. But the fanatic loyalty demanded by Milosevic in return for a modest role in governing Kosovo, though allowing the Roma for the first time in the history of Kosovo and Serbia, to enjoy some authority, turned out to be too high a price. Few Roma gained from the alliance and most remained politically "mute."

Regardless, many Kosovor Albanians viewed the Roma as Serb allies and felt a deep betrayal, since Roma have lived beside and gone to school with Albanians. What particularly angered some

Kosovors, particularly in Priština, which had a large Muslim Roma population, was that the Roma seemed to flaunt their pro-Serb feelings. The *New York Times* (June 24, 1999), for example, reported that at the height of the ethnic cleansing campaign, Priština's Roma organized "a parade of their own police unit."

Ibrahim Makolli, the head of the Council for the Defense of Human Rights and Freedoms in the Kosovor capital, defended the Roma. He said that many of the Roma were drafted by the Serbs and possibly forced to behave the way they did. The Serbs, he noted, often forced the Roma to do the "worst jobs," such as collecting and burying the bodies of the dead. Regardless, he explained, many Kosovors would "find it hard to forgive the apparent [quickness] with which many Roma looted, burned, and wielded weapons during the last months" of the ethnic cleansing campaign. He added that testimony existed reporting that some Roma took part in the Serb atrocities against Kosovo's Albanians. Other Roma, he explained, "took people from refugee columns, they demanded identification papers, they took action in the same way that the Serbian forces did." Makolli said that the Albanians expected such behavior from the Serbs, not from the Roma.

There were many Roma, though, who did not support the Serbs and who suffered from Serb abuse. Some Muslim Roma were driven out of their homes throughout Kosovo by Serbian police, and there is some evidence of Serbian policemen raping Roma women before the NATO air campaigns began. Roma refugees reported that in some cases, the Serb police forced them to loot and burn Kosovor homes to ensure that the Roma would be blamed for the destruction. Yet the Serbs were not the only ones who mistreated the Roma. Roma refugees reported numerous instances of threats and murders by the Kosovo Liberation Army (KLA) and mistreatment by Albanians.

Once the fighting ended and the hundreds of thousands of Kosovors who had been driven from their homes returned, they took revenge on the remaining Serbs and Roma. Any town or village with a Roma quarter was attacked, looted, and burned. In fact, even before the Kosovors returned home, they attacked Roma in refugee camps in Albania and Macedonia. As Albanian refugees returned to Kosovo, the attacks against Roma and Serbs intensified to the point that by the end of July 1999, there were few Roma left in Kosovo.

The intensity of the attacks shocked human rights groups and Roma organizations. The International *Romani* Union (IRU) in Berlin decried unsubstantiated press accounts in France, Italy, and Kosovo that pointed to Roma attacks against Albanians. The IRU statement also criticized the use of the word *cigány* and Gypsy in the press, since both words were laden with prejudicial meaning.

By mid-August 1999, there were only twenty thousand to twenty-five thousand Serbs left in Kosovo, out of a population that had numbered almost two hundred thousand only months earlier. Almost all of Kosovo's Roma had fled the province. Yet unlike so many other refugees in Europe's Balkan wars over the past decade, the Roma have no ethnic homeland they can look to for refuge like the Albanians, Croats, or Serbs. The Roma probably will, as they have in the past, quietly drift back into Kosovo once the current ethnic hatred dies down. Roma resiliency may well assure that they will have a presence in Kosovo's future.

BIBLIOGRAPHY

Bernadac, Christian L. *Holocaust oublié: Les Massacre des tsiganes.* Paris: Editions France-Empire, 1979.

Cahn, Claude and Tatjana Peric. "Roma and the Kosovo Conflict," *Roma Rights* no. 2 (1999): 1–3.

Commission on Security and Cooperation in Europe, 104th Congress, Second Session (July 21, 1998). *Romani Human Rights in Europe* (Hearing before the Commission on Security and Cooperation in Europe). Washington, D.C.: United States Government Printing Office, 1998.

Crowe, David M. *A History of the Gypsies of Eastern Europe and Russia.* New York: St. Martin's Press, 1994, 1996.

European Roma Rights Center. *A Special Remedy: Roma and Schools for the Mentally Handicapped in the Czech Republic.* Budapest: European Roma Rights Center, 1999.

Gall, Carlotta. "Albanians Loot and Burn, Aiming Wrath at Gypsies," *New York Times*, 24 June 1999, sec. A14.

———. "Kosovo War Over, Gypsies Find Themselves Alone," *New York Times*, 11 July 1999, sec. A6.

Hancock, Ian. *The Indian Origin and Westward Migration of the Romani People.* Manchaca, Tex.: International Romani Union, 1998.

Human Rights Watch/Helsinki Watch. *Roma in the Czech Republic: Foreigners in Their Own Land.* New York: Human Rights Watch, 1996.

———. *Struggling for Ethnic Identity: Czechoslovakia's Endangered Gypsies.* New York: Human Rights Watch, 1992.

Kenrick, Donald and Grattan Puxon. *The Destiny of Europe's Gypsies.* New York: Basic Books, 1972.

———. *Gypsies Under the Swastika.* Hertfordshire: Gypsy Research Centre and University of Hertfordshire Press, 1995.

Latham, Judith. "Roma of the Former Yugoslavia," *Nationalities Papers* 27, no. 2 (June 1999): 205–226.

Malcolm, Noel. *Kosovo: A Short History.* New York: Harper Collins, 1999.

Open Society Institute, Forced Migration Projects. *Roma and Forced Migration: An Annotated Bibliography.* 2d ed. New York: Open Society Institute, 1998.

Perlez, Jane. "Boxed In by Bias, Czech Gypsies Look to Canada," *New York Times,* 31 August 1997, sec. A3.

Rohde, David. "Kosovor Attack on Gypsies Reveals Desire for Revenge" *New York Times,* 7 June 1999, sec. A12.

David M. Crowe

RWANDA AND BURUNDI: CULTURE, HISTORY, POWER, AND GENOCIDE

In 1994 the central African nation of Rwanda erupted into genocide. For six weeks in April and May, between five hundred thousand and one million ethnic Tutsi were massacred by their Hutu neighbors. Over seventy-five percent of the Tutsi living in Rwanda were killed, and between ten and one hundred thousand sympathetic Hutu were also executed. By July, between thirty-five to forty percent of the Rwandan population had been killed or fled the violence. The killing was highly organized and rapid—most of the slaughter was finished two weeks after it began. Carried out with low-tech weapons, including machetes, spears, and machine guns, executions were quick and brutally violent.

As the violence escalated, hundreds of thousands of refugees poured out of Rwanda and into neighboring countries such as Zaire (now the Democratic Republic of the Congo) and Tanzania. When the Tutsi resistance gained the upper hand and overthrew the Hutu government responsible for launching the attacks, Tutsi refugees returned and it was the Hutu who fled, fearing retribution. Among the Hutu refugees were many of those responsible for orchestrating the Tutsi murders; they were fleeing from responsibility and biding their time to return to power. They used the Hutu refugee camps as a staging area for guerrilla attacks on Rwanda's fledgling Tutsi government, which struggled to restore order and peace to the country. Tanzania, tired of being in the middle of the fighting, asked the refugees to return home. Between 1996 and 1997, about 1.3 million Hutus returned to Rwanda. Thousands suspected of participating in the Tutsi massacres were arrested, and the Rwandan government, in an attempt to bring about justice and reconciliation, planned to put the killers on trial.

THE CONFLICT

Traditional economic and tribal divisions in Rwanda and Burundi—divisions that identified specific individuals and groups based on physical characteristics and livelihood—were exacerbated during colonization by Belgium. The best jobs, education, and religious leadership were given only to Tutsis, a minority group in Congo. While this changed after Rwanda gained independence, anger and distrust continued. In 1994 fears of being cheated out of the political and economic largess caused some Hutu to incite others to kill. Between five hundred thousand and one million Tutsis were brutally killed by their Hutu neighbors.

Economic

- Historically, the majority Hutu made their living off the land, a less prestigious occupation than the cattle-owning Tutsi. When Rwanda was colonized, Tutsi were given preference for jobs and education. Little of the class system still exists, though the frustration and anger at the economic discrimination still does.

Ethnic

- While there is no biological evidence of difference races, many Rwandans perceive that Tutsi and Hutu are of different races. This view was popularized when Rwanda was colonized: Tutsi were thought to be tall, with thin lips and noses, and a generally Caucasian appearance; Hutu were thought to be shorter, broader, with think lips and flat noses.

Political/Ethnic

- Political forces within Rwanda incited Hutu to kill their neighbors. This was done for many reasons, including fear that they were about to lose political power.

CHRONOLOGY

1853–1895 Kigeli IV Rwabugiri, the Great Tutsi Conqueror, begins extending Tutsi power throughout Rwanda by conquering Hutu empires while using Hutu foot soldiers in his armies. Tutsi, Hutu, and Twa share the land and co-exist, despite efforts by both Hutu and Tutsi kingdoms to expand.

1895–96 Rutalindwa, the son designated by King Kigeli IV Rwabugiri as heir, ascends the throne. One of his co-mothers, Kanjogera, is chosen Queen Mother and conspires to overthrow Rutalindwa.

1896 Queen Mother Kanjogera to cause King Rutalindwa's death in a palace coup d'etat. She selects King Yuhi V Musinga, her biological son.

1897–1916 German Colonial Period of "indirect rule," strengthens King Yuhi V Musinga's grip on power.

1926–1931 Les reformes Voisin. Governor Charles Voisin, a Belgian official, creates the myth of Tutsi racial superiority and the purging of Hutu chiefs from top-level administrative positions as the seeds of ethnic conflict are sown.

1932–1940 Belgium creates modern Rwanda with centralized authority, Roman Catholicism, and heavy tax burdens.

1945–1959 Alex Kagame and African intellectuals agitate for independence.

1959–1990 The "Hutu Republic" (Muyaga). The Tutsi are increasingly oppressed.

1990–1991 Civil War and French intervention. The Tutsi-dominated Rwandan Patriotic Army (RPF) invade Rwanda, using Uganda as a staging area.

1991–1992 Multi-party electoral politics are introduced, creating Hutu fear of losing power and of renewed Tutsi domination.

1993 Groupe des Observateurs Militaires Neutres (Neutral Military Observer Group or GOMN) is set up by the OAU (Organization of African Unity) to monitor the application of the Dar es Salaam cease-fire agreement following the February war between the Tutsi dominated RPF (Rwandan Patriotic Front) and the Hutu dominated FAR (Forces Armees Rwandaises or Rwandan Army).

1994 Hutu massacre between 500,000–1,000,000 Tutsi in a planned and well-coordinated manner.

1995–2000 Paul Kagame and the RPF seize power and many Hutu are killed in "revenge." Approximately 750,000 exiled Tutsis return from Burundi, Uganda, and Tanzania to claim land and power.

During the Tutsi massacre, deaths occurred at a rate three times faster than the execution of Jews during the Holocaust. In a country where Tutsi and Hutu lived side by side for years in relative peace, why did this outbreak of violence occur so rapidly and so brutally? Some journalists claimed that primeval tribal hatreds had spilled over into modern politics, triggering the worst violence in Rwandan history. Many factors other than traditional hatreds, however, influenced the massacre, including overpopulation, a shortage of jobs and farmland, the myth of Tutsi racial superiority, the introduction of multi-party politics, and the quest for personal power.

HISTORICAL BACKGROUND

The country of Rwanda covers 26,338 square kilometers, or 10,169 square miles. It is about the size of its neighbor to the south, Burundi, or the U.S. state of Maryland. Rwanda has a total population of nearly eight million people, averaging 745 people per square mile. By contrast the heavily urban state of Maryland has 561 people per square mile. Rwanda's population doubles every twenty years and, despite the recent widespread slaughter, it remains one of the most crowded nations in Africa.

With nearly half its land occupied in agriculture and an expanse of rugged uplands and hills, Rwanda is an overwhelmingly rural country. Tension over land ownership in this densely populated region is explosive. Most of the population is traditionally engaged in farming and land is in short supply. Many families work small plots of land of no more than an acre or two, and with each generation the land shortage becomes more severe. Farmers are generally able to grow enough food to feed themselves and their families, with little remaining to sell on the market. Agricultural technology in the country is not improving fast enough to feed the growing population, and Rwanda lacks enough industries to absorb all the people in its cities. The government, consequently, has encouraged people to stay on their land. At the same time, the scarcity of land prompts many to head for the cities, creating a crowded and tense political and social situation.

Pre-Colonial Rwandan Culture

Three African ethnic groups inhabit Rwanda. The tall, slender Tutsi form fourteen percent of the population. Traditionally herdsmen, Tutsi males went through initiation ceremonies from childhood to adulthood that stressed courage, valor, and stoicism. Warrior traditions were encouraged, since they helped protect family herds and national wealth. Cattle were viewed as a symbol of prestige and status. The larger the herd, the greater was the prestige and status. Tutsi folklore claims that they are a Nilotic-speaking group who arrived in Rwanda from the north during the fifteenth and sixteenth centuries. After their arrival, they gained dominance over the ethnic Hutu population, who made up the majority population in the region, and established a monarchy.

The agricultural Hutu people claim to be descendents of Bantu speakers from the west, probably Cameroon, and they form eighty-five percent of Rwanda's population. They claim status as Rwanda's first "settler" population. The Hutu migrated to the area of present day Rwanda in the fourteenth century, conquering the native Twa, cave-dwelling Pygmy hunter-gatherers, and imposing their language and culture. Surplus grains traditionally served as the Hutu measure of wealth and status. The larger the surplus, the greater was the volume of trade. As surpluses and trade increased, so did a family's prestige and influence.

The Twa, physically small in stature, form one percent of Rwanda's current population. Well before 800 B.C. their ancestors inhabited the area. They lived by hunting, gathering, and foraging. For a fee, the Twa served as assassins for both Tutsi and Hutu kings, and the elite of both groups feared them. They also served as court jesters for Tutsi kings. Today the Twa, making up such a small percentage of the population, are marginalized from society, disenfranchised, and denied access to education.

From the seventeenth century to the mid-twentieth century the Tutsi and Hutu coexisted in

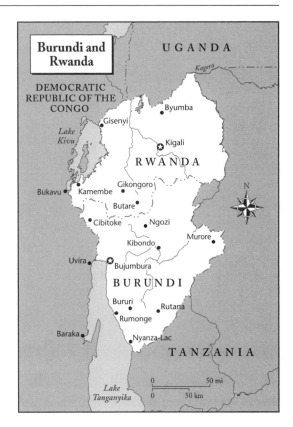

MAP OF RWANDA AND BURUNDI. *(XNR Productions Inc.)*

a highly stratified, monarchical society. Tutsis were the dominant ethnic group and held the highest social status. That status, however, was fluid. A Hutu could advance to the status of a Tutsi, and a Tutsi could fall to the lower strata of the Hutu. The *mwami*, or king, and his appointed leaders, however, were predominantly ethnic Tutsis, as were those at the very tops of the society. The general population intermarried, lived in ethnically mixed communities, fought in the same army, and shared the same religion and the same political and social cultures.

Tutsi monarchs enjoyed greater success at capturing and consolidating power over land and people than did Hutu kings. Their symbol of office was a large drum, known as the *Kalinga*. It was a ceremonial drum decorated with the genitalia of slain enemies of the Tutsi empire, a stern warning to anyone thinking of revolt. To revolt against a Tutsi king was considered sacrilegious. A system known as *ubuletwa*, or public interest, prevailed. Under this system a patron would give his or her client cattle to care for. Tutsi kings rewarded brave Hutu and Tutsi soldiers with cattle when they defended the kingdom against external aggression,

RWANDA'S IMAGINED OR MYTHICAL PAST

European explorers, including John Hanning Speke, (1827–1864) were impressed by the fact that Rwandans had powerful, divine-like kings. Speke believed that most black Africans were rude "savages." It was unthinkable to him that African could reach Rwanda's level of political and religious sophistication. He speculated that the rulers in Rwanda were "pastoral invaders" from the north, probably Ethiopia. They were descendants of lost tribes of Europeans and were not simply racially different but actually superior to the black agriculturists whom they conquered. European-featured Tutsi with narrow noses, thin lips, narrow chins, tall lanky frames, and long narrow faces were believed to be natural-born rulers, while their Negroid-featured Hutu neighbors with dark skin, short stocky builds, round faces, flat noses, thick lips, and square jaws were deemed destined to lives of servitude. In reality, some Tutsi were short, dark, and round faced and some Hutu were tall, with lighter completions, and thin noses, faces, and lips.

From Speke's observations arose the myth of Tutsi racial superiority and Hutu racial inferiority. Speke referred to this myth as his "Hamitic Hypothesis," and his theory became part of the history of anthropology. According to this theory, all high culture, civilization, and technological advancement in Africa had been introduced from outside Africa. A taller, sharp-featured race of European descent created these complex states in Africa. Thus, Ethiopia was created by descendents of King David, who were vastly superior to the local Negroid races whose labor they directed in Rwanda, the Sudan, and in Pharaonic Egypt. Racism masqueraded as so-called race science. The charade worked for a time. Modern anthropologists consider this myth "wild fantasy."

European colonial authorities latched onto this theory to justify educating Tutsi youth and training them to become Roman Catholic priests, while depriving Hutu youth of similar opportunities. When Belgian colonial officers took over from the German overlords they put this theory of racial superiority into practice by removing competent Hutu chiefs and replacing them with Tutsi chiefs. By increasing the power of the Tutsi, Europeans hoped to make it easier to collect taxes to support themselves. Belgian officials also issued identity cards to each Rwandan listing their ethnic identity as Tutsi, Hutu, or Twa. Belgian colonialism created apartheid-like systems that discriminated against the Hutu; these systems were rooted in the myth of Tutsi racial superiority and hereditary privilege. Collective national identity was destroyed.

---

expanded the kingdom, or stole cattle for the king from non-Rwandan ethnic groups. Cattle, traditionally connected to the Tutsi, were a sign of good breeding, power, and wealth. The gift of cattle, therefore, created a type of upward mobility for a Hutu. Since the cow could reproduce, future cattle were shared between patron and client. Once enriched with cattle, a Hutu family ascended to the higher social ranks of the Tutsi. If riches were lost, a Hutu or a Tutsi could lose stature politically and socially. Thus, a Tutsi could also descend to the ranks of a Hutu.

The ethnic divisions described endured throughout the twentieth century, though in an altered form. Pre-colonial Tutsi monarchs did much to assimilate the Hutu for centuries. As a result, all three Rwandan ethnic groups recognize a single nationality, *Banyarwandan*, and speak a common language, *Kinyarwanda*, though French and English are also recognized as national languages. The Tutsi elite is most closely associated with the English language, since many Tutsi exiles lived in English-speaking Uganda for thirty years, from 1959 until 1991, until they returned to Rwanda with a conquering army.

Authoritarian State Traditions

King Kigeri IV Rwabugiri (1853–1895), a Tutsi leader, demanded absolute obedience from his subjects—Tutsi, Twa, and Hutu alike. By this time Tutsis had advanced from a single hilltop kingdom to domination of most of what is currently the country of Rwanda. In Rwanda the king was semi-divine and disobeying him was not just a crime but also a sin. People considered the *mwami* infallible.

In 1899 German forces entered Rwanda. After withstanding slave raiders and hostile neighbors for centuries, the Tutsi kingdom was conquered. Indirect rule by the German colonizers ensured that Tutsi society, culture, and power would change little under European rule. The

Germans accepted Tutsi dominance in the social structure of the region and racial superiority began, perhaps, as a convenient method of dividing and ruling Rwandans.

The Germans actually heightened societal and cultural divisions by issuing ethnic identity cards, promoting Tutsi chiefs and demoting Hutu chiefs, and advancing Tutsis in schools, hospitals, churches, government offices, and the military. The Tutsi manipulated German beliefs to their own advantage in the area, helping Tutsi kings conquer the remaining independent Hutu kingdoms. When Germany was defeated in World War I, Rwanda and its neighbor Burundi became League of Nations Mandate Territories entrusted to Belgium (1923). Belgium later administered them as United Nations Trust Territories. After World War II, both nations were administered as international U.N. Trusteeships until independence.

The Belgians, like their German predecessors, were largely ignorant of local culture, history, and politics, and had strong beliefs in race and hierarchy. In 1926, the Belgians instituted a classification system for the population. A native person was to be classified as either a Tutsi or a Hutu. No mobility between the two groups was allowed. Pockets of autonomy that had existed in the region prior to colonial times were quashed, including several Hutu-controlled areas. This served to further elevate the preferred Tutsi class, and, under Belgian oversight, Tutsi chiefs gained a near perfect monopoly on power.

Belgian officials also redesigned the system of forced labor, which contributed to repression of the Hutu and Twa. Exhausted from road construction or plantation work, these peasants, perceived now by both the Tutsi and the Belgians as inferior, were too tired to cultivate their own fields. As a result, crop production declined, and under the rigid new system there was little hope for advancement.

Those closest to the ones in power, the Tutsi, benefited greatly from this system. The Tutsi in Rwanda and the Ganwa royalty in Burundi were granted jobs and positions in the colonial government. Both argued that they were racially superior to the Hutu, and both succeeded in attaining a special social and political status in the colony. Taking advantage of their power and position, local chiefs in Rwanda abused their authority, seizing Hutu cattle and punishing any who opposed them.

Belgian reforms and policies greatly contributed to the modern Rwanda: a nation highly centralized, efficient, and brutal. Men were obligated to engage in forced labor, which consumed fifty to sixty percent of their time. Failure to comply met with harsh treatment. Belgian brutality was so notorious that a United Nations mission in 1948 discovered that of 250 peasants interviewed, 247 had been beaten. The excess of brutality and repression in Rwanda led to the country's first mass migration to the more humanely administered British territories, notably Uganda in the north.

World War II vastly expanded the cash economy in Rwanda and the old patron-client system of *ubuletwa* was falling into disuse. By 1959 new economic systems had created a Hutu elite that rivaled that of the Tutsi. Tutsi of noble lineage were among the first to adopt the notion of equality between the races, and they advocated the devolution of power and self-government. In addition, many communist nations championed Rwandan independence. This, in combination with Tutsi talk of self-government, led Belgium to suspect the Tutsi of radical leftist sympathies. The support for independence encouraged Belgium to shift its backing to the emerging Hutu elite. This created a new strain in the Belgian-Tutsi relationship. The Belgians considered the Hutu easier to control, since they would welcome relief from oppression. In 1959 the Hutu attacked Tutsis in ethnic clashes in which many Tutsi homes were burned and three hundred Tutsi were killed. Symbolically, Hutu leaders asked that the Tutsi *Kalinga* drum be destroyed, as it was a reminder of past subjugation.

Shortly thereafter, in 1960, Belgian colonial officials began systematically replacing Tutsi chiefs with Hutu chiefs. Their positions were reversed. Tutsis became objects of public ridicule and persecution. United Nations efforts to ally the tensions and create a reconciliation between the sides failed, and over seven hundred fifty thousand Tutsi migrated to Uganda and Tanzania.

Belgium granted early independence to Rwanda, ensuring a Hutu electoral victory. On July 1, 1962, Rwanda became an independent state. The Hutu rulers claimed that they represented the numerical majority and that they were merely protecting the interests of the impoverished Hutu majority. The Tutsi were portrayed as a wealthy alien racial minority, little different from the European minority who once used the apartheid policy to legally segregate and discriminate against South Africa's African majority.

From 1962 to 1973 Gregoire Kayibanda governed the newly independent Rwanda. He was overthrown in a bloodless coup d'etat in 1973 by General Juvenal Habyarimana. Habyarimana, a Hutu, ruled as a dictator for the next twenty years. During that time, he showed great preference for his own tribe and kept a close circle of advisors. This circle was called the *Akazu*, or "little house," and its members controlled most major government institutions. Habyarimana kept a tight grip on the economy, depending on foreign aid to prop up a country with little industry, poor infrastructure, and few natural resources. As president, he doled out aid money and influence to a select group, ensuring the continued support of the elite and the continued decline of the general population.

Rigid ethnic quotas were established. Since Tutsi were nine percent of Rwanda's population, he reasoned, they could only have nine percent of the students in schools, and nine percent of jobs and government contracts. Formerly over-represented in schools, the Tutsi switched from government jobs to private sector employment. Educated Hutu enforced these quotas hoping to take for themselves places in schools and in academic life once monopolized by Tutsi.

Habyarimana continued to require that citizens carry identity cards noting their ethnicity, a practice begun under the Belgians. Discrimination against Tutsis was rampant. Beginning in 1973 Tutsis were expelled from politics, government, business, and schools. Many Tutsi left Rwanda for neighboring countries, such as Uganda, Zaire, and Tanzania. This exodus created a strain on Rwanda's neighbors, who were hard pressed to absorb the flood of refugees. In the late 1980s and early 1990s they attempted to open negotiations between Rwanda's Hutu government and Tutsi refugees, with little progress.

The Rwandan Patriotic Front

The oppressive measures against Tutsis under Habyarimana's regime gave rise to the Rwandan Patriotic Front (RPF), a group of Tutsi rebels based in Uganda since 1979. The RPF regularly launched raids into Rwanda in an attempt to destabilize the government. The official Rwandan media referred to the RPF as *inyenzi*, or cockroaches, and the term was soon used publicly to describe all Tutsis. The media incited ethnic divisions and hatred through the consistent use of vehement anti-Tutsi rhetoric. This rhetoric and Habyarimana's determined efforts to shut the Tutsi out of Rwandan society gave the RPF support from exiled Tutsis and from those remaining in the country.

The RPF was also supported by Yoweri Museveni, a Tutsi and the president of Uganda. Many RPF members fought in Ugandan conflicts during the 1970s and 1980s and Museveni allowed them to operate in Uganda without interference. With this support and experience, the RPF continued to grow more sophisticated and effective in its attacks on Rwanda.

Fighting and the Prospect of Peace

Paul Kagame led the RPF in the early 1990s and through the Rwandan massacre of the Tutsi in 1994, and he attempted to broaden the group's appeal by including Hutu fighters and political figures. This attempt was not wholly successful. Backed by years of government propaganda Rwanda's Hutu were not ready to revolt against Habyarimana's corrupt regime. They feared the Tutsi-dominated RPF too much to support it.

In 1990 RPF forces crossed the Ugandan border into Rwanda and overran the government garrison at Kakituimba. Using armored vehicles, they raced half way to the capital, Kigali, before encountering serious resistance. Government propaganda claimed that Tutsi invaders hoped to reinstate forced labor and feudal servitude. The RPF asserted that it wanted to share power among all Rwandans and accused Habyarimana's government of being undemocratic and corrupt. The fighting intensified.

Rwanda's army grew ten-fold during this conflict, between 1990 and 1993. Habyarimana's government was firmly backed by Belgium and France. France sent weapons and troops to support Rwandan government forces and a French officer was allegedly commander of the Rwandan Army and counterintelligence. French troops also manned roadblocks and served as military advisers to Rwandan field commanders.

Negotiations for a settlement took place on and off between 1990 and 1994. In 1991 Habyarimana agreed to a new constitution that would allow multi-party politics, a limited presidential term, and separate branches of government. He also announced that the requirement of ethnic identity cards would cease, though this was never implemented. Within one year, twelve political parties were participating in Rwanda's government. In mid-1992 the government and the RPF agreed to form a representative interim government. They planned extensive reforms. The methods of implementing these plans, however, remained contentious.

THE UNITED NATIONS FELT COMPELLED TO USE FORCE IN THE RWANDAN CONFLICT; ONE OF ITS ARMORED VEHICLES IS ON PATROL IN SOUTHWEST RWANDA. *(Corbis. Reprinted by permission.)*

In 1993 Tanzania was host to the Arusha Agreement. It allowed all Tutsi refugees to return to Rwanda. Tanzania, Uganda, the Democratic Republic of the Congo (formerly Zaire), and Burundi would grant full citizenship to those who chose not to return. Under the accord, Habyarimana and the RPF agreed to form a transitional government, including the twelve Rwandan political parties, and to hold multi-party elections in 1995. Habyarimana's *Mouvement Revolutionnaire pour le Development* party (MRND) would have six of the twenty-two posts in the transition government, including the presidency. The RPF would have five seats, including the prime minister's office. The other Rwandan political parties would

share the remaining seats allotted under the Arusha Agreement. In addition, a new national army would be created with fifty percent of the officers and forty percent of the soldiers coming from the RPF.

With this promise of peace the United Nations issued a U.N. Assistance Mission in Rwanda (UNAMIR). A deployment of 2,500 troops from several nations arrived in Rwanda in November 1993, to monitor the peace settlement. The Rwandan military, however, strongly opposed the settlement and stepped up its attacks against Tutsis. Opposition also came from Habyarimana's own party, the MRND, and the Committee for

TUTSI REFUGEES WERE ABLE TO RETURN FROM THEIR EXILE IN TANZANIA AFTER THE RWANDAN PATRIOTIC FRONT (RPF) ROSE TO POWER. *(AP/Wide World Photos. Reproduced by permission.)*

the Defense of the Republic (CDR), a Hutu extremist organization. Habyarimana's grip on power was tenuous. Though he succeeded in splitting key opposition parties he made little effort to reign in CRD actions and, in fact, aligned his own party closely with the extremist group, bringing into question his sincerity in pursuing peace negotiations.

The RPF did its part to continue the fighting as well. Weapons continued to be distributed to RPF forces and the group's media organization regularly encouraged violence against Habyarimana's supporters. Neither side backed away from fighting, even when laying the foundations for a coalition government. The UN peacekeeping force, faced with such opposition, could not keep a peace that had never existed, but they did not pull back, and remained as witnesses to what was to come. It is difficult to say the intentions of the RPF and Habyarimana were ever serious.

The answer to that question will remain unknown. On April 6, 1994, Habyarimana flew to Dar es Salaam, Tanzania, for another round of peace talks. His plane was shot down en route. Habyarimana and Burundi's President Cyprien Ntaryamira were killed. The circumstances surrounding the assassination remain unclear, but the death of Rwanda's dictator served as a stick of dynamite to a powder keg.

Genocide

The Hutu extremists in Rwanda, including the military and the CRD, quickly mobilized. They used Habyarimana's death as an excuse to mount a no-holds-barred offensive against the Tutsi, though the perpetrators of the president's assassination remain unknown. Government offices across Rwanda gave mayors, *Interahamwe* (militias), and "zero networks," or death squads, the order to start the killing. It began with the assassination of every Tutsi in the cabinet. Death lists were established and everyone on them was hunted down and killed. In an obvious note of premeditation, victims' homes had been previously marked with red paint for easy identification.

The speed and level of the violence was shocking. Hutu gangs armed with swords, spears, and machetes attacked Tutsis, hacking, clubbing, or beating them to death. No Tutsi was safe. Keith Richburg, a correspondent for the *Washington Post Dispatch*, described standing at the Rusomo Falls bridge on the Kagera River weeks after the worst killing had ended and seeing the river so bloated with human bodies that it seemed to be a river of people instead of water. Richburg witnessed babies torn from their mother's arms and tossed onto spears. Mothers were disemboweled, their arms and legs cut off.

From this horror, the Tutsi fled, gathering in central locations—hospitals, churches, and stadiums. This originally gave the Tutsi an advantage. They were able to overwhelm their poorly organized and simply armed Hutu attackers by sheer size. Within a week after the killing began, however, reinforcements arrived in the form of the national army, Presidential Guard, and national police. These new troops came bearing rifles,

GENOCIDE

Genocide may be an ancient practice. Some anthropologists speculate that the sudden disappearance of the Neanderthals, or cavemen, thirty-five hundred years ago might be because modern man, or Homo sapiens, murdered them all. Britain killed all of the Tasmanians when fighting to seize control of Tasmania in Australia by poisoning all fresh water supplies. Nazi Germany attempted to implement Adolf Hitler's Final Solution for the Jews, killing six million Jewish people in the process. Turkey's Muslims killed over one million Christian Armenians. Americans killed an estimated twelve million Native Americans during the conquest of the United States. The Khmer Rouge killed some three million Cambodians, and Rwanda's Hutus killed an estimated one million Tutsi.

Social scientists don't agree on specifically what constitutes genocide. Regardless of the terminology, there are shared characteristics of mass killings, such as the massacre of the Tutsi in Rwanda in 1994. Many religious, racial and ethnic groups live comfortably beside each other. Many others live with hatred of others daily, but do not act violently toward others. The Nazi soldiers killed Jews on orders from their superiors, as did the Hutu militias. People often live peacefully beside other groups until they feel threatened. The Hutu felt threatened by the introduction of multi-party elections in Rwanda.

People must be persuaded that their neighbors or friends are evil. Rwandan radio encouraged this perception prior to their genocide. In addition, an elite that plans genocide must persuade the population that the target group is out to get them, so killing the target group is merely be an act of self-defense. To the Hutu elite, it seemed that the invading Tutsi would conquer Rwanda and retaliate against Hutus—killing them first. Psychological preparation to kill Jews was master minded by Joseph Goebels, Hitler's Minister of Propaganda. He showed Germans pictures of rats, then pictures of Jews; then people killing the rats, implying what they must do to the Jews. Similarly, in Rwanda, Tutsi were dehumanized and killed.

Mass killings must be taught and organized. In Rwanda, this role was played by the extremist element in the Hutu Power elite and the CDR radicals. Their Hutu Manifesto played a major role. People have to be trained and mobilized, as happened with the *Interhamwe* in Rwanda. Moreover, appeals must be made to identify with the "superior" group. Hitler appealed to the ideal of the German super race; the Hutu claimed racial superiority over the Tutsi.

Many Hutu became convinced that the Tutsi represented a perpetual threat. Defending the Hutu way of life justified killing Tutsi. To this day, many are not remorseful and believe that they did the right and necessary thing.

grenades, and machine guns. The Tutsi advantage became a trap.

Hutu militias threw hand grenades into the buildings housing the Tutsi. Anyone who ran out was shot. Tear gas canisters followed the grenades. Tutsis remaining alive inside who made a noise were hacked to death. Those who survived the killings were often mutilated—fingers, arms, and legs cut off. Some survived by the "luck" of being hidden under the fallen bodies of their tribesmen. It is estimated that over twenty thousand people died per day in the slaughter.

The worst atrocities occurred in the southeast and southwest of the country. Tutsis in the north had either fled to Uganda or were protected by the RPF. The killing was without prejudice. Moderate Hutus were often killed to discourage other Hutu

from sympathizing with Tutsi victims. Others were forced under threat of death or torture to kill their Tutsi neighbors. Between thirty thousand and one hundred thousand Hutu were dead by the massacre's end.

The Tutsi responded in several ways to the killings. Some sat outside their homes and waited patiently for their murderers to arrive and kill them. Others hid in filthy latrines, in roofs, in the mountains, and in caves until the RPF liberated their area. A few Tutsis fought with sticks, stones, and broken bottles. By mid-June 1994 over seventy-five percent of the Tutsi in Rwanda had been killed.

The slaughter convinced the RPF that it had to defeat the Hutu government or face total extermination. RPF leader Paul Kagame gave orders

TRYING CRIMES AGAINST HUMANITY

In the summer of 1998, delegates from 160 countries gathered in Rome, Italy to draft and ratify a statute that would establish a permanent International Criminal Court (ICC) to try war crimes, crimes against humanity, genocide, and acts of international aggression. This court would have a different mandate than the United Nations' International Court of Justice in the Hague (ICJH). While the ICJH prosecutes nations, the ICC would charter a new course in international law by prosecuting individuals. Advocates believe this distinction is essential to the protection of human rights worldwide.

The idea of an international court for criminal prosecutions has been around since World War II. Originally proposed following the Nuremberg War Trials, which tried German Nazis for their crimes, the ICC was stalled for decades by the Cold War between the United States and the former Soviet Union. When the Soviet Union dissolved, and, more importantly, when ethnic conflicts broke out in a number of countries, interest in the ICC was rekindled. Its most immediate predecessors have been the tribunals established by the United Nations to prosecute war crimes in the former Yugoslavia and in Rwanda. Both courts have struggled with the same problems that will face the ICC.

The International Criminal Tribunal for the Former Yugoslavia (ICTFY) was created in 1993. Seven years later, sixty-seven of the ninety-four public indictments are still outstanding. Plagued by continuing unrest in the region and by varying levels of cooperation from local governments, many whose leaders have been listed in the indictments, the tribunal has been criticized for its slow progress and costs which have exceeded $300 million. Supporters of the court point to the convictions it has made and stress that great care must be taken as important legal precedents are being set.

The International Criminal Tribunal for Rwanda (ICTR) was established in December 1994 to prosecute the persons responsible for the 1994 genocide of Tutsis by the Hutus in Rwanda. To date, twenty-nine indictments have been issued against fifty individuals. Several judgements have been delivered including one against former Prime Minister Jean Kambanda—the first ever by an international court for the crime of genocide. ICTR prosecutors are satisfied with the convictions thus far but worry that the reasoning they use to achieve the convictions may conflict with that of the Yugoslav Tribunal. If the resulting case law from both courts differs too much, it would effectively nullify any precedents being set for the ICC.

Critics of the proposed ICC believe, at the very least, it will be ineffectual, incapable of navigating the contrary interests of participating nations. At its worst, it would threaten national sovereignty as its prime directive is to focus on the individual rather than the nation, thus eliminating the protection behind which many a former despot has stood. Human rights activists belittle these fears and point out that the ICC has been hamstrung before it tries its first case by the fact that it must have the permission of any given state to prosecute its citizen. Even with that safeguard, many nations vigorously opposed the resolution to create the ICC. Turkey abstained from voting because terrorism was left off the list of crimes to be prosecuted. China voted against the resolution after its bid to limit the powers of the prosecutor was rejected. The United States voted against it after the U.S. was unable to secure the guarantee that U.S. servicemen and agents would not be liable for crimes committed while on official duty. In spite of these objections, the ICC was approved by a vote of 120 to seven.

not to kill Hutu survivors, but as the RPF began to win the fight, Tutsis whose families had suffered from Hutu massacres often sought revenge. The killing of Hutus by the Tutsi was on a far smaller scale than the Hutu initiated massacre, but the cycle of violence did not end.

By July the RPF had captured the capital, Kigali, and the second largest city, Butare. Gisenyi and other towns fell rapidly. Only the French-held zone remained unconquered. By late July 1994 the RPF controlled essentially all of Rwanda.

The war ended on July 16, 1994. The RPF established a government in accordance with the principles outlined in the Arusha Agreement, with Pasteur Bizimungu serving as president of Rwanda. Bizimungu was a Hutu, and his election as president was designed to initiate national reconciliation. Paul Kagame was appointed vice president, though he in fact held much of the power. Many Hutu fled from the RPF's triumph. Fearing reprisals and full of the Hutu government's propaganda of Tusti-supported mass murders, over two hundred thousand Hutu crossed the border into Zaire. Overall, more than two million refugees poured into Zaire, Burundi, and Tanzania. The masterminds behind the Tutsi massacre went with them.

The fighting did not completely stop. Just as the RPF had launched incursions into Rwanda from its locations in Uganda, so did Hutu extremists initiate attacks from the refugee camps in Zaire. Though the massacre was over, the killing was not. In February 1996 a series of cross-border attacks occurred in the west and south of Rwanda. Attacks from both sides were carried out sporadically through much of 1995, 1996, and early 1997.

The new Rwandan government was faced with a country in collapse. Millions of its citizens were now refugees and thousands were dead. The scars of such violence and upheaval would not heal quickly. In July President Bizimungu called the mass murders of Tutsi "premeditated prepared operations implemented in cold blood by the MRND and its militia, a section of the army, the CDR and other extremist factions." Bizimungu also invited refugees to return home, though most, fearing renewed fighting, did not immediately come back. By 1997 about 1.3 million Hutus had returned to Rwanda.

The United Nations Assistance Mission in Rwanda (UNAMIR) had never completely left the country, and as the new government established itself the size of UNAMIR increased. The peace-keeping force maintained a presence in the country until March 1996. In July 1994 the United Nations authorized a commission to investigate genocide in Rwanda and an international court was established to try those suspected of the crime. A few months later, in November, the United Nations established an international tribunal to try the accused.

RECENT HISTORY AND THE FUTURE

As refugees returned to Rwanda thousands were arrested on suspicion of participating in the genocide. By mid-1995, a year after the war ended, an average of fifteen hundred Hutus were

IN REVENGE FOR HUTU-SPONSORED GENOCIDAL ATTACKS ON THE TUTSI PEOPLE, TUTSI DESTROYED HUTU AND THEIR HOMES (LIKE THIS ONE IN KAMENGE, BUJUMBURA, BURUNDI) AFTER THE RWANDAN PATRIOTIC FRONT (RPF) ROSE TO POWER. *(Corbis. Reprinted by permission.)*

detained and imprisoned each week. Conditions in prisons were unhealthy, overcrowded, and harsh. Many prisoners contracted tuberculosis or died from other illnesses. By August 2000 forty-three of those considered to be the ringleaders of the genocide had been apprehended by the U.N. International Criminal Tribunal for Rwanda and were awaiting trial.

Rwanda has struggled to absorb the millions of refugees that have returned to the country since the war and the genocide ended. This influx has taxed Rwanda's fragile infrastructure and economy. With thousands of displaced people and a government and society trying to reconcile the atrocities of the past few years and live together again in peace, the road ahead is shaky. The northwest region of the country is still subject to insurgent attacks from rebels based in the Democratic Republic of the Congo (formerly Zaire), and in November 1999, the Rwandan government suspended cooperation with the U.N. International Criminal Tribunal. While the tribunal was established to bring about justice after the genocide, the RPF's leader and Rwanda's current prime minister, Paul Kagame, claimed that, after an overturned indictment, the court could not be considered impartial. In addition, the United Nations human rights operations in Rwanda were suspended in 1998 by a decision of the Rwandan government.

The international community, as represented by the United Nations, has been pushed out of Rwanda. The government has systematically distanced itself from the international organization and clearly asserted that much of the responsibility for the genocide lies with the international community, which failed to react quickly and decisively early on. Whether or not anything could have been done to staunch the violence can not be known. What is certain is that the restructuring of Rwanda—the rebuilding of its economy, society, and national identity—lies with the country's current leadership. Paul Kagame, once a leader of a rebel faction, must now lead a nation. Only time will tell in which direction he will steer this troubled land.

BIBLIOGRAPHY

Albright, Madeleine K. *Focus on Africa: Excerpts from Testimony, Speeches and Remarks by US Secretary of State Madeleine K. Albright on Africa.* Washington, D.C.: United States Department of State. Bureau of Public Affairs, 1999.

Bourmand, David. "France in Africa: African Politics and French Foreign Policy," *Issue: A Journal of Opinion.* 13, no. 2 (1995): 58–62.

Browning, Christopher. *Ordinary Men: Reserve Police Battalion 101 and the Final Solution in Poland.* New York: Harper Collins, 1992.

———. *The Path to Genocide: Essays on the Launching of the Final Solution.* New York: Cambridge University Press, 1996.

Buckley, Stephen. "In Zaire, Good Intentions Yield Tragic Effects," *Washington Post,* 10 November 1996, sec. 33A, 38A.

Chossudovsky, Michel. "Economic Genocide in Rwanda," *Economic and Political Weekly,* 13 April 1996, 938–941.

Chretien, Jean-Pierre. *Rwanda; les medias du genocide.* Paris: Karthala, 1995.

Des Foges, Alan. *Leave None to Tell the Tale.* New York: Human Rights Watch, 1998.

Destexhe, Alain. *Rwanda and Genocide in the Twentieth Century.* New York: New York University Press, 1995.

De Waal, Alex, and Rakiya Omaar. "The Genocide in Rwanda and the International Response," *Current History,* April 1995, 156–161.

Edgerton, Robert B. *Sick Societies: Challenging the Myth of Primitive Harmony.* New York: Free Press, a Division of Simon and Schuster, 1992.

Edwards, Mike. "Central Africa's Cycle of Violence in Focus," *National Geographic* 191, no. 6 (June 1997): 124–133.

Fossey, Dian. *Gorillas in the Mist.* Boston: Houghton Mifflin, 1983.

Gourevitch, Philip. *We Wish to Inform You that Tomorrow We Will be Killed With Our Families: Stories From Rwanda.* New York: Farrar, Straus and Giroux, 1998.

Gutman, Roy. *Crimes of War: What the Public Should Know.* New York: W.W. Norton, 1999.

Human Rights Watch. *Shattered Lives: Sexual Violence during the Rwandan Genocide and Its Aftermath.* New York: Human Rights Watch, 1996.

Jefremovas, Villia. "Contested Identities: Power and the Fictions of Ethnicity, Ethnography and History in Rwanda," *Anthropologica* XXXIX (1997): 91–104: 1997.

Karnik, Niranjan, ed. *Great Lakes Crisis Briefing Packet.* Washington, D.C.: Association of Concerned Africa Scholars, 1996.

Kuper, Leo. *Genocide: Its Political Uses in the Twentieth Century.* New Haven, Conn.: Yale University Press, 1981.

———. The Prevention of Genocide. New Haven, Conn.: Yale University Press, 1985.

Kuperman, Alan J. "Rwanda in Retrospect," *Foreign Affairs* 79, no. 1 (January/February 2000): 94–118.

Lampman, Jane. "Taming the Desire for Revenge," *Christian Science Monitor,* 4 November 1999, 15–16.

Lemarchand, Rene. *Burundi: Ethnic Conflict and Genocide.* Cambridge: Cambridge University Press, 1998.

Malkki, Liisa H. *Purity and Exile: Violence, Memory, and National Cosmology among Hutu Refugees in Tanzania.* Chicago: University of Chicago Press, 1995.

Mamdani, Mahmood. "From Conquest to Consent as the Basis of State Formation: Reflections on Rwanda," *New Left Review* no. 216 (March/April 1996): 3–36.

Monga, Celestin. "A Theory of Disenchantment and Violence: Rwanda and Other Tragedies. " In *The Anthropology of Anger: Civil Society and Democracy in Africa.* London: Lynne Rienner Publishers Inc., 1996.

Newbury, Catharine. "Background to Genocide: Rwanda," *Issue: A Journal of Opinion* 13, no. 2 (1995): 12–17.

———. *The Cohesion of Oppression: Clientship and Ethnicity in Rwanda, 1860–1960.* New York: Columbia University Press, 1998.

Pottier, John. "Relief and Repatriation: Views by Rwandan Refugees: Lessons for Humanitarian Aid Workers," *African Affairs* 95 (1996): 403–429: 1996.

Prunier, Gerard. *The Rwanda Crisis: History of a Genocide.* New York: Columbia University Press, 1995.

Richburg, Keith B. *Out of America: A Black Man Confronts Africa.* New York: Basic Books, Harper Collins Publisher, 1997.

Rieff, David. "Abort Mission: The Humanitarian Mission That Wasn't," *The New Republic,* 9 December 1996, 9–10.

Shalom, Stephen R. "The Rwanda Genocide: The Nightmare That Happened," *Z Magazine,* April 1996, 25–36.

Speke, John Hanning. *Journal of the Discovery of the Source of the Nile.* New York: Mineola: 1863, 1996.

Twagiramariya, Clotilde. "Women as Victims of Power Conflicts: The Case of Rwandan Refugee Women," *ACAS Bulletin* no. 45–46 (Winter/Spring 1996): 13–18.

Uwechue, Raph, ed. *Africa Today.* London: Africa Books, 1996.

Williams, Gavin, ed. *Africa South of the Sahara.* 29th ed. London: Europa Publications, 1999.

Dallas L. Browne

SERBIA AND NATO: THE 1999 WAR

THE CONFLICT

During 1999, the North Atlantic Treaty Organization (NATO) conducted an extensive bombing campaign against the Federal Republic of Yugoslavia (FR Yugoslavia, comprised of Serbia and Montenegro). Yugoslavia, a former Communist country, had been a federation of several provinces that each had some level of autonomy. FR Yugoslavia had been, off and on for almost ten years, at war with provinces that had declared their independence. In 1999 FR Yugoslavia attempted to keep the former autonomous province of Kosovo from seceding from the union.

Ethnic

- Kosovo is largely Albanian and Muslim, and Serbia is largely Serbian and Orthodox Christian. The Albanians generally want to secede from FR Yugoslavia because they feel inadequately represented and protected. The Serbians generally want to preserve the larger union, which they feel is part of an historic empire.

Political

- NATO appears to feel pressure to prove itself, and to establish its role in the international community.

- Europe and the U.S. appear haunted by their inaction during the Holocaust during World War II. They appear to feel that they cannot let situations that might be construed as "ethnic cleansing" happen in Europe.

- NATO, and the West in general, is worried that, if it doesn't protect and defend Albanian Muslims, the Albanians will look to Islamic countries such as Iraq and Afghanistan for support. A potentially hostile country would be located in Europe.

Economic

- Kosovo and other Albanian areas are, generally, much less developed than Serbian areas.

Operation "Allied Force," the bombing campaign by the North Atlantic Treaty Organization (NATO) against the Federal Republic of Yugoslavia—Serbia and Montenegro, referred to as Serbia or FR Yugoslavia—was the largest campaign by U.S. troops in Europe since World War II. The seventy-eight-day air campaign from March 24 to June 10, 1999, was also the largest use of military force in NATO's history and the first military intervention into the former Yugoslavia without a United Nations mandate. Yet, despite doing extensive damage within Serbia proper it did not resolve the "Kosovo issue." Since June 1999 American and NATO troops have occupied the province under a U.N. mandate, but hardly a week has gone by without violence in Kosovo appearing in international headlines.

This is not the first time that the United States, NATO, and the United Nations have intervened in the region. The United Nations and the European Community (EC) were present at the beginning of the conflict in 1991, in attempts to negotiate an end to the fighting. After the failure of the EC, United Nations, and other organizations to mediate the conflict, the United States intervened. American troops were stationed in the region as part of U.N. missions in Macedonia from 1993 to 1999 and were in Bosnia beginning in 1995. NATO's first ever use of military force occurred in the form of air strikes against the Bosnian Serbs in 1995, a move intended to force the Bosnian Serbs to agree to peace negotiations and to retaliate for Serbian attacks on civilians.

While the cause of conflict and the motivation for intervention will continued to be debated, it seems most likely that economic tensions in the former Yugoslavia were played upon by politicians to

CHRONOLOGY

1914–18 World War I. Twenty-five percent of the Serb population dies. Many Serbs demand primary status in new state, since they suffered the most during the war.

1919 Royal Yugoslavia is founded.

1941 The Nazis invade Yugoslavia; the Croatian Ustasa faction sides with the Nazis.

1944–45 Communist Yugoslavia is formed.

1948 Tito and Stalin split. Yugoslavia becomes "unaligned" with either the United States or the Soviet Union.

1974 New constitution grants Kosovo and Vojvodina autonomy, and decentralizes power to the republics.

1980 Tito dies.

1981 Government begins discussing major economic reforms. Albanian protests break out. The unemployment rate in Kosovo is nearly three hundred percent higher than the national rate.

1982–1989 The living standard falls rapidly in all of Yugoslavia.

1987 Milosevic gaines national attention by defending Serbian rights.

1989 Milosevic removes Kosovo's (and then Vojvodina's) autonomy and institutes martial law. The fall of the Communist regimes in Eastern Europe begins while inflation is at two thousand percent.

1990 Slovenia withdraws from Communist party elections in Slovenia and Croatia. Tudjman takes power in Croatia.

June 1991 Slovenia and Croatia declare independence. Fighting between JNA and Slovene militias.

September 1991 Albanians declare Kosovo independent.

November 1991 United Nations begins attempts at a cease-fire in Croatia.

December 1991 Serbs in Krajina declare independence from Croatia. Serbs in Bosnia declare "Serbska Republika" independent from Bosnia.

January 1992 United Nations brokers a cease-fire in Croatia. UNPROFOR mission begins in Croatia.

February–March 1992 The majority of Croats and Muslims vote for independence. Bosnia declares independence. Skirmishes break out in Sarajevo.

June 1992 Serbs control about seventy percent of Bosnian territory.

October 1992 No-Fly Zone declared in Bosnia.

1993 The United Nations and the European Community attempt negotiations on the Vance-Owens plan to end the violence in Bosnia.

April 1993 NATO planes begin to enforce No-Fly Zone at the U.N.'s request.

March 1994 The United States brokers an agreement between Muslims and Croats against the Serbs.

May 1995 Croatians overrun western Slovenia; thousands of Serbs flee. NATO bomb Serb artillery; in response, Serbs take 350 U.N. troops hostage.

August 1995 Serbs shell market in Sarajevo, killing dozens of civilians. Major NATO air strikes in Bosnia against the Serbs.

December 1995 Dayton Peace agreement is signed between Croats, Muslims, and Serbs in Bosnia.

July–August 1998 KLA offensives bring approximately forty percent of Kosovo under their control.

October 1998 NATO authorizes and threatens bombing. Milosevic agrees to pull out of Kosovo.

November 1999 U.N. and U.S. investigators suggest that the death count and anti-Albanian atrocities are much lower than stated.

February 2000 Attacks on Serbians in Kosovo continue.

create an atmosphere of distrust. Inconsistent, contradictory, and often sloppy international policies did nothing to stop the outbreak of war in Yugoslavia. The speed of intervention in Kosovo was most likely motivated by the dismal showing of intervention in Bosnia and a desire to not make the same mistakes again.

CROATIAN SERBS, BOSNIAN CROATS, AND SERBIAN MUSLIMS

One of the confusing things about the former Yugoslavia is the presence of national minorities in nearly all areas—Serbs in Croatia and Bosnia, Muslims in Serbia and Kosovo, Hungarians in the Vojvodina. Part of the complexity is due to various historical events. The Krajina region of Croatia was once part of the "Military Border" of the Austrian Empire, and Serbs were settled here by the Austrians to defend against the Turkish Ottomans. The Turkish minority (and the conversion of many Bosnians and Albanians to Islam) is a product of Ottoman rule. As a result, there are simply no clear "ethnic borders" in much of Croatia, Bosnia, the Vojvodina and Kosovo.

However it is worth noting that most of Europe was much more ethnically diverse as recently as two hundred years ago. This changed when governments organized programs of national assimilation, and climaxed after World War I and World War II when millions of people moved, often unwillingly, as new borders were drawn. Though it does not excuse the campaigns of ethnic cleansing today, it is only fair to note that these are just the most recent examples of brutal population transfers—some of which the United States conducted against Native Americans (such as the expulsion of the Cherokee in the 1830s), and some of which (such as the Highland Clearances in Scotland) inspired tens of thousands to emigrate to America.

HISTORICAL BACKGROUND

The media often invoke history in an attempt to explain "why things went wrong" in Yugoslavia and why fighting continues after years of war. During the Cold War the West saw Yugoslavia as the most progressive of the communist regimes. Yet its history since 1989 is by far the bloodiest in Eastern Europe. Accordingly, it is sometimes suggested that this violence is linked to a history of "ancient hatreds." These are said to be related to the cultural and religious differences between the groups: Croatians and Slovenes are Catholic; Macedonians, Montenegrins and Serbs are Orthodox Christians; Bosnian Muslims are Muslims; and Kosovo Albanians are largely Muslim (though many are Catholic or Orthodox Christian). Each group, this theory claims, has a legacy of bitter hatred nursed for centuries—hatred that communism

eclipsed but did not eliminate—and that the recent violence is just the latest manifestation of centuries of conflict.

While there were ethnic tensions in the former Yugoslavia, however, there was little overt hatred: People intermarried, worked, lived beside and befriended members of other ethnic groups, particularly in the cities. Even in rural Kosovo where the divide between the Serbs and Albanians was perhaps the worst in the country, the level of violence was relatively low. Although there were historic conflicts between the peoples of Yugoslavia, this is also true of United States or Europe. The French and English, or, for that matter, the United States and Great Britain, have fought more wars against each other in the past five hundred years than have the Croats and Serbs.

What is different about the current conflicts is that in the past ten years nationalists in the former Yugoslavia have used history to inspire hatred and fear, fueling the atrocities and crimes performed by each group. A good example is the use by some nationalists of the medieval Serbian defeat by the Ottoman Turks in 1389 and the subsequent five hundred years of the "Turkish yoke." This story is used to incite anger against Muslims, who are accused of sharing a "collective guilt" for the acts of the Turks. Croatian President Franjo Tudjman's role in downplaying the role of the World War II Croatian *Ustache*'s killing of at least a quarter of a million Serbs, Jews, Roma, or Gypsies, and Bosnian Muslims is also quite typical, invoking strong emotions in both Croats and Serbs. The "ancient tensions" were exploited during and after the breakup of the former Socialist Federal Republic of Yugoslavia, hereafter referred to as the former Yugoslavia, in 1991.

Politics, Economics, Decline and War

When Josip Broz Tito, the leader of the wartime partisan movement, founded modern Yugoslavia in 1945, he faced the challenge of reconciling ethnic and political groups that been at odds not just during World War II, but over the 1919–41 life span of the Kingdom of Yugoslavia. The new Socialist Republic of Yugoslavia, with nearly identical borders (the city and surrounding area of Triest and several islands were acquired from Italy), from the onset stressed that communism and the partisan heritage of the war was "above" ethnicity. Although the history of the communist Yugoslav government is complex—especially after the "Stalin-Tito split" of 1948, when Yugoslavia left the Soviet bloc—the overall pattern is one of careful balancing between regional interests and a focus on economic development. In the 1950s and 1960s there was hope that socialist planning would lead to economic prosperity and the decline of nationalism.

Despite considerable growth in the post-World War II years, by the late 1960s it was becoming clear that progress was uneven. While all regions were better off than they had been, the "haves"—primarily Slovenia and Croatia, but also Vojvodina and Serbia proper—were still much wealthier than the "have-nots" in Bosnia-Herzegovina, Montenegro, Macedonia, and, in particular, Kosovo. This gap in levels of economic development was actually increasing over time, as the rich got richer. Although large investments were made in the less developed regions they were often badly planned and managed—money was typically spent on prestige projects that could not successfully compete with industries in the more developed regions.

By the 1970s there were clear signs of growing disaffection between the two groups. The developed regions resented giving money to the federal government to be squandered on political gestures while the less developed regions envied their prosperity. Sharp crises broke out in Slovenia in 1969 and in Croatia in 1971 over economic issues, which could have led to secession if Tito had not intervened. The resulting reforms, including the 1974 constitution of Yugoslavia, gave a high degree of control over economic issues to the republics, as well as granting autonomous status to Vojvodina and Kosovo—the most and least industrialized regions of Serbia. While placating the more affluent regions, the reforms tended to encourage economic separatism between the republics—money generated in one region now tended to stay there—created resentment in the less developed regions. Continuing economic problems also led to thousands of Yugoslavs, chiefly Croatians and Slovenes, working abroad in Germany and Western Europe.

By the late 1980s economic problems were at a crisis point. In response, the federal government of Yugoslavia turned abroad for loans for development. The use of external loans to fund industrial investment in the 1970s meant a rise in Yugoslavia's foreign debt from $3.5 billion in 1971 to $20.5 billion in 1981. The government faced increasing problems making loan payments, in part because the economy slowed during the 1980s. From 1982 to 1989 the standard of living fell by roughly forty percent. Even as the price of food and consumer goods rose by alarming levels, with annual inflation reaching 2000 percent in December 1989, there was widespread unemployment, particularly of the

young, which was complicated by the return of many guest workers from Germany. Economic woes served to increase tensions between the haves and have-nots: Many Slovenes in particular argued that the region was being pulled down by the poor economies of the less developed areas.

By 1981 there were calls within the federal government for widespread economic reforms but since this implied the centralization of economic planning such reforms were unacceptable to the regional governments. By the end of the decade the federal government under Prime Minister Ante Markovic attempted a series of drastic reforms and enjoyed some initial success in restoring order, but Markovic lacked firm international support and was undercut by opposition from new political elites at the provincial level.

The Rise of the Ultra-Nationalists

Economic problems in the 1980s led to increasing disenchantment with the Communist Party—particularly in Slovenia and Croatia—and a rising tide of nationalism manipulated by new political figures. Nowhere were the new conditions more apparent than in Kosovo.

Kosovo was the least economically developed region of the former Yugoslavia. Nonetheless, Kosovo embarked on an ambitious series of local economic and educational projects after 1974, when it received autonomy within the Republic of Serbia under a new Yugoslav constitution. The decision to grant autonomy was in part to recognize the complaints of the Albanian population and to encourage the support and loyalty of Albanians to the federal government. Kosovo's autonomy may also have been intended to weaken the Republic of Serbia in its relations with the federal government. The failure of development in Kosovo by the 1980s, however, left thousands of young Albanians with university degrees but no suitable jobs. Within a year of Tito's death in 1980, ethnic tensions were on the rise as Albanians protested what they saw as the privileged position of Serbs and Montenegrins living in Kosovo and demanded further autonomy from Belgrade.

The poor economic prospects of Kosovo increasingly encouraged tens of thousands of Serbs to leave in search of work in the industrial cities of Serbia proper. The exodus of the Serbs combined with the high Albanian birth rate—a high birth rate encouraged both by poverty and by the low status of women—meant that the Albanian population of the province increasingly dwarfed that of Serbs. The threat that Serbs would soon be marginalized within

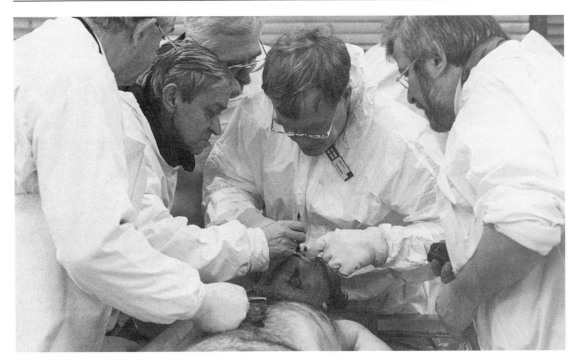

AUTOPSY TEAMS IN KOSOVO EXAMINE THE VICTIM OF A SERBIAN MASSACRE TO IDENTIFY THE BODY AND DIS-COVER THE CAUSE OF DEATH. *(AP/Wide World Photos. Reproduced by permission.)*

Kosovo was troubling for those who considered the region to be an integral part of Serbia and an important historical landmark. Albanian dissatisfaction soon turned to protests and riots, which were severely suppressed by Yugoslav security forces and police, leading to further alienation. Serbs claimed that Albanians were attempting to drive out the Serbian population through hate crimes; Albanians insisted that the government systematically discriminated against them. The increasingly volatile situation provided the springboard by which Slobodan Milosevic rose to national prominence in 1987 by insisting on Serb rights in the region.

Kosovo thus became a crucial element in the breakup of Yugoslavia. For Milosevic Kosovo was not only a potential means to bolster Serb nationalism and obtain political power, but it was an issue where many Serbs felt grievances: The constitution of 1974 had "stolen" the region from Serbia, and the politics of the federal government favored Albanians attempting to force the remaining Serbs to leave. During 1987 to 1989 Milosevic became one of the most powerful political figures in the republic of Serbia. The Slovene and Croatian regional governments mistrusted Milosevic's Greater Serb politics and saw little reason to foot the bill to establish Serb control over Kosovo. Nevertheless, Milosevic enjoyed much support from the Yugoslav

National Army (JNA) and the media, which saw him as a supporter of a strong central Yugoslav government. When on March 28, 1989, Milosevic and his supporters in the Assembly of the Republic of Serbia eliminated the region's autonomy and reintegrated Kosovo, and, a few days later, Vojvodina into Serbia many Serbs interpreted this as a correction of the faults of the 1974 constitution. Slovenes and Croats, however, saw it as an aggressive move to crack down on the aspirations of a national minority.

The rise to power of Franjo Tudjman and the nationalist Croatian Democratic Alliance in the Croatian elections of April 1990 was a reaction to Milosevic and to Serb nationalism within Croatia. Tudjman, however, heightened tensions by resurrecting the national symbols of the Croatian fascist government of World War II and by passing a series of discriminatory laws and measures against Croatian Serbs. Tudjman defended these laws by claiming that they rectified the over-proportion of Serbs in government positions. The response by Croatian Serbs in Krajina was to arm and deny the authority of the new Croatian government, and armed clashes between Croatian police and rebels broke out in 1990. Croatian attempts to restore order were met with the threat of intervention by the JNA.

At the same time, a broad coalition in the Slovene government demanded further decentralization of the Yugoslav government or independence to pursue economic interests, and in January 1990 the Slovene delegation withdrew from the Yugoslav Communist Party. All this served to legitimize Milosevic, who was increasingly seen as a figure that could not only restore Serb rights but also maintain the faltering Yugoslav state, despite the fact that much of the Serbian political leadership had previously backed liberal reforms. During the republican elections in 1990, political parties based on ethnicity won elections in every republic, and polls showed that Slovenes, Croats, and Albanians were increasingly critical of federal institutions and the concept of a strong, united Yugoslavia.

The World and the Wars of Yugoslav Secession

Although the breakup of Yugoslavia was propelled by economic factors and erupted when nationalist movements arose in the republics, international events and the foreign policies of other countries helped shape the breakup. Perhaps the most crucial event was the end of the Cold War. Since 1948 Yugoslavia had enjoyed an unusual position in Europe. Although a communist country, it was not a member of the Soviet bloc and was courted by both Moscow and Washington through loans, military aid, and diplomacy.

The fall of communist governments throughout Eastern Europe in 1989 put an end to Yugoslavia's strategic position. The threat of invasion by NATO or the Warsaw Pact helped bind the Yugoslav factions together, but this threat was now removed. International organizations and foreign countries were not prepared for a violent Yugoslav breakup. Although there were early indications that armed conflict might erupt in Yugoslavia, Washington and the European capitals were focused on the questions of German reunification, the events in the Soviet Union/Russian Federation, the transition of Eastern Europe from the Communist bloc to democracies in a market economy, and the 1991 Gulf War in Iraq. Further, the end of the Cold War and U.N. success in the Gulf suggested a "New World Order" where diplomacy and negotiation would replace military conflict.

Early Involvement by Europe

By the middle of 1991, however, European leaders were becoming increasingly worried that Yugoslavia was headed for a violent breakup. With the United States and the Soviet Union both focused on internal issues, leadership fell to the Euro-

SLOBODAN MILOSEVIC

1941– Slobodan Milosevic is the former president of the Republic of Serbia, and the current president of the Former Republic of Yugoslavia (Serbia and Montenegro). His wife, Professor Mira Markovic, is leader of the Yugoslav United Left Party and his chief political advisor.

Milosevic was born August 29, 1941 in Pozarevac, Yugoslavia. While a law student at Belgrade University, he joined the League of Communists of Yugoslavia (LCY). After graduating in 1964, Milosevic began a career in economic administration, serving as head of the state-owned gas company, and later as president of a major bank. In 1984 he became the local leader of LCY.

In 1987 Milosevic began promoting Serbian nationalism, and was elected leader of the Serbian Communists. He became president of Serbia in 1989 and was reelected in 1990 and 1992. After the secession of Croatia and Bosnia-Herzegovina in 1991–92, Milosevic backed insurgents in both republics. He won removal of U.N.-imposed economic sanctions against Serbia by signing the Bosnian peace agreement in 1996. He became president of Yugoslavia (Serbia and Montenegro) in July 1997. In 1998 and 1999, Milosevic launched offensives against secessionist ethnic Albanians in Kosovo. On May 27, 1999 the U.N. War Crimes Tribunal indicted him for atrocities committed during the conflict.

pean Community, which in June 1991 offered financial aid to assist in the restructuring of the Yugoslav economy. In addition, the EC announced that any unilateral decision by Slovenia and Croatia to declare independence would not be recognized.

Despite these efforts Slovenia declared independence on June 25, 1991, and despite previous agreements to the contrary, seized control of the customs service offices on the borders. To the surprise of most observers, when the JNA was dispatched to retake control of the customs facilities the Slovene forces beat the larger and better-armed Yugoslav troops in ten days of fighting. The EC was instrumental in negotiating the cease-fire and withdrawal of the JNA, which raised hopes that negotiations led by the European Community could resolve the crisis.

There was a lack of consensus among the members of the EC, however, over the best policy regarding the increasing strife in Yugoslavia and over

A PROUD CIVILIAN GIVES THE SERB THREE-FINGERED SALUTE WHILE BEING HELD BACK BY PEACEKEEPERS IN THE CITY OF KOSOVSKA MITROVICA. *(Archive Photos. Reproduced by permission.)*

the nature of the conflict itself: Was Yugoslavia an emerging civil war or were Slovenes and Croats merely defending themselves against Serb aggression? Alarmingly for many Serbs, the strongest supporter for recognition of Slovene and Croatian independence was Germany, with Austria, the Vatican, Hungary, and Italy also favoring recognition—these were the same allies of the fascist Croatian government of World War II. Despite earlier announcements that declarations of independence would not be considered, the EC declared only a short-term, three-month moratorium while brokering a cease-fire in Slovenia under the Brioni Declaration. This change was largely due to a diplomatic offensive by Helmut Kohl's administration in Germany, under internal pressure from Croat sympathizers and the strong domestic Catholic lobby.

Many commentators have since criticized the EC action, since the EC could have informed the Slovene and Croatian governments that recognition would not be forthcoming until they had resolved secession with Belgrade in Serbia and ensured equality of minorities. In addition, the EC interpreted the ten-day conflict in Slovenia as an invasion of the republic by the JNA, but failed to establish that the EC would not tolerate similar fighting between the JNA and Croatian forces. Finally, despite the existing ethnic tension in Croatia, the EC failed to recognize that once

Slovenia and Croatia were recognized, Bosnia-Herzegovina and Macedonia were likely to declare their independence. Accordingly, the EC failed to create a policy on recognition for these two states that might have prevented future conflict.

When fighting broke out between the Croatian police and military forces, and the JNA and local Croatian Serb irregulars in July 1991, neither the EC nor the various other European security organizations were prepared to attempt to enforce peace in Yugoslavia. Although over a dozen EC cease-fires were negotiated and declared from July to December 1991, each was broken by the Croatian military or JNA. The ongoing German pressure for European recognition of Croatia also undermined the potential for a lasting cease-fire, since Serbian forces began to view the EC as sympathetic to the Croats and since Croatians expected rapid recognition of their independence. The conflict grew and in late 1991 the EC invited the United Nations to attempt to negotiate a cease-fire. The U.N. team, led by special envoy Cyrus Vance, arranged for a cease-fire in Croatia and the establishment of U.N. troops in Croatia to monitor it. Although EC members continued to aid mediation efforts between the warring parties, as with the Lisbon Accords of 1992, which attempted to solve the question of Bosnian stability before fighting broke out—and Cyrus Vance and David Owen continued to participate in the 1993 and 1994 negotiations to settle the fighting, but the chief agent of intervention was now the United Nations.

The United Nations

The success of the United Nations in brokering a cease-fire between Croatia and the federal government was part of a broad trend of increased U.N. activity around the world. With the end of U.S.-Soviet conflicts and the success of the U.N. coalition in the Gulf War, the United Nations began to play a greater role in settling international conflicts and civil wars. Accordingly, in 1992, the United Nations was involved in mediating disputes in Somalia, Angola, Iraq, the Western Sahara, El Salvador, Cambodia and Mozambique, as well as in the former Yugoslavia. The U.N. Protection Force (UNPROFOR) mission was established in 1992 with the intention of increasing the United Nations' role: monitoring the cease-fires, supervising the withdrawal of the JNA from Croatia and providing humanitarian aid to civilians. At the same time, the United Nations declared an embargo of the sale of weaponry to Bosnia and put economic sanctions on the FR Yugoslavia for its support of military activities to the Bosnian Serbs. By 1995 it was clear that the United Nations and the European Union (formerly the EC) had not been able to negotiate an end to the fighting in Bosnia, nor to enforce peace on the different factions.

The first problem was one of impartiality—each warring party was opposed to U.N. intervention when it interfered with their goals and welcomed intervention when it was in their best interests. The Bosnian Serbs were opposed to U.N. aid to cities and regions they were besieging. The United Nations' failure to protect Serb-populated U.N. Protected Areas in Croatia led many Serbs to suspect that intervention was directed against them. In addition, the series of peace treaties negotiated by the EU and U.N. teams were criticized in Sarajevo and in Washington, DC, as too accommodating to the Bosnian Serbs, whose tactics of "ethnic cleansing"—brutal attacks, killings, and terror to drive a specific ethnic group from a village—had turned international opinion against them.

The United Nations lacked the money and peacekeeping troops to make good on all of its commitments. From 1988 to 1995 it was involved in no less than twenty-three different operations in seventeen countries, several missions involving human tragedies just as terrible as the war in Bosnia but with less international interest. Further, in Bosnia the United Nations was subject to "mission creep." The initial goal in September 1992—to

ACRONYMS

FYROM: The Former Yugoslav Republic of Macedonia. Due to Greek objections over the name "Republic of Macedonia," the country is officially referred (by the U.N. and U.S. government, among others) as FYROM.

IFOR/SFOR: Implementation FORce and Stabilization FORce. Established by U.N. mandate 1995, IFOR was intended to monitor the cease-fire in Bosnia and assist in rebuilding; with the completion of the original mission in 1996, it was given a new mandate by the U.N. and renamed SFOR. Participants include all NATO countries, as well as troops from Albania, Austria, Argentina, Bulgaria, Estonia, Finland, Ireland, Latvia, Lithuania, Morocco, Romania, Russia, Slovakia, Slovenia, Sweden and Ukraine.

JNA: Yugoslav National Army.

KFOR: Kosovo FORce, established by U.N. mandate and comprised primarily of German, Italian, French, British and American troops with a small Russian contingent and assistance by other NATO countries.

KLA: Kosovo Liberation Army.

NATO: North Atlantic Treaty Organization.

UNMIK: The United Nations Interim Mission in Kosovo

UNPREDEP: U.N. Preventative Deployment force, stationed in Macedonia since 1995.

UNPROFOR: U.N. PROtection FORce, since 1992; initially, this included deployments in Croatia and Macedonia as well as Bosnia, but later was refined to focus on events in Bosnia.

provide aid to refugees—gradually required more troops to protect aid convoys, increasing the size of the U.N. force stationed in the area. To protect the refugees the United Nations eventually enacted restrictions on military action (the "no fly" zone) and established safe areas in 1992 and 1993 in Croatia and Bosnia. Yet, the United Nations lacked the resources and military force to carry out the expanded mission. Not only had the Unite Nations lost the trust of many Bosnian Serbs, but it was also increasingly obvious that that it was unable to back up its threats. By the middle of 1993 there were the first tentative moves in the United States to allocate NATO aircraft to enforce the U.N. mandate in Bosnia.

NATO and the United States

Much of the weakness of the United Nations was due to the changing foreign policies of the United States. As late as 1991 the Bush administration did not have a clear foreign policy in Yugoslavia, despite the fact that the Central Intelligence Agency (CIA) had by November 1990 predicted the violent collapse of Yugoslavia within eighteen months. Through much of 1991 the United States voiced its support for the continued unity of Yugoslavia, without any tangible material aid. Part of this disinterest was due to disagreement in the U.S. government about post-Cold War foreign policy and by a focus on Iraq and the Soviet Union/Russia. Some disagreement was also probably due to the upcoming presidential campaigns of 1992, in which foreign policy issues were unlikely to play well with the public. Despite the outbreak of violence, the United States deferred leadership in international mediation and intervention to Europe.

When U.S. President Bill Clinton took office in early 1993 he advocated a stronger role for the United States abroad and supported intervention for humanitarian issues in Yugoslavia, Africa, and Latin America. This included pressuring Serbia and the Bosnian Serbs to agree to negotiations, tightening sanctions on the FR Yugoslavia and supplying food and supplies to Bosnian Muslims. Diplomatic relations with Bosnia and Croatia were strengthened, and U.S. foreign policy became increasingly hostile to what it saw as Serb aggression. Clinton was unwilling, however, to support the introduction of American troops in Bosnia. This may have been due to the failure and withdrawal of the U.S. mission in Somalia in October 1993, which demonstrated the American public's lack of support for military intervention without a clear goal. There was widespread opposition within the commanders of the U.S. military against any use of ground troops, since the conflict was feared to be a potential Vietnam, lacking a coherent strategy or reachable goal for the U.S. military. At the same time, the NATO allies opposed the possibility of U.S. air strikes, since several countries had contributed ground troops to the U.N. operations and these would be the first targets of any retaliation.

While unwilling to intervene directly in the conflict, the Clinton administration was also reluctant to support the EU/U.N. efforts to create a negotiated peace. This was because the various peace plans of 1992–94—the Lisbon Agreement, the Vance-Owen Plan and the Owen-Stoltenberg Plan—were seen as rewarding the Bosnian Serbs with a disproportionate amount of Bosnian territory, and because the plans effectively called for the division of the country into ethnic enclaves with a loose central government. The United States instead pressured Zagreb and Sarajevo to improve their relations and to create an alliance against the Bosnian Serbs, reclaiming lost territory on the battlefield.

The significance in these moves was that, unlike the previous EC and U.N. interventions, the United States saw the conflict as one in which clear villains could be identified. Much of this was likely due to television coverage of the Serb military in Bosnia, which led to a generally anti-Serb public opinion. The war, however, was much more complex than a simple Serb versus Croats and Muslims dynamic—not only did Croat and Muslim factions fight each other, but there were numerous cases of temporary local alliances of two factions against the third. In certain cases there were even divisions with ethnic groups: The Bihac offensive of 1995 by the government in Sarajevo was against the local Bosnian Muslim leader, who subsequently formed an alliance with Bosnian Serbs and Croatian Serbs in Krajina.

By 1995 U.S. policy was increasingly antagonistic toward the Bosnian Serbs. Air strikes were finally launched from August to September 1995 in retaliation for artillery attacks on civilians in Sarajevo and continued Bosnian Serb offensives. During the strikes the United States encouraged the Croat-Muslim coalition to make offensives into Serb territory even while the United States called for negotiations. Ironically, the agreement signed at Dayton, Ohio, in December 1995, by the representatives of all three groups was not far removed from the earlier EU/U.N. peace plans. Although agreements were made for a moderate central government with some autonomy for each group, much of the reform and rebuilding of the central government has been completed and there may be a *de facto* partition of the country, despite the presence of troops and a U.N. mission to rebuild the country.

Intervention in Kosovo

It was in the mold of NATO intervention in Bosnia that involvement in Kosovo would be cast. Surprisingly, while Kosovo had been the scene of the fiercest ethnic tensions in the 1980s, the region did not erupt into open warfare in the early 1990s. Though Albanian separatists had declared Kosovo's independence from FR Yugoslavia in September 1991, Serbia was preoccupied with the conflicts in Croatia and Bosnia.

By 1996, however, the emergence of Albanian separatist terrorist and resistance groups had led to

ALBANIANS SHOW THEIR DISPLEASURE WITH SERB CONTROL OF PARTS OF KOSOVO WITH A MARCH THROUGH THE CITY OF MITROVICA. *(AP/Wide World Photos. Reproduced by permission.)*

attacks on police officers of the Serbian Interior Ministry (MUP). From 1997 to 1998 the Kosovo Liberation Army (KLA) emerged and was engaging in constant clashes with MUP police, establishing control over nearly one-third of Kosovo. The conflict undermined the power of moderate Albanians such as Ibrahim Rugova, and threatened to unleash another major episode of warfare. In response, in April 1998 the International Contact Group that had worked to arrange the Dayton Accords imposed new sanctions on the FR Yugoslavia and pressured both groups into a series of negotiations.

During the negotiations Yugoslav forces made significant progress in the offensive against the KLA, despite agreements to a cease-fire. Reports of civilian deaths prompted threats of NATO air strikes in October 1998 unless Milosevic allowed international observers to monitor the cease-fire. By the end of November both sides had violated the cease-fire and fresh fighting broke out in December. Mounting civilian casualties resulted in another threat of air strikes and a new round of negotiations.

Although both sides agreed to participate in the February 1999 talks in Rambouillet, France, the FR Yugoslav negotiators balked at the NATO demand to station ground troops in Kosovo to monitor a peace agreement. Faced by continuing refusals from Belgrade, the NATO air campaign

OPERATION FLASH AND STORM

In a move that was largely overlooked in the Western media, in May and August 1995 the Croatian army undertook Operations Flash and Storm in Krajina. Thousands of Croatian Serbs were killed in fighting and hundreds episodes of ethnic cleansing. Perhaps as many as two hundred thousand Croatian Serbs fled to Serbia or to Bosnia. The Croatian government viewed these moves as simply the extension of legitimate control over regions that Serbian rebels had illegally attempted to seize while they drove out Croatian residents in an attempt to form a "Greater Serb" state.

However, the United Nations had previously declared much of Krajina as a "United Nations Safe Area." The U.N.'s inability to protect the Serbs seemed, to some, to emphasize the ineffectiveness of the U.N. In addition, Serbs charged that the West applied a double standard to war crimes: one standard for crimes against Bosnian Muslims and another for crimes against Serbs. The Serb charge was upheld in part, perhaps, when the International Tribunal in the Hague, Netherlands ruled, in 1999, that there was evidence of ethnic cleansing by the Croatian army and police.

began on March 24 with the stated goal of hindering the Yugoslav Army and security forces' ability to take the offensive against the KLA.

Publicly, the Clinton administration called for the negotiations on a humanitarian basis, to stop increasing violence and to prevent the possibility of ethnic cleansing on the scale of Croatia or Bosnia. It is likely that international considerations also played a hand—the fear that massive ethnic cleansing, driving tens of thousands of Albanians south into Albania and Macedonia, could destabilize the Macedonian government's relations with its own Albanian minority and lead to the scenario of the FR Yugoslavia intervening in Macedonia to pursue guerrillas and of Greece intervening to prevent Albanian refugees from crossing the Greek border. If this occurred, it was judged likely that Bulgaria and possibly Turkey could become involved in what would rapidly expand into a wider Balkan war. It was this possibility that had originally led to the establishment of a small number of U.S. troops in Macedonia in 1993. There have been accusations, however, that intervention was essentially a matter of prestige for the United States and a forum in which

NATO could be transformed and maintained after the Cold War.

What does seem likely was that the Clinton administration and NATO allies expected the war to last for only a few days. Although the expectations and thoughts of both remain unclear, it seems that they expected Milosevic to back down in the face of force, as had the Bosnian Serbs in 1995. Serbian resistance came as a surprise, and NATO was forced to provide additional aircraft and supplies. Despite this, it was still largely unable to prevent Serbian forces from forcing an estimated 200,000 Albanians out of Kosovo in reaction to the air strikes, and killing between five thousand to ten thousand civilians.

Worse, NATO rapidly discovered that it was extremely difficult to target the dispersed and hidden Serbian forces in the province, and soon turned to attacks on infrastructure and economic targets in Serbia proper (with some, but fewer, attacks on Montenegro). This seems to have been intended to pressure the civilian population to oust Milosevic by bringing the war "close to home," but instead resulted in widespread support for Milosevic's policies. While Serbia did eventually back down—possibly due to the threat of a ground campaign, which Clinton had originally ruled out—the NATO air campaign was largely unable to stop widespread killing and expulsions by Serbs or to destroy the Serbian army in Kosovo. In addition, it severely disrupted the civilian economy and took the lives of many civilians in Kosovo and Serbia. The civilian death toll is estimated by some international human rights groups at roughly five hundred, though the Serbian government claims far more and the U.S. government claims far less. Ultimately, Kosovo Force (KFOR) troops were sent in to halt future violence, but no clear exit strategy or a time frame for the removal of troops was established. Furthermore, as of mid-2000 there was no agreement regarding the ultimate NATO mission: An independent Kosovo? Partition? A multi-ethnic Kosovo within the FR Yugoslavia?

Part of the difficulty of intervention in Yugoslavia has been the problem of determining "who wears the black hats." Although it is easy to find individual villains, it is less easy to determine which is the "wrong side." Even more confusing, intervention in Bosnia was undertaken to prevent ethnic fragmentation, while in Kosovo it has largely served to promote the possibility of autonomy or independence. While there is evidence that the majority of the atrocities committed in Bosnia and Kosovo were committed by Serbs, many were committed by Croatians and Muslims. There is the danger of demonizing Serbs and of believing that these events cannot happen elsewhere. The dilemma of Bosnia and Kosovo for the United States was that wars rarely happen simply by accident, and that it is almost impossible to impose peace from outside by military force without taking sides.

It is also worth noting that the wars in the former Yugoslavia were "media wars." By highlighting certain aspects of fighting (such as Serb atrocities) and downplaying others (such as Serb opposition to Milosevic) the media played a crucial role in shaping public opinion in the United States and western Europe. Intervention in Kosovo was fueled in part by the widespread opinion that the Serbs had raped, plundered, and massacred thousand of Bosnians, and would do the same in Kosovo.

This perception is especially dangerous because nationalist hysteria fueling ethnic violence is not confined to Serbia, as Croatian and KLA activities attest. The breakup of British India into modern India and Pakistan in 1947 saw similar levels of violence, which still occasionally flares back to life in the Punjab and Kashmir regions, where ethnically or religiously mixed populations remain. There are also similar examples in U.S. history—anti-immigrant and anti-Catholic sentiment in the nineteenth century, or, to a lesser extent, the wave of "Japanophobia" that struck during the 1980s recession. It seems clear that nearly any ethnic group anywhere in the world can be manipulated by racism and nationalism—not just in the Balkans.

Some Serbs, frustrated with what they see as American interference in Kosovo, draw an interesting parallel with Mexican immigration to California. What would happen if, achieving a majority of the population, Mexican Americans voted for the state to break away from the United States and unite with Mexico? Would the U.S. government allow them to leave, or use the military to intervene? California was part of Mexico until the United States conquered it in 1848. The irony that California was part of Mexico until the 1848 conquest is unintentional—much as some Kosovar Albanians claim to be resisting an unfair conquest, many Mexicans might well see a union of California as reversing American imperialism!

RECENT HISTORY AND THE FUTURE

It is unclear exactly what the future holds for the former Yugoslavia. The history of U.N. and

FILMS ON THE YUGOSLAVIAN CONFLICT

The tragedies of Yugoslavia have inspired a number of superb films. These tend to be dark comedies and are intended for mature audiences only. The films can provide a number of insights into the complexity of the conflict. The films noted below are all available in the United States and are available on videocassette. Each of the films addresses the question of "ethnic conflict."

- Dragojevic, Srdjian. *Pretty Village, Pretty Flame.* 125 min. Fox Lorber, 1999. Videocassette.

- Kusturica, Emir. *Underground.* 167 min. New Yorker Films, 1999. Videocassette.

- Manchevski, Milcho. *Before the Rain.* 112 min. Polygram Video, 1999. Videocassette.

NATO intervention in Bosnia, however, suggests that the return of peaceful co-existence may be much more difficult than is commonly estimated by American politicians and suggested by the media. Within Serbia proper the extensive damage to bridges, factories, power plants and the like has devastated the economy. The G17 group, an independent body of Serbian economists, has estimated that without outside aid Serbia may need as much as fifteen years to recover from the war. Unemployment has risen from about twenty-five percent before the bombing to thirty-two percent in 1999, and industrial production and the living standard continue to diminish from 1989 levels. Estimates on the cost of rebuilding war damage vary, but are in the $6 to $7 billion range for a country with an economy crippled by war, sanctions, internal corruption, and crime. It is unclear to what extent these factors might bring about the fall of the Milosevic regime—still the stated goal of the American government. Even before the air strikes, as much as seventy percent of the population of FR Yugoslavia was at the poverty level, and the country continued to suffer widespread unemployment, corruption, and inflation.

In Montenegro, NATO intervention has encouraged divisions within the country and there is the possibility that President Milo Djukanovic may push for independence from Belgrade, severing the last union between the republics of Tito's Yugoslavia. Such a move, however, could well bring about conflict with Serbia or spark a civil war between those favoring independence and those preferring continued ties with Serbia.

For Yugoslavia's neighbors the Kosovo intervention is part of continuing economic problems caused by the isolation of Belgrade, which was an important trading partner for all of its neighbors. The seven years of sanctions have hurt economic growth in Macedonia, Hungary, Romania and Bulgaria, and the destruction of bridges over the Danube River has blocked a major transportation route for the region. Although each government at least tacitly supported NATO's actions, continued economic sanctions and strife in Kosovo may lead to disagreements with U.S. policy.

Finally, the NATO strikes may possibly change international politics outside the Balkans. For the first time, NATO intervened in a foreign country, violating the principles of "sovereignty"— that a national government is the paramount source of authority and must agree to direct intervention by foreign governments. The United States has intervened in such a fashion previously, in Latin America, but not in Europe.

Although NATO justified the strikes on humanitarian grounds, there is widespread disagreement over their legality under international law and whether such actions are prohibited under the U.N. charter. There has been sharp criticism of U.S. and NATO actions by countries such as China and Russia that face similar "Kosovo"-style conflicts within their borders, and worsening relations between Washington, DC, Moscow, and Beijing.

Within the United States itself, although there was generally a high degree of sympathy for the Albanians and support for humanitarian efforts, there was not the same level of support for intervention. If the American presence continues to be drawn out, or if—as in Somalia—there are significant casualties, there may be a shift in the American public's willingness to support future intervention. The fact that the air campaign was conducted without a single combat casualty may raise expectations that future interventions be "bloodless," while the high cost of intervention, estimated at about $10 billion, and the possibility that the United States and Europe will need to supply $30 to $40 billion for rebuilding in Kosovo and FR Yugoslavia may discourage such campaigns in the future.

The dominant American role in Kosovo underscores the continuing problems faced by western Europe in foreign and military policy. On three separate occasions—in 1991–95 Croatia, 1992–95 Bosnia, and in 1999 Kosovo—the countries of the European Union have been unable to take the lead in resolving the crisis. As of June 1999 the European Union decided for the first time to begin to create a military force separate from NATO that could be used for future peacekeeping operations, which could possibly lead to greater independence from the United States in matters of foreign policy.

It is unclear what the future holds for Kosovo itself. Under the terms of the U.N. mandate for NATO occupation, the province is still legally a part of the FR Yugoslavia, but the arrival of KFOR troops has undermined the government's position in the region. Revenge attacks by Albanians—including looting, house burnings, and killings—had by early 2000 killed as many as thirty Serbs, Roma, and Albanians a month. This is roughly the same number as were killed each month in the fighting between the KLA and Yugoslav security forces before the air strikes. KFOR does not seem to have been prepared to police the province, and killings by Albanians immediately after the air strikes have done little to assure Serbs of NATO impartiality. The KFOR response to the massacre of fourteen Serb farmers on July 23, 1999—possibly by members of the KLA—was sharply criticized by Serbs and some human rights groups as inadequate.

With much of the remaining Serbian population removed to the north of the province, or to Serbia and Montenegro, the situation in Kosovo appears prone to declarations of independence by radical Albanians and possibly the partition of the province. In such a case the effect on neighboring Macedonia may be devastating. The Macedonian government has, generally, ensured a wide measure of rights for an Albanian minority that makes up as much as one-third of the population. With the Albanian population concentrated in the northwest of the country, and with possible influence from Kosovars, Albanians could conceivably hope to unite Kosovo, western Macedonia, and Albania and, in doing so, destabilize the Macedonian government.

BIBLIOGRAPHY

Banac, Ivo. *The National Question in Yugoslavia*. Ithaca, N.Y.: Cornell University Press, 1984.

Chomsky, Noam. *The New Military Humanism: Lessons from Kosovo*. Monroe, Maine: Common Courage Press, 1999.

Holbrooke, Richard. *To End A War*. New York: Random House, 1998.

Judah, Tim. *Kosovo: War and Revenge*. New Haven, Conn.: Yale University Press, 2000.

KFOR Online. http://www.kforonline.com (29 February 2000).

Kosovapress. http://www.kosovapress.com (29 February 2000).

Lampe, John. *Yugoslavia: Twice There Was a Country*. 2d ed. New York: Cambridge University Press, 2000.

Malcolm, Noel. *Kosovo: A Short History*. New York: New York University Press, 1999.

Mayak, James ed. *The New Internationalism: the U.N. Experience in Cambodia, the Former Yugoslavia and Somalia*. Cambridge: Cambridge University Press 1996.

Mertus, Julie. *Kosovo: How Myths and Truths Started a War*. Berkeley, Calif.: University of California Press, 1999.

Ramet, Sabrina. *Balkan Babel: The Disintegration of Yugoslavia from the Death of Tito to the War for Kosovo*. 3rd ed. Boulder, Colo.: Westview Press, 1999.

Roberts, Walter R. *Tito, Mihailovic and the Allies, 1941–1945*. New Brunswick, N.J.: Rutgers University Press, 1973.

SFOR Online. http://www.nato.int/sfor/index.htm (29 February 2000).

Thomas, Raju G.C. and H. Richard Friman, eds. *The South Slav Conflict: History, Religion, Ethnicity and Nationalism*. New York: Garland Publishing, 1996.

Todorova, Maria, "The Balkans From Discovery to Invention," *Slavic Review* 53 (1994): 453–482.

Woodward, Susan L. *Balkan Tragedy: Chaos and Dissolution After the Cold War*. Washington, D.C.: Brookings Institution, 1995.

James Frusetta

THE SOVIET UNION: COLLAPSE OF THE USSR AND FORMATION OF INDEPENDENT REPUBLICS

THE CONFLICT

Economic and political conflict led to increasing tension within the Soviet Union (USSR) in the late 1980s. Economic stagnation led to frustration with the centrally managed system. Political pressure to end (or win) the war in Afghanistan led to military frustration with the political regime. In addition, the member countries of the Soviet Union, including the Balkans, the Soviet bloc, and Chechnya and Georgia experienced a resurgence of nationalism. Soviet leader Mikhail Gorbachev tried to engineer a gradual liberalization of the country. While this was initially successful, Soviet citizens ultimately rebelled, and the Soviet Union was broken into many smaller countries, many of which experienced internal ethnic/national conflict.

Territorial

- The Soviet Union believed it had sovereignty over the member countries of the Soviet Union—and their land. At a minimum, it believed it had the right to rule those countries that were part of historical Russia.

- The member countries of the Soviet Union often did not have histories of independence.

Economic

- Many of the most fiercely contested areas following the break-up of the Soviet Union were areas of significant potential resources or trade.

Political/Ethnic

- Much of the emerging national identification was around ethnic-linguistic groups. This was complicated by the fact that there was a lot of internal migration in the Soviet Union, and there are now a lot of Russians in Georgia, and a lot of Armenians in Azerbaijan.

In March 2000 Russian troops claimed to have pushed rebel forces out of their strongholds in Chechnya, a Russian republic in the south. The Russian army treated this as a significant victory. The Russian military action in Chechnya took place against a background of economic decline and political uncertainty as long-time Russian president, Boris Yeltsin, transferred power to his successor, Vladimir Putin. Further to the south, the mandate of Russian peacekeepers in the Abkhaz region of Georgia was extended to keep warring factions apart. The former Soviet republics of Armenia and Azerbaijan rejected yet another proposal for peace in a long series of Russian-mediated discussions over the status of Nagorno-Karabakh, while Tajikistan held its first presidential elections after years of civil war.

On December 7, 1991, three leaders from Russia, Ukraine, and Belarus signed an agreement for the creation of a Commonwealth of Independent States (CIS) and rejected the legitimacy of a 1922 treaty that was the corner stone of the Union of Soviet Socialist Republic (USSR), also referred to as the Soviet Union. Within a week this agreement was ratified by the parliaments of Russia, Ukraine, and Belarus. Fearful of being left out of the new organization, leaders of the five Central Asian republics declared their intention to join the CIS in the following days. By December 21, the process of the Soviet collapse was complete as leaders from 11 republics signed the Almaty Declaration on the foundation of the CIS. Signatories to the declaration were Armenia, Azerbaijan, Belarus, Kazakhstan, Kyrgyzstan, Moldova, Russia, Tajikistan, Turkmenistan, Uzbekistan, and Ukraine. Georgia and the three Baltic states of Estonia, Latvia, and Lithuania refused to join the CIS. The

CHRONOLOGY

1922 Establishment of a treaty that is the foundation of the USSR.

1940 The Molotov-Ribbentrop Pact, between Moscow and Nazi Germany, gives the Baltic states of Estonia, Latvia, and Lithuania to the Soviet Union.

1985 Mikhail Gorbachev is appointed first secretary. He launches *perestroika* (a major restructuring of the economy) and *glastnost* (a new policy of openness).

1989 Gorbachev orders the withdrawal of the Soviet Union from Afghanistan. For the first time in nearly sixty years, the Soviet state allows more than one candidate to run for office.

1989 Armenia and Azerbaijan go to war over Nagorno-Karabakh.

1991 Leaders of Russia, the Ukraine, and Belarus sign the Almaty Declaration for the creation of the Commonwealth of Independent States (CIS). Later Armenia, Azerbaijan, Kazakhstan, Kyrgyzstan, Mol-

dova, Tajikistan, Turkmentistan, and Uzbekistan sign the agreement, and the Soviet Union ceases to exist. Lithuania, Estonia, and Latvia declare independence, and the army moves in to suppress the independence movements. There is an attempted coup, which is repulsed, but shortly thereafter, Gorbachev resigns. Chechnya declares its independence by staging a coup against Communist leaders in Chechnya.

1992 Russia goes to war with Moldova to protect the large numbers of Russians living within Moldova. The war ends with the promise of a special autonomous unit within Moldova for Russians. Abkhazia, an autonomous region with Georgia, declares independence, resulting in war with Georgia.

1994 War between Georgia and Abkhazia has ceased, but the status of Abkhazia remains unclear. Russia invades Chechnya.

2000 Russians take Grozny, the capital of Chechnya.

Soviet Union officially ceased to exist at 12:00 P.M. December 21, 1991.

The Soviet collapse was not accompanied by widespread conflict. With the exceptional case of Armenia and Azerbaijan, there were no border clashes between emerging states. This was largely due to the Soviet federal structure. By the 1980s all member republics of the Soviet Union had a clearly demarcated territory that was to reflect the traditional homeland of the largest ethnic community that gave its name to the territory. Latvians were the titular community in Latvia and Uzbeks in Uzbekistan, although this did not exclude other ethnic groups from living there. These republics also had all the trappings of sovereign states. They had a republican parliament, a council of ministers, and their own national flags. The real power, however, resided with the Communist Party of the Soviet Union (CPSU) and its leadership in Moscow, the capital of Russia. But once the Communist Party was removed from power, and independence was made possible, real leadership fell to the existing administrative structures. Thus, the Soviet collapse did not result in a power vacuum.

The smoothness of the transition to independence was remarkable, especially given the speed of events. Many greeted the disintegration of the Soviet Union with disbelief. Although signs of decline were visible, no one expected the Soviet empire to crumble so rapidly. The causes of its collapse, as well as the rise of nationalistic fervor, ethnic bloodshed, and the emergence of a new system, often referred to as the post-Communist or post-Soviet system, has occupied political scientists and specialists in Soviet studies.

HISTORICAL BACKGROUND

The Soviet System

By the late 1970s it was clear to Soviet leaders that the political and administrative system was encountering difficulties. Although these difficulties were not severe enough to cause extreme alarm, they did threaten political stability and undermined the superpower status of the Soviet Union. These issues challenging the Soviet system included the economy's capacity to expand, the ability of Soviet leaders to maintain and increase the level of spend-

COMMUNIST AND CAPITALIST ECONOMIES

Throughout a significant majority of the twentieth century, the people of the USSR lived under the Soviet economic system that prescribed that wealth be distributed equally among all. In keeping with communist theory, Russian citizens were provided housing and jobs by a centralized government to which they "paid" their salaries. Consumer goods, while not available in great variety, were accessible at regulated prices. While some resented the level to which the government control extended, most Russians were able to lead somewhat economically solid lives.

However, when Boris Yeltsin took control of the Russian government and independent states were formed from former Soviet republics in the early 1990s, the Russian public faced great uncertainties. The end of the Soviet Union meant the end of the guaranteed supply line. Prices were released from government control, and, in response to market demand, the price of products soared. Without the government to fund many unprofitable businesses, workers went unpaid or lost their jobs. The Russian economy spiraled downward, bringing the average standard of living down and inflation rising unchecked. Despite the increase in freedoms, especially those of expression, the Russian people have faced great economic hardships and look to for some time to come.

ing on the arms race with the United States, and the question of the political legitimacy of the Soviet regime.

The root of these issues may be found in the system of government, established during the 1920s and 1930s. The system created under Josef Stalin (1929–53) was highly centralized—the government attempted to control every facet of public life and was largely successful. A multi-layered bureaucracy planned all economic activities, complete with production targets and the prescribed quality and quantity of finished goods, sold at fixed prices in state-run outlets. This extensive system, which operated throughout the Soviet Union and extended across eleven time zones, promised to bring uniformity and equality to all citizens. It appealed to a sense of equity. In practice the system was too disengaged from the public to be responsive to its needs. This led to miscalculations and mistakes. At times, for example, all shoes in state-run stores were in size ten because the order to produce other sizes had not reached the shoe-making factory.

The Soviet economic system was also weighed down by defense expenditures and the allocation of the best resources to the military sector. The arms race with the United States, which started after World War II, escalated in the 1950s and 1960s after the Soviet Union developed its own nuclear bomb and again in the 1980s after the Soviet invasion of Afghanistan (1979) and the coming to office of President Ronald Reagan (1981) in the United States. Soviet leaders in Moscow felt it critical to keep apace of technological advances and to upgrade the imposing Soviet Army to discourage aggression from the North Atlantic Treaty Organization, or NATO, and to maintain the superpower status of the Soviet Union. So many resources were being spent on the military that there was little left over to improve the people's lifestyle. This commitment placed a heavy burden on the Soviet economy and its citizens.

The defense and military priorities of Soviet leaders and the inefficient system of economic planning meant that the needs of Soviet citizens were not being met. Soviet leaders first came to power in 1917 with promises of a better, more equitable life for the people, but the system they built had little concern for the needs of ordinary citizens. The rift between promise and practice, between the people and their leaders, between private life and public, was very wide. The political system that emerged in the 1920s and 1930s was based on the assumption that the Communist Part of the Soviet Union, or CPSU, was the only legitimate political association. This assumption was clearly set out in Article Six of the constitution in 1977. Consequently the system of one-party rule gave the CPSU a free hand in dominating all state organs. There was no separation of powers between the legislative, executive, and judiciary branches of the state. All fell under CPSU control.

The political system in the Soviet Union, therefore, did not reflect the wishes of its citizens. This does not mean that Soviet citizens did not go through formal electoral motions. Regular elections were held for local, republican, and all-Union—which covered the entire Soviet Union—assemblies. But, as a rule, there was only one candidate for every seat and that candidate was nominated by the CPSU. The media were under tight control so that all discussions preceding elections, as in other times, were tightly regulated and guided. The CPSU controlled public life, and there was little chance for the airing of concerns and demands without its endorsement.

MIKHAIL GORBACHEV

1931– Mikhail Sergeyevich Gorbachev was born March 2, 1931 in Privolye, Russia, and spent most of his young life working on farms. He received his law degree in 1955; the next year he married Raisa Titorenka.

Gorbachev continued his education, and graduated as an agronomist-economist. He became the youngest member of the Politburo (the policymaking body of the USSR), in 1980. He became head of state on March 11, 1985, when elected general secretary of the Communist Party.

Gorbachev's original goals were soon eclipsed by more drastic reform policies such as *glasnost* (openness) and *perestroika* (restructuring). He signed a pact with the U.S. in 1987 to limit nuclear weapons, and was elected to retain the presidency by the newly created parliament in 1988. When non-Communist governments came to power in former Soviet-bloc countries, Gorbachev withdrew Soviet troops. He was awarded the Nobel Peace Prize in 1990.

After being held under house arrest in August 1991 during a brief coup attempt, Gorbachev quit the Communist party. On December 25, 1991, Gorbachev resigned as the president of the Soviet Union, which subsequently ceased to exist. Although a 1996 re-

MIKHAIL GORBACHEV. *(UPI/Bettmann. Reproduced by permission.)*

election bid garnered less than one percent of the vote, Gorbachev continues to be involved in Russian politics and environmental and educational foundations.

Because the system was not meeting or representing the people's needs, a rift emerged between the rulers and the ruled. Neither Soviet leaders nor the system enjoyed the trust of Soviet citizens. Soviet leaders were aware of the erosion of their political legitimacy and the need to reform the system. After the death of Leonid Brezhnev, the long time party leader and head of state (1964–82), an unsuccessful attempt was made by his aging successor, Yuri Andropov (1982–1984), to breath life into the ailing Soviet system. But Andropov died in 1984 before he could achieve anything tangible. Konstantin Chernenko (1984–1985) succeeded Andropov but died just over a year after taking office. The responsibility of rejuvenating the Soviet system fell to Mikhael Gorbachev, who, with the exception of Stalin, was at age fifty-four the youngest man to hold the most powerful post in the Soviet Union. He was appointed first secretary of the CPSU in March 1985. It was ironic that Gorbachev's reforms, which were designed to re-

vive the stagnating Soviet economy and regenerate public trust in the country's leadership accelerated the Soviet decline and led to its total collapse.

The Gorbachev Years

Mikhail Gorbachev's policies of reform affected all spheres of Soviet life. The reforms were initiated in 1996 and began with the Soviet economy, but it was soon clear to Gorbachev and his reformist colleagues that the Soviet political system and its foreign relations would also need to be revisited. The success of economic reforms depended on a comprehensive overhaul of the Soviet Union.

Gorbachev identified economic stagnation as his most pressing challenge and launched successive campaigns against the waste of resources, human and material. He invited industrial managers and the workforce to show initiative and address corruption, apathy, and drunkenness at work. Gorbachev, however, realized that without a major re-

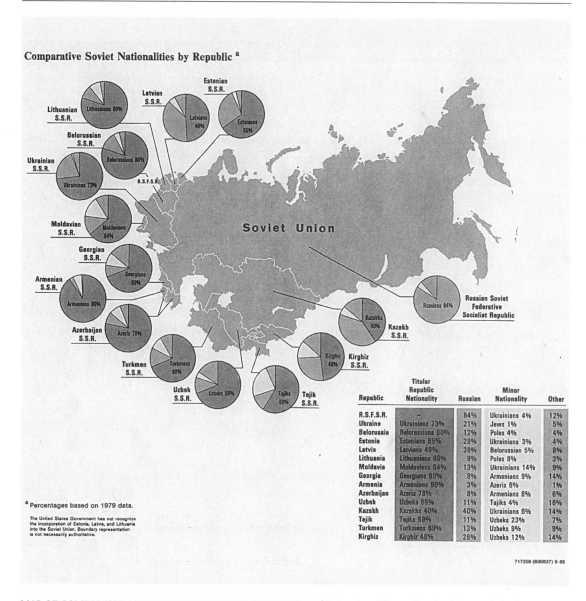

Comparative Soviet Nationalities by Republic [a]

[a] Percentages based on 1979 data.

The United States Government has not recognize
the incorporation of Estonia, Latvia, and Lithuania
into the Soviet Union. Boundary representation
is not necessarily authoritative.

Republic	Titular Republic Nationality	Russian	Minor Nationality	Other
R.S.F.S.R.	–	84%	Ukrainians 4%	12%
Ukraine	Ukrainians 73%	21%	Jews 1%	5%
Belorussia	Belorussians 80%	12%	Poles 4%	4%
Estonia	Estonians 65%	28%	Ukrainians 3%	4%
Latvia	Latvians 49%	38%	Belorussian 5%	8%
Lithuania	Lithuanians 80%	9%	Poles 8%	3%
Moldavia	Moldavians 64%	13%	Ukrainians 14%	9%
Georgia	Georgians 69%	8%	Armenians 9%	14%
Armenia	Armenians 90%	3%	Azeris 6%	1%
Azerbaijan	Azeris 78%	8%	Armenians 8%	6%
Uzbek	Uzbeks 69%	11%	Tajiks 4%	16%
Kazakh	Kazakhs 40%	40%	Ukrainians 6%	14%
Tajik	Tajiks 59%	11%	Uzbeks 23%	7%
Turkmen	Turkmens 69%	13%	Uzbeks 9%	9%
Kirghiz	Kirghiz 48%	26%	Uzbeks 12%	14%

717208 (B00837) 9-89

MAP OF COMPARATIVE SOVIET NATIONALITIES BY REPUBLIC. *(University of Texas. Reprinted by permission.)*

structuring of the economy, called *perestroika*, and a freeing up of resources from defense commitments, and an immediate injection of funds in the dilapidated industrial sector his plans for rejuvenating the Soviet economy would achieve very little. But withholding funds from defense and rechannelling them to civilian industries was an impossible task while in the midst of an arms race with the United States. The matter was made even more complicated by the Soviet Army's involvement in Afghanistan. This led Gorbachev to take unprecedented steps to remove tensions in East-West relations and repair Soviet relations with the West.

In May 1989 Gorbachev ordered the withdrawal of Soviet forces from Afghanistan, a major step in removing a point of contention between the United States and the Soviet Union. In Europe Gorbachev abandoned the traditional Soviet commitment to its East European allies. He ordered Soviet forces stationed in Eastern Europe not to interfere in the internal affairs of their host states. This reformist foreign policy, dubbed "New Thinking," was a drastic departure from traditional Soviet practice. It laid the groundwork for a wave of political upheavals in Eastern Europe, which swept communist governments aside and brought to power leaders with anti-Russian, pro-Western orientations. The new approach resulted in the celebrated unification of East and West Germany (1990) and had major ramifications for the Soviet Union and the global political environment.

Gorbachev declared his commitment to a "common home" in Europe to reduce tensions between East and West. If tensions were reduced the Soviet Union could more comfortably decrease military spending. Gorbachev's initiatives appeared to pay off. By February 1991 the Soviet Union and the United States had signed a number of treaties for a thirty percent reduction in their strategic nuclear arsenals.

On the home front Gorbachev was aware of the Communist Party's legitimacy crisis. He responded by to easing control over public life and presenting a more open, responsive, and "democratic" image for the CPSU. The policy of openness, *glasnost*, was effectively implemented a few weeks after the Chernobyl nuclear accident in April 1986. Soviet media started running stories about the disaster and its casualties; this kind of "negative reporting" would never have been allowed by Soviet authorities before *glasnost*. This openness was gradually broadened and reports about crime, corruption, and prostitution—taboo subjects until that time—began to appear in the press.

Gorbachev's philosophy was to win public trust by showing the people that the CPSU deserved their allegiance. This was an ambitious project and required a radical shake-up of the system—*perestroika* was to be extended to the political system. Gorbachev invited the CPSU to forgo its monopoly on power. In the 1989 parliamentary elections, for the first time in nearly sixty years, the Soviet state allowed more than one candidate to compete for a seat. With Gorbachev at the helm, the elected body—now called the Congress of People's Deputies—became the first Soviet assembly in sixty years to witness uncensored debate over issues. It also adopted legislation to promote *glasnost* and *perestroika*. The spirit of reform was on the rise in 1989 and 1990.

Gorbachev encouraged the formation of public organizations, independent of the CPSU. This new tolerance was greeted with the sprouting of a kaleidoscope of social and political clubs and associations. These popular clubs often adopted titles such as *perestroika*, or In Defense of *Glasnost*, indicating their support for Gorbachev's policies of reform and putting pressure on Gorbachev's critics within the ruling party. These popular clubs were among Gorbachev's allies in his power struggle with CPSU hardliners who did not view reforms as necessary or suitable for the Soviet Union.

But popular clubs had a major limitation—they could not register as political parties, hence they could not nominate candidates in elections.

BORIS NIKOLAEVICH YELTSIN

1931– Boris Yeltsin was born February 1, 1931 in Siberia. Once, as a schoolboy, he was expelled for arguing. Shortly after he received an engineering degree from Ural Polytechnic Institute in 1955, he married fellow engineer Naina Girina, with whom he had two daughters.

After working in construction he joined the Communist party (CPSU) of the Soviet Union in 1961, and rose through the local party ranks. Selected to serve as the mayor of Moscow in the mid-1980s, he promoted reform but was forced to resign after criticizing party leaders. In March 1989 he was elected to the new Congress of People's Deputies, and became the speaker of the Congress in May 1990.

During the August 1991 attempted coup, his popular support grew when he climbed onto an advancing tank to address the army. After the coup failed, Yeltsin renounced the CPSU and won Russia's first democratic presidential election. Although his first term was marked by the breakup of the Soviet Union, economic recession, internal strife, and a heart attack, he was reelected in July 1996. During his second term, tensions in Chechnya increased, and Yeltsin's health continued to suffer. In 1998 he dissolved his cabinet, although many were later reappointed. Yeltsin resigned as president December 31, 1999.

Article Six of the Soviet constitution needed to be revised before these informal political associations could be formally registered. Under pressure from growing popular clubs and mindful of his public image, Gorbachev allowed the CPSU's constitutional monopoly to be removed in 1990.

Ramifications of Reform

The Soviet Union was made up of numerous republics. The new public organizations in non-Russian republics of the Soviet Union were often concerned about reviving their cultural heritage and resisting Russian influence on their culture and traditions. In nearly seventy years of Soviet rule, Russians and the Russian language had become dominant throughout the Soviet Union. Non-Russians interpreted Gorbachev's reforms, with the promise of openness and freedom of social action, as permission to reclaim their history. Non-Russians, especially in the Baltic states and the Caucasus, challenged the myth of a united Soviet nation as they rejected the official version on their

SOVIET ART THEFT CONTROVERSY

When the Axis forces fell after World War II, Soviet troops secretly took works of art from Germany that the USSR claimed had been taken from its country when Nazi forces invaded. It wasn't until 1990, with the establishment of Russia and the Commonwealth of Independent States, that details of the Soviet plunder began to surface; the art had been stored in museums throughout the former Soviet Union for over forty years. Among them was the "Treasure of Priam," a find that German archaeologist Heinrich Schliemann considered to be from the ancient Greek city of Troy. When it became known that the treasure was in the former Soviet Union, Germany, Turkey, and Greece issued calls for its return to its rightful owner—though who that rightful owner was under debate between the three parties.

Russia, however, disputed the requests for the return of plundered art. Claiming that the trophy art was compensation for the high losses sustained by the Soviet Union during World War II, the Russian parliament passed a bill in March 1998 nationalizing the trophy art. President Boris Yeltsin, however, refused to sign it. In early May 2000 the bill was once again put forth and it passed the lower house of the Russian parliament with a unanimous vote. Whether Russian president Vladimir Putin will sign the bill if it comes to him remains to be seen. As the determination to nationalize Soviet plunder would violate several international agreements, among them the 1970 UNESCO Convention and three separate Hague Conventions (1899, 1907, and 1954), Putin's decision could have significant international implications. With its economy in transition, Russia can ill afford to make enemies of other members of the global community.

"voluntary" admission to the Soviet Union. Popular fronts were growing in strength; their demands for culture revival and a reassessment of their history were only a logical step away from calling for greater autonomy, even independence. In 1990–91 that threshold was crossed.

Growing pressure forced Gorbachev to agree to a new Union Treaty to replace the original 1922 document, because the old treaty was rejected as biased against non-Russian republics. The draft of the new treaty provided extensive rights to all republics. Gorbachev's tolerance for dissent and willingness to appease nationalist demands, however, were not acceptable to conservative members of the CPSU. Reforms had undermined the authority of the Communist Party both internally and externally. The CPSU no longer enjoyed a monopoly on public life. Gorbachev's conciliatory gestures toward the West had cost the Soviet Union its allies in Eastern Europe. Negotiating a new Union Treaty threatened to cap all this by undoing the Soviet Union itself. Conservative members of the CPSU and the armed forces complained that reforms had gone too far.

Trying to calm these fears, Gorbachev assured the conservative members of his party that his reform program was necessary for the preservation of a viable Soviet Union. In support of this, he took a hardline approach to demands for independence in the Baltic and Transcaucasia. In Lithuania fifteen people died as the Soviet army moved to suppress the republic's move for independence in January 1991. Gorbachev's bouts of conservatism did not appease the hardliners and were seen as insufficient to maintain the Union. At the same time, independent clubs and associations lost faith in Gorbachev's commitment to reforms. On August 19, 1991, two days before a new Union Treaty was to be signed, the hardliners, among them the vice president, ministers of internal affairs and defense, and the commander-in-chief of ground forces, attempted a coup. Tanks rolled into Moscow streets, but the coup was badly organized. Reports circulated about soldiers without live ammunition and commanders reluctant to order more killings. The army failed to prevent communication that allowed contact among anti-coup activists. The army also failed to storm the Russian republic's parliament—not to be confused with the Soviet federal parliament. The Russian parliament, under the leadership of Russian president Boris Yeltsin, defied coup plotters. Boris Yeltsin managed to stay in touch with his followers and inspire mass demonstrations against the coup. By nightfall August 21, 1991, the attempted coup had unravelled.

Whose Loss? Whose Gain?

The August coup plotters sought to return the Soviet Union to the old system. Instead, they expedited the process of change. The winners of the coup were primarily the nationalist forces of the republics. In addition, the August coup debacle benefited the democratic forces headed by Russian President Boris Yeltsin.

Boris Yeltsin was himself a former party boss who was expelled from the leadership (1987) because of his outspoken remarks about the slow pace of reforms. Yeltsin remained an active proponent of reforms and in 1990 was elected speaker of the newly formed Russian parliament. In June 1991 he ran in the presidential elections and won a popular mandate, the first Russian leader to stand in direct elections—not even Gorbachev had risked

RUSSIA'S CONTROVERSIAL CONFLICT WITH CHECHNYA HAS HAD CATASTROPHIC EFFECTS ON THE CHECHEN POPULATION; HERE A REFUGEE WATCHES WARILY AS RUSSIAN TANKS PATROL THE CHECHEN BORDER. *(AP/Wide World Photos. Reproduced by permission.)*

popular elections. Yeltsin's courage in August 1991 brought him and his team of reformers even more popularity and international recognition.

Yeltsin capitalized on his popularity and pressed ahead with radical reform policies. Immediately after the attempted coup, his government banned the CPSU and confiscated its assets. It also began the process of price liberalization and privatization to distribute state assets to the populace. The pillars of the Soviet economy were rapidly dismantled.

Russian economic reforms were masterminded by Yegor Gaidar, who became acting prime min-

ister in June 1992 and popularised the term "Shock Therapy." The underlying assumptions were that the rapid implementation of economic reforms would speed up the pace of economic recovery. Not all citizens of Russia, however, were in a position to benefit from privatization and economic reforms. Existing industrial managers and Soviet administrators, dubbed *apparatchiki*, used inside knowledge and connections to secure productive and lucrative positions in various industries. Soviet managers were transformed overnight into capitalists: a new class of *nouveau riche*, with extensive influence and connection with the new Russian government.

POPULAR RUSSIAN PRESIDENT VLADIMIR V. PUTIN SIGNS AUTOGRAPHS NEAR THE CITY OF GROZNY. *(AP/Wide World Photos. Reproduced by permission.)*

Gains made by the democratic forces and economic reformers were at the expense of the CPSU leadership, particularly Mikhail Gorbachev. The August coup was a humiliating experience for Gorbachev, who was on holiday in Crimea at the time and was caught unprepared when trusted members of his government sought his overthrow. Upon returning to Moscow after the attempted coup Gorbachev denied the CPSU's involvement in the plot and rejected calls for banning the party. He was subsequently subjected to a harsh televized verbal attack by Boris Yeltsin. Gorbachev had lost credibility and could not stop the tide sweeping over the country. A defeated man, Gorbachev resigned from the presidency of the Soviet Union on December 25, 1991, one week before it ceased to exist.

The disintegration of the system and the implementation of new policies resulted in triple-digit inflation and price hikes, an unprecedented experience for Russians. The inflation and rise in prices radically undermined living standards for the majority of the population. The new Russian state was unable to collect taxes from privatized industries, partly because it had not developed the necessary taxation mechanism and partly because new owners evaded taxes. The crisis was deepened by a fall in industrial production. The government found it increasingly difficult to pay its employees. The plight of wage earners was compounded by the privatization of services, including housing, childcare, and retail shops, which deprived citizens of subsidized government social services. Economic reforms following the Soviet collapse resulted in an unprecedented imbalance in the distribution of wealth in Russia in the twentieth century. At the same time, Soviet republics began to take advantage of the central government's loosening grip and assert their own rights to power.

The Emergence of Nationalist Politics

Nationalist supporters justified the disintegration of the Soviet Union into fifteen separate entities as a natural and inevitable process. They argued that every nation had an ordained right to govern itself. Nationalists saw national sovereignty and statehood as inalienable rights, withheld from them by the repressive Soviet regime. *perestroika* and *Glasnost* made it possible for nationalist aspirations to be propagated and take hold, and the Soviet collapse made their independence possible.

Some republics within the Soviet Union claimed that they had a national right to statehood, which was violated by the Soviet regime. The three Baltic states of Estonia, Latvia, and Lithuania enjoyed independence in the period between World War I and World War II. It was only after the Molotov-Ribbentrop Pact, a secret deal between the Soviet Union and Nazi Germany, that the Baltic territory was annexed by Moscow in June 1940. Memories of independent statehood remained vivid in the Baltics, however, which explained the strength and popularity of nationalism there.

In other parts of the Soviet Union it was more difficult for non-Russians to have memories of independence. External borders of the Soviet Union were almost identical to those of Czarist Russia and, with the obvious exception of the Baltics, remained so until its collapse in 1991. Non-Russian nationalist groups, therefore, had no real experience with independent modern statehood. Transcaucasia and Central Asia were colonized by Czarist Russia in the nineteenth century. Before that, Transcaucasia was ruled by the Persian Empire in the south, and Central Asia was divided between rival local *khanates*, or chieftans. Belarus and Ukraine were located at the heart of the Czarist Russian empire, with Moldova at its periphery.

Soviet policy on nationalities, ironically, facilitated the emergence and consolidation of nationalist feelings. The formal allocation of territories to ethnic groups and the formation of ostensibly "self-ruling" national republics germinated the ideal of national sovereignty. This national ideal, however, was contradicted by the reality of Soviet politics. It was clear that real power was concentrated in Moscow, exercised by the Russian-dominated CPSU, and it was difficult for non-Russians to distinguish between Soviet and Russian rule. Consequently, their anti-Soviet national feelings invariably took on anti-Russian overtones once the Soviet Union collapse. This was especially true in the Baltics.

Anti-Russian sentiments in the Baltics influenced post-Soviet legislation and voting rights were denied to Russian residents in Estonia and Latvia. In Moldova, nationalist fervor was in favor of Moldovan unity with Romania, reverting back to borders of the early nineteenth century, which caused extreme anxiety among Russians in the country. A war between Russians and Moldovans ensued in 1992. The war ceased after Moscow pressed and achieved a special autonomous status for Russians within Moldova.

Anti-Russian feelings were not always so blatant. Language laws in all successor states, for instance, made the titular language the official language of the state, causing anxiety for Russian settlers in non-Russian republics, many of whom did not speak the local language. Under Soviet rule, the Russian language was effectively the official language throughout the Soviet Union. Russian settlers in Latvia and Uzbekistan, for instance, had no compelling reason to learn Latvian or Uzbek, although Latvians and Uzbeks had to learn Russian in order to improve their career prospects. It was clear that the implementation of language laws after independence was an exercise in national self-assertion by non-Russians. It caused an exodus of Russians from these republics back to Russia. This experience complicated relations between Russia and the newly independent states.

Nationalist politics heightened tensions in Transcaucasia. All three Transcaucasian republics experienced armed conflict directly linked to competing nationalist aspirations. In the case of Armenia and Azerbaijan the two states went to war over the mountainous territory of Nagorno-Karabakh. In Georgia, the state was forced to suppress aspiring nationalist claims by its ethnic minorities.

Conflict in Nagorno-Karabakh

Armenia and Azerbaijan went to war in 1989 over Nagorno-Karabakh (Mountainous Karabakh in Russian). Conflict between Armenian and Azeri communities in the late 1980s preceded the war, but conflict between the two communities and the two states may be dated still further back. In the confusion that succeeded the fall of the czarist empire (1917), the British and the Ottoman Empires competed for a foothold in the Transcaucasus. Their policies helped create the two states of Armenia and Azerbaijan. The enclave of Nagorno-Karabakh, with its predominantly Armenian population, was given to Azerbaijan. This was not acceptable to Armenia, leading to a full-fledged war between the two new states, which only stopped when Russians (now under Soviet rule) regained control of Transcaucasia in November 1920.

Soviet rulers, however, could not find a satisfactory resolution to the Nagorno-Karabakh issue. Soviet policies on the "nationalities question," in fact, made the issue more complicated. This policy gave credence to the principle of autonomous self-government for each ethnic group. The policy could even be interpreted as a justification for nationalist demands for independent statehood, a demand that stirred the Armenian population in Nagorno-Karabakh.

Following the establishment of Soviet rule in the Transcaucasus and the formation of the two Soviet republics of Armenia and Azerbaijan, Nagorno-Karabakh was initially given to Armenia. This decision reflected the Soviet nationalities policy because it did not allow the geographic separation of Armenia and Nagorno-Karabakh to hamper the unity of the Armenian people under a single administration. Pressure from Azeris, who could not accept a break in their territorial integrity, and protests from Mustafa Kemal, head of the provisional government in Turkey, forced a reversal of this decision. In 1921 Nagorno-Karabakh was reassigned to Azerbaijan, and in 1923 it was turned into an autonomous region within Azerbaijan. This autonomy gave the population of Nagorno-Karabakh a degree of freedom to promote their own culture, conduct education in the local language, and attend to local affairs independently, while remaining part of Azerbaijan.

This compromise, however, could not be a permanent solution. Armenians in Nagorno-Karabakh continued to press for a complete break from Azerbaijan. In 1968 and again in 1977, the capital of Nagorno-Karabakh was rocked by ethnic clashes between the Armenian and Azeri communities. Given this history, it was not surprising that the policy of reform and reconstruction that was initiated by Mikhail Gorbachev was seen by Armenians in Nagorno-Karabakh as a fresh opportunity for their nationalist aspirations.

In July 1988 the regional council of Nagorno-Karabakh voted unanimously for secession from Azerbaijan, causing renewed tension between the two communities. The Soviet government in Moscow assessed the situation as critical and stepped in to relieve tensions. Nagorno-Karabakh was placed under direct rule from Moscow in January 1989, but Moscow withdrew its direct rule before the year's end. This experience only made Armenians more determined in their quest for secession. In December 1989 Nagorno-Karabakh was declared reunited with Armenia proper in a "United Armenian Republic." This put Armenia and Azerbaijan on a collision course once again.

A formal peace between Armenia and Azerbaijan has, as late as mid-2000, not been achieved. A series of talks, mediated by the Organization for Security and Cooperation in Europe, have only achieved a temporary ceasefire. The status of Nagorno-Karabakh remains uncertain.

Conflict in Georgia

Georgia experienced a turbulent political crisis after the Soviet collapse. A bloody civil war threatened to tear the state apart. This crisis was linked to the politics of nationalism. At the time of independence Georgia contained three autonomous administrative regions: Abkhaz, Ajar, and South Ossetia. These autonomous regions were created under Soviet rule to represent the ethnically distinct populations of these localities. In Abkhazia, for example, the Abkhaz language and culture were promoted by the regional administration, reinforcing the message that Georgians and Abkhazians were not the same people.

The policy, consistent with the Soviet regard on nationalities, was accepted and encouraged by Moscow. Georgian nationalists in Georgia's capital of Tblisi, however, dismissed the Soviet policy on promoting Abkhaz, Ajar, and South Ossetian cultures as misguided and detrimental to the cohesiveness of the Georgian state. Ethnic minorities responded by accusing Georgians of trying to assimilate them into Georgian culture and appealed to Moscow for protection. Tensions over cultural identity in Georgia were relatively subdued until 1990–91 when Gorbachev's policy of *Glasnost* made possible public debate on and mobilization around issues of cultural revival and autonomy.

A Georgian nationalist coalition led by Zviad Gamsakhurdia, a political dissident under Soviet rule who had links to the Georgian church, won fifty percent of the seats in the republican parliament (November 1990). In the following months

Gamsakhurdia was elected chair of the parliament and then president (May 1991). The Georgian nationalists were very popular in the region's first direct elections in nearly sixty years, attesting to the popularity of the nationalist message.

During Gamsakhurdia's short term in office, Georgia adopted nationalist postures both internally and externally. Internally his government disputed the need for education in minority languages, and externally it rejected the Commonwealth of Independent States (CIS) as another Russian-dominated structure. Tbilisi's nationalist postures caused anxiety for ethnic minorities in Georgia. Non-Georgians felt increasingly marginalized. Now that Georgia was not joining the CIS, there could be little hope of appealing to Moscow to act as the arbiter in Georgian-Abkhazian disputes. National self-assertion seemed to be the only venue open to Abkhazians, South Ossetians, and Ajars. Thus they asserted their national self-interest, though with varying degrees of intensity.

In July 1992 Abkhazia declared independence and tried to obtain international recognition as an independent nation-state. This course of action seemed only natural to Abkhazians. The idea of cultural autonomy and political self-rule for every culture was popularized under the Soviet leadership and was now primarily taken for granted. If there was going to be a state for the Georgian people, why not one for Abkhazians? This was not a purely ideological proposition, but had practical implications. A state was seen in Abkhazia as the only way to stop the Georgianization of that territory, both culturally and demographically. The settlement of Georgians in Abkhazia, with the support and encouragement of Tbilisi, had reduced the proportion of the Abkhaz population in their own "home land" by half. For that reason, Abkhazian nationalists targeted Georgian settlers as agents of Georgian colonization.

The ensuing conflict brought Georgia to the brink of collapse. It was clear that Tbilisi could not manage the crisis by itself and needed help to quell unrest. Assistance from Russia, however, would undermine Georgia's nationalist postures. At the same time, Gamsakhurdia was forced out of office by a palace coup. Edward Shevardnadze, a seasoned politician and former Soviet foreign minister in Gorbachev's government, took the helm. Shevardnadze was concerned that Moscow might encourage separatism in Abkhazia and in other parts of Georgia, leading them to exert pressure on Tbilisi. To avoid this he changed Georgia's external nationalist position, and Georgia entered the CIS.

Georgia's entry into the CIS satisfied a major Russian condition for assistance. In return, Russia sent peacekeepers and mediators to conflict zones in the former republic. By mid-1994 war between Georgians and Abkhazians had ceased, but the status of Abkhazia remained uncertain. This uncertainty has justified the continued presence of Russian forces in Georgia.

At the turn of the twenty-first century, both Nagorno-Karabakh and Georgia had reached temporary settlements, but long-term prospects for peace remained uncertain. Nagorno-Karabakh and Abkhazian demands for self-rule, the first through unification with the republic of Armenia and the second through independent statehood, respectively, remain unacceptable to the governments of Azerbaijan and Georgia. Azerbaijan and Georgia, however, cannot challenge the underlying logic of minority nationalist self-determination because they resorted to that very same logic to justify the legitimacy of their two states.

Minorities in Russia

The Russian state, the largest and the most populous out of Soviet-successor states, was not immune to nationalist fervor. Russian nationalist forces grew in strength and popularity as the shock of the Soviet break gave way to disillusionment. Russia's economic demise meant an increasing dependence on foreign aid. Citizens of the once-mighty Soviet Empire were now at the mercy of aid from the United States, the European Union, and Japan. The experience of discrimination against Russians in the Baltics, Moldova, and elsewhere outside Russian borders were treated with indignation by Russians everywhere. Russians turned to their own state as the champion of their interests and a pillar of their identity.

Not all citizens of Russia, however, identify with Russian nationalism. Over eighteen percent of Russia's population are non-Russians, some of whom live in their own ethnically designated territories. Russia contains twenty autonomous ethnic republics, created under Soviet rule to generate the illusion of self-rule among ethnic minorities. The growth of Russian nationalism threatened to undermine the administrative and cultural autonomy of these ethnic territories, making minority ethnic groups wary. At the same time the emergence of independent states from Soviet republics served as an appealing model to be followed.

The republic of Chechnya declared independence under the leadership of Dzhokhar Dudayev. Moscow would not allow one of its minority ethnic territories to leave Russian sovereignty, in case it should set an example for other autonomous republics. Russian armed forces challenged Chechen separatists in December 1994 in what was designed to be a quick operation. Instead, the mission was a failure. Chechen forces used guerrilla tactics to force the withdrawal of Russian troops. Although Dudayev was killed, Chechnya retained its semi-independence from Russia. In late 1999 Moscow felt strong enough to tackle Chechnya again. The matter of Chechen independence appeared urgent, especially after reports that separatist forces in Dagestan, another ethnic autonomous republic neighboring Chechnya, were trying to emulate Chechnya. A swift victory in suppressing the separatists in Dagestan and Chechnya was expected. Moscow's military strategy may be seen as flirtation with Russian nationalism, as the military victory was expected to boost national pride among Russians and rekindle popular trust in President Yeltsin and his team. In March 2000 the Russian military operation in Chechnya was declared a success, though the war was not over.

The International Community and the Disintegration of the Soviet Union

The Soviet break-up was greeted with feelings of euphoria and anxiety in the West. The Soviet collapse was considered to be a testimony to the supremacy of the Western democratic system. For example, Francis Fukuyama, in his celebrated book, *The End of History* (1992), argued that with the fall of the Soviet alternative, there remained no obstacle to the universal spread and adoption of the "liberal democratic" model of government. Fukuyama concluded that ideology would no longer determine international politics. This belief in the ultimate victory of liberal democracy underpinned a sense of euphoria in the West. At the same time, the political vacuum in the post-Soviet region was regarded as dangerous and an opportunity for exploitation by extremist forces and rogue states. The West was especially concerned about the spread of Islamic radicalism and the influence of Iran in the Muslim Soviet-successor republics—Azerbaijan and the five Central Asian republics of Kazakhstan, Kyrgyzstan, Tajikistan, Turkmenistan, and Uzbekistan.

The concern with post-Soviet Central Asia and Transcaucasia was not only about religion. The rich deposits of oil, gas, and other minerals in this region made it highly prized. Central Asia and Transcaucasia appeared to be pulled in three directions. The West, including the United States, the European Union, and Turkey have been trying to establish close diplomatic and economic ties with the region to benefit from its alternative source of cheap fuel and also to prevent the spread of Islamic radicalism. The West was aided in this goal by the linguistic and ethnic proximity of Turkey and many Turkic communities in Azerbaijan and Central Asia.

Central Asia and Transcaucasia were also pulled by Iran. The ethnic and linguistic closeness of Iranians and Tajiks facilitated close cultural ties between the two states. But the Tajik civil war (1992–1997) complicated relations when Iran was accused of harbouring opposition leaders. Despite the West's fear that Iran would export its brand of Islam, however, the Persian nation remained focused on economic relations with its northern neighbors. The secondary importance of Islamic considerations meant that Iran felt it was prudent to side with the Christian state of Armenia, against the Muslim state of Azerbaijan in their territorial conflicts. Additionally, Iran's weak economy has not allowed it to play a serious part in the region.

The third and the more important pull was exercised by Russia. Moscow has never accepted that its former Soviet republics should have complete freedom from Russia. Even under the leadership of President Yeltsin, who was praised in the West as Russia's champion of democracy, the terminology of the "near abroad" was developed to emphasize the special relationship between Russia and other Soviet-successor states. Behind this terminology was an assumption that the near abroad remained a zone of special interest to Moscow and that Russia should retain its influence over the post-Soviet region. Just as Georgia had feared, Russian-dominated CIS economic and security organizations were used to maintain Russian influence.

RECENT HISTORY AND THE FUTURE

Nationalism was a major force in all Soviet-successor states. The nationalist forces in Russia and the republics were often in competition and could not be reconciled. Political self-rule for one community within a given territory could be achieved only by the violation of that right for another community. At times this obvious clash of interests led to open conflict. Examples of such nationally inspired conflicts included the dispute over Nagorno-Karabakh and the Georgian civil war. Within Russia, competing nationalist aspirations have caused conflict between Moscow and the Chechen community, as each strove to establish its own sovereignty.

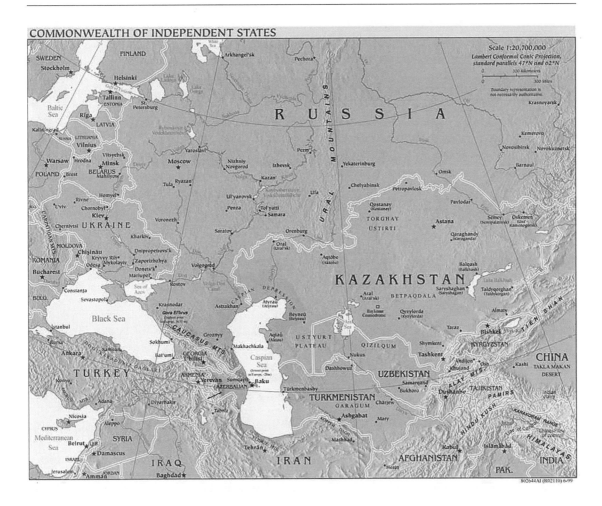

MAP OF COMMONWEALTH OF INDEPENDENT STATES. *(Central Intelligence Agency. Reprinted by permission.)*

It is ironic that the very same nationalist forces that caused the collapse of the Soviet Union are now threatening to destabilize Soviet-successor states. The Abkhaz community, for example, questioned that the Georgian claim to statehood should be any more legitimate than that of the Abzhaz. Nationalism assumes that cultures deserve to be regenerated and perpetuated through autonomy and self-rule. Political self-rule is the ultimate form of defending, institutionalizing, and perpetuating cultures.

Yet, competing national interests are not always expressed openly, especially when they are likely to antagonize a powerful neighbor. Although language laws were clearly designed to boost national self-esteem among the predominate nationality of a republic, the laws were viewed by the Russians living there as discriminatory. Soviet-successor states have, on the whole, refrained from making that obvious connection for fear of offending Moscow. Russia remains an influential power in the post-Soviet region. Though the West or Iran may pose as a counterforce to Russia, they may lack the determination, the resources, or the overwhelming interest in the region to wrench the Soviet-successor states from the Russian orbit.

BIBLIOGRAPHY

Ian Bremmer and Ray Taras, eds. *New States, New Politics: Building the Post-Soviet Nations.* New York: Cambridge University Press, 1997.

Khazanov, Anatoly M. *After the USSR: Ethnicity, Nationalism and Politics in the Commonwealth of Independent States.* Madison, Wisc.: The University of Wisconsin Press, 1995.

Miller, John. *Mikhail Gorbachev and the End of Soviet Power.* New York: St. Martin's Press, 1993.

Sakwa, Richard. *Russian Politics and Society.* 2d ed., London & New York: Routledge, 1996.

Shahram Akbarzadeh

SUDAN: SLAVERY AND CIVIL WAR

THE CONFLICT

Slavery re-emerged in the Sudan as the civil war continued. The government has armed one tribal group, the Baqqara, and allowed them to hold Dinka women and children as slaves.

Religious
- The Islamic north wants to impose *shari'a* law (Islamic law) on the Christian south.

Economic
- With the discovery of oil in southern Sudan, the south became crucial to the economic health of the north. In addition, there are conflicts over water and grazing rights.

The civil war in Sudan, which has raged in various stages of intensity for forty years, has given rise to allegations of slavery—men, women, and children taken from their homes and forced into labor or, for some, forced into conscription in the army. Human rights groups have volubly protested the reemergence of slavery in Sudan. Pictures of enslaved children have appeared in the western media and horrified the public. In the western world, the word "slavery" immediately brings forth volatile emotions and issues that reflect the struggle to end slavery and to develop racial equality, a struggle in which the West—particularly the United States—is still engaged. Tradition and modern day warfare fuel slavery in Sudan in the late twentieth and early twenty-first century.

Sudan's slavery is often described in terms of race and religion. Religious differences are aggravated by the extended civil war. The north of the country is populated predominantly by Arab Muslims who speak Arabic and advocate that Islamic law, *shari'a*, govern the country. The south consists largely of black Africans, speaking a variety of languages, whose beliefs are Christian or Animist and who prefer a secular government to a religious-based one. These differences are a few of the factors that have contributed to the fighting.

Ancient tribal practices in the area of southern Sudan include the abduction of women and children from rival tribes. Victims were often held for ransom and only released when relatives were able to buy their freedom. The civil war helped revive tribal animosities and the practice has resurfaced. In a letter from the Council on American-Islamic Relations, the Sudan Foundation describes just this situation and offers, "What looks like the purchase of slaves is actually the redemption of pris-

CHRONOLOGY

1821–25 Turco-Egyptian invasion of Sudan and subsequent expansion of colonial rule into what is now southern Sudan.

1898 Defeat of Khalifa Abdullahi and establishment of the Anglo-Egyptian Condominium.

1922 Passports and Permits Ordinance, the start of the "Southern Policy," which separates the administration and people of northern and southern Sudan.

1955 Rioting of strikers at Zande and mutiny of troops in Equatoria. The beginning of the north/south conflict.

1956 Sudan gains independence from Great Britain.

1963 Anya Nya, the southern insurgent group, is founded.

1969 Colonel Jafaar al Nimieri seizes power in a coup.

1972 Addis Ababa Accord establishes qualified autonomy for the south.

1983 President Nimieri proclaims the *shari'a*, or Islamic, law.

1983 Civil war resumes, this time the Dinka SPLA/SPLM are among the major insurgents.

1985 Nimieri is removed from power.

1987–88 The first reports of contemporary slavery in the south.

1989 Coup brings Colonel Omer al Beshir and Dr. Hasan al Turabi to power.

oners of war," proposing that while to the western world this appears to be slavery, to the tribes in southern Sudan it is a tradition of tribal conflict.

What can, with little equivocation, be termed slavery is the action of government-backed militia groups raiding southern villages and abducting men, women, and children. The targets of these attacks are primarily Dinka civilians in the Bahr El Ghazal region. The Dinka people are closely identified with the Sudan People's Liberation Movement/Army (SPLM/A), the main faction fighting the Sudanese government. Once captured, the abductees are forced into labor. Women and children are used as domestic slaves, and women may also be forced to serve as concubines. Men have been forced into conscription in the army.

The lives of slaves are difficult. They are kept in poor living standards, sleeping on floors, receiving little food, denied access to education and their own languages and culture. They are forced to work at whatever task their captors demand—be it manual labor, fighting in battles, or prostitution. Captors have been known to rename their slaves, giving them Arabic names and sometimes forcing them to adopt Islam, the dominant religion of the north. As justification, some believe that the Dinka culture is inferior and that they, the captors, are actually helping the slaves into a better culture and way of life.

Whatever the motivations behind the abduction and captivity of another human being, the end result is the same—enslavement. While Sudan's civil war wages, these practices continue, and human rights groups around the globe struggle to bring attention to the degradation and devastation wrought by slavery. Both sides of Sudan's war have committed human rights violations. Both are willing to go to great lengths to achieve their ends. No matter what side ultimately wins, it is the people themselves who are losing.

HISTORICAL BACKGROUND

Sudan is the largest country in Africa, encompassing almost nine hundred seventy thousand square miles. Sudan stretches from Egypt and the Red Sea in the north and east, to the Democratic Republic of Congo and Uganda in the south, and Chad in the west. In total, Sudan borders nine countries and the Red Sea. In keeping with its huge size, Sudan contains all major ecosystems of tropical Africa within its boundaries. The Sahara lies in the northern and western portion of Sudan, the middle zone of the country is sahelian grassland, and in the south rainfall reaches levels capable of sustaining tea and coffee cultivation in Equatoria province.

Sudan matches its geographic diversity with its ethnic variety. Literally dozens of ethnic groups re-

THE SEPTEMBER LAWS

Sudan's struggle with *shari'a,* the Islamic holy law, has become a highly politicized issue in their ongoing civil war. First introduced in 1983 by Colonel Jafaar al Nimieri, frozen by Sadiq el Mahdi in 1986, and reintroduced by General Omer Beshir in 1991, the *shari'a* has caused peace negotiations to break down and resulted in the civil war being declared a *jihad,* or holy war, by the north.

The *shari'a* is based on the Koran, the sacred book of Islam. While only eight percent of the Koran's 6,236 verses deal with mores of behavior, it has spawned a richly detailed body of law and customs that govern how Muslims speak, dress, and interact with each other and with non-Muslims. Included are instructions that range from how often to pray and how much to give to charity to prohibitions against drinking alcohol and mingling with the opposite sex in public. For certain crimes, punishment is very specific and harsh. Murderers are publicly beheaded. A thief's hand is amputated. Stoning and flogging punish adultery and fornication. According to opponents of the system, these punishments are medieval and barbaric. Proponents say they are fair and just as the most specific punishments are only applied to crimes that are very narrowly defined and stringently prosecuted. Under *shari'a,* shoplifting is not stealing if the goods are not under lock and key, and stealing in order to eat is not punishable. Circumstantial evidence is strongly discounted in favor of eyewitness accounts or, when possible, confessions. Even if those conditions are met, the proscribed punishment is not always administered. A convicted murderer will be imprisoned rather than executed if just one of the victim's heirs objects to the beheading.

Like most legal systems, *shari'a* is only as good as its enforcers and this has differed widely depending on the country, the judges, and the underlying political atmosphere. Saudi Arabia and Iran have the longest histories using the *shari'a* law and have adopted the harshest punishments. Nigeria and Pakistan are the most recent countries to turn away from secular law and it is still unclear how much of the law they will implement. When Nimieri instituted the *shari'a* in the Sudan in September 1983, he did so in order to deliver "instantaneous justice." He argued that the *shari'a,* known in the Sudan as the September Laws, diminished suffering because only the criminals were punished. In a secular system when a criminal is imprisoned, the family suffers as well. Nimieri's motives for replacing the existing legal system were undoubtedly political. His critics argued that he was manipulating public attention away from the country's many problems and increasing pressure on the non-Muslim opposition whose members could now be arrested for anti-Islamic convictions. Because of Nimieri's underlying motivations, the Sudanese *shari'a* was applied unevenly and unfairly. After Nimieri was overthrown, cases were still tried under *shari'a* and lesser offenses were still punished. However, punishment of the more serious offenses was suspended because of the court's irregularities. Shortly before Mahdi's government was toppled, the Criminal Bill of 1988 was drafted. It suggested the reintroduction of the *shari'a* in the northern half of the country. Defendants in the south could also request to be judged by either secular or Islamic law. In January 1991, Bashir reinstalled the *shari'a* throughout the country regardless of whether or not the accused was Muslim. Bashir has taken the *shari'a* one step further. In addition to reinstituting all punishments, his government now calls for neighboring countries to adopt the *shari'a* as well. Only then he claims, can peace in the region be achieved.

side within both the north and south confines. Sudan is not simply a country occupied by Arabs and Africans—the country contains many people, all of whom, including Arabs, are African.

In contemporary Sudan the majority of northern Sudanese consider themselves to be Arabs. Arabs in Sudan are distinguishable because Arabic is their primary language. Non-Arab groups in the north include the Nubians of the far north who are also found in Egypt, and the Beja of the east who are related linguistically to the Afar, Issas, and Somalis of Djibouti and Somalia respectively. In the west live people, such as the Fur and Zaghawa, who are ethnically related to people in the countries of Chad, Central African Republic, and Niger. In the Nuba mountain region of the north live the Nuba, who relate to the people of southern Sudan and who are also engaged in a struggle against the current government.

Although there are great variations in facial features and hair texture, the vast majority of northern Sudanese people would be considered black by the social standards of current U.S. society. It should also be noted that although non-Arab Sudanese speak languages other than Arabic in their homes, Arabic is the *lingua franca*—the common language—of the north and is the dominant trade or market language of the south. Due to the dominance of Islam, most Muslim northerners claim some Arab ancestry whether they identify themselves as Arab or not. In addition, northern Sudan has a large minority of people of northern Nigerian origin who primarily live in the central cotton-growing region of the country.

In the southern third of Sudan, people from the Nilotic group of languages are dominant. The Nilotic southern people include the Dinka, Shilluk, and Nuer, traditional pastoralists—people who depend primarily on their herds for sustenance. The Azande, another prominent southern group, live along the border with the Democratic Republic of the Congo.

Traditionally in Sudan most people lived along the Nile River by agrarian or pastoral means. Currently, Sudan has more active pastoralists, or herdsmen, than any nation in the world. Pastoralism, along with religious difference, is at the root of the controversy over slavery in southern Sudan. The southwestern region of Sudan known as Bahr al Ghazal (Gazelle River) was traditionally an area where the southernmost Arab groups, the Baqqara came into contact with the Dinka. Baqqara means cattle, and the Baqqara people kept and often rode cattle, since their region is too moist for camels. Both groups are cattle pastoralists who require similar land for the maintenance of their herds; consequently, there has been ongoing conflict over resources. In addition, religious and physical differences between the groups served as justification for conflict, and the tribes have resorted to the tradition of kidnapping members of rival tribes and holding them for ransom.

Throughout most of their history, the Baqqara and Dinka had been evenly matched in terms of strength or in their capacity to inflict harm on each other. This began to change after 1821, when an Egyptian governor of Ottoman (Turkish) Albanian origin, Muhammad Ali, occupied Sudan. Ali's regime and successors established the Turco-Egyptian period of rule in Sudan. During this time the Egyptians aggressively expanded southward and established *Zaribas*, armed encampments that served as slave stockades and trade warehouses. Sudanese Arab groups like the Baqqara were re-

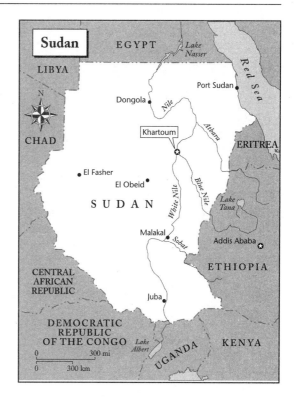

MAP OF SUDAN. *(XNR Productions Inc.)*

cruited into these slave-trading networks and began to use their newly acquired technological advantages—guns—to capture and exploit their Nilotic neighbors.

During the period of Turco-Egyptian rule (1821–85), many indigenous people of Sudan suffered at the hands of a government that was concerned only with exploiting the resources of the country. The non-Muslim population suffered extensively among Sudan's people because they were subject to widespread slave raiding.

The Turco-Egyptian period came to an abrupt end in 1885 with the appearance of Muhammad Ahmad. Ahmad came out of the west of the Sudan and declared himself the *Mahdi*, or rightly guided one—a figure called by God to reestablish the proper order of the Islamic world. The movement founded by Muhammad Ahmad overswept the occupying regime, and Sudan was able to maintain independent rule until 1898. The emergence of the *Mahdi* and his government, the *Mahdiyya*, had a profound affect on the political culture of northern Sudan; it indelibly marked the national identity of the north with an aggressively Islamic foundation. The south remained primarily Animist in its beliefs, with small pockets of Christianity.

The *Mahdiyya* was destroyed in 1898 by a joint force of British and Egyptian troops. After the

THE PRACTICE OF SLAVERY IS RAMPANT IN SUDAN. AN ARAB TRADER EXCHANGES THE EQUIVALENT OF $13,200 WITH A MEMBER OF CHRISTIAN SOLIDARITY INTERNATIONAL FOR THE PURCHASE AND FREEDOM OF 132 SLAVES. *(AP/Wide World Photos. Reproduced by permission.)*

Sudanese were defeated a new leadership known as the Anglo-Egyptian Condominium was established. The political rule was known as the condominium because the law of the territory was divided between the two powers or *co-domini*. Although the Egyptians were formally equal partners with the British, they had no significant power. The northern Sudanese were absorbed into the government as low ranking soldiers and bureaucrats, but were also subject to many restrictions.

One of the most profound restrictions placed on Sudan was the establishment of the Passports and Permits Ordinance in 1922. This law placed substantial barriers on the movement of northern

Sudanese to the south. Consequently, the ability of northern Sudanese to work as (Islamic) missionaries in the south was reduced considerably. Instead, Christian missionaries were encouraged by the British to establish institutions in southern Sudan. In the minds of many northern Sudanese this policy was instrumental in magnifying the estrangement between the two segments of the country—north and south. Another policy ensured that very few southerners were able to receive appropriate western education, thus making it difficult for them to compete for skilled jobs in the colonial structure. Subsequently, the region was left in isolation while portions of the north underwent considerable development in order to produce cotton for the British textile industry.

Occasionally during the Condominium period, it appeared that southern Sudan might be separated from the north and joined to another British territory such as Uganda. This, however, did not happen because after World War II, nationalist politicians in the north began agitating for Sudanese control of the entire country—north and south. Northerners also demanded Sudanization, or that all jobs in the government be given to Sudanese as soon as possible. Since there were few educated southerners, this policy led to friction. In 1955 strikes broke out among workers in the Zande region of the south, and troops mutinied in the far south province of Equatoria. Within a few years of independence in 1956 and the increasing imbalance of power between the north and south, southern Sudan was engaged in a full-scale civil war against the government in Khartoum. The breakdown of political relations between the north and south was hastened by the first military coup in post-independence Sudan, led by General Ibrahim Abboud in 1958. Under the new military government children in the south were given Muslim names and encouraged to convert to Islam without prior consultation with their parents.

The negative response to this and similar treatment was evidenced by the first wave of refugees fleeing Sudan for neighboring countries like Kenya, Uganda, and Ethiopia. Many dissidents eventually formed an organization known as the Sudan African Closed Districts National Union. The leaders of this movement were Joseph Oduhu and Friar Saturnino Lohure. During the initial civil war, most of the leadership of the rebel movement was known as the Anya Nya and was based in the Equatoria region of southern Sudan. The Dinka, who would be much more important in the conflict in the 1980s, were marginal at the beginning of the initial civil war.

Certain defining elements of the southern movement were beginning to take shape. Specifically, the southern movement found a great deal of leadership in the Christian church, the sole source of education in southern Sudan, since the British had not previously established public universities there as they had in the north. Although the struggle between the north and south has been as much about access to government positions and resources as anything else, the prominence of religious figures in the south, and later the north, has further emphasized the religious and ethnic aspects of the conflict.

JAFAAR MOHOMMAD AN-NIMEIRI

1930– Jafaar Mohommad an-Nimeiri was born in Omdarman, Wad-Nabawi, near Khartoum, Sudan, on January 1, 1930. He attended the Sudan Military College and trained in Egypt, where he became a follower of Egyptian president Gamal Nasser. In 1966 he graduated from the U.S. Army command college in Fort Leavenworth, Kansas. He returned to the Sudan, and in 1969 led a military coup against the civilian government. He installed himself as the head of the army and the government, and established a Revolutionary Command Council, a political-military organization, to enforce his rule.

Nimeiri banned political parties and jailed anyone considered politically active. He survived several attempts to overthrow him in the first two years of his regime. In 1971 he declared himself president. In 1972 he attempted to stop the seventeen-year-old civil war between north and south Sudan with the Addis Ababa Agreement. This granted autonomy to the non-Muslim, southern parts of the Sudan, and temporarily brought peace and stability to the region.

However, the agreement didn't change the economic conditions of southern Sudan. Many southern Sudanese felt alienated and threatened by the introduction of *shari'a* (Islamic) law throughout the country. Although Nimeiri was twice re-elected president, his regional policies and attempts to impose strict Islamic law made his regime unpopular, and while visiting the United States in 1985, he was deposed in a military coup. He now resided in Egypt, and has written a book on military strategy.

Political Leaders

For all but ten years of its volatile modern history Sudan has dealt with an ongoing civil war in its southern region. This constant state of war has weakened Sudan's civil society and encouraged a cycle of alternating civilian and military command. Because of the difficult environment, politicians looked for alternative approaches to alleviate Sudan's problems. Dr. Hasan al Turabi emerged during the fall of Sudan's military dictatorship in 1964 and began a period of elected government. Turabi was head of the Muslim Brothers, an organization founded in Egypt in 1928. The organization seeks to find a traditional Islamic approach to the demands of the contemporary world. Turabi

DR. HASSAN AL-TURABI

1932– Turabi, considered one of the leading Islamic political philosophers of modern times, was born February 4, 1932, into a conservative, religious family in the eastern Sudanese town of Kassala. He joined the law faculty of Khartoum University at the age of nineteen. He received a Ph.D. in law from the University of London in 1957, and a Ph.D. in emergency law from the Sorbonne in France in 1964.

He returned to Khartoum University as its chancellor, but resigned in 1965, and became a political leader, forming the Islamic Charter Front, and running as its candidate in elections. He brokered an Islamic Constitution for Sudan, which he described as "liberal and fair." This constitution had much popular support in the (mostly Muslim) north, but before it could take affect, the process was pre-empted by Jaafar Nemeiri's military coup.

The May 1969 coup resulted in the suspension of all political activities. However, Turabi continued to organize, and was arrested in 1970. He served more than seven years in prison. Under pressure from the politically strong Muslim Brotherhood, the government released Turabi and appointed him to a governmental position; however, he was re-arrested and sent back to prison by Nimeiri in 1985, a few months before Nimeiri was deposed.

After Nimeiri left Khartoum, Turabi was released from prison and formed the National Islamic Front, and worked toward a coalition government. In June 1989, General Omer al-Bashir led a military takeover of Sudan, and Turabi was once again thrown into prison. In 1990 Turabi left prison, and pledged to work to work for the new regime, declaring its goals identical to the Islamic Front. However, leadership tensions mounted throughout the 1990s. In 1998 Turabi was elected to the post of secretary-general of the National Congress and speaker of parliament. However, at the beginning of 1999, President Bashir declared a state of emergency, allowing him to dismiss Turabi and his supporters from their Cabinet posts.

played a major role in the government during the re-emergence of the slave trade in southern Sudan.

In 1969 the electoral government of Sudan was overthrown and Colonel Jafaar al Nimieri emerged as the country's new president. Nimieri ruled Sudan until 1985; his tenure was marked by shifts in his political allegiances in order to main-

tain his power. Early on, Nimieri allied himself with the Sudanese Communist Party and other leftist groups. In the process he acted harshly against the traditional parties of Sudan, in particular the Ansar party that had its roots in the Mahdi family. In March of 1970 the government killed over ten thousand Ansar members at Aba, an island outside of Kosti, Sudan. Within a year of attacking his mainstream opponents, Nimieri purged his government of its communist supporters after they attempted a coup against him. He proclaimed himself a nationalist Arab leader similar in style to Jamal Abdul-Nasir of Egypt or Moammar Qaddafi of Libya.

After fortifying his position in Sudan Nimieri concluded one of the most important political agreements of Sudanese history, the Addis Ababa agreement of 1972. At the same time that Nimieri battled his enemies in the north, he put together an effective army that limited the ability of southern troops to gain territory. Nimieri's initial communist connections also allowed him to place two southerners, Abel Alier and U.S.-educated John Garang, into his government. Nimieri used his southern connections to persuade the emperor of Ethiopia, Haile Selassie, to facilitate negotiations between the Sudanese government and Joseph Lagu, the most powerful of the southern leaders. The two sides reached an agreement on March 28, 1972, providing for an autonomous status for the southern districts of Sudan—southern Sudan would have significant independence within the country. The Addis Ababa agreement was honored until 1983.

By the early 1980s a number of partisan changes had occurred in Sudan that altered the political climate of the country. First, there was exploration for oil in southern Sudan. When oil was discovered in the Bentiu district the government attempted to change the boundaries so that Bentiu would be in the north. When this maneuver failed, the government attempted to pipe the oil to the north and then to the Red Sea without involving southerners in the processing of this valuable resource. During the first civil war, the center of anti-government activity was in the far southern province of Equatoria; during the 1980s the Dinka region was involved. The central government saw the Dinka, the single largest ethnic group in Sudan, as a serious threat.

Civil Issues and Law

In addition to the issue of oil, the possibility of completing the Jonglei canal project also upset many Dinka. The Jonglei canal was a planned waterway that would connect the Bahr al Ghazal with the White Nile. A river of such caliber would drain much of the marshland that has been the traditional dry season pasture for the Dinka. The canal project also spawned rumors that land in Bahr al Ghazal would be made available to northern Sudanese farmers or the fellahin, or peasants, of Egypt.

Another facet of the civil war stemmed from the fatal maneuvering that Nimieri engaged in to maintain power. Having allied himself with all other political parties at one time or another, in 1983 Nimieri found himself allied with the National Islamic Front (NIF) and Dr. Hasan al Turabi. This alliance led to the proclamation of *shari'a*, the traditional law of Islam, and its traditional punishments, the *hudud*, which include such sentences as amputations for theft and flogging for drinking alcohol and fornication. When *shari'a* was announced as the legal code for the entire nation, including the overwhelmingly non-Muslim south, it was taken as a direct assault on the Addis Ababa agreement.

After the establishment of *shari'a* the south, led by the Dinka, rebelled. The man who emerged as the head of the Dinka was John Garang, the former cabinet minister then on staff at the University of Khartoum. Garang headed the Southern Peoples Liberation Army (SPLA). The SPLA and the Southern People's Liberation Movement (SPLM) have been at the center of the southern struggle for the past two decades, though new groups are emerging.

RECENT HISTORY AND THE FUTURE

With the renewal of war in the south, the position of Nimieri became weak and he was overthrown in 1985. In his place Sudan made another attempt at parliamentary democracy under the leadership of Sadiq el Mahdi. The Mahdi government was unable to make any significant progress to overcome Sudan's problems. In particular, the government was reluctant to revoke *shari'a* for fear that it would be perceived as anti-Islamic. A military coup struck in 1989, led by General Omer Beshir. General Beshir's government was strongly committed to the Islamist philosophy of Dr. Hasan al Turabi and the NIF. Under this rule, the Sudanese leadership has characterized the war with the south as a *jihad*—holy war. In the atmosphere of increased Islamization, immediately before and after the coup of 1989, reports of renewed slave trade began surface in southern Sudan.

THE SUDAN PEOPLE'S LIBERATION ARMY (SPLA) HAS HISTORICALLY BEEN ONE OF THE MAJOR INSTIGATORS IN THE SUDANESE CIVIL WAR. ONE OF ITS SOLDIERS EXAMINES THE SITE OF AN SPLA AMBUSH ON THE SUDANESE GOVERNMENT. *(AP/Wide World Photos. Reproduced by permission.)*

In order to gain support the government armed the Baqqara neighbors of the Dinka, giving them a huge advantage in the competition for pasture. Furthermore, the government permitted the Baqqara to hold Dinka children and women as captives. This practice developed into a slave trade where boys were sold as manual labor and girls were used both as laborers and as wives or concubines. In addition to the slave trade, refugees fleeing north to the large cities of Khartoum, Khartoum North, and Omdurman, were captured and placed in

DESPITE THE EFFORTS OF INTERNATIONAL HUNGER RELIEF ORGANIZATIONS, FAMINE AND CIVIL WAR HAVE TAKEN THEIR TOLL THROUGHOUT SUDAN. THESE CHILDREN ARE DYING IN THE CITY OF AJIEP. *(AP/Wide World Photos. Reproduced by permission.)*

camps where, reportedly, food was used to encourage their conversion to Islam.

Nongovernmental organizations (NGOs) have entered Sudan to engage in relief work with refugees in the south and in adjacent countries. Many of these agencies have been traditional groups such as Medecins Sans Frontieres (Doctors Without Borders) and the Red Cross. Missionary groups have also come to Sudan, however, with the express purpose of propagating Christianity. These organizations aggressively brought the issue of slavery to the attention of the world media. Religious groups such as Freedom House, a subsidiary of World Vision, have gained considerable attention by fostering slave buy-back programs—they purchase the slaves in order to free them. Some groups, such as UNICEF, criticize the slave redemption programs as both legitimizing and encouraging slave raiding among the cash-strapped Arab populations, as the slave traders would capture more people in order to make more money. But the groups encouraging the buy-backs insist that gaining the freedom of captives under any circumstance is worth the effort. Most of the religious hierarchy of southern Sudan, including the Dinka bishop, Macram Gassis, supports the redemption policy.

In the foreseeable future, Sudan's slave raiding—and its conflict—will likely continue. In the late 1990s Sudan's NIF government provoked its neighbors Eritrea and Uganda to such a degree that the adjacent countries were willing to allow substantial attacks on Sudan from their borders. Sudan benefited politically, however, from a 1998 attack that U.S. President Bill Clinton ordered on a Khartoum pharmaceutical plant in retaliation for the bombing of the U.S. embassies in Nairobi, Kenya, and Dar es Salaam, Tanzania. Since the actual connection of this facility to biological or chemical warfare agents was tenuous at best, many countries have softened their stance toward the Islamist government of Sudan. As a result Sudan has been able to secure funding for oil pipeline projects from investors in Canada and China. Although these projects will provide the Sudanese with improved funding to pursue its war, it is doubtful that this aid will provide a sufficient inducement to actually end the current conflict and help free the Sudanese people from the specter of slavery.

BIBLIOGRAPHY

Allen, Tim. "Full Circle?: An Overview of Sudan's 'Southern Problem' Since Independence," *Northeast African Studies* 11, no. 2 (1989).

"CBS and Allegations of Slavery in Sudan." http://msanews .mynet.net/MSANEWS/199902/19990204.8.html (29 August 2000).

Daly, Martin and P.M. Holt. *A History of the Sudan.* London: Longman, 1988.

Deng, Francis Mading. *The Dinka of the Sudan.* Prospect Heights, Ill.: Waveland Press, 1984.

Ibrahim, Abdullahi Ali. " A Theology of Modernity: Hasan al-Turabi and Islamic Renewal in Sudan," *Africa Today* 46, no.1 (Winter: 1999).

Mintier, Richard. "The False Promise of Slave Redemption," *Atlantic Monthly* 284, no.1 (July 1999).

Robinson, B.A.. "Slavery in Sudan." http://www.religious-tolerance.org/sla_sud.htm (29 August 2000).

Rone, Jemera. "HRW Background Paper on Slavery and Slavery Redemption in Sudan." http://www.igc.org/hrw/backgrounder/africa/sudan1.htm (29 August 2000).

Voll, John, ed. *State and Society in Crisis.* Bloomington, Ind.: Indiana University Press, 1991.

Anthony Q. Cheeseboro

SYRIA AND ISRAEL: NEGOTIATIONS FOR PEACE

THE CONFLICT

Syria and Israel have been at war off and on since the establishment of Israel in 1948. Both have occupied parts of Lebanon in an effort to protect their borders. In recent years they have been—sporadically—negotiating for peace.

Religious

- Muslim Syria and Jewish Israel both believe that they have a religio-historical right to Palestine, the site of many important religious places.

Political

- Syria has not, historically, recognized Israel's right to exist.

- There have been numerous wars between Israel and neighboring Arab countries, including Syria.

- Prior to its division by France, Syria included today's Syria, Jordan, Lebanon, and Palestine (Israel).

Economic

- Conflict over fishing and water rights.

The conflict between Israel and Syria poses one of the most complex challenges to achieving a comprehensive peace in the Middle East. The modern history of the Israeli-Syrian conflict began with the creation of the state of Israel in 1948. Yet it was after Israel's defeat of Syria during the Six-Day War in 1967 that the conflict between the two became exceptionally tense and violent. During that war, Israel captured the Syrian-held Golan Heights, a strategically important area for both countries.

The 1999 election of Israel's prime minister, Ehud Barak, increased optimism for a peace treaty between Israel and its Arab neighbors. Barak declared his willingness to negotiate a resolution concerning the Israeli-occupied Golan Heights. Although talks between Israel and Syria resumed in December 1999, they were quickly suspended. To understand why negotiations failed, it is important to understand that Syria's struggle with Israel is inextricably intertwined with the entire Arab-Israeli conflict. For years, regional and global pressures have influenced Syria's activities regarding Israel. Although the two states are not currently in a phase of "hot war" they frequently play out their battles in Lebanon.

HISTORICAL BACKGROUND

The Creation of Israel and Its Aftermath

Prior to World War II, Syria had been under French control. Until 1920 the region known as "Syria" encompassed today's Syria, Lebanon, Israel and Jordan. After World War I, the French divided Syria into smaller units to prevent the areas from unifying against them. By 1946 Syria had gained its shaky independence, though it still retained dreams of "Greater Syria."

CHRONOLOGY

1800s Jewish groups, known as Zionists, advocate a Jewish state in the Biblical land of Israel.

1915–1916 The Husayne-McMahon correspondences, between the British and the Arabs, specify that if the Arabs help the British defeat the Ottomans, the British promise to support the Arabs' request for independence after World War I. At the same time, the British negotiate the Sykes-Picot agreement with the French, which divides up the Middle East between the French and the British. The country known as "Syria" encompasses today's Syria, Lebanon, Israel, and Jordan.

1917 The Balfour Declaration by the British states that Great Britain favors the establishment of a national home for the Jewish people in Palestine.

1920 The San Remo Peace Conference gives Britain a mandate over Palestine, Transjordan (known as Jordan, today), and Mesopotamia (modern day Iraq). The French receive control of Lebanon and Syria.

1947 The U.N. General Assembly votes to partition Palestine between the Jews and the Arabs.

1948 David Ben-Gurion declares the creation of the state of Israel. The following day, the first Arab-Israeli war begins. When it ends, Israel has more land that it started with—and more than was promised them under the U.N. resolution.

1949 Syria signs an armstice agreement with Israel.

1966 A radical faction of the Ba'ath party comes to power. Egypt enters into a defensive pact with Syria.

1967 The Six-Day War.

1970 Jordan has thousands of Palestinian refugees within its borders—some conducting raids on Israel—and Israel retaliates. In "Black September," King Hussein massacres three thousand Palestinians and expels thousands of others.

1973 The 1973 (Yom Kippur) War.

1975 Civil war erupts in Lebanon.

1975–99 Negotiations proceed slowly and sporadically.

1999 Newly elected Israeli president Ehud Barak enters negotiations with Syrian's foreign minister Farouk al Shara.

2000 Israel unilaterally withdraws from Lebanon.

In 1948 Syria opposed the creation of Israel, perceiving it as part of a Western plot to maintain regional domination and divide the Arabs. Syria also participated in the first Arab-Israeli war, fought to control the area allotted to Palestinians under the 1947 United Nations partition and to prevent Transjordan (now Jordan) from acquiring the land. The 1947 U.N. partition divided Palestine between Israel and the Palestinians, providing an independent state for each. The war resulted in Israel, Egypt and Jordan occupying the territories designated for the Palestinians. Syria signed an armistice (peace agreement) with Israel in July 1949. Israel hoped this pact would lead to a permanent border settlement. Syria, however, was not interested in peace with Israel, although some scholars argue that there were missed opportunities for agreements. In May 1949, Husni Za'im, Syria's leader, offered to meet with the Israelis to discuss settling some Palestinian refugees in his country. Israel's prime minister, David Ben-Gurion, rejected the overture by attaching stringent conditions to any preliminary discussions.

Hostilities between the two countries continued to mount during the 1950s. A key source of tension involved the demilitarized zone (DMZ) created by the agreements of the late 1940s. Both states interpreted the legal standing of the DMZ differently. Israel insisted that it ruled the zone, while Syria maintained that neither party had freedom of movement, and the matter remained a point of contention. In addition, many disagreements stemmed from fishing rights in the Sea of Galilee (Lake Tiberias). There were several tense incidents in which Syria fired on Israeli fishermen from the Golan Heights. Likewise, tension mounted when Israeli patrol vessels tried to prevent Syrian use of the lake. The United Nations attempted to resolve the disputes, but hostilities continued.

MAP OF SYRIA AND ISRAEL. *(XNR Productions Inc.)*

Competition for resources intensified during the 1960s. Since water is scarce in the Middle East, improper use of it by any party involved can lead to all-out fighting. When Israel began to pump water from the Sea of Galilee, the Syrians constructed diversion canals to prevent the water from reaching the Jewish state. Viewing the struggle over water as crucial to its survival, Israel retaliated by bombing Syria.

Previously, in 1955, the United States sponsored a plan to regulate water use between Jordan and Israel. The Johnston plan, named for the American emissary Eric Johnston, established a method for both states to share Jordan River waters to irrigate their fields. Jordan rejected the proposal, believing that its acceptance would connote recognition of Israel. Israel, however, decided to build a national water carrier and utilize the water allocated to it under the plan. By tapping into the Jordan waters, Israel energized and united the Arab states against it. In 1963 Syria called on other Arab countries to compel Israel to end its water diversion efforts. A year later, Egypt's president, Gamal Abd al-Nasser, invited Arab heads of state to Cairo to discuss diverting the tributaries of the river, thereby halting Israel's construction of its national water carrier. These actions were precursors to the Six-Day War between Israel and its neighbors in 1967.

Internal Syrian politics also had an impact on the outbreak of the Six-Day War. In 1966 a more radical faction of the Ba'ath Party, also known as the Arab Socialist Renaissance Party, came to power in Syria. This new faction, headed by Saleh Jadid, espoused the idea of Arab nationalism, which called for a single Arab political community. Under this ideology, the presence of a Jewish state in the midst of this region was untenable. Under Jadid's leadership, Syria established itself as one of the most radical nations in the Middle East. It advocated war with Israel to regain control of the whole of Palestine and led the attempt to divert the Jordan River's tributaries. To help achieve its goal of destroying Israel, Syria armed various factions of the Palestinian Liberation Organization (PLO) and allowed Palestinian guerrillas to launch attacks on Israel from its territory. A connection between Fatah, the main branch of the PLO, and the ruling Ba'ath Party greatly facilitated terrorist and guerrilla raids from Syria. Border infiltration continued despite Israeli warnings of retribution.

At the same time, Egypt feared that Jadid would pull it into a war for which it was unprepared. Not only was the USSR withholding weapons that Egypt required to engage Israel but Egyptian troops were also involved in Yemen's civil war. To restrain Syria, Nasser entered into a defensive pact with officials in Damascus, the capital of Syria, in November 1966. Yet hostilities between Israel and Syria continued, involving infractions in the DMZ, Palestinian raids from Syrian territory, and Israeli reprisals. In April 1967 Israel shot down six Syrian planes during an aerial battle, thereby intensifying the already strained situation. Syria had hoped that, in light of their defensive pact, Egypt would respond, but it did not. From Israel's perspective, the march to war was becoming inevitable.

Six-Day War

According to Israel, Syria's aggressive actions contributed greatly to its decision to execute a preemptive strike on June 5, 1967. Yet global politics also played a large role in the outbreak of the Six-Day War. By supporting Syria with money, arms and advisers, the Soviets hoped that Jadid would establish a communist state. However, Jadid's unstable regime concerned the Soviets, who worried about losing a key Middle Eastern client. They knew that his actions—including allowing Palestinian raids to originate from Syrian territory—would provoke massive Israeli retaliations, ones that Jadid could not repel. The Russians thus concluded that to maintain their influence they needed to curb Israel's propensity to retaliate.

By encouraging a military alliance between Egypt and Syria, the Russians theorized that Israel would think twice before bombing Syria and destabilizing an already tenuous regime. According to the Soviets, the Israelis would presume that reprisal raids against Syria would provoke an Egyptian response. Hence, the Soviets pushed for the defense pact between Syria and Egypt. When Egypt did not respond to the aerial battle in April, the Soviets passed false information to the Egyptians claiming that Israel was amassing troops on the Syrian border. Unfortunately, the USSR's attempt to prevent increased fighting instead led directly to it. President Nasser acted on the information believing that, in the event of hostilities, he would have full Soviet support. He removed U.N. forces from Egyptian soil, closed the Gulf of Aqaba to Israeli shipping, and called for Israel's destruction. Israel, prepared for quick action against any Arab threat to its sovereignty, was aware of Egypt's intent and launched a devastating preemptive strike on Egypt and Syria. This strike, coupled with Israel's defeat of Jordan when that nation also joined the war, shattered Arab confidence.

Despite the U.N.'s demand for a cease-fire, Israel continued fighting until it had captured the Golan Heights on June 10. Following the war, Israel controlled Jordan's West Bank, Egypt's Sinai Peninsula and Gaza Strip, and Syria's Golan Heights. Controlling the latter allowed the Jewish state full access to the Sea of Galilee and the Banyas, an important water source. As soon as the fighting ceased, the Soviets attempted to push a resolution through the U.N. General Assembly finding Israel the aggressor in the war and calling for a return of all lands taken during the fighting. Approval of this resolution by the United Nations would have meant an unconditional withdrawal of Israeli troops from the occupied lands. The Israelis, convinced they needed to retain the territories as bargaining chips for a comprehensive peace with the Arabs, considered unconditional withdrawal out of the question.

Over time, Syria hardened its position and refused any diplomatic solution. In August 1967 Syria boycotted a meeting of Arab nations in Khartoum, Sudan, to discuss the results of the war. Arab leaders resolved that they would not negotiate directly with Israel, make peace, or recognize Israel, although they did agree that a political solution was acceptable. By contrast, the Israelis were adamant that direct negotiations with the Arab states were the path to peace. Despite this, Israel further entrenched itself in the disputed territories. It built settlements, deported suspected terrorists, and annexed East Jerusalem.

In November 1967 the United Nations finally passed Resolution 242, calling for the withdrawal of Israel from the "territories occupied in the recent conflict" and "respect for and acknowledgement of the sovereignty, territorial integrity and political independence of every state in the area." This resolution has since become the basis for all negotiations between Israel and the Arab states.

The 1973 War (Yom Kippur War)

The Soviets began rearming Syria and Egypt almost immediately after the Six-Day War and the United States sent new weapons to Israel. Although the United States and the Soviet Union recognized the need to contain a Middle East war from erupting into a superpower conflict, the growing arms race was pushing them in that direction. The race abated somewhat after the U.S.-Soviet détente or "easing of tensions" in the early 1970s. This thaw in superpower relations convinced the Egyptians that resolution of the Middle East conflict was losing importance.

When Egyptian president Anwar Sadat assumed power in 1970, he improved the Egyptian army to resuscitate interest in the region and to retain a military option to recapture the occupied territories. Part of his plan involved a Syrian attack on Israel from its northern border. Syrian president Hafez Assad, who had assumed power in 1970, was willing to use force to regain the Golan Heights. Yet both Egypt and Syria recognized waning Soviet support in the early 1970s and attempted to court the United States by moderating their stance toward Israel. But the lukewarm American response frustrated the Arab states. Egypt decided to pursue its military option.

On October 6, 1973, Egypt and Syria initiated a surprise attack against Israel on two fronts. Israel came dangerously close to losing this war until an American airlift replenished ammunition. Israel retained control of the territories it had acquired during the 1967 war and advanced further into the Golan. The United States orchestrated disengagement agreements at the end of this most recent conflict andconvinced Israel to withdraw from part of the Golan Heights in return for a U.N. buffer zone. Moreover, Syria's Assad agreed to curtail Palestinian guerrilla attacks from his country. From 1973 until 1982, Israel's border with Syria was its most quiet. Although the war was not a military victory for the Arabs, it was a political and psychological one. Israel was no longer viewed as the unbeatable military force it was following the 1967 war.

The Lebanese Connection

The Syrian-Israeli conflict is intricately connected to events in Lebanon, as is the Palestinian-Israeli conflict. Oftentimes Israel and Syria have played out their conflicts within Lebanon, a nation that was embroiled in civil war for many years and a country to which many Palestinians fled after the formation of Israel. As opposed to fighting in their own lands, Israel and Syria often used Lebanon as their battleground. Both countries invaded the infrastructurally weak Lebanon in an attempt to maintain a balance of power. Israel withdrew its troops from Lebanon at the end of May 2000, hoping to forge a lasting peace with both Syria and Lebanon.

As Syria and Israel fought on Lebanese land, Palestinian guerrillas continued to use border countries to launch attacks against Israel. When the Israelis successfully quashed the PLO activities emanating from the West Bank and Gaza by the late 1960s, many of the guerrillas went to other Arab nations to carry out their assaults—Jordan was a popular choice. The Israelis, who were not interested in a full-fledged war with Jordan, conducted reprisal raids to counter guerrilla activities launched there and sent its leader, King Hussein, the message that attacks from within his state were his responsibility. Eventually Jordan concluded that the price of allowing the Palestinian guerrillas to remain in its territory was too great. In 1970 Jordan's intolerance of the Palestinian situation culminated in Black September, during which King Hussein massacred three thousand Palestinians and expelled thousands of others.

It was not simply Israel's military undertakings into Jordanian territory that prompted Jordan to rid itself of its Palestinian population. Hussein was apprehensive about the growing number and increasing power of the Palestinians within his kingdom. He feared they would eventually gain control of his country. As a consequence of Jordan's action, the PLO required another country from which to initiate its attacks against Israel. The most logical choice was Lebanon, which had a weak, decentralized government and conveniently bordered Israel. Prior to Black September, there had been a large buildup of guerrillas in Lebanon. This increase, most noticeable in 1969, led the Israelis to suspect that the insurgents were looking to establish a new base. Palestinians continued to attack Israel from Lebanon and send terrorists to infiltrate its northern border. Israel responded with reprisal raids, creating more tension between the Christian-dominated Lebanese government and the Palestinians.

In 1975 a civil war erupted in Lebanon. Although the causes of the war are multifaceted, it was primarily a war between Christian and Muslim factions vying for power. The French, who had controlled the area earlier, had established a gov-

ernment in which Christians held the majority of power. With demographic changes, Sunni and Shiite Muslims grew in number and demanded a proportional change in authority. Many Muslims, along with the Palestinians, felt excluded from public life. As such, the PLO sided with the Muslims. When Syria sent troops to Lebanon in 1976, it supported the existing Christian-dominated government. Initially Syria objected to any action that strengthened the PLO, since that would have lessened its control over the organization. Furthermore, Syria feared that an unstable Lebanon would invite an Israeli invasion. When a cease-fire was worked out, a group of Arab states authorized a deterrent force to keep the peace. The force was dominated by Syrian troops. Although the Syrians had supported the Christians, they eventually made alliances with certain factions of the PLO and the Muslims.

Syrian fears about Israeli interference were warranted. Israel began training and arming some of the predominantly Christian Lebanese militias. It also allowed the Christians in the south of the country to work and trade in Israel; more importantly, Israel warned Syria to stay out of southern Lebanon. This had the obvious effect of dividing the country between Syria and Israel. Syria had placed surface-to-air missiles in Lebanon, and despite Israel's warnings, refused to remove them. As the PLO continued its attacks from Lebanon, Israel retaliated by bombing Palestinian strongholds. In 1978 Israel entered Lebanon to create a security zone and only withdrew its troops reluctantly after the United Nations sent a buffer force. This withdrawal was to be short-lived. After frequent rocket attacks on its northern towns, Israel invaded Lebanon again in 1982. Although Israel's stated goal was to push the PLO out of southern Lebanon, its undeclared aim likely was to destroy the organization. As such, the Israeli military continued all the way into Beirut to battle PLO forces. During this incursion, Israel destroyed many of the Syrian missile encampments that had so concerned it. The United States attempted to get the parties involved to agree to a withdrawal and to disarm the militia groups but it was not until 1985 that Israel decided to pull out of Lebanon. Even then it retained troops and influence in its buffer zone in the south. Syria also remained fully entrenched in the country with thirty-five thousand troops.

In 1991, while much of the world focused on the Gulf War, Syria signed the Treaty of Cooperation and Brotherhood with Lebanon, allowing Syria control over Lebanon's internal security and foreign affairs. Israeli prime minister, Yizthak Sha-

SOLDIERS PASS BY THE REMAINS OF A SYRIAN TANK, A REMNANT OF THE SIX-DAY WAR. *(Corbis. Reproduced by permission.)*

mir, was aware of Syria's quiet takeover of Lebanon. Shamir continued to finance the South Lebanon Army in the hopes of using the Christian militia to enforce the Israeli security zone in the south of the country.

Peace Process: Madrid

In August 1990 Iraq's president Saddam Hussein ordered an invasion of Kuwait. A U.S.-led coalition forced Iraq to withdraw from its tiny neighbor. After the Gulf War of 1991, the U.S. government pressed Israel and the Arab states to attend an international peace conference. The goal of the meetings was to begin to develop a comprehensive peace settlement and bring closure to the Arab-Israeli conflict. The United States believed that its new credibility after the Gulf War, especially among Arab states, would enable it to play a significant role in the negotiations. Bringing Syria into the discussions was a challenge but eventually changes in the global arena coupled with the newly-won status of the United States proved successful. With the collapse of the Soviet Union Syria lost a major financial backer and thus sought a warmer relationship with the United States. As such, the U.S. government was able to coax Syria to the Middle East Peace Conference by threatening to "cool" relations if it did not attend. Additionally, the United States encouraged the wealthier nations

of the Persian Gulf to send financial aid to Syria. Israel also needed significant prodding to join the conference. By linking aid to participation in the conference, the United States pressured Israeli Prime Minister Shamir to attend. Notwithstanding U.S. urging, Israel also believed that Arab attendance at an international conference would mean the recognition of Israel's existence.

The conference had several tracks. It consisted of a multilateral track where the parties involved discussed major issues including the division of resources, arms control, environmental questions, refugees, and economic development. The second track was a bilateral one that included direct negotiations between Syria and Israel. Syria refused to participate in the multilateral talks until some progress was made on the bilateral level. Israel also boycotted several of the multilateral working groups because Palestinians from outside the West Bank and Gaza were participating. Shifting the stance of Arab-Israeli relations from angry rhetoric, armed attacks and reprisals was an arduous task.

After Israel's election of Prime Minister Yitzhak Rabin in 1992, the negotiations advanced slowly. Rabin indicated that he would be willing to give back some or all of the Golan Heights in return for a normalization of relations. Despite this announcement, the talks did not proceed, as Syria

ORTHODOX JEWS PROTEST ISRAEL'S NEGOTIATIONS WITH SYRIA OVER A POSSIBLE WITHDRAWAL FROM THE GOLAN HEIGHTS. *(AP/Wide World Photos. Reproduced by permission.)*

demanded Israel's full withdrawal from the Golan Heights before it would discuss its definition of "peace." Again, there was minimal movement on bilateral talks.

Another challenge to the peace process occurred in 1993 when Israel's northern border saw increased violence. Hizballah, or "Party of God," armed by Iran, continued to attack Israeli soldiers and their allies in its security zone in southern Lebanon. Israel retaliated harshly, causing many civilians to flee their homes. The United States entered into negotiations to establish a cease-fire. Because Syria controlled supply routes to Hizballah, the United States and Israel were convinced that without Syrian acquiescence, Hizballah would not be restrained. Therefore, U.S. Secretary of State Warren Christopher shuttled back and forth between Syria and Israel to convince both sides to restrain Hizballah. With a cease-fire in place, the groups looked forward to another round of talks.

RECENT HISTORY AND THE FUTURE

Israeli Prime Minister Yitzhak Rabin's Labor Party brought with it a new approach to the peace process. During his tenure, Syria recognized the

opportunity for negotiations. Syria received messages from Rabin that Israel would be willing to return the Golan Heights if it received proper assurances regarding security but a peace treaty remained illusive.

When Rabin was assassinated in 1995 by a Jewish extremist, the new prime minister, Shimon Peres, attempted to keep the negotiations alive. However, after the 1996 election of a more right-wing Israeli prime minister, Benjamin Netanyahu, optimism for a settlement with Syria faded. The Likud Party assumed power and was less inclined to make a deal with the Syrians than was the Labor Party. A four-year break in the negotiations between Israel and Syria followed.

After Israeli Prime Minister Ehud Barak assumed power in 1999, Israel and Syria resolved to restart talks, hoping to finalize an agreement by July 2000. Still, Syrian leader Assad refused to consider normalization of relations with Israel until he was guaranteed a full return of the Golan Heights. He seemed less interested in diplomatic or economic ties than in regaining Syria's lost territory.

Ehud Barak entered negotiations with Syria's foreign minister, Farouk al Shara. Syria insisted that the negotiations take place with the United States serving as intermediary. The talks broke down quickly when the Israeli press leaked a working paper prepared by the United States on the status of the talks. The paper described Israel's view of maintaining some settlers in the Golan Heights even after a treaty was signed. Syria believed that its acceptance of this position would be seen as a capitulation to Israeli demands, and was unwilling to go further.

After negotiations stalled, Syria, angered by the press leak, allegedly gave permission for Hizballah to carry out attacks on Israeli soldiers in its security zone in southern Lebanon. For Syria, continued Israeli occupation of Lebanon would allow it a key bargaining chip. It could offer to restrain violent activity on Israel's northern border as part of a deal for the Golan Heights. A unilateral withdrawal would rob Syria of this leverage.

Yet that is exactly what Barak decided to do. With the suspension of Israeli-Syrian talks, he declared that Israel would withdraw from southern Lebanon in July 2000. He had hoped that an exit from Lebanon would help restart peace negotiations with Syria. As opposed to viewing this as a step in the right direction, however, the other Arab states responded negatively to Israel's announcement. They said they could not ensure the safety of Israeli troops as they withdrew and could not restrain Hizballah and PLO factions from continuing to launch attacks from that border. Again, Syrian and Israeli talks appeared deadlocked. Israel continued with its plan and withdrew its troops from southern Lebanon by the end of May, earlier than expected. Although Israeli troops made it out of Lebanon safely, the situation remained tense.

In June 2000, shortly after the Israeli withdrawal from Lebanon, Syrian leader Hafez Assad died, stalling any further peace talks indefinitely. Assad was succeeded by his son, Bashar Assad. Young and politically inexperienced, yet reportedly more liberal than his father, Bashar will have to consolidate his power before turning an eye toward negotiating a solid and lasting peace with Israel. Crucial issues remain to be resolved, including the creation of new borders, access to resources, and the normalization of relations. The fate of seventeen thousand Jewish settlers is also in question.

Negotiations with Syria have proven more intractable than those with other Arab states. Israel signed a peace treaty with the Palestinians in 1993, followed by an agreement with the Jordan in 1994. Although Hafez Assad wanted to regain control of the Golan Heights, he was not willing to compromise on many issues. He expected Israel to commit to a full return of the territory before negotiating security arrangements. This position could change under Bashar Assad. For its part, Israel wants specific security pacts before agreeing to final borders, as it views the delineating of borders impossible without also considering security issues. From its perspective, boundaries differ depending upon the type of security arrangements. For example, Israel wants to guarantee its security by maintaining control over all of the Sea of Galilee while Syria has insisted on a return to pre-1967 borders, granting it access to the Sea. Israel's reluctance to return to pre-1967 borders without alterations likely stems from its earlier confrontations with Syria over rights in the Sea of Galilee.

The United States remains committed to helping both sides come to an agreement. Since Syria has refused to speak with the Israel without the presence of a third party, the United States maintains a large role in the process. Several proposals have been discussed regarding security for Israel and Syria. One thought is that a special U.N. force be stationed between Israel and Syria. Others have argued that the United States should provide monitoring or troops as a buffer between the two. As yet, none of the proposals has proven sufficient for the two parties.

Although the idea of a peace treaty is attractive, especially since other Arab states have concluded agreements, it seems increasingly likely that Israel and Syria will not find common ground. In that case, it is incumbent upon both sides to maintain the "no war, no peace" situation that has existed since 1973. Since Israel has withdrawn from Lebanon, it is in Syria's interest to assist in maintaining a tranquil border with Israel. Through its attacks on northern Israel, Hizballah has attempted to draw both Syria and Israel into a war. Another round of fighting would be costly in lives and finances for both sides, not to mention the possibility of unleashing unconventional, destructive weapons, such as biological or chemical weapons. Ultimately peace is an option in the best interests of both nations.

BIBLIOGRAPHY

Bickerston, Ian J. and Carla L. Klausner. *A Concise History of the Arab-Israeli Conflict.* 2d ed. Upper Saddle River, N.J.: Prentice-Hall, 1995.

Khouri, Fred. *The Arab-Israeli Dilemma.* 2d ed. Syracuse, N.Y.: Syracuse University Press, 1976.

Rabinovich, Itamar. *The Brink of Peace: The Israeli-Syrian Negotiations.* Princeton, N.J.: Princeton University Press, 1999.

Rubenstein, Alvin, ed. *The Arab-Israeli Conflict: Perspectives.* 2d ed. New York: HarperCollins Publishers, 1991.

Safran, Nadav. *Israel: The Embattled Ally.* Cambridge, Mass.: Harvard University Press, Belknap Press 1981.

Seale, Patrick. *Assad of Syria: The Struggle for the Middle East.* Berkeley, Calif.: University of California Press, 1989.

Smith, Charles D. *Palestine and the Arab-Israeli Conflict.* 3rd ed. New York: St. Martin's, 1996.

Ruth Margolies Beitler

Taiwan and China: Unification and Nationalism

The Conflict

Taiwan was once part of China; more recently, Taiwan was ruled by Japan. During the Communist revolution in China, nationalist forces retreated to Taiwan. Taiwan has acted as an independent country since that time. With a tradition of capitalism and orientation to the West, Taiwan does not want to be subjected to China. China claims the right to the province, resulting in threats of war.

Political

- China believes Taiwan is simply a renegade province that must be brought in line.

- Taiwan does not want to be subjected to China and China's limitations on political choices, free speech, and free travel.

Economic

- Taiwan is much more developed than China and has a tradition of capitalism.

- Taiwan would like access to the large Chinese market, and to be able to develop businesses in China.

In the early spring of 2000, Taiwan voters gathered to elect a new president. While the campaigning was generally peaceful, Taiwan watchers in mainland China became increasingly concerned. Although leaders in the Chinese capital of Beijing maintained an official neutrality toward the Taiwan elections, China's state-run newspapers made it very clear that Chen Shui-bian (Chen Shuibian), the favored candidate, was unacceptable and encouraged voters to reject him. Chen had previously challenged Beijing's long-held belief that Taiwan was a renegade province of China that would eventually be united, either peacefully or through force, with the "motherland." Top Chinese officials believed that by electing Chen, Taiwan voters would, in effect, approve his pro-independence platform. Mahlon Larmer and Brook Meyer reported the warnings of China's prime minister, Zhu Rongji, to Taiwan voters in "Moment of Truth," "the Chinese people [were] ready to shed blood and sacrifice their lives defending the sovereignty and the territorial integrity of the motherland." Chen's rivals in Taiwan attempted to capitalize on the resulting fear, claiming that if Chen was elected, the cold relationship between Taiwan and the mainland would heat up considerably.

Despite such rhetoric, thirty-nine percent of Taiwan's electorate voted for Chen Shui-bian, enough to defeat his political rivals. Immediately upon winning the election, Chen offered an olive branch to authorities in Beijing. "In the future we will use the most positive and friendly gestures to build a constructive dialogue with Mainland China," president-elect Chen declared, adding that "peace and security in the Taiwan Strait is our goal, our promise...and our hope" (Larmer and Meyer 2000).

CHRONOLOGY

1683 Taiwan is effectively subjected to Chinese control.

1885 Taiwan is made a province of China.

1895 Taiwan is ceded to Japan following the Sino-Japanese War.

1911 Sun Yat-sen's Kuomintang party (KMT, Guomindang, or "Nationalists") overthrows the last Chinese emperor, hoping to establish the Republic of China (ROC).

1927 Chiang Kai-shek, Sun's successor, militarily unites the country under Kuomintang rule.

1937 The Kuomintang and the Chinese Communist Party (CCP) unite to fight against the Japanese invasion.

1945 The Japanese are defeated and Taiwan returns to Chinese control.

1946 Despite their cooperation battling against the Japanese, Chiang's KMT troops begin fighting with Mao Zedong's CCP troops.

1947 The KMT-appointed governor of Taiwan launches a ruthless suppression of Taiwanese dissidents. Thousands are killed.

1949 Chiang and his ROC troops retreat to the island of Taiwan. Mao establishes the People's Republic of China (PRC) on the mainland. Both sides see the cessation of hostilities as temporary.

1950 Engulfed in the Korean War, the United States send the Seventh Fleet to protect Taiwan from a mainland attack.

1953 The United States and the ROC sign a mutual defense pact.

1964 China detonates its first atomic bomb.

1966 Mao launches the Cultural Revolution, creating chaos in China that lasts for the next decade.

1971 President Nixon announces his intention to travel to Beijing. China joins the United Nations and Taiwan is expelled. Various nations sever their diplomatic ties with the ROC.

1975 Chiang dies. His son, Chiang Ching-kuo (Jiang Jingguo) succeeds him.

1976 Mao dies. Deng Xiaoping eventually emerges as the political leader of the People's Republic.

1979 The United States recognizes the PRC and severs ties with the ROC.

1984 Beijing and London agree to terms for the return of Hong Kong to Chinese control.

1988 Chiang Ching-kuo dies and Lee Teng-hui (Li Denghui) assumes Taiwan's presidency.

1989 Student demonstrators in Beijing's Tiananmen Square are brutally suppressed.

1996 During presidential elections in Taiwan, China holds military exercises in the Taiwan Straits. Lee is reelected president in Taiwan.

1997 Hong Kong returns to Chinese control. The same year, Deng Xiaoping dies and Jiang Zemin becomes the leading political figure in China.

2000 Lee steps down from Taiwan presidency. Taiwanese pro-independence candidate Chen Shui-bian is elected.

The furor coinciding with the election of Chen Shui-bian is just the most recent example of the tenuous and volatile relationship between Taiwan and the People's Republic of China (PRC). To appreciate the importance of these recent events, it is necessary to understand the contentious history between these two entities over the past several decades.

HISTORICAL BACKGROUND

Taiwan's History to 1945

Taiwan's relationship with China has always been tenuous. The island of Taiwan covers an area of 13,844 square miles and lies approximately one hundred miles off the southeast coast of China. As early as the seventh century, immigrants from the mainland began moving to the island. It was not until 1683, however, that Taiwan came under the control of court authorities in Beijing, and in 1885 the island became an official province of the mainland government. By that time, the people of Taiwan had developed linguistic, religious, and social systems distinct from the mainland.

Chinese rule over the province, however, was short-lived. Following Japan's 1895 defeat of China in the first Sino-Japanese War, Japan took control of Taiwan. For the next fifty years, Taiwan was a Japanese colony. During this period the residents of the island learned Japanese, integrated their economy with Japan's, and increased their cultural differences from the mainland. By 1945 most people living in Taiwan had a rather limited knowledge of China.

China's History to 1949

With the defeat of the Japanese and the end of World War II, Taiwan reverted to Chinese rule. By that time, however, the political situation in China was chaotic and unpredictable. In 1911 Sun Yat-sen (Sun Yixian) and his revolutionary followers had overthrown the last Chinese emperor, bringing an end to more than two millennia of dynastic control. Sun's political party, the Kuomintang (KMT, Guomindang, or "Nationalists"), established the Republic of China (ROC) in 1912. Sun never obtained effective control over the country, as regional military leaders, or "warlords," ignored his authority and expanded their power within their respective regions. Consequently, the nation fell into a prolonged state of fragmentation and chaos.

Though Sun died in 1925, his revolutionary party survived under the guidance of its premier military leader, Chiang Kai-shek (Jiang Jieshi). Chiang soon realized that to unite the entire country under KMT control he would have to rely on the help of other competing parties, especially the Chinese Communist Party (CCP). Under the influence of Mao Zedong (Mao Tse-tung), the CCP had grown in power and prestige, particularly in China's rural countryside. Though the CCP agreed to assist Chiang and the Nationalists in forming a unified state, cooperation between the two sides was never complete, as mistrust and suspicion colored the relationship. In 1928 Chiang succeeded in unifying the country and established a new capital in Nanjing. By that time he had decided to turn against the CCP, and for much of the next decade Chiang attempted to eradicate the vestiges of communism from China. Chiang's actions forced Mao and his band of followers to temporarily abandon

national politics and retreat instead to an isolated and barren area around the northwest city of Yen'an (Yunan).

The 1937 Japanese invasion of China provided a respite for the CCP in its battle against Chiang and the Kuomintang. Faced with a common enemy, the CCP and the KMT agreed to set aside their differences, form a new united front, and wage total war against the Japanese invaders. During the course of the war both Chiang and Mao's troops suffered losses, but because the CCP used a guerrilla style of warfare, its losses were not as significant as the KMT's. Furthermore, Mao retained control of vast areas in northwest China, while Chiang retreated far up the Yangzi River valley.

After eight years of fighting, and with the assistance of the United States, the combined Chinese forces defeated the Japanese military. The Japanese not only evacuated the Chinese mainland, they also surrendered control over their Taiwan colony. Both the CCP and the KMT rushed to occupy formerly Japanese-held positions, realizing that the old antagonisms separating the two sides would soon reemerge. While Mao and his Communists spread through the countryside, Chiang's forces gained control of virtually every major city. The Kuomintang also moved in and took control of the island of Taiwan.

Not all of the island's residents welcomed the return of Taiwan to China. Kuomintang officials treated the Taiwanese as conquered subjects who should be grateful for their liberation from Japan. Corruption and inefficiency eroded support for the newly arrived Chinese authorities and in February 1947 antigovernment riots broke out. Kuomintang soldiers responded by firing into the ranks of the Taiwanese demonstrators, killing many. For the next several weeks, the KMT-appointed governor suppressed all opposition, arresting and executing thousands of Taiwan's important leaders.

Kuomintang leadership suffered the same fate on the Chinese mainland. Skyrocketing inflation, rampant corruption, and a failure to push for rural reform all weakened the prestige of Chiang's government. American mediators tried to convince Chiang to broker an agreement with the competing Communists, but Chiang refused. By mid-1946, civil war appeared inevitable.

Although the KMT had every military advantage, the civil war quickly turned in the Communists' favor. Chiang's demoralized troops were no match for Mao's inspired forces, and in 1949 the Communist armies captured city after city as the

CHIANG KAI-SHEK

1887–1975 Chiang Kai-shek, the leader of the Nationalist Chinese Party (Kuomintang), was born in the Zhejiang Province in 1887. He received his military education in China and in Tokyo, where he joined the Kuomintang. Chiang's education continued in the Soviet Union; upon his return to China he was appointed as head of China's most prestigious military academy, and in 1926 took control of the Nationalist Army. In 1927, Chiang married Soong Mei-ling, a graduate of Wellesley College in Massachusetts, and shortly thereafter converted to Christianity.

Chiang established the National Government of China in 1928. His attempts to improve and consolidate economic and political institutions were thwarted by the Japanese invasion of China in 1931. To defend China, the Nationalists united with the Communists (led by Mao Zedong) in 1937; Chiang assumed full military power as Generalissimo. After the defeat of Japan in 1945, the Nationalists and the Communists fought for power within China. By the end of 1949, Chiang and the Nationalist Army had been driven from the Chinese mainland to the island of Taiwan. There, Chiang established Taipei as his capital, and took full military and civil control, serving as president until his death in 1975.

CHIANG KAI-SHEK. *(Library of Congress)*

KMT retreated further to the south. Faced with certain defeat, Chiang and two million of his supporters fled the mainland to the island of Taiwan, where they hoped they could regroup, strengthen their forces, and eventually return to reengage the CCP. Recognizing that total victory was imminent, Mao declared the founding of the People's Republic of China (PRC) on October 1, 1949.

Various factors explain the failure of Chiang's KMT forces in China. Corruption, inflation, and the military's abuse of the peasantry all combined to undermine public confidence in the Nationalists' army. Large sections of the urban middle class that had been the backbone of the Kuomintang organization eventually deserted Chiang's regime. On the other hand, rural reform, an appeal to nationalism, and an efficient administration helped sway millions to the Communists' cause. For these reasons, the CCP achieved a stunning victory despite staggering odds and with little international assistance.

China–Taiwan relations, 1949–1971

After arriving in Taiwan, Chiang quickly reestablished the structure of the Republic of China (ROC), which claimed to be the official government of China in exile. Owing to the 1947 clash between the KMT army and local citizens, relations between the newly arrived "mainlanders" and the long-settled "Taiwanese" remained tense. Nonetheless, they viewed the situation as only temporary, since both the Communist government in Beijing and the Kuomintang government in Taiwan vowed to renew hostilities at the earliest possible moment.

With the outbreak of the Korean War in 1950, Taiwan-China relations took a new turn. Dedicated to "containing" communism in Asia, U.S. policymakers determined to protect Taiwan at all costs. Consequently, President Harry Truman ordered the U.S. Navy Seventh Fleet to patrol the Taiwan Straits against any possible Communist

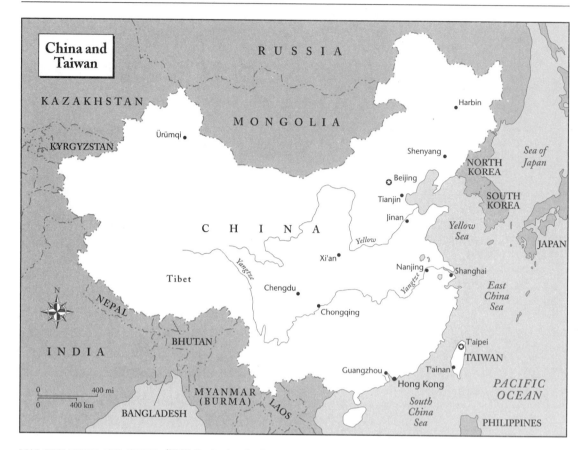

MAP OF TAIWAN AND CHINA. *(XNR Productions Inc.)*

invasion. Additionally, the United States sent Chiang's regime military supplies and economic aid. It did not take long for the Taiwan government to assemble an impressive fighting force of more than six hundred thousand men. In 1953 U.S.-ROC cooperation became official as the two sides signed a mutual defense pact. While small-scale fighting continued on the tiny offshore islands in the Taiwan Straits, all participating parties understood that such activities did not represent a serious threat to the status quo. In fact, the shelling of the islands eventually slackened to an every-other-day schedule, with each side civilly taking a turn firing upon the other. By the end of the 1950s, what was originally a temporary divide between the PRC and the ROC seemed much more permanent.

This "competing Chinas" predicament had obvious international ramifications. Leaders in both Beijing and Taiwan insisted that their respective regime was the legitimate government for all of China. Therefore, members of the international community had to choose whether they would recognize the PRC or the ROC. The U.S. government, with its anti-Communist stand, chose to rec-

ognize Chiang's power in Taiwan, exchanging diplomats and other high-level representatives. Most U.S. allies also established ties with the ROC, while the Communist-bloc countries forged ties with the PRC. With the assistance of its allies, the United States impeded the mainland government from taking a seat in the United Nations, reserving it instead for Chiang's delegate from Taiwan. For over twenty years, until 1971, the United States succeeded in blocking the PRC's entry into the United Nations. Beyond the question of U.N. representation, the existence of "two Chinas" created confusion and embarrassment at virtually every international gathering, from scholarly conferences to the Olympic games.

Besides shoring up its international position, ROC leaders sought to govern the local Taiwanese population effectively. To this end, they adopted a two-pronged approach. First, they hoped to create a loyal citizenry through education and propaganda. They then enforced this loyalty with martial law. Government officials allowed no dissension as they quickly disbanded all competing political parties and imprisoned the offending lead-

MAO ZEDONG

1893–1976 Mao Zedong, poet, philosopher, and leader of the Chinese Communists, was born in 1893 in Hunan province, into a peasant family. Although poor, Mao distinguished himself intellectually. In 1918 while working as a librarian, he became interested in Communism; in 1921 he and eleven others formed the Chinese Communist Party in Shanghai. In 1934 Mao led his forces on a six thousand mile trek, The Long March, to escape extermination campaigns that had been launched against them by the Nationalists. The journey gained Mao popular support, and molded the survivors into a disciplined force under his leadership.

After uniting during World War II to defend China, the Nationalists and Communists returned to their civil war after Japan's defeat. (During this time, Mao married former actress Jiang Qing.) After defeating the Nationalists in 1949, Chairman Mao began programs to expand agricultural and industrial production. After the failure of The Great Leap Forward, Mao resigned as Chairman of the People's Republic, although he maintained control of the Communist party. Throughout the 1960s, he encouraged young Red Guards to condemn Chinese who favored social changes. In the early 1970s, Mao met with several western leaders, which improved China's relations with non-Communist countries. Mao Zedong died in 1976, after a long illness.

MAO ZEDONG. *(UPI/Bettmann. Reproduced by permission.)*

ers. From the mid-1960s to the mid-1970s, ROC authorities arrested, detained, and tortured thousands of would-be protestors. Moreover, they limited freedom of the press and banned the dissemination of all Communist material.

Despite this heavy-handed approach, the KMT did make several notable concessions to the local population. The government increasingly allowed Taiwanese to fill local government positions and occasionally placed local-born individuals into the highest levels of the government, including the cabinet and the legislature. Effective economic planning, including progressive land reform programs and capital investment incentives, placated the island's inhabitants. At the beginning of the 1970s, the ROC benefited from an expanding economy and a stable government. Fewer and fewer Taiwanese were interested in retaking the mainland and the island continued to develop independently of PRC control.

China-Taiwan Relations, 1971–1988

Notwithstanding its apparent position of strength, the ROC's international standing disintegrated in the early 1970s. In the summer of 1971, U.S. president Richard Nixon announced that he would travel to Beijing and meet with leaders of the PRC. Within months of the announcement, U.N. delegates at the United Nations admitted the PRC to their organization. By this point, the chain reaction was unstoppable as nation after nation, including the United States, severed ties with the government in Taiwan and officially recognized the People's Republic. In each case, Beijing insisted that the PRC was the only legitimate government for China and bilateral agreements between Taiwan and other states were unacceptable. At the same time, officials reaffirmed their commitment to one day reunite the renegade Taiwan province with the mainland, though the United States encouraged the PRC to rely on peaceable means to accomplish this goal.

THE THREAT OF CHINESE MILITARY ACTION AGAINST IT HAS CAUSED TAIWAN TO INTENSIFY ITS MILITARY PREPAREDNESS AS IS EVIDENCED BY THESE TANK MANEUVERS. *(AP/Wide World Photos. Reproduced by permission.)*

Such a rapid turn of international events was certainly understandable, if not predictable. In the early 1970s, Taiwan's population was less than two percent of the PRC's. Furthermore, the continued military development of the PRC, including the detonation of an atomic bomb in 1964, made it impossible to ignore Beijing. Still, many in Taiwan were shocked and felt abandoned by the international community. By the mid-1980s only twenty-two countries maintained official ties with the ROC government in Taiwan.

During this period of international readjustment, the leadership of both the PRC and the ROC underwent fundamental changes. With the death of Chiang in 1975, followed the next year with the death of Mao, the first generation of the Chinese civil war came to a symbolic end. Both men had been committed to the eventual reunification of the nation, but it was left to their successors either to follow or abandon their plans.

Led by Deng Xiaoping, the next generation of PRC leaders continued to emphasize reunification with the ROC. They contended that the island of Taiwan, like the British colony of Hong Kong and the Portuguese colony of Macao, was an integral part of the Chinese nation-state waiting to be returned "to the motherland." In 1982 authorities in Beijing began negotiations with their counterparts

in London for the return of Hong Kong. Not wanting to upset the enormously profitable Hong Kong economy, PRC leaders promised to grant Hong Kong special administrative status for fifty years. They assured Hong Kongers that they would maintain the freedoms they were accustomed to, including freedom of the press, freedom of religion, and freedom of demonstration. They would also retain their own currency and membership in international organizations. Nevertheless, sovereignty, including the power to make foreign policy and maintain a defense force, would reside in Beijing. Shortly thereafter, PRC authorities made a similar "one country, two systems" proposal to the Portuguese colony of Macao, which followed Hong Kong's lead and accepted it.

This "one country, two systems" plan did not satisfy everyone. Still, Deng Xiaoping and other PRC leaders hoped it could be a model for the eventual return of Taiwan. Many Chinese patriots looked forward to the scheduled return of Hong Kong and Macao, while others saw these as merely preludes to the return of Taiwan. In Beijing's Tiananmen Square, workers set up a large clock, counting down the days, hours, and minutes leading to the return of Hong Kong. Next to the clock, bright banners proclaimed, "China is eagerly welcoming the return to the motherland of Hong Kong, Macao, and Taiwan." The successful and smooth transition of Hong Kong and Macao, officials believed, would reassure Taiwan's residents of the sincerity and magnanimity of China's offer.

Yet while the PRC was achieving stunning successes with Hong Kong and Macao, Chiang's successors in the ROC government were increasing the political and cultural divide between the island and the mainland. Under the direction of Chiang Ching-kuo (Jiang Jingguo), the son of Chiang Kai-shek and heir to the Kuomintang mantle, the Republic of China experienced remarkable changes. First, Chiang Ching-kuo actively sought to place Taiwanese in higher positions in the government and even groomed a local-born individual, Lee Teng-hui (Li Denghui) as his successor. To complement this "Taiwanization" policy, Chiang Ching-kuo reversed many of his regime's restrictive measures in the hope of creating a more liberal, democratic society. Indeed, before Chiang Ching-kuo's administration, Taiwan was similar to mainland China in regard to civil liberties and political participation. In 1987, Chiang Ching-kuo abolished martial law, allowing the residents of Taiwan to exercise the promised rights the government had for so long suspended. Simultaneously, "loyal opposition" parties came into existence. One of those new parties was the Democratic Progressive Party (DPP), which was dedicated to making Taiwan an independent state from China.

With the death of Chiang Ching-kuo on January 13, 1988, leadership of the ROC passed to the Taiwanese vice-president, Lee Teng-hui. The transition was smooth and relatively uneventful. Few international observers fully appreciated the significant changes Chiang had brought to Taiwan, and they could not predict the ramifications of these changes.

China-Taiwan Relations, 1988–2000

The inauguration of Lee Teng-hui in Taiwan represented a new era in ROC-PRC relations. During the early years of Lee's first term, interaction between Taiwan and the mainland flourished. After lifting the ban on cross-straits travel, hundreds of thousands of Taiwan's residents began visiting the PRC. Initially, Taiwan's septuagenarian "mainlanders" traveled to visit long-lost relatives and friends, but increasingly, Taiwanese residents also took advantage of the chance to visit the PRC. With this added familiarity, and with the implicit consent of the ROC authorities, Taiwan businessmen began looking at the mainland as an investment opportunity, pouring millions of dollars into Chinese factories and plants.

Nevertheless, sightseeing tours and increased trade did not lead to talks of political unification. To the contrary, with a better understanding of the mainland, Taiwan's residents became confident of their own economic might, an awareness that led to a desire for greater political prestige. Building on this popular sentiment, Taiwan's pro-independence DPP party increased in notoriety and influence. This forced the more conservative KMT to respond by asserting its own independence from mainland control. To this end, in the spring of 1996, ROC president Lee Teng-hui offered the financially strapped United Nations one billion dollars in exchange for a seat for Taiwan. Although the U.N. declined, the offer demonstrated the determination of KMT politicians to reassert Taiwan into the international arena.

Not surprisingly, such moves only angered government officials in Beijing. Still committed to the policy of unification, Communist leaders on the mainland viewed Lee's actions with wariness. As Taiwan prepared for its first-ever presidential elections in 1996, Lee's popularity soared. Leaders in Beijing, meanwhile, were determined not to let pro-independence sentiment escalate. In the days leading up to the election, Communist officials stationed 200,000 troops directly across the straits from Taiwan and launched several "test" missiles around Taiwan's harbors. Hoping to defuse the situation, the United States sent a naval carrier group to the straits. Despite the PRC's actions, Taiwan's voters disregarded the implicit threats and overwhelmingly reelected Lee as president.

Facing his last term in office, Lee continued to push for greater Taiwan independence. Lee realized that a declaration of independence would bring military reprisal from the mainland. He also realized that he could not count on the United States and other nations to provide military support. Instead, he opted for a new path, namely, maintenance of the status quo. Since Taiwan enjoyed de facto independence, Lee saw no imminent need to alter the international situation. Instead, he began obliquely discussing a special "state to state" relationship between Taiwan and the People's Republic of China.

With each of Lee's comments, policymakers in Beijing became more firmly committed to retaking the offensive and countering Taiwan's moves toward de facto independence. The death of Deng Xiaoping in 1997 reminded many PRC officials that the second generation of leadership had ended and the Taiwan issue was still unresolved. The subsequent third-generation leaders, represented by President Jiang Zemin and Prime Minister Zhu

Rongji, determined to resolve the Taiwan dilemma within their lifetime. Therefore, they viewed Taiwan's spring 2000 presidential elections as a vitally important step toward reunification.

RECENT HISTORY AND THE FUTURE

Although Lee Teng-hui exasperated Beijing, mainland policymakers still preferred him to many of his political rivals. For that reason, PRC leaders such as Jiang and Zhu hoped Lee's chosen successor, KMT candidate Lien Chan, would defeat his DPP rival, Chen Shui-bian, in the 2000 elections. Because the DPP platform included a plank detailing Taiwan's independence from China, Jiang and Zhu viewed the possible election of the DPP candidate as tantamount to insurrection.

In the days leading up to the election, China's state leaders issued a white paper (a policy statement) titled "The One-China Principle and the Taiwan Issue." In the statement, China reiterated its determination to unify Taiwan with the mainland under the "one nation, two systems" arrangement previously implemented in Hong Kong. It also set forth new requirements it expected Taiwan's leaders to follow. Whereas in the past China declared it would use military force against Taiwan only if Taiwan declared independence or if a foreign state invaded, the new white paper, according to the Taiwan Affairs Office, added that if Taiwan indefinitely postponed unification talks-in essence maintaining the status quo-then, "the Chinese government [would] only be forced to adopt all drastic measures possible, including the use of force, to safeguard China's sovereignty and territorial integrity." The PRC military followed up the white paper by publicly announcing in the *Liberation Army Daily* that it would "spare no effort in a blood-soaked battle" to protect the territorial integrity of the PRC, including the renegade province of Taiwan.

By electing Chen, Taiwan's voters sent a message to Beijing. As one Taiwan political scientist explained, "Taiwanese voters want to tell Beijing that 'we want to decide our own future.' They're not trying to provoke China, they just feel that Beijing has nothing to offer Taiwan" (Andrew Yang as quoted in Larmer and Meyer 2000). Ray Chen, president of computer manufacturer Compal, summed up the feelings of many Taiwanese when he explained "[we] want peace with China, [but we] don't want it at the cost of becoming like Hong Kong, which is easily threatened and controlled by Bejing" (Young 2000). Still, the Taiwan

presidential elections involved much more than simple posturing regarding China. In fact, before the election Chen softened his pro-independence platform, using language that was nearly indistinguishable from that of his KMT rival. Chen's popularity was bolstered not only by his promise to end government corruption and by his progressive reform proposals, but also by his views on cross-straits relations.

Since the election, Chen has continued to pacify his mainland counterparts by further lifting travel restrictions between Taiwan and the mainland. He has invited PRC delegates to discussions in Taiwan and has volunteered to travel to Beijing. While all sides have adopted a "wait-and-see" approach, the situation remains unpredictable.

At present, there appear to be at least five possible scenarios for future cross-straits relations. The most obvious solution for the PRC would be a military attack on Taiwan. Currently the PRC does not maintain sufficient amphibious resources to attempt an invasion of Taiwan. Instead, it would need to rely on a barrage of missile attacks. Assuming such a barrage is possible, Beijing must still consider a variety of other factors. For example, while a missile attack would debilitate Taiwan, it would not necessarily lead to a quick victory but would instead usher in a long, drawn-out engagement.

American military involvement is another factor China must consider. The U.S. administration has maintained a policy of intentional ambiguity, leaving both China and Taiwan unclear as to what America's response would be to a military crisis. Such ambiguity, policymakers hope, will cause both sides to proceed with caution. On the other hand, while U.S. involvement is indefinite, international condemnation of an armed attack is certain. A violent invasion attempt would discredit China in the eyes of the world, and its status in various international organizations would falter. Besides suffering internationally, the PRC would need to pour huge amounts of military and economic resources into the engagement, thus running the risk of domestic upheaval. Nevertheless, by repeatedly issuing military threats, China's leaders may be forced into action by popular sentiment. Still, it seems unlikely, though not impossible, that Beijing will use military force in the near future.

The second scenario—the opposite of a violent reunification—would be a peaceful declaration of Taiwan's independence. In the past, the DPP has called for a plebiscite (popular vote) on the issue, believing that popular support is behind independence. Advocates of independence point out

THE NEWS OF THE DAY IN CHINA IS AN INCREASE IN THE COUNTRY'S MILITARY PREPAREDNESS DUE TO IN-CREASING TENSIONS WITH TAIWAN. *(AP/Wide World Photos. Reproduced by permission.)*

that in the past century Taiwan has been under the control of the mainland government for only four years. The language, politics, and economics of Taiwan, they add, are distinct from those of the mainland, and whatever cultural ties might exist are weakening with each passing year. According to a recent poll noted by Larmer and Meyer in "Moment of Truth," forty-five percent of Taiwan's residents consider themselves Taiwanese rather than Chinese. Still, Chen and vice president-elect Annette Lu won the election with only thirty-nine percent of the vote, while the more conservative candidates captured sixty percent. Taiwan watchers should not interpret the DPP victory as a popular mandate for immediate and formal independence from China.

Naturally, China's leaders would prefer a third possible scenario: peaceful rapprochement and re-unification under the one-nation, two-systems policy. If China can combine saber rattling with an impressive performance in Hong Kong, Taiwan's residents may view reunification as inevitable and perhaps even desirable. Nevertheless, Taiwan's situation is very different from Hong Kong's, and unification under the one-nation, two-systems program offers very little to Taiwan that the island does not already enjoy.

This is not to say that peaceful reunification is impossible. A fourth scenario entails unification under Taiwan-issued guidelines. In 1990 Taiwan's president Lee Teng-hui suggested that unification would be possible when China had achieved a higher degree of democracy and economic development, and when it protected its citizens' basic civil liberties. Most important, he argued, any unification must be to the mutual benefit of both sides and with the consent of peoples in both China and Taiwan. While Lee is no longer in power, it is conceivable that Taiwan's current administration could issue a similar set of reunification guidelines. Detractors on the mainland contend that Taiwan's past unification policies were merely delay tactics, while skeptics on Taiwan suggest that China will never make radical changes in its political regime. Nevertheless, Taiwan's residents have shown that rapidly switching from a one-party dictatorial regime to a multiparty democracy is possible.

For the immediate future, it appears that the fifth scenario, a continuation of the status quo, is the most likely. Neither side has made drastic concessions toward the other, nor are any such concessions on the horizon. With the PRC attempting to strengthen its position in the international arena (including joining the World Trade

Organization and similar bodies), it does not want to antagonize potential allies with a risky cross-straits war. Nor do Taiwan's residents, who currently enjoy a high standard of living and a burgeoning democracy, see any need to alter their position concerning the PRC. Assuming wise leadership prevails, residents on the mainland and in Taiwan will continue to interact and appreciate the common heritage they share. Cooperation will undoubtedly lead to strong economic ties and mutual respect, even if each side maintains its distinct and separate political system.

BIBLIOGRAPHY

Cabestan, Jean-Pierre. "Taiwan's Mainland Policy: Normalization, Yes; Reunification, Later," *The China Quarterly* (December 1996): 126–1283.

Chao, Linda and Ramon H. Myers. *The First Chinese Democracy: Political Life in the Republic of China on Taiwan.* Baltimore, Md.: The Johns Hopkins University Press, 1998.

Clough, Ralph N. "Taiwan-PRC Relations." In *Taiwan in World Affairs.* Boulder, Colo.: Westview Press, 1994.

———. *Cooperation or Conflict in the Taiwan Strait?* Maryland: Rowman and Littlefield, 1999.

Cooper, John. *A Quiet Revolution: Political Development in the Republic of China.* Washington D.C.: Ethics and Public Policy Center, 1988.

———. *The Taiwan Political Miracle: Essays on Political Development, Elections, and Foreign Relations.* Maryland: East Asia Research Institute, University Press of America, 1997.

Eckholm, Erik. "China Army Renews Threat Against Taiwan Separatism," *New York Times,* 7 March 2000.

http://www.nytimes.com/library/world/asia/030700china-taiwan.html (12 April 2000).

Huang Kun-huei. *The Key Points and Content of the Guidelines for National Unification.* Taipei: Mainland Affairs Council, 1991.

Klintworth, Gary. *New Taiwan, New China: Taiwan's Changing Role in the Asia Pacific Region.* New York: St. Martin's Press, 1995.

Larmer, Brook and Mahlon Meyer. "Moment of Truth: With Chen Shui-bian's Historic Victory, a New Taiwan is Born. Will an Angry Beijing Spoil the Party?" *Newsweek,* 27 March 2000. http://newsweek.com/nw-srv/printed/int/asia/a17615-2000mar20.htm (12 April 2000).

Meyers, Ramon. "A New Chinese Civilization: The Evolution of the Republic of China on Taiwan," *China Quarterly* (December 1996): 1072-1090.

Platt, Kevin. "US, China, and Taiwan Keep the Lid on Tensions," *The Christian Science Monitor,* 31 March 2000.

Pomfret, John. "China Assails Taipei Again," *International Herald Tribune,* 10 April 2000. http://www.iht.com/iht/today/mon/in/taiwan.2.html (12 April 2000).

Stolper, Thomas E. *China, Taiwan, and the Offshore Islands.* New York: M.E. Sharp, 1985.

Wu Hsin-hsing. *Bridging the Strait: Taiwan, China, and the Prospects for Reunification.* Hong Kong: Oxford University Press, 1994.

Young, Stuart. "Taiwan's Chen Treads Carefully: President-elect Yesterday Said 'Eternal Peace' with China is the Goal, but Held Firm to his Own Terms," *The Christian Science Monitor,* 23 March 2000.

David L. Kenley

U.S. Militant Separatist Movements: Freedom Fighters or Terrorists?

The Conflict

Militia movements—and militant individuals—have violently attacked people and groups in the United States. Government officials, especially the U.S. government, and specifically the Federal Bureau of Investigations (FBI) and the Bureau of Alcohol, Tobacco and Firearms (ATF) have countered the militias' actions.

Religious

- The stated beliefs of the militia groups are often based in Christianity. The militia groups often regard the U.S. as overrun with and under the control of Jews and "godlessness."

Political

- The militia groups often believe that the U.S. government is unjustly taxing them, limiting gun ownership, and inflicting regulations and restrictions on them.

Economic

- Militias grew in the wake of the farm crisis of the early 1980s.

Ruby Ridge. Waco. The Oklahoma City bombing. Militia groups. "Patriot" Groups. Covenant Communities. Freeman. Posse Comitatus. Christian Identity. Aryan Nations. Y2K. One World Government. New World Order. These terms are among those used by the media to describe both key events and many of the groups that are linked to modern militant separatist movements in the United States today. The fears and anxieties of some people in the United States have prompted them to militant action. These militant separatists often say they are "defending themselves" against a government they believe is against them; or that they are "defending their rights," or even that they are trying to "re-establish" their rights. In any case, militant separatist groups have come into conflict with the U.S. federal government and law enforcement officials.

The debate about how the Federal Bureau of Investigation (FBI), the Bureau of Alcohol, Tobacco, and Firearms (ATF), and other federal agencies have dealt with some of these modern militant separatist groups continues in the media, the courtrooms and within the government itself. There is also a large amount of material in a variety of media (short wave radio, the Internet, alternative media papers/magazines) that is concerned about not only past problems, but also how to deal with future confrontations. The FBI and ATF have been criticized for the handling of Ruby Ridge and Waco in particular, because in both cases people lost their lives.

In 1992 in Ruby Ridge, Idaho, an ex-Green Beret and white supremacist named Randy Weaver and his family moved to the top of a remote mountain to separate themselves from a society and government they believed discriminated against

CHRONOLOGY

1865 Ku Klux Klan is founded.

Late 1980s Militia groups begin to increase around the United States.

1992 Confrontation between the Federal Bureau of Investigation (FBI) and Randy Weaver and his family leave Weaver's wife and son and a federal agent dead.

1993 A standoff between the Branch Davidians of Waco, Texas and the FBI results in the deaths of more than eighty people. Subsequent investigations fail to calm suspicions that the FBI was to blame. There is a dramatic rise in the number of militant separatist groups.

1995 The Oklahoma City bombing of the Alfred P. Murrah Federal Building kills 168 people. Timothy McVeigh and Terry Nichols, who had some history with militant separatist movements, are convicted.

2000 The new millennium—the year 2000—had special meaning for many separatists, who believed it would be marked by chaos and the proclamation of martial law.

whites, was infiltrated by Jews, and was anti-Christian. In fact, Weaver used the term "ZOG," which stands for Zionist Occupational Government, to describe the government. An undercover federal agent asked Weaver to make a sawed-off shotgun, and then the federal agent tried to have Weaver become an informant, instead of prosecuting him for producing an illegal weapon. Weaver refused to become an informant and he did not appear in court after being charged. The entire Weaver family was put under careful surveillance because it was thought to be armed and well trained in the use of weapons. When Weaver, his son, and a friend who was staying with them came across some of the agents who were watching them, a gunfight ensued. There is still debate as to who shot first. However, the result of the gunfight was that a federal agent died, and Vicki and Randy Weaver's son, Sam, was killed, along with his dog.

After the firefight, the federal agents called in for backup, explaining they had been attacked. This resulted in a siege—the federal government surrounded the house and watched the family's activities. The following day, Vicki Weaver was killed by an FBI sniper while she was holding her infant.

During the ten-day standoff, James (Bo) Gritz, well known in the militant separatist community, provided mediation. Eventually the family was convinced to surrender. The FBI sniper who fired the shot that killed Vicki Weaver was prosecuted, and it was revealed that an unprecedented "shoot to kill" order had been given to agents in the field. The sniper, Lon Horiuchi, was not convicted, but a civil suit by Randy Weaver as a result of the killing led to a multi-million dollar settlement by the government. The standoff at Ruby Ridge and the actions of the FBI in dealing with the Weaver family became very important to many different groups in the United States. Many groups believed it was the beginning of what they believed would be a nationwide persecution of gun owners, separatists, and those who claimed to be "true Christians."

HISTORICAL BACKGROUND

Early Militant Separatist Movements

Well before the Ruby Ridge incident, there had been confrontations between the federal government and militant separatists. One noted researcher, James Corcoran, reports that the current radical militia strategies of armed resistance date to the early 1970s. The militant separatists who began to get media and law enforcement attention after Ruby Ridge had their roots in earlier movements, such as the Posse Comitatus, the Ku Klux Klan, and various Neo-Nazi groups (including the Order, also known as Bruders Schweigen). A central part of the beliefs of many of these militant separatists is that their "way of life" is being taken away or changed by something or someone. These groups exploit fears related to the economy, social change, or political movements that they believe are trying to persecute them. Many of these groups believe in a conspiracy to take away rights bit by bit, and that, eventually, a One World Government will establish a New World Order. Many groups link this belief in a conspiracy to doctrines within Christianity, and see the conspiracy as part of the persecution that is foretold in the Book of Revelation in the New Testament. The groups these militant separatists blame, and the details of their beliefs are complex, but a common point is a mistrust of "big government." Many of the militant separatists believe the government is taking rights away, especially those relating to guns. They view gun control legislation, including the 1968 Gun Control Act, the Brady Law, and the 1994 Crime Bill, as taking away their right to bear arms.

The Ku Klux Klan was founded in 1865, and was at its most popular during the 1920s when between three and four million Americans were members; which makes it one of the oldest and best known militant groups in the United States. Although it is often portrayed as a Southern institution because it was founded in Pulaski, Tennessee, the Klan has members across the United States. Although its numbers have never again reached the levels of the 1920s, the Klansmen in their robes and hoods are highly visible symbols of the extremist subculture. The Klan claims to be defending white rights and has often used violence as part of its message. A primary component of the Klan's recent message is an integration of beliefs that include the idea that the government is trying to take away rights of white people.

A group that mixes a defense of rights and a subtler racist message is the Posse Comitatus (Latin for "power of the county"). This group of believers, founded in 1969, asserts that the United States was founded as a Christian Republic, and that individuals are sovereign actors who have biblically and constitutionally guaranteed freedoms. They believe that the Articles of Confederation (the document that established a pre-U.S. Constitution government with limited federal powers) were biblically based. Furthermore, the Constitution was taken from the Articles, showing that the government formed is meant to be a "Christian" institution. They extend this belief to include the idea that only white Christian men are true citizens of the United States, and all others are "Fourteenth Amendment" citizens. (The Fourteenth Amendment to the U.S. Constitution grants citizenship to "all persons born or naturalized in the United States and subject to the jurisdiction thereof.") The Posse Comitatus' interpretation of this amendment is that they are "original" Constitutional citizens and thus are not "subject to the jurisdiction" of the United States, but should be treated as individuals who may or may not choose to follow the rules and laws of the federal government. Therefore, no law enforcement body, except the county sheriff, has the ability to control "original" citizen's actions. Since the county sheriff is often directly elected, he is likely to be sympathetic to local citizens. The Posse believe that if a sheriff fails to perform his duties satisfactorily then by "natural law" the Posse has the right to act in the name of the sheriff.

Perhaps the most notorious member of the Posse Comitatus was Gordon Kahl. Kahl was on probation for his refusal to pay income taxes, due to his hatred for the "Jewish-controlled" banks. The desperation of many farmers and small town businesses due to the severe economic problems in the early- to mid-1980s had led to an influx of mem-

JAMES "BO" GRITZ

1938– Former Green Beret James Gordon "Bo" Gritz is a leader of the Survivalist Movement. Some consider him a patriot, who has served his country with distinction. Many, concerned by his connection to white supremacist groups and his anti-Semitic statements, consider him a dangerous bigot.

Gritz was born in 1938, and raised in Oklahoma. He was decorated sixty times over the course of his twenty-two-year military career. After the war in Vietnam, he returned to the United States, and began training commandos in Leesburg, Florida. Gritz prepared a private army for secret missions into areas of Indochina he believed American POWs (prisoners of war) were still being held. Although he lead four rescue missions, gained the support of Clint Eastwood and Ronald Reagan, and inspired the Rambo movies, he never found any American prisoners.

Bo Gritz ran briefly for Vice President on the Populist Party ticket with former Ku Klux Klan leader David Duke, but withdrew to run his own presidential campaigns in 1988 and 1992. Federal officials have consulted with him during standoffs with separatists. In 1998 he formed a Christian Patriot community, known as "Almost Heaven," in northern Idaho. Currently, he directs survival seminars and teaches home school.

bers to extremist groups, and the Posse was most successful in the mid-1980s. The economic downturn was blamed on bankers and big government, and was seen by some as part of a larger plan to break down the "traditional" American society represented by American farming. In February 1983, Gordon Kahl and his son were confronted at their farm in North Dakota by four U.S. marshals and a deputy sheriff, who had come to arrest him for violating his probation. A shootout followed; Kahl's son Yorie was shot, the deputy sheriff and two U.S. marshals were killed, and the other two marshals wounded. One of the marshals, wounded in the initial gunfight, was killed when Kahl fired two shots at point blank range into his head. Kahl fled and became a nationally sought fugitive. He was tracked to Arkansas, where he killed a county sheriff who attempted to apprehend him. Kahl's run from the law ended when the house he had sought refuge in was burned to the ground by a law enforcement team and Kahl himself was killed after a prolonged shootout. Extremist groups hailed Kahl as a martyr.

The neo-Nazi groups, including such groups as the Aryan Nations, White Aryan Resistance and National Alliance, believe in the supremacy of whites. Some neo-Nazi groups also believe that whites are the only true citizens. Some groups espouse a religious belief, Christian Identity, which explains that whites were created to be superior, and Jews and minorities are seen as either "mud people" that were created before Adam as "creatures" who are less than white men (who come directly from Adam) or are the result of Eve having sexual relations with Satan (or Adam with Lilith, depending on the interpretation); others believe the separation between the races is from the lineage of other Old Testament figures (i.e. Ham and Shem or Cain and Abel). Some Identity followers trace out the belief that after the fall of the Temple in Jerusalem, the Tribes of Israel spread out and founded European countries, and that modern Jews are actually descended from a "thirteenth" tribe who were not Jews by lineage, but by conversion. These ideas serve to further the belief that white men are not only created superior, but are in fact the "true" chosen people, and Jews are actually imposters who are claiming a false heritage.

One group of Identity believers was guided by Robert Matthews, and was called the Order. Matthews believed in Christian Identity and was also an Odinist (a pre-Christian religion based on Nordic gods) and his followers were very militant. Members of the Order robbed armored cars, counterfeited money, and used machine guns to murder Alan Berg, an outspoken Jewish talk-radio host, outside his home in Denver in June 1984. Another group of Identity believers, the Covenant, Sword and Arm of the Lord (CSA), had their compound in Arkansas raided on April 19, 1985. Law enforcement officials found automatic weapons, explosives, an LAW (a Light Anti-tank Weapon), directions on how to build bombs, large quantities of poison, and targets in a "simulation city" that were painted to look like state troopers with Stars of David—a symbol of Judaism—painted on their chests. The raid took place after a number of incidents tied the group to illegal weapons, and it was discovered that members of the Order were hiding out in the CSA compound. Law enforcement surrounded the compound with almost two hundred federal, state and local police, but the confrontation ended peacefully when the CSA members surrendered.

Militias

Modern militia groups began to arise in various states during the late 1980s, justifying their existence with the U.S. Constitution's Second Amendment: "A well regulated militia, being necessary to the security of a free State, the right of the people to keep and bear arms, shall not be infringed." Historically, militias were made up of all able-bodied men and were commissioned and funded by the state. This function is now generally considered to be the role of the National Guard, under direction of the state government. Article I, Section 8 of the Constitution that states Congress shall "provide for calling forth the Militia to execute the Laws of the Union," and Article 2, Section 2 proclaims the "President shall be Commander in Chief of the Army and Navy of the United States, and of the Militia of the several States." The modern militia movement is made up of groups of individuals and was raised by private sources, not recognized or commissioned by the state. However, some militant separatists view the U.S. Constitution as justification for stockpiling weapons and conducting military training.

An important part of the beliefs of many of the existing militant separatist groups is a common fear of policies and programs that were established to bring equality to minority groups. After Ruby Ridge, different groups that previously had little to do with each other began to use Ruby Ridge as a common point to discuss their ideas and fears. The idea that the federal government had overstepped its authority by trying to take away or limit the ownership of guns when laws such as the 1968 Gun Control Act and the Brady Bill were passed, and that federal officials and agencies were trying to attack militant separatists, began to spread. A year after Ruby Ridge, the Branch Davidians, who lived outside of Waco, Texas, became the next tragedy that helped the modern militant separatist movement to grow.

The Branch Davidians at Waco

The Branch Davidians, led by Vernon Howell, who changed his name to David Koresh, were a separatist religious group that split off from a branch of Seventh-Day Adventism. An important part of their beliefs was that the End Times, or Armageddon, was near. This belief is tied to the Book of Revelation in the New Testament, which describes Tribulation, or the persecution of Christians by the Antichrist and the agents of "Babylon." Because of this belief, the group collected guns on their property to defend themselves if they were to become targets of "Babylon," which they saw as represented by modern American society.

The Davidians' property was raided by the ATF in 1993 because of reports of illegal weapons, and a firefight broke out, during which four agents were killed and twenty were wounded. Six Davidians were also killed in the ninety-minute assault. The FBI was called in after the initial confrontation and a fifty-one day standoff resulted, with federal government agents outside of the compound and the Davidians inside. Twenty-one children and two women left the compound in the first week, followed by a few others during the next few weeks. The siege ended on April 19 when the FBI sent in armored vehicles to tear gas the people remaining inside the buildings. A fire broke, killing more than eighty people, including two-dozen children. Nearly everyone remaining inside the compound was killed. Surviving Davidians blamed the fire on the FBI, and the government blamed the fire on Koresh and the Davidians. During later trials and investigations the government provided infrared videotapes showing that fires broke out in multiple places and audio tapes of Koresh asking if his followers had set them yet; however, these findings did not convince the Davidians. A test in March 2000 was designed to disprove the claims by Davidians that flashes seen on an infrared surveillance tape were of agents shooting at Davidians as they tried to escape the fire. The tape showed that, in fact, the "flashes" were actually reflections off of pieces of metal strewn on the ground.

Ruby Ridge and Waco, occurring within just a year of each other, were very important to the militias, patriot groups, and other militant separatists who believed the federal government was starting a campaign of persecution. Experts noted a dramatic rise in militant separatist groups, and the media began to report on their spread across the country. E-mail, faxes, short wave radio and "free" presses began to send out information that the government was infiltrated by such groups as Freemasons, the Illuminati, or "Zionists" and that there was a plan to give control of the country to the United Nations and form a New World Order. (The "free" press is a term the separatists use to distinguish their presses from mainstream newspapers and magazines, which the separatists believe are controlled either by the government or by the groups that have infiltrated it.) Militant separatist groups have different ideas on why this takeover will occur: some thought the takeover of the United States was being guided by the Antichrist to persecute "true" Christians, while some thought it was an attack by "mud people" against "white America" (pointing to the 1992 Los Angeles riots to "prove" whites were being singled out for attacks). Still others were more concerned with practicalities like new gun control measures and having to pay taxes to a "false" government. The movements against

THE MILITIA MOVEMENT HAS BEEN A CONSTITUTIONAL TRADITION IN THE UNITED STATES; PEOPLE LIKE THIS SKINHEAD HAVE HISTORICALLY BEEN PROTECTED BY LAW. *(Corbis. Reproduced by permission.)*

the federal government were scattered in their ideologies, but more than ever before the different groups were communicating and sharing ideas.

Communication, among militant groups and individuals has been increasingly important. The rise of the Internet, where e-mail and Web sites can easily pass ideas to large audiences is an especially important method of communication. Anyone can post a Web site and spread ideas in the United States (as long as they do not directly threaten a particular person or place). The electronic medium has become a potent tool in the spread of beliefs.

The Oklahoma City Bombing

On April 19, 1995, ten years after the raid on the Covenant, Sword and Arm of the Lord compound in Arkansas, and two years after the FBI raid of the Branch Davidians, a truck bomb of fuel and fertilizer exploded in front of the Murrah Federal Building in Oklahoma City. One hundred and sixty-eight men, women and children were killed in the blast, and over five hundred were injured. Timothy McVeigh and his accomplice, Terry Nichols, were convicted of the crime, and at McVeigh's trial it became evident to many experts that the hatred and fears that had been building against the government by militant separatists had resulted in direct actions. McVeigh is believed to have visited and contacted a militant Christian Identity group in their compound in Elohim City (on the Oklahoma border) in the weeks prior to the bombing. Richard Wayne Snell, a member of the white separatist militant group known as the Covenant, Sword and Arm of the Lord (CSA) was executed on the same day as the bombing, and it is reported he had threatened that his execution would be marked by a bombing. An ex-leader of the CSA has noted that members of the CSA had traveled to Oklahoma City and considered blowing up the federal building there as early as 1983. Another reason Oklahoma City may have been targeted was a story that can be traced back to the 1970s which experienced renewed interest in 1992 (spread in part by a member of James "Bo" Gritz's campaign for president, as well as militia groups in Montana and Michigan). The story was that Oklahoma City would be the "central processing point" for a round-up of "troublemakers" by Federal Emergency Management Agency (FEMA). "Black helicopters" and pre-positioned foreign military equipment would be used by groups of international troops who would invade the United States to round up those who were hindering the plans to create a One World Government and establish the New World Order. These ideas are considered by experts to be part of the reason for the bombing.

Another belief of many militant separatist groups is racially motivated hatred. A book that gained increased attention after Oklahoma City was *The Turner Diaries*. *The Turner Diaries* was written by William Pierce, under the pseudonym Andrew Macdonald, in 1978. Pierce is the leader of the neo-Nazi group called the National Alliance. The novel describes a race war—a war against people of other races—in the United States that is led by an underground group called the Order. The hero of the novel is initiated into the underground and they begin a series of attacks against the government in response to the enaction of repressive gun laws and the persecution of white citizens. The book specifically mentions a truck bomb made up of fertilizer and explosives being set off at the FBI headquarters in Washington, DC. Timothy McVeigh was said to have read the book, sold it at gun shows, and recommended the book to other people. The call for a race war is part of the beliefs of many militant separatist groups. Militant separatists include white supremacists who call for a race war in the United States and "Ten Percenters" who advocate that a five-state region in the Northwest should be split off from the United States and only whites allowed in. These beliefs often tie into a

"constitutional" argument about the citizenship of minorities or a religiously held belief such as Christian Identity.

The Oklahoma City bombing led to a public outcry against militant extremists. Militia groups began to divide themselves between those who adhere to views of the government as oppressor and with those who advocated working with the federal government and agencies to try to ensure their rights were not taken away. The experts today believe that since 1995 there has been a change in the makeup and motives of militant separatist groups: one part of the movement has been more open with their beliefs and ideas and another part has become more secretive. Leaders of some militant separatist groups have even called for followers to stop joining larger groups, because they can be infiltrated too easily by law enforcement informants and undercover agents. A new, dangerous trend has arisen, guided by an important essay by a white supremacist named Louis Beam. This idea is that "cells" should be formed that are not tied to a larger militant group, and "lone wolf" attacks better serve the cause of militant extremists by not indicting an entire group. This concept of "leaderless resistance" is not new, but is has become an important part of the militant separatist movement.

The Freemen

The federal government has tried to find better ways to address confrontations with militia groups so that violence and death are not the end results. Some new tactics were used in a standoff between the FBI and the Montana police, and a group of extremists known as the Freemen in Justus Township, Montana, in 1996. Justus Township is the name the Freemen gave to their piece of land in Jordan; it is a play on Justice and "just us." This confrontation did not end with violence, and the state and federal agents involved in the incident tried to talk to the group and understand their motivations. The Freemen believed they were "free men" who were not citizens under the federal system, but instead are "free" agents with guaranteed rights granted to them by the Bible and guaranteed under the Constitution. One such right is the freedom to travel, so the Freemen did not believe they needed to have driver's licenses or register their vehicles. The Freemen also believe that they do not have to pay taxes to the federal government and they do not believe that any government law enforcement beyond the county level has a right to control them—that federal and state laws do not apply to them as individuals. The Freemen began a series of filing liens against officials' property, using fraudulent money orders, and even issuing death threats against local judges and law enforcement officials. The peaceful resolution of the standoff with law enforcement did not end the Freemen's resistance to the government. During the trials of the Freemen, the defense disputed the validity and power of the federal government and the presiding judge. For example, a U.S. flag hung in the courtroom and the flag had a gold tasseled fringe. The Freemen argued that this constitutes an "admiralty" or military flag; thus the court they were in was not a "civil" court but a military court. For the Freeman this confirmed their beliefs that the government is actually working under wartime provisions (the military instead of civilian court) and they were not bound by the decisions of the "admiralty" courts. The various legalistic maneuverings of the Freemen and other, newer groups have led to a crisis in many smaller courts. These groups and their followers file numerous complicated legal documents and liens against law enforcement and judicial figures that can tie up their personal finances and credit ratings.

RECENT HISTORY AND THE FUTURE

Y2K

The year 2000 (Y2K) is also an important part of many militant separatist groups' beliefs. As 1999 was coming to an end, some groups believed the Y2K "bug" would be used to cause a collapse of society that could only be cleaned up by declaring martial law. This would be the excuse to impose a One World Government that would establish a New World Order and initiate a round-up of troublemakers. Some believers felt that like-minded people should gather together into "covenant communities." These communities were designed to be separatist enclaves that were self-sufficient and away from government interference; a covenant among members is set forth as the means whereby a person's constitutional rights will be guaranteed. James "Bo" Gritz and Robert K. Spear are two notable militant separatists who advocated the "covenant community" ideal. When January 1, 2000 came and went with no major problems, some experts thought it might cause more people to turn away from militant separatist beliefs. However, some believers point out that Y2K stands for "Year Two Thousand" and there is a whole year for these events to occur. The FBI released a report, titled "Project Meggido" (a reference to the meeting place described in the Bible where Armageddon—or the "final conflict" between good and evil—will take place). The report detailed the history of militant separatism and responses to it by law en-

LOUIS BEAM

Louis Beam, an ex-Ku Klux Klansman and a leader of the Aryan Nations, started early efforts to spread extremist beliefs through computers, faxes, and short wave radio. Beam created an early BBS (computer bulletin board), called Aryan Nations Liberty Net. This BBS was a computer network dedicated to spreading neo-Nazi beliefs. Beam also created a "point system" that gave a "point" value to killing or attacking minorities or leaders of civil rights groups. Beam is perhaps best known for expanding and promoting the idea of "leaderless resistance." The concept is that instead of one big movement, independent "cells" all work towards a common goal without a central leadership. Because of the implementation of this idea of small, independent groups, the militant separatist movement has been very hard for law enforcement agents to monitor.

forcement. The report concluded that there might be actions taken in the year 2000, and it warned that caution should be taken by law enforcement officials at all levels.

According to a press release in mid-March of 2000, the overall number of smaller hate factions may be declining in the United States, but larger, hard-line groups are gaining in power. According to a report by a hate crimes monitoring group, the Southern Poverty Law Center, "the smaller groups that were less active are joining the more serious and potentially dangerous groups." But some scholars disagree, saying the extremist groups are far less dangerous today than they were in almost any decade in the last century. "Hate groups had greater influence in the past," said Brian Levin, a criminology professor at California State San Bernardino. "The movement today has not coalesced in any meaningful way." Levin said he feels the most potentially dangerous are the "freelancers," independent individuals who do not belong to a particular group, but draw inspiration from different groups and the essay by Louis Beam.

Militant separatists in the United States have mainly used traditional weapons—bombs and guns, for example. The attack against a Tokyo subway with a form of nerve gas in 1995 by a religious cult, Aum Shinrikyo, may be a foreshadowing of the greatest fears of law enforcement. This fear is that a militant or extremist group will release a chemical, nuclear, or biological agent. The U.S. Army and law enforcement have collaborated on a project that keeps a group of specialists on call at all times, ready to be sent to any attack that may involve weapons of mass destruction. This type of attack could result in thousands of deaths or injuries.

The recent history of militant separatist groups in the United States has included violent actions, legalistic maneuverings, and threats. Though the economy at the end of the twentieth and early twenty-first century is doing well and there appears to be more contentment with the government as a whole, law enforcement officials fear that groups could be losing "weekend warriors" for "hardcore" believers. As the leaders of militant separatist groups begin to age, and there have been little or no "revolutionary actions" or direct confrontations, some law enforcement officers fear that younger followers may splinter off to form groups that advocate more action. As militant separatist groups work to bring in new, younger members, these recruits may pose future problems for law enforcement.

BIBLIOGRAPHY

Abanes, Richard. *American Militias: Rebellion, Racism & Religion.* Downers Grove, Ill.: InterVarsity Press, 1996.

Aho, James. *The Politics of Righteousness: Idaho Christian Patriotism.* Seattle, Wash.: University of Washington Press, 1990, 1995.

Bushart, Howard L., John R. Craig, and Myra Barnes. *Soldiers of God: White Supremacists and Their Holy War for America.* New York: Kensington Books, 1998.

Coates, James. *Armed and Dangerous: The Rise of the Survivalist Right.* New York: Hill & Wang, 1987, 1995.

Corcoran, James. *Bitter Harvest: The Birth of Paramilitary Terrorism in the Heartland.* New York: Penguin Books, 1990, 1995.

Dees, Morris with James Corcoran. *Gathering Storm: America's Militia Threat.* New York: HarperCollins, 1996.

Ezekiel, Raphael S. *The Racist Mind: Portraits of American Neo-Nazis and Klansmen.* New York: Penguin Books, 1995.

Macdonald, Andrew (nee Pierce, William). *The Turner Diaries.* Hillsboro, W.Va.: National Vanguard Books, 1978, 1980.

Noble, Kerry. *Tabernacle of Hate: Why They Bombed Oklahoma City.* Prescott, Ontario, Canada: Voyageur Publishing, 1998.

Serrano, Richard A. *One of Ours: Timothy McVeigh and the Oklahoma City Bombing.* New York: W.W. Norton & Co., 1998.

Stern, Kenneth S. *A Force Upon the Plain: The American Militia Movement and the Politics of Hate.* New York: Simon & Schuster, 1996.

Stock, Catherine McNicol. *Rural Radicals: Righteous Rage in the American Grain.*

Walter, Jess. *Every Knee Shall Bow: The Truth and Tragedy of Ruby Ridge & the Randy Weaver Family.* New York: HarperCollins Publishers, 1995.

Brian Marcus

VENEZUELA:
NEW MILITARY POPULISM

On December 6, 1998, former paratrooper Hugo Chávez Frías was elected president of Venezuela with a decisive majority of the popular vote. This resounding support, however, masked some serious concerns. Chávez had come to office on the strength of a campaign that targeted corrupt political parties and corrupt politicians for stealing the wealth of the nation from its people. How, he demanded, could a nation rich in petroleum reserves be home to so many poor citizens? Many Venezuelans believed that once he became president, Chávez would follow through with his promises to restore the nation's wealth to its people. After all, he had a rather impressive record of acting decisively against corruption. In 1992 then-lieutenant colonel Hugo Chávez had spearheaded an attempt to overthrow President Carlos Andrés Pérez Rodriguez, though the military coup d'état, or rebellion, failed. The Venezuelan congress impeached Pérez on corruption charges and removed him from office the following year. While Chávez's election in 1998 brought hope to the poor, his opponents warned that Chávez was reviving a Latin American tradition of populism—representing the common people—by making irresponsible promises to the working class in order to win elections. Critics of populism argued that the special benefits granted to workers in exchange for their political support, and the measures taken to assure state control of key industries, created bloated bureaucracies that ultimately thwarted economic development. In the 1970s, the economic crisis faced by populist presidents, coupled with the fear of communist revolution, brought right-wing military dictatorships to power in much of Latin America. Thus, while some hoped the election of Hugo Chávez would result in a more just distribution of the nation's wealth, others feared that he would lead Venezuela into even more violence and poverty.

THE CONFLICT

In 1998 Venezuela elected an officer of the military, Hugo Chávez Frías, president. During his campaign, Chávez promised the poor more economic equity and greater security and order. His election revived a tradition of military populism in Latin America.

Economic

- Economic tensions encourage support of strong leadership, in this case, the military.

Political

- The military, through its strong presence, discourages free election.

- Chávez made promises to the poor in order to be elected—promises on which he could never deliver. He played on the poor people's fears in order to win the vote.

CHRONOLOGY

1920s Venezuela is the world's leading exporter of oil.

1958 A military coup deposes President Pérez Jiménez.

1960s–1970s Military dictators replace many populist presidents in Latin America, but not in Venezuela.

1980s The price of oil drops and Venezuela goes into an economic crisis.

1988 Carlos Andrés Pérez Rodriguez is reelected to the presidency. When the Pérez administration increases bus fares, rioting ensues.

1992 Hugo Chávez leads an effort to overthrow Venezuelan president Carlos Andrés Pérez Rodriguez. The effort is unsuccessful and Chávez spends two years in prison.

1998 Chávez decides to run for and is elected president of Venezuela.

Once in office, President Chávez quickly took steps to design a new constitution to govern the new Venezuela. On July 25, 1999, Venezuelans elected a constitutional assembly to draft the new law of the land. Once again, the president's immense popularity became apparent at the polls. His leftist coalition and its radical political position won a sweeping victory, claiming well over 90 percent of the assembly seats. Venezuelans overwhelmingly approved the constitution in a referendum vote on December 15, 1999. This set the stage for a "mega election" to take place on May 28, 2000, when virtually every elective office in Venezuela would be up for public vote. Few doubted that Chávez would win a resounding victory in the presidential contest until, in the early months of 2000, Governor Francisco Arias Cárdenas challenged Chávez for the presidency. Like Chávez, Arias had participated in the 1992 coup attempt against President Pérez. He, too, campaigned against corruption; but he now urged Venezuelans to move away from the empty speechmaking of the Chávez administration to a more competent administration he would lead.

HISTORICAL BACKGROUND

The homeland of South American revolutionary Simón Bolivar, Venezuela led the way in the independence movements of the early nineteenth century. After separation from Spain, however, Venezuelans found it difficult to establish the republican nation envisioned by Bolivar. Like much of South America, Venezuela was ruled by a series of military strongmen called *caudillos* in the nineteenth and early twentieth centuries. By the 1920s, British, Dutch, and American investment in Venezuela's petroleum reserves had made Venezuela the world's leading exporter of oil. Revenue from this new industry funded the building of railroads and shipping networks, contributing to the nation's apparent prosperity.

Only after World War II, however, did party politics replace *caudillo* rule. For the first time in 1945, the president in power was backed by a political party, the Democratic Action Party, or AD, which was supported by a majority of the people. A new constitution was written, and Venezuelans became actively involved in a reform movement to share the benefits of oil with a wider range of citizens. Opposition to these reforms prompted a military coup that eventually brought to power Marcos Pérez Jiménez, another military *caudillo*. After almost ten years in power, evidence of corruption in his administration spurred a military coup that deposed President Pérez Jiménez in 1958. The AD returned to power, this time cooperating with the Christian Democratic Party (COPEI). Since 1958 presidents chosen in free elections have governed Venezuela.

Despite military coups and political corruption, Venezuela escaped the first round of populist governments in Latin America. In much of the region, the Great Depression in the early 1930s had reversed a period of economic prosperity built on export commodities. In Brazil, for example, the slump in international demand for coffee contributed to an economic crisis that led to a successful military coup. Getúlio Vargas, the man who became president with support from the military, implemented a program that focused on internal economic development as he courted the vote of the working class. Throughout Latin America, a new breed of politicians joined the tradition of *caudillo* rule to attract the vote of a new urban working class. The example of Argentina is perhaps best known.

In 1943 Colonel Juan Domingo Perón joined with other military officers to overthrow a corrupt president who supported the interests of a conservative few. In the aftermath of the coup, as secretary of labor, Perón encouraged workers in Argentina's capital city, Buenos Aires, to form unions and lobby the government for legislation that would provide them with more of the profits from their labor. Perón's popularity soared among members of these new unions. When he ran for the presidency in 1946, he won an impressive victory. Argentina, a neutral nation during the World War II, had accumulated significant treasury surpluses by selling wheat and beef to the aggressive nations. During his first administration, Perón redistributed some of those wartime profits to the working class. Salaries rose, working hours shrank, and more and more workers enjoyed the benefits of paid vacations and quality health care. A strong supporter of nationalist independence, Perón also challenged foreign control of key sectors of the Argentine economy. For example, he used treasury surpluses to pay for nationalizing foreign-owned railroads and utility companies. As a result, the role of the state in the economy grew.

Perón's wife, Eva Duarte de Perón, a young radio and screen actress, also courted the workers. From a humble background, she empathized with the plight of the new urban working class and created a foundation to help provide for their most basic needs. The poor came to love "Evita" (as they called her) for all the tangible things she gave them. Her personal connection to the workers strengthened their support for her husband. But many of the new benefits had been funded by wartime treasury surpluses. Perón's policies, furthermore, had frightened off investors. Once treasury surpluses were spent, Perón was forced to cut back on his commitments to workers. After Eva Perón's untimely death in 1952, Juan Perón's political position rapidly deteriorated. His one-time allies felt betrayed when budget constraints forced him to renege on some of his earlier promises, and his opponents seized the opportunity to challenge his rule.

In 1955 a military coup deposed Juan Perón. Yet the presidents who followed were unable to remedy the severe political and economic crises. In the 1960s radical Argentine youth inspired by Fidel Castro's revolution in Cuba came to believe that Juan Perón was their best hope to lead a government that would restore a measure of social justice to Argentina. Military leaders, on the other hand, feared that a new Perón administration would bring communists to power. When Perón finally was permitted to return from exile in Spain in 1973, he was again elected president. But his short term in office failed to restore economic growth or political peace. His new wife, Maria Estela (known as Isabel) was elected vice president in 1973, and succeeded him in the presidency after his death in 1974. Her time in office witnessed further deterioration of the Argentine economy as political vio-

PRESIDENT HUGO CHAVEZ. *(AP/Wide World Photos. Reproduced by permission.)*

lence escalated. The military stepped in again in 1976, this time determined to restructure Argentina by eliminating the Marxist threat of socialism (the government ownership and management of goods) and promoting conservative economic development. The cruelty that accompanied their program resulted in the imprisonment and death of tens of thousands of Argentines who disagreed with their politics.

Not only in Argentina, but also throughout Latin America, military dictators replaced populist presidents in the 1960s and 1970s. Venezuela and Colombia were, in fact, the only two nations in South America not governed by military officers in the 1970s. Military governments sought to reestablish ties to the international trade community that had been disrupted by the protectionist policies of populist presidents. These policies had given protection to domestic companies through restrictions on foreign competitors. To encourage business investments, the military governments repressed unions and slashed workers' benefits, implementing "austerity measures" recommended by the International Monetary Fund in order to make their export products more competitive on the international market. However, frustrated by declining living standards and angered by the continued repression that kept military dictators in power,

MAP OF VENEZUELA. *(© Maryland Cartographics. Reprinted with permission.)*

South Americans launched massive protest movements that restored democracy to the region in the mid-1980s. Popularly elected presidents now faced the challenge of promoting economic growth while distributing their nations' wealth more equitably.

For much of the twentieth century Venezuela was perceived as a "great exception" to the general trends governing Latin American development. At a time when a leftist guerrilla, or rebel, movement triumphed in Cuba, and the struggle between left and right brought right-wing dictatorships to many other Latin American countries, Venezuelans moved toward consolidating democracy when they ousted President Marcos Pérez Jiménez in 1958. The military dictator fled first to the Dominican Republic, then to Miami, Florida, but he was returned in 1963 to stand trial in

Venezuela on corruption charges. While other South American nations were succumbing to repressive military dictatorships, Venezuela moved toward truly representative government under the rule of law. Venezuela was also an exception in the source of its export wealth. Now the third largest oil producer in the world, Venezuela possessed the largest petroleum reserves in the Americas. As a founding member of the Organization of Petroleum Exporting Countries (OPEC), Venezuela's oil revenues quadrupled following the Arab-Israeli War of 1973, when the war between Israel and its neighboring states kept them from exporting large amounts of oil. At a time when oil-poor Latin American countries were borrowing money to help meet their oil needs, wealth from oil exports fueled economic and political development in Venezuela. Carlos Andrés Pérez, elected president in 1973, became extremely popular as Venezuelans enjoyed the benefits of the oil boom. The need to oversee this oil bonanza, however, fostered state-controlled development marked by bloated bureaucracies and costly corruption; during the 1970s, a handful of politicians and their cronies amassed enormous wealth.

When the great oil surge of the 1970s busted in the 1980s, the pretense of wealth faded in Venezuela. By the late 1980s, Venezuela's once sizeable middle class was slipping below the poverty line. In the early 1990s, perhaps as many as 80 percent of Venezuelans lived in poverty. By 1988, with government income cut in half, once rich Venezuela was having trouble meeting interest payments on its foreign debt. At this time of crisis, Carlos Andrés Pérez was reelected to the presidency in December 1988. Many Venezuelans, remembering his time in office during the oil boom years, hoped he would restore economic prosperity. Instead, he implemented hardship measures that, he claimed, would provide a sounder basis for economic growth. Many Venezuelans suspected that the president and his friends were getting rich while most of their countrymen suffered. When the Pérez administration increased the price of bus fares, rioting and looting erupted in Caracas, the capital city. Army troops sent in to quell the demonstrations killed hundreds of citizens.

This economic downturn, and the way the government chose to deal with the situation, made abundantly clear the sad reality that oil-rich Venezuela harbored too many poverty-stricken citizens. Outraged military officers, among them lieutenant colonel Hugo Chávez, organized a coup in 1992 to depose President Pérez. Chávez was a devoted admirer of Simón Bolivar. He saw in Bolivar an army man who fought to liberate his people from the despotic and corrupt control of Spanish officials. Chávez believed that Venezuela had once again become a country stolen from its people. In his mind, the only explanation for widespread poverty in such a wealthy country was the selfish corruption of greedy politicians. Chávez admired the measures Cuban president Fidel Castro had taken in the late 1950s to liberate Cuba from the control of foreign investors and corrupt Cuban leaders. And so he helped organize the Bolivarian Revolutionary Movement, named after his hero Simón Bolivar, to restore freedom and prosperity to the Venezuelan people. The coup attempt came in the midst of riots and strikes protesting the scandals that indicated widespread corruption in the Pérez administration. Pérez forces succeeded in putting down the uprising, but at least eighty people were killed in street combat. Chávez spent two years in prison for his role in the attempted coup. In 1993 after investigating Pérez for fraud, Venezuela's congress voted to impeach the president and removed him from office. When Hugo Chávez was released from jail in 1994, he visited Cuba and was welcomed at the airport by Fidel Castro. Upon his return to Venezuela, he traveled the country on horseback and on foot, observing firsthand the plight of his countrymen.

When he decided to run for the presidency in 1998, Chávez based his campaign platform on the need to end the corrupt practices of traditional politicians. Only then, he claimed, could the wealth of the nation be returned to its people. He also argued that neo-liberal free-trade policies allowed foreigners to cheat Venezuela. (Neo-liberal free-trade policies encouraged the free flow of goods between countries without protective tariffs and quotas.) Thus, he seemed to adopt the old populist rhetoric: a military man would save his nation by looking out for the interests of the working poor, curbing the foreign presence, and sweeping out political corruption. His campaign addressed very specific issues as he courted the vote of the workers. He proposed to seek a suspension on the foreign debt payment, arguing that the Venezuelan people's needs should be met before the demands of international banks. He criticized the trend toward privatizing state companies (putting organizations previously under government in the hands of private developers), wary that private citizens, and even foreigners, might buy up important sources of the state's wealth. Petroleum investments, he argued, should be cut back, thus reducing the international oil glut and raising oil prices. He also promised that, as Venezuela's president, he would nationalize land, capital, and national resources in such a way that the wealth of the nation could be used for the good of the people. And he was determined to keep key industries in state hands. But he tempered this strong-state rhetoric by also claiming to welcome foreign investment. As for workers' benefits, Chávez promised to raise the minimum wage, to fund social programs, to reduce the budget deficit, and to convene a popular assembly to write a new constitution. Many of his advisors were leftist intellectuals, causing some concern that his government would not respect the free flow of international capital. Chávez tried to soothe these concerns by expressing his admiration for British Prime Minister Tony Blair's emphasis on the need to follow a "third way" between capitalism (free enterprise) and socialism (an economy directed by the government).

RECENT HISTORY AND THE FUTURE

Clearly, Chávez's program appealed to many Venezuelan voters. In December 1998, he was swept to the presidency with an astonishing 56.5 percent of the popular vote. His strongest opponent, businessman Henrique Salas Romer, won a mere 39.5 percent of the vote. Chávez received more popular support than any other Venezuelan presidential candidate in forty years. While many voters rallied behind him, investors expressed concern about the effect his policies would have on economic growth. This skittishness on the part of investors had serious consequences for Venezuela. In 1999 the economy contracted by 7.2 percent as foreign investment fell by $1.7 billion and capital flight reached $4.6 billion. Yet Venezuelan voters did not abandon their president. Many believed that he was sincerely committed to righting old wrongs by fighting corruption. They were willing to give him a chance to put his ideas to work even if it meant greater hardships in the short run.

Evidence of the president's continued popularity came with the July 1999 elections to the constitutional assembly. The voters rejected well-known politicians, including ex-President Carlos Andrés Pérez. Individuals associated with the Christian Democratic Party or the Democratic Action Party won not a single seat in the assembly. Instead, the Patriotic Pole, a coalition of parties that supported Chávez, captured 121 of the 128 contested seats. The two individuals who received the most votes were Chávez's wife, Marisabel, and his former chief of staff, Alfredo Pena. About twenty former military colleagues were also elected, as were five of his former ministers. Although only forty-seven percent of eligible voters turned out for this election, those who chose to vote demonstrated continued confidence in the president. The figures are particularly impressive given the fact that the decline in investments following Chávez's election had already produced a sharp economic downturn, including the loss of about six hundred thousand jobs nationwide since he had taken office. This loyal devotion of working-class Venezuelans brought to mind the committed support Latin American workers elsewhere had given to populist presidents in the 1940s, 1950s, and 1960s.

Venezuela's new Asemblea Nacional Constituyente (ANC) got to work immediately and produced a new constitution in November 1999. On December 15, 1999, the Venezuelan electorate ratified the constitution with seventy-two percent approval of those who voted (less than 50 percent of the voters, however, went to the polls). Among its more important provisions, the constitution extended the presidential term from five to six years and allowed a second consecutive presidential term; created the office of vice president, an individual to be chosen by the president and approved by the legislature; eliminated the senate, making the legislature a single lawmaking body; forbade the state to finance political parties; gave voters the right to remove elected officials and labor leaders by referendum; extended social security and labor benefits while reducing the workweek from forty-four to forty hours; permitted the president to promote military officers without legislative approval; and forbade the privatization of the state-owned oil company. This new constitution, with its provisions favoring a strong president supported by the working class, seemed to some to confirm the emergence of populism in Venezuela.

As was to be expected, the new constitution encountered opposition. Business interests, for example, expressed fears that it returned Venezuela to a state-controlled economy, jeopardizing any chance of long-term economic recovery. Businesspeople worried that the costs of granting more benefits to workers would further reduce company profits. The new constitution did little to attract investors. Even outside the business community, some claimed the document was drawn up too quickly, with too little discussion, and that many of its provisions were hopelessly idealistic. To them, the drafting of the constitution confirmed concerns that Chávez was a typical populist, a charismatic *caudillo* determined to promote more of the very centralized government control responsible for Venezuela's current problems. Still others feared that although Chávez meant well, he had little time to deliver on his promises of prosperity before workers and military men became disgruntled and organized yet another coup attempt.

On the one hand, Hugo Chávez appeared to be committed to improving the lot of poor Venezuelans, even if that meant challenging international and elite interests. But the path to prosperity is not an easy one. Even nature, at times, seemed to conspire against Chávez's success. In December 1999, as the country was preparing to vote on the new constitution, torrential rains provoked flooding and mudslides in much of Venezuela's central Caribbean coast. At least five thousand (and possibly more than thirty thousand) people died, while hundreds of thousands lost their homes in what has been called one of the worst natural disasters in the history of Latin America. The plight of Venezuela's poor became frighteningly apparent as the Chávez administration sought to deal with the devastation.

Venezuela's oil continued to be a source of promise, but also of potential conflict. Before becoming president, Chávez had questioned his country's policy of large oil production, arguing that low prices for oil hurt Venezuela. After his election, he immediately cut oil production. His predecessor, President Rafael Calderas, had tried this tactic with disastrous consequences. In 1998 Venezuela had cut its oil output by two hundred thousand barrels per day. When the international price of crude oil fell from $15.50/barrel to under $12.00/barrel, Venezuela's budget faced a shortfall of millions of dollars. But under Chávez, Venezuela's minister of energy (and president of OPEC), Ali Rodriguez Araque, helped to orchestrate the reduced output that sent oil prices soaring during the winter of 1999. Higher oil prices brought a welcome infusion to the Venezuelan treasury. Though oil-producing countries wanted to keep production low and prices high, oil-dependent countries like the United States pressured OPEC for an increase in production to bring down the costs consumers paid for gasoline, diesel, and heating oil. President Chávez's administration needs to carefully navigate the complicated waters of international oil interests.

Chávez also faced challenges from within. On May 28, 2000, a Venezuelan "mega election" was to determine who would occupy almost every elected office, from members of congress, to mayor, to president. Few doubted in the early months of 2000 that Hugo Chávez would handily win the presidency. But, with the emergence of challenger Francisco Arias Cárdenas, it appeared that there might actually be a true contest. Like Chávez, Arias has struggled against the corruption of traditional politicians. He, too, was imprisoned and stripped of his military rank for his role in the 1992 coup attempt against President Pérez. Arias was twice elected governor of the oil-rich state of Zulia, where he earned the reputation of devoted public service even at personal cost. His claims that he would go beyond the "empty words" of Chávez to actually implement a more efficient administration, coupled with his personal record, made him a serious contender for the presidency. Although he lost some supporters to Arias, Chávez maintained his appeal among the vast majority of the Venezuelan poor. Then, on May 25, three days before they were scheduled to take place, Venezuela's high court postponed the elections due to "technical problems." At first the Chávez administration blamed these problems on the North American

WHILE THE POPULARITY OF HUGO CHAVEZ WOULD SEEM TO BE HIGH GIVEN THE NUMBER OF POSTERS ON THIS WALL, ELECTIONS TO DETERMINE MANY HIGH-RANKING OFFICES ARE IMMINENT. *(AP/Wide World Photos. Reproduced by permission.)*

company that was hired to set up the computerized balloting. On May 29, however, the five-member National Electoral Council appointed by Chávez's coalition, resigned amidst charges of incompetence and mismanagement. Despite these setbacks, Chávez remained poised to win the presidency by a comfortable margin.

It is unclear whether or not Hugo Chávez points to the return of military populism in the region. During the past fifty years, Venezuela has developed a strong tradition of an informed, participant electorate. Since 1958, Venezuelans have lived through periods of prosperity and periods of economic hardship without resorting to populism or to military dictatorship. They have seen irrefutable evidence of corruption in high places, and have dealt with it through the courts. Venezuelans know the history of their region. They are well aware of the grim aftermath of populist governments in South America. While Chávez does remind some of Juan Perón (including his wife's popularity among voters), others suspect he may turn out to be more like Peru's Alberto Fujimori or Argentina's Carlos Menem, realists who recognized the need to also court business interests. The example of Venezuela in the late twentieth century highlights the frustration many Latin American voters feel as the promises of free trade fail to bring prosperity to the region. It remains to be seen whether solutions will once again be sought along the failed populist path, or whether creative politicians will forge a new way into the twenty-first century.

BIBLIOGRAPHY

Coronil, Fernando. *The Magical State: Nature, Money, and Modernity in Venezuela.* Chicago: University of Chicago Press, 1997.

Enright, Michael J., Antonio Frances, and Edith Scott Saavedra. *Venezuela: The Challenge of Competitiveness.* New York: St. Martin's Press, 1996.

Ewell, Judith. *Venezuela: A Century of Change.* Palo Alto, CA: Stanford University Press, 1984.

———. *Venezuela and the United States: From Monroe's Hemisphere to Petroleum's Empire.* Athens, Ga.: University of Georgia Press, 1996.

Marquez, Patricia C. *The Street is My Home: Youth and Violence in Caracas.* Palo Alto, Calif.: Stanford University Press, 1999.

Joan E. Meznar

THE WORLD TRADE ORGANIZATION: THE BATTLE IN SEATTLE

On the last day of November 1999, representatives of the 135 member countries of the World Trade Organization (WTO) gathered in Seattle, Washington, for the start of what most hoped would be the launch of a new round of talks aimed at further liberalizing global trade. Those hopes would soon be dashed. In scenes reminiscent of the late 1960s, protestors poured into the "Emerald City's" streets to demand an end to what they saw as the ugly effect of globalized commerce. For the next four days, the world would watch not the triumphant birth of a new era of free trade but the startling images of street violence, clouds of tear gas, and rampant vandalism.

The trade ministers, commerce secretaries, politicians, and other delegates who assembled in Seattle for the first American gathering of the WTO had planned to debate the rules for ensuring the smooth, predictable, and free flow of trade into the new century. Indeed, organizers had ambitiously labeled the talks the "Millennial Round." Seattle, home to such commercial giants as Microsoft and Boeing and the largest city in the country's most trade-dependent state, would be an ideal location to negotiate a range of issues from labor standards to agricultural subsidies to trade in genetically altered foodstuffs. The plan was that after vigorous discussions and concessions leading to an agreement, U.S. President Bill Clinton would address the delegates, laud the virtues of free trade, and seal another victory over protectionism and other barriers to transnational commerce.

There were, however, others with their own plans in Seattle on Tuesday, November 30. Environmentalists, human rights activists, labor unions, consumer lobbies, farmers, feminists, anarchists, and others had orchestrated a "mobilization

THE CONFLICT

In Seattle, Washington in 1999, protestors fought in the streets in protest of the World Trade Organization (WTO). Police fought the protestors, and protestors were arrested and jailed. This was the most violent of several recent protests against organizations that support global development, including the IMF in Washington, DC and the Organization of American States in Detroit, Michigan.

Political

*   Protestors change that the WTO undermines domestic human rights and workers' rights around the world.

Economic

*   Protestors believe the economic development initiatives of the WTO damage economies of developing nations.

*   The WTO supports economic development initiatives around the world.

CHRONOLOGY

1944 Bretton Woods Conference. Forty-four countries lay out rules and institutions to govern post-World War II international trade and monetary relations.

1948 Establishment of the General Agreement on Tariffs and Trade (GATT). Twenty-three countries sign the charter in Havana, Cuba, to reduce customs tariffs.

1950 U.S. Congress fails to act on ratification of a proposed International Trade Organization.

1963 The Kennedy Round of multilateral trade negotiations takes place. Forty-six countries reduce tariffs by an average of thirty-five percent. Talks ended in 1967.

1964 United Nations Conference on Trade and Development (UNCTAD) is created to press for trade measures to benefit developing countries.

1973 Round of multilateral trade negotiations takes place in Tokyo, Japan. Ninety-nine countries agree to reduce tariffs by an average of thirty-four percent. Talks end in 1979.

1986 Another round of multilateral trade negotiations take place, this time in Uruguay. One hundred twenty-eight countries agree to largest-ever package of market access concessions. Tariffs are reduced further, with agreements covering agriculture, textiles, clothing, services, and intellectual property rights. Talks end in 1994.

1994 GATT ministers meeting in Marrakesh, Morocco, establish the World Trade Organization (WTO).

1996 First ministerial meeting of the WTO is held in Singapore.

1998 Second WTO ministerial conference in Geneva, Switzerland.

1999 Third WTO ministerial summit in Seattle, Washington, in the United States is held from November 30 to December 3; protestors disrupt talks.

against globalization." Unified, perhaps, only by their anger that under WTO stewardship economic efficiency has often appeared to supercede social and political concerns, some thirty-five thousand protestors assembled to air their grievances. The presence of so many demonstrators caught no one by surprise. Seattle Mayor Paul Schell and the city's political leadership had decided to welcome the inevitable onslaught of protestors in an effort to encourage lively but peaceful debate on world trade. The city had budgeted six million dollars for police overtime and tear gas and considered itself prepared for the largest meeting on international trade ever held on American soil. Events would soon show that Schell and the city's political leaders were wrong.

Day 1

The "Battle in Seattle" began in the early morning hours of the first day of the WTO conference, commencing one of the bleakest weeks in Seattle history. Global Action, Direct Action Network, Earth First, and other anti-globalist groups organized a "Shut Down the WTO—Mass Nonviolent Direct Action" rally at 6:00 A.M. The relative calm

of this event would stand in sharp contrast what soon followed. Indeed, three hours later, protestors blocked WTO delegates from attending the conference's opening ceremonies at the Paramount Theater, forcing a one-hour postponement of the event and ultimately its cancellation. On the streets adjacent to the main conference venues, crowds swelled and pockets of protestors turned violent. Some demonstrators allegedly locked themselves to metal pipes and concrete blocks, others cut off key intersections, and still others escalated their protest by smashing windows and slashing tires on police cars and city buses. By 10:00 A.M. police in full-body armor had begun firing tear gas in efforts to disperse the crowds and allow delegates safe passage to official WTO events. Their efforts were largely unsuccessful. The police then advised all WTO delegates—including U.S. Secretary of State Madeline Albright and U.S. Trade Representative Charlene Barshefsky—to remain in their hotels. With United States and foreign dignitaries cordoned off in their hotels, the frenzied first hours of the crisis grew more violent. Protestors broke windows, looted, and otherwise inflicted damage on Seattle's downtown commercial district: McDonald's, Bank of America,

THIS GROUP OF PROTESTORS SITS QUIETLY AFTER BEING ARRESTED FOR ENTERING A "NO-PROTEST ZONE" SET-UP BY SEATTLE POLICE DURING THE WORLD TRADE ORGANIZATION MEETING. *(AP/Wide World Photos. Reproduced by permission.)*

Banana Republic, FAO Schwartz, Warner Brothers, Nike Town, Planet Hollywood, and Starbucks were among the worst hit. Defiant in the face of mounting opposition and with much of the world now watching on live television, WTO officials at noon announced the conference would go on. Barshefsky, who chaired the ministerial summit, warned, "Failure is not an option."

While the conference organizers struggled to jumpstart the meeting with a 2:00 P.M. plenary session at the Seattle Convention Center, demonstrators continued to converge on the city's central business district. Setting garbage cans ablaze and hurling glass bottles at police, protestors were met by repeated volleys of tear gas from officers who, by 3:00, had depleted their supplies of pepper spray. Informed by Clinton administration officials that failure to clear the protestors from the downtown area would result in cancellation of the WTO meeting, Mayor Schell called Washington Governor Gary Locke to ask that he send in the National Guard and state troopers; Locke concurred and gave the order. With protests continuing to gain in intensity, the mayor declared a state of emergency at 4:30 and announced a 7:00 P.M. to 7:30 A.M. curfew for downtown Seattle (the first in Seattle since World War II). Only hours before Clinton's scheduled arrival, National Guard troops

and police reinforcements swept into the business district and mounted a forceful effort to evict the combative demonstrators. By day's end police had arrested sixty-eight protestors and injuries had sent more than thirty people (including two WTO delegates) to the hospital for treatment. Figuratively, as well as literally, the WTO had its eye blackened on the first day of the Seattle meeting.

Days 2–4

The final three days of the WTO ministerial summit did little to repair the damage. On the second day of the conference (Wednesday, December 1, 1999), delegates attempted to press ahead with scheduled meetings. Outside, with most businesses closed, demonstrators mobilized. Mayor Schell responded by banning all protests in a fifty-block area and by banning the possession of gas masks (with the exception of police who were allowed to wear gas masks). Protestors defied the bans and throughout the day battled police who, on horseback, motorcycles, and in armored vehicles, fired tear gas, rubber pellets and concussion grenades into the crowds. By the end of the day and with a second night of curfew in place, 504 opponents of the WTO had been arrested. Nine months of security planning by the Seattle Police Department had disintegrated into full-scale crisis.

USING NON-LETHAL FORCE, RIOT POLICE ARREST A WOMAN FOR PROTESTING DURING THE WORLD TRADE ORGANIZATION MEETING. *(AP/Wide World Photos. Reproduced by permission.)*

On the WTO summit's third day, many of the protestors and much of the media attention shifted to focus on tough police behavior and a perceived mismanagement of the crisis by city authorities. With by then six hundred people locked up in King County Jail, Seattle Police Chief Norm Stamper (who would announce his retirement only a week after the debacle) came under fire with allegations of beatings in jail, business owners tear-gassed without warning outside their stores, innocent bystanders arrested, and peaceful protestors silenced. Groups assembled outside the jail and blared their demands over megaphones: immediate release of all protestors, drop all charges, issue a public apology, and an end to the WTO. While authorities did not give in to the protestors' demands, they did arrest only two additional anti-WTO protestors on December 2.

The new Director-General of the WTO, Mike Moore, had said on the ministerial conference's first day that "the Seattle meeting is doomed to succeed because too much is at stake." By the fourth day, however, the Seattle meeting was simply doomed. Protests continued outside the county jail. Business owners and community leaders roundly condemned the mayor. Talks inside the conference venues had made little substantive progress, and by mid-afternoon hopes of reaching any major agreement had slipped away. At 10:30 P.M., U.S. Trade Representative Barshefsky announced a suspension (what she strategically deemed a "time out") of the Seattle round of WTO talks. The first American meeting of the WTO had failed, and it had failed in an excruciatingly public fashion. Distancing themselves from the destruction wrought by some protest groups, anti-globalist forces claimed victory. "The outcome in Seattle," according to the *Washington Post*, "was quickly dubbed a fiasco, a debacle, a disaster for free trade—or a stunning victory by the activists who had come to Seattle to frustrate the negotiations." Seattle, which had beaten more than forty U.S. cities to win the rights to host the meeting (with one of the determining criteria being security arrangements), finally came to the end of its week of misery.

HISTORICAL BACKGROUND

The apparent failure of the Seattle conference stands in contrast to the more than half century of progress in the field of multilateral trade liberalization. To more fully understand the event that captured so many headlines at the end of 1999, it is necessary to recognize the WTO's deep historical roots, to describe the organization's current stated mission, and to identify the sources of its opposition.

AGREEMENT ESTABLISHING THE WORLD TRADE ORGANIZATION (WTO)

Signed in Marrakesh, Morroco, on April 15, 1994

The Parties to this Agreement,

Recognizing that their relations in the field of trade and economic endeavour should be conducted with a view to raising standards of living, ensuring full employment and a large and steadily growing volume of real income and effective demand, and expanding the production of and trade in goods and services, while allowing for the optimal use of the world's resources in accordance with the objective of sustainable development, seeking both to protect and preserve the environment and to enhance the means for doing so in a manner consistent with their respective needs and concerns at different levels of economic development,

Recognizing further that there is need for positive efforts designed to ensure that developing countries, and especially the least developed among them, secure a share in the growth in international trade commensurate with the needs of their economic development,

Being desirous of contributing to these objectives by entering into reciprocal and mutually advantageous arrangements directed to the substantial reduction of tariffs and other barriers to trade and to the elimination of discriminatory treatment in international trade relations,

Resolved, therefore, to develop an integrated, more viable and durable multilateral trading system encompassing the General Agreement on Tariffs and Trade, the results of past trade liberalization efforts, and all of the results of the Uruguay Round of Multilateral Trade Negotiations,

Determined to preserve the basic principles and to further the objectives underlying this multilateral trading system,

Agree as follows . . . The World Trade Organization (hereinafter referred to as "the WTO") is hereby established.

From Postwar Settlement to the General Agreement on Tariffs and Trade (GATT)

During the first half of the twentieth century the world experienced a massive global economic depression in between two world wars. Reacting to the apparent unreliability of the international system in the 1920s and 1930s, most countries adopted postures and policies of intense economic nationalism. Distrustful of one another's motives and perceiving the increasingly uncertain environment as one in which only the strongest would survive, many states saw competition rather than cooperation as their only course of action. The impulse to compete led, in the economic realm, to the erection of barriers to foreign trade, such as tariffs and quotas, to protect local industries from an influx of foreign goods. Following the 1929 stock market crash and subsequent Great Depression, the U.S. Congress, for example, passed the highly protectionist Smoot-Hawley Tariff Act, which raised the effective rate of U.S. tariffs by almost 50 percent from 1929 to 1932. The act provoked retaliation by a number of America's trading partners, with the net result being a decrease of nearly two-thirds in U.S. exports in the two years following passage of the act. Many historians, economists, and political scientists regard the policies pursued by the major industrial powers as a major factor in deepening and perpetuating economic depression. The economic depression, in turn, made the

ground fertile for the rise of extremists such as Adolf Hitler and Benito Mussolini who promised self-reliance and a return to national greatness. Among the painful lessons of the period was that protectionism breeds neither economic nor political salvation.

In an effort to avoid past mistakes, leaders of the victorious allied powers launched major projects designed to craft a postwar world built upon cooperation and interdependence rather than competition and nationalist protectionism. In July 1944 in the New Hampshire resort community of Bretton Woods, representatives of forty-four countries met to construct the rules and institutions that would govern international trade and monetary relations after the war. The so-called "Bretton Woods System" established the principles of an open international economy—free markets—with little government intervention and few barriers to private trade and flows of capital. Bretton Woods created what later came to be known as the International Monetary Fund (IMF) and the World Bank. These two international organizations would help countries maintain stability in their currencies and finance economic growth. The architects of this new international economic order at the time also envisaged the creation of an International Trade Organization (ITO), a specialized United Nations agency that would permanently manage economic relations and

JOHN SELLERS

Thirty-three-year old John Seller is the director of the Ruckus Society, one of the groups in Seattle that protested the WTO summit. After studying at school, Sellers joined Greenpeace. His work protesting globalization led to difficult situations: he was sailing on Greenpeace's ship, the Rainbow Warrior, when he was blown out of a dinghy by a stun grenade fired by the French navy. Sellers helped lead "Globalize This!" training sessions for protestors outside Seattle in preparation for the WTO conference.

The Berkeley, California-based Ruckus Society advocated nonviolent civil disobedience in support of environmental and human rights goals. In an interview with "Telegraph" magazine, Sellers said, "We're not opposed to globalism we welcome it. But we want it to be a just, humane globalism."

rule in defense of open and nondiscriminatory world trade. The 106-article 1948 "Havana Charter" christening the ITO, however, failed to secure ratification by enough signatories (including its chief sponsor, the United States).

With the ITO abandoned, advocates of trade liberalization turned to the only remaining international instrument laying down rules accepted by nations conducting most of the world's trade: the new General Agreement on Tariffs and Trade (GATT). The GATT began as a set of tariff-reduction (tax-reduction) negotiations among twenty-three countries, which met in Geneva, Switzerland, in 1947. These negotiations resulted in some 45,000-tariff concessions impacting ten billion dollars (or about one-fifth) of the world's trade. The tariff concessions and rules governing their implementation became known as the General Agreement on Tariffs and Trade and came into force in January 1948.

Less an international organization with enforcement powers than an evolving set of intergovernmental agreements for negotiating reductions in trade barriers and equality of market access among "contracting parties," the GATT led to a series of further multilateral tariff negotiations throughout its forty-six-year history. Early rounds were held in Annecy, France, in 1949, Torquay, United Kingdom, in 1951, and Geneva in 1955–56, resulting in relatively modest tariff reductions but bringing the total number of contracting countries to thirty-three. A fourth round, dubbed the "Dillon

Round" after the U.S. Undersecretary of State who proposed the talks, took place in 1960–61 following the creation of the European Economic Community in 1957. The Dillon Round resulted in still more incremental tariff concessions. It was not until the Kennedy Round (1963–67), however, that the momentum toward a genuinely liberal and expansive trade regime began to crest. With membership of the GATT reaching seventy-four countries by the end of the Kennedy Round, the contracting parties agreed to an impressive average tariff reduction of thirty-five percent in industrial products by developed countries. All told, in a matter of two decades the GATT sessions had contributed to an exponential expansion in the value of world trade and had successfully created a system of relatively peaceful economic interdependence among the leading industrial powers.

The GATT would witness two more rounds of multilateral trade negotiations before transforming itself into the WTO in 1994. Ninety-nine countries participated in the Tokyo Round (1973–79), which focused less on reductions in tariffs and more on the elimination of non-tariff barriers or NTBs—trade restrictions that discriminate against imports without direct tax levies, often in the form of government health and safety regulations used to deny equal treatment to the products of other countries adhering to the GATT system. While the Tokyo Round broke new ground in the area of NTBs, it failed to come to grips with emerging problems in global trade including America's expanding trade deficit with Japan, the preferential treatment accorded products and services (especially in agriculture) produced within the European Community and other regional trading blocs, the perceived threats posed by low-cost exports from the newly industrializing countries, and the sensitive issue of intellectual property rights (such as copyrights on computer software, movies, and music). The United States, in particular, had come to believe that it had the only truly open market and that only it truly played by the GATT rules. The Uruguay Round of negotiations (1986–94) attempted to tackle many of these seemingly intractable concerns. Early projections of a four-year round of talks proved false, as the United States and then twelve-member European Community reached impasse after impasse over the American proposal to phase out all agricultural subsidies and farm trade protection programs. At the end of the protracted, eight-year process the more than one hundred participating countries agreed to only limited rules on subsidies and market access in the agricultural sector and made modest inroads in the areas of copyrights, patents, and trade secrets.

PROTESTORS AT THE WORLD TRADE ORGANIZATION MEETING REPRESENTED A NUMBER OF DIFFERENT INTEREST GROUPS; ALL WERE MET WITH STIFF RESISTANCE IN THE FORM OF TEAR GAS FROM SEATTLE RIOT POLICE. *(AP/Wide World Photos. Reproduced by permission.)*

Indeed, the Uruguay Round could likely have been remembered as a disappointing failure were it not for the bargain struck in April 1994 to create the World Trade Organization and so greatly expand the reach of trade policies.

From GATT to WTO

One of GATT's weaknesses had been that it lacked an effective enforcement mechanism—it lacked "teeth." When disputes arose among its contracting parties, GATT findings were not binding. Because of the proposal for the ITO had not been approved in the postwar period, there had been no genuine international organization for trade of equal standing to the IMF or World Bank as had been envisioned at Bretton Woods. The absence of such an organization with an effective means to enforce decisions on member states meant that throughout the GATT era, states often bent if not broke the rules. GATT negotiators, in 1994, sought to rectify this shortcoming through the creation of the World Trade Organization. Trade ministers signed the Uruguay Round's Final Act in Marrakesh, Morocco, on April 15, 1994 and the WTO became the top court of the global economy in 1995.

Headquartered in Geneva, the 135-member WTO administered and enforced trade agreements signed by member countries, facilitating the freer flow of goods and services worldwide. The WTO Secretariat has around five hundred staff and is headed by a director-general, currently Michael Moore. Its rulings are law among members. If, for example, the United States and the European Union clash over Caribbean-grown bananas, hormone-treated beef, or the right to do business in what some deem to be pariah states such as Cuba or Libya, then it is the WTO that acts as both judge and jury to this dispute. The WTO is empowered to enforce standing GATT rules (as well as newly constructed ones in the fields of trade, services, and intellectual property) with a legal process backed by substantial sanctions.

Key decisions are made by a ministerial conference of all members, which meets at least once every two years. The first such conference took place in Singapore in 1996, sparking agreements among forty members for tariff-free trade in information technology products. In 1997 seventy members reached a financial services deal covering ninety-five percent of all trade in banking, insurance, securities and financial information. The WTO's second ministerial conference occurred in Geneva in May 1998, where members grappled with trade issues arising from global electronic commerce. While opposition challenged each of the WTO's first two ministerial meetings, the protests were nothing like those that met the delegates at the third meeting in Seattle in 1999.

Indigenous Peoples' Seattle Declaration

On the occasion of the third ministerial meeting of the World Trade Organization from November 30–December 3, 1999

We, the Indigenous Peoples from various regions of the world, have come to Seattle to express our great concern over how the World Trade Organization is destroying Mother Earth and the cultural and biological diversity of which we are a part.

Trade liberalization and export-oriented development, which are the overriding principles and policies pushed by the WTO, are creating the most adverse impacts on the lives of Indigenous Peoples. Our inherent right to self-determination, our sovereignty as nations, and treaties and other constructive agreements which Indigenous nations and Peoples have negotiated with other nation-states, are undermined by most of the WTO Agreements. The disproportionate impact of these Agreements on our communities, whether through environmental degradation or the militarization and violence that often accompanies development projects, is serious and therefore should be addressed immediately.

The WTO Agreement on Agriculture (AOA), which promotes export competition and import liberalization, has allowed the entry of cheap agricultural products into our communities. It is causing the destruction of ecologically rational and sustainable agricultural practices of Indigenous Peoples. Food security and the production of traditional food crops have been seriously compromised. Incidents of diabetes, cancers, and hypertension have significantly increased among Indigenous Peoples because of the scarcity of traditional foods and the dumping of junk food into our communities. Small-scale farm production is giving way to commercial cash-crop plantations further concentrating ancestral lands into the hands of few agri-corporations and landlords. This has led to the dislocation of scores of people from our communities who then migrate to nearby cities and become the urban homeless and jobless . . . .

Mining laws in many countries are being changed to allow free entry of foreign mining corporations, to enable them to buy and own mineral lands, and to freely displace Indigenous Peoples from their ancestral territories. These large-scale commercial mining and oil extraction activities continue to degrade our lands and fragile ecosystems, and pollute the soil, water, and air in our communities. The appropriation of our lands and resources and the aggressive promotion of consumerist and individualistic Western culture continue to destroy traditional lifestyles and cultures. The result is not only environmental degradation but also ill health, alienation, and high levels of stress manifested in high rates of alcoholism and suicides . . . .

Finally, the liberalization of investments and the service sectors, which is pushed by the General Agreement of Services (GATS), reinforces the domination and monopoly control of foreign corporations over strategic parts of the economy. The World Bank and the International Monetary Fund impose conditionalities of liberalization, deregulation and privatization on countries caught in the debt trap. These conditionalities are reinforced further by the WTO.

In light of the adverse impacts and consequences of the WTO Agreements identified above, we, Indigenous Peoples present the following demands: We urgently call for a social and environmental justice analysis which will look into the Agreements' cumulative effects on Indigenous Peoples. Indigenous Peoples should be equal participants in establishing the criteria and indicators for these analyses so that they take into consideration spiritual as well as cultural aspects . . . .

Opposition to the WTO

By certain measures, the historical record suggests that the GATT/WTO system has produced tangible benefits, not the least of which have been the expansion of world trade and the securing of a system of peaceful economic interdependence. Total trade at the end of the 1990s was more than fifteen-times the level of 1950. Moreover, it could fairly, if humorously, be said that no two countries with McDonald's restaurants operating within their borders had ever gone to war against one another (or at least until NATO air strikes against Serbia in 1999). Globalization was good. Efforts to globalize and liberalize global trade have, according to proponents, stood in stark but pleasant contrast to the zero-sum nature of economic nationalism in the first half of the twentieth century.

Alongside the GATT/WTO, IMF and World Bank stand other examples of institutionalized cooperation: the United Nations, the North American Free Trade Agreement (NAFTA), the European Union, Asia-Pacific Economic Cooperation (APEC), and others. Technological advancements (computers, telecommunications, transport) have facilitated economic interdependence and the mobility of goods, services, people, and capital across national borders. Cooperation, once institutionalized, has caused new and related forms of cooperation in other areas. This process of "spillover" has given some the sense that globalization is both inevitable and irreversible. The collapse of communism in the Soviet Union and Eastern Europe is, for example, seen as a vivid indicator of the triumph of both democracy and capitalism and an ultimate convergence of people. However, the proliferation of nongovernmental organizations (NGOs) seeking to protect and defend the environment, culture, consumers, workers, indigenous people, children, the poor and others represents a trend counter to that of commercial globalization. Globalization creates uncertainty: in a global market prices may be less reliable, countries have a more limited ability to erect trade barriers for humanitarian reasons, and commercial development can damage the long-term needs of the environment. Globalization challenges assumptions about security and predictability in people's lives. The anxieties that have spurred the growth of defensive NGOs represent a force that could collide with globalization. The Battle in Seattle, for many, represents just such a collision.

The more than three hundred groups arrayed on the streets of Seattle from November 30 to December 3, 1999 embodied a mix of opposition to the global market and opposition to potent international institutions. For some, the global market meant roving multinational corporations (MNCs) from wealthy countries setting up shop in poorer countries, systematically exploiting the population for cheap labor and the environment for raw materials, and then leaving when both have been thoroughly plundered. Free trade meant the loss of rainforests, the erosion of habitats for wild animals, and the spilling of chemicals into water supplies and the atmosphere, as well as other forms of pollution. Free trade meant evicting indigenous peoples from their ancestral lands in pursuit of raw materials. Free trade meant child labor and sweatshops. Free trade means sacrificing consumer safety to the priorities of corporate profits. Others said that the global market is inherently biased in favor of the existing rich, industrial countries because poor countries do not have the level of manufacturing infrastructure to enjoy the benefits of free trade. Collectively, such attitudes suggest that the presumed triumph of the market would not endure unchallenged.

Other opponents of the WTO saw the WTO as one of a number of increasingly intrusive, unaccountable international organizations and that too many areas of national life were falling under control of trade rules. Many of the protesters expressed the concern that the WTO—in the name of free trade—has the power to undermine laws passed by individual countries to promote health, food safety, environmental protection, and workplace safety. For these protesters, free trade meant the manipulation of national political processes by business interests bent on profit at any price. Free trade meant the erosion of national independence, as argued by,

among others, conservative commentator and presidential candidate Pat Buchanan. Buchanan praised the anti-WTO protestors in Seattle, calling the global trade organization an "embryonic monster." To these protesters, free trade meant closed ministerial summits where trade representatives cloistered away in meeting rooms make decisions that have important impacts on the lives of everyday citizens. The WTO, for such activists, represented the opposite of democracy. The solution, according to groups such as the Ruckus Society leading the charge in Seattle, is simple: shut down the WTO. In response U.S. President Clinton spoke frequently in Seattle of the need to "put a human face on the global economy."

RECENT HISTORY AND THE FUTURE

In the immediate aftermath of the Seattle riots, some observers questioned the viability of the WTO and raised the specter of a reversal of the globalization process. Fears arose in some quarters that the United States—a country where sentiment for isolationism and protectionism still exists—might turn its back on multilateral trade arrangements. Indeed, in early March 2000 a group of conservative members of the U.S. House of Representatives announced their intention to introduce legislation demanding that the United States quit the World Trade Organization. The effort, led by Rep. Ron Paul (Republican-Tex.), guaranteed a vote within ninety days on withdrawing from the WTO. In a statement, Paul, a longtime foe of the WTO, said he submitted the resolution because the WTO "is an egregious attack upon our national sovereignty, and this is the reason why we must vigorously oppose it." Under the 1994 legislation that authorized U.S. membership in the newly created WTO, Congress required the administration to submit a progress report after five years of WTO membership about the costs and benefits to the U.S. For the WTO's supporters, an American exit from the WTO would clearly represent the worst-case scenario. U.S. withdrawal would almost certainly mean the end of the WTO.

A more likely scenario is that the WTO emerges from the humiliation of Seattle prepared to make enough reforms (some substantive, some cosmetic) to regain a measure of public trust—yet ultimately uncertain as to how exactly to go about doing so. A thorough democratization of the WTO by allowing greater participation of interest groups and nongovernmental organizations in its deliberations, for example, is one possible avenue for reform. Such a move would almost certainly complicate trade negotiations in the future. WTO officials are expected to mount a campaign to more effectively sell skeptical public on its merits. A vigorous public relations campaign would include the message that the WTO is not some form of world government; the campaign would, moreover, describe the virtues of the WTO and what the consequences of its demise might be.

Almost all observers recognize Seattle as a seminal moment in the history of globalization. Anti-WTO activists will be buoyed and emboldened by the talks' collapse, promising to turn out in equal if not greater numbers at the next possible ministerial summit. WTO supporters, while admitting that the organization is in the midst of a crisis, seize optimistically upon USTR Barshefsky's characterization of the adjourning of the Seattle meeting as a "time out" rather than a definitive and failed end to the negotiations. If nothing else is certain, it is clear that the next U.S. city to host a WTO event be under intense pressure to "avoid another Seattle."

BIBLIOGRAPHY

Grady, Patrick and Kathleen Macmillan. *Seattle and Beyond: The WTO Millennium Round.* Toronto: Global Economics Ltd., 1999.

Hoekman, Bernard M. and Michel M. Kostecki. *The Political Economy of the World Trading System: From GATT to WTO.* Oxford: Oxford University Press, 1995.

Irwin, Douglas A. *Against the Tide: An Intellectual History of Free Trade.* Princeton, N.J.: Princeton University Press, 1996.

Kaiser, Robert G. and John Burgess. "A Seattle Primer: How Not to Hold WTO Talks," *The Washington Post,* 12 December 1999.

Kirshner, Orin, ed. *The Bretton Woods-GATT System: Retrospect and Prospect After Fifty Years.* Armonk, NY: M.E. Sharpe, 1996.

Krueger, Anne O. and Chonira Aturupane, eds. *The WTO as an International Organization.* Chicago: University of Chicago Press, 1998.

Marcus, Nolan. "Learning to Love the WTO," *Foreign Affairs* 78 (September 1999): 78–92.

Nader, Ralph, ed. *The Case Against Free Trade: GATT, NAFTA and the Globalization of Corporate Power.* Berkeley, Calif.: North Atlantic Books, 1993.

Wallach, Lori and Michell Sforza. *Whose Trade Organization? Corporate Globalization and the Erosion of Democracy.* Washington, D.C.: Public Citizen Inc., 1999.

———, and Ralph Nader. *The WTO: Five Years of Reasons to Resist Corporate Globalization.* New York: Seven Stories Press, 2000.

Zeiller, Thomas W. *Free Trade, Free World : The Advent of the GATT.* Chapel Hill, N.C.: University of North Carolina Press, 1999.

William M. Downs

CONTRIBUTORS

Shahram Akbarzadeh (M.Soc.Sci. Birmingham; Ph.D. La Trobe) is a lecturer in international politics at the School of Sociology Politics and Anthropology at La Trobe University in Australia and Honorary Research Fellow of Arts Faculty at Monash University, Australia.

ENTRIES: The Soviet Union: Collapse of the USSR and Formation of Independent Republics

R. William Ayres is an Assistant Professor in the Department of History and Political Science at the University of Indianapolis, where he is also coordinator of International Relations programs. He has published articles on violent ethnic conflict in the *Journal of Peace Research, Nationalism and Ethnic Politics,* and *International Politics.* He is also a contributor to the book *The Persian Gulf at the Millennium* (1997), and has published work on the role of perception in conflict mediation. He received his M.A. and Ph.D. from Ohio State University, and his B.A. from Williams College.

ENTRIES: Chechnya and Russia: A War of Succession; Kashmir: War in the Himalayas

Ruth Margolies Beitler was an Assistant Professor of International and Comparative Politics at the United States Military Academy at West Point from 1993–98 and is currently an Adjunct Professor in the Department of Social Sciences. From 1993–98, she directed the Middle East Program. Her publications include "The Intifada: Palestinian Adaptation to Israeli Counterinsurgency Tactics," in *The Journal of Terrorism and Political Violence* and contributions to *Understanding International Relations: The Value of Alternative Lenses* (1994). She is a member of the Council on Foreign Relations.

ENTRIES: The Gaza Strip and West Bank: Statehood and Security; Syria and Israel: Negotiations for Peace

Brian Black teaches history and environmental studies at Altoona College of the Pennsylvania State University. He is the author of *PETROLIA: The Landscape of America's First Oil Boom* (2000) as well as numerous articles for scholarly journals and popular magazines. After recently completing a book on nineteenth cen-

tury whaling, Black is now researching the New Deal for a book about the Tennessee Valley Authority and environmental planning.

ENTRIES: Oil: Protectionist Pricing and Fuel Dependence

Michael P. Bobic earned his B.A. in Political Science from Berea College (1985) in Kentucky. He earned his M.A. in 1992 and Ph.D. in 1996 in Political Science from the University of Tennessee, specializing in national institutions and research methods. Dr. Bobic is currently employed at Emmanuel College in Franklin Springs, Georgia, as an Assistant Professor of Political Science and as the Director of Institutional Research. He and his wife live in upstate South Carolina. Dr. Bobic was assisted in the research and writing of "The Afghan Taliban: Emerging Government Or Civil Rights Tragedy?" by his students: Laquisha Hazel, a member of Pi Gamma Mu Honor Society; Tim Curry, a member of the Emmanuel College History Club; Joy Suza, an Honors Graduate of Emmanuel College (2000) and a Recipient of the U.S. Minority Achievement Award, 2000; Martha Mengistu, a recent graduate of Emmanuel and a recipient of Recognition for Academic Achievement from Columbus State University; Kathryn White, a member of Phi Gamma Mu; Dena Bush, the recipient of the College Award for Academic Excellence, Pre-Law (2000); Angelen Brookshire, a junior at Emmanuel College majoring in Communications.

ENTRIES: The Afghan Taliban: Emerging Government or Civil Rights Tragedy?

Dallas L. Browne is Chairman of the Department of Anthropology at Southern Illinois University-Edwardsville. He is also president of the St. Louis Council on Foreign Relations and Chairman of the CFR Board of Directors. He is under consideration to become Honorary Counsel for the Republic of Tanzania. He is completing a book-length biography of Allison Davis, the first African-American ever awarded tenure on any faculty in the United States.

ENTRIES: Rwanda and Burundi: Culture, History, Power, and Genocide

T. Timothy Casey is an Assistant Professor of Political Science at Mesa State College in Grand Junction, Colorado. His teaching and research interests include international relations and political theory.

ENTRIES: Deforestation of the Amazon: Economics and Biodiversity

Anthony Q. Cheeseboro is an Assistant Professor at Southern Illinois University at Edwardsville. He has published in the *Northeast African Studies* journal and the *Journal of the Illinois State Historical Society,* as well as the *Historical Encyclopedia of World Slavery.* He received his B.A. from the University of Georgia, his M.A. from the University of South Carolina, and his Ph.D. from Michigan State University.

ENTRIES: Sudan: Slavery and Civil War

James Ciment received his Ph.D. from City University of New York in 1992. His publications include the *Encyclopedia of American Third Parties* (1999), the *Encyclopedia of Conflicts Since World War II* (1998), and "The Kurds: State and Minority in Turkey, Iraq, and Iran" and "Angola/Mozambique: Post-Colonial Wars in Southern Africa" in *Crisis and Conflict in the Post-Cold War World.*

ENTRIES: The Kurds in Turkey: The Capture of Ocalan

David M. Crowe is a Professor of History at Elon College. He is a member of the Education Committee of the United States Holocaust Memorial Museum in Washington, DC and is president of the Association for the Study of Nationalities at the Harriman Institute at Columbia University. His publications include *A History of the Gypsies of Eastern Europe and Russia* (1994, 1996), *The Gypsies of Eastern Europe* (1991), with John Kolsti, and *The Baltic States and the Great Powers: Foreign Relations 1938–1940* (1993).

ENTRIES: Roma in Eastern Europe: The Wall in the Czech Republic

Barbara DeGorge is an Assistant Professor of African Studies in the Department of Humanities at the State University of New York College at Old Westbury. She received her doctorate in modern world history, specializing in Islamic African politics, from St. John's University in Jamaica, New York. Dr. Degorge has also taught history at St. John's University, the United States Merchant Marine Academy, and Iona College.

ENTRIES: Liberia in Civil War: Haven for Freed Slaves Reduced to Anarchy

William M. Downs (Ph.D. Emory University, 1994) is Assistant Professor of Political Science at Georgia State University. His research and teaching interests comprise comparative politics, European politics with emphases on western and northern Europe, and regional economic integration. He is the author of *Coalition Government, Subnational Style: Multiparty Politics in Europe's Regional Parliaments* (1998), and has published in the *Journal of Legislative Studies, Publius: The Journal of Federalism, Regional and Federal Studies, Electoral Studies,* and *West European Politics.* Downs has held academic appointments at Aarhus University (Denmark), Odense University (Den-

mark), and the Center for European Studies at Harvard University.

ENTRIES: The World Trade Organization: The Battle in Seattle

Paul du Quenoy is a doctoral candidate in history at Georgetown University.

ENTRIES: Humanitarian Aid: Compassion and Controversy

Mark A. T. Esposito is a Ph.D. candidate from West Virginia University who specializes in international relations. He has contributed numerous articles to various reference works and is presently completing a doctoral dissertation on U.S. relations with Japan during the 1970s.

ENTRIES: Nagorno-Karabakh: Self-Determination and Ethnic Identification

James Frusetta is a doctoral candidate in modern European history at the University of Maryland-College Park, focusing on Southeastern Europe in the early twentieth century. He has been an NSEP Graduate Fellow holder in both the Republic of Macedonia and in Bulgaria, and is currently working on the dissertation, "Bulgaria in Macedonia: Intersection between Bulgarian and Macedonian National Identity."

ENTRIES: Serbia and NATO: The 1999 War

Charles Hauss teaches political science at George Mason University in Fairfax, Virginia, and is Political Science Guide at About—The Human Internet.

ENTRIES: Iraq: Economic Sanctions

Sandra Fullerton Joireman is an Associate Professor of Political Science at St. Bonaventure University and Wheaton College. She is the author of *Property Rights and Political Development in Ethiopia and Eritrea* as well as numerous articles on the Horn of Africa.

ENTRIES: Ethiopia and Eritrea: Border War

David L. Kenley (Ph.D., University of Hawaii) specializes in modern Chinese history, and is particularly interested in overseas Chinese communities and Chinese intellectual history. His publications include such articles as "The May Fourth Movement in Singapore: Studying May Fourth from a Diaspora Perspective" and "Publishing the New Culture: Singapore's Newspapers and Diaspora Literature, 1919–1933." Dr. Kenley is currently an Assistant Professor of History at Marshall University where he teaches courses on modern Asia.

ENTRIES: Taiwan and China: Unification and Nationalism

Michael Levy is an Assistant Professor of Political Science at Southeast Missouri State University (Cape Girardeau). He specializes in European politics, political parties and identity politics, having published articles on the transformations of the British Labour Party, the history of Labour Party political thought, American third parties, and the role of identity groups in the American political process.

ENTRIES: German Right Wing Extremism: Anti-Foreigner Violence in the Country of the Holocaust

DeeAnna Manning is an historian of Latin America who specializes in Chile and Mexico. Her dissertation is entitled "Economic Nationalism in Comparative Perspective: The Mexican and Chilean Copper 'Nationalizations.'" She holds a B.A. in Humanities from Arizona State University, an M.A. in History from Washington University in St. Louis, and is completing her Ph.D. from Washington University. She taught as a Visiting Lecturer in Latin American History and Ethnic Studies at the University of Nebraska-Lincoln from 1998–2000 and is currently revising her dissertation for publication. She is researching the environmental impacts of copper mining in Mexico and Chile.

ENTRIES: The Extradition of Chilean General Augusto Pinochet: Justice Delayed?

Brian A. Marcus received his B.A. from the University of Albany (SUNY) and his M.A. from the J.M. Dawson Institute of Church-State Studies at Baylor University. Currently a Ph.D. student at Drew University, he is also editor of *e-Vigilance* (a quarterly journal produced by HateWatch at http://www.hatewatch.org).

ENTRIES: U.S. Militant Separatist Movements: Freedom Fighters or Terrorists?

Joan E. Meznar completed a Ph.D. in History and Latin American Studies at the University of Texas at Austin. A specialist in the history of Brazil, she is a member of the Department of History, Political Science, and Philosophy at Eastern Connecticut State University. She has received two Fulbright awards to research and teach in Brazil. A contributing editor to the *Handbook of Latin American Studies* since 1995, her work has also appeared in scholarly journals such as the *Hispanic American Historical Review*, the *Journal of Social History, The Americas*, and the *Luso-Brazilian Review*.

ENTRIES: Venezuela: New Military Populism

Carlos Pérez received a Ph.D. in History from the University of California, Los Angeles, in 1998, for his dissertation "Quinine and Caudillos: Manuel Isidoro Belzu and the Cinchona Bark Trade in Bolivia, 1848–1855." He is currently an Assistant Professor in the Department of Chicano and Latin American Studies at California State University, Fresno. He has published numerous articles, including "Caudillos, comerciantes y el Estado-National en la Bolivia decimonovena" and "The Export Roots of Bolivian Caudillo Politics: The Cinchona Bark Boom and Belzu's Jacquerie." He also contributed to the following books: *Encyclopedia of Historians and Historical Writing, A Global Encyclopedia of Historical Writing, Historical Dictionary of the Spanish Empire*, and *Historical Dictionary of European Imperialism*. He received a Fulbright Fellowship, 1988–89, to conduct research at the Archivo y Biblioteca Nacionales de Bolvia, Sucre, Bolivia, the Archives of La Paz, and other Bolivian archives.

ENTRIES: The Chiapas Rebellion: Indigenous People's Rights in Mexico

Anne Pitsch is in her fourth year as Project Coordinator for the Minorities at Risk Project, housed at the Center for International Development and Conflict Management at the University of Maryland. The project tracks ethno-political conflict on a global basis and provides researchers and practitioners with profiles of 275 ethno-political groups as well as raw data related to their economic, political and cultural status within the countries in which they reside. In addition to the management duties of the project, she has regional expertise in Sub-Saharan Africa and has largely been responsible for research on the more than seventy groups of that region. While at Maryland, Ms. Pitsch has also done consulting work for research organizations and government agencies, including PIOOM and USAID. Prior to entering the Ph.D. program at Maryland, she was in the Peace Corps for two years in Mauritania, West Africa and also worked for a short time in both Ghana and Rwanda. She also has an M.A. in Political Science from the University of Nebraska and a B.S. in Psychology from Viterbo College in La Crosse, Wisconsin.

ENTRIES: The Democratic Republic of Congo (Congo-Kinshasa): The African World War

Thomas D. Reins received his Ph.D. in 1981 from Claremont Graduate School and currently teaches at California State University, Fullerton. Previously, he has taught at the University of California, Riverside, California State University, Los Angeles, and Chapman University. His research interests include the global drug trade and drug trafficking in Asia, especially in China. He has published reviews, articles, and chapters in the *Journal of Asian Studies*, the *Journal of Third World Studies, Modern Asian Studies, China Review International, Magill's Guide to Military History*, and other publications.

ENTRIES: Colombian Drug Wars: Guerrillas, Paramilitary Groups, and the Government

Thomas E. Skidmore is the Carlos Manuel de Céspedes Professor of Modern Latin American History and Director of the Center for Latin American Studies at Brown University. He is also a member of the Department of Portuguese and Brazilian Studies at Brown. He received a B.A. from Denison University, a B.A. and an M.A. from Oxford University (Magdalen College) and a Ph.D. from Harvard University. Professor Skidmore has held fellowships from the Kellogg Institute (Norte Dame), the Guggenheim Foundation, the Social Science Research Council, Harvard University, and the American Philosophical Society. He has received Fulbright Fellowships to study at Oxford and to conduct research in Brazil and Argentina. He has also been a consultant on Latin America to the Ford Foundation. Among his many written contributions are: *Brazil: Five Centuries of Change, Modern Latin America, Brazil Visto de Fora, The Politics of Military Rule in Brazil, 1964–1985*, and *Black Into White: Race and Nationality in Brazilian Thought*. He was President of the Latin American Studies Association in 1972 and in 1989 won the Association's first Bryce Wood Award for his Politics of Military Rule in Brazil. He was also President of the New England Council of Latin American Studies in 1996.

ENTRIES: Brazil: Racism and Equality

Michael Tkacik earned his Ph.D. in Political Science from the University of Maryland. His M.A. in Political Science is from Columbia University. He also holds a

J.D. from Duke University School of Law. His publications include: *Nuclear Deterrence, Arms Control, and Multipolarity: An Argument for Incremental Policy Change, Armed Forces and Society, World Trade Organization Dispute Settlement: Substance, Strengths, Weaknesses, and Causes for Concern, International Legal Perspectives, Islam and Democracy: Toward Creating a User-Friendly Environment,* and *An Evolutionary Approach Toward Drafting Autonomy Agreements: Applying Theory to Reality in the Search for the Resolution of Ethnic Conflict.* Tkacik is currently an Assistant Professor of Political Science at Stephen F. Austin State University in Texas. His research and teaching interests include international relations, international security, international law, and ethnic conflict resolution.

ENTRIES: Cuba and the United States: Revolution, Nationalism and Enemies Next Door

Robert H. Whealey, Ph.D., University of Michigan, 1963, is an Associate Professor at Ohio University. His many publications include *Hitler and Spain: The Nazi Role in the Spanish Civil War 1936–1939,* "Foreign Intervention in the Spanish Civil War" in *The Republic and the Civil War in Spain,* "Anglo-American Oil Confronts Spanish Nationalism, 1927–31: A Study of Economic Imperialism," in *Diplomatic History,* and "Give Ronald Reagan Credit for Ending the Cold War? What Cold War? The Myth the Politicians Manufactured" in *Tom-Paine.common sense A Journal of Opinion.* He has also written several papers on U.S. president Bill Clinton's policy toward the Bosnian civil war, including the "1992 Presidential Campaign: Presidential, Congressional and Journalistic Pressures."

ENTRIES: Bosnia-Herzegovina: Civil War

GENERAL BIBLIOGRAPHY

This bibliography contains a list of sources, primarily books and articles, that will assist the reader in pursuing additional information on the topics contained in this volume.

A

Amstutz, Mark R. *International Conflict and Cooperation: An Introduction to World Politics.* New York: McGraw-Hill Companies, 1998.

Arrighi, G. *The Long Twentieth Century.* New York and London: Verso, 1994.

Atlas of World History. New York and London: Oxford University Press, 1999.

Avruch, Kevin. *Culture and Conflict Resolution.* Washington, D.C.: U.S. Institute of Peach Press, 1998.

B

Bairoch, Paul. *The Economic Development of the Third World since 1900.* Berkeley, Calif.: University of California Press, 1975.

Bartlett, C. J. J. *The Global Conflict: The International Rivalry of the Great Powers.* New York: Addison-Wesley Longman, 1994.

Bercovitch, Jacob and Richard Jackson. *International Conflict: A Chronological Encyclopedia of Conflict Management, 1945–1995.* Washington D.C.: Congressional Quarterly, 1997.

Best, Geoffrey. "Where Rights Collide with Duties," *Times Literary Supplement* (22 September 1995): 11–12.

Bothe, Michael and Horst Fischer, et al. *The Handbook of Humanitarian Law in Armed Conflict.* New York and London: Oxford University Press, 1999.

Brown, Michael E. *Ethnic Conflict and International Security.* Princeton, N.J.: Princeton University Press, 1993

———. *The International Dimensions of Internal Conflict.* Cambridge, Mass.: MIT Press, 1995.

C

Clark, Robert P. *The Global Imperative.* Boulder, Colo.: Westview Press, 1997.

Costello, Paul. *World Historians and Their Goals: Twentieth-Century Answers to Modernism.* De Kalb, Ill.: Northern Illinois University Press, 1994.

D

Deudney, Daniel H. and Richard A. Matthew, eds. *Contested Grounds: Security and Conflict in the New Environmental Politics.* Albany, N.Y.: State University of New York Press, 1999.

Diamond, Jared. *Guns, Germs and Steel.* New York: W.W. Norton, & Co., 1997.

Diehl, Paul and Nils Gleditsch. *Environmental Conflict.* Boulder, Colo.: Westview Press, 2000.

E

Encyclopedia of World History. New York and London: Oxford University Press, 1999.

F

Fukuyama, Francis. "Rest Easy. It's Not 1914 Anymore," *New York Times,* 9 February 1992.

G

Gall, Susan B., ed. *Worldmark Chronology of the Nations.* Farmington Hills, Mich.: Gale Group, 2000.

Gall, Timothy L., ed. *Worldmark Encyclopedia of Cultures and Daily Life.* Farmington Hills, Mich.: Gale Group, 1997.

Ganguly, Rajat and Raymond C. Taras. *Understanding Ethnic Conflict: The International Dimension.* New York: Longman, 1998.

Goldstone, Jack A., Ted Robert Gurr and Farrakh Mashiri. *Revolutions of the Late Twentieth Century.* Boulder, Colo.: Westview Press, 1991.

Gottlieb, Gidon. *National Against State: A New Approach to Ethnic conflicts and Sovereignty.* Washington, D.C.: Council on Foreign Relations, 1994.

H

Haass, Richard N. *Conflicts Unending: the United States and Regional Disputes.* New Haven, Conn.: Yale University Press, 1990.

Hobsbawm, Eric. *Nations and Nationalism Since 1780: Programme, Myth, Reality.* Cambridge, England: Cambridge University Press, 1993.

Hodgson, Marshall G. S. "World History and a World Outlook." In *Rethinking World History: Essays on Europe, Islam and World History.* New York: Cambridge University Press, 1993.

Hoffman, Stanley. *World Disorders:Troubled Peace in the Post Cold War Era.* Lanham, Md.: Rowman & Littlefield, Publishers, 2000.

Homer-Dixon, Thomas F. *Environment, Scarcity, and Violence.* Princeton, N.J.: Princeton University Press, 1999.

J

Jones, E. L. *Growth Recurring: Economic Change in World History.* New York and London: Oxford University Press, 1993.

K

Kakar, Sudhir. *The Colors of Violence: Cultural Identities, Religon, and Conflict.* Chicago, Ill.: University of Chicago Press, 1996.

Kanet, Roger E. *Resolving Regional Conflicts.* Urbana, Ill.: University of Illinois Press, 1998.

Katz, Richard S. *Democracy and Elections.* New York and London: Oxford University Press, 1998.

Keegan, J. *A History of Warfare.* New York: Vintage Books, 1994.

King, Anthony, ed. *Culture, Globalization and the World-System: Contemporary Conditions for the Representation of Identity.* Minneapolis, Minn.: University of Minnesota Press, 1997.

Khalilzad, Zalmay and Ian O. Lesser, eds. *Sources of Conflict in the 21st Century.* Santa Monica, Calif.: Rand, 1998.

Kohn, Hans. "Nationalism," *International Encyclopedia of the Social Sciences* 11: 63–39.

L

Lambert, Richard D., Alan W. Heston, and William Zartman. *Resolving Regional Conflicts: International Perspectives.* London: Sage Publications, 1991.

Landes, David S. *The Wealth and Poverty of Nations: Why Some are So Rich and Some are so Poor.* New York: W.W. Norton, 1999.

M

Mazlish, Bruce and Ralph Buultjens, eds. *Conceptualizing Global History.* Boulder, Colo.: Westview Press, 1993.

McNeill, W. H. *Plagues and Peoples.* New York: Anchor Books/Doubleday & Co, Inc., 1998.

Meadows, et al. *Beyond the Limits: Confronting Global Collapse, Envisioning a Sustainable Future.* Mitts, Vt.: Chelsea Green Publishing, 1992.

Miall, Hugh and Tom Woodhouse, et al. *Contemporary Conflict Resolution: The Prevention, Management and Transformations of Deadly Conflict.* Malder, Mass.: Blackwell Publishers, 1999.

Mitchell, C. R. *The Structure of International Conflict.* New York: St. Martin's Press, 1990.

N

Nash, Gary B., Charlotte Crabtree, and Ross E. Dunn. "In the Matter of History." In *History on Trial: Culture Wars and the Teaching of the Past.* New York: Alfred A. Knopf, 1998.

Nye, Joseph S. *Understanding International Conflict: An Introduction to Theory and History.* New York: Addison-Welsey Longman, 1999.

P

Prendergast, John. *Frontline Diplomacy: Humanitarian Aid and Conflict in Africa.* Boulder, Colo.: Lynne Rienner Publishers, 1996.

R

Ramsbotham, Oliver and Tom Woodhouse. *Humanitarian Intervention in Contemporary Conflict: A Reconceptualization.* Oxford, England: Blackwell Publishers, 1996.

Ratcliffe, Peter. *Race, Ethnicity, and Nation: Ethnicity and Nation International Perspectives on Social Conflict.* London: UCL Press, 1994.

Ray, James Lee and Charles W. Kegley, et al., eds. *Democracy and International Conflict: An Evaluation of the Democratic Peace Proposition.* Columbia, S.C.: University of South Carolina Press, 1995.

Rayner, Caroline, ed. *Encyclopedic World Atlas: Country-by-Country Coverage.* New York and London: Oxford University Press, 1994.

Rieff, David. "A Just War is Still a War," *Newsweek,* 14 June 1999.

Rochards, Andrew. "Meaning of 'Genocide'," *Times Literary Supplement,* 15 May 1998.

Rothchild, Donald and Dave A. Lake, eds. *The International Spread of Ethnic Conflict: Fear, Diffusion, and Escalation.* Princeton, N.J.: Princeton University Press, 1998.

S

Sachs, Wolfgang. *Global Ecology: A New Arena of Political Conflict.* London: St. Martin's Press, 1993.

Schlesinger, Arthur Meier. *The Disuniting of America: Reflections on a Multicultural Society.* New York: W.W. Norton, 1998.

Schnaiberg, Allan and Kenneth Alan Gould. *Environment and Society: The Enduring Conflict.* New York: St. Martin's Press, 2000.

Shawcross, William. *Deliver Us from Evil: Peacekeepers, Warlords and a World of Endless Conflict.* New York: Simon and Schuster, 2000.

Shrire, C. *Past and Present in Hunter-Gatherer Societies.* London: Academic Press, 1985.

Simmons, I. G. *Changing the Face of the Earth: Culture, Environment, History.* 2d ed. New York and London: Oxford University Press, 1993.

Smith, David A. and Steven Topik, eds. *States and Sovereignty in the Global Economy.* New York: Routledge, 1999.

Snooks, Graeme Donald. *The Dynamic Society: Exploring the Sources of Global Change.* New York: Routledge, 1996.

Stearns, Peter N. "Nationalisms: An Invitation to Contemporary Analysis," *Journal of World History* (Spring 1997): 57–74.

Strayer, Robert. *Why Did the Soviet Union Collapse? Understanding Historical Change.* San Diego, Calif.: Greenhaven Press, 1994.

Sulimann, Mohamed. *Ecology, Politics and Violent Conflict.* New York: St. Martin's Press, 1998.

V

Van Evera, Stephen. *Causes of War: Power and the Roots of Conflict.* Ithaca, N.Y.: Cornell University Press, 1999.

W

Walter, Barbara F. *Civil Wars, Insecurity, and Intervention.* New York: Columbia University Press, 1999.

Waterfield, Larry W. *Conflict and Crisis in Rural America.* New York: Praeger, 1986.

Weart, Spencer R. *Never at War.* New Haven, Conn.: Yale University Press, 2000.

Wippman, David. *International Law and Ethnic Conflict.* Ithaca, N.Y.: Cornell University Press, 1998.

Worldmark Encyclopedia of Nations. Farmington Hills, Mich.: Gale Group, 1998.

Wolfe, Patrick. "Imperialism and History: A Century from Marx to Postcolonialism," *The American Historical Review* 102 (April 1997): 388–420.

Worsley, Peter. *The Three Worlds: Culture and World Development.* Chicago, Ill.: University of Chicago Press, 1989.

General Bibliography

INDEX

Page numbers in boldface refer to a topic upon which an essay is based. Page numbers in italics refer to illustrations, figures, and tables.

D

X

Y

Z